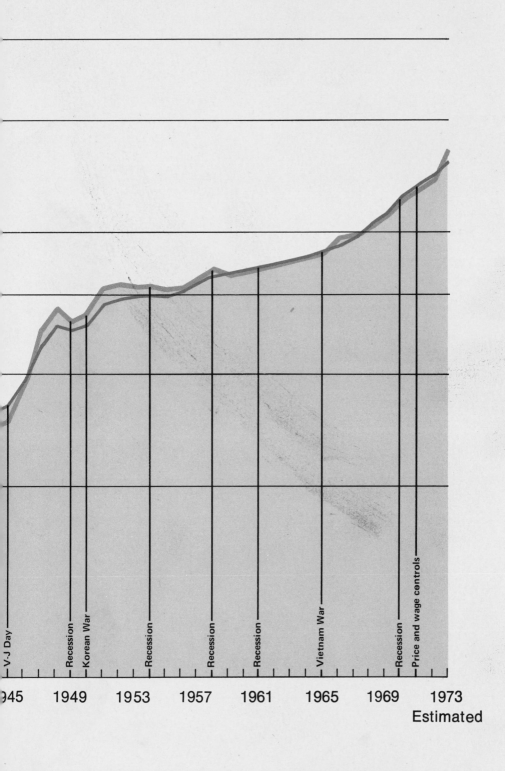

V-J Day
Recession
Korean War
Recession
Recession
Recession
Vietnam War
Recession
Price and wage controls

945   1949   1953   1957   1961   1965   1969   1973
Estimated

Introduction to business
a societal approach

Prov. to form
How raise begin cap'tl
How make decision to
those profits
what liability of founders
what terminates the business
relationship
participation in manag.
by "Founders
assessment rights
of company onto
Founders

Introduction to business
a societal approach

Walter W. Perlick
Colorado State University

Raymond V. Lesikar
Louisiana State University

Revised edition   1975

BUSINESS PUBLICATIONS, INC.   Dallas, Texas   75231

Irwin-Dorsey International   London, England   WC2H 9NJ
Irwin-Dorsey Limited   Georgetown, Ontario   L7G 4B3

Revised Edition
First Printing, April 1975

ISBN 0-256-01690-9
Library of Congress Catalog Card No. 74–27542

Printed in the United States of America

Learning Systems Company—
a division of Richard D. Irwin, Inc.—has developed a
Programmed Learning AID
to accompany texts in this subject area.
Copies can be purchased through your bookstore
or by writing PLAIDS,
1818 Ridge Road, Homewood, Illinois 60430.

To students who remain unknown,
To friends who go unnamed, and
To our wives, Arlene and Lu, whose
love and support was unfaltering
during the arduous months of
writing this book.

Preface

Writing a text for a course on Introduction to Business is a complex and difficult undertaking. When we wrote the first edition several years ago, we set for ourselves the ambitious goal of writing a text that was both relevant and interesting. Our own experiences in teaching this course convinced us that Introduction to Business was a vital course in college curriculums, and that with the proper text could continue to provide a valuable "first look" at the world of business for countless students.

We recognized then, and we recognize now, that writing a "relevant" text is a complex project. For as we all know, relevance is a constantly changing phenomenon. Nonetheless, the airing of timely issues, and an attempt to point out the importance of past events in shaping future problems and opportunities, stood as a primary objective in this revision.

Similarly, we redoubled our efforts to make the text readable and understandable to all students. We recognize that students in Introduction to Business cover the full spectrum of talents and abilities. They come from varied environments and are enrolled in educational programs ranging from the smallest part-time activities to those of the large, multidimensional universities. To communicate with all of these students, we have concentrated on using a controlled vocabulary and short, concise sentences and paragraphs. At the same time, however, we have made every effort to assist the student in the development of a broad business vocabulary. Greater effort has been made to define all new terms when they are introduced, as well as including them in the Glossary. The net result, we believe, is a text written at a reading level commensurate with the abilities of most students and yet one that attempts to enrich the student's understanding of the language of business.

Several significant changes will be found in this edition of *Introduction to Business: A Societal Approach*. We have added a completely new chapter on economics and business at the very start of the text. In this chapter, the private enterprise system is discussed, the basic points of economics so necessary to understanding the profit system are developed, and comparisons are made with other systems. The chapter on business philosophies has been given a new dimension, primarily through a better discussion of the great economists of times past. The marketing chapters have been heavily revised and updated to include the latest concepts of that discipline. The government/business relations chapter examines the anti-trust problem in depth, and the multinational business firm is the subject of extensive discussion in the chapter on international business. Finally, the Appendix on careers in business has been expanded and updated.

In other respects, the text continues to reflect the basic structure of the first edition. The basic division into three parts: one stressing the historical and philosophical background of business; a second stressing the functional aspects of business; and the third stressing business and society relationships, remains as before. New biographical sketches, new mini-cases and new discussion questions abound in this edition. All in all, we believe this edition of the text represents an improvement over the highly successful first edition. We trust you will agree with this belief.

March 1975   WALTER W. PERLICK
                                                                 RAYMOND V. LESIKAR

Acknowledgments

As we reflect on the extensive work which has gone into this revision, we cannot help but feel a heavy debt of gratitude to all who helped us. There were many. Some of them played a formal role in our work, and these we are able to recognize individually in the paragraphs that follow. But there were others whose relationships were rather informal—such as those who passed along suggestions to us at professional meetings, through correspondence, in telephone conversations, and the like. To this group we extend our sincere thanks. Even though we cannot recall them specifically, their contributions were significant.

Among those who formally contributed to our work, we must first acknowledge those scholars in the field who reviewed the book. Don Porterfield, The University of Texas at San Antonio; Donald D. Myrold, North Dakota State University; and Rhae M. Swisher, Jr., Troy State University, reviewed the first edition and made many valuable suggestions for improving the work. Jack Hill, University of Nebraska at Omaha, and Gary Falkenberg and Henry Gram, both of Oakland Community College, very ably reviewed the revised manuscript. In addition, Sonja Brett, Andrew Lonyo, and Edward Laube, all of McComb Community College, reviewed various parts of the completed work. And Tom Hendrick, University of Colorado, reviewed the chapter on operations/production management, which is the area of his specialization. The contributions of all of these most competent people appear liberally throughout the book.

Special thanks are due Wilma Jean Alexander, Illinois State University, and Dave Adams, Oakland Community College, who are the authors of the *Student's Guide to Learning Experiences,* which accompanies the book. In addition to their workbook roles, they also served as reviewers. Their many valuable suggestions contributed significantly to the revision. And to Robert Ristau, Eastern Michigan University, goes our appreciation for his professional review of the workbook material.

We must acknowledge, also, the informal reviews, comments, and suggestions made by certain key users of the first edition. Louis Hoekstra, Grand Rapids Community College; Donald Nelson, College of DuPage; J. H. Foegen, Winona State University; and Carl Nielson, Wichita State University, were especially helpful. Deserving of special recognition for their suggestions for innovative techniques in using the text are Phil Swensen, Wisconsin State University, and Caroline Boyer, University of Cincinnati.

We owe a note of very special thanks to the New York Life Insurance Company for permitting us once again to use their classic brochure on business careers. As they did in the first edition, we are confident that students will find this material to be genuinely helpful.

In addition, each of us made use of a wide assortment of our friends and associates. At the Baton Rouge end of our partnership, we are indebted to Karen Arnold and Danny Worrell for their research assistance. Likewise, Gloria Armistead receives our appreciation for her expert secretarial assistance.

At the Fort Collins work scene, we are indebted to Eliot Waples, Chairman, Department of Finance and Real Estate, and to Dean Don Dobler for their support and encouragement. Our appreciation is also due Debra Atkinson for her typing assistance. And to teaching colleagues A. J. Wedell and Linda Bates goes a very special thanks for their ideas, suggestions, questions, and other contributions too numerous to mention. Finally, a word of thanks is due John Sorbie, professor of art at Colorado State, for his advice on the art design of this book.

Last but far from least, we are indebted to our wives. To Arlene Perlick and Lu Lesikar for their patience, encouragement, love, and understanding throughout the ordeal of the revision we are truly and forever grateful.

March 1975   WALTER W. PERLICK
                                               RAYMOND V. LESIKAR

Contents

part one Perspectives on American industry

This study of business begins with a brief look at the essentials of economics, and a look at the economic characteristics that distinguish American business. In this review, we examine the energy crisis, and note its impact on American business. Following this necessary introduction, we continue our analysis with a study of American business history.

Although we recognize that the study of history does not necessarily endear itself to students of business administration, we must begin here. For without a solid understanding of where we have been, we cannot expect to know where we are going.

Next, we study the social and economic philosophies of business. We do this so that we can understand the *why's* underlying our business growth; *why* business expanded and took the form it did; *why* it has been criticized for some of its actions; and *why* the dilemmas and predicaments that confront the businessman exist and are worthy of our attention.

Given these perspectives on American industry, we will be prepared to pursue the examination of the structure and functions of business enterprise.

Adam Smith
(1723–1790)

The first great economist

Adam Smith was a Scottish economist and philosopher whose famous work *Inquiry into the Nature and Causes of the Wealth of Nations* is responsible for his being known as the first great economist. Born in early 1723, Smith was educated at the University of Glasgow, and later at Balliol College in Oxford. In 1748 he began lecturing at the University of Edinburgh. In 1751 he was appointed professor of logic at Glasgow University and in 1752 he assumed the chair of moral philosophy. During these years, Smith befriended another great philosopher, David Hume, who became a life-long friend. Smith began lecturing and writing letters on the subject of economics, particularly on what he called "the obvious and simple system of natural liberty," which later was to become the basis for *The Wealth of Nations*.

In 1763, Smith resigned his professorship to assume the lucrative position as tutor to the young duke of Buccleuch. In this post, Smith traveled a great deal in France, where he had the chance to meet and know such intellectual leaders as Turgot, D'Alembert, Morellet, Helvetius, and Francois Quesnay. Their influence caused Smith to resume work on his magnum opus, and during the next ten years, Smith worked on his ideas of political economy. In 1776, Smith's ideas became known to the World, as *The Wealth of Nations* was finally published. In it he expounded many of the ideas of free enterprise and nonintervention in the affairs of business by government that were to become imbodied in the American economic system.

Adam Smith died in 1790, following a long and painful illness. Unfortunately, much of his later works were destroyed shortly before his death. It is thought that Smith was working on two other major treatises, one on the theory and history of law and one on the sciences and art. These, however, have been lost forever.

1

Economics and business: The relevant issues of our time

Business: The oldest of the arts, the newest of the professions.

——A. Lawrence Lowell

INTRODUCTION

It may seem a bit strange to find a text beginning with a chapter that is titled as modestly as "Economics and Business: The *Relevant* Issues of OUR Time." Several people will probably read that title and say to themselves, "Nothing like a little conceit on the part of these authors." Hopefully, however, those persons will actually read this chapter (and ideally, the 20 that follow it) before passing final judgment on the issue of our conceit. Because if they do, hopefully the full meaning of that title will manage to come forth in all its force. For business and economics *are* the relevant issues of this day. Nothing is accomplished in the world today that does not intimately involve the world of business and economics.

Nor can any business or economic decision be made without having major impact on the lives of someone—or even everyone—in the world. Thus, for those of us about to embark on a study of the business system, it behooves us to first make sure we understand the basics of what business and economics are all about.

Why economics and business are "the relevant issues"

Think, for a moment, of the most serious problems facing the world today. If we were to ask the average people to name them, no doubt they would list quite a variety of problems. But almost certainly their list would include (*a*) inflation, (*b*) jobs, (*c*) urban redevelopment, (*d*) finding food to feed the world's population, (*e*) war and peace, and (*f*) ecology or environmental concerns. Each of these issues involves, essentially, those related to business and economics.

Inflation   Inflation, in very simple terms, refers to a condition of rising prices for goods and services. If prices rise faster than incomes of people, it results in these people being able to acquire fewer and fewer goods with their money. Money seems to be losing value; that is, it buys less tomorrow than it does today, and it buys less today than it did yesterday. Inflation is the culprit.

Inflation is caused by a wide variety of factors, but essential to all of them are pressures in the economic or business systems. Economic systems such as those found in the United States are based, essentially,

FIGURE 1–1

Inflation affects corporations, too (corporate earnings retained by businesses, in 1965 prices)

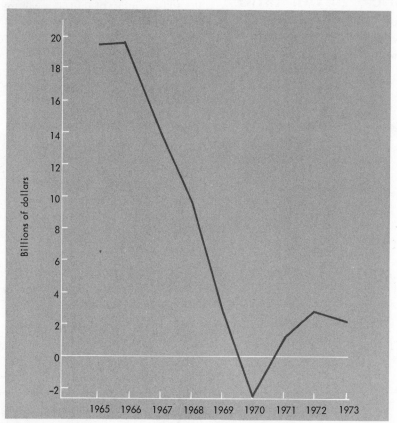

Source: Machinery and Allied Products Institute, as reported in *The Wall Street Journal*, February 21, 1974.

on the laws of supply and demand. That is, the price we pay for goods depends on the supply of those goods available for purchase, and the demand for those goods by potential consumers. If demand is greater than supply, prices will rise. Similarly, if supply happens to fall off, much like gasoline supplies did in the summer of 1973–74, prices will also rise. Whether inflation is caused by rising demand or falling supply, however, is not of particular concern here. What is important to understand is that business is intimately involved in the problem, no matter which factor (rising demand or falling supply) is causing the problem. For no matter what else happens, business is the institution that ultimately produces the goods for sale. Changes in the supply and demand for goods operate directly on the business firm.

Jobs There is little doubt that the issue of employment is intimately related to the subject of business. Indeed, the question of employment looms large in the minds of many students, particularly when they see upward of 6 percent of the nation's work force going unemployed.

Why business allows some people to go unemployed, and what forces are at work in the economy that determine whether there shall be unemployment, is a complex, but very relevant question. In many ways, business is both the culprit and the hero insofar as employment is concerned. New technology is responsible for many of our cherished goods, and accounts for a great part of our high living standard. It also accounts for some of our unemployment, as people are replaced by machines at increasing frequencies. True, the production of these machines creates, in many instances, more jobs than the machines themselves replace. But the new jobs require new knowledge and skills—training that older and unskilled workers do not have. These people become victims of the technological revolution we are presently facing. Business faces a major part in trying to help resolve this problem.

Urban redevelopment The role of business in resolving urban problems is much more difficult to explain and justify than is its role in providing jobs. Everyone is aware of the fact that government and various charitable organizations have tried to resolve this problem, and have met with only limited success. But what about business?

Actually, business has been one of the most active—if not well-publicized—institutions in the nation when it comes to involvement in this area. Companies such as Xerox, IBM, Eastman Kodak, SKF Inc., and many, many others, have spent vast sums of money and devoted countless hours of human energy helping to resolve this problem. For the most part, these efforts have been modestly successful. As for a reason *why* they have done this, well, perhaps a quote from the most famous American capitalist, John D. Rockefeller, summarizes it best: "If a man has succeeded, he has brought upon himself corresponding responsibilities, and our institutions devoted to helping men to help themselves need the brains of the American businessman as well as part of his money." Business leaders know that if they are to continue to have an environment in which business can grow and prosper, the social structure must be such that large segments of the population do not feel deprived of their basic share of prosperity. As Kenneth Clark, noted black psychologist has said, "If business doesn't help, who will?" In this text, Chapters 19 and 20 are devoted to a closer examination of the role of business in resolving social problems.

Feeding the world   At first glance, the problem of finding adequate sources of food for the peoples of the world sounds like a problem for farmers and agricultural specialists, and not business executives. Today, however, the distinction between farmers and business leaders is not nearly as great as it may have once been. Farm management today is big business. Many of the larger farms are actually corporate farms, owned and operated by business corporations. Moreover, the research in new seeds, insecticides and pesticides is all the result of private industry. Even the farm machinery and implements are produced by corporate structures. Because of the productive genius of the American business system and the farmer, the American farmer is the most efficient and productive in the world. Business has done an admirable job in assisting in this great accomplishment. What is needed now is a continued effort on the part of business to help find a solution to this difficult problem.

War and peace   Few issues are more basic to our organized world than the issue of war or peace. Governments, obviously, are the prime makers of war and peace. And yet, the motivation behind nations that go to war are more often than not, economic motives. When nations lack raw materials that are vital to their survival, and those nations that do possess these materials refuse to trade under reasonable terms, war usually results. President Ford warned of this problem in a speech to the United Nations shortly after assuming office. The president directed his remarks at that time to the oil-producing nations of the world, warning that increasing prices and continued restriction of production would cause havoc in the industrial economies of the world. He noted that, in the past, when nations of the world attempted to use their natural resources as weapons in the world, war usually resulted. Ford dramatized his point by noting that if war were to occur again, it might well be for the last time.

Clearly, the challenge to the business community is there. If industry can, for example, successfully learn to extract oil from the oil shale found in the western states, and if it can learn how to extract the coal deposits from the earth without causing too much damage, the nation may again become self-sufficient in energy. Certainly this development would go a long way toward easing international tensions.

Unfortunately, much of industry's efforts at extracting coal and oil

FIGURE 1–2

Number of farms and workers dwindle as farm production soars

The revolution on the farm: Much greater efficiency...

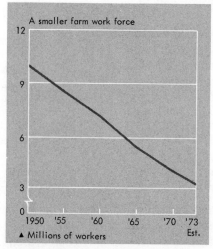

A smaller farm work force

▲ Millions of workers

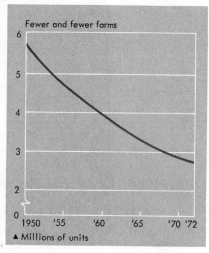

Fewer and fewer farms

▲ Millions of units

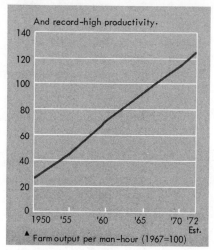

And record-high productivity.

▲ Farm output per man-hour (1967=100)

Source: Data, Agricultural Department.

from the ground have sparked other problems. Most noteworthy of these is the problem of ecology and environmental preservation.

Ecology and the environment Certainly one of the most publicized problems facing the world today concerns the environment in which we live. Air and water pollution, strip mining, oil spills, noise, waste—these are but a few of the concerns that fall under this heading. Business, of course, is intimately tied to both the problems and the possible solutions

to those problems. Many people fault business for having caused pollution—and indeed, business *has* caused pollution. But so has government, at all levels. And so have people. One estimate has more pollutants
being caused by cigarette smoking than from the automobiles on the
streets of New York!

Actually, the relationship between economics and ecology is a lot
closer than most people realize. Indeed, the very words "economics" and
"ecology," originate from the same Greek word. Ecology refers to the
science of natural life. Economics, on the other hand, refers to the science
of human life. In our complex society, the above two fields must, of
necessity, progress together. For we cannot long have anything resembling an advanced society if we fail to protect the natural environment
surrounding us.

ECONOMICS: WHAT IT'S ALL ABOUT

In the preceding paragraph, economics was defined as the science of
human life. That is, "economics is the study of how men and society
choose, with or without the use of money, to employ *scarce* productive
resources, which could have alternative uses, to produce various commodities over time and distribute them for consumption, now and in the
future, among various peoples and groups in society."[1] Admittedly, this
is quite a complex definition, but it does do a good job of summarizing
economics. For no society can exist without *someone, somewhere,*
answering the following questions:

a.   Given a limited amount of resources, *what* should we produce?
b.   Given the size and complexity of our society, for *whom* shall our
     resources be used?
c.   What short- and long-term goals do we as a society choose to strive
     for? That is, *why* should we choose to produce one good instead of
     another?

Why economic systems vary

In any organized society, it is necessary that some individual or group
of individuals exercise the responsibility for making the decisions that
ultimately answer the foregoing questions. Just who it is that does make
that decision depends, to a great extent, on the political system that
operates in the economy.

If we were to look at the world's political systems, and try to categorize
them, we could probably develop a breakdown that resembles that shown
in Figure 1–3. Admittedly, this is an oversimplification, but the break-

---

[1] Paul Samuelson, *Economics,* 7th ed. (New York: McGraw-Hill Book Company, 1967),
p. 5.

FIGURE 1–3

The spectrum of economic and political systems

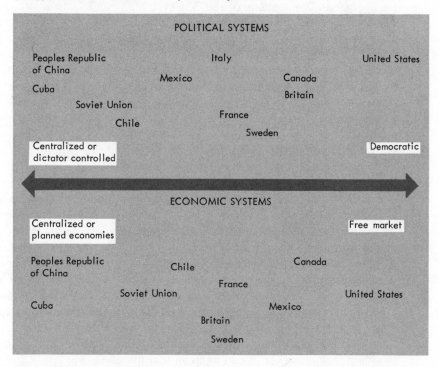

POLITICAL SYSTEMS

Peoples Republic of China

Cuba

Soviet Union

Chile

Italy

Mexico

France

Sweden

Canada

Britain

United States

Centralized or dictator controlled

Democratic

ECONOMIC SYSTEMS

Centralized or planned economies

Free market

Peoples Republic of China

Cuba

Soviet Union

Chile

France

Britain

Sweden

Mexico

Canada

United States

down is useful nonetheless. As Figure 1–3 shows, a strong relationship exists between the type of political system in a country and the kind of economic system in that country.

It has already been noted that Figure 1–3 is an oversimplification. That is, no economy in the world today is purely democratic, with all of the basic economic decisions being made by the open market. Similarly, it is doubtful that any economy in the world is totally dictated to from a small group of people. For example, the U.S. economy is not totally determined by a "free market." Many economic decisions are made or influenced by government edict. And it is unlikely that every economic decision in the People's Republic of China is determined by central authority. Undoubtedly, small peasant farmers have some leeway in deciding what crops will be produced and where. Despite these obvious situations, however, we can generalize and state that in countries where decisions are made only by a handful or either elected or self-appointed leaders, the economic decisions tended to be centralized also. Under a dictatorship, for example, one person might make the important economic decisions. As sole ruler, he and he alone has the power to make these decisions.

Similarly, under a Communist form of government a small group of controllers determines priorities as to how productive resources should be allocated. The leaders of the Soviet Union, for example, arbitrarily decide how much money to spend on the exploration of outer space. Their decision is assumed to have already considered the military and political consequences of the action, as well as the economic activity that must be delayed because of a limited national budget. In effect, the trade-off of "guns for butter" is determined by a central authority and is not usually subject to revision by other forces. With each of these forms of government, however, priorities are decided somewhat arbitrarily, with political and military considerations often carrying more weight than considerations relating to the economic welfare of the people.

By way of contrast, the economic decision-making process in democracies tends to reside not with central authorities, but with the people themselves. Generally speaking, in democracies, each individual is free to produce, within limits, whatever he or she wants, and in whatever way he deems most appropriate. The person may join with other individuals in the formation of large economic units called *businesses,* which can compete with other businesses for the sale dollars of the consumers. Sometimes individuals become quite successful at providing goods and services for a reasonable price, and the institutions they create grow to be large industrial firms. Other times the business ventures end in failure, simply because the product or service that was being provided or the price that was being charged was unsatisfactory to potential customers. In either case, however, it can be seen that the combined effect of many suppliers of goods and many buyers of goods, when joined together create a *marketplace* where the economic decisions of the society are finally determined. Those producers that are successful are those that have manufactured goods that the market of buyers wanted. Those that failed did so because the total market of buyers decided to forego that particular product in favor of something else. Thus, one can summarize by saying that in democracies the major economic decisions are determined by the market forces of supply and demand.

The American economic system

In the United States, most economic decisions are made by the market forces of supply and demand. There are some decisions, however, which are not made by the marketplace, but instead come from governmental bodies. The decision to produce automobiles, for example, was determined solely by individuals operating in the marketplace. They thought such a product would be in demand by the public, and they were right. They profited handsomely, as a result of making a decision with which the free marketplace agreed. The decision to put seat belts in those cars, however, did not emanate from the marketplace. Rather, the decision was imposed on the automobile manufacturers by government, which insisted that safety features be incorporated into the cars. We can find countless other examples of both privately determined and governmentally determined economic decisions. How our system decides whether government or private enterprise shall be the decision maker for any particular product or service, consequently, is an important one, and is a feature that has distinguished our economic system from most other systems in the world.

Economic decisions in a free enterprise system In a free enterprise system, decisions as to what shall be produced, how it shall be produced and for whom, are normally decided by those persons or organizations that control the *factors of production.* There are, essentially, four factors of production: (*a*) land, (*b*) labor, (*c*) capital, and (*d*) entrepreneurship.

The factors of production

Land Land is required, obviously enough, for any economic activity to exist. The land on which the activity takes place may be owned by the operators of that activity, or it may be rented from others. In either event, land is a requirement for the production of goods and services to occur. To the classical economist, land was the indestructible gift of nature.

Labor Labor is the contribution, mental or physical, of human beings (employees or workers) to the economic activity. In some situations, labor may be supplied by only one or two people. Or, as is sometimes the case, thousands and thousands of people may be required to perform the activity. With the growing number of service industries in existence today, labor is an extremely important factor of production. For some firms, however, automation has replaced manual labor at many tasks.

Capital Capital refers to all of the nonhuman factors found in the production process. It might be called the nonhuman work force that is needed to produce the economic activity. Thus, capital includes such things as machinery and equipment, tools, the building, and so on. Capital also includes, quite logically, the money or financial resources needed to perform the activity. Thus, it is easy to see that the more capital that can be accumulated for a particular economic activity, the more complex and larger the unit performing that activity can become. In business, the growth of a company is directly related to the capital resources available to that firm.

Entrepreneurship Entrepreneurship refers to the managerial skills and talents that are necessary to bring the other three factors of production together. Thus, entrepreneurship can be looked upon as a catalyst. It represents the skill that is necessary to get the economic activity performed. The entrepreneurs originate economic activity. They take risks, particularly financial risks. They hire workers, assemble capital and machines, sell goods and services, and receive any profits that may result.

As has been noted, in a free enterprise system, the holder or possessor of these factors of production determines to a great extent what shall be produced. Usually, private individuals possess these factors of production; that is, individuals possess title to most of the land in our country. Individuals also possess the labor to do work, and they alone determine what work they are willing to perform. Individuals also possess most of the financial wealth in the country. Many times they agree to put their financial wealth in institutions called banks, for which they receive a reward, usually called interest. The bank in turn "rents" the use of this money to others, and charges them interest. The money, however, is still owned by private individuals. Finally, individuals are the ones that willingly take risks by agreeing to invest their money in such ventures known as businesses. These ventures sometimes make the risk takers (or entrepreneurs) very rich. Sometimes, they make them very poor. But whichever occurs, it is usually the individual that performs the vital task of entrepreneurship.

Even in a free enterprise system, however, there are occasions when the various factors of production are assumed by the various governmental bodies. For example, the Constitution allows the government to create and maintain an armed force. The purpose, of course, is to provide protection for society, from foreign aggressors. The government accomplishes this task by ordering individuals to provide a few years worth of labor to the government. (This was the function of the draft.) Or, it acquires the needed labor force by bidding for it in the marketplace. That is, the government offers wages, career opportunities, education, and so on, to all who will agree to work for the government by being a soldier.

The government also acquires the needed land by purchasing it from its previous owners. This land is then converted to military bases. To acquire the land, and to pay the wages of the work force, the government has been provided with the power of taxation. The government taxes people (another way of saying it charges the people for the service their tax money will provide) and uses the tax revenue to pay for the labor and land. Finally, some of the people it hires perform the management function. In the case of the armed forces, this management function is performed by the generals and admirals.

Thus, we can see that in the free enterprise system, even the government must bargain for much of the factors of production necessary to perform an economic activity. This fact is a distinguishing factor between free enterprise and dictatorships, or other countries which do not allow freedom of choice and ownership. In these other countries, individuals do not have a choice of whether they will "rent" or "sell" their factors of production to the government. The government in these other countries simply seizes whatever it needs.

How the law of supply and demand works

The law of supply and demand works through what is known as the competitive price system. That is, all of those people or institutions that possess a particular factor of production, decide for themselves what they will do with that factor. Some possessors of a factor of production will decide to keep the factor, and perhaps try to obtain the other factors necessary for them to produce some good or service. Thus, the holder or owner of a skill (labor)—for example an auto mechanic—may decide to seek out someone who will rent or sell a location (land) and possibly a building (capital). Also, the mechanic may seek financial assistance (capital) in order to acquire the tools needed to perform the job. The mechanic, if successful, may try to perform the management (entre-preneurship) tasks necessary to make a success of his endeavor.

Other holders of a factor of production may decide to sell or rent their factors to someone else. Because the factors of production are limited in their total supply, there are often several people or institutions that desire those factors. When this happens, the holders of those factors offer them to the highest bidder. Whoever pays the most gets the use of the factors of production. This explains how the *supply* of factors of production gets allocated.

The institution or person acquiring a factor of production realizes a price must be paid for those factors that are not owned outright. The price they are willing to pay for the use of any factor depends on several things. First, the price depends on the total available supply of that factor. The more abundant a particular factor of production is, the lower the price that need be paid for it. Second, the use to which that factor will be put often determines the price that will be paid for it. That is, if the producer or supplier of a particular good or service in society needs the factor badly enough, and feels that the product will still be in demand on the marketplace even if the price is raised (because of the price of the factor) the producer or supplier may willingly pay more for the factor. On the other hand, if the producer of a product does not think the product can command a price that is high enough, he or she will refuse to bargain for the expensive factor of production—and may cease to produce the product. Thus, we find that the *demand* for factors, as well as the *demand* for the ultimate product or service produced by those factors, plays a vital role in our system.

The historical role of supply and demand in America The laws of supply and demand are perhaps the most basic aspect of our economic system. Yet, throughout our history, either supply or demand has played an extremely important part in shaping our economic and social structure.

In the 19th century, for example, one of our major economic concerns centered around the *supply* problem. Wars were waged with Mexico, treaties were signed with Spain and France, and so forth, all of which helped provide us with one particular factor of production; namely, land. Immigration was encouraged, partly to stimulate the availability of still another factor; namely, labor. The abundance of resources, and some unusually bright and ambitious individuals, helped to build large industries, which both required and produced capital. Finally, concurrent with the development of these large businesses was the development of a new breed of business leaders. Management—or entrepreneurship—came of age, as the United States emerged from the Industrial Revolution as the most powerful economic nation in the world.

In the 20th century, the emphasis on supply and demand underwent a swift and dramatic change. Henry Ford's mastery of mass-production techniques suddenly meant that several of the factors of production changed significantly in importance. Labor tended to diminish in importance, while the demand for capital increased severalfold. Given sufficient capital resources, an almost unending stream of goods could be produced. Indeed, supplying goods no longer was the major problem. Instead, finding enough *demand* for all that could be produced became the paramount problem. To help stimulate the demand for goods, advertising came of age. New products were constantly introduced, and old products were designed in such a way as to limit their usefulness. The age of planned obsolescence was upon us.

ENERGY AND RAW MATERIALS: A REEMERGENCE OF A SUPPLY PROBLEM

The latter half of this century has seen a dramatic reversal of trends once again. After a half-century of "conspicuous consumption" of goods of all kinds, the United States has suddenly found itself with a shortage plagued economy, once again. This time, however, the shortage is of a different kind. Whereas the supply problem of the 1800s was because of a primitive production economy—one which was unable to satisfy demand—the new supply crisis involves a lack of natural resources. Quite simply, the United States and the rest of the world found themselves running out of the raw materials needed to produce the goods their respective economies required. Nowhere was the problem more in evidence than in the most basic of all resources: that of energy.

THE ENERGY CRISIS

At the present time, the United States has approximately 6 percent of the world's population. That 6 percent, however, consumes over 35 per-

FIGURE 1–4

U.S. domestic energy demand

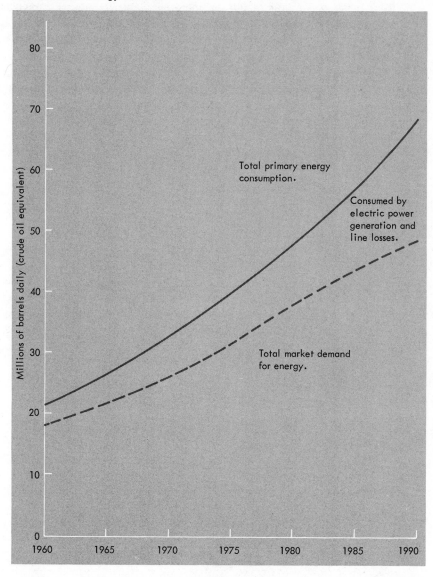

cent of the world's total energy output. The average American uses as much energy in just a few days as half the world's population uses, on an individual basis, in one year.[2] Moreover, as Figure 1–4 shows, the

[2] Statistics are abstracted from A Report on the Joint Committee on Atomic Energy, "Understanding the National Energy Dilemma" (Washington, D.C.: The Center for Strategic and International Studies, Georgetown University, 1973).

growth in the usage of energy by this country has shown no signs of
slowing down. Given the fact that virtually all of our energy originates
from fossil or natural resources materials, and in most cases is non-
replaceable in the short run, it was inevitable that at some point in time,
the world would simply run out of energy sources. The 1970s saw a realization of that fear.

   Where our energy comes from   America's energy resources are, and
have been, essentially fossil-fuel based. Some part of our energy, of

FIGURE 1–5

U.S. energy sources 1950–70

1950: 16.1 million barrels per day = 100%   1960: 21.2 million barrels per day = 100%

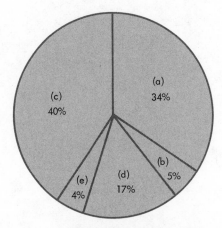
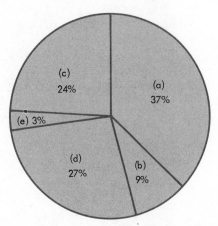

1970: 32.5 million barrels per day = 100%

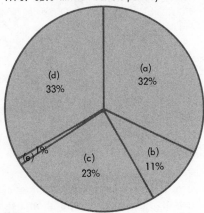

Key:
(a) Oil—Domestic
(b) Oil—Imports
(c) Coal
(d) Gas
(e) Hydropower and other

course, comes from nuclear and hydropower sources, but these have been minor sources. Figure 1–5 shows the major sources of energy over the past 30 years. Naturally, these energy sources have had a major impact on the development of our economy. The automobile, for example, was built around an engine that could burn petroleum products. As a consequence, shortages in the supplies of these fuels can have a major impact on our continued economic growth. Unfortunately, shortages in the energy field have been focused primarily on these fuels. A closer look at each of the major sources of energy will, perhaps, put the energy crisis in better perspective.

Oil   Without question, the major source of energy for the United States is oil. Most of the world's oil is, of course, found in the Arab nations of the Middle East. The embargo imposed by the Arab nations in 1973, and the agreement by the Organization of Petroleum Exporting Countries (OPEC) to limit production has put the industrial nations of the Western world in a bind. America has, in some ways, been fortunate because it has a reasonably large reserve of oil within it own boundaries. But even here, the amount of oil that the United States can produce falls far short of what is needed. It is estimated that oil needs of the United States will approximate 21.5 million barrels per day by 1980, of which just about half will need to be provided by foreign sources.

Part of the problem with a heavy reliance on foreign fuel sources, of course, is the threat that the resource will be used as a political weapon by the nation or nations controlling that resource. Thus, the United States would prefer, if at all possible, to become as self-sufficient in its energy needs as it can. A reemphasis on oil exploration by this country is most certainly one possible answer. However, time becomes a critical factor. Oil industry experts project that it takes from one to three years to complete the geophysical work relating to oil discovery. It takes another five to seven years to build a refinery. If the oil is discovered in offshore waters, it takes from four to seven years to complete the drilling and building of a platform. Add these time factors to the obvious cost problems and to the uncertainty that anywhere near enough oil can be found, and we can see that a better answer to the oil shortage might be to find alternative energy sources. One such source is natural gas.

Natural gas   Natural gas has been a major source of energy for some time. Back in the 1950s, gas was one of the cheapest of fuel sources, partly because we had a large number of gas wells in production, and partly because the Federal Power Commission kept the price of gas at very low levels. Indeed, the price of gas was kept so low that it tended to discourage further exploration for gas. Gas transmission companies, unable to obtain more and more gas from the gas fields, began to restrict their deliveries, forcing many customers to turn to oil instead. Oil companies, given a restricted supply and increasing demand, began to produce additional heating oil and also cut back on gasoline production. This led directly to the gasoline shortages of 1973. Many proposals have been made to allow the developers of natural gas to charge what the market will bear. Such action, it is argued, will encourage more exploration for natural gas, and help alleviate our pressing needs for more energy. To date, these steps have not been taken.

Coal   Coal is one of our oldest energy sources. The United States is extremely fortunate in this respect, for it is estimated that over 20 percent of the world's coal deposits lie within the continental United States. If all available or known coal deposits were mined, and consumed at present rates, it would last for over 300 years. But problems exist in the use of coal. The biggest problem, of course, is environmental in nature. Strip mining is a popular and economical means of mining coal. But all too often, strip mining has left permanent scars on the countryside. Moreover, burning coal tends, in many instances, to violate the Clean Air Act of 1970. Much of the coal deposits in the United States are high in sulfur, a noxious pollutant when burned. One big hope is to turn coal into oil and gas, but economical ways for effecting that conversion have not yet been developed.

Nuclear reactors   Nuclear energy has been one of the great hopes for resolving our energy crisis and also one of our great disappointments. The combination of skyrocketing costs (a doubling in the past three years), fears of environmental contamination, and a lack of coordination in the building of reactors have been the primary reasons for the dis-

Where America's energy goes

	Percentage of all energy used in U.S.
Running Industry...................................	37.3
Powering transportation..........................	24.8
Driving cars.....................................	13.2
Driving trucks and buses.......................	5.5
Flying planes....................................	3.2
Driving farm and other off-road vehicles.........	1.2
Fueling ships and boats........................	1.0
Fueling trains..................................	0.7
Heating homes and offices.......................	17.9
Providing raw materials for chemicals, plastics....	5.5
Heating water for homes and offices..............	4.0
Air-conditioning homes and offices...............	2.5
Refrigerating food...............................	2.2
Lighting homes and offices.......................	1.5
Cooking food....................................	1.3
Other uses......................................	3.0

Source: Office of Science and Technology; Chase Manhattan Bank.
Note: Figures may add to more than 100% because of multiple uses of various energy forms.

appointing results. At the present time, it takes from five to ten years to build a reactor. To date, there has been a total lack of design coordination. Each new attempt at developing a nuclear plant has, consequently, required approval from more than 30 agencies. Progress, as previously stated, has been disappointing, and nothing that has happened thus far indicates that it will get any better in the future.

Shale oil One of the more interesting and promising sources of energy is shale oil. The western states of Colorado, Wyoming, and Utah contain the world's largest known reserve of a particular kind of rock—shale. This rock can be processed, and oil can be extracted from it. It is estimated that full development of the shale oil deposits could yield from 3 to 5 million barrels per day. However, problems exist here, also. Full development of the shale oil deposits would require using up all of the available water supply in those three states. Development of shale oil would also cause permanent environmental damage. Shale is unique in that the waste product that results is actually larger in volume than the shale rock was before processing out the oil. The waste, moreover, has the consistency of talc, is totally worthless, and will grow nothing. There is only one known place to put it: in the natural canyons of the Rocky Mountains. Environmentalists, of course, are absolutely opposed to any such move. And the volume of that waste is no small amount. It is estimated that to produce just 1 million barrels of oil would result in the removal of 1.7 billion tons of shale rock. By contrast, the entire coal production of the United States in 1973 amounted to only 0.6 billion tons.

We can see, therefore, that the problem of finding energy sources in sufficient quantity and at a price that will enable the American economy to grow and prosper without the threat of inflation, is a challenging one indeed. As it develops, business is the one institution that can possibly resolve this problem. Government can provide financial assistance and tax breaks, and research laboratories of nonprofit foundations may accomplish some needed research. But it will take the combined managerial, financial, marketing and production know-how of business to make a solution feasible. This is but one reason why business is "where the action is," and why business today must be considered one of the real "relevant" institutions in society.

THE RAW MATERIAL SHORTAGE

Energy sources, however, are not the only shortage problem confronting the American economy. Shortages of virtually all raw materials are developing, causing a whole maze of problems for business and the consumer. Where once the United States was almost self-sufficient in many raw materials, now it is dependent on others. The Mesabi iron range of Minnesota has been virtually depleted of the rich iron ore deposits that were once the envy of the world. The Keweenaw Peninsula of Michigan is barren of the virgin copper that once was extracted in huge boulders. And the softwood forests of the East and the Midwest have long since been logged off.

At first glance, it might seem one easy solution to the problem exists. One might ask, for example, What's so terribly wrong about finally being dependent upon the rest of the world for many of our needed raw materials? The answer, of course, is that in and of itself, there is nothing wrong about the nations of the world becoming mutually dependent on each other. As we shall see in Chapter 21, the idea of trade among nations, if carried to its ultimate, will result in a better way of life for all. However, in the world as we know it, we are a long way from accomplishing that feat. Nations of the world still have nationalistic tendencies. They still tend to first regard the growth of their own countries—even at the expense of other nations—as their first priority. Moreover, the United States faces a particularly troublesome problem. For years, the United States has had a higher wage schedule than most nations of the world; that is, we paid workers more per unit of work produced than anyone else. We could do so because we were able to obtain our raw materials at lower cost than most other nations could. Now this has all changed. For the first time, the United States must pay the same high prices for its raw materials as other nations have had to pay. But we, alone among nations, also pay our working force a higher wage than other countries do. As a result, American products tend to cost more to produce, and therefore, are more expensive on the world market. Consequently, American companies are losing more and more of the world market. This trend, if allowed to continue, may well result in a lowering of our standard of living in years to come.

A closer look at the materials shortage   Raw materials, as most people realize, exist in the world in a limited amount. As these resources are used up, the remaining supply diminishes. Moreover, the more industrialized the nations of the world become, the greater becomes their demand for more and more raw materials, thus making the resulting supply even smaller. Since World War II, the world has seen an unprecedented growth in industrialization. This has meant that the world's demand for raw materials has increased at ever-faster rates. The United States alone has consumed—from 1940—more raw materials than was consumed by all humanity in previous history! And the demand is increasing today at even faster levels. Obviously, such demand and consumption of basic resources cannot continue forever; sooner or later we are going to run out of basic elements. It appears that the shortage of raw materials is going to be sooner than most of us would like to believe.

The problem of a shortage of raw materials first became really apparent with the energy crisis of the early 1970s. When the supply of oil was suddenly restricted, the U.S. economy suffered through a whole series of apparent "shortages." Suddenly synthetic fibers were in short supply, primarily because they are developed from oil-based products. Dacron and nylon tricot (used in lingerie and hosiery) became scarce. In an effort to substitute, some manufacturers turned to cotton and wool. But foreign nations had been buying cotton and wool in larger and larger amounts, thus causing a shortage of supply in these areas.

The same thing happened with steel. Steel manufacturers in the United States were operating at almost full capacity. When the fuel shortage hit, they were forced to slow down production. As a result, less steel was available for the construction of electric generating plants (which construction would have helped alleviate the energy problem) and for the construction of oil refineries, which were in dire need. Also, bailing wire became in short supply. Farmers needed bailing wire to bail the hay they fed to their cattle. Normally, farmers could turn to a substitute, such as plastic or sisal fiber. But a drought halfway around the world sharply cut the production of sisal, and plastic, of course, required oil-based products, which were not available. Some farmers tried to obtain bailing machines, but these were constructed from steel, which was in short supply. The examples go on and on. Aluminum is in extremely high demand and short supply, partly because of material users switching from steel and plastics to aluminum, but more importantly, because aluminum also requires a great input of energy. Paper is in short supply, partly because timber is getting scarce, but also because milling companies require a large amount of energy. Fertilizers are in short supply, primarily because they rely heavily on nitrogen, and other natural gases.

As matters now stand, the problems promise to get worse before they get better. The rest of the world is demanding these same raw materials at even greater rates of increase than the United States. No doubt, American businesses will have to learn to cope with material shortages at an ever increasing scale in the years ahead. And this will not be easy. As can be seen in Figure 1–7, the United States consumes the lion's share of the

TABLE 1–2

Percent of world's resources consumed by the United States

Raw material	Percent consumed in late 1960s	Percent consumed in year 2000 (projected)
Crude steel	26.7	17.1
Iron ore	21.3	13.0
Sulfur	29.5	26.5
Aluminum	40.4	33.5
Copper	29.0	22.3
Zinc	26.6	21.0

world's natural resources now, and projections to the year 2000 indicate that the trend will continue.

Moreover, indications are that the United States will become even more dependent in the future on foreign nations for much of those resources. Figure 1–8 shows the development over the past 20 years of how the U.S. reliance on foreign sources for raw materials has grown.

THE CHALLENGE TO BUSINESS

The foregoing discussion should amply illustrate the challenge facing the business community. With a shortage of raw materials, business must find new ways of producing the products and services that are demanded by everyone. Moreover, it must do so at a cost and price that make it all worthwhile. With the energy crisis that we have just begun to recognize, the challenge becomes even greater, since most of our more advanced products and technology demand increasing levels of energy.

The challenge is compounded, moreover, by the fact that the world will become increasingly competitive in the demand for the raw materials that remain. Many of the newly developed countries are only beginning to appreciate a higher standard of living. Consequently, the pressure by their populations for more and more goods will increase to a point where we in the United States may have to make some difficult choices.

This problem, namely, the increasing competition for raw materials by other countries, has been growing for a long time, and actually is a by-product of the Industrial Revolution. Prior to the Industrial Revolution, there was no measurable difference in the living standards among the

TABLE 1–3

U.S. imports of resources

Resource	Percent of total consumption imported in	
	1950	1970
Aluminum	71	86
Chromium	100	100
Cobalt	92	96
Iron ore	6	14
Lead	59	40
Manganese	77	94
Mercury	92	38
Nickel	99	91
Petroleum	8	22
Platinum	91	98
Tin	100	100
Titanium	32	47
Tungsten	80	40
Zinc	37	60

world's nations. By 1850, the gap between the nations' living standards was as high as two times. That is, there were some countries where the standard of living was twice that found in some other countries. By 1950, the gap increased to ten times. By 1960 it was 15 times. It is estimated that by the year 2000, the difference between living standards may be as high as 30 times. These differences pose serious problems for those countries fortunate enough to have one of the better standards of living. For whenever the differences between peoples' ability to enjoy the good life gets far enough apart, that is, whenever there is formed a large body of people who are not enjoying the finer things in life, instability begins to rock the earth. Nations fall victim to revolution, and wars begin to break out. We in the United States may find ourselves to be one of the more vulnerable nations to this kind of threat. And yet, there is a solution. The potential cure for that problem lies in an enlightened business community; one which makes a legitimate and honest effort at becoming international in scope. Only by assisting other nations in their quest for a higher standard of living, can be the business executives assure themselves of an economy and a society, in which they can profitably function in the years ahead.

This then, is the challenge facing business. In the chapters of this text that follow, we will go back in time and trace the development of the American business system. We will examine its philosophical heritage, look at its growth, and examine its function. We will conclude by examining the way business presently interacts with the rest of society, including the role of business internationally. Hopefully, when completed, a better understanding, if not appreciation, of the American business system, will be had.

DISCUSSION QUESTIONS

1 Why do the authors call business and economics, "The relevant issues of our time"?

2 What is inflation? In your opinion, is inflation always bad? Is it always good? Explain.

3 The text quotes John D. Rockefeller as saying, "Our institutions devoted to helping men to help themselves need the brains of the American businessman as well as part of his money." In your opinion, what was Rockefeller referring to?

4 Everyone knows that industry is the source of much of our pollution. Suppose that business agreed to stop all production activities that resulted in pollution. What do you see happening to our society as a result?

5 Study the definition of economics given in the text. Why do you suppose the emphasis in that definition is on the words "choose" and "scarce"?

6 The text makes the statement that no nation in the world has a purely market-determined economy. Can you think of any instance in our history when the United States did, in fact, have a "free" economy?

7 What are the factors of production?

8 The law of supply and demand and the price system go hand in hand. Explain what each is, and how they relate to each other.

9 Examine Figure 1–4. Do you see anything on that graph that could present a challenge to the users of energy, that would help alleviate the energy problem? Explain.

MINI CASE

David and Joan Smith were students at a large midwestern university. Their class on basic business was examining alternative economic systems and the historical development of each. As their part in the class project, Dave and Joan were asked to explain why the United States was finding the energy problem so difficult to deal with. Their professor urged them to give special consideration to explaining why the Soviet Union wasn't facing the same problem.

As they pondered their response to this question, Dave and Joan noted that there were two important factors that needed to be considered in answering. These were:

1. The state of industrialization of both the United States and the Soviet Union, and the degree to which each of the respective economies are dependent on various types of energy; and

2. The way decisions are reached in each of their respective systems.

1. *How would you react to each of the two points raised by Dave and Joan?*

2. *Are there any other considerations that need to be evaluated?*

Dave and Joan thought about the similarity between the oil industry then, and the natural gas industry now.

1. *What parallel do you see between the two situations?*

2. *Are there any other industries the parallel might apply to?*

Elias Howe was one of the more important individuals to come upon the scene in America's "age of inventions." Although he was a man of modest means, Howe's invention of the sewing machine helped to speed the industrialization of New England, and with it raise the standard of living for all Americans.

Howe was born in Spencer, Massachusetts, on July 9, 1819. Although he attended school occasionally, Howe's fondness for machines, plus his family's need for income resulted in his spending much of his time working on a farm and at a local sawmill. After short stints at several jobs, Howe eventually went to work for a Cambridge watchmaker. Because his employer was a skilled and respected inventor, Howe was exposed to some of the finest minds and equipment in Massachusetts.

One day Howe overheard his employer state that he would construct a machine that could sew cloth. Given his own knowledge of milling machines and sewing techniques, Howe immediately set to work building his own machine. After five long years of work, Howe successfully completed his task, and received U.S. Patent No. 4750 for his sewing machine on September 10, 1846. To Howe's great dismay, however, his machine received little attention in the United States. Disappointed, Howe eventually went to England, where he sold British rights to his machine for £250. The money didn't last, however, and Howe found himself forced to sell his model and patent papers in order to obtain funds to return to America. In the ensuing years, Howe saw more and more American businessmen copying his machine. Angry, Howe instituted a patent infringement suit against them. The suit, one of the largest such suits in American history, was resolved in Howe's favor in 1854. From then until his death in 1867, Howe was never again poor, receiving royalties which sometimes amounted to as much as $4,000 per week.

Elias Howe
(1819–1867)

Inventor of the sewing machine

2

The development of American business

I find the greatest thing in this world is not so much where we started, as in what direction we are moving.

——*Oliver Wendell Holmes*

Our purpose in discussing business history is to provide a framework for the understanding of why business in America developed in the way it did. We want to describe also, the social atmosphere surrounding that development. To do so, however, requires that we first establish a "beginning" for the study of American business history. This, it develops, is not an easy thing to do. For instance, it would be easy to think of the founding of the United States in 1776 as the beginning of America's business history. This, however, would overlook the roots of our business history in England, where commerce and trade flourished for hundreds of years before the founding of the United States. Moreover, commerce was not unique to the British Isles. It had thrived for centuries on the European continent and, in fact, was engaged in by the Greeks, Egyptians, Sumerians, the Arabs, and the peoples of all the lands bordering the Mediterranean, the North Sea, and the Atlantic. Mention of commercial activity can be found in the Bible, the Koran, and even in the works of Aristotle and Plato.

To simplify our task, therefore, our discussion will begin with the period of industrial development that began in the early 1800s. This period, more than any other, seems to set the stage for the kind of economic structure America was eventually to develop.

A LITTLE BACKGROUND

The growth of the United States in the years following the Revolutionary War was nothing short of spectacular. From a simple, agricultural community, America grew quickly to become a recognized industrial nation in the world. Partly this was caused by an ever-increasing supply of labor. People in Europe heard about the "New World," and decided, in increasing numbers, to come to the United States and seek their fortunes. Thus, labor was always available for the small industries that had formed in the East, and plenty of farmland lay to the West for those who preferred to stake out their own claim.

Assisting this ever-increasing labor supply, moreover, was the relative freedom the United States had from the other nations in the world. England and France were feuding with each other, and Spain also had its problems. Thus, the United States was free to embark on a course of independent growth. Given the vast natural resources that were found in the United States, an industrious people, and a strong desire to grow and be prosperous, the United States grew to become one of the world's more formidable countries in just a few years.

The growth of sectionalism

Primarily an agricultural nation that depended on others for its manufactured goods, America developed quickly into three regional economies. The South, blessed with an ever-favorable climate and fertile land, became a leading supplier of cotton and tobacco. When Eli Whitney invented the cotton gin in 1793, the South's supremacy in world cotton markets became unquestioned. Trade rapidly developed with both England and the northern states. Southern plantations grew and prospered, and the South continued as a one-crop region for the next several decades.

The Midwest quickly became the breadbasket of America. Corn, wheat, and other grains were grown on the fertile lands of the Ohio Valley. Later, as westward expansion moved across the Mississippi, the Midwest brought new industries to the fore. One of the most prominent was the meat-packing industry. Cincinnati, for example, quickly became the center for the processing of much of the pork that was later transported to the population centers of the East.

The East, meanwhile, became known as the financial center of America. Because of its earlier colonization, and because many of the cities of the East were also major seaports, merchants found it easy to settle their financial business in the ports from where their goods were to be shipped. Thus, the East developed the financial markets for the country. However, when the War of 1812 broke out, money that had previously gone into the financing of foreign trade was turned inward, and instead was used to build manufacturing businesses at home. As a result, the East soon began developing into a manufacturing center as well.

The economy and the country grew in both size and complexity, and an atmosphere of innovation and invention permeated the land. As mentioned, Whitney's cotton gin pushed the South into the premier position in a world where cotton was king. Similarly, the invention of the steamboat by Robert Fulton in 1807 gave indications of things to come; by 1819 steam engines were in use as far west as St. Louis. Within 20 years, the steam engine was to find use on ships, and ultimately in locomotives, and the world of transportation was to undergo a drastic change.

THE IMPACT OF INNOVATIONS IN TRANSPORTATION AND COMMUNICATIONS

Given the regional development of the United States, it is fairly easy to see how the simultaneous development of the steamboat and the railroad had a profound impact on the developing country. Coupled with the extensive network of rivers and canals, the steamboat made it possible for goods to travel from the Midwest to the East coast via the Mississippi, the Gulf of Mexico, and the Atlantic Ocean.

Yet, as promising as the steamboat was, the growth of river and inland waterway traffic was largely overshadowed by the simultaneous development of the railroad. The steamboat, after all, was limited to the waterways in existence in the United States, plus the interconnecting canals. All too often, however, the various canals differed in size, so that the larger ships could pass through some of the canals but not through all of them. With the development of the railroad, however, goods of varying quantities could be shipped without concern for the size of the carrying vessel. Moreover, such goods could usually be shipped with greater frequency as well as more easily and faster than by steamboat.

The growth of the rails

The development of the railroads in the United States was undoubtedly one of the great events of the 1800s. For without that development, it is doubtful that the nation would have witnessed the tremendous growth in both population and industry that it did. To understand this statement, consider that building a railroad requires the following three things in very large quantity: (a) people, (b) physical capital, and (c) financial capital.

Rail expansion occurred well before the concepts of automation and mass production were known. Consequently, it took a large work force to lay even a few miles of track. One estimate had the railroads employing up to 1,000 people for every 100 miles of track laid. When one considers the statistics on tracks laid during these early years (see Table 2–1), one can appreciate how the railroads quickly became one of the leading employers in the land. This availability of many jobs, moreover, helped to attract large numbers of immigrants to this country, all of whom had heard about the great opportunities in the United States.

Along with people, the railroads were also in need of large amounts of physical capital. Physical capital can be thought of as all of those items actually needed in the construction of the railroad. This would include picks and shovels, steel rails, railroad engines and cars, lumber and construction materials, to name but a few. Since most of these items were needed at the point of construction, it was necessary that these industries

TABLE 2–1

Railroad mileage in existence, 1830–60

Year	Miles of track
1830	23
1832	229
1834	633
1836	1,273
1838	1,913
1840	2,818
1842	4,026
1844	4,377
1846	4,930
1848	5,996
1850	9,021
1852	12,908
1854	16,720
1856	22,076
1858	26,968
1860	30,626

Source: U.S. Bureau of the Census (Washington, D.C.).

"develop" right along with the railroads. Moreover, the increasing needs of the railroads meant that innovation in each of these industries was required. As this innovation occurred, more new products became available, more businesses started up, and still more people were put to work.

Finally, the railroads were in need of massive financial assistance. Workers had to be paid, supplies had to be purchased, and equipment was always in demand. The United States, however, was in a financial predicament. The government was in need of additional revenues for its various purposes, and other businesses were also in need of financing. Unfortunately, not enough funds were available here at home. As a result, a great deal of railroad financing occurred with the help of foreign lenders. Indeed, it has been estimated that a substantial portion of the total financing needs of the railroads was met by European banking interests alone. Moreover, much of the domestic financing that occurred developed only because the railroads were ingenious at developing new financial instruments. The wide variety of notes and financial instruments, combined with the European financial interests in the railroads, were indirectly responsible for an early development of stock exchanges, brokerage firms, and law firms that specialized in financial matters.

TABLE 2–2

Federal land grants to railroads, by state

State	Total reported acreage in state	Federal land grants (acres)	Percent of state area
Alabama...................	33,029,760	2,747,479	8.3
Arizona...................	72,901,760	7,695,203	10.6
Arkansas.................	33,985,280	2,586,970	7.6
California................	101,563,520	11,585,393	11.4
Colorado.................	66,718,080	3,757,673	5.6
Florida...................	37,478,400	2,218,705	5.9
Idaho....................	53,476,480	1,320,591	2.5
Illinois...................	36,096,000	2,595,133	7.2
Iowa.....................	36,019,200	4,711,328	13.1
Kansas...................	52,656,640	8,234,013	15.6
Louisiana................	31,054,720	1,375,000	4.4
Michigan.................	37,258,240	3,134,058	8.4
Minnesota................	53,803,520	9,953,008	18.5
Mississippi...............	30,538,240	1,075,345	3.5
Missouri..................	44,591,360	2,328,674	5.2
Montana..................	94,168,320	14,736,919	15.6
Nebraska.................	49,431,680	7,272,623	14.7
Nevada...................	70,745,600	5,086,283	7.2
New Mexico..............	77,866,240	3,355,179	4.3
North Dakota.............	45,225,600	10,697,490	23.7
Oregon...................	62,067,840	3,655,390	5.9
Utah.....................	54,346,240	2,230,085	4.1
Washington..............	43,642,880	9,582,878	22.0
Wisconsin................	35,938,560	3,666,062	10.2
Wyoming.................	62,664,960	5,749,051	9.2
Total............	1,217,269,120	131,350,533	9.3

Source: Robert S. Henry, "The Railroad Land Grant Legend in American History Texts," *The Mississippi Valley Historical Review*, Vol. 32, No. 2 (September 1945).

One final factor that certainly helped or contributed to the development of the railroads was the active assistance of the federal government. In order to encourage the railroads in the expansion westward of their rail lines, the government offered them "land grants." Essentially, land grants amounted to "free" land rights provided the railroads constructed their facilities through the land given them. As Table 2–2 reveals, a large portion of many western and southern states were awarded to the railroads if they would expand westward. In later years, the railroads were to attract many settlers to the various parts of the country, by offering

FIGURE 2–1

The railroads pushed hard to get their land grants developed

Courtesy of The Bettmann Archive.

them the opportunity to purchase land from the railroad. Prices for such land varied from $2 to $5 per acre. (See Figure 2–1.)

Improvements in communication

Another innovation that had tremendous impact in the 1800s was the telegraph. Samuel F. B. Morse first developed this unique means of communication in 1835, but it took another ten years to refine it for commercial use. Once established, however, the telegraph and the railroads complemented one another. The railroad managers found the telegraph a useful aid in controlling operations, and the telegraph promoters were quick to utilize the railroad's right-of-way for the establishment of their lines. The development of these new methods of communication and transportation had a significant impact on the economic development of the nation. Farmers in the interior of the land were able to get prices for their goods that were competitive with prices in the eastern markets, while the new communications media greatly simplified the problem of keeping the nation uniformly advised about events and policies of interest to everyone.

Finance remains a problem   Still, however, the nation faced one critical problem in its economic development: the problem of developing a sound financial system. International trade had long been hampered by the uncertainty of others regarding the solvency of the United States.

Even at home, American merchants were more willing to accept European currencies in payment for goods than they were the various state notes that had been issued. This whole problem, moreover, had at its core a basic mistrust of banks and bankers by both the general public and the politicians. How the banking system started and faltered, and the financial problems the young nation encountered are, therefore, deserving of study.

EARLY BANKING IN THE UNITED STATES

The state of finance in the early days of the Republic was in total confusion. As president, Washington authorized the minting of both gold and silver coins as the official currency of the United States. Washington realized, however, that many merchants were distrustful of the "value" of this new currency, so he authorized the use of foreign currencies as well. After all, a nation's currency is only valuable if people will accept it as payment for debts. By allowing citizens to deal in all the major foreign currencies as well as the new American one, Washington hoped to convince the citizenry that the U.S. dollar was just as good as any other currency. The result was that merchants were commonly accepting British pounds, French francs, and Spanish dollars, or pieces of eight, along with the new American gold and silver pieces.

The individual state governments, moreover, had been given a great deal of freedom in managing their own affairs. In order to promote economic development, each of the states authorized the establishment of local state banks within their jurisdiction. These banks began issuing notes to represent coin left on deposit with them by individuals. Soon, bank notes of all sizes and descriptions were circulating in the economy. While the notes themselves did represent actual gold and silver deposits made with the banks, they were only redeemable for gold and silver when presented to the bank that issued them. As a result, the farther from the originating bank a note traveled, the less people tended to honor it. A merchant in Boston, for example, was much more likely to accept a note from a Boston bank than he would a note from a Philadelphia bank. As a consequence, the practice of *discounting* notes became widespread. Discounting is the practice of offering less than the face value for a financial instrument (such as a note). The difference between the face value and the amount offered (i.e., the discount) generally is related to the general marketability of the note itself. Thus, the merchant in Boston might give only 70 cents on the dollar for the Philadelphia bank note, while he would readily give 100 cents on the dollar (or par) for the Boston bank note. In effect, the value of the various notes became directly related to the distance between the issuing bank and the merchant receiving the note.

The result of all this confusion, of course, was that merchants began to have more faith in foreign currencies (whose value tended to remain stable throughout the country) than they did in the various American bank notes. Foreign countries, too, were increasingly reluctant to sell goods to the various states except for gold or some European currency. The state notes were too unpredictable in value for these countries to readily accept them.

Such a condition was intolerable for the Founding Fathers. It was imperative that the United States have a currency that would be treated with equality in international and domestic trade, and not one that was looked on as being inferior to other currencies. Washington knew he could not prohibit the states from issuing their own bank notes. The distrust in the old English central banking system had carried over to this country and many people feared the concentration of financial power in the hands of a central authority. Washington, however, realized that the United States was in need of some type of central banking facility. Some means of stabilizing the value of America's currency was needed. Moreover, the new government had to have some way of gathering gold and silver bullion for the minting of its coins, as well as the facilities for the collection of import duties, the handling of foreign exchange, and the financing of government operations. Alexander Hamilton, therefore, proposed that a bank of the United States be established to engage in general commercial banking and to conduct monetary transactions for the central government. After much debate, the Bank of the United States was established in 1791 with a 20-year charter. At the conclusion of 20 years, Congress would have to renew its authorization if the bank were to continue.

The first Bank of the United States   For the most part, the first Bank of the United States successfully executed the functions Hamilton had said it would. The various branch offices of the bank collected the import duties for the government. The bank also gathered gold and silver bullion for the mint, sold government bonds to help finance the debt incurred after the Revolutionary War, and even provided the state banks with emergency loans to help them remain solvent. Despite these many useful functions, however, the charter of the first Bank of the United States was not renewed in 1811. Some members of Congress were concerned about the constitutionality of the bank. Others, worried about the growing influence of the central bank, pictured the bank as a financial monster, controlling the nation's economic growth. Finally, the local state bankers waged a major lobbying effort to prevent renewal of the charter. Despite the many benefits the local banks received from the central bank, the state bankers were jealous of the huge federal deposits that were kept by the central bank. They reasoned that if the charter was not renewed, these deposits would have to be kept with the various state banks, thereby enabling the state banks to increase their profitability. In any event, this combination of reasons and pressures was sufficient to bring the first Bank of the United States to an end.

Following the demise of the Bank of the United States, state banks witnessed an unprecedented growth. With this growth, however, came another phenomenon to the American financial scene. We have already noted the tendency of merchants to discount out-of-town bank notes by paying something less than face value for them. As the number of state banks increased, so too did the number of outstanding bank notes. The result was the development and growth of a group of merchants that specialized in buying and redeeming these state bank notes. Known as *rag merchants,* these men traveled up and down the country, buying out-of-town bank notes at the going price, and redeeming these notes at the banks that issued them. Thus, the rag merchant would buy Philadelphia bank notes from merchants in Boston at a substantial discount and redeem them in Philadelphia. In Philadelphia, the rag merchant would buy those notes issued from banks in and around Boston, which he would redeem on his trip back north. Although the rag merchants performed a valuable service in keeping the value of the various state notes reasonably near their stated value, they did not maintain their importance for long, for the country was again ready to attempt to develop a central banking system.

The second Bank of the United States   When the War of 1812 broke out, the government again attempted to finance the war by selling government bonds. In earlier times, the government had relied on the first Bank of the United States to provide the marketing of its bonds. This time, however, there was no central bank. Plagued by a large debt, a mismanaged money supply, and runaway inflation, Congress quickly agreed to the establishment of a second Bank of the United States and chartered it in 1816. This bank, like its predecessor, was given a 20-year charter. Like its predecessor, too, it again proved successful at accomplishing the various functions assigned to it. Moreover, under the capable leadership of Nicholas Biddle, the second Bank of the United States went even further in establishing control and order in the financial sector. For one thing, Biddle loaned funds to the federal government at favored rates when it needed such aid. He also undertook the regular redemption of state bank notes, thus depriving the rag merchants of their source of livelihood. He also began issuing national bank notes, thus establishing a truly national currency for the first time. Finally, Biddle realized that the cyclical nature of the economy—moving from periods of prosperity to depression at infrequent intervals—had some relationship to the supply of money in circulation in the economy. Biddle thus became the first economist in this country to actively attempt to regulate and stabilize America's monetary policy. Indeed, the ultimate compliment was probably paid to Biddle and his efforts by Spain. So impressed were the Spanish with "Biddle's Bank" that they used it as a model for their own banking system.

The second Bank of the United States, however, was to face the same fate as the first. Andrew Jackson was an up-and-coming politician from the "western" state of Tennessee. Coming from a frontier state, where money was scarce and debts were high, Jackson did not approve of Biddle's controls over the money supply. As a consequence, Jackson ran for president on the issue of the bank. He charged the bank with being a tool of the monied East and called for its abolishment. Jackson's own popularity, combined with the powerful enemies that Biddle had made over the years, proved too strong for the banking interests to overcome. Jackson was elected and reelected, and the bank charter was not renewed in 1836. For the next 30 years, finance and banking fell into ruins in the United States. All banking was taken over by state-chartered institutions and in many states degenerated into "wildcat" banking. Banks would open with little more than the promise of remaining in business. Public acceptance was often obtained by duping some well-known individual into becoming a partner in the bank. After deposits had been received, the "bankers" would suddenly disappear, only to open a similar bank elsewhere in a few days. Meanwhile, the depositors had lost their savings. Only the fantastic growth of the industrial sector, and the widening split between the North and South, kept the issue of central banking from surfacing again.

THE INDUSTRIALIZATION OF AMERICA

The economic growth of the United States from 1820 to 1860 was nothing short of phenomenal. We have already noted the impact of Whitney's cotton gin and Fulton's steamboat on the growth of American commerce. From 1835 to 1860, however, still more invention and innovation were generated. In 1839, Charles Goodyear discovered the principles of vulcanized rubber, and the tire and rubber industry was born. In 1846, Elias Howe invented the sewing machine and made a lasting impact on the economy of New England. Factories appeared where once the manufacture of textiles had been done in small shops. Within a decade, the factory concept was to spread to other vocations; and by the mid-1850s, guns, watches, and textiles were all being manufactured in factories. The factory, of course, required new concepts in the treatment of labor and personnel. Labor had certain grievances to be resolved, and when management refused recognition of their rights, unionization began. Similarly, the concentration of many workers in one place of business called for new concepts of management, and over the next 30 years, the germ of America's managerial genius was born.

The railroads, America's first large businesses, were expanding at tremendous rates. The Pennsylvania, the New York Central, the Illinois Central, the Erie, and other railroads all ranked among the largest firms in the industrial world. By 1856, railroad service reached as far west as California, and by 1860, Chicago was the railroad capital of the United States. The expansion of the railroads gave further impetus for the development of new industry. Moreover, it helped bring about the rise of some of the great social grievance associations and movements in America's history. The Grange, the Populists, the National Labor Union, and others owed their start to the practices of the railroad magnates. Only the outbreak of the Civil War prevented the unrest that culminated in the 1880s and 1890s from occurring 30 years earlier.

Europe's contribution to America's growth

The rapid expansion of the pre-Civil War period was due in large part to the influence of Europe on the American economy. Left alone while Europe warred, the American nation was able to devote its energies to the fulfillment of individual aspirations and goals. The American spirit of inventiveness, bolstered by a strong puritan ethic which encouraged hard work and thrift and, operating in an atmosphere of religious and political freedom, was establishing a way of life that inspired hope all over the world. Soon immigrants, particularly from Europe, were pouring onto America's shores. Between 1790 and 1820, the population of the United States increased two and a half times. Between 1820 and 1860, it more than trebled—to a grand total of about 31.5 million. Business leaders became gravely concerned about the ever-expanding population; large populations in a society unable to support them tended to lead to anarchy, revolution, and destruction. The business executives, not wanting to see their life's work lost, grew disturbed at the threat of a population explosion. Consequently, they rationalized a means of "helping" to curb this threat by limiting the wages paid for work. An "iron law of wages" emerged as a doctrine of business.

Essentially, believers in the iron law of wages held that workers should be paid a subsistence wage and no more. The vast working population of America was schooled in the preachings of the Protestant or Catholic ethic. Such ethics taught people the dual virtues of having offspring and providing for their welfare. If workers could afford to have more children, it was considered appropriate for them to have a large family. On the other hand, if workers could not support a family, it would be sacrilegious for them to have one. Thus, business leaders argued, we should pay our workers a low, barely subsistence wage, which would have the effect of limiting the development of large families and would ease the threat of a population explosion.

Actually, business leaders did have one very sound reason to be concerned about an exploding population. Industry was still in the production-oriented stage; the major problems facing the business executives involved building enough product to satisfy the demand. The market of buyers was plentiful; all one needed was to perfect a way of producing enough product. If a population explosion were to occur, the populace might grow dissatisfied with its economic institutions and institute an alternative economic system. Such was the lesson of history, and business leaders were well aware of it. By following policies intended to limit population growth, executives saw themselves as helping to secure the continuation of the newly created American enterprise system. Ironically, this fear of a population explosion was the reason why business leaders applied the "iron law of wages," and which helped bring about the creation of organized labor. Today, many executives might well question the "wisdom" shown by some of the early business leaders in practicing this philosophy.

The combination of a large and growing supply of labor (many of whom were skilled or semiskilled) and the active pursuit of a wage policy that stressed payment of a minimal wage, resulted in a rapid increase in the profitability of manufacture. Workers could be had at low cost. The inventiveness of America at this time, coupled with this favorable labor market, saw a rapid expansion in business opportunity develop. This expansion in turn attracted capital investment—Europe's other major contribution to America's industrial development.

Concurrent with America's rapid surge of economic growth was the general slowing down of Europe's major economies. The ravages of war and the stifling attitudes of governments dominated by monarchs and kings, combined to create an interest in American business by European financiers. More and more capital shifted from Europe to the United States. Large banking houses, such as the J. P. Morgan bank, began to develop in the United States, often with established contacts in London and Paris, to further aid the credibility and desirability of investment in the New World. By 1860, European capital accounted for almost one fifth or 20 percent of the total investment in manufacturing and transportation enterprises in the United States.

THE DEVELOPMENT OF MODERN INDUSTRY

The industrial life of America changed drastically after the conclusion of the Civil War. The factory system had penetrated all aspects of America's industry. The railroads and the steamships had tied together sections of the country that had previously been kept apart by geographic factors. The United States was changing from a rural, agricultural society to an industrialized, urban one. Moreover, with the new improved means of transportation now available, business found itself confronting a national market for its goods rather than the regional or local ones they had previously served. Meeting the demands of this new market required that businesses change their very structure and operations. No longer could small shopkeepers satisfy their customers. They now needed distribution systems, production lines, transportation, and storage facilities and a host of new managerial skills. The ship of commerce had entered new waters, and business executives faced unprecedented challenges and opportunities. A new breed of "captains of industry" was needed to navigate the course for business.

The period from 1870 to 1900 saw the business structure evolve into a system comprising several giant commercial enterprises. Where once a multitude of business firms had competed for the sales dollars of the consumer, now only a handful competed effectively in each of the major industries. Through shrewd calculation, foresight, innovation, and occasional conspiracy, business power shifted into the hands of a few "business titans." Men like Andrew Carnegie, John D. Rockefeller, Jay Gould, J. P. Morgan, and a host of others all accumulated vast wealth and power from their industrial enterprises. Perhaps the best way to illustrate business during this phenomenal period of America's history, however, is to look at a few cases in point.

Industrial growth: Some examples

As has been noted, the period of 1870 to 1900 witnessed a massive transformation of industry from small, single-owner shops to multi-factory, corporate complexes often spanning several industries. Frequently, this growth occurred because of new technology—technology developed by the business entrepreneur. A case in point is the development of the meat-packing industry, and in particular, the development of Swift & Company.

Meat-packing Gustavus F. Swift, founder of Swift & Company, began his business career as a butcher and cattle dealer in New England. At the time, fresh beef could only be obtained in the urban East by transporting live cattle to the city, where butchers—like Swift—would slaughter and prepare the beef for sale. Often, large portions of the carcass were discarded as waste; indeed, too frequently the cattle died in transit because of erratic transportation service. Swift saw that this problem could be resolved by butchering the cattle in large slaughterhouses located near the stockyards and the railroad. The problem, however, was shipping butchered meat hundreds of miles. No way had yet been developed for preserving fresh beef. Accordingly, Swift began experimenting with ways of developing refrigeration, particularly for use in freight cars. When one of Swift's engineers hit on the concept of circulating air as applied to refrigeration, the problem was solved. In 1878, Swift and his brother began to market fresh beef, slaughtered in the West, to the markets of the urban East.

Immediately, Swift encountered organizational problems. The problem of the refrigerated car had been resolved; but still remaining was the need for a refrigerated warehouse located at the stockyards for storage of the beef until it was ready for transporting. He also needed to establish refrigerated warehouses and distribution centers in all the major cities of the East. Finally, he needed to develop efficient butchering facilities and to develop ways of profitably utilizing more of the carcass of the slaughtered animals.

Even beyond these problems, however, was the problem of marketing the beef. Swift soon encountered stiff opposition to his sale of "fresh" beef. Local butchers, suddenly confronted with this new competition, argued that the meat was unsafe, and even tried to enlist the railroads' aid in boycotting Swift's refrigerated cars. The idea of a plentiful supply of beef proved too overpowering, however, and Swift won out. By 1900, Swift had major operations in Omaha, St. Louis, and Chicago, and many other western cities.

Swift's success in reaching his goals was soon duplicated by other meat-packers. From beef, they soon branched to pork and lamb. New industries developed as a result of research into uses for various parts of the animal. Soap, pet food, resins, and a host of industries developed in the next few years. (Dial soap, for example, the largest selling soap in America, was a product of the Armour meat-packing company.) At one time, Augustus Swift was heard to remark, "Now we use all of the hog except his squeal." In effect, the meat-packers created what today is called a "fully integrated" business—one which encompasses all phases of product handling, from the cow in the field to the beef on the platter.

Petroleum   The discovery of oil at Titusville, Pennsylvania, in 1859 signaled the birth of one of the great industries of all time, the oil industry. From the very beginning, the oil industry was plagued with overproduction, numerous producers, and vicious competition. If ever an industry was in need of some semblance of order, the oil industry was it. Such order was soon forthcoming, however, due largely to the activities of one John D. Rockefeller.

Rockefeller entered the oil business in 1862 in partnership with several other individuals. Realizing the catastrophic consequences that awaited virtually everyone in the business because of the fierce competition, Rockefeller set out to organize the industry. By effecting a series of mergers and combinations—not all of which were voluntary—Rockefeller soon eliminated many of the small producers of crude petroleum. He then broadened his control to include the retailing of oil to the ultimate consumers as well. By exercising his influence with other business leaders, Rockefeller was able to obtain favorable railroad rates for his oil, vis-à-vis the exorbitant rates his competitors had to pay. Moreover, Rockefeller ruthlessly cut prices on his oil well below cost in order to drive other competitors out of business. Competitors soon realized that their choice was merger with the Rockefeller interests or destruction through his unmerciful competitive practices. As a consequence, Rockefeller's oil empire grew to phenomenal size.

To further establish control and order in the industry, Rockefeller developed the "trust," an arrangement whereby the ownership of Rockefeller's company and that of several leading competitors was consolidated under one managerial team. This team could then determine the most efficient way of dividing up the market, thereby assuring all of the agreeing parties of maximum profits. The abuse of power that this Standard Oil trust engaged in, however, led the Supreme Court to declare the trust to be illegal in 1892. By then, however, the Standard Oil Company was worth substantially more than $100 million. Although the company was later broken up, Rockefeller's influence remained. The limited competition observed in the oil industry today stands as a reminder of this influence.

Steel In steel, Andrew Carnegie created a similar empire. Following a meeting in the 1870s with the developer of the Bessemer steel-making process, Carnegie became convinced that steel was destined to be a great industry of the future. Through shrewd dealing, Carnegie gained control over large coal deposits and (through an alliance with Rockefeller) iron ore deposits. Using Bessemer's new process, Carnegie quickly became the largest producer of steel in the United States. Carnegie, however, had visions of something even greater. He sought to make his steel company even larger by extending his business into the area of specialty steels and finished steel products. By 1900, the company was producing one quarter of all the steel in the United States. These possibilities, however, also intrigued J. P. Morgan, who controlled many of these specialty companies. Morgan arranged to buy the Carnegie Steel Company, and proceeded to combine it with several other companies. Carnegie received $250 million in bonds and retired from the steel business. The new company was renamed the United States Steel Corporation, which remains the largest steel producer in the United States today.

Other industries saw similar consolidation take place. In tobacco, James B. Duke utilized the automatic cigarette-making machine to establish control over that industry. He acquired several competing brands, and extended his business from the tobacco fields to the retail selling of the finished product. His American Tobacco Company soon became undisputed leader in the field. In later years, it took the Supreme Court's enforcement of the Sherman Antitrust Act to bring about a dissolution of the company and thereby assure some type of competition in this field.

A summary of industrial development

We can see then how the growth and expansion of the United States led to a corresponding growth and consolidation of business enterprises. In the relatively short period of time from the end of the Civil War to 1890, the development of General Electric, Westinghouse, International Harvester, Singer Sewing Machine, and the Pullman Company, among others, occurred. In the ensuing years, these firms quickly rose to prominent positions in American commerce (see Table 2–3).

The heads of the great corporations came to be recognized as the undisputed captains of industry. Their quest for power and profits, however, led to the abuse of the rights of the individual man. The economy went through periods of unprecedented turbulence, as the management

TABLE 2–3

America's largest companies in 1909*

1. U.S. Steel
2. Standard Oil
3. American Tobacco
4. International Harvester
5. Amalgamated Copper (Anaconda)
6. Central Leather
7. Pullman
8. Armour & Company
9. American Sugar
10. U.S. Rubber
11. American Smelting & Refining
12. Singer Manufacturing Company
13. Swift & Co.
14. Pittsburg Coal
15. General Electric

* Asset size.

policies pursued led first to overproduction, then to the firing of workers, thereby denying them the means to buy the products that had been produced. Business leaders cut prices, eliminating the weaker of their competitors, raised prices to maximize profits, and again overproduced. The depression of 1873 was particularly severe, and criticism of business practices began growing more and more vocal. By the late 1880s, Congress knew something had to be done. Its response was the Interstate Commerce Commission Act of 1887, an act designed to overcome the abuses suffered by the farmers at the hands of the railroad titans. Three years later, Congress acted to halt the growth of monopolies and trusts by passing the Sherman Antitrust Act. Thus did an era of unrestricted business consolidation come to an end.

THE DEVELOPMENT OF ORGANIZED LABOR

Labor was very slow to organize in the United States. Some authorities have argued that the availability of new opportunity in the developing West caused people to move rather than fight to overcome the hardships imposed by industry. Others have argued that the puritan ethic and the philosophy of the day dictated against the development of such a movement. In fact, it is probable that both of these factors were contributing causes. Coupled with these factors, moreover, was the matter of ethnic discrimination. The vast numbers of immigrants to the United States in the 1800s tended to form isolated subcultures, even to a larger extent than they do today. These various ethnic groups were extremely reluctant to sacrifice their individuality and communal interests in order to create an effective union with other groups.

Still, however, some attempt to form worker associations or unions did occur. Skilled craftsmen successfully organized associations known as *guilds,* in which the craftsmen established certain minimum standards under which they would work. The unskilled workers, however, faced different conditions. As the factory system of production came into widespread use, the unskilled workers found themselves working in "sweatshop" conditions—often for only pennies a day. A sweatshop was so named because of pressure tactics used by businessmen to "sweat" increased production out of workers. As a consequence, the nonskilled workers attempted to organize unions similar to the guilds of the skilled craftsmen, but they were quickly stopped. Management had devised various techniques to impede the spread of unionism, among which the *blacklist* was most infamous. The blacklist was a list of the names of all individuals known or suspected of being sympathetic to the cause of unionism. It was circulated among all of the business executives of an area, thereby assuring that union sympathizers would be unable to find work in the community. Adding to the problems facing unionism, moreover, was the fact that the courts had unanimously declared the idea of unionism to be a conspiracy, and that unions were, therefore, illegal. Given these conditions, then, it is easy to see why unionization was such a long time coming to this country.

The first major labor movement

Although there were labor organizations as far back as 1794, the first national organization was the National Labor Union, formed in 1866. This union was comprised of various and sundry organizations, associations, and guilds from across the country. Created after the Supreme Court had reversed itself on the legal status of unions, membership quickly rose, until the union boasted a membership of over 500,000 people. Indeed, in 1868, the National Labor Union even campaigned for an eight-hour workday for federal employees. However, its attempts at aiding labor failed, and it lost out as a labor organization, becoming political instead. It became defunct in 1872.

The progress of the labor movement was further impeded by the severe depression of 1873. It was one of the economic characteristics of early unionism that when times were bad, unions tended to lose membership. Workers were reluctant to join them at a time when unemployment was high. If management discovered workers belonged to a union, those workers stood a good chance of losing their jobs.

The Knights of Labor

Another labor organization that developed even before the demise of the National Labor Union was the Noble Order of the Knights of Labor. The Knights started as a secret organization but came out into the open in 1879. The Knights of Labor managed to capture the imagination of the workers. In 1886, while still a secret organization, the Knights of Labor pulled the dramatic move of calling a strike against the Wabash, Missouri-Kansas-Texas, and Missouri Pacific railroads, controlled by the notorious Jay Gould. When the union proved successful at this endeavor, it received widespread publicity. News that a once secret union had waged and won a labor dispute against Gould was news indeed! Membership in the Knights of Labor grew from fewer than 20,000 to over 700,000, in just a few years.

The Knights of Labor soon encountered organizational difficulties and were defeated in a number of strikes. Admission was open to both skilled and unskilled workers. When the union became large and powerful, however, the interests of the skilled and unskilled workers moved in different directions. The resulting split in the ranks of the union proved disastrous. Membership declined until in 1893 the Knights could only muster 75,000 members.

The American Federation of Labor

Following the decline of the Knights of Labor, only one organized union remained intact—the American Federation of Labor. Under the able leadership of Samuel Gompers, the AFL grew steadily in size. Still, however, the strength of the workers and their union was slow in coming. Throughout the remainder of the 1800s, labor continued to be treated as another factor of production, something management used to achieve higher production. It took the growth of labor in the early 1900s and the discovery of the principles of personnel management for labor to begin to achieve any real gains.

THE CONTINUING PROBLEMS IN FINANCE

Following the demise of the second Bank of the United States, the financial system of the country fell into a chaotic state. State notes of varying size and description circulated throughout the economy, and two national coins, one of silver and the other of gold, were in use as the currencies of the day. Both of these conditions created monumental problems for commerce in the pre-Civil War period.

The state bank notes

With the end of the second Bank of the United States, state banks increased from a total of 330 in 1830, about fivefold in the next 30 years, as can be seen in Table 2–4.

TABLE 2–4

Growth of state banks, selected years

Year	Number
1830	330
1835	704
1840	901
1845	707
1850	824
1855	1,307
1860	1,562

The real difficulty with the state banks was, as mentioned earlier, the lack of regulations and safeguards surrounding their activities. Recall that the state bank notes were only redeemable when tendered to the bank that originated the note. Many of these bankers, therefore, saw a means of getting rich quick. After opening up for business, and taking in large deposits of gold and silver in exchange for their notes, the bank would suddenly disappear. The founders of the bank would secretly move the bank to a new location in some other town, thereby preventing the holders of its notes from ever finding them. In this way, the banker could avoid paying out the gold and silver he had in his vaults. Then, too, other unsound practices abounded, such as issuing notes with little or no security and stretching credit beyond reasonable limits. Consequently, the public was caught in a never-ending wave of bank failures. This condition lasted until well into the 1840s, when many states began passing banking legislation to control state banking operations.

The bimetallic monetary system

Another problem that faced the country in the 1800s was the continued use of two metals—gold and silver—in its currency. When the minting of gold and silver coins was first authorized by Congress, the ratio or percent of gold or silver that each dollar was to contain was fixed by law. Thus, in 1837, the dollar was required to contain 23.22 grains of gold or 371.25 grains of silver. This was fine as long as the value of gold and silver remained unchanged. However, a market soon developed in gold and silver, and soon the prices of the two metals began to fluctuate. Thus, on any given day, the value of gold was worth more or less than an equivalent measure of silver. This fluctuation had its effect on the currency in circulation. Suppose, for example, that the price of gold increased vis-à-vis the price of silver. Gold dollars suddenly became worth more than silver dollars. Accordingly, merchants began to hoard the more valuable of the two coins and would pay out only the other of the coins in change for purchases. In effect, the cheaper money tended to drive the more expensive money out of circulation. Gresham's law, "Bad money drives out good money," was operating and the result was causing mass confusion in the domestic economy. People began to refuse payment for debts in one metal or the other, depending on the respective values of each. Some parts of the country were literally cash poor, as all of the currency in the area disappeared from circulation. All in all, confusion reigned supreme.

The crisis reached critical proportions several times, but each time new gold and/or silver deposits were discovered, thus driving the market prices for the two metals back into balance. As a result, the United States lived with the problem throughout the remainder of the century.

Lincoln brings monetary reform

With the outbreak of the Civil War, it became imperative that some order be brought to the financial sector of the economy. Lincoln obtained authorization from Congress to charter national banks—none as powerful as the second Bank of the United States, but national banks nonetheless. He then invited the state banks to change their charters from state charters to national ones. The state bankers balked. The only thing they had to gain by a national charter was prestige. The price, however, was national control. Since Lincoln proposed much more restrictive controls over the national banks than most of the state banks were operating under, the state bankers reasoned that they would suffer by converting. Lincoln, however, forced their hand by imposing a 10 percent tax on the issuance of all state bank notes. This tax was sufficiently high so as to create an unbearable burden on the state banks. Robbed of their most profitable activity, many state banks switched to national charters. Having finally achieved a uniform banking community in the country, Lincoln then was able to begin the issuance of the "greenback"—federal paper money— as the major currency of the day. The problem of gold versus silver backing for the greenback, however, remained a problem until the close of the century, when it finally culminated in the presidential election campaign of 1900. In that campaign, William Jennings Bryan and his famous "cross of gold" speech represented the silver interests, while William McKinley and his followers advocated the gold standard. McKinley won and for the next 40 years, the issue of gold versus silver was resolved.

The money trust

As has been seen, the industrial growth of the United States from 1860 to 1900 was phenomenal. Industries grew overnight, as the spirit of innovation and experimentation permeated the land. To facilitate the rapid expansion of business during that time, a new breed of banker came into being. This banker was known as an *investment banker,* and his job was to assist large businesses in obtaining the finances necessary for expanding their activities. Essentially, the investment banker would arrange the purchase of large amounts of the bonds and stocks of companies that were attempting to raise cash. The banker would then arrange to resell these securities to others, for a slight profit. In this way, a fairly efficient flow of money from investor to business firm took place.

Some of the investment bankers of the day were quite adept and skilled at their profession. Jay Cooke, for example, soon became the largest investment banker in the country specializing in the sale of government bonds. However, Cooke overextended himself in financing an expansion of the Northern Pacific Railroad and went bankrupt.

Following Cooke's passing, the reins of power among investment bankers passed to J. P. Morgan. Morgan helped arrange a particularly risky financing venture in France and, because of his success, established a highly enviable reputation. Businesses flocked to his offices seeking aid. Morgan was quick to capitalize on his success and parlayed his banking practice into the greatest accumulation of wealth ever controlled by one man. It was known as the "money trust."

Morgan's chief interest was in the financing problems facing the railroads. Many railroad organizers were careless about their financing and soon found themselves in serious trouble. Morgan would volunteer to come to their rescue by acquiring the necessary securities to finance the railroad. The price he asked was control over the railroad for a period of five or six years. Faced with the choice of bankruptcy or temporary loss of control, the railroad leaders gave in and Morgan achieved control. He then passed this control over the railroads to a group of fellow bankers in whom Morgan had confidence (and whom he could control) who were delegated to manage the business. This "money trust" would proceed to reorganize the railroad, such that when the voting trust ended, the railroad was again solvent. Upon reorganization, however, Morgan saw to it that he or one of his associates remained on the board of directors of the company—thus assuring Morgan of a substantial, if not controlling, voice in the management of the firm.

Morgan's influence grew. Soon, other bankers were joining with

Morgan in the development of the "money trust." Morgan's control spread from industry to industry. So powerful did he become that *twice* he bailed the United States Treasury out of a financial crisis!

Morgan's power was not without a price, however. Criticism grew as the charge arose that Morgan was causing the economic depressions that rocked the country around the turn of the century. By causing businesses to fall upon hard times, Morgan was able to acquire still more control at a very small price. Despite the criticism, however, Morgan's influence remained a dominant voice in American finance until Congress formed an investigation into the existence of the "money trust" in the early 1900s. By then, however, Morgan had major interests in over 110 corporations, including U.S. Steel, American Telephone & Telegraph, General Electric, 10 railroads, and 13 percent of the banking resources of the world!

The development of the United States in the late 1700s ushered in the Industrial Revolution. Given the freedom of the democratic form of government and the belief in the principles of noninterference by government in the affairs of business, commerce grew at an unprecedented rate. Despite problems of war, a mismanaged money supply, the growth of the business titan, and the continued oppression of the laboring classes, America's industrial power grew until, in 1900, America could boast of having the most industrialized economy in the world.

DISCUSSION QUESTIONS

1 The railroads are often thought to be the primary reason for America's rapid economic development. Explain how the industries of meat-packing, steel, oil, and agriculture benefited from this means of transportation.

2 What do you consider to be the first evidence of government interference or intervention into the private sector of business?

3 Examine Table 2–3. What changes would you expect to see if a similar table were constructed of the largest business in 1974?

4 What do you feel was the most significant innovation in business or commerce in the pre–Civil War days? Why? What was the most significant development in the post–Civil War days? Why?

5 Envision yourself as a business leader operating in 1865. The population of the country has more than tripled in 45 years. Would *you* be concerned about a population explosion? Why or why not? Does your argument have any application to today's society?

6 What impact did the increasing number of immigrants to the United States have on the inability of organized labor to get started in this country?

7 In 1860, almost 20 percent of America's industry was being financed by Europeans. Do you see a parallel anywhere in the world today?

8 Develop an argument that justifies the business practices of the 1800s. Develop an argument that criticizes those same practices.

9 What was the blacklist and why was it effective?

10 Discuss Gresham's law. What does it mean to say that "bad money drives out good money"?

11 Why study business history?

MINI CASES

June Blaisdell was a freshman at Chambersville Junior College. Her professor in Introduction to Business had just assigned term paper topics to each student in class. June's subject was "The rise and fall of bimetallism in the United States." June pondered over her subject. "Why," she asked herself disgustedly, "did I have to get such a boring, dull, and irrelevant subject?"

At any rate, June proceeded to write about the problems the United States faced during the 1800s with gold and silver. She concluded the report with the presidential election of 1900, and the defeat of the silver interests and William Jennings Bryan.

The professor asked her to present her paper in class. Upon completing the presentation, the professor asked June to compare the problems of America in the 1800s with those that were currently happening in the United States in the present-day international community. June hesitated, and then acknowledged her inability to do so.

1. *In what ways was June wrong in her attitude about history?*

2. *Suppose that June had been asked to write about (a) the development of the oil industry, (b) the impact of immigration on America's work force, or (c) the importance of government in the development of the railroads. Would her statement about the "irrelevance" of her subject be more valid?*

Eliot and John Waples were students in a business history class at Central Wisconsin State College. The lecture of that day had concerned the development of the railroads, and the causes of the passage of the Interstate Commerce Commission Act in 1887. Their professor had given them an assignment, namely, to discuss two questions in depth, the following day. The questions were: (a) should the railroads have been regulated in 1887? and (b) should the railroads be regulated today?

Both John and Eliot knew that the Interstate Commerce Commission Act was originally passed to regulate the actions of the railroads. And, as

Eliot pointed out, much of the reason for the passage of the act was due to the practices of the railroads during that time. The railroads took unfair advantage of the farmers by charging them exorbitant rates for shipping their products to market. Thus, they were inclined to say "yes" to question (*a*).

Still, question (*b*) bothered them, and in some ways, they weren't very happy with their answer to question (*a*). John phrased their problem very precisely when he commented about the Penn-Central Railroad. Would the Penn-Central, he pondered, have collapsed if it had been free from regulation?

1. *How would you answer questions (a) and (b) above?*
2. *What would your response be to John's comment about the Penn-Central collapse?*

At an early age, Henry Ford displayed the mechanical aptitude which was to shape his career. At 16 he ran away from home and found employment in a machine shop. Here he gained first-hand a foundation knowledge of production.

Henry Ford's interests in things mechanical continued into early adulthood. In 1893, he built his first "gasoline buggy." In the following years, he continued to experiment with automobile designs. Then, in 1896, he quit his job with an electric company to begin manufacturing automobiles.

After various experiences with pioneer manufacturing companies, Henry Ford founded the Ford Motor Company in 1902. From the beginning, his strategy was to produce large quantities at small profits. Concentrating all its efforts on one model, the Model T, the company achieved tremendous success. By 1913, Henry Ford's dream of a fast-moving assembly line was a reality.

In addition to developing the assembly-line production method, Henry Ford was a trailblazer in other areas of modern industrial planning and production. He was first to construct large floor spaces without dividing walls. He used the one-story rather than the multistory factory for reasons of economy and safety. He gave his workers a variety of company benefits— medical, welfare, profit sharing. In 1914, he shocked the industry by introducing the eight-hour, $5 day, more than doubling wages. His system of high wages and mass production worked, dropping the price of a Model T from $850 in 1908 to $284 in 1926.

In the 1920s, Ford refused to accept the fact that marketing had become more important in the automobile industry than production. Ford sales dropped sharply. In 1927, the Company shifted to the Model A in desperation. In the process, Henry Ford performed feats of production his critics said were impossible. The company, of course, continues to this day.

Henry Ford
(1863–1947)

He changed the world of production

3

The history of American business from 1900 to date

Recession is when the other fellow is unemployed, but you are not; Depression is when you are both unemployed.

——Anonymous

BUSINESS AT THE TURN OF THE CENTURY

"As the twentieth century dawned, the American businessman was at the height of his power. His decisions, made free from governmental restraints or with positive governmental aid and encouragement, had revolutionized the economy, and with it, society."[1] By 1900, America had become the foremost industrial nation in the world. No nation could match its growth—in production, average income, and productive resources. America changed from a small, underdeveloped nation to the world's richest and most productive. With it America retained a mobile, free society, continuing to welcome with open arms all those who desired a new lease on life in the New World.

Yet, this growth did not occur without creating problems. True, by 1910 America had far outdistanced all other countries of the world in output of manufactured goods. Moreover, most of this production went for domestic consumption, meaning that the benefits of the industrialization accrued to its citizens— though not in equal proportions. But many problems remained unsolved. No solution had been found, for example, to correct the problems of America's financial system. For almost 80 years following the collapse of the second Bank of the United States in 1836, America suffered from the lack of a central banking system. Then too, the great wealth that

---

[1] Arthur M. Johnson, *Government-Business Relations* (Columbus, Ohio: Merrill Books, Inc., 1965), p. 404.

had developed as a result of industralization was not finding its way to all citizens in equal proportion. Recurring periods of depression and unemployment meant that people lived at or near the subsistence level. Labor still worked long hours under conditions which, at times, were scarcely better than those of medieval days. The quality of education was uneven, and many failed to receive it. The giant industrial empires, begun in the latter part of the 1800s—the oil empire of Rockefeller, the steel empire of Carnegie and Morgan, and the various railroad empires—were, at the turn of the century, using their monopoly powers to the detriment of society. Concentration of economic power in the hands of a few proceeded unchecked, and the need for some form of government regulation to restore and protect free, competitive enterprise became pressing.

The development of regulation   In the 1890s and early 1900s, people became more and more distrustful of the growing concentration of power in corporate hands. Pressure increasingly was brought to bear on the government to curb the misuse of corporate power. In 1901, Theodore Roosevelt entered the White House. During his administration, he put an end to the era of unrestrained freedom that big business had enjoyed and abused. Roosevelt became the first president to openly declare war on the industrial monopoly, and he set about "trust busting."

Although Roosevelt's administration lasted only eight years, the antitrust enforcement continued on. In 1911, Rockefeller's Standard Oil Company was ordered to dissolve into smaller units. The Supreme Court held that the company, as it was constituted then, was in violation of the Sherman Antitrust Act. That same year, the American Tobacco Company was also found guilty of violating the Sherman Act and it too, was forced to dissolve into smaller units.

In spite of these successes, however, the courts found the Sherman Antitrust Act difficult to interpret and enforce. For example, the act declared as illegal all acts by "every person who shall monopolize, or attempt to monopolize, or combine or conspire with any other person or persons, to monopolize any part of the trade or commerce among the several states. . . ." Did this mean that an individual could not be a member of the management of two competing companies? How did it apply to an individual that served as a member of top management for companies that enjoyed a customer-supplier relationship? This and other provisions created confusion among business leaders and in the courts as to the intent of the Sherman Act. In an attempt to clarify various parts of the Sherman Act, Congress passed the Clayton Antitrust Act in 1914. Considered an amendment to the Sherman Act, the Clayton Act attempted to specify those practices that, in the eyes of Congress, tended to encourage collusion and monopolization. (Both the Sherman Antitrust Act and the Clayton Act are discussed more fully in Chapter 18.)

After the successful prosecution of the Standard Oil and American Tobacco Company cases, antitrust enforcement slowed considerably. Much of the slowdown, of course, was because of American involvement in World War I. The last thing Congress wanted during the war was to break up any highly efficient monopoly that was providing war material, just so competition could thrive. Besides, a new industry—the automobile industry—had just come into being, and its impact promised to remake virtually the entire American economy.

The turn of the century saw urban America approaching a critical stage in its development: the transportation facilities of the horse-and-buggy age no longer met the needs of the thousands that inhabited our central cities. Horse-drawn carriages and bicycles were just not satisfying the transportation needs of the growing population. What was needed was a new form of transportation, one which would be more versatile than the horse and buggy. The development of the "horseless carriage" seemed to some to be the answer to the problem.

THE AUTOMOBILE INDUSTRY

Its early development

There is probably no industry that better illustrates the dynamics of American business in the early 1900s than the automobile industry. Interestingly enough, the automobile was first developed in Europe and soon came to the attention of several noted bicycle makers and carriage makers in this country. Many of these "entrepreneurs" (people who create new businesses or provide the capital for new business ventures) were convinced that prosperous Americans would find the "horseless carriage" a novel, if not useful, means of transportation. They began exploring the commercial possibilities of developing and producing automobiles. Among the early pioneers to explore the potential of this market were Charles and Frank Duryea, Henry Ford, and Ransom E. Olds. When Olds succeeded in selling over 500 of his "Reo's" in 1900, all doubt was removed about the market. Competition quickly formed. Among the men who became leaders in the infant industry were George N. Pierce, William C. Durant, the Studebaker Brothers, Walter Chrysler, and Henry Ford. Of these famous men, three in particular played instrumental roles in the development of the industry. These three were Henry Ford, William C. Durant, and Walter P. Chrysler.

Ford stresses internal efficiency   Henry Ford, self-trained as an engineer early in life, felt that the answer to success in the automobile industry was to develop a product that could sell at a price low enough to enable a large number of people to buy one. Accordingly, he began improving the methods of producing cars, particularly by combining various production phases. Ford reasoned that improved manufacturing methods were especially important, since speedier production would increase output, which would in turn lower the cost of producing each car. This would enable him to reduce prices, and thereby capture the market.[2] As a consequence, Ford strived to become a master of internal efficiency. He pioneered assembly-line, mass-production techniques. His skill at developing a large and efficient productive capability proved so overwhelmingly successful that the Ford Motor Company became one of the leading firms in the industry.

There was, however, another popular method of growing in market share other than by becoming more efficient. That method was to grow by buying out the competition. This was the path chosen by William C. Durant.

Durant stresses acquisitions Durant was a businessman who had made a fortune in the bicycle and carriage business. When he entered the automobile market, then, he had a ready-made sales organization. Since Durant was convinced that success depended on which firm was able to capture the largest portion of the market first, he began to buy out his competition. These acquired companies were then merged into Durant's own organization, the Buick Motor Company. In 1908, Durant reorganized his companies into one large corporate organization, which he called the General Motors Corporation.

Durant accomplished his acquisitions of other companies by offering their founders a combination of partial ownership in his company and cash. Like Ford, he was eminently successful, and soon General Motors boasted a percentage of the market second only to Ford's. Durant was so intent on gaining control over the entire industry that he even approached Ford about the possibility of buying him out. One authority described the effort as follows:

> Durant realized there had to be stabilization (in the auto industry). Early in 1908 he proposed to Ford, Couzens, Briscoe and Olds a consolidation of Ford, Maxwell-Briscoe, Reo and Buick.
>
> Ford and Couzens played with the idea, matched wits against the wits of the others, and when Durant appeared more hopeful they tossed in this stipulation: "We will go in only on condition that we receive $3,000,000 in cash."
>
> Not to be outdone by the Ford and Couzens ultimatum, R. E. Olds got to his feet and pronounced sentence on the consolidation: "If you do that for Ford you have got to do likewise by Reo. We will expect three millions in cash also." Durant waved his hands. The meeting ended. The project was abandoned.[3]

---

[2] See Alfred D. Chandler, Jr., *Giant Enterprise: Ford, General Motors, and the Automobile Industry* (New York: Harcourt, Brace & World Inc., 1964), p. 11.

[3] Federal Trade Commission, *Report on the Motor Vehicle Industry* (Washington, D.C., U.S. Government Printing Office) 1939.

The automobile comes of age

The growth of the auto industry during the first 15 years of its existence was phenomenal. Annual production soared from zero at the turn of the century to well over 100,000 automobiles by 1910, and to over 1 million by 1917 (see Table 3–1). This growth occurred even before the

TABLE 3–1

Comparison of number and proportion of passenger motor vehicles sold by the principal manufacturers during alternate years from 1911 through 1929

Year	Total number passenger motor vehicles sold by all manufacturers	Chrysler Corporation sales (units)	Ford Motor Co. sales (units)	General Motors Corporation sales (units)	Subtotal, Chrysler Corporation, Ford Motor Co., General Motors Corporation passenger-car sales (units)	Subtotal, Hudson, Nash, Packard, Studebaker passenger-car sales (units)
1911........	199,000	—	39,640	35,459	75,099	30,524
1913........	462,000	—	182,311	56,118	238,429	44,004
1915........	896,000	—	342,115	97,937	440,052	57,998
1917........	1,746,000	—	740,770	195,945	936,715	75,348
1919........	1,658,000	—	664,482	344,334	1,008,816	107,187
1921........	1,518,000	—	845,000	193,275	1,038,275	120,459
1923........	3,624,717	—	1,669,298	732,984	2,402,282	308,491
1925........	3,735,171	134,474	1,494,911	745,905	2,375,290	515,066
1927........	2,936,533	182,627	273,741	1,277,198	1,733,566	551,945
1929........	4,587,400	375,381	1,435,886	1,482,004	3,293,271	563,405

Source: U.S. Department of Commerce, *Statistical Abstract of the United States.*

development of consumer credit and convenient time payment plans had taken place. All of the automobile manufacturers sold their products on a cash only basis and depended on the cash received from these sales to pay for raw materials and labor that went into the production of the cars.

In 1910, the economic growth of the United States suffered a slight downturn. The recession that accompanied this interruption of economic growth resulted in just enough of a slowdown in the demand for automobiles to cause problems for Ford and Durant. Durant's policy of using all available funds for acquisition of other companies had left General Motors short of cash. When the demand for automobiles slackened, Durant and General Motors found themselves in a bind. Durant was able to obtain a multimillion dollar loan for General Motors, but the price included the stipulation that Durant step down as president for a five-year period, during which time the corporation was to be managed by a banking trust. Ford also suffered from the downturn in demand, but his policy of internal improvement and expansion, financed out of the company's own accumulated funds, worked in his favor. Such internal expansion is less costly than external expansion. Ford had carefully been preserving his profits over the years and therefore did not need to seek bank loans. As a result, Ford was able to weather the storm without difficulty, remaining independent of banker's control.

Durant was still to be heard from in the automobile industry, however. Having been removed from General Motors by the banking trust, Durant teamed up with a noted racing driver of the day, Louis Chevrolet, and they began a new company. With the financial backing of the Du Pont family, Chevrolet grew into a thriving company. But Durant still had plans for General Motors, and with the profits of Chevrolet, he secretly began to buy General Motors stock. He then proceeded to startle the investment world by offering General Motors' stockholders the chance to swap their stock for Chevrolet stock. Since most of GM's stockholders knew of Durant, and had profited handsomely when he created General Motors, they willingly agreed to the exchange. Through these combined maneuvers, Durant was able to regain control of General Motors in the fall of 1915. Upon regaining control, he reorganized the company, incorporating Chevrolet into the General Motors corporate structure.

In the following five years, Durant embarked on a massive building and expansion program. His need for capital was so great that he again ran short of cash and had to call on the Du Pont family for financial aid. When the post–World War I depression hit, he was caught in a financial squeeze. Remember, Durant's success, and likewise General Motors', was dependent upon being able to buy out other companies and expand. To buy out other companies, Durant usually used the lure of cash and stock. When the stock market began to drop, potential merger candidates began to lose interest in acquiring General Motors stock. To save both the company's fortunes and his own, Durant began the desperation move of buying General Motors stock himself, in an attempt to buoy the price up. The depression proved stronger than Durant's financial strength, however, and soon the Du Ponts were forced to come to his rescue again. This time, in association with a famed banking house, the House of Morgan, the Du Ponts removed Durant from control of GM, and Pierre Du Pont replaced him. Three years later, Pierre Du Pont retired, but before leaving saw to it that the young founder of one of Durant's earlier acquisitions, Alfred Sloan, was appointed president of General Motors.

Ford, for his part, was able to survive the post–World War I depression. He mercilessly cut prices and forced his dealers to buy cars and store them—even though they had no immediate customers for the cars. As a result, he came through the depression relatively unscarred, and in

1921, Ford Motor Company actually had over 50 percent of the entire automobile market.

New developments alter the industry   The decade of the 1920s, however, presented Ford with new problems. Whereas the preceding ten years had been years in which production innovations were rewarded, the 1920s were years in which marketing skills became the key to continued success. Ford's success in the early years was directly attributable to assembly-line mass production of a single product—the black, Model T Ford. When the market began stabilizing in the 1920s, Ford's share of the market began to drop. Ford, however, was blinded by the success of the early years and failed to see that people were tiring of a product that was virtually unchanged since its introduction in 1908. Indeed, so stubborn was Ford, that it wasn't until 1928 that he finally introduced a second car, the Model A. By that time, even though he had sold 15 million Model T's in the 20-year period, Ford had lost his share of the market to the more aggressive and imaginative tactics of General Motors' young chief executive, Alfred Sloan.

When Sloan was appointed president of General Motors, he knew that to capture a larger share of the market, he was going to have to innovate—to introduce marketing techniques and appeals that Ford was overlooking. He began by consolidating control of the many automobile companies that Durant had acquired. Each company was still allowed to produce its own cars for particular markets, and Sloan even authorized the painting of cars colors other than black, in order to appeal to those customers who were tiring of the color. Further, he began offering different options on the cars and assisting his dealerships in the marketing of General Motors' products. Sloan also introduced the concept of installment buying to the auto industry. Although this concept had been in use in the furniture industry for some time, its advent in the auto industry had tremendous impact for both GM and Ford. For the first time, people were able to buy a car without worrying about having cash on hand to pay for it. A poor individual that could only afford a Ford could now afford a Cadillac—on time payments. The result was a tremendous increase in General Motors' share of the market. By 1929, General Motors had become the largest and most profitable of the automobile companies—a position which it has never since relinquished.

Chrysler enters the picture

Another development which helped to cut into Ford's dominance in the auto market was the emergence of a third major competitor. In 1910, the United States Motor Company was formed by merging the Columbia Motor Company, the Dayton Motor Company, and the Maxwell-Briscoe Motor Company, as well as several other smaller companies. Most of

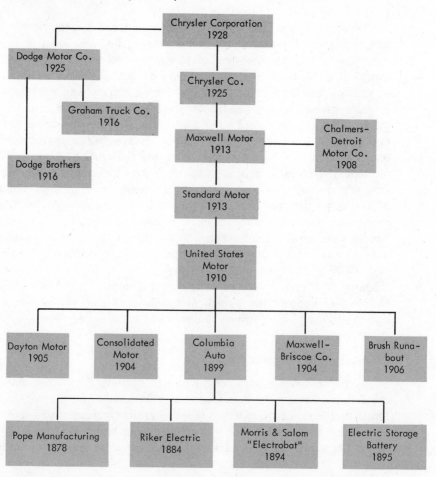

these companies, remember, were discussants and possible participants
in the possible merger in 1908 that Durant had tried to arrange. When
those talks fell through, these smaller companies discussed merger
among themselves, a development which occurred two years later. Still,
the United States Motor Company remained financially weak, and in
1913 was reorganized as the Standard Motor Company. Shortly thereafter, the name was changed again to the Maxwell-Briscoe Motor Company, since the Maxwell-Briscoe cars were the best sellers in the
company.

During the early 1920s, the company was still struggling, and a decision was subsequently made to hire a vice-president from the General
Motors Company as president of Maxwell Motor Company. That new
president was Walter P. Chrysler. On June 6, 1925, Maxwell was re-

FIGURE 3–1

Development of the Chrysler Corporation

organized as the Chrysler Corporation. In 1928, Chrysler acquired the much larger Dodge Motor Company, in an acquisition that one author likened to "a minnow swallowing a whale." At that time, Dodge had one of the most popular of the low-priced cars. Thus was put together the third of what we know of as the "Big Three." With the establishment of Chrysler, the Big Three accounted for approximately 80 percent of all of the nation's auto production.[4]

THE DECADE OF THE TWENTIES

The decade of the 1920s was a period of vast change in American business and industry. The automobile had come of age—sales of cars rose from just over 1.5 million in 1921 to more than 4.5 million by 1929. With the automobile had come all of the related products and industries —businesses that supplied, among other products, glass, rubber, chemicals, parts, and gasoline for automobiles. Other industries grew because of the demands created by the use of the car—notably the cement industry, which became a growth industry as a network of concrete highways came into being.

Still another important aspect of the growth of the automotive industry was its impact on mass passenger and freight transportation. In the 1920s, the development of paved roads enabled trucks to compete successfully with the railroads. Trucking, like the auto industry, soon consolidated into a few large firms. Recognizing the potential of the new form of long-distance as well as local transportation, General Motors bought out the Yellow Truck Company, while Ford started its own company. Railroads were slow to react to the threat of the trucking industry primarily because most trucks were used only for short-distance hauls. When the trucks began moving across the nation, however, the railroads found themselves at a disadvantage competitively and have had increasing difficulty in competing ever since.

The bus, too, was a radical development. The development of the bus triggered one of the most significant changes ever to occur in the area of education, for as the school bus came into being, the one-room country schoolhouse gave way to the more centralized county schoolhouse. This concentration of school facilities enabled many school districts to greatly improve the quality of education offered.[5]

Other fundamental changes took place in the utility, chemical, and steel industries. Steel, for example, was such a vital component of automobiles that the steel companies found themselves hard-pressed to keep up with the auto industry's ever-increasing demand. Thus, the late 1920s

---

[4] See Thomas C. Cochran, *The American Business System: An Historical Perspective, 1900–1955* (New York: Harper & Row, Publishers, 1957), p. 40.
[5] Ibid., p. 43.

saw the steel industry radically change its productive processes in order to meet the increased demand for the steel sheets needed in making automobiles.

Chemicals likewise became a growing industry. Spurred on by the demands of the military during World War I, the chemical industry underwent a period of great expansion during the postwar decade. Indeed, some writers are now pointing to the assistance given this industry by the military during World War I as marking the beginning of what has become known as the "military-industrial" complex.

The growth of all of these automobile-related industries had a tremendous effect on the consumption of power by industry, leading to a corresponding expansion in the electric utility industry. Faced with this tremendous increase in demand, the utility industry began a massive investment program. So great was the investment by this one industry, that the total dollars spent from 1900 to 1930 was greater than the total amount invested in the steel industry during the 60 years preceding 1900.

The end of an era

From a consumer standpoint, the 1920s represented a dream come true. The increased use of installment buying ended having to wait years to enjoy the finer things in life; now consumers could buy on time, paying the debt off a little at a time. The result was a revolution in consumption patterns for consumer goods—a revolution that was to have repercussions in industry within a few short years.

In other ways, too, the consumer's way of life was being altered considerably. The 1920s saw airmail service become a reality. In 1927, Lindbergh astounded the world by making a solo, nonstop flight across the Atlantic. This feat foreshadowed a rapid expansion of the new airline industry.

In a more subtle manner, Madison Avenue was making its presence felt. As consumers found it possible to purchase more and more goods, industry was forced to begin refining its productive structure in a way that would help it to meet this demand. Since industry had no way of knowing what would be demanded and by whom, it turned increasingly to the advertising industry for the preselling of its products. Companies would develop advertising campaigns, and then produce large amounts of goods which would be offered for sale at the precise time the advertising campaign made the consumer aware of its availability.

All things considered then, the decade of the 1920s probably witnessed more dramatic changes than any other decade. But the real significance of the 1920s can be found in the financial events of the decade —those events that culminated in the worst economic collapse this country has ever witnessed—the Great Depression of 1929.

BANKING AND FINANCE

The years surrounding the turn of the century represented a turbulent time for banks and the monetary system. People were becoming increasingly suspicious of the "money trust," a group of bankers that joined together for the common purpose of consolidating economic power through their control over the country's monetary system. The slight economic depression associated with the panic of 1907, which caused the stock market to drop rather sharply, further convinced people of the existence of the money trust. People believed that bankers deliberately caused the stock market decline and the recession which followed by refusing to give businesses loans. Then, when the businesses began to lose money, their stock would drop. When it dropped far enough, the bankers would begin to buy in and thus would eventually gain control of the business enterprise.

Such feeling grew so strong that Congress was prodded into action. In 1912, Congress established the Pujo Committee (named after its chairman, Congressman A. P. Pujo of Louisiana) to investigate the reports of a "money trust." The committee reported to Congress in February of 1913, and the results of the investigation confirmed the suspicions of many people. The Pujo Committee found that there was such a trust and that it was exercising an unhealthy degree of control over the nation's money and credit. In dramatic interrogation before the committee, J. Pierpont Morgan and his associates were revealed to be the main culprits. They were shown to hold over 340 directorships in more than 110 corporations, with assets totaling more than 22 billion dollars.[6] Unfortunately, Morgan died the following month, and with his death much of the excitement that surrounded the Pujo Committee findings died also. However, the publicity that accompanied the hearings helped create an atmosphere favorable to the passage of the Federal Reserve Act in 1913 and, incidentally, the Clayton Antitrust Act in 1914. Congress at last was willing to create the long-needed central bank for the United States. Such a central banking system, it was now agreed, would sufficiently control such money trusts in the future.

The Federal Reserve System

Late in 1913, President Woodrow Wilson signed the Federal Reserve Act into law. The act created the first central bank since the demise of the second Bank of the United States in 1836, during the administration of Andrew Jackson. It differed, however, from the earlier central banks in its basic structure. Instead of establishing a single central bank, the

---

[6] Ross M. Robertson, *History of the American Economy,* 2d ed. (New York: Harcourt, Brace & World, Inc., 1964), p. 322.

FIGURE 3–2

The Federal Reserve System

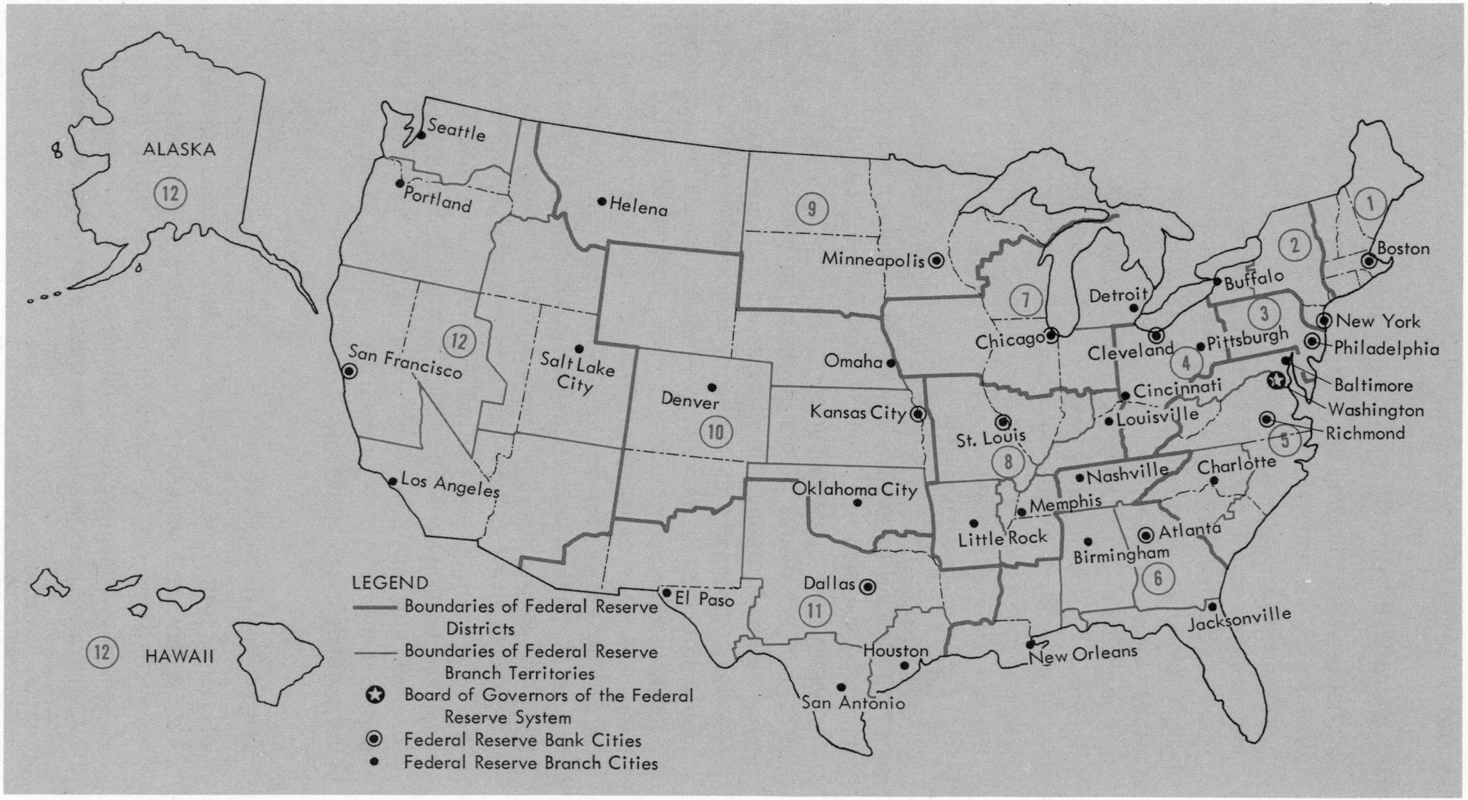

Source: Board of Governors, Federal Reserve System, *The Federal Reserve System: Purposes and Functions* (1963), p. 16.

Federal Reserve Act divided the country into 12 districts, with a central bank located in a major commercial bank in each of the districts (see Figure 3–2).

The purpose of the Federal Reserve System was really quite simple and straightforward. Essentially, the Federal Reserve was instructed by the Congress to control the money supply of the nation. That is, the charter of the Federal Reserve System stipulated that the Federal Reserve would:

a. Supervise and regulate member banks so as to establish a sound banking system.
b. Create an elastic currency, that is, a currency whose supply will expand or contract, depending on the needs of business and consumers.
c. Assist banks in clearing checks, by acting as a "clearinghouse." In effect, this meant the Federal Reserve would assist banks in getting checks written on each bank, returned to those banks as quickly as possible.

To enable the Federal Reserve to meet these objectives, Congress gave it certain powers, or tools. These tools enabled the Federal Reserve to control the supply of money in circulation in the economy, assist local banks in getting funds whenever they found themselves in financial difficulty, and also to control the amount of money banks had available to lend to customers.

In order to overcome the deep-rooted suspicions and fears many people had about giving too much power to a central bank, the Federal Reserve Act provided for a unique division of influence. Overall policy and supervisory authority were given to a Board of Governors, which was located in Washington, D.C. The Board itself comprised seven individuals, all appointed by the president with the advice and consent of the Senate. Each member of the Board served for a term of 14 years, with one member's term expiring every two years. The members would not be eligible for reappointment.

In deciding on this term of office for the Board members, Congress tried as best it could to remove all political influence from the decisions these men would make. Congress felt that if a man or woman were appointed for a 14-year, nonrenewable term, that person would be less likely to give in to political pressures—whether the pressures came from the president or anyone else. Yet, by having the terms expire at two-year intervals, any particular president would be able to appoint individuals whose philosophy was at least compatible with his own. And to prevent one particular segment of the country from becoming too influential (many people feared that Wall Street bankers would dominate the Board), Congress provided that no two members of the Board of Governors could come from the same Federal Reserve District (see Figure 3–3).

FIGURE 3–3

The Federal Reserve System: Organization

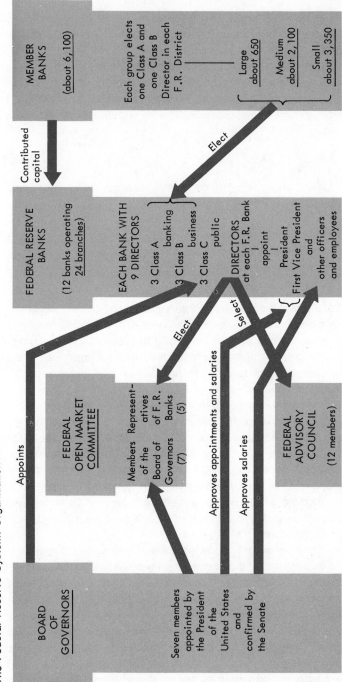

Source: Board of Governors of the Federal Reserve System, *The Federal Reserve System: Purposes and Functions.*

A similar division of influence was purposely imposed on each of the 12 regional Federal Reserve Banks. Each of these banks was governed by nine directors. These nine directors were divided into three groups, or classes. Class A directors numbered three, and were to represent the banking interests in the particular district. Class B directors, also numbering three, were to represent the business and agricultural interests. The remaining three directors, Class C directors, were to represent the public, or the nonbusiness, nonbanking interests of the community.

The six Class A and Class B directors are elected by the banks in the district that belong to the Federal Reserve System. To prevent any group of banks from exercising undue influence, the law provided that two of the directors—one Class A director and one Class B director—were to be elected by the small banks in the district. Similarly, two of the directors were to be elected by the medium-sized banks, and the remaining two directors were to be elected by the large banks. The three Class C directors are appointed by the Board of Governors in Washington, one of whom is appointed chairman of the directors for that particular bank (see Figure 3–3).

To assist the Board of Governors in its policy-making deliberations, the law established a 12-member Federal Advisory Council, consisting of 1 member from each of the 12 Federal Reserve banks. While the Council has little formal power, it does assist the Board by advising it periodically of conditions in each of the districts.

A second additional body that was created to assist policy making was the Open Market Committee. The Open Market Committee is really the most powerful operational body of the Federal Reserve System. It is within this group that responsibility lies for increasing or decreasing the money supply of the country. It does this by buying and/or selling U.S. government securities on the open market. For example, if the Committee feels there is too much money in circulation, it will sell securities on the open market. In exchange for these securities, it will receive cash. This cash is retired, or removed from circulation, thus accomplishing the objective of reducing the money supply. Similarly, if the Committee decides to increase the money supply, it will buy federal securities on the open market, paying cash for those securities. The Open Market Committee is comprised of the seven members of the Board of Governors plus representatives from 5 of the 12 regional district banks. A representative of the New York Federal Reserve Bank is always present on the committee, a privilege accorded that bank by virtue of its position as a leading international money center.

The system is rounded out by its thousands of member banks. All national banks must belong to the Federal Reserve System and state-chartered banks may join if they meet the requirements of the system. Each member bank of the system is required to invest a small portion of its capital (ownership funds) in the Federal Reserve System. In exchange for the use of this money, each bank receives a small dividend, and also has the right to elect the Class A and Class B directors for its Federal Reserve District bank.

Overall, the System helped remove the fears of many people of a concentration of too much power over the money supply being vested in one place. At the same time, the country received the central banking system that was so necessary for financial stability.

One of the primary reasons why Congress gave the Federal Reserve the power to control credit and the money supply was that it was seeking ways of preventing the epidemic of bank failures that periodically plagued the country. Traditionally, banks kept only a small fraction of their deposits in their vaults as a reserve against withdrawals; the remainder was loaned to individuals and to businesses. At any time business conditions or decline in confidence in the bank led to more requests for withdrawal than the reserves would satisfy, the bank was in trouble. It could close its doors or it could start foreclosure on outstanding loans, both of which actions would have adverse effects on the economy. Panic in one bank might lead to runs on others. Later it was found that the only way to halt a rash of bank failures was to declare a bank holiday.

After its establishment, the Federal Reserve System succeeded in softening several financial and commercial crises and in bringing greater stability, at least for a time, to the banking system. Member banks of the Federal Reserve were required to keep a specified percentage of their deposits in reserve, in the form of deposits with the Federal Reserve bank or in vault cash. Thus, the banks could not so easily become vulnerable to panic.

Adding further to bank stability, the Federal Reserve allowed all member banks to borrow, within the established policy, from the Federal Reserve bank in their district. This often enabled them to meet the demands of depositors without calling in outstanding loans, thereby reducing failures.

Thus, the establishment of the Federal Reserve System, with the powers made available to it, appeared to mark a period of control over the financial structure of the United States. Such control, however, was to prove more illusory than real.

Prelude to the crash

At the conclusion of World War I, the American economy emerged as the strongest in the world. Business in America was booming, and its success was evident everywhere. Europeans were buying large amounts of American-made goods. These goods were being purchased with European currencies which the U.S. Treasury was promptly converting to gold. Thus, as our gold reserves increased, the reserves of the European countries dwindled. This shrinking of the gold reserves of the European countries caused a general weakening in their financial systems which carried over into their economic systems. As a consequence, a group of European bankers, including England's Chancellor of the Exchequer, Winston Churchill, urged the United States to change its monetary policy in a way which would remove the pressure from Europe's economies. It was widely believed that the gold drain Europe was suffering would halt if the prices of American goods began rising. And, it was reasoned, the best way to cause an increase in the price of American goods would be to encourage the Federal Reserve to increase the money supply and make it easy for people to borrow money. The more money in circulation, the more people here in America would spend, thus driving up the prices of goods in general.

In 1927, the Federal Reserve agreed to the request, and lowered the discount rate to 3½ percent. The effect was to keep interest rates fairly low. The Federal Reserve also began buying back some of the few outstanding government bonds. Unfortunately, these and other Federal Reserve policies tended to overexpand the money supply, overextend credit, and encourage excessive speculation on the stock market.

As the speculative fever drove stock prices up and up to dangerously high levels, the Federal Reserve began to apply the brakes. But it was too late. The crash by then was inevitable, and when it came, the reverberations were felt around the world, particularly in the highly industrialized nations of the Western world.

THE GREAT DEPRESSION

The year 1929 was destined to become imbedded in the minds of people for all time. Throughout that year, the stock market moved in an upward spiral. By late fall, the market was at a dangerously high level. Then came the crash. Its initial impact was reflected in newspaper headlines on October 30, 1929 (see Figure 3–4). Stocks plummeted rapidly, beginning on October 29. Some lost as much as one-half of their value in a single day! When it was all over, the stock market was down over 80 percent from its highs, and thousands of people saw their savings, their hopes, and aspirations wiped out.

What caused the crash, and the subsequent depression? This is a question which may never be completely answered. There are, however, certain things which can be singled out as contributing causes. First, there was an overproduction of all types of consumer goods, spurred on by the increased use of installment buying and by people spending the windfall fortunes they were reaping in the stock market. This, in turn, led to an overambitious expansion program by business in the early and mid-

FIGURE 3–4

Headlines of *The New York Times,* October 30, 1929

1920s. When business realized that it had, in fact, overexpanded, it reacted by suddenly ceasing all expansion quite suddenly. The sudden halt in borrowing by business caused banks to become even more willing to lend to individuals for stock market speculation. This compounded the problems that led to the market crash.

Similarly, the unfortunate concentration of business power in the hands of the "holding companies" helped to bring about this reduction in new investment. Holding companies are corporate entities that do not produce products for resale, but rather invest their money in the stocks of other companies, holding these stocks as their assets. The income earned by holding companies consists primarily of dividends paid by the companies whose stock they own. Since holding companies generally hold a large portion of a company's stock, they are able to compel management to pay large dividends instead of reinvesting the profits of the business in new equipment. The year 1929 witnessed an unprecedented amount of power being exercised by such holding companies. This concentration of power tended to further hasten the halt in corporate expansion in the late 1920s.

Then, too, the financial condition of Europe, as mentioned, was a contributing factor. Without Europe's encouragement, it is doubtful that the Federal Reserve would have lowered the discount rate in 1927, thereby unleashing the great speculative fever that swept the land in those few years.

Finally, the attitude of the people themselves was a contributing factor. Many individuals firmly believed they were living in some kind of utopia. All across the land, people were proving (on the basis of the stock market's performance in the decade of the 1920s) that small investments made early in life virtually assured that every man, woman, and child would eventually retire a wealthy person. People were literally convinced that stock prices were going to go up indefinitely. Moreover, often only 10 or 20 percent down was sufficient to buy stock.[7] As a result, many people willingly invested savings and emergency funds in common stocks— money they simply could not afford to lose. When the crash came, these people were hurt far worse than they could afford to be, and the resulting consequences were tragic.

The aftermath

The years of the Great Depression, which lasted from the crash in 1929 to the early 1940s—were unprecedented in American history. The amount of poverty, tragedy, and wholesale unemployment that prevailed (see Table 3–2 and Figure 3–5) has never been equalled.

The years of 1930 to 1939 were difficult ones for the American people. The hopes and aspirations millions of people had formulated in the prosperous 1920s dissipated in the same discontent and despair that John Steinbeck so vividly expressed in his novel *The Grapes of Wrath.* At the peak of the depression there were 16 million people without jobs, and in the years 1929–33, the gross national product (the total dollar value of all goods and services produced in a given period) declined from about $103 billion to around $55.5 billion.

It is hard for many of us who did not witness the tragedy of the Great Depression to really appreciate its consequences. When Franklin D. Roosevelt became president in 1932, the economic structure of our nation was virtually paralyzed.

The New Deal President Roosevelt immediately moved to put into effect a series of reforms that he labeled the "New Deal." These reforms

---

[7] In contrast, margin requirements today vary between 50 and 70 percent as a general rule.

TABLE 3–2

Estimated unemployment, 1929–43

Year	Average annual unemployed, (in thousands)	Percentage of labor force unemployed
1929.........	1,550	3.2
1930.........	4,340	8.7
1931.........	8,020	15.9
1932.........	12,060	23.6
1933.........	12,830	24.9
1934.........	11,340	21.7
1935.........	10,610	20.1
1936.........	9,030	16.9
1937.........	7,700	14.3
1938.........	10,390	19.0
1939.........	9,480	17.2
1940.........	8,120	14.6
1941.........	5,560	9.9
1942.........	2,660	4.7
1943.........	1,070	1.9

Source: Bureau of Labor Statistics, Washington, D.C.

were designed to deal with three major problems of the day: (*a*) the banking crisis, (*b*) unemployment, and (*c*) the defaulting of home mortgages.

To correct the banking situation, Roosevelt declared "bank holidays," and closed all of the banks. When a bank was certified as sound, it was allowed to reopen. In order to prevent people from converting their dollars into gold (which, until that time, had been legal), Roosevelt decreed it to be illegal for individuals to hold gold without government permission.[8]

FIGURE 3–5

Another view of unemployment

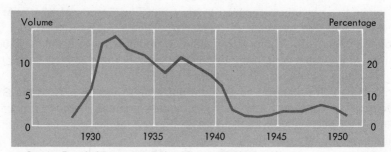

Source: Board of Governors, Federal Reserve System.

---

[8] Gold was required as backing for the paper dollars in circulation. The more gold that was in the Treasury, the more flexibility the government had to regulate the dollars in circulation. If, however, people converted their dollars to gold, the U.S. Treasury would soon run out of gold, thereby causing others to question the safeness and soundness of the backing behind the dollars still outstanding.

Unemployment proved harder to combat. Two of the famous "Alphabet Acts," the Civil Works Administration and the Public Works Administration, were created. Because of the huge number of acts that were passed during this period, everyone referred to them by their initials. These agencies hired the unemployed for tasks ranging from street repairs to Post Office construction. Still, however, unemployment persisted at an extraordinarily high level.

To assist the homeowners, many of whom were in danger of losing their homes because of their inability to meet mortgage payments, Roosevelt developed the Home Owners Loan Corporation. Over one million homes were saved because of the guarantee provided by the federal government under this act.

The two remaining problems that Roosevelt had to cope with involved the falling price level and the labor situation. To push prices back up again, and thereby stimulate domestic production, Roosevelt ordered a devaluation of the dollar to $35 dollars per ounce of gold. This successfully reversed the previously falling price level, by making the dollar suddenly worth less in purchasing power than it had been previously.

Roosevelt resolved the labor problem by initiating the passage of major legislation that was to aid labor development during this period. During the 1930s, the Wagner Act was passed, giving labor unions the legal right to bargain collectively with management. The 40-hour workweek was established later in the decade, via the Fair Labor Standards Act of 1938.

Slowly the economy began to recover. Social security came into being in 1935, giving the retired a guaranteed retirement income. The Rural Electrification Act brought electrical power to the thousands of rural families that had been passed over in the preceding 30 years' development. Finally, the Securities and Exchange Commission was established to oversee and provide direction and stability to the depression-tattered stock market. Still, however, the effects of the depression stubbornly hung on, while the economy slowly tried to recover. Not until World War II, however, did the American economy finally rid itself of the effects of this granddaddy of all depressions.

The war years

Without question, World War II was largely responsible for lifting America from the throes of the depression. This was accomplished because of the simultaneous occurrence of several factors. First, unemployment dropped rapidly as large numbers of men and women were drafted into the Armed Forces and as business received a huge influx of government contracts for war materials. The workers the army removed from the labor force and the jobs that government purchasing created soon eliminated the problem of unemployment. Indeed, unemployment gave way to a shortage of some skilled workers, such that companies found wage requirements rising rapidly, thus causing a minor problem in the area of prices.

Second, business received added encouragement to expand its facilities in the form of tax benefits. In an effort to increase the productive capacity of the country, the government had offered tax advantages for those companies willing to expand their productive capacities. The result was a new wave of industrialization throughout the country, but particularly in the South.

New industries were also created during this period of time. Again, because of the needs of the government, massive assistance went into the establishment of an aluminum industry, which was transferred to private ownership as soon as possible after the conclusion of the war.

The managed economy

In retrospect, it is easy to see how World War II gave birth to what we know now as the "managed economy." During the period of the war, government expenditures accounted for almost one third of our gross national product. The national debt climbed from less than $100 billion to over $300 billion in just a few short years. To prevent a runaway inflation from taking place, the government instituted price controls on the economy. Such inflation was a definite threat because of the rapid rise in government expenditures that had taken place. The added money the government was pumping into the economy was finding its way to consumers, who were now able to buy all sorts of goods. With our productive capacity so largely devoted to providing the government with war material, it was impossible to also produce enough to keep up with consumer demand. Prices eventually began to rise. The result was a need for some type of control, and in 1942, Congress gave the Office of Price Administration authority to fix maximum prices. Ceilings were placed on prices for most commodities and on rents, and certain consumer items were rationed.

At the beginning of the war, the National Defense Mediation Board was already in existence to deal with strikes in the defense industry. But it proved ineffective for overall control, so the National War Labor Board was established in 1942 to keep wages in line. The WLB developed a basic wage stabilization program, which restrained but did not "freeze" wages. Wages continued to rise throughout World War II. The WBL did focus with some success on the settlement of labor disputes, and wages did not rise as much as they would have without the stabilization program.

Under conditions other than those of a national emergency, it is doubtful that the American people would have submitted to the restrictions imposed on them by the government during this time. Prices were strictly controlled, wages were stabilized, choices of purchase in the economy were severely restricted. Some products became virtually impossible to acquire. The "controlled economy" became a reality, and at the conclusion of the war, the attempted removal of the controls caused still more problems for the still shaky economy.

During the war, both industry and the consuming public had to make sacrifices on behalf of the war effort. For business, these sacrifices were easily arranged—the government helped stabilize wages and settle labor disputes and it set price ceilings. Companies could seek out substitute raw materials for those the government restricted. (For example, Lucky Strike cigarettes changed the color of their package from green to white as their contribution to preserving the green dye which the government needed for the war effort.)

The consuming public faced sacrifices of a somewhat different nature, however. Certain commodities such as gasoline, fuel oil, sugar, coffee, rubber, meat, radios and other products were suddenly rationed or allocated by some government formula. Others, such as automobiles, which were not manufactured during these few years, were in short supply. Thus, people found themselves with wages they could not spend.

When the war ended, the country faced a problem which posed serious threats to our efforts at stabilizing the economic system. The U.S. Treasury, faced with the need to sell a large number of "war bonds" as a means of paying the tremendous bills the government had incurred during the war, was hoping the Federal Reserve would keep interest rates low. By doing so, the Treasury hoped to sell the bonds for as low an interest rate as possible, thereby lowering the interest payment the government would have to make each year on the bonds.

The Federal Reserve, however, saw the large amount of money that consumers had been forced to save (for lack of anything to purchase) during the war. It knew that at the first opportunity people would begin buying things they had denied themselves for the preceding four years. As a result, it desired to keep interest rates high, in the hope that people would keep their money in savings in order to earn the high rate of interest.

The Federal Reserve System, however, had underestimated the extent of the buying pressure that had been suppressed during the war. As a result of the excessive demand for goods—a demand which industry found impossible to meet—prices of goods climbed rapidly. Demands for wage increases followed, and unemployment began to rise. The resulting downturn in the economy lasted until 1950, when the Korean War involvement created new demands for goods.

The Korean War period The inflationary impact of the Korean War, which began in June 1950, was immediate. Remembering the effects of World War II, consumers rushed to buy up available goods, labor fought for bigger wage increases, and producers started overtime production. Naturally, prices shot up. President Truman did not invoke wage and price controls soon enough to stop the wage-price inflationary spiral. They were, however, eventually put into effect, and a Wage Stabilization Board was created to exercise authority over voluntary wage adjustments and, later, some control over disputed cases. Actually, wage control never worked very effectively during the Korean War.

The prosperous fifties With the conclusion of the Korean War, the United States embarked on its most productive decade in over 40 years. Indeed, one author succinctly put it:

> . . . the Great Depression eventually became only a vague childhood experience to the young men who were gradually assuming positions of power. Only after this memory of economic calamity had faded and was replaced by expectations of continued prosperity was an affluent society, as John Kenneth Galbraith labeled it, created.[9]

And an affluent society it was! The war had resulted in tremendous scientific advances which were beginning to find application in the business world. Aluminum, for example, brought great changes in providing a light, tough new material used in autos, airplanes, kitchenware, and siding for houses. Similarly, the development of radar made television practicable, and further refinements made TV an almost universal household possession. The development of the jet plane led to the introduction of high speed commercial travel. As a result Americans became the most traveled people in the world. This sudden accessibility to the remote corners of the earth greatly increased the influence of American products overseas. Indeed, some European nationals expressed concern over the impending invasion of American technological and marketing skills into their country, thus forever capturing the economic structures of their economies.

The 1950s, however, were not without their share of problems. Foremost of these was the old problem of the business cycle. In 1955, the economy witnessed a rising price level, primarily because of the continued increase in consumer demand for goods and continued pressure for wage increases. As the prices of goods moved upward, the President's Council of Economic Advisers urged quick action to head off the inflationary threat. The Federal Reserve quickly put a tight-money, high-interest-rate policy into effect, but they unfortunately left the policy in effect too long. The result was a recession (a mini-depression) in 1958. The economy slowly recovered throughout 1959 and 1960, but the fear of a stagnant economy helped put John Kennedy into the White House in 1960.

---

[9] Joseph W. McGuire and Joseph A. Pichler, *Inequality: The Poor and the Rich in America* (Belmont, Calif.: Wadsworth Publishing Co., 1969), p. 16.

The 1960s   The election of John F. Kennedy ushered in a new era in American life. No longer content with the slow, somewhat spasmodic growth of the 1950s, Americans became an impatient people. They began longing for new purposes, goals, and ideals. People seemed to have become satiated with the abundance of material wealth that most possessed, and desired new drives to keep the system, and themselves, moving.

Much of the reason for this changing attitude could be found in the changing composition of the population itself. America was a nation of youth-oriented people and the proportion of the young in the population was growing. Midway through the 1960s, America boasted a population one half of which was under the age of 25. The young people were not motivated by the same goals and ideals as their parents. Their parents had had the goal of economic survival, and for the most part, had successfully met that goal. The young, however, lacked that motivation. To them, depression was a word found in dictionaries or read about in history books, not something that several unfortunate generations had to live through. The young needed a new sense of purpose—a new reason to push on and a new goal they felt worthy of their full attention. They found their challenges in the form of new areas of concern, namely, the attainment of racial equality, the elimination of poverty, and the improvement and protection of the environment.

Business was greatly affected by these changing goals. For years, the sole purpose of the business firm was universally considered to be economic. Business was expected to make profits by providing goods and services to the public. Jobs were created, but these were expected by business leaders to be earned; they were not an inalienable right of all people. Thus, the shift in society's goals had major repercussions on the business community. Business benefited by the increased expansion of federal housing programs, civil rights actions, medical care programs, and job training, but all was not well. Many people, particularly young people, grew increasingly critical of the reluctance of business to get totally involved in these programs. Moreover, as unemployment dropped because of the new infusion of government-aid programs, more and more people acquired the means to buy more and more goods. The result was a straining of the ability of businesses to meet the added demand. Many businesses were forced to operate beyond their peak efficiency levels to produce these goods, and the result was a higher cost of production. This led directly to higher retail prices—an event for which business was thoroughly criticized, particularly since it tended to offset the gains that employment had finally brought to the poverty-stricken people of the land.

The space program was also having an effect on business. The job of landing a man on the moon led to the development of a gigantic space industry, employing thousands and spending billions of dollars of federal money each year. Moreover, the fringe benefits of the space program for society were only starting to become apparent as the decade closed. The largest single benefit was COMSAT, the Communications Satellite Corporation developed by business and the federal government. This unique company is owned by both the federal government and private citizens and corporations as a joint endeavor. With the establishment of COMSAT, instantaneous worldwide communications became a reality.

The combined efforts of the government and business in the space program brought to a head a growing concern over a "military-industrial" complex. Such a complex had been growing for many decades (one *New York Times* writer has traced the growth of the military-industrial complex back to World War I).[10] With the unpopularity of the war in Southeast Asia and the huge expenditures for military and space programs taking larger and larger portions of the federal budget, less and less was left for domestic programs. The result was a growing fear about the social implications of a military-industry combine, a fear that did not subside until the termination of that war.

In one way, the concern over a military-industrial complex was only a reflection of other serious trends in business. The decade of the 1960s saw more merger activity than any other period. Small businesses were combining with other small businesses to form larger ones; large businesses were combining with other large businesses to form gigantic ones. Companies like Ling Temco Vought Corporation and Litton Industries grew from fledgling companies to among the largest in the land—all through mergers. This merger wave touched off a serious debate in Congress over the implications of this apparent concentration of economic power that the mergers seemed to portend. Indeed, not until the recessionary years of 1969–70 did the merger wave slow down. Unfortunately, the ten years of mergers only added to the mounting criticism of business practices.

Finally, the massive expenditures for the space programs, the military programs, and the domestic programs, together with the effort of business to expand in order to meet the needs of the consuming public, caused instability in the financial sector. Prices began moving rapidly upward, and by 1969, a full-scale inflationary spiral was under way. Unemployment also began increasing, as companies began cutting back payrolls to meet rising costs. Throughout 1969 and 1970, prices and unemployment continued upward. A recession had finally ended one of the greatest decades of prosperity the nation had ever known.

The 1970s We are still in the midst of the 1970s, but already events have occurred which promise to make this an interesting decade. When Richard M. Nixon entered the White House in 1968, he found himself

---

[10] Frank Bailinson, "Complex Traced to World War I," *New York Times*, Sunday, March 22, 1970, p. 25.

confronted with an unpopular war abroad and an inflationary[11] economy at home. He immediately set to work to resolve these two problems.

In the international scene, Nixon began a phased withdrawal of American forces in Southeast Asia. Although his efforts to extricate the United States from Vietnam were warmly applauded, they had other, less fortunate, effects. Over a quarter million troops were brought home. These people, newly released on the labor market, aggravated an already serious problem of unemployment. The inflationary cycle at home had grown so feverish that businesses began to cut back on investment. Unemployment had begun climbing. By 1971, it had reached over 6 percent of the labor force.

Moreover, the vast amount of foreign aid the United States had poured into Southeast Asia, Japan, and Europe since the end of World War II began to take its toll of U.S. financial stability. Other nations, notably Japan and Germany, saw their economies grow and prosper. As American dollars in the form of foreign aid and tourism continued to pour into these countries, foreign claims on the U.S. gold supply began to grow. The dollar gradually grew weaker in international markets, as speculators began anticipating the day when the United States could no longer pay gold for dollars at the rate of $35 per ounce. In mid-1971, consequently, Nixon took the historic step of removing the U.S. dollar from the gold standard. In effect, this action told the world that the U.S. dollar was no longer redeemable for gold. Rather, its value henceforth would be its exchange value for American goods and services.

At home, the domestic economy proved to be resistant to all of the minor inducements that were used to stimulate recovery in earlier years. As a consequence, Nixon imposed a wage-price freeze, to be followed by a series of economic steps that came to be known as Phase 2, 3, and later 4 measures. One of these measures even included wage and price controls over much of the economy. It was hoped that these measures would have the psychological effect of breaking the fears of people of continued inflation.

Unfortunately, the goals of control were not achieved. In part, the failure was caused by the hesitancy on the part of the administration to stick with the controls first adopted in Phases 1 and 2. The controls may or may not have cured the inflationary psychology—that we may never know. But the uncertainty in Washington about the effectiveness of con-

---

[11] An inflationary economy is one in which the value of the dollar or monetary unit, is continually decreasing. In other words, if the same goods cost more today than they did last year, the economy has seen its price level "inflated," or raised. Another way of expressing increases in prices is to say the dollar has declined in value relative to its purchasing power.

In a deflationary economy, just the opposite occurs. Under deflation, the dollar actually buys more today than it did previously. In other words, prices fall over time, thus increasing the purchasing power of the dollar.

trols did little to alleviate the fears and suspicions that began to pervade society. In the early 1970s, inflation soared to unprecedented heights. By early 1974, the annual rate of inflation was over 12 percent.

This unprecedented level of inflation was due to a wide variety of factors. Economists generally agree, however, that two of the major causes were the large and sustained levels of government spending that occurred throughout the 1960s, and the quadrupling of the price of oil by the Arab nations of the Mideast. The resulting increase in the price of energy resulted in increases in the prices of all goods, thus adding fuel to the inflation already running rampant in the economy.

To compound the problem, unemployment was also creeping up. In early 1975, the unemployment rate reached 7.0 percent of the working force. Added to the problems of the economy, moreover, were the tragic political consequences of Watergate. The American public's confidence in the ability of government to solve the nation's domestic economic needs waned, and the country waited to see what new solutions and cures to its economic woes would be forthcoming from the Ford-Rockefeller administration.

SUMMARY

The growth of the United States in the years following World War II created a truly affluent society. This affluency, however, had an interesting effect on the mores and attitudes of the American people. "The average American citizen [had been] depicted as acquisitive and materialistic . . . a person who wanted desperately to get ahead, to climb the social pyramid. At the same time, he had become 'other directed' and had therefore lost the drives that had moved his forefathers forward and upward."[12] It was this new society that the business leaders of the 1960s found themselves thrust into. To the average business executive, it seemed that a revolution had taken place!

What had happened was indeed a revolution of sorts. An affluent nation had ceased to put increased materialism at the top of its priority list. This change was most evident among the young, who had grown up accustomed to prosperity, and who therefore tended to value it less than those who had known harder times. Instead, the energies of the young particularly were increasingly being directed toward solving the problems of racial equality, urban renewal, population control, and environmental control, among others. Whether this change in attitude is a permanent one or only temporary remains to be seen. In any event, however, the impact of the last decade's events have had a lasting impact on American business.

---

[12] McGuire and Pichler, *Inequality: The Poor and the Rich in America*, p. 17.

Why should business care? The impact of this shift in emphasis has presented several challenges to the business community. The questions of pollution, of racial equality, or urban renewal are all problems that need, indeed require, the participation of business. Business, however, faces the very difficult problem of reconciling a profit-oriented organization—and profit-oriented owners—with nonprofit-oriented expenses. For example, a pollution filter on a smokestack offers no additional sales revenue for the company buying the filter, but it does cost money to acquire. How a firm is to reconcile such activity to the satisfaction of the stockholders of the firm is a question that is now confronting business. Indeed, how business is to actively engage its resources toward social goals, and still achieve its built-in goal of profit is, perhaps, the ultimate challenge. For business to continue to play an active role in the shaping of our national destiny, however, it must find a way to compromise these goals. It is to help provide an understanding that will facilitate this search that this chapter and the previous one have been written, and it is this question that we shall confront in the coming chapters.

DISCUSSION QUESTIONS

1 What was Henry Ford's most significant contribution to American business?

2 Look up the term *entrepreneur* in the Glossary. How does this term fit the role of Olds, Durant, Ford, and Chrysler in the developing auto industry?

3 What major contribution did Alfred Sloan make to American business that is alluded to in the text?

4 Why did the railroads—America's first form of intercontinental transportation—have difficulty competing in the 1920s?

5 What was the Pujo Committee? Why was it formed?

6 In your opinion, what were the major causes of the Great Depression?

7 In a period of economic depression, what policy should the Federal Reserve take regarding the purchase and sale of government securities? Why?

8 The authors discuss what they feel is the major issue facing business in the coming years. What is it? Do you agree with them? Why or why not?

9 A fairly well-established economic theory states that the level of unemployment in society and the rate of inflation in society are trade-offs; that is, that as one (say inflation) increases, the other

(unemployment) decreases. Do you feel this relationship still holds? Why or why not?

10 When President Nixon removed the U.S. dollar from the gold standard, the effect was to make the dollar worth only what it could purchase in the way of goods and services. How did this "new value of the dollar" differ from the "old value of the dollar"?

MINI CASES

One of the great calamities of America's business history took place in the years of 1929–33—the years of the Great Depression. Over the past 30 years, many experts have attempted to isolate the reasons for, or causes of, this tragic event. Perhaps the most significant debate over these causes and their possible remedies, however, occurred during the presidential election campaign of 1932. Then, President Hoover and would-be president Franklin D. Roosevelt, engaged in a sharp debate over what actually caused the depression and how it could best be resolved.

Hoover felt that recovery depended on the revival of the international financial system—that a restoration of Europe's financial system would alleviate the problems here at home. Roosevelt disagreed sharply with Hoover's analysis. He felt that the depression was largely a result of domestic problems, stemming from a production system that suddenly found itself able to produce products faster than people could consume them. Moreover, he felt the financial system of the country had contributed to the problem by a careless disregard for financial security in its loan policies. When companies found themselves unable to sell all of their goods, they began firing people, and the whole economic structure came tumbling down.

> *What justifications can you point to that would support Hoover's conclusion regarding the proper remedy for the causes of the depression? Following Roosevelt's argument, how far back in history can you trace the beginnings of the problem as Roosevelt saw it?*

We have seen how many business leaders of the past were able, in their own lifetimes, to become fabulously wealthy by pursuing business vocations. For example, Henry Ford, although he began as a fairly wealthy young man, became one of America's richest men before he died. Similarly, Andrew Carnegie became the leading industrialist of his day, amassing a fortune of several hundred million dollars—this despite his beginnings as a penniless immigrant.

In your opinion, do similar opportunities for wealth accumulation exist today? In what ways are conditions today (a) more conducive to wealth accumulation, and (b) less conducive to wealth accumulation, than they were at the turn of the century?

Adolph Coors Co.

The beer that won the West

Nestled in the Rocky Mountains just to the west of Denver, Colorado, sits the largest brewing facility in the world. In this brewery, one of the world's most famous beers is brewed: Coors Banquet Beer. Coors is world reknown, and the stories that exist about it have become legend. Former President Eisenhower used to have it airlifted by Air Force jet to the White House. One individual used to rent a refrigerated truck and drive from Denver to North Carolina every weekend with a truck load of Coors, which he resold at $1 per can! And another individual is on record as having motorcycled from Ohio to Kansas City (the nearest location where Coors was sold) just to have a few beers.

Coors is perhaps unique in several respects. It is, first of all, sold only in 11 Western states. It is the number-one selling beer in ten of those states. It is the fourth largest selling beer in America; the three larger selling beers are sold in all 50 states.

Coors is a unique company in more than one respect, however. The chief officers of the company work in spartan headquarters; no fancy frills, no private secretaries. The company offers no bonuses and no stock options. All promotions come from within. And the employees are free to drink all the beer they want while on the job.

The company is almost entirely self sufficient. It has its own construction crew working on expansion of the brewery; does its own advertising; manufactures its own beer cans; and provides for its own energy needs through recycling. It has long been known for its concern for the environment, and despite all of this, has never borrowed a penny in its 100-plus year history.

Expansion plans? Those in the Eastern United States can forget about it. Coors is expanding at a rate of about 20 percent per year, and can't meet the growing demand for its product in the 11 states in which it now operates!

4

Social and economic philosophies of business

The philosophy of one century is the common sense of the next.

——*Henry Ward Beecher*

The American economy has existed as an organized economy for several hundred years. While this is not very long so far as the history of nations is concerned, the achievements that this particular economic society have realized are most remarkable. Born with English heritage, and nurtured under a democratic form of government, the American economy grew from its humble beginnings to become the greatest economic structure the world has ever seen.

The question might well be asked then, as to what aspect of America's business system has been most responsible for this accomplishment. What is it about the American "capitalistic" economy that has generated this vast amount of material wealth? More significantly, perhaps, are the questions that arise concerning the social implications of business. Has business as an institution been philosophically consistent with the values and standards of the American people? Or has business developed, as some people have charged, as the instrument of a select few, to be used for the exploitation of the masses of the United States? All of us are aware of the stigma attached to the word *capitalist.* Is the criticism justified? In this chapter an attempt shall be made to show how changes in social standards and values have influenced the attitude and philosophy of the business establishment. The development of capitalism shall be traced from its traditional economic interpretation to what appears to be a more responsible, if not enlightened, approach in today's contemporary society.

THE CLASSICAL FOUNDATION OF AMERICAN CAPITALISM

‎As an economic doctrine, *mercantilism,* had reached its zenith when America became an independent republic. Mercantilism was an economic doctrine which tended to regard precious metals or money as identical with wealth. Mercantilism stressed the accumulation of such wealth, and looked upon it as the source of power for the national government.

Under the rigid rules of mercantilism, nations of the world vied with one another to acquire gold and silver bullion through the manufacture of goods to be sold abroad. They sought to build up large stores of bullion in the national treasury. Thus, history shows us that the great colonial empires were established by the countries of Western Europe, particularly England and France, partly to fulfill these mercantilistic goals. Control over the colonies enabled the governments to restrict purchases of goods from their colonies to necessary raw materials. Sales of goods manufactured in the mother countries resulted in increasing the gold and silver in the national treasury; purchases of goods had the opposite effect. When goods were purchased from others, gold and silver flowed out of the country, thereby lessening the monetary wealth, and consequently, in their view, the power, of the nation doing the purchasing. Thus, the mercantilistic nations sought to establish captive markets for their goods, and when purchases were necessary, to limit them to raw materials. Under mercantilism, the development of agriculture and the extractive industries, such as mining, at home was neglected.

Finally, mercantilism did not concern itself with the problem of economic concentration at home. If a business leader controlled or monopolized an entire market, the government expressed little concern, so long as it received its fair share of the executive's profits in the form of taxes. Indeed, government often encouraged the consolidation of industries under a single producer, in the belief that this would improve efficiency and remove the duplication of efforts caused by competition. As a consequence, a form of exploitation of the citizens of all the mercantilistic countries occurred with regularity. People paid high prices for their goods, businesses made large profits, and the government collected huge tax revenues. A perpetuation of wealth for a few and poverty for many was thus forced on the people, for mercantilistic policies tended to encourage the formation of barriers for individual incentive and improvement.

With the coming of the 18th century, however, concern began to be expressed about the effects of mercantilism on the well-being of average people. The Protestant Reformation had, in the 16th century, introduced England to the Calvinistic doctrines which brought the message that hard work and industry were the ways toward salvation. Many began to wonder whether mercantilism allowed or encouraged such virtues, particularly given the monopolistic tendencies of business leaders that were so common. Among those who questioned mercantilism was a man destined to become known as the first great economist, Adam Smith.

Adam Smith and laissez-faire

Adam Smith was one of the more prominent 18th-century critics of the economic policies of mercantilism. Smith believed that man's natural tendency was to be industrious and work hard and that value was created by the use of labor in production. He thus looked with disfavor on the business practices that had been allowed to flourish under mercantilism. He saw the existence of monopolies in various trades as tending to stunt the natural tendencies of people to seek advancement and progress. Moreover, Smith felt that monopolies were directly related to the influence of the government in industry. If government would leave business alone, he reasoned, more competition would result, prices would fall, and the plight of the average worker would thus improve. Thus, Smith was actually criticizing the very heart of the mercantilistic philosophy, namely, that a nations' wealth was measured by the gold and silver in its treasury. Rather, Smith felt that the quality of life enjoyed by the citizenry was a more fundamental measure of wealth, and that the good life could be best achieved if government practiced a laissez-faire[1] philosophy—an attitude of nonintervention by government in the affairs of business. (See Adam Smith biographical sketch which precedes chapter one.)

Smith summarized his economic philosophy in a book which has become one of the classics of economics titled *An Inquiry into the Nature and Causes of the Wealth of Nations,* more popularly called the *Wealth of Nations.* This book, almost 1,000 pages in length, had the noted distinction of being one of the two great documents that were published in 1776 that called for the freedom of choice for human beings. The other, of course, was the American Declaration of Independence.

In *The Wealth of Nations,* Smith voiced certain economic principles for the first time. For example, Smith defined national wealth in terms of a nation's output and productivity (much as we do today when we speak of gross national product) instead of the accumulation of gold and silver. Smith also became a proponent of free trade, a concept viewed as being akin to heresy by mercantilists. Smith felt that by trading goods with other nations, each nation could thus specialize in producing those goods that it was uniquely suited to produce. This argument, which was later taken

---

[1] Literally translated, this means to "leave free," or in an economic context, to leave free from governmental intervention.

ADAM SMITH
(1723-1790)

"Every individual endeavors

to employ his capital so that

its produce may be of greatest

value. He generally neither

intends to promote the public interest, nor knows how much he

is promoting it. He intends only his own security, only his

own gain. And he is in this led by an *invisible hand* to

promote an end which was no part of his intention. By pursuing

his own interest he frequently promotes that of society more

effectively than when he really intends to promote it."

Source: Adam Smith, *The Wealth of Nations* (1776).

---

up by David Ricardo is discussed in more depth later in this text. Perhaps, however, the most famous aspect of *The Wealth of Nations* and one that is still heard on occasion today, was Smith's concept of an "Invisible Hand" that would assure efficiency in business.

To Smith's way of thinking, the path to national wealth required that government avoid interfering in the affairs of business. Smith felt that people were basically devoted to and capable of improving themselves. This attitude, of course, was entirely consistent with the ideas introduced by Calvin in the 1500s and which were still exerting a strong influence. Because of the urge to better himself, man as a consumer of goods would tend to work hard in order to maximize his own wealth. Whenever people purchased goods or services, they would be inclined to buy from the merchant offering the lowest prices, if given a choice. For example, if three merchants all offered the same goods at different prices, people would buy from the merchant with the lowest prices, until the other merchants—forced by the "invisible hand" of competition—lowered their prices. Competition, therefore, was the key. If government stayed out of the affairs of business and allowed people to compete freely for the dollars of the consumer, competition would ultimately see to it that prices were kept low, that the right goods would be produced, and that wealth would be maximized. Indeed, argued Smith, rather than encourage monopolization (as had been done under mercantilism), the proper role of government was to see to it that monopolies did not come about as the result of the unscrupulous actions of some business executives. The unscrupulous executive was the only reason Smith advocated *any* government involvement in business at all.

The impact of Adam Smith on both the economic structure of our society and our social beliefs surrounding business-government relations cannot be overstated. Today, Smith's views are still being heralded by a large segment of the population. Indeed, in 1964 one candidate for the presidency of the United States openly stated his admiration for the principles of laissez-faire and found over 30 million Americans who agreed with him.

The formation of capitalism as an economic doctrine

Smith's views on a new economic order were further extended and refined by David Ricardo. Ricardo formulated a "law of rent" and refined

---

DAVID RICARDO

(1772-1823)

"The reason then, why raw produce rises

in comparative value, is because more

labour is employed in the production of

the last portion obtained, and not because a rent is paid to

the landlord. The value of corn is regulated by the quantity

of labour bestowed on its production on that... land."

[Author's note: In this passage, Ricardo is attempting to

explain or show that the value of products produced would be

determined almost solely by the amount of labor needed for the

production of the last item produced. In other words, as de-

mand for a product increased, the need for labor to produce

that product would increase. So too, would the cost of labor,

since the holder of that "factor of production" would demand

a greater price.]

Source: David Ricardo, *Principles of Political Economy and Taxation* (London: George Bell & Sons, 1891).

a theory that based value on labor. He demonstrated that a distribution of income far more efficient than that attainable under mercantilism could be achieved if the market were allowed to work its own will. Each individual possessed certain skills or property that were essential for a productive economy. These included the ownership of land and the possession of some labor ability. The individuals possessing these "factors of production" could sell or rent the use of these factors to others. The scarcer the particular factor, the more the owner of the factor would receive for its use. In essence, Ricardo showed that the laws of supply and demand would result in the same efficiencies among individuals in society as *producers* of goods that Smith showed would result for the *consumers* of those goods. In summary, the combined analyses of Smith and Ricardo established the basis for contemporary American capitalism.

EARLY THOUGHTS ON THE SOCIAL ACCEPTABILITY OF CAPITALISM

Given the economic logic formulated by Smith and Ricardo, it was only natural that other thinkers would attempt to determine the impact of capitalism on the social aspects of the economy. For example, the capitalistic economy advocated by Smith required that individuals seek to improve themselves. This improvement could be measured in terms of the profits earned by business leaders. Ricardo, too, assumed that individuals sought to increase their personal wealth and could accomplish this by bargaining away the use of their productive resources. Both Ricardo and Smith assumed that these tendencies were natural and proper—after all, they were in keeping with the Protestant ethic. What neither explained nor considered, however, was whether in fact other forces could arise which might restrict or prevent the operation of this neat system. This question was left for others to explore.

The mobility of labor and the equality of man

Adam Smith emphasized that social influences determined the development of the individual. He possessed an ethical concern for the average person and a social insight along with his belief in the power of individual self-interest to regulate things. He saw that wealth, education, and subsequent exposures to opportunities determined to a large extent what occupation or trade individuals would assume and what their station in life would be. John Stuart Mill and his contemporary, John Cairnes, continued this line of thought one step further. Mills sounded a note of humanitarianism approaching socialism. In so doing, he uncovered what he believed would be an obstacle to the system Smith envisioned. This was the relative immobility of labor.

The perspective of both Mills and Cairnes on labor showed a keen sensitivity to economic and social change. They perceived that humans' ingenuity would cause advances in the technology used in business. This new technology would probably require new skills on the part of labor. They saw this as creating a problem, for people were, they felt, incapable of changing jobs with the degree of flexibility that the new technology might require of them. Moreover, workers who lacked a skill or education (as was particularly true among the masses in Mill's time), would soon be restricted in the jobs they could perform, the wages they could earn, and the standard of living they could attain. That is, they would soon reach the point where they could no longer improve their station in life, but instead would be forced to remain in their present position—or worse —forever. This possibility loomed as a serious threat to Smith's economic system, for the operation of the system required a continuous motivation on the part of man. How did you motivate a person who had no future? In later years, John Cairnes likened this problem of labor's immobility to a flight of stairs, each landing representing some social impediment to further advances on the occupational staircase.

Two observations on how the works of Mill and Cairnes influenced the development of capitalism in America are worth noting here. First, one can see how the concept of free, public education came to be regarded as an essential ingredient of an economic system by the Founding Fathers of this country. The argument of Mill, in particular, was given serious consideration in early America and led to the belief that a broadly based system of education was essential to the success of the American capitalistic system.

Second, and perhaps a bit more philosophically, it is interesting to note the degree of social consciousness that was expressed by these early economists. We often tend to think of "social responsibility" and "social awareness" as being relatively new concepts. Yet, here were two of the foremost early economists deeply concerned with the social problem that they perceived was being created under capitalism—a concern that was to reappear in the New World. Most significantly, the problem they envisioned was one which exists in modified form today—that of the hardcore unemployed in society.

THE JUSTIFICATION FOR PROFITS

Another aspect of the laissez-faire economic system that caused considerable discussion was the issue of profits. Under the teachings of Calvinism, God worked His will through humans; therefore the best way for people to serve God and thereby attain everlasting salvation was to practice to the fullest their chosen vocation. Consequently, the earning of profits by a business leader was not considered sinful; indeed, it was viewed as the mark of a successful individual and was, therefore, admired. Calvinism also preached, however, that the earning of profits just for the sake of living an extravagant life was inherently sinful and should be avoided. People were expected to be prudent, show discretion in their personal life; they were not to live extravagantly on their accumulated wealth. Since God instructed the people to earn profits and to spend them prudently, only one thing could result: many successful business leaders began *saving* large sums of money. These accumulations of wealth were then reinvested in the business, thereby expanding the economic productivity of the nation. Saving followed by investment was the process by which one succeeded to the fullest at his chosen vocation of business. That the business leaders earned still more profits as a result of the investment was just further proof of their success.

We can see, therefore, how the phenomenon of modern capitalism came into being. People were urged by their religious beliefs to work hard and save their wealth, investing it only in those works that would further the successful execution of their own vocations (and thereby add to the glory of God). The result was a methodical accumulation of wealth by successful businessmen in the country and the investing of these accumulations in new industries. Indeed, some authorities have called this steady accumulation of wealth the most important characteristic of modern capitalism. For *capitalism* has been around as long as humans have had civilized societies. American capitalism, however, also stressed accumulation of wealth. This phenomenon helps explain why men like Carnegie, Rockefeller, and Vanderbilt were able to accumulate the massive fortunes they did, and yet, in the best tradition of Charles Dickens' Scrooge, still lead rather spartan personal lives. Moreover, it explains how the ruthless managers of the early factories in America could work small children 14 hours a day for just pennies a day in wages, thereby perpetuating the poverty that the families of these children found themselves in. At the same time, they were counted among the most ardent churchgoers on Sunday and among the churches' best supporters. What would seem to us today to be a moral contradiction really was consistent with the prevalent beliefs of early puritanism.

An economic justification

Economists, however, sought to find another justification for profits. How was the charging of a price in excess of cost justified by those making the product? This question was probably best answered by John Stuart Mill, who attributed the existence of profits to the "surpluses produced by labor." After labor had been paid its wages, that which was left was "surplus" or profit. Business leaders were justified in receiving this

---

[2] *Capitalism* is a term that tends to defy definition. In a broad sense, however, we can liken it to individual's quest for wealth through the sale of goods or services.

JOHN STUART MILL

(1806-1873)

The cause of profits..."is that labor

produces a surplus. As the wages of

the labourer are the remuneration of

labour, so the profits of the capitalist are properly,...the

remuneration of abstinence."

Source: John Stuart Mill, *Principles of Political Economy*
(Ashley ed.; London: Longmans, Green, 1920), p. 405.

profit for two reasons. First, the profit represented payment for the risks incurred in establishing the business. Second, profits represented the owner wages for supervising the production.

Little controversy arose over the legitimacy of these reasons, although Karl Marx was later to seize upon Mill's "surplus-of-labor" theme as the basis for his attack on the capitalistic system. Early evidence of the acceptability, desirability and righteousness of earning a profit can be seen in the following passage from Benjamin Franklin's *Advice to a Young Tradesman:*

> Remember that time is money. He who could make ten shillings a day through his work, but goes walking half the day or idles in his room, even if he spends for his amusement only a sixpence, may not count this alone (as a loss), but he has, in addition, given up five shillings, or rather thrown it away. Remember that credit is money. If anyone leaves money with me after it falls due, he makes me a present of the interest.[3]

EARLY AMERICAN CAPITALISM

The economic philosophy of laissez-faire advocated by Adam Smith and refined by Ricardo and Mill achieved popularity at the very time this country was developing as an independent nation. This economic philosophy was adopted in the United States and formed the philosophic basis for the Industrial Revolution in the Western world.

Early American society probably came as close to realizing the ideal

---

[3] Benjamin Franklin, *Advice to a Young Tradesman.*

of pure laissez-faire as did any economic period in modern history. Prior to the 1800s, very little government regulation over commerce existed (although government was a significant influence in the levying of tariffs and import duties). Most industry was small (although the development of the railroads and the establishment of corporations as an economic necessity hinted of things to come). Entry and exit into or out of any business was open to all. Given the westward expansion of the nation geographically, Americans found themselves willingly accepting the role of "masters of their own destiny." Those who braved the West and established farms and small shops found themselves existing in little "laissez-faire" communities with others. No government bothered them; no large businesses controlled their lives. Not until the nation ran out of new lands to explore, and more and more people moved into the towns and villages established by the settlers, did the need arise for a redefining of the roles of business and government. And not until the abuses of big business threatened the way of life of the American people did business find itself confronted with the need to justify its status in society.

Moreover, the doctrines and teachings of puritanism kept people in the more urban East working hard to improve their stations in life. The Industrial Revolution had been ushered in by the introduction of a vast array of new machines and inventions, all of which created new opportunities for wealth and advancement. The Horatio Alger story had not yet become a reality, but the possibilities of it occurring were more numerous than at any other time. Not until the pressures of industrialization, the growth of big business, and the realization of growing inequalities of income that separated America into classes based on wealth did business undergo a decline from its position of unquestioned eminence in our society.

A CHANGING PHILOSOPHY OF BUSINESS

With the development in the 1840s and 1850s of the railroads and other large business organizations, the fears of Adam Smith began to become apparent. Said Smith: "People of the same trade hardly meet together even for merriment and diversion but the conversation ends in a conspiracy against the public, or in some contrivance to raise prices." This, indeed, was what was happening in 19th-century America. Large business combinations were in the making, and business leaders seemed to know no bounds in the extent they would go to keep competition away.

Large industrial empires grew, and some men became fabulously wealthy in the process. Andrew Carnegie, for example, the emigrant son of a poverty-stricken Scottish family, worked his way up the ladder of business until he became the multimillionaire leader of the steel industry.

His wealth was so great that before he died he gave an estimated $350 million to various charitable, educational, and cultural organizations. John D. Rockefeller, Cornelius Vanderbilt, and many others accumulated great fortunes as a result of their business ventures. Among the masses, however, poverty remained widespread. Many people questioned the way the multimillionaires got to the top and asked for a justification for being there. People began asking, "Why them and not me?" "Why should they be allowed to enjoy the benefits of fabulous wealth—often at my expense"? The business executive's answer came, strangly enough, from the world of anthropology and sociology, and the teachings of Charles Darwin and Niccolo Machiavelli.

Social Darwinism as a business philosophy

In 1859, Charles Darwin published his now famous work entitled *"The Origin of Species by Means of Natural Selection."* In this book, Darwin advanced the hypothesis that all living creatures evolved from lower, more primitive life, and that through the evolutionary processes of time, the strongest of the species managed to survive. Although Darwin's work created a social storm, particularly among religious and educational groups, it made a major contribution to establishing a new business philosophy. This was primarily due to the interpretation of Darwin's thesis by Herbert Spencer, a noted English philosopher of the times.

Spencer tried to apply the concept of Darwin's ideas of "evolution of the species" and "natural selection" to society. He labeled the latter idea "survival of the fittest," and in so doing, he hit upon the very justification the business titans of the day were seeking. Spencer argued that the existence of the business titan was not only compatible with, but logically extended from, Darwin's thesis. The business titan, argued Spencer, rose to his position of preeminence in society because he was "most fit." Other would-be competitors were destined to be snuffed out by the natural law of the survival of the fittest. It didn't matter what methods were used to achieve a superior position in commerce; the ends justified the means. Moreover, argued Spencer, the process that determined who should rise to be a "captain of industry" was a natural process, directly related to the natural evolution of superior creatures. The business titan was literally preordained to a position of eminence in society. This theory of social Darwinism was quickly embraced by the business leaders of the day. Indeed, it was hard to refute at that time, for the logic of it extended so directly from what seemed to be a natural, biological phenomenon.

Machiavelli and The Prince   The strength underlying the acceptance of social Darwinism stemmed to some degree from the historical precedents that seemed to support it. One such forerunner was *Il Principe* (*The Prince*) written by Niccolo Machiavelli more than 300 years before

Darwin's *Origin of Species* and published in 1532, 5 years after Machiavelli's death. In this well-known book, the Florentine author and statesman told of the problems a prince had in ruling the people of his kingdom. *The Prince* describes in great detail the methods by which a ruler may gain and keep power, and it justified means to this end, including some that we would regard as amoral or tyrannical. For example, Machiavelli cited the problem of keeping one's subjects "united and obedient," and he went on to show how any means used were justified if the desired ends were accomplished. Business leaders, already supported in their positions of eminence and wealth by social Darwinism, seized upon these conclusions of Machiavelli to justify the sometimes harsh methods they employed to attain their ends, namely, higher profits. If harsh, cruel means were required for a business executive to succeed, they were justified, for without the employment of such devious tactics, one's survival in the world of commerce was highly questionable.

It seems difficult to believe that people of that time would accept such teachings as adequate justification for some of the practices of the day. Yet accept them they did, and from the Civil War until the depression of 1873, business executives were largely free from government curbs on their business methods, however ruthless they might be.

THE CHANGING NATURE OF PROFITS

During this period, a change occurred also in the way profits were justified. Through the influence of social Darwinism, profits evolved from a "just due" to a "moral obligation" of business. Recall that in the days of Adam Smith, David Ricardo, and John Stuart Mill, profits were viewed as a payment to the business leader for services rendered, an interest payment for the use of capital, and a surplus produced by the labor employed by the business leader. None of the early economists and social commentators quarreled with the right of the business executive to a profit. None, in fact, worried about an executive making "too much profit"—for the invisible hand of competition was supposed to prevent any such occurrences. Social Darwinism, however, brought about a marked change in the structure of business, and in so doing, altered markedly the attitude toward profits.

The social implications of profit

In the latter part of the 19th century, as we noted, a change took place in the competitive structure of business. In Chapter 2, for example, we saw how the giant industrial empires of Swift, Carnegie, and Rockefeller were created, each effectively eliminating or minimizing the competition it faced from others.

As business grew in size, the concentration of power that Adam Smith had feared became a reality. In many cases, competition no longer existed. The "invisible hand" concept broke down. Nothing existed to prevent large, even excessive profits from being earned. Moreover, with the popularity of social Darwinism and the Machiavellian attitude of business managers, the earning of large profits became an obsession. The extent to which this obsession had developed was evidenced in the famous "Acres of Diamonds" speech of Russell Conwell, a noted Methodist minister of the late 1800s. The excerpt below certainly needs no elaboration.

> I say you ought to be rich; you have no right to be poor . . . I must say that you ought to spend time getting rich. You and I know there are some things more valuable than money; of course, we do. Ah, yes . . . Well does the man know who has suffered that there are some things sweeter and holier and more sacred than gold. Nevertheless, the man of common-sense also knows that there is not any one of those things that is not greatly enhanced by the use of money. Money is power. Love is the grandest thing on God's earth, but fortunate the lover who has plenty of money. Money is power; money has powers; and for a man to say, "I do not want money," is to say, "I do not wish to do any good to my fellowmen." It is absurd thus to talk. It is absurd to disconnect them. This is a wonderfully great life, and you ought to spend your time getting money, because of the power there is in money.[4]

Economic implications

Even economists, who, as we saw earlier in our discussions, strived to find a practical justification for profits instead of a more philosophical one, were swept up in the reverence and tribute paid to the earning of profits. Alfred Marshall, for example, in his *Principles of Economics,* excused the quest for excessive profits by saying: "It is probable that those businessmen who have pioneered new paths have often conferred on society benefits out of all proportion to their own gains, even though they have died millionaires."[5] Thus were profits, and the earning of profits, raised to new levels of importance in business and society. From an initial status as a "surplus produced by labor," profits came to enjoy a position of respect second only to Godliness, and in some cases, no doubt, above it.

PRAGMATISM AND THE "GILDED AGE"

The public during the period from 1870 to 1900 became increasingly distrustful, discontented, and in general disenchanted with business. The

---

[4] Agnes Rush Burr, *Russell H. Conwell and His Work* (Philadelphia: John C. Winston Co., 1917), pp. 414–15. As quoted in Clarence C. Walton, *Corporate Social Responsibilities* (Belmont, Calif.: Wadsworth Publishing Co., 1968), p. 39–40.

[5] Alfred Marshall, *Principles of Economics* (London: Macmillan & Co., Ltd., 1946), p. 598.

rich became richer; the poor became poorer. Great depressions in the 1870s and 1890s convinced many that business leaders were seeking profits—regardless of the costs to others—just for the sake of profits. Surely, it was argued, this was not the way life was meant to be. Accordingly, many began to take a second look at the doctrine of social Darwinism and to question the premise of survival of the fittest as justifying the ruthless practices of the business titan. Quite literally, people began to believe that, rather than being manipulated by the economic environment that surrounded them, they should be able to affect that environment and change it to suit their needs. A philosophy of *pragmatism*—essentially a belief that the truth of a proposition or the validity of a course of action could best be measured by its practical results—began to take hold.

It is ironic that the demise of social Darwinism as an accepted business philosophy was probably due largely to the pushing to extremes of the philosophy itself. Social Darwinism preached that an individual's fate was determined by natural forces—for better or worse—and that one could do nothing to change it. This tendency to accept ruthless struggle as ordained by God, combined with a laissez-faire attitude on the part of government, permitted a few "Captains of Industry" to reap riches far beyond the expectations of most people. The resulting glaring inequities in income aroused such a degree of discontent in the average person that he finally rebelled at his inferior status. Thus, business leaders, operating under a premise and philosophy that they themselves pushed to excesses, laid the groundwork for a demand for legislation that would restrict their actions.

Influences from literature and philosophy

The pragmatic school of philosophy was fortunate in having among its leading thinkers two men able to present the new ideas in appealing literary form—the psychologist William James (1842–1910) and the educator and philosopher John Dewey (1859–1952). Just as Harriet Beecher Stowe's *Uncle Tom's Cabin* had mobilized public indignation against slavery, such works as James's *Principles of Psychology* (1890) and Dewey's *School and Society* (1899) helped to provide a pragmatic justification for efforts aimed at creating a more just society. Henry George's classic book, *Progress and Poverty,* was published in 1879, and it sold millions of copies all over the world. It seemed to offer finally a reasonable explanation for continued poverty amidst vast increases in the nation's riches. George said it was due to the unearned increases in land values, created by the many, but shared in only by the few. His answer to the problem was a single tax—a tax only on land, not on the fruits of labor and capital—which would support all government activity.

FIGURE 4–1

"The American beauty rose can be produced in all its splendor only by sacrificing the early buds that grow up around it," said John D. Rockefeller, Jr.

Father's Picture; Son's Word's. At a time when the monopolistic practices of Standard Oil company were being violently attacked, John D. Rockefeller, Jr., casually—but unfortunately drew an analogy, in a speech before the Brown University YMCA, between business consolidation and the process of developing a rose by pruning. The press lost no time in lifting this figure of speech from its context.

Cartoon by Spencer, 1905. Reprinted with permission from The World of Business, *Edward Bursk et al., eds. (New York: Simon & Schuster, Inc., 1962).*

In 1873, Mark Twain wrote *The Gilded Age* in collaboration with Charles Dudley Warner. This was a satirical novel that mercilessly pictured the business society of the time as truly the product of a "gilded age," all shiny outside but lacking true substance within. While the novel itself made but a passing contribution to the times, the title of "The

FIGURE 4–2

The caricaturist and . . . Jay Gould

SANCTUS JAY-GOULDUS.

Reprinted with permission, from *The World of Business*, Edward C. Bursk *et al.*, eds.
(New York: Simon & Schuster, Inc., 1962).

Gilded Age" was soon used by others to describe the conditions of the day.

In the 1890s and early 1900s, newspaper editorials and cartoons also began to criticize the business tycoon. When John D. Rockefeller, Jr., casually drew a comparison between the consolidation of businesses under a single trust and the need to prune a rose bush to make it beautiful, the cartoonists lost no time in providing a graphic interpretation (see Figure 4–1). Other business tycoons, including the notorious Jay Gould, were also the subject of ridicule and criticism in the press, as can be most vividly seen in Figure 4–2.

BUSINESS PHILOSOPHIES IN THE 20TH CENTURY

The rise of pragmatism as a philosophy of business occurred at a time when science was beginning to play an increasingly important role in business. Science-related industries had developed, and experimentation with new ideas and concepts in management became widespread. People realized that the scientific technology which was giving humans increasing control over the environment could also be applied to business management. Moreover, the management of many of the early companies in America began passing to another, more scientifically inclined and trained, generation. These new "professional managers" often lacked the zeal and obsession for personal wealth that the creators of the business had had. Instead, they were more concerned with securing the futures of the business enterprises they headed. Consequently, they were more open to change and experimentation. To these people, the development and application of sound principles of management was of primary importance. Indeed, the culmination of the pragmatic philosophy, as far as business is concerned, can be found in the application of science to the art of management, which is best exemplified in the work of Frederick W. Taylor.

The development of scientific management

Frederick W. Taylor (1856–1915) is sometimes called the father of scientific management. He is best known for his pioneering work in the area of time and motion analysis. Extremely annoyed at the unnecessary motions he observed being made by most workers, Taylor set about experimenting on ways of setting standards based on studies that revealed the shortest and speediest combinations of motions. His techniques and ideas were soon copied throughout all industry. The "speedup" was widely hailed by management, which saw Taylor's techniques as enabling them to greatly increase the productivity and hence the profitability of their operations. It also became a factor in competition, particularly in the auto industry. Labor, however, did not share management's enthusiasm for this new breed of "efficiency experts." To labor's way of thinking, the net result of this stress on mechanical efficiency was to make management more impersonal than ever, and further increase the conflict between the goals of the worker and the goals of management.

A PHILOSOPHY OF SOCIAL RESPONSIBILITY DEVELOPS

As business became more and more obsessed with the impersonal application of science to management, it became obvious that concern would have to be given to the human needs and motivations of the worker. The factory worker could not, without negative results, continue to be viewed exclusively as another machine or cog in the giant productive processes of industry. He was a human being, and as such was subject to feelings, moods, and other psychological conditions which affected his productivity. The existence of this factor was made conclusively apparent to business leaders by experiments in which Western Electric Company and the Harvard Graduate School of Business Administration collaborated.

The Hawthorne experiments

These experiments were conducted in the 1920s by a team of researchers under the leadership of Professor Elton Mayo of Harvard.[6] They formed the groundwork for what was to be known as the human relations movement. The Harvard researchers explored human responses to changes in environment at the Hawthorne plant of the Western Electric Company. During the course of the experiments (which were an attempt to isolate and analyze the causes of increases in the productivity of workers), the researchers caused a series of changes to be made in the working environment of a select number of workers. To their amazement, they found that almost inevitably, production increased whenever a change in the environment was made—even if the change was for the worse! Thus, they found that even when the hours worked were increased, productivity of the workers also increased. When they decreased the number of hours worked, productivity again increased! Clearly, they concluded, the answer was not so much in the environmental conditions surrounding the workers as it was in the human responses of the workers themselves. The researchers concluded that the sudden feeling of importance gained by the group of workers being tested was the key to their strange behavior; the sudden awareness and treatment of the workers as human beings and not as machines gave a new sense of pride and accomplishment to the workers, and caused them to work harder. This

---

[6] The experiments were reported in detail in F. J. Roethlisberger and W. J. Dickson, *Management and the Worker* (Cambridge, Mass.: Harvard University Press, 1939).

and other findings of the researchers eventually led to a new interest in the human relations aspects of management. It was seen that paying attention to workers as human beings in a social environment could pay off in increased production and fewer personnel problems. The field of personnel management was thereby given birth, and a whole new philosophy of regard for the individual worker as a member of society was initiated.

The spectacular success of the Hawthorne experiments should not obscure the fact that some business executives had been quite adept at managing their personnel for many years. Henry Ford, for example, initiated an unheard of $5 working day as early as 1914—nearly double the going wage rate of the time. Workers were so satisfied with Ford's policy that Ford wasn't organized by a labor union until well after the other major auto makers.

Similarly, Montgomery Ward initiated group life insurance for its employees as early as 1912, and Sears, Roebuck installed a profit sharing plan as early as 1916. Yet, these were isolated instances. It was not until the findings of the Hawthorne experiments found their way into management literature and practice that human relations was fully recognized as meriting an emphasis equal to that of scientific technology in industry.

Pragmatism, science and the social critics

With the rise of pragmatism as a social and business philosophy, and with the ever-increasing emphasis on scientific management, it was only to be expected that social commentators would find some fault with the developing American business environment. One noted critic of the times was Thorstein Veblen (1857–1929).

Thorstein Veblen was an embittered, eccentric, and brilliant economist and social philosopher. His personal life was a string of unfortunate circumstances, possibly accounting for some of the bitterness that he displayed in his outlook on society and business in particular. Yet, his criticisms of society have stood the test of time, for many of them are still being trumpeted today.

Veblen was one of the first social scientists to call attention to what he felt was a wasteful use of our productive resources. In his classic work, *The Theory of the Leisure Class* he depicted people's social and economic lives as being directed by a group of wealthy aristocrats—individuals who had no need of work but rather engaged in living lives of leisure. (Veblen was not alone in viewing the "leisure class" with disdain. Even Theodore Roosevelt once called them the "idle rich.")

Veblen saw these "idle rich" as flaunting their status by acquiring exaggerated status symbols—huge mansions, yachts, Rolls Royces, and so on—and displaying their riches through what he referred to as "con-

THORSTEIN B. **VEBLEN**

(1857–1929)

"The motive that lies at the root of
ownership is emulation; and the same
motive of emulation continues active
in the further development of the institution to which it has given
rise and in the development of all those features of the social
structure which this institution of ownership touches. The possession
of wealth confers honor; it is an invidious distinction..."

Source: Thorstein B. Veblen, *The Theory of the Leisure Class*
(New York: The MacMillan Company, 1912).

spicuous waste." The tragedy, in Veblen's opinion, was that this impelled the worker to emulate or imitate the idle rich. The rich bought automobiles; therefore, the way for the worker to appear successful was to also buy an automobile, even if it meant foregoing expenditures for more basic needs. The resulting attitude of "keeping up with the Joneses" was, in Veblen's mind, essentially wasteful. He felt the only way to correct this was to take a more enlightened approach to the production of goods in society—to introduce "social engineering." Thus, Veblen held to the hope that more responsible leadership would assume command of America's economic institutions. Although he held no hope for a "worker's revolution," he did believe in the possibility that an engineering class woud emerge that would properly plan the course of future economic development.

Veblen's ideas might have gained more support if they had come at a different time. He died, however, on the eve of the greatest economic calamity of modern history, the Great Depression.

A NEW ECONOMIC PHILOSOPHY EMERGES

The depression of 1929–33 severely shook people's faith and confidence in the workability of a laissez-faire approach to business. Granted, government had been active in commerce for almost 40 years, beginning with the passage of the Interstate Commerce Commission Act in 1887.[7]

---

[7] This date merely signifies the beginning of actual intervention. Government aid to business can be traced all the way back to the Founding Fathers.

However, such regulation had been designed to correct certain specific business abuses—particularly the malpractices of the railroads—and was not intended to set up broad economic guidelines for business behavior. With the coming of the Great Depression, however, people clearly realized that something more was needed. The thinker who was to have the greatest influence on the postdepression era was the brilliant English economist, John Maynard Keynes. (1883–1946).

Keynesian economics

 Keynes' famous work, *The General Theory of Employment, Interest, and Money,* was published in 1936, and immediately captured worldwide attention. When *The General Theory* came out, England was in the midst of a ten-year depression and was urgently in need of a program that would resolve its economic woes. Keynes' work provided that program.

In *The General Theory,* Keynes discussed the problems of unemployment, interest rate determination, and money supply, with emphasis on the problem of unemployment. In his text, Keynes showed how government, through its fiscal powers (the power of taxation and government spending programs) and its monetary powers (determination of the amount of money to be allowed to circulate in the economy), would be able to alleviate the problems that were plaguing the world's economies. Some of his recommendations were followed in both England and the United States, contributing to partial recovery.

Keynes' philosophy represented a sharp departure from the laissez-faire economics of Adam Smith. Where Smith had advocated nonintervention by government in the affairs of business, Keynes advocated intervention and manipulation by using the monetary and fiscal policy tools available to government.

Keynesian economics, as his policy recommendations have come to be called, won both admirers and critics. One author has stated that if Keynes had written *The General Theory* ten years earlier, World War II might have been avoided, for Hitler would never have been able to assume power in Germany; all would have been well in Europe, thereby eliminating the need for Hitler's "New Order." Others, however, were strongly critical of the "evils" of Keynesian economics. It was "socialism," said the critics, and would spell the end to the greatest economic system the world had ever seen, namely the American system of free enterprise. Even President Herbert Hoover once compared Keynes with Hitler and Mussolini as comprising the three greatest threats to civilized society in the world.

To this day, of course, Keynes' philosophy is a much debated topic. It is true that Keynes said little in *The General Theory* that hadn't been said before. Keynes, however, did put it all together in a manner which

JOHN MAYNARD KEYNES

(1883-1946)

"In some...respects, the [General] theory is moderately conservative in its implica- tions. For whilst it indicates the vital importance of establishing certain central controls in matters which are now left in the main to individual initiative, there are wide fields of activity which are unaffected. The State will have to exercise a guiding influence on the propensity [i.e., willingness] to consume, partly through its scheme of taxation, partly by fixing the rate of interest, and partly, perhaps, in other ways."

Source: John Maynard Keynes, *The General Theory of Employ- ment, Interest and Money* (New York: Harcourt, Brace & World, 1965), Chapter 24.
Note: Bracketed insertions are this author's, and are in- tended only to clarify certain words used by J. M. Keynes.

enabled politicians and other economists to see the complexities of na- tional economic policies more clearly. Moreover, he had the good fortune of writing *The General Theory* at the precise time when the nations of the world were searching for a new economic doctrine. His theories have since been modified and few adherents of pure Keynesianism exist today.

Business philosophy undergoes a change

Keynesian economics was ushered in with the New Deal of Franklin D. Roosevelt. Massive government aid and regulatory programs were passed (see Chapter 3), all in an attempt to lift the economy out of the massive depression. One result of these programs was to cause a shift in the attitudes people had about business. The programs also changed business attitudes about the role of government in society.

During the boom years of the 1920s, business prestige had been at an all-time high. As Frederick Lewis Allen put it, it was "a time . . . when one could pay his clergyman high praise by telling him he had delivered his sermon in a businesslike manner."[8] The depression years of the 1930s, however, badly tarnished the image of the business executive. Laissez-fairism had failed, and it required massive government aid to get the business community back on its feet.

People began to lose faith in the underlying principles of free enterprise, wondering instead whether such a system of business could ever again achieve the goals of the American people. Thus, the decade of the 1940s saw business undertake a massive program to resell the free enterprise system to the American public. William Whyte's book, *Is Anybody Listening?* presents an interesting and entertaining discussion of this campaign.

Business soon came to realize, however, that the fears of an early end to the free enterprise system were largely unfounded. True, government was not about to remove itself from its position of influence in the economy, but neither was it about to drastically increase that role. Henceforth, business would have to accept the role of government in the economy. The era of the partially managed economy had arrived.

A DOCTRINE OF SOCIAL RESPONSIBILITY

The last 20 years have seen the development of what appears to be a new philosophy of business, namely, that of social responsibility. This philosophy is characterized by corporate concern for, and dedication to, the solving of some of the major social problems of today. For example, following the principles of a philosophy of social responsibility, many businesses have aided in the hiring and training of the hardcore unemployed. Other businesses have made efforts at improving housing and other urban ills, have provided support for the arts and other cultural activities, and have made an effort at providing the consuming public with more information about the products it purchases. Some of these activities have been voluntary; others have been mandatory. Government, pushed by various groups to alleviate these social ills, has passed laws requiring certain actions by the business community.

Regardless, however, of the manner in which "socially responsible" acts happened to come about, the question of real importance remains, "Why?" Why has business in the past 20 years become so concerned about establishing a philosophy seemingly so foreign to its economic basis? All of the earlier social philosophies of business attempted to explain or rationalize the existence of the business firm as a profit-making institution in society. The philosophy of social responsibility, however,

---

[8] Earl F. Cheit, "The New Place of Business: Why Managers Cultivate Social Responsibility," as found in Earl F. Cheit (ed.), *The Business Establishment,* (New York: John Wiley & Sons, Inc., 1964), p. 153.

would tend to subordinate the unrestricted earning of profits to the performance by business of a worthwhile role in society. Indeed, profitable firms are often those most severely criticized today, in the belief that too profitable a firm must not be doing its share of work in the "public interest."

Why a philosophy of social responsibility?

People do not agree as to the reasons underlying the development of a philosophy of social responsibility. Some have argued that business' new found "social responsibility" is really an attempt to resell the American people on the virtues of an unrestricted free enterprise system. Business, they argue, has not been able to regain the prestige it lost when the Great Depression hit, and that this new "corporate conscience" is really just another effort to win friends and followers.

Others have advanced the idea that the philosophy of "social responsibility" is an outgrowth of a new environment, one in which the public has assumed a role of substantial importance for the first time. Given the advances in communication and education in the postwar years, the public has become increasingly aware of the inequities in our society and is increasing its demands that the major institutions of society be reformed. As one of these major institutions, business has felt the power that public opinion can wield in determining survival and has consequently responded with an increasing social awareness both inside and outside the firm.

Finally, some have viewed business' new attitude as arising from the increased power and status of the corporation itself. They point out that corporations and corporate managers today are in the enviable position of wielding power without owning property. Adolf Berle, noted business philosopher, historian, and critic, has perhaps been most responsible for advancing this line of thought. Berle has argued that business today finds itself in the awkward state of possessing immense wealth and power, and that this has all transpired solely because of our modern, large corporate structures. To justify their existence, and put a stamp of "legitimacy" on it, these companies have adopted a paternalistic attitude toward society in general. With others, however, Berle shares the view that only the force of public opinion can keep this new "social conscience" operating in a manner beneficial to society.

Which reason or reasons are correct is a most difficult judgment to make. As is true of any contemporary development, the real meaning and importance of social responsibility as a corporate philosophy can only be answered in hindsight. We can state, however, that all of these reasons probably contain elements of truth in them. For example, the successful development of a "socially responsible" business and labor community would certainly advance the cause of free enterprise as the best economic system yet devised by man. That this is the underlying motive to this new philosophy, however, is questionable. If business and labor were truly that concerned about the social acceptability of the free enterprise system, it seems logical that greater efforts would have been forthcoming voluntarily from these two institutions. Truth-in-Packaging laws and Truth-in-Lending laws would hardly have been necessary; business would have taken steps to remove these problems on its own. Indeed, the inflationary spiral that began in the late 1960s and early 1970s would have ended long ago. In the realization that inflation causes more social damage than any other action, business and labor leaders—if they were truly concerned about the survival of the free enterprise system—would have taken the necessary steps to bring the inflation to a halt.

Similarly, there is little doubt that the force of public opinion is a powerful one and often influences business' actions in society. The success of Ralph Nader, for example, is ample evidence of how public opinion can be effectively used to bring changes in business' role in society. Yet, here, too, the argument that it is the power of public opinion alone that is effecting this change in corporate philosophy does not stand up. Many businesses are active in providing cultural and educational opportunities for people in their communities. Doesn't it seem logical that if public opinion were business' prime motivator, business would make a much greater effort than it has to influence public opinion by advertising or publicly announcing such things? Yet, how many people ever hear of these developments?

Finally, we have the argument that business' unique wealth and power have forced it to seek legitimacy in our contemporary society. Again, the wealth and power of American business cannot be denied. A very recent study ranked the wealthiest corporations in the free world. Table 4–1 shows the staggering wealth of America's largest corporations vis-à-vis the world. As the table clearly shows, of the 11 corporations that had sales in 1973 in excess of $10 billion, 9 of them were American-based firms.

Yet, even the wealth of American business is not unlimited, nor is its power so great that it need act defensively to protect it. The American textile industry, the shoe industry, and even the steel industry, face severe competition from abroad. The airline and aircraft manufacturing industries are also in trouble, as the recent government loan guarantee to Lockheed Aircraft evidences. (Lockheed, you may recall, was under contract to build several major new planes. The costs got out of hand, and Lockheed almost went bankrupt. Even bankers refused to loan money to Lockheed, for fear the company would never be able to make a profit on its planes, and consequently, never be able to repay the loans. Only after the federal government agreed to guarantee payment for the loans was

TABLE 4–1

The world's largest companies 1973 (in millions of dollars)

Company	Sales	Assets	Income
1. General Motors...........	$35,798,289	$20,296,861	$2,398,103
2. Exxon....................	25,724,319	25,079,494	2,443,286
3. Ford Motor...............	23,015,100	12,954,000	906,500
4. *Royal Dutch/Shell*........	18,672,150	22,797,257	1,789,248
5. Chrysler.................	11,774,372	6,104,898	255,445
6. General Electric..........	11,575,300	8,324,200	585,100
7. Texaco..................	11,406,876	13,595,413	1,292,403
8. Mobil Oil................	11,390,113	10,690,431	849,312
9. *Unilever*..................	11,009,559	5,675,732	423,284
10. IBM.....................	10,993,242	12,289,489	1,575,467
11. I.T.&T...................	10,183,035	10,132,571	527,837

Note: Italicized companies are foreign owned or headquartered.
Source: *Fortune* Magazine, August 1974, p. 185.

Lockheed able to get the money it needed to stay in business.) If American business were all-powerful, would problems like these exist? One would hardly think so.

Thus we find that all of these reasons, although true in part, lack sufficient credibility to adequately resolve why business has become, or is becoming, "socially responsible." Perhaps the answer lies—as it always has—in the meaning of *profit,* and the new interpretations that this motivating force has undergone.

PROFITS IN CONTEMPORARY SOCIETY

A final explanation for the development of a philosophy of social responsibility is founded in the profit motive of business. This argument states that business is acting in a socially responsible manner simply because in the long run, this is the most profitable way to do business. By acting to correct social inequities now, business is helping to assure that an environment it can profitably function in will still exist 30 and 40 years from now. Thus, by training and educating the poor and hard-core unemployed, business is helping to create a new supply of labor for the future and new consumers for its goods. This argument has a strong relationship to the economic functions of business. Business, in its purest sense, is an institution designed to efficiently allocate resources within the economy. Its primary function is to produce *things*—things demanded by the people of the society. Thus, actions which further enable it to accomplish this goal are economically justified. Certainly this line of reasoning—the seeking of long-run profit maximization—is consistent with the economic principles of business.

What, however, explains business' involvement in causes that are not economically justifiable? For example, the training and educating of the poor creates a work force that can help business function. What contribution to its own survival does business make, however, when it subsidizes an opera? It might be argued that "cultural enrichment" is as necessary to the development of good workers as is on-the-job training. This argument, however, becomes tenuous if one is seeking to justify the practice from an economic standpoint. What makes more sense from an economic standpoint is the acknowledgment that *profit* no longer has the same restrictive meaning it once had. Where profit was once strictly defined to mean an economic, material gain, it may now be that profit just means gain—either material or aesthetic. Businesses still strive for a dollar profit; their stockholders require that. However, more and more of them are becoming concerned with earning a "sufficient" dollar profit instead of a "maximum" dollar profit. Interestingly enough, these same firms are becoming more and more active in pursuing other objectives—objectives that provide more of an aesthetic profit than a dollar one. Quite possibly American society may be on the threshold of an era where material prosperity is sufficiently plentiful that earning still more material wealth is becoming secondary to "earning" a better quality of life.

Criticisms of social responsibility

Although the idea of a "socially responsible" business community has a great deal of appeal, the arguments *against* such a philosophy are substantial. Economists, for example, have questioned whether the entire economic fabric of our society might not collapse as a result of too much emphasis on "social responsibility" by business. The function of business, it is argued, is to satisfy society's needs for goods and services. It does this through the capitalistic system. The market exchange mechanism that is determined by the laws of supply and demand achieve a rather efficient system for satisfying these economic needs. Business, it is argued, has this function and responsibility and no more. Involvement in causes which focus on things other than the principle of profit maximization will only succeed in making the allocation of goods and services less efficient than it once was. Perhaps the argument against a philosophy of social responsibility was best summarized by the University of Chicago's eminent economist, Milton Friedman: "Few trends could so thoroughly undermine the very foundations of our free society as the acceptance by corporate officials of a social responsibility other than to make as much money for their stockholders as possible."[9]

As the evidence clearly shows, the merits and demerits, the strengths and weaknesses, of a philosophy of social responsibility are far from

---

[9] Milton Friedman, *Capitalism and Freedom* (Chicago: University of Chicago Press, 1962), p. 133.

having been finally determined. Why such a philosophy developed is not yet entirely clear, although insights into various contributing factors are available. Whether, in fact, such a trend spells further success or doom for our capitalistic economy still remains to be seen. Certainly, advocates of a philosophy of social responsibility are impatient for further advances. Also certain, however, is the concern being expressed by those opposed to this development about the speed with which business has already responded. If nothing else, the development of this philosophy does reveal one thing: business as an institution is highly susceptible to changes in response to society's wants and demands. Whether those wishes of society are for more and better goods, or for a more refined and enlightened attitude by its managers, business has been quick to respond. For today, just as was true 200 years ago, business functions as an institution *within* society, and as such, must naturally be affected by changes that occur for the society as a whole.

DISCUSSION QUESTIONS

1   "Laissez-faire" as an economic philosophy is widely heralded as being the primary reason for America's rapid growth. In reality, however, the principles of laissez-faire were violated early in our nation's history. What is the earliest activity you can point to that violates these principles?

2   Examine the quote by Adam Smith, found on page 88. This quote, as you can see, is the one that discusses the "invisible hand" for the first time. However, in this quote, the "invisible hand" is used in a different context than was used in the text. How is Adam Smith using the concept in that short paragraph?

3   What was Mill referring to when he mentioned the "relative immobility of labor"?

4   Discuss the principles of social Darwinism.

5   Many people have argued that the unusual stability witnessed in the United States during the early 1800s was due primarily to the opening of the West. They argued that the West served as an "escape valve" for discontented labor. Discuss the merits of this argument in light of the philosophies of the time.

5   Among recent social critics of business, the names of Vance Packard, John Kenneth Galbraith, and Ralph Nadar stand out. Compare the work of any of these men with social critics of previous eras. Who do they most resemble? Why?

6   Define "social responsibility." Compare your answer with that of a fellow classmate. Are they the same? If not, why?

7   Can a "socially responsible" firm be a profitable one? Can it be an unprofitable one? Explain.

8   Reexamine the argument of Professor Milton Friedman, as found near the end of this chapter. Why do you suppose Friedman feels a "socially responsible" attitude, that is, one that emphasizes things other than making a profit, could undermine the foundation of a free society?

MINI CASES

Oftentimes, the question of right and wrong, or "ethical" and "unethical" are subject to a great deal of personal feeling. Such is the case with a large ranch in the southwestern part of the United States. This particular ranch employed large numbers of illegal Mexican immigrants —commonly known as "wetbacks"—in its daily operations. This practice was fairly common among ranches in this part of the country; indeed, it was almost a necessity. The "wetbacks" would perform physical labor that most Americans would refuse to do, and they would work for low wages—another necessary factor for the profitable maintenance of some of these ranches.

The owner of this particular ranch, however, had a long-standing interest in politics and, indeed, had announced his intention to run for governor of that state. Thus, the newspapers had a major story when the U.S. Immigration Department announced that a raid on this man's ranch revealed the widespread employment of these illegal immigrants.

The opposition candidate for governor immediately seized on this issue in his campaign. He charged the rancher with a certain callousness and unconcern for American workers, because the rancher willingly employed "wetbacks" when there were Americans who could not find work. The rancher/politician protested, noting that it was not illegal to employ "wetbacks," and that although many Americans were unemployed, the unemployed people were not found in rural areas. Rather, they were in the big cities of the North, and as such, beyond his scope of business. He also stated the low pay the immigrants were paid amounted to eight to ten times per month more than they could earn in their own country.

1. *Comment on the ethical nature of the rancher's problem.*
2. *Was the rancher acting in a socially responsible manner?*
3. *Is there such a thing as an "international social responsibility"? How would the rancher's position be affected by the existence of an international responsibility?*
4. *Does the fact the workers were economically better off justify this practice?*

(Author's note: Late in 1974, the U.S. Congress was debating a bill to make it illegal for employers to hire "wetbacks." As of this writing, however, the bill had not yet become law.)

One of the interesting phenomenons of our business heritage is the shifting that occurs in our standards of conduct. John D. Rockefeller, Cornelius Vanderbilt, Jay Gould, and many other "business titans" achieved success through all types of business practices—some ethical and others not so. Regardless of the method, however, that was employed, these men gained fame and fortune that lived on well beyond their times.

Interestingly enough, it took the passing of only a few years for attitudes on business practices to change. J. P. Morgan, for example, was thoroughly criticized for his role in forming the banking trust. Yet, his method of operation was certainly no worse than that practiced by the forementioned business titans.

1. *How do you explain this change in society's attitude?*
2. *Do you see a parallel in today's society?*

In late 1972, the noted psychologist B. F. Skinner introduced a "new theory" designed to improve the performance of workers in industry. Skinner's theory is known as "behavior modification," or "positive reinforcement." Simply stated, it holds that individuals' behaviors can be influenced by changing their environment and by praising their performance.

Essentially, Skinner's theory requires management to use praise, recognition, and a regular feedback system to tell employees how they are doing on the job. Several companies have attempted to put Skinner's theory into practice, and have been pleasantly surprised at the results. Critics, however, charge that the technique amounts to "mollycoddling" of the employees, and in some cases amounts to an invasion of privacy and/or manipulation of the worker.

1. *Given your understanding of earlier philosophies of business, do you feel Skinner's theory is a "new" business philosophy? Why or why not?*

Theodore Vail, the managerial genius behind the growth of the American Telephone and Telegraph Company, was born near Minerva, Ohio, on July 16, 1845. While he was still a young boy, his family moved to New Jersey. By the age of 19, Vail was working for Western Union. A short time later, he became a telegraph operator for the Union Pacific Railroad. His adroitness at handling the mail service soon gained him a reputation, and by 1873, Vail was serving in Washington, D.C., as the assistant superintendent of railway mail service.

In the meantime, Alexander Graham Bell had invented the telephone, and a man by the name of Gardiner Greene Hubbard began to organize the telephone business. Recognizing Vail's talents, Hubbard hired him as general manager of the Bell Telephone Company. Between 1878 and 1887, Vail merged many of the local exchanges into Bell. He acquired the Western Electric Company, which until then had been part of Western Union and turned it into the manufacturing arm of Bell. Vail also connected all of the operating companies and exchanges by means of a long-distance telephone system. In 1885, he incorporated the A.T.&T. company and became its first president. In 1889, tired and exhausted, Vail retired.

Vail's retirement was short-lived, however. The Bell system's patents had begun expiring in 1883–84, and hundreds of small companies were formed. The directors of A.T.&T. appealed to Vail to return. In 1907, Vail was again elected president. He immediately began a massive public relations campaign, and formed an alliance with Western Union. The federal government, however, threatened to take over A.T.&T. and turn its operations over to the Post Office. Vail quickly backed down and dissolved the tie with Western Union. Nonetheless, A.T.&T. remained the dominant phone company in America. Vail retired from the presidency in 1919, one year before his death.

Theodore N. Vail
(1845–1920)

"One phone company was enough!"

5

The Structure of American business

If a man can write a better book, preach a better sermon, or make a better mouse trap than his neighbor, though he builds his house in the woods, the world will make a beaten path to his door.

——*Ralph Waldo Emerson*

This chapter begins an in-depth study of how business actually functions. To this point, attention has been focused on the role of economic systems in modern societies on one of the major "crises" that face virtually all societies, and something on the historical and philosophical background of American business. In this chapter, we shall examine the significant types of business organizations found in the United States, discuss the reasons for their existence, and also discuss the implications of these various business structures to the American society's further development. At the conclusion of this chapter, you should have a reasonably solid foundation of American business as we begin our discussions of the business functions in Part two of the text.

THE EVOLUTION OF AMERICA'S BUSINESS STRUCTURE

At first glance, it may seem rather strange to begin a chapter by discussing the evolution of our business structure. Yet, such an approach is both necessary and logical. Most of us, for example, have heard of a "corporation"; and most of us have heard of a "partnership." Thus, one might ask, Why study the evolution of these institutions?

The answer, of course, is that an understanding of why these institutions exist, and what caused them to come into being, is necessary if we are to understand and/or appreciate what kinds of institutions might come into being in the future. As an example, consider the institution of the corporation—the really big modern-day corporation!

Corporate institutions of the magnitude of a GM or an A.T.&T. are phenomena of the 20th century. Imagine, for example, a single business firm employing almost 1 million people, selling more goods and services than most countries produce, earning profits upward of $2 billion a year, and paying taxes that account for as much as 7 percent of all the corporate income taxes collected by the federal government! That's General Motors—a truly colossal firm! Fifty years ago, firms of that magnitude and profitability were nonexistent. Indeed, people no more believed such firms could actually exist one day than they believed that the fiction in Jules Verne's novels *Twenty Thousand Leagues under the Sea* and *From the Earth to the Moon* could become factual in the submarine and in moon landing.

The corporation itself was just coming into being about the time North America was colonized. The trading companies chartered by the Crown played a major role in colonization. But in colonial America most of the industrial work was done in small shops located around the country. The corporation, however, did not develop the form that characterizes it today until much later in history. The giant corporation is even more recent, and in a sense, the corporate form of business is still a relatively new development.

MAJOR FORMS OF BUSINESS ORGANIZATION

It is interesting to note that, of the 12 million plus business organizations in the United States, the vast majority of them are of one of three types: they are either *sole proprietorships, partnerships,* or *corporations.*

The sole proprietorship

The sole proprietorship is the oldest, and still the most popular, form of business organization. Its origins trace back thousands of years, to the days of the Phoenicians, Greeks, and Romans. Basically, the sole proprietorship is characterized by the existence of a single owner, or proprietor, who both owns and operates the business. Sole ownership of the business; sole right to the profits of the firm; singular authority, with the right to open and close when so desired—these are some of the unique features of this form of business organization. To elaborate:

Characteristics of the sole proprietorship

Ease of entry and exit	Taxation benefits
Sole managerial authority	Limited life
Right to all profits	Limited size
Unlimited liability	

Ease of entry and exit Without question, sole proprietorships are the easiest form of business to create. There is a minimal amount of paper work or legal compliance to go through in order to become a sole proprietor. Only in cases where regulation, inspection, or licensing are required does the sole proprietor really encounter any regulatory restrictions.

Related to this advantage is the ability to go out of business with equal speed and simplicity. In many cases, all one need do to go out of business is to lock the door and hang a sign in the window saying "Closed."

Part of the reason for such ease of entry to and exit from the sole proprietorship, of course, stems from the early history of this nation. When this country was formed, sole proprietorships were practically the only type of business organization. Given the desire of the Founding Fathers to remove the influence of government from the everyday lives of the people, it is understandable that the sole proprietorship was left without rigid controls and requirements.

Sole managerial authority One characteristic of sole proprietorships that at first glance appears to be a distinct advantage for motivated individuals is the right to be the sole managerial authority. As sole proprietor, the owner and only the owner exercises managerial power. The business operates according to his or her preconceived ideas and wishes.

As attractive as this "right" may seem, it frequently develops that this is one of the characteristics that qualifies as a major cause of failure for sole proprietorships. (See Figure 5–1.) As sole owner and

FIGURE 5–1

Major mistakes causing business failures

1. Lacking a clear-cut comprehension of what is to be achieved.
2. Failing to develop a program of future activities.
3. Starting without facts and research information about the business and its market.
4. Going in the business without adequate experience in it.
5. Making poor selection of employees and failing to motivate them.
6. Underpricing or overpricing goods and services.
7. Underestimating competition.
8. Expanding too rapidly.
9. Having too little capital to start.
10. Starting with an excessive amount of capital and spending it unwisely.
11. Buying too much on credit.
12. Ignoring the building up of a reserve for contingencies.
13. Giving insufficient attention and effort to the business.
14. Failing to keep adequate and accurate records and reports.

Source: George R. Terry, *Principles of Management,* 5th ed. (Homewood, Ill.: Richard D. Irwin, Inc., 1968), p. 7.

manager, he ("he" being understood to include females as well as males) is required to be the sales manager, purchasing agent, accountant, lawyer, public relations manager, and custodian all at the same time. Very few people possess the necessary talent to adequately perform these many and varied tasks. Thus, sole proprietorships frequently suffer from managerial deficiencies and occasionally go out of business because of them. Indeed, the inability to enjoy a division of labor is one of the primary disadvantages for sole proprietorships.

Right to all profits   As sole owner of the business, the proprietor is entitled to full ownership of all profits earned by the business. Also, however, he is responsible for the debts of the business and must bear the losses suffered by the business.

Frequently, many people desire to start their own business simply because of the right to full ownership of all profits. The limited size of most sole proprietorships, however, tends to severely limit the profitability of this type of business organization.

Taxation benefits   Assuming that the sole proprietorship is successful at earning a profit, the owner may enjoy still another advantage. This concerns the tax liability of the firm. Individual proprietorships are not taxed directly; the law does not distinguish between an owner of a proprietorship and his business. Thus, the profits earned by the business are considered, for tax purposes, as having been earned by the owner. The owner pays taxes on the profits at the regular rate for individual taxpayers. As we shall see, this rate can be significantly lower than the tax rate paid by corporations. Profits of corporations are taxed directly, and again indirectly, by the taxes paid by individual stockholders on their dividends.

Limited life   One of the major weaknesses of a sole proprietorship is the limited period of time the business will remain in existence. Sole proprietorships exist only so long as the sole proprietor lives. When he dies, the business comes to an end.

Occasionally, a sole proprietorship appears to continue in business even after the death of the owner. Really, what has happened is that a new sole proprietorship has been created. The business may seem the same—indeed, it may be the same—in all respects except one. That is the identity of the owner, the sole proprietor of the firm.

Limited size   The sole proprietorship is limited in the amount of capital usually available to it. In a sole proprietorship, all ownership investment comes from one individual—the sole proprietor. To the extent that the proprietor is wealthy, a substantial initial investment in the firm may be possible. Most owners, however, are not so well endowed financially, and therefore are required to limit the size and scope of their business venture.

Then, too, partly because of the limited life factor, sole proprietorships rarely get very large. It takes a good many years to accumulate enough profits to really become big. Also, most business executives find it desirable to borrow money on occasion—sometimes for rather long periods of time. Sole proprietors who are middle-aged or older, may find that it is exceedingly difficult to borrow money for long-run expansion. Creditors would fear the owner's demise before the company's growth could be realized or the loan repaid. Thus, we can see that a limitation capital is directly responsible for the inability of many sole proprietorships to get very large.

Unlimited liability   Finally, sole proprietors face the prospect of unlimited liability for the debts and obligations of the business. Consider a business that is forced into bankruptcy, or against which a lawsuit is filed. If the court finds the complaint to be valid, the owner may lose not only whatever the business is worth, but may also be liable to the full extent of his personal wealth for those debts. As a result, of course, extremely wealthy people rarely continue a business as a sole proprietorship. A simple act of negligence or carelessness in the business may result in a judgment against the business, and endanger the personal wealth of the owner.

Despite these drawbacks, however, sole proprietorships are still the most popular form of business organization. The desire for independence, to be one's own boss, and to reap the profits from one's toil combine to

FIGURE 5–2

Types of business organizations

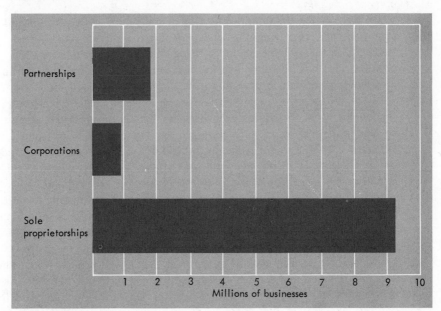

keep this a particularly popular form of business organization. Figure 5–2 shows the relative popularity of sole proprietorships.

Partnerships

A second form of business organization is the partnership. The partnership, as the name implies, is a business organization with two or more owners. In most other respects, the partnership resembles a sole proprietorship in that it possesses a limited life, provides unlimited liability for certain partners, and generally tends to be smaller in size than corporations.

Characteristics of partnerships

Ease of entry	Two or more owners
Division of labor	Limited life
Tax benefits	Unlimited liability

Ease of entry   Creating a partnership is only slightly more complex than creating a sole proprietorship. To form a partnership, agreement must be reached among the various partners regarding such things as how profits are to be shared, the circumstances under which new partners may be admitted, where the business will locate, and so on. Such agreement is the basis for the partnership contract and may be either written or oral. When they are written, they are called the *articles of copartnership.*

Division of labor   Recall that one of the major disadvantages of the sole proprietorship was the need for the owner to be a jack-of-all-trades, possessing legal skills, knowing bookkeeping, salesmanship, purchasing, and having other talents. A desire to overcome this particular disadvantage of sole proprietorships was, in fact, one of the major reasons for developing the partnership form of business. In a partnership, responsibility for the various tasks in the firm can be spread among the several partners. Thus, one partner may handle the legal and book-keeping chores, another may be the chief sales representative, and so on. The ability to divide the labor—to specialize on managerial skills—is one of the strengths of the partnership form of organization.

Tax benefits   Partnerships have the same tax treatment advantages that sole proprietorships enjoy. Again, the partnership is not subject to direct taxation. That is, in the eyes of the law, income earned by a partnership is considered to be earned by the respective partners, according to the way in which the partners split those profits. Accordingly, the partners are taxed on their respective share of the earnings at the lower, personal income tax rate, rather than at the higher business (corporate) tax rate. In the absence of any agreement on the splitting of profits by a partnership, it is assumed that all partners share the profits equally.

Two or more owners   Partnerships are characterized by the existence of two or more owners, at least one of whom is known as a *general partner*. It may also have several other classes of partnership, ranging from *limited partnership* to *secret* and/or *silent partnership*.

General partners are those partners that enjoy all of the benefits of the partnership (i.e., managerial authority, share in the profits, and so on) and are subject to all of the shortcomings or liabilities of partnership (unlimited liability, possible mistrust among the partners, and so on). Normally, general partners are active in the management of the business, while other types of partners tend to limit their role in the operation of the business.

Limited partners are partners whose managerial voice is limited to certain aspects of the business. Similarly, the extent of liability for each such partner is also limited. For example, a lawyer or accountant might be a limited partner.

Silent partners likewise tend to have limited liability within the firm. Silent partners are those partners who do not desire to take an active role in the management of the company, but who are willing to let their name be used as one of the partners of the firm.

Secret partners may or may not have limited liability, depending on the extent of their participation in the business. Secret partners are partners who play an active role in the management of the partnership, but who, for one reason or another, desire to keep their status as a partner secret from the public. Frequently, if a partner enjoying limited liability by virtue of his status as a secret partner should lose that secrecy, he may also lose the limitation on his liability he had enjoyed as a secret partner. Once the secrecy is removed, nothing remains to distinguish the secret partner from the general partners. As a general rule, there is no upward limit as to how many partners a firm may have, although cooperation, coordination, and general trustworthiness between and among the partners tend to decline with increases in the number of partners.

Limited life   Partnerships face an even more uncertain life than do sole proprietorships. In sole proprietorships, if the owner dies, the proprietorship comes to an end. In a partnership, however, if any of the general partners die, or becomes mentally or psychologically incapacitated, the partnership ends. Indeed, depending on the nature of the relationship, the death of even a limited partner may bring the entire business to a close. Thus, with many partners in a partnership, it becomes apparent that the length of life of the business is rather tenuous.

Unlimited liability   As has already been indicated, all general partners in a partnership have unlimited liability for all of the debts of the business, and actions taken by one partner are binding on the others. Thus, a partnership of five general partners will find each of those partners liable for all of the debts of the firm. In the case of a lawsuit, if one partner is exceptionally wealthy and the others are relatively poor, the one wealthy partner may be forced to bear a disproportionate share of any loss. Otherwise, the loss will probably be spread evenly among the various general partners.

Because of the restrictions mentioned, and the general inability of people to get along well with one another, partnerships tend to be considerably less popular than the other forms of business organization. The possibility that the actions of one partner may cause all of the other partners to lose their entire personal fortunes is not a pleasant prospect and tends to sharply limit the popularity of this form of business organization.

Corporations

The third major type of business organization is the corporation. The corporation is, perhaps, the best known and yet least understood of all business structures. In the United States, the corporation is responsible for approximately 80 percent of the national output and employs vast numbers of people. On the international scene, the corporation has become the single most important symbol of American capitalism.

The corporation: What is it? Chief Justice John Marshall of the United States Supreme Court, in the famous *Dartmouth College* case of 1819, defined a corporation as "an artificial being, invisible, intangible, and existing only in contemplation of law."[1] That is, a corporation is a legal person, possessing most of the same rights, privileges, and obligations of ordinary people.

Corporations are unique among the business organizations found in this country. Because they are recognized in law as an "artificial person," they possess a wide variety of powers and obligations. For example, a corporation is required to pay taxes on its profits, even though the shareholder-owners of the corporation are required to pay taxes on their dividends paid from the same profits. Corporations can initiate lawsuits, and can in turn be sued—even by their shareholders. In a broader sense, we can even find parallels to marriage and divorces of individuals in corporate mergers and spin-offs. More on this, however, will be discussed later in the chapter.

A corporation can be created by permission of a state government, or in rare cases, by permission of Congress. Such permission is granted upon approval by the state of the corporation's *charter* and *bylaws*. The corporate charter specifies the purpose for which the corporation is being organized, the nature of its business, who its founders are,

---

[1] *Dartmouth College* v. *Woodward*, 17 U.S. 518.

FIGURE 5–3

The importance of the corporate form of business

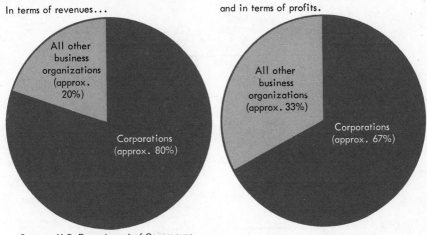

In terms of revenues...   and in terms of profits.

All other business organizations (approx. 20%)

Corporations (approx. 80%)

All other business organizations (approx. 33%)

Corporations (approx. 67%)

Source: U.S. Department of Commerce.

and how many shares of ownership the company desires to issue.

The corporate bylaws provide the rules regarding the election of officers and directors, the location of the annual meeting, and other rules that have a meaning to the formation of the company. Upon approval of the charter and bylaws, and the payment of the various corporation fees and taxes, the state can then approve the establishment of the corporation.

The requirements for the formation of a corporation vary considerably from state to state, with some states having more stringent requirements than others. For example, Delaware charters or authorizes the creation of many more corporations than states like California or New York, simply because its requirements are much more lenient.

Types of corporations Corporations can be classed as *private corporations* or *public corporations.* Private corporations are those that have been organized by and for various individuals in society. U.S. Steel, General Motors, and A.T.&T. are private corporations (see Figure 5–4).

In contrast, public corporations are those owned and/or operated by some governmental body. Thus, the Tennessee Valley Authority is a public corporation, as are most major cities around the country.

Recent years have witnessed the development of quasi-public corporations—that is, corporations whose ownership is both public and private. COMSAT, the Communications Satellite Corporation, is an example of a quasi-public company. It is half owned privately and half owned by the federal government. Amtrack, the newly created National Railway Passenger Corporation, is also a quasi-public corporation.

FIGURE 5–4

Types of business corporations

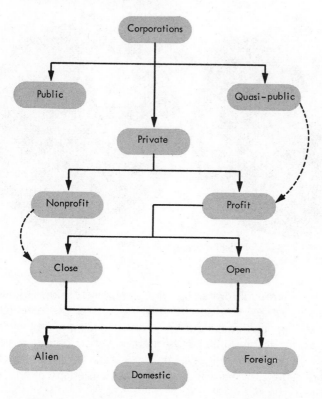

Corporations can be formed for either *profit* or *nonprofit* purposes. Business corporations usually are profit oriented, while churches may be organized as nonprofit-oriented corporations.

Corporations may in turn be classified as either *open corporations* or *close corporations.* An open corporation is one whose stock can be readily acquired on the open market. In contrast, close corporations are usually owned by small groups, families, or by a few individuals. Stock in these companies usually cannot be acquired on the open market and usually does not have a fluctuating and known market value. Stock in most professional sports teams, for example, is usually closely held, while stock in the large industrial corporations is usually available for purchase on the open market.

Finally, corporations may be classed as *domestic, foreign,* or *alien.* Domestic corporations are companies operating in the same state in which they were chartered. Foreign corporations are corporations that have been chartered by one state but do business in other states. Alien corporations are corporations doing business in the United States but which have been chartered by a foreign government. Volkswagen, for example, is an illustration of an alien corporation, when conducting business in the United States.

Characteristics of corporations

Corporations possess characteristics which overcome some of the major deficiencies of sole proprietorships and partnerships. They also possess, however, characteristics which are much more restrictive than the characteristics of either of the other two forms of business organization. Specifically:

Characteristics of corporations

Unlimited life	Division of labor
Right to transfer ownership	Limited liability
Ease of expansion	Double taxation
Organizational expense; lack of privacy	

Unlimited life As has been seen, one of the primary difficulties with the sole proprietorship and the partnership form of business organization is the limited life expectancy of each. During the early 1800s, entrepreneurs realized that the limited life expectancy of these organizational forms would severely limit the expansion and growth of both their businesses and the economic growth of the nation. To overcome this limitation, it was necessary to adopt still another form of business organization. This was the corporation.

Corporations possess, for the most part, an unlimited life expectancy. This is because the death of any of the owners of the business does not affect the corporate structure itself. Ownership in a corporation is signified by legal possession of a certificate of ownership, a stock certificate. If one owner dies, his beneficiaries become legal owners of his share of the business. Because the corporation is considered a legal person, its legal survival is not dependent upon the survival of any one of its owners. Indeed, the only restriction on the life of a corporation is the life expectancy stated in the charter. Thus, if a corporate charter specifies a life of 99 years, after that time the corporation will cease to exist. Such a restriction, however, is rarely if ever found. First, if a corporation desires, it can amend its corporate charter to lengthen its legal life expectancy. Second, more and more corporations are filing for permission to possess a perpetual life, meaning in effect, an indefinite life expectancy.

Right to transfer ownership It has already been noted that one reason for the indefinite life of a corporation is that the life of the business is not dependent on the lives of the owners of the business. In a corporation, the possession of stock certificates is proof of part ownership in the firm. These stock certificates possess the useful characteristic of being negotiable, meaning that they can be transferred from one

FIGURE 5–5

A stock certificate represents ownership in corporations

person to another. Thus, when a person dies, the trustee of the estate will determine who shall assume the ownership of the securities. Similarly, if a stockholder tires of ownership, the stock can be sold on the open market for whatever price that can be obtained. Transfer of ownership by sale and/or purchase has grown to such enormous proportions that among the largest financial institutions in the country today are the stock exchanges, especially the New York Stock Exchange, where transfer of ownership of stock certificates takes place.

Ease of expansion Another limitation of sole proprietorships and partnerships that is overcome by the corporate form of business organization is the ability to expand with ease. Sole proprietorships, you will recall, are limited in their sources of capital to whatever the sole proprietor can contribute from his own funds or borrow. Partnerships, although capable of adding additional partners as the firm grows, are limited to some extent by the difficulties arising out of having too many partners involved in the business and by the uncertain life expectancy of the business.

Corporations face none of these problems. To expand its ownership base, it need only meet the legal requirements to issue more stock.[2] As

---

[2] It should be noted that the issuance of stock involves complex financial considerations and often results in weakening the value of the original owners' shares. These considerations are discussed more fully in Chapters 14 and 15.

more stock is issued and sold to new stockholders, more owners are created, more ownership funds are brought into the business, and the easier it becomes (as we shall see later) to borrow money.

The only limitation imposed on the issuing of more stock by a corporation is the amount of stock authorized by the state of incorporation and stated in the corporate charter. Again, however, this is a relatively minor problem and can usually be overcome by amending the charter.

Division of labor   Corporations enjoy the ability to divide the management of the business among various specialists within the firm. We have seen how sole proprietors are required to be "generalists," managing everything from selling to bookkeeping to custodial services. Even partnerships, although able to divide the labor to some extent, cannot usually achieve the degree of specialization possible in a corporation.

In a corporation, it usually happens that the owners of the business are not the managers of the business. This characteristic is an extremely important one, for it is one of the most important factors distinguishing corporations from other forms of business organizations. The ability to transfer ownership in a corporation has resulted in widespread ownership of most of America's largest corporations. Owners, or stockholders, of

FIGURE 5–6

The organizational structure of
a corporation

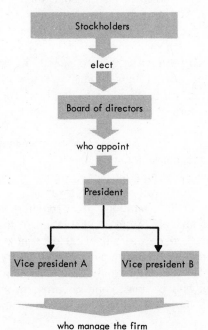

these firms reside all over the country and in some instances, all over the world. It would be impossible for these people to exercise managerial control over their businesses. Rather, these stockholders elect professional managers—known as the *board of directors* of the corporation— and entrust the managing of the firm to them (see Figure 5–6).

Periodically, these managers report to the stockholders on the performance of the company over the preceding period. (A detailed discussion of the relationship of the stockholders and the board of directors of the corporation can be found in Chapter 7.)

The board of directors has wide latitude in determining the degree to which a division of labor shall be exercised. They can create or abolish jobs almost at will. They are required only to protect the owners' investment and to try as hard as possible to earn a satisfactory return for the owners. Often, the difference between a successful firm and an unsuccessful one is the people on the board of directors.

Limited liability   Because of the legal nature of the corporation, its stockholders are not subject to the same liability risks as owners of the other organizational forms of business. Rather, stockholders have a "limited liability" extending only to the amount of their investment in the business. Thus, if a corporation is sued for some reason, and happens to lose the suit, the *company* could be liable for an amount equal to its total value. However, if the suit asked for damages in excess of the value of the corporation, the amount could not be paid. All that can be asked from a corporation in a lawsuit is an amount equal to the value of the business. The stockholders cannot be asked to pay additional funds for the corporation's bills.

You may ask yourself why this condition exists. The reason, of course, is based on that original definition of a corporation as "a legal person." In the eyes of the law, the corporation is treated exactly as an individual would be. As a result, the corporation's debts are the responsibility of the corporation, not the corporation's stockholders. This is the basis for the limited liability feature of the corporate form of business organization.

Double taxation   Although the corporation as a form of business organization possesses many desirable characteristics, there are a few undesirable traits that tend to lessen its popularity. Chief among these unfavorable characteristics is the feature known as double taxation.

When a corporation earns profits on its operations, it is required to pay income taxes on that profit. This tax rate is quite substantial. At the present time corporations are required to pay a rate of 30 percent on the first $25,000 earned, and 48 percent on everything earned thereafter. Thus a corporation like General Motors—earning several billions before taxes each year, pays almost half of this to the government as taxes. Corporations pay dividends to their owners out of remaining income. These dividends are considered to be income for the stockholders, and consequently are subject to personal income taxes! In effect, two taxes are paid on income earned by the corporation. One is paid by the corporation earning the income, and the other is paid by the stockholder receiving the dividends. Corporations are the only institution in this country whose profits are subject to two income taxes in this way.

The reason underlying this double taxation, of course, can be traced to the definition of Justice Marshall. He declared corporations to be "legal persons," subject to the same rights and privileges and obligations as real people. One of these obligations, unfortunately, is to pay income taxes. Thus, corporations—as "legal persons"—are required to pay an income tax. Similarly, the stockholders—as real people—are also required to pay taxes on their income. To the extent, then, that stockholders receive the company's profits as dividends, these profits become subject to double taxation.[3]

Organizational expense and lack of privacy A final characteristic of corporations that causes some business leaders to reject this form of business organization concerns the legal expense required to organize a corporation, and the lack of privacy that must be endured once the corporation is created.

Corporations are legal creations, and as such require a considerable amount of legal processing in order to come into being. This legal processing is not only time-consuming but is expensive as well. Incorporation fees, state taxes, and lawyers fees all need to be paid. It is not unusual for this initial processing expense to run into the tens of thousands of dollars.

Moreover, once created, the corporation is required to file numerous reports and financial statements with the state government that has chartered it. If, moreover, the corporation engages in interstate commerce (does business in more than one state) it will be required to file statements with the U.S. Department of Commerce and the Securities and Exchange Commission. Since these are departments of the federal government, the filings are open to inspection by the public, including competitors. There is small wonder that some business leaders prefer not to incorporate. The resulting loss of privacy could destroy their competitive position in the industry.

These various advantages and disadvantages of the corporate form of organization combine to create an interesting situation. As we have seen, sole proprietorships and partnerships are far more numerous than corporations. However, they are not nearly as important in terms of out-

---

[3] Actually, individuals are allowed to receive from domestic corporations $100 in dividend income annually without paying taxes on it. On a joint return, $200 may be excluded when the securities are jointly owned. Only dividend income in excess of these amounts is subject to double taxation.

put, wages and salaries paid, or in capital investment. Indeed, Figure 5–3 gives a view of the relative importance of the corporate form of American business and tends to explain why we will be concentrating on this institution through most of the remainder of this text.

THE GROWTH OF BIG BUSINESS

The last half century has witnessed not only an increase in the number of business corporations but also in the size of these corporations. Indeed, some of the more challenging questions for consideration today involve this very matter of size. Can a corporation, for example, get too big? What is the economic meaning of "bigness" in business? To answer these questions, we first need to examine the ways business grows and to evaluate the impact of these growth patterns.

Businesses can grow larger in size in either of two ways. They can grow internally, increasing their efficiency of operations and subsequently, their profits, and use these profits to grow still larger. Or they can grow by buying out other firms or establishing smaller, subsidiary companies whose profits are returned to the original company. Recall the discussion in Chapter 3 of the growth techniques. Ford grew through internal expansion, constantly reinvesting his profits. Durant, on the other hand, expanded by buying out competing firms and restructuring them as divisions of the parent company, the General Motors Corporation.

Durant's action is of particular interest because his acquisitions involved restructuring the actual economic fabric of our society. As Durant reduced the number of companies in competition with General Motors and as Ford grew to giant size, very few companies in the country remained to produce automobiles. Most of the others either failed to compete with Ford or were acquired by GM. Moreover, the trend in recent years towards larger and larger business combinations has important international implications. Thus, an understanding of the whys and wherefores of big business—by whatever method it attains giant size—becomes essential if we are to develop an understanding of American business practices in its world setting.

Reasons for business combinations

Business combinations occur in many different ways and for many different purposes. Sometimes businesses combine because they can realize certain *economies of scale* by doing so. This means that they can increase output faster, and at lower cost, than would be possible if they did not combine. One company may have excess production capacity, while another firm has excess orders but a shortage of production facilities. By merging, the two firms can increase their combined output at little extra cost and thereby generate an increase in profits.

Companies also combine in order to assure themselves of a supplier and/or customer for their product. Thus, a paper mill may combine with a newspaper publisher, thereby assuring the mill of a buyer for its paper and simultaneously guaranteeing the publisher of a supply of paper.

Businesses also combine in order to eliminate fluctuations in their incomes. Thus, a manufacturer of ski equipment may combine with the manufacturer of swimming pools. In this way, one division will have peak sales during the summer months, while the other will be busiest during the winter months. Assuring itself of a steady stream of sales, and therefore income, throughout the year not only will improve employee morale but can aid the business in financing, production, and other basic business functions.

Finally, businesses may combine in order to reduce competition. Thus, many of the daily newspapers in the country have disappeared, having been merged into one of the larger daily papers in the respective city. Such a justification for combining, however, runs the risk of running afoul of the antitrust laws in the country. Over the past 80 years, Congress has been continually watchful lest some business executives gain effective control over a market by acquiring all or most of their competitors.

TYPES OF BUSINESS COMBINATIONS

There are several major classifications or types of business combinations, each having a particular meaning for the combining companies.

FIGURE 5–7

Types of business combinations

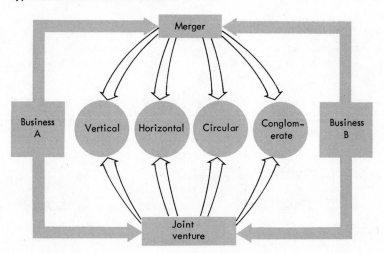

These classifications depend upon such things as the reasons for combining, the product lines of the respective companies and the competitive structure of the industry after the combination occurs.

As Figure 5–7 indicates, the major classifications of business combinations are mergers and joint ventures.

Mergers

A merger occurs if two or more companies combine in such a way that one of the firms remains in business after the combination is effected. That is, if Company A and Company B agree to combine, such that Com-

FIGURE 5–8

The Growth of Warner-Lambert Co.

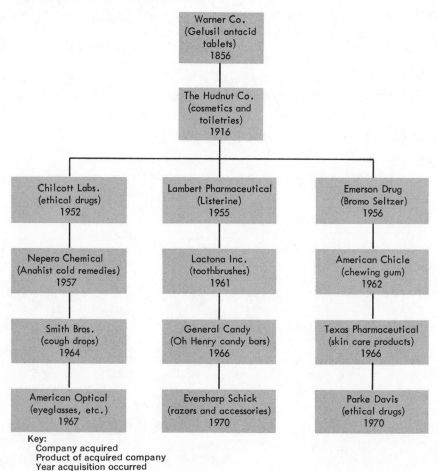

Key:
   Company acquired
   Product of acquired company
   Year acquisition occurred

pany A will still exist after the combination, but Company B will not, then a merger is said to have occurred. Company B has become part of Company A.

Figure 5–8 illustrates several mergers, all of which relate to one particular company. The Warner-Lambert Pharmaceutical Company has engaged in several mergers over the years. Notice in particular that in 1962, the company merged with the American Chicle Company, makers of Chiclet Chewing Gum. In 1964, the company merged with Smith Brothers, makers of the famous Smith Brothers Cough Drops. In each of the cases, the surviving company was Warner-Lambert. The other company may have continued to exist in name. That is, Smith Bros. may still make and sell cough drops. However, the company no longer exists as a separate company. It is now a division of the Warner-Lambert Company.

A merger

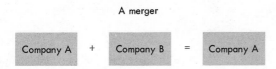

Company A   +   Company B   =   Company A

Mergers take on still other characteristics, depending on the nature of the relationship that exists between the combining firms. These characteristics usually result in a combination being called a *horizontal combination,* a *vertical combination,* a *circular combination,* or a *conglomerate combination.*

Horizontal combinations   A combination is said to be horizontal if the result is to eliminate a competitor firm from the industry. Thus, a merger between two steel mills or two grocery stores would be considered a horizontal merger, since one less steel mill or one less grocery store would exist after the merger occurred. Another way of viewing horizontal mergers is to consider them to be mergers between companies operating at the *same level* in the channel of distribution of goods in an industry (see Figure 5–9). Thus, the merger between the National Steel Company and the Granite Steel Company was a horizontal merger, since both were in the steel business, and the merger resulted in eliminating a competitor firm from the industry.

Vertical combinations   Vertical combinations are the "twin sister" of horizontal combinations. Rather than combine businesses at the same level of distribution, however, vertical combinations result from the combining of firms *within* the channel of distribution. In the example given in Figure 5–9, a merger between any two companies operating at *different* levels but in the same channel of distribution would be a vertical combination.

FIGURE 5–9

Horizontal and vertical mergers

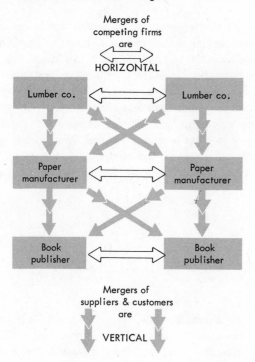

Vertical combinations, then, result in combining a customer with a supplier. In contrast, horizontal combinations result in the combining of competitor with competitor, thereby eliminating competition between them.

Circular combinations If two or more companies that are both operating in the same general industry combine, the result may be called a circular combination (see Figure 5–10). Care must be taken here in distinguishing between "general industry" and "channel of distribution." As general industries one might consider the food industry, the transportation industry, the heavy equipment industry, and so on. Thus, the 1969 merger of Holiday Inns and TCO Industries, Inc., owner of Continental Trailways, Inc., and Delta Steamship Lines, Inc., can be viewed as a circular merger. The acquisition greatly broadened the activities of the Holiday Inns, Inc., in the field of transportation-accommodation.

Conglomerate combinations When a merger or combination occurs between companies operating in totally different industries, it is called a conglomerate merger. Thus, the merger of RCA and Hertz Rent-a-Car was a conglomerate merger, as was the merger of British-American Tobacco Company with Gimbel Brothers, Inc.

FIGURE 5–10

Circular and conglomerate mergers

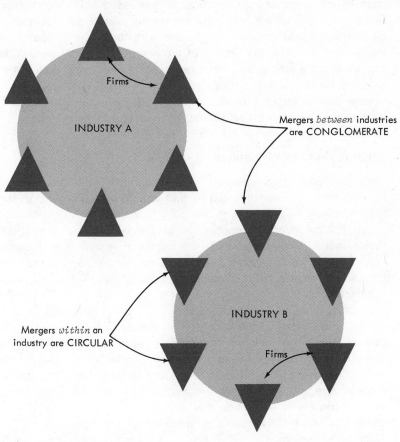

Recent years have seen widespread growth of conglomerate mergers. Indeed, some of the largest firms in the country today are basically conglomerate companies, operating in a wide variety of fields. Among the better known of these firms are Litton Industries, International Telephone and Telegraph, Walter Kidde, and Gulf and Western Industries.

Joint ventures

The last of the three major types of business combinations to be considered here is the jont venture. Frequently, two or more firms will agree to combine forces to undertake a particular action. They agree to split profits, expenses, and managerial responsibility for this single venture. In these circumstances, the undertaking might be called a joint venture. In essence, it is a partnership of two or more corporations. To qualify as a joint venture, however, it is necessary that the specific purpose of the combined undertaking be spelled out, so that the Justice Department will not suspect collusion on the part of each company. Two oil companies, for example, might agree to form a joint venture in the exploration for oil at the bottom of the ocean. The venture might be too expensive for a single firm, but by combining resources, both firms hope to gain. Under joint ventures, both firms remain as competitive businesses; the cooperative venture is limited to the agreed-on purpose, and terminates when the objective has been accomplished.

Other types of combinations

On occasion, businesses will form still other types of combinations. For example, it is not unusual to find conglomerate firms operating as *holding companies.* A holding company is a firm that does not maintain active control over the operations of the businesses it controls, but rather, merely owns the stock of the captive company. The dividends received on its stock become the income for the holding company. Banks frequently use the holding company concept when engaging in other businesses.

Another type of business combination found primarily in financial circles is the *syndicate.* A syndicate is similar to a joint venture, except that its purpose for being is usually of a much shorter duration. Thus, a group of banks may agree to join together to make a one-year loan of several hundred million dollars to a large corporation. After the loan is made and repaid, the syndicate comes to an end. Again, such organizations are quite rare outside the investment banking and corporation finance fields, where they are in common use.

Occasionally, a firm will establish a *subsidiary* company to further its exposure to a particular market. The subsidiary may even compete with the parent company for its share of the business, on the premise that by tolerating some overlap in its competitive position, a firm can actually increase sales. Thus, Richard D. Irwin, Inc., produces and sells textbooks for use in colleges across the United States. So does Business Publications, Inc. Business Publications, however, is a subsidiary of Richard D. Irwin.

Frequently, the result of a merger will be to merely change one of the merged companies into a subsidiary of the other. Several examples of such a situation can be found in Figure 5–8, the diagram showing the growth of the Warner-Lambert Company.

A more recent development in the area of business combinations is the *franchise.* A franchise is a licensing agreement between an operator of a business and the owner of a particular idea and distribution center.

Each operator buys the right to open, say, a Burger King or McDonald's in a particular area. He then receives instruction on the proper way of managing the business, is sometimes given bookkeeping assistance, and has the use of the name, goodwill, reputation, and operating methods of the franchise chain. In return, the operator agrees to give a percentage of the income earned each year to the franchisor and may sign agreements on buying supplies from the franchiser as well. Franchises have realized a tremendous growth in popularity in recent years, as is evidenced by their popularity in the fast-food carry-out business.

We have seen, then, that a wide variety of techniques for growing larger are available to business firms. Each of these techniques, moreover, tends to have certain distinctive characteristics. By carefully blending internal growth and external expansion, business firms in the United States have grown to immense size. Whether some American businesses are, in fact, too big is a question that requires special attention.

WHEN IS A BUSINESS "TOO BIG"?

What makes a business "too big"? Is it physical size, monetary worth, profits, or some other characteristic? These are questions that are not easily resolved, primarily because they require too many explicit definitions of what "big" really means. An investigation of several cases will reveal the complexity of the question.

Some illustrative examples

In terms of total sales, General Motors is the largest industrial corporation in the world. It employs almost 1 million people, has a monetary value of approximately $13 billion, and earns in excess of $3 billion a year, before taxes. In 1973, GM's sales revenue was over $35 billion and its net profit was almost $2.5 billion. It is the largest manufacturer of automobiles in the world, and the largest manufacturer of diesel engines in the United States. It is even the largest manufacturer of cigarette lighters in the United States. It is so big that it pays more in taxes each year than most other industrial companies earn in profits. It has approximately 700,000 owners, and consistently earns a higher profit per dollar of sales than the industry average. Question: Is General Motors "too big"?

Or consider the Exxon Corporation. Exxon is the largest integrated oil company in the United States. At the present time, Exxon ranks among the largest oil companies in the world, and probably is the largest privately owned oil company. (Several oil companies exist that are owned by several foreign governments, and may actually be larger in absolute size than Exxon.) At the present time, Exxon ranks second to General Motors in terms of sales, but ranks first in terms of profits. Exxon

TABLE 5–1

The largest corporations—1973

Rank	Company name	Sales (000)	Income (000)	Employees
1	General Motors......................	$35,798,289	$2,398,103	810,920
2	Exxon...............................	25,724,319	2,443,286	137,000
3	Ford Motor Co........................	23,015,100	906,500	474,312
4	Chrysler Corp........................	11,774,372	255,445	273,254
5	General Electric.....................	11,575,300	585,100	388,000
6	Texaco..............................	11,406,876	1,292,403	74,918
7	Mobil Oil............................	11,390,113	849,312	73,900
8	IBM.................................	10,993,242	1,575,467	274,108
9	I.T.&T...............................	10,183,035	527,837	438,000
10	Gulf Oil.............................	8,417,000	800,000	51,600
11	Standard Oil–Calif...................	7,761,835	843,577	39,269
12	Western Electric.....................	7,037,290	315,305	206,608
13	U.S. Steel...........................	6,951,905	325,758	184,794
14	Westinghouse........................	5,702,310	161,928	194,100
15	Standard Oil–Ind....................	5,415,976	511,249	46,589

earned about $100 million more in profits in 1973 than did GM. Question: Is Exxon Corporation "too big"?

And finally, consider the International Business Machines Corporation—IBM. Those initials are known the world over as meaning computers. IBM is the largest manufacturer of computers and related equipment in the world. No other company in this business even comes close to it in size. It is so big that it dwarfs in size all of the other computer manufacturers in the United States combined! IBM's stock is worth more money than the stock of any other U.S. corporation—well into the billions of dollars.

Yet, as recently as 30 years ago, IBM was virtually unheard of. A small, disorganized computer company, it was dwarfed in size by the Rand Corporation. Twenty years ago, the name in computers was "Univac." How many remember Univac today? Question: Is IBM "too big"?

Each of these three companies present an interesting situation. Many people would probably respond to the above questions by saying that, yes, General Motors is too big and should be broken down in size. Given the headlines over the past few years regarding automobile safety and costs, a large portion of the American public has come to suspect that the fault lies in the inability of other companies to effectively compete with GM. People believe that competition means little to a company that big and powerful.

As for Exxon and IBM, many people probably haven't given them much thought. Indeed, many people don't realize the size and growth rate that IBM enjoys. By 1980, if it maintains its present growth rate, IBM will be the largest industrial company in the world—surpassing even General Motors. Moreover, this will have been accomplished in half the time it took GM to get that big! But let's get back to our question—are these two firms "too big" also? To put this question in better perspective, let us consider IBM and the computer industry. Starting a computer company is much different from opening a service station, an auto company, or even a steel company. Building computers requires the great skill and technical know-how of mathematicians, engineers, and workers from other highly skilled professions. The services of such people are in short supply and do not come inexpensively. Small wonder that computers today sell for anywhere from several thousand dollars to several million dollars—each.

Finally, technological innovation is costly and uncertain. No sooner does one computer manufacturer come out with a newer, faster model than the competition uncovers new technology that makes the new computer obsolete. In the early 1960s, IBM gambled an investment of $5 billion in the development of a family of computers known as System 360. It was a gamble because at the time IBM didn't know if someone else might uncover still newer and better concepts that could make System 360 computers obsolete even before they were manufactured. Again, the question reemerges—is IBM too big? Or is it necessary for a successful computer company to be that large? Would we have had System 360 if IBM hadn't been large enough to invest the huge sum of money necessary to bring this achievement about?

We can even raise the case for General Motors. What other country in the world boasts a standard of living so high that two or more cars per family is a common occurrence? Don't forget, we saw in Chapter 3 just how important the growth of the auto industry in the early 1900s was to our economic development. Would the development have been the same if we had had 12, 13, or more manufacturers of autos, instead of 5 or 6? An interesting speculation, to say the least.

Then, too, consider the variety of makes and models of cars offered by General Motors. Cadillac competes with the higher priced Buicks and Oldsmobiles, Pontiac competes with Chevrolet, and so on. Would the market structure be any better if these were manufactured under different ownership instead of one? Indeed, it may be that the very fact of GM's size enables it to enjoy certain economies and consequently sell cars at lower prices than would otherwise be the case. The case has its merits, and deserves some consideration before we condemn GM as being "too big."

When might a company be "TOO big"?

The argument regarding "too big" has its negative side also. In recent years, more and more spokesmen have been asking Congress and the

Courts to establish some guidelines regarding "bigness" in business. They have argued, quite legitimately in some cases, that the very size of some business firms has given those firms a degree of power in society that often works to the disadvantage of society as a whole. For example, in the years immediately following President Nixon's reelection in 1972, the International Telephone and Telegraph Company (I.T.&T.) was rather severely criticized for its purported role in planning a revolution in Argentina, and for its purported role in trying to land the Republican National Convention for San Diego in 1972. Moreover, many people have expressed anger and outrage at the oil industry, for what seems to be

FIGURE 5–11

Can business get "too big"?

The 500 largest business firms in America account for . . .

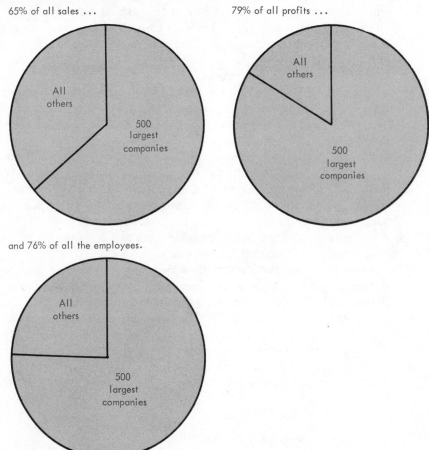

65% of all sales . . .

79% of all profits . . .

and 76% of all the employees.

Source: *Fortune* Magazine, May 1974, p. 231.

a monopoly over the supply of oil and gasoline. Most people are sure to remember the "summer of 1973," when gasoline was almost impossible to get. Later, when prices increased by a substantial amount, it seemed that all the gasoline anyone wanted was available. Many people claimed—and still claim—that the "shortage" of gas that year was really a hoax—an attempt by the oil companies to get higher prices, and consequently, larger profits.

Finally, the argument has been made that healthy business requires a certain degree of competition. Some have argued that IBM would be a better company—certainly society would be better off—if one company did not have such total and absolute control over an entire industry. IBM today controls approximately 70 percent of America's computer market. Moreover, it controls similar positions in the computer markets in other countries around the world! (See details in Chapters 18 and 21.) It is small wonder that IBM has been the object of a great deal of investigation by the Justice Department, and why so many other computer companies have launched legal suits against IBM.

The issue of bigness remains an elusive one. Can a firm get too big? James Roche, former chairman of the board of General Motors, speaking on a nationally televised news program in 1971, said no. He said that a firm should be allowed to grow as large as it can, so long as it continues to provide a product or service that is desired by the consuming public. He felt, in the best laissez-faire tradition, that as soon as a company became so large as to become inefficient, competition with the company's products would automatically arise.

To the extent that competition can form—that is, that entry into the market is not prohibitive—his statement is probably true. However, we have seen that the expense of initially entering some of these businesses is extremely high. For industries like steel, automobile production, and computers, to name but a few, it may not be possible for the free market to operate in the manner conceived by Mr. Roche. Laissez-faire competition implies free and easy entry into a given market. For industries like these, the exceptionally large initial investment required may make the idea of "freedom of entry" and "ability to compete," moot questions. In such a situation, one needs to give serious thought to the question of bigness and to put the question into its proper perspective in the ever-changing evolution of business structure.

DISCUSSION QUESTIONS

1 Why are sole proprietorships so popular? Can they compete with larger corporations and still survive?

2 In your opinion, what is the chief disadvantage of a partnership? Why?

3 Discuss the principle of "double taxation" as it applies to corporations. In your opinion, is the principle a fair one?

4 Distinguish between domestic, foreign, and alien corporations. Can you think of examples of each?

5 What makes a business "big"? Is General Motors too big? Explain the reasoning behind your answer.

6 Distinguish between vertical mergers, horizontal mergers, circular mergers, and conglomerate mergers. In the mid-1960s, PepsiCo, maker of the soft drink, merged with Frito-Lay, a major producer of snacks, such as potato chips and Fritos. Classify that merger as to type. Explain your reasoning.

7 What is a syndicate? What is a joint venture? How are the two different? How are they similar?

8 The question regarding bigness in business is a complex one. In a recent interview, two business executives made the following points.

   a "Bigness is not automatically a great thing for the consumer. Look no further than U.S. Steel to make that point. They are so bogged down by red tape that they are unable to change direction or products."

   b "It takes a large company with a lot of money and good people to develop better products."

   Which of these two statements do you agree with? Why?

MINI CASES

In the mid-1950s, a large conglomerate corporation acquired controlling interest in one of the two largest manufacturers of scouring pads. Upon gaining control, the company engaged in an extensive survey to find out why consumers preferred the competitor's product over theirs. The conclusion was that the color of the soap in the pad gave consumers a feeling of poor quality—the soap in the pad was red and when applied to pans gave the impression of rust. Accordingly, the manufacturer changed the color of the soap to blue. Within a few short years, the company's sales had grown to the point that it was now the largest manufacturer of scouring pads in the country.

The other large manufacturer of scouring pads, however, was determined to hold onto its market share. Accordingly, it developed a scouring pad made of synthetic materials which it claimed were superior to the steel fiber used in the traditional pads. Soon, other companies also began producing scouring pads using the synthetic fibers. The result was a multitude of new products on the market—most of which sold at prices lower than did those in existence just a few years earlier.

In the early 1960s, however, the U.S. government dropped a bomb-shell on the industry. It ruled that the acquisition seven years earlier of one of the two large scouring pad manufacturers by the conglomerate was, in fact, illegal, since it "lessened competition." The government argued that the conglomerate would have developed its own product had it not been able to acquire this company. Consequently, the government said, there might have been three major producers of scouring pads in-stead of the two now in existence.

1. Comment on the government's case. Do you agree with its initial assertion?
2. What was the effect of the merger on the competitiveness of the scouring pad industry?

Tom and Marvin were two fraternity brothers who happened to be en-rolled in a course on introduction to business at the same time. Dur-ing the past week, their class had been discussing horizontal, vertical, and conglomerate mergers. They saw, for example, how the government's policy had been to discourage horizontal mergers of all types, on the premise that these types of mergers resulted in a lessening of competition. Moreover, they also saw how the government was tentatively discour-aging some conglomerate mergers, on the grounds that large firms tended to restrict competition more than did small firms. Thus, by prohibiting growth by acquisition, the government could prevent the growth of these large, diversified companies.

Tom and Marvin began to discuss this facet of their course one evening. Tom argued, for example, that he couldn't quite see the logic behind the government's attitude. He questioned, for example, whether size was a fair criterion to use in determining competitiveness. More-over, he questioned whether having a large number of businesses com-peting with one another was actually in the public's best interest. Might it not be true, he thought, that having a limited number of businesses might result in more benefits to society than having a large number of businesses?

1. Comment on Tom's observation about size of business and the issue of competition.
2. Do you agree with his observation on "number" of businesses and the public interest?

One of the popular criticism's of very large businesses stems from the fact that when one of these large businesses gets into financial difficulty, it generally is able to avoid the usual result of bankruptcy that would befall any typical company. For example, when Lockheed Aircraft Corporation got into difficulty, the U.S. government granted the company a $250 million loan to continue in business. The government argued that Lockheed was too important—both as a defense supplier and as an employer of people in the Pacific Northwest—to allow collapse. Smaller businesses, particularly those that compete with Lockheed in various areas, have argued that this amounts to unfair competition.

1. *Do you agree?*
2. *What alternative or alternatives do you see the government following that could alleviate this problem?*

part two Functional aspects of American business

Business is activity. It consists of people doing things—performing the functions that achieve the goals of business. It is to these functions of business that this review of business now turns.

The following discussion of business functions begins with an examination of the organization itself, for the organization is the environment in which the functions take place. Then it looks at how the organization is managed, including the management of its personnel and its machines. Next it explores the broad field of labor relations. In logical succession it examines the functions of marketing, accounting, and finance. Finally the review covers the more technical work done in business—the work involving quantitative methods and computers. Hopefully, this summary of functions will give you an appreciation of the kinds of work done in business. Perhaps it will help you to select the one career that will be right for you.

147

A sociologist, political writer, and economist, Max Weber helped build the foundations of modern sociology and of organization theory. He wrote extensively on leadership, law, music, religion, and many other topics. One of his main purposes was to develop a methodology for the social sciences.

His "ideal-type" method for studying society examines the elements of social institutions and studies how each relates to the other. Weber was the first to discuss the process of organization, providing a systematic theory of bureaucracy.

In his *Protestant Ethic and the Spirit of Capitalism* (1920), Weber argued that certain Protestant religious beliefs, especially the teachings of Calvinism, created an attitude toward life which favored the development of modern capitalism. Particularly fascinated that capitalism had not emerged in China as it had in the West, Weber noted that sanctification of tradition was a feature of the Chinese social structure. In contrast, the West's Calvinist belief in hard work and avoidance of conspicuous consumption promoted expansion of business. Economic success so achieved proved that a man was a chosen child of God.

Born in Erfurt, Germany, in 1864, this brilliant scholar was the son of a well-to-do lawyer. Following in his father's footsteps, Weber studied law at Heidelberg. He also concentrated upon economics and history, receiving a Ph.D. in 1889. He taught at the universities of Freiburg, Munich, and Heidelberg. Stricken with illness in 1897, Weber was never able to resume his regular teaching duties at Heidelberg. He did gradually recover, and taught briefly at the University of Munich until his death in 1920. Meanwhile, an inheritance received in 1907 enabled him to live as a private scholar.

Max Weber
(1864–1920)

Pioneer organization theorist

6

Internal business organization

No organization can hope to hold its members that does not consider not only the welfare of the organization as a whole, but also the welfare of the individuals composing that organization.

——*Frank and Lillian Gilbreth*

Before you begin the study of the functions of business, it is important that you know what they are. It is equally important that you know how business functions are related, both to each other and to groups outside the business. As you will see, these relationships are vital to your understanding of how business operates and the role of business in our society.

AN EXPLANATION OF BUSINESS FUNCTIONS

As used here, *business functions* are the activities that take place in a business organization. It may help you to understand them by looking at a business organization as a group of people working together for a common purpose —or more specifically, a business purpose.

Thus, a business organization consists of people doing things—things such as giving orders, storing goods, selling goods and services, keeping records, making products, hiring workers, and financing operations. All of these activities combine to enable the business to achieve its goals. Modern management scholars look upon these combined activities as a system. That is, they see the activities as all related and working together, much like the parts of a machine.

So numerous are these activities that one has to group them in order to talk about them meaningfully. This part of the book presents such a grouping for review. These particular groupings of business functions are quite broad. But they are ones commonly used and ones that have proved to be most useful in the study of business.

Relationships within the business system

Although the following review takes up the business functions separately, you should keep in mind that they are closely related to each other. Often they affect each other and are dependent upon each other. Executives do not perform them independently. Instead, they work to coordinate them; that is, they strive to consider each function in relation to the other functions, so that each can contribute as much as possible to the success of the business system.

The foregoing point may be made clear by example; so let us analyze the case of a business which makes and sells chairs. It is easy to see that this business would have to coordinate its functions of production (making chairs) and marketing (selling the chairs). These two functions are closely related. In fact, they depend upon each other. Obviously, the business simply could not afford to produce more chairs than it can sell; nor could it afford to sell more chairs than it can produce. Or, for another example, in this same business the function of hiring workers should be coordinated with both marketing and production. The business needs just the right number of salespeople and production workers to handle its output—no more, no less. And so it is with relationships between the other functions. All must be coordinated to make the business run efficiently and effectively.

Effects on other businesses

The business functions also are related to groups outside the business. Especially are they related to other businesses. If you were to take an overall view of businesses in the world, you would see that everyone has its place in the whole scheme of business activity. Some make goods, some sell goods, some store goods, some provide services, and so on. Together they form a system which works to provide for the world's needs for goods and services. The individual businesses compete with each other, of course, but they also serve each other. And actions taken by one of them can affect others. For example, when one company grants a pay increase or lowers prices, its competitors may be forced to follow suit. When one business develops a new product or service, others may have to change their operations in order to compete or to make use of the product or service. Or when one uses a new and successful sales plan, others may have to work to overcome its effects.

Cooperation with the outside world

Perhaps even more significant is the relation of business functions to the rest of the world. All the world forms a giant system, and business is only a part of it. There is also the land, the waters, the air, and plant and animal life. And perhaps most important of all, there is human life and all that humans beings have developed—culture, institutions, governments, religions, technology, and such. Often what business does affects parts of the world system, and these parts often affect business. Thus, if we are to have the best possible quality of life, business must consider the effects of its actions on the outside world. And because business has a place in the world and contributes to the quality of life, the rest of the world must consider its effects on business. It is upon this logical reasoning that the societal approach of this book is based.

APPROACHES TO THE STUDY OF MANAGEMENT

To begin the study of how business functions, management is a logical first subject. By *management* is meant everything executives do in running an organization. It is a broad function covering all the other functions of business (marketing, finance, accounting, and so on) which are discussed in the following chapters. As you will see, it is the function that brings together all the other functions to make the business operate.

How best to discuss management depends much on the viewpoint one takes toward the subject. Over time, many such viewpoints have developed. They fall into five general categories (see Figure 6–1).

The first to develop was the authoritarian (or autocratic) viewpoint. This is the viewpoint that holds that the administrator (boss) is a strong ruler—that it is the duty of all under him to obey without question. Or more precisely, it is the viewpoint that holds that the task of the administrator is to make the decisions, give the orders, administer justice, and generally to run the organization. The administrators are in complete command. Their goal is to make as much money as possible for their business. Although some of those who developed this viewpoint felt that administrators should take care of the needs of the workers, others disagreed.

Around the beginning of the 20th century, the second major viewpoint took form. Called scientific management, this viewpoint places the manager in the role of a technician seeking the most efficient way to do the organization's work. After finding the best way, the manager's task is to teach the technique to the employees and to make certain that they practice it.

Third in the succession of management philosophies came the human

FIGURE 6–1

The management viewpoints illustrated

relations approach. Gaining general support in the 1930s, this viewpoint holds that the manager's work centers around handling people. The human relations group sees the manager as a counselor, as a therapist, and in general, as a practicing psychologist. The manager's task, they believe, is to achieve the organization's goals through the proper handling of people.

In recent years, the changing concepts of management have led to a fourth and a fifth viewpoint. The fourth is organization theory, which is described in some detail later in this chapter. The fifth, decision theory, is perhaps a continuation of the scientific management school.

FIGURE 6-2

A relic of the autocratic management period

EIGHT RULES FOR OFFICE WORKERS IN 1872

1. Office employees each day will fill lamps, clean chimneys and trim wicks. Wash windows once a week.
2. Each clerk will bring in a bucket of water and a scuttle of coal for the day's business.
3. Make your pens carefully. You may whittle nibs to your individual taste.
4. Man employees will be given an evening off each week for courting purposes, or two evenings a week if they go regularly to church.
5. After thirteen hours of labor in the office, the employee should spend the remaining time reading the Bible and other good books.
6. Every employee should lay aside from each pay day a goodly sum of his earning for his benefit during his declining years so that he will not become a burden on society.
7. Any employee who smokes Spanish cigars, uses liquor in any form, or frequents pool and public halls or gets shaved in a barber shop, will give good reason to suspect his worth, intentions, integrity and honesty.
8. The employee who has performed his labor faithfully and without fault for five years, will be given an increase of five cents per day in his pay, providing profits from business permit it.

Source: *Boston Herald,* October 5, 1958, p. 50.

The decision theory viewpoint of management activity holds that the manager is a skilled technician making decisions based on mathematical models. In a sense, managers are partners to the computer. They feed it information, extract information from it, and apply the output to the company's problems. They are highly trained and competent practitioners who apply their skills in a professional manner.

In a very real sense, all of these viewpoints have a place in the practice of management. All are evident in business today. Thus, our approach in this and following chapters will be a consolidated one. We shall include parts of all. From each we shall extract that which appears most useful in explaining how management really functions in business.

THE NATURE OF ORGANIZATIONS

Our efforts to understand management begin with a study of the organization. (A business, of course, is an organization.) This approach appears logical, for it is the organization which managers manage. Certainly, if we are to understand management we must know the organization—how it is structured, how it works, and how it sometimes does not work.

Why we study organizations

As obvious as this analysis appears to be, only in recent times has the study of organizations received much emphasis in management circles. Previously, business management was heavily based on a "how-to-do-it" philosophy. Administrators concentrated on what they believed to be the rules of management. They believed there was a set of guidelines or principles for all areas of management activity. The manager's task was to learn them and plug them into his situation. Good management would then result.

Much of this how-to-do-it material worked. It still works. In fact, much of it appears in this book. But these practical approaches have been broadened with a new dimension—the study of the organization itself.

Known as organization theory, this new approach to management equips managers to cope with the organizational complexity that exists today. In today's complex organization, managers must know more than the rules or principles of management. They must also know and understand the operations of their organizations. They must look beyond their immediate subordinate groups and try to see the effects their decisions have on other managers and other departments. And conversely, they must understand the effects the decisions of others have on their operations. They must know and understand the overall operations and workings of the whole organization. And especially with the growing concern for the welfare of humanity, they must know the effects the actions of their organizations have on the larger organization of society.

Organizations defined

A formal organization is "a system of consciously coordinated activities or forces of two or more persons."[1] Analysis of this commonly accepted definition reveals the essential ingredients for the beginning of an organization. First, two or more people must have a common purpose. They must have a willingness to work together to achieve this common purpose. And they must be able to communicate with each other. "The elements of an organization are therefore (1) communication, (2) willingness to serve, (3) common purpose."[2] As illustrated in Figure 6–3, the presence of these ingredients results in organized group effort. The absence of any one of them results in disorganization.

By this definition, all of us are a part of countless organizations. They range in formality from the simplest to the most complex. For example, hardly a day goes by that we do not agree to combine efforts with someone to perform a routine task—such as moving a desk, pushing a stalled car, or building a fence. On each such occasion we form an organization. Then all of us are members of the more formal types of organization—those with long-range objectives. These include such groups as civic clubs, athletic teams, classes in school, and political parties. To this

---

[1] Chester I. Bernard, *The Functions of the Executive* (Cambridge, Mass.: Harvard University Press, 1938), p. 73.

[2] Ibid., p. 82.

latter list we could add our church and any organization for which we might work, such as a firm or a government agency.

Perhaps your thought at this point is that this definition of organization is much too broad. Why not limit our discussion to the formal, structured business organization? Why include as organizations the trivial and almost casual relationships of people? Our interest is in business organizations. And business organizations are not informal cooperative groups. They have structure—that is, a hierarchy. They are organized with some people serving as bosses to others. The explanation is that all organiza-

FIGURE 6–3

The nature of disorganization and organization

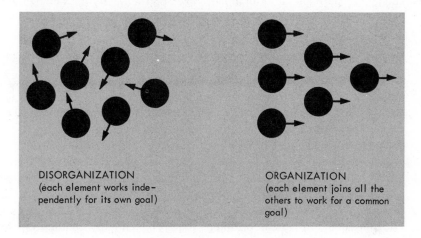

DISORGANIZATION
(each element works inde-
pendently for its own goal)

ORGANIZATION
(each element joins all the
others to work for a common
goal)

tions, regardless of size or purpose, have much in common. They are structured relationships between people. All of them are subject to much the same problems that occur whenever people do things together. Thus, that which we learn about the functioning of organizations in general will apply to the business organization.

From an extension of the definition we can conclude further that organizations live and die. Just as organizations form when a common purpose exists, they end when their purpose ends. This point is illustrated by the case of a simple, everyday organization formed by neighbors for the purpose of putting out a brush fire. The effort of the organization begins quickly when the fire is detected; it ends abruptly when the fire ends. So it is with all organizations, including business.

Business firms, of course, are created usually to be continuous organizations. So when a business or other administrative organization finds that its purpose no longer exists, it must either find a new purpose or die. For example, a manufacturer of after-shave lotion may find its product no longer needed as beards become the vogue; a medical research center created to find a cure for a disease may discover a cure; or a company formed to make a synthetic material may suddenly find competition from a superior and less costly material. So it is that organizations must continually be aware of the reality of their purpose; and they must make repeated adaptations to new purposes. If they do not, they die.

Similarly, an organization also ends when it fails to accomplish its goal. People do not work indefinitely for an impossible purpose. How long the organization will try unsuccessfully to reach its goal will vary with the scientific circumstances involved. A group effort to move a boulder may end abruptly after one maximum effort fails to budge the object. On the other hand, a more persistent group may try again and again. To some extent, business organizations may react similarly. Fortunately (or perhaps unfortunately), how long they try to achieve their purpose is determined by how much money they have to spend.

Organizations throughout society

Perhaps the most meaningful contribution of organization theory to the study of management is the concept of the firm as one in the total structure of organizations in society. We human beings have created many other organizations in our efforts to exist in our society. Organizations are a vital part of our way of doing things. We organize in the first place because we are cooperative social beings and prefer to do things with others. Our second reason for organizing is that we are also competitive animals[3] and know that only the efficient can compete successfully. We strive for greater efficiency. We have learned from centuries of experience that we can do things more efficiently by banding together with others.

In forming our organizations to achieve any one of our goals, we have some freedom to operate. But we must keep in mind the goals of other organizations in society.[4] We must consider, also, the needs of the whole of society, which is the largest of all organizations and has its own goals. More specifically, in making decisions, administrators must recognize the needs of all the groups involved—their employees, other businesses, and the public. Their decisions must not be made in the vacuum of their one organization.

Essentials of effective organization

In order to determine how best to manage an organization, administrators should understand what makes an organization work. A close observation reveals certain essentials of successful organization. It is

---

[3] Fremont E. Kast and James E. Rosenzweig, *Organizations and Management: A Systems Approach* (New York: McGraw-Hill Book Co., 1970), p. 5.

[4] Ibid., p. 29.

the administrator's duty to fully understand them and to do what is necessary to maintain and promote them.

Coordination   The first and foremost of these essentials is coordination. It is the first principle of organization and all others are subordinate to it.[5] Without coordination, effective organization cannot take place. Unless each member of the whole organization does his part toward the total effort, the organization's effort will fall short of its goal. Thus, the task of administrators is to work out and put into effect the most efficient effort possible.

Authority   A second essential is authority. An organization is not likely to manage itself. Someone must take charge. Someone must direct the coordination of efforts. Without authority in the hands of someone, there could be no coordinated effort.

Commonality of interest   A third essential of successful organization is commonality of interest. Ideally, the members of the group should consciously work for the same goals; and it is the manager's job to see that they do. How managers best maintain a commonality of interest varies with the case. But always they will need to make certain that their group's objectives are sound. If they are not, the managers will need to adjust them. Also, they will make good use of their best communication abilities to explain and persuade so that the organizational goals are clear to all.

Objectives   Vital to all coordinated effort is the fourth essential, objectives. Always there must be a goal. It is not even necessary that the goal be a logical one for an organization to exist. All that is necessary is that the group accept it and be willing to work for it. In a business organization, the manager's job involves determining and appraising the organization's goals. The goals selected must be the right ones. If they are not, the organization could suffer, perhaps even fail.

Discipline   The fifth essential of organization is discipline. For any organization to reach its goal, all members must function properly. Because the members of organizations are human beings, they are not by nature disciplined workers. Thus, in the successful organization there must be sufficient control over the members' efforts to ensure success. In a business organization the task of managers is to effect this control. They must discipline their workers to most effectively achieve the organization's goals. And because they, too, are a part of the organization, they must discipline themselves.

Classification of organizations

As has been noted, organizations take many forms; and for all practical purposes, they are infinite in number. So that some order may come

---

[5] James Mooney and Alan C. Reiley, *The Principles of Organization* (New York: Harper & Bros., 1939), p. 5.

out of this confusing picture, a means of classifying organizations is needed.

As with any such complex area, a number of means of classification are possible. For our purposes, however, those organizations that managers manage are most important to us. Thus the following classification[6] includes only such types. And because management is concerned with what an organization does, this classification also is based on this consideration.

Service Those organizations which exist to serve people without requiring full compensation from those receiving the service (government agencies, charities, civic organizations).

Economic Organizations which produce and distribute goods and services for some form of payment (corporations, partnerships, sole proprietorships).

Religious Groups which serve the spiritual needs of the membership (churches, sects, orders).

Protective Organizations having the duty to protect the populace (fire departments, law enforcement agencies, military services).

Government Those organizations engaged in governing a unit of population (national, state, county, city governments).

Social Organizations which strive to fulfill the social needs of their members (fraternities, clubs, amateur athletic teams).

Certainly the list is not all inclusive; and it contains some overlap. Nevertheless, it covers the major groups with which managers are concerned. Our main interest, of course, is the economic group, which includes all forms of business firms. A skilled manager, however, would find his administrative talents easily transferred from one type of organization to another.

THE STRENGTHS AND LIMITATIONS OF ORGANIZATIONS

In general, organizations are the most efficient means we have of reaching certain goals. Thus, they have specific advantages over independent effort. Unfortunately, they also have disadvantages. Effective managers should understand these strengths so that they can use them to the maximum in their management activities. Likewise, managers should understand fully the disadvantages of organization.

Advantages of organization

Compress and expand time A major advantage of organized activity is that it makes it possible to compress and to expand the time available.

---

[6] Herbert G. Hicks, *The Management of Organizations* (New York: McGraw-Hill Book Co., 1972), p. 16.

Simply stated, to compress time is to reduce the time period in which an activity is performed. To expand time is to lengthen this time period.

For example, assume that Mr. Smith, a manufacturer of bottles, is faced with a deadline for producing a certain quantity of bottles. He could meet his goal by hiring additional workers. (We are assuming, of course, that no improvement in method of manufacturing is possible.) Specifically, assume that Mr. Smith now employs 400 workers and that it would require 60 workdays per worker to manufacture the desired quantity of bottles. He needs them in 30 days. Assuming that he could get the same output per worker (not likely), he could get the job done by hiring an additional 400 workers.

Assume again that instead of an early production deadline, Mr. Smith now has insufficient orders for bottles to keep all 400 workers busy. In fact, for the next 60 days he has need to produce only half the quantity his 400 workers could produce in that time. Ignoring the ethics involved, it would be possible for Smith to meet his goal by reducing employment to 200.

Perhaps you have suspected that this illustration ignores some very practical considerations in the case, such as cost and availability of labor and loss of efficiency. Your suspicions are well founded. But the illustration does explain the point. Through organizations, time available can be compressed, and it can be expanded to meet the needs of the organization.

Overcome limitations Another primary advantage of organizations is that they can overcome the limitations of the individual human being. By organizing, we can do many things more efficiently than if we did them alone. And through organization we can do some things which we cannot do alone.

To illustrate, an individual worker is capable of building tables, chairs, and the like, assuming that he or she has the tools, materials, and skills. The job could be done more efficiently, however, if others joined the worker in the task. Each member would then make a specialized contribution, and by coordinating the activities, the group could build furniture more efficiently than the one could build alone.

Specialization A third basic advantage of organization is specialization. The term is so well known to us that it is truly a household word. Even so, it is appropriate that we reflect on its meaning as it applies to modern organizations.

In an organizational sense, *specialization* is simply the division of labor. Each job or project to be completed by the organization is broken down into its basic tasks. These tasks are then assigned to different workers. As these workers have limited assignments, they can become highly proficient at them. That is, they become specialists. As a result, the total effort of the organization is done more skillfully.

Economies of scale   A major advantage of organization that applies primarily to business organizations is that organization can result in economies of scale. *Economies of scale* means that as larger and larger numbers of units of a given product are produced, the cost per unit declines. The decline is not likely to continue indefinitely but will to a point. Thus, the organization's efficiency is enhanced.

As an illustration of this principle, take the case of a manufacturer of automobiles. It is well known that the costs of plant, equipment, engineering, and such for producing automobiles is high. Assume that one highly competent individual has all these production facilities. It would be possible for this person to manufacture an automobile single-handedly. As the cost of the automobile would have to include all the costs of production, it would be astronomical. Now, using the same production facilities, suppose that this worker could employ ten persons to help. Together they would produce a number of automobiles. The cost per automobile would be lower; but still it would be high. By adding more and more workers, this organization would produce more and more automobiles. Until the ideal number of employees was reached, the cost per automobile would decrease.

Disadvantages of organization

On the disadvantage side, four stand out. On first glance they may appear to fit organizations in general more than business organizations in particular. Closer analysis reveals, however, that they apply to all organizations, and managers should know them in order to understand the organizations they manage.

The two-sidedness of organizations   The fact that an organization tends to bring together its members and to alienate them from those outside the group is one disadvantage. In other words, organizations develop a spirit of comradeship and of belonging. This closeness of feeling, however, sets members of the ingroup apart from those outside the group. And these outsiders are inclined to react by opposing the group.

One of the best illustrations of this tendency is one of the largest forms of organizations we have—a national state, such as the United States, Russia, and France. The members develop strong loyalties for these organizations. They love them. They are willing to fight and die for them. On the other hand, those outside these national states have feelings that are far less positive. These feelings may range from complete indifference to extreme hatred.

To a lesser degree, similar feelings develop within and among the organizations in the business world. Members of one department may develop a strongly favorable feeling among themselves. They may have different feelings for members of other departments. Members of craft groups (welders, machinists, diemakers, carpenters, and so on) likewise may develop a kindred feeling for other members of their groups. Their opinions toward outsiders may be quite different. So it is with all the many organizations within business.

Increasing unfavorable internal-external environment A second disadvantage is that as organizations grow, their relationships among their workers (internal environment) and with their consumers (external environment) tend to become unfavorable. The explanation is obvious. As a new organization grows, it gets more and more customers. Also, more and more competition comes in, and this competition also gains more and more customers. In time, the number of additional new customers to be gained becomes low. Competition increases; growth slows down, or even stops.

Similarly, the organization's internal relationships become less favorable with growth. As the organization gains in size, it becomes more and more difficult for the members to communicate. Workers tend to find it difficult to communicate their needs to top management. And top management finds it difficult to communicate with those below them.[7] Throughout the organization communication suffers.

Desire for homogeneity A desire for *homogeneity*—a tendency to resist change or the introduction of jarring elements—is a deterrent to the growth of almost all organizations.[8] Members of organizations have a tendency to keep their organizations pure—that is, to keep out all alien units. The result is to restrict growth. Members of a labor union, for example, will tend to restrict their membership in various ways. A manufacturing organization will tend to limit its production to one product— the one which the original membership has the know-how to produce. A social organization will limit its membership to a select few.

Fortunately, the desire to keep the organization homogeneous frequently is offset by a desire for growth. Because they want to grow, or perhaps because they must do something to keep from deteriorating, organizations will choose to bring in outside members. As an illustration, a manufacturer of cigarettes may see its market decreasing because of new evidence on the health hazards of its product. Rather than watch its sales and profits decline, the company may decide to expand into another area—say, the manufacture of chewing gum. Some of the old members of the organization may grumble a bit, but the organization strengthens its position.

Individual versus the organization A fifth limitation of organizations is that they make requirements on the individuals which are contrary to

---

[7] Adapted from Kenneth E. Boulding, *The Organizational Revolution* (New York: Harper & Bros., 1953), pp. 10–29.

[8] Ibid., pp. 20–29.

the development of the individuals' personalities. Usually business organizations have a pyramidal structure, with top executives over second-line executives, second-line executives over third-line executives, and so on down to the lowest workers. Thus, organizations place members in positions which force them to be dependent, subordinate, and submissive. Such relationships are inconsistent with the personalities of most healthy human beings. They are placed in work situations opposed to the development of their personalities. People simply are not inclined to accept such roles; so they resist. The result is conflict within the organization.

ORGANIZATION STRUCTURE AND ITS DEVELOPMENT

Structure is the next topic in this analysis of the organization. Included also are some of the explanations of why it must be as it is. As the word is used here, structure means the working relationships among the members of an organization. All organizations must have it. For an organization to exist, each member must play a role in the organization's work. Each must have certain duties. Each must have relationships with others in the group. The total of these work and relationship activities is the structure of the organization.

The organization chart

The usual means of describing the structure of a business organization is the *organization chart.* This chart is a schematic diagram showing the administrative relations of the members and divisions of the organization. Typically they are pyramidal in shape with the president at the top and successively larger levels of people below him. Corporations might have stockholders and a board of directors above the president. For a small corporation the top of the pyramid might appear as in Figure 6–4.

By examining the chart, we can learn much about the firm and its operations. At the top of the structure are the stockholders—those people who own the company. The chances are they are only investors and have neither the ability nor the desire to run the organization. Below them is the board of directors. The directors are responsible to the stockholders. But in large corporations (such as RCA, General Motors, and Union Carbide) the responsibility largely is a moral one. Stockholders of such corporations are so numerous and spread out that they have little effective power. In general, the board of directors acts as a committee to determine broad policy issues, to make major appointments, and generally to serve in an advisory capacity to the company.

Below the board of directors is the company president. He is the one charged with the responsibility for running the organization. More specifically, he is in charge of overall operations. He is responsible for achieving company objectives. He makes plans for the company's future. In general, he is responsible to the board of directors for the conduct of the firm.

At the next level are the three departments through which the president carries out the organization's goals. In this instance, the department titles tell us that this probably is a manufacturing company. There is a production manager who is responsible for all the work involved in making the company's products. There is a marketing manager who has the assignment of directing the efforts to sell the products produced. Finally, there is a financial manager. In general, the goal of the finance depart-

FIGURE 6–4

Organization chart of a small company

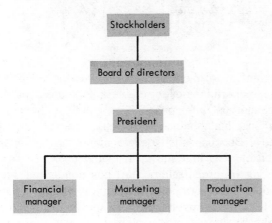

ment is to appraise the work of the other two departments by keeping the financial records on their operations. It supplies the information to those at the top of the structure which is needed to provide people with a measure of how well the organization is being run.

Remember that this is a relatively small organization with a simple organization chart. Larger organizations need a more complex structure. For example, assume that this same company continues to grow. As it grows, it hires more and more workers. It trains them. In time, it dismisses some and loses some. All of these personnel activities mean time-consuming work for each of the departments, for there is no separate department to do it. As the work mounts, a personnel department is created. And we now have a fourth department. In this personnel department there would be specialists skilled in interviewing, testing, selecting, training, and counseling.

Similarly, growth could lead to the development of other departments. A progressive, technological organization may find need for a separate

FIGURE 6–5

The organization for a typical large firm

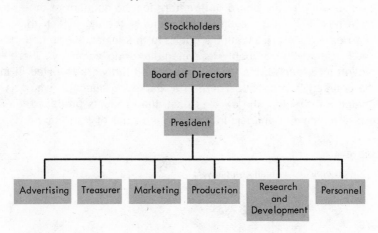

research and development department and an engineering department. A company with overseas operations might create a separate department to handle this work. Numerous other possibilities exist for the growing company—public relations, maintenance, production control, and purchasing, to name a few. Because such developments are common, a more likely organization chart is that shown in Figure 6–5.

So far, this analysis of the organization chart has concerned the top of the pyramid. You could take any one of the departments or divisions mentioned above and trace the structure down to the individual worker. The production department, for example, might have the organization as described in Figure 6–6.

As you can see, a production manager heads the department. Reporting to the manager are three supervisors, perhaps each handling a separate process or operation. Ten workers report to each supervisor.

FIGURE 6–6

Organization of a production department in a large firm

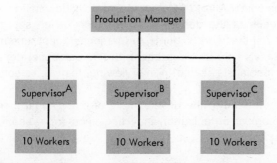

If the company produces a line of products rather than a single product, its organization of the production department would be quite different. (Also it would likely be a larger company.) Possibly its top organization chart would appear something like that shown in Figure 6–7. Under the production manager are three general supervisors, each in charge of a different product of the product line—that is, products, X, Y, and Z. Each general supervisor has three supervisors reporting to him. Each is in charge of a different production process. In short, the supervisors of processes A, B, and C produce product X. Similar arrangements could be shown for products Y and Z.

FIGURE 6–7

Organization of a production department
by products (X, Y, Z) and by processes
(A, B, C)

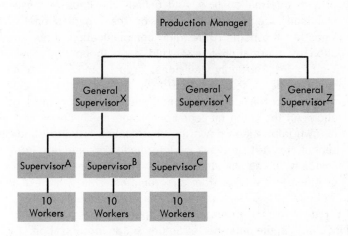

At this point it is important to remember that this grouping process is possible only as long as the division of labor is reasonably clear-cut. In other words, workers performing the same operations generally would be grouped together, and possibly under one manager. Except in small businesses, it would not be desirable to organize a company by placing marketing people under the production manager or vice versa.

Authority-accountability relationships As you may have inferred from this discussion, the organization chart shows the authority and accountability relationships within the firm. The boxes in the chart represent either a position (title of job occupied by a person) or a department. In either case, the person or position is superior to that which falls below it.

Thus, in a very real sense the organization chart reflects the structure of the organization. It shows who reports to whom. Every person in the firm can tell at a glance who is the boss. Supervisors and other managers can tell precisely who are their subordinates. They can tell, also, how their departments fit into the whole operating plan of the organization and how they relate to other departments.

Communication and information flow   The lines connecting the boxes in the chart illustrate another characteristic of the organization. In a sense, the lines are indications of connections or "hookups" between departments or positions. Like the wires in an electric circuit, they show the direction of movement.

In all organizations, especially the large-scale ones, information and communication are essential to the satisfactory performance of administrative work. Managers at all levels need records, orders, instructions, reports, and the like. Without such myriad forms of information, they could not make intelligent decisions; nor could they plan or do the other things managers do. Thus, for efficient administration, the organization needs networks of information flow. And usually the lines in these networks are practically identical to the lines on the organizational chart. In fact, the lines are the paths over which communication should travel.

The direction of information flow should be both up and down the organization structure. Certainly decisions, orders, and other administrative communications must be handed down from superior to subordinate. And reports, records, and other operating information must go up the organization. All too often management is too much concerned with the flow of its own information down the organization structure and pays too little attention to certain types of information it can get from the bottom. Specifically, management often fails to encourage the upward flow of suggestions and advice from subordinates. This source of information can be most valuable in achieving the organization's goals.

Formal versus informal structure   Not apparent from a view of the organization chart is the informal structure of an organization. By *informal organization* is meant the organization's structure that arises out of the socialization process and is based primarily on feelings and attitudes. Usually it is not that structure established in the company's organization chart. Informal organizations exist in virtually all businesses.

Informal organizations develop through the personal relations of the workers. For example, workers may respect and follow a fellow worker more than the person management places in an administrative position over them. Thus, on the job the fellow worker may be the leader rather than the person appointed by management. For another example, workers may band together to press a grievance. In the process they may form an organizational structure quite different from that on the organization chart. And this structure may become quite real in the company's operations. In addition, an organizational structure may develop off the job through social contacts. Then it may be carried back to the job. In general, this informal structure can come about through any of the relationships between people that make some people look up to others.

Line and staff relationships

In analyzing the structure of an organization, sometimes it is useful to understand the kind of authority each part has. Specifically, we may need to know whether a department or a position has line authority or staff authority.

FIGURE 6–8
Line and staff authority illustrated

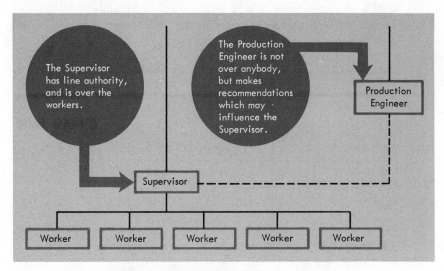

Line authority means superior-subordinate authority. This is the authority which a boss has over the workers under him. On the other hand, *staff authority* is the authority which a person or department has in an advisory capacity.

Illustrating this difference are the positions of a supervisor in a typical industrial organization and a production engineer (see Figure 6–8). The supervisor has line authority. He has workers under him to do his bidding. Supervisors make decisions and enforce them within the department. The production engineer holds a staff position. He is an expert in his field and from time to time is called on to advise the supervisor on procedures. But he does not make decisions. Usually he does not have subordinates working under him.

The power of staff people typically is greater than that implied in the example above. Frequently staff members make recommendations which flow upward to top management. And the fact that top management frequently heeds this advice and directs lower levels of management also to heed it often gives staff members more authority than the organization chart implies.

The line and its function   The function of the line is to do the work that directly contributes to doing what the organization was set up to do. In a business organization, the line tasks are likely to concern producing, selling, and financing. In such organizations, line authority for production typically runs directly down from plant manager, to supervisors, to foremen, to workers. Similarly, for the sales activity line authority typically flows from a general sales manager, to regional sales managers, to the salepeople.

Perhaps the paths of line authority are explained best by example. The three organizations shown in the following listing are among the best known for clean line relationships.[9]

Army	*Government*	*Roman Catholic Church*
Commander in Chief	Chief of State	Pope
Army Commander	Minister	Cardinal
Corps Commander	Service Director	Archbishop
Division Commander	Office Director	Bishop
Regimental Commander	Bureau Director	Priest
Battalion Commander	Division Director	
Company Commander	Section Chief	
Platoon Leader	Unit Chief	
Squad Leader	Group Leader	
Private		

This structure clearly shows the distinction between supervisor and subordinate. The supervisor exercises authority, and the subordinate accepts it. Final responsibility in each organization rests with the person in the top position. In such large organizations, however, the persons at the top would have an impossible job personally assuming responsibility for all that goes on below them. Thus they must decentralize authority. That is, since the people at the top are responsible for more authority than they can handle effectively, they must delegate some of it downward.

The staff and its function   Staff positions in industrial organizations are products of the development of large-scale organizations. Probably the first staff people were clerks, copiers, or couriers who assisted in the paper work of the earlier firms. As business firms became more and

---

[9] Bertram M. Gross, *Organizations and Their Managing* (New York: Free Press, 1968), p. 221.

more complex, with many specialized departments, they needed people with expertise to advise the managers in the areas of specialization. Those hired for this purpose became the staff members of the organization.

In today's business world, staff assistants are commonly used to help executives in their work. Primarily, they perform facilitating functions— that is, they give advice, conduct research, make fact-finding investigations, and the like. Regardless of what service they perform, their main distinction from line personnel is that they do not have the authority to command. Indeed, often they have everything except command and can wield strong power in the firm. This they can gain through effective suggesting, pleading, cajoling, or the like. To some degree their knowledge itself conveys power. In a sense, staff members are salespeople selling their knowledge to the organization. Their strengths in the organization depend on how effectively they can sell the line executives on the logic or appropriateness of their objectives.

Staff assistants may be of many kinds. They may be personal staff assistants such as secretaries who keep track of business engagements, answer routine letters, and decide on what information should be given the executive. They may be highly specialized workers such as ghost writers who compose the speeches busy executives must make. They may be administrative assistants who do a large part of an executive's routine work, or lawyers who give legal opinions when management needs them. And they may be tens of other kinds of workers.

Staff assignments need not be thought of in terms of only individuals. They may be given to entire departments. In fact, in the larger organizations this is the rule rather than the exception. Commonly in the large organizations there are departments of research, accounting, personnel, legal matters, public relations, and advertising, to name a few. None of these departments is directly involved in introducing or selling products or services. All operate in a supportive or advisory capacity.

Such departments, however, are not totally staff in their operations. Their own internal structures may follow a line pattern. In a typical accounting department, for example, structure of authority is evident. At the top we are likely to find a chief accountant; and directly below we may find several junior accountants and bookkeepers. The relationships between these two levels truly is line. But when the department as a whole renders its services to the firm, we have a staff relationship.

Span of management

A major question to be answered in setting up the structure of an organization is that of how many subordinates each manager should manage. The question is a vital one, for there is a limit as to how many subordinates a given manager can supervise effectively. To use the terminology of management, there is an ideal *span of management* for each unique situation.

Span of management for a given position is determined by human limitations. A human being can do only so much and do it effectively. Or, as one management writer explained it, the human brain can manage only a limited number of other brains. Certainly, managing one person requires some work. Managing two requires more work. And managing three requires still more. Eventually, we reach a point at which managers are supervising just the right number. Were they to supervise fewer, managers would have time to spare; were they to supervise more, they would not do the work efficiently. This point represents the ideal span of management for the position.

Just how many subordinates a manager can supervise effectively is not easily determined. Even the experts do not completely agree on the matter. Most agree, however, that the number is determined by the frequency and intensity of the relationships required between manager and subordinates. More specifically, how often managers need to contact subordinates and how much time they must give them on these contacts are the determining factors. The requirements for each managerial position must be determined separately.

Levels of supervision The frequency and intensity of contacts vary considerably from the top to the bottom of the organization chart. In fact, there appear to be two levels of supervisors, both of which require different rules governing the number of subordinates that a supervisor can control.[10]

At the lowest level (first-line supervisors in a manufacturing plant), a supervisor's duties mainly are physical. There is little need for mental activities. Thus a supervisor can effectively manage a relatively large number of workers—15 to 20, according to most authorities.

Applying to all executives above the level of first-line supervisor is the span of executive control. It is a narrower span limiting effective supervision from three to five managers (perhaps to seven in extreme cases). The reason for this extreme limitation for the higher position should be apparent. The higher executive spends much of his time planning and organizing activities. This type of work is largely mental. Mental work is more demanding and time-consuming than physical activity.

Flat versus tall organization The concept of span of control generally is accepted in business. Even so, companies vary widely in their applications of it. The result is a wide assortment of organization structures, even for similar businesses.

At one extreme are those organizations that believe in a very narrow

---

[10] Waino W. Suojanen, "The Span of Control—Fact or Fable," in Max D. Richards and William A. Nielander (eds.), *Readings in Management* (Cincinnati, Ohio: South-Western Publishing Co., 1958), p. 571.

span of control. Because of this belief, their structures have many layers of management, and their organization charts take on a tall or peaked appearance (see Figure 6–9). At the other extreme are those companies that believe managers can supervise larger numbers of subordinates. Their organizations take on a flat appearance. Obviously, the flat plan costs less, for it requires fewer management salaries. But whether it is more effective or efficient is a matter upon which business people do not agree.

In American business, the tendency is toward a more peaked design. On the other hand, many foreign businesses favor flatter arrangements. In recent years, however, there has been some tendency toward a flatter arrangement in American business. One leader in this trend has been Kaiser Alumium Company, which flattened its organization in order to weather an industry recession in the early 1970s. The direction business will take on this matter in the years ahead is not clear.

The bases of structure

In a very real sense, the organization chart for a firm is an orderly arrangement of the work the firm does. Thus, we may look upon organization as a division of work.

A logical first step in dividing the work of a firm is to determine its primary goals. Specifically, we must decide what is the purpose of the firm. Is it to manufacture? To sell? To provide a service? Then with this question answered, we move to the question of what are the logical working divisions which will enable the firm to accomplish this purpose? The possibilities here are numerous. Among the possibilities, three are most commonly used: division by function, by product, and by process. As these three are by far the most popular, they shall be reviewed briefly in following paragraphs. But there are others which may be useful in a given case, such as division by location of work done, by the kinds of equipment used in the work, and by the time sequence of the work.

Function A division by function breaks down the organization's work into broad categories of similar activities. A manufacturing concern may have the primary functions of production, marketing, and finance. A sales organization needs only major divisions of marketing and service. In both examples, a large organization might include secondary work areas such as research, advertising, law, public relations, and purchasing.

After determining the primary divisions, we may further divide each into logical subareas of work. For example, the production department of the firm mentioned above might be further divided into departments of fabrication, assembly, tooling, production control, and quality control. And its marketing department might be made up of divisions of selling, advertising, and sales promotion. At the next step in the organization

FIGURE 6-9

Variation in peakedness of organization

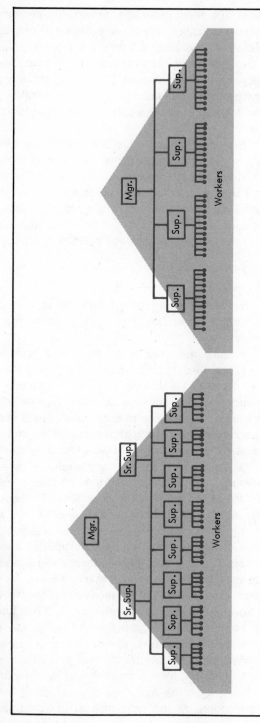

This organization is more peaked. Here the workers are organized into eight departments, each with a supervisor. One senior supervisor is over each supervisor. A manager has authority over the two senior supervisors. Thus, there are three levels of management above the workers.

This is a flatter organization. The workers are divided into four larger departments. Each department has a supervisor. The supervisor is directly under the manager. This plan has only two levels of management above the workers. Five people do the work assigned to 11 in the other plan.

chart, each of these subdivisions would be further subdivided into narrower work areas. These successive divisions would continue as long as necessary to meet the organizational needs of the firm.

Product The large firm manufacturing a number of products may logically organize by product. Likewise, a service organization or a sales organization may structure its work by the products it handles. "Grouping by product has the advantage of bringing together and coordinating in one place major activities required to make a particular product."[11] For example, a company manufacturing fertilizers, tractors, and insecticides might have a group of products that would serve a similar market; but it would find the manufacturing work to be vastly different for each. Such clear differences in work would make organization by products a logical possibility.

Process Some forms of manufacturing involve activities which logically are organized by process—that is, by the nature of the work being done. A manufacturing firm might organize by processes such as tooling, fabricating, assembling, inspecting, packaging, and shipping. Or a textile mill could be arranged on the basis of its operational sequence: spinning, weaving, bleaching, dyeing, inspecting, boxing, and shipping. In each case, the arrangement is an effective and logical means of organizing the company's personnel for a coordinated effort.

Concept of authority

Our study of organizations would be lacking in thoroughness were we not to discuss the concept of authority. Authority is a key concept to understanding organizations, and if we are to manage organizations, we should understand it clearly. We should know what it is, and what it is not. We should know how it comes about, and how it works.

Probably we all have a reasonably clear concept of what authority is. Nevertheless, we are likely to confuse it with power. We can avoid this confusion if we think of *power* as the *ability* to do something. On the other hand, *authority* is the *right* to do something. The two are distinctly different; but they are related, as the following discussion illustrates.

From these definitions it should be clear that one can have the authority to do a thing but not have the power to do it. Likewise, he may have the power to do a thing but lack the authority. For example, a manager may be given formally the authority to make certain purchases for the organization. A strong administrative assistant, however, may have total influence (power) over all such actions and in fact may make the decisions. Or a strong personality in a department may be the one to

---

[11] Earnest Dale, "The Division of Basic Company Activities," in Harold Koontz and Cyril O'Donnoll, *Management: A Book of Readings* (New York: McGraw-Hill Book Company, 1964), pp. 170–79.

whom the members look for advice and leadership. The department head, who has the formal authority and power for most personnel actions, may follow the course of action suggested by this leader. Where, then, does the effective power lie? These two opposing situations occur in organizations; and they are as much a part of the organization as those relationships shown on the organization chart.

The examples given above raise the question as to the source of authority. How does one get it? As we noted, authority is formally recognized and awarded when the organization is given its structure (when the organization chart is made). But this is not the only way in which it is given. Some feel that authority and power grow over time—that an old boss has them because he has earned them. Another point of view holds that they are products of trial. That is, if a person exercises his authority and those concerned accept it, he has gained authority. Or to use the words of one management writer, ". . . we must concede, whether we like it or not, that Might has often made Right."[12]

With some organizations, authority is shown by status symbols, such as fancier office furniture, preferred parking space, telephones, washroom keys, and such. In the military, visual symbols—uniforms, stars, stripes—clearly tell all involved the degree of authority and power held. Rank and title in all organizations are intended to represent different degrees of authority. Then there is the belief that authority rests with the characteristics of the individual manager. If he or she has qualities of leadership, expertise, or special ability, they tend to gain in authority.

There are other explanations, but these are the principal ones. Which of them are correct, are partially correct, are incorrect, is not clearly evident. Probably all of them are valid to some extent.

DISCUSSION QUESTIONS

1 What viewpoint of management do you believe is practiced at your school? What viewpoint should be practiced? Defend your decision.

2 Select an organization to which you belong and explain how it is like and unlike a business organization.

3 Three men who operate one—employee, tie manufacturing businesses are thinking about going together to form one business. Point out the advantages and disadvantages their proposed form of organization would have.

4 Construct an organization chart for some organization with which you are familiar (your school, a local business, a social club, or the like). Explain and evaluate it.

---

[12] Gross, *Organizations and Their Managing*, p. 91.

5 Assume that you are the manager of a department and that one of your subordinates has more control over the other subordinates than you do. What has happened? What would you do to overcome this problem?

6 Can one position have both line and staff relationships? Explain using examples.

7 Discuss the differences in span of management in supervising the following types of workers:
 a Department supervisors.
 b Welders.
 c Door-to-door interviewers.

8 Select a local business and discuss the possibilities of organizing it by function, by product, by process.

9 Can a manager have power without authority? Authority without power? Explain using illustrations.

MINI CASES

Quincy Manufacturing Company is a typical, moderately large American business. Its organization chart is somewhat peaked in much the same way as other businesses of its size and type in the United States.

Recently the company was purchased by Mr X, a wealthy foreign business leader. Mr. X also owns a number of similar businesses in his native land. All of his businesses have been highly efficient and have given him very good profits. In his homeland, Mr. X is considered to be an exceptionally good manager.

Soon after acquiring the Quincy Manufacturing Company, Mr. X began making changes in its organization. Because his businesses back home worked so well with about half the number of supervisory personnel, he expanded the span of management throughout his new company. Immediately he received a storm of protest from his new employees—management and workers alike. Morale dropped; and so did production. Mr. X's new business not only did not increase profits, it actually lost money.

 1. *Explain these results.*
 2. *What should Mr. X do now?*
 3. *What would you do if you had bought a foreign company and found its organization inefficient by American standards?*

In the shipping department of the Green Valley Manufacturing Company, coffee breaks have been scheduled at 10 a.m. and 3 p.m. At these times all ten employees stop work, drink coffee, and talk. Obviously, all work stops.

Susan Hollas, who is in charge of the department, feels that it would run more smoothly if the workers staggered their rest periods so that no more than three would be on a break at one time. So she decides to make a basic change.

This morning she initiated the change by calling each worker into her office. She explained the reasons for the change to each worker. And with one exception, from each worker got a verbal assurance that the new policy would be all right. The one dissenting worker was Larry Cornwell.

During the lunch hour, the workers all discussed the matter; and Larry Cornwell brought his position before the group. Shortly after lunch, Larry Cornwell walked into the office of Susan Hollas and delivered this message: "Me and the boys have been talking about your new coffee break plan. We don't like it. In fact, we're 100 percent against it. You're going to have to change it."

Susan Hollas changed the policy.

1. *Analyze this situation from an organizational point of view.*
2. *What should Susan Hollas do to correct the problem?*

Assume that you have accepted the assignment as campaign chairman of the annual United Fund campaign for your campus. You have at your disposal 35 volunteer student workers. (You may adjust this number upward or downward, depending on the size of your school.) Your task primarily consists of publicizing the campaign and of collecting contributions through a door-to-door solicitation.

1. *What activities would you need to consider in organizing this campaign?*
2. *Draw the organization chart you would use in this case.*

Mary Parket Follett lived during the heyday of efficiency experts in management. Through her deceptively simple philosophizing she was able to provide the link between the scientific management and the human relations period which followed. Possibly in reaction to the coldness and dehumanizing aspects of scientific management, she gave less attention to the individual and placed more emphasis on the group in industry. She saw management as a social process and the organization as a social system. Her viewpoints were sharp departures from those held by most management scholars of her time. But interestingly enough, many of her viewpoints have since been supported by the findings of research.

Born in 1868 in Boston and trained in philosophy and political science at what is now Radcliffe College, Ms. Follett became keenly interested in the new field of social psychology. The management discipline did not discover her until she was in her fifties, at a time when she had already achieved international fame as a political philosopher. This occurred in 1925 when she was invited to give a lecture series to business executives. While she was making these presentations, her main area of philosophical interest changed from politics to business.

From 1925 onward she was much in demand as a lecturer in the United States and England. And she became quite active in consulting work, especially on matters relating to selecting and maintaining cooperation among people in business. Although only five years of her life were devoted to business, her contributions form a landmark in management literature. She was the first to adapt meaningfully the social sciences to industry, and in doing this, she developed a new concept of management and of relations within industrial groups. Even today her contributions continue to influence the thinking of management practitioners and scholars.

Mary Parker Follett
(1868–1933)

Philosophical sage of management

7

Management of the organization

Management is getting things done through people.

———*Mary Parker Follett*

The preceding review shows us how the people in a business are organized to do the work of the business. Especially does it show us the structure of its managers—that is, of who bosses whom and who has authority over what. The next logical step is to turn to the work managers do in their positions in the organization. Thus, a review of the activities of management follows.

THE MANAGEMENT PROCESS

Let us begin our review of the work of management by defining the term. As we shall view it, *management* is the process of planning, organizing, leading, and controlling the coordination of resources used by the firm so as to achieve stated objectives.

The key words in this definition form a base for understanding management. First, note that management is described as a process; that is, it is not a static thing but a procession of events. It is a continuous activity, and continually suggests change. Perhaps no word better characterizes the functions of managers than this one—*change.* The managers strive to achieve the objectives of the organization; and always they are under the pressure of change.

Next among the key words in the definition are those which describe what managers do. They coordinate the resources of the organization; that is, they coordinate all that the organization has to operate—its people, equipment, and money. They do all of this coordinating by performing the basic managerial functions: planning, organizing, leading, and controlling (see Figure 7–1). Each of these functions shall be discussed later in this chapter. But two general observations about them should be made at this point.

First, these functions are not separate and distinct activities, as a listing of them may imply. As has been noted, the work of managing is a continuous process. All of these activities are related and interwoven in this process. In fact, so interrelated are these functions that often it is difficult to separate them. They are discussed separately mainly for the purpose of studying them.

The second observation about managers' activities is that all managers perform all of the functions. Of course, some managers specialize in

FIGURE 7–1

How the management functions work

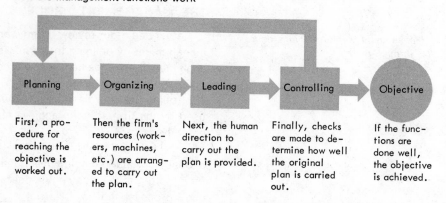

one or more of these activities; and certainly some managers' jobs will require that they do more of one activity than another. But all managerial effort, if it is a truly managerial effort, incorporates all of the managerial functions. A review of these functions should make this point quite clear.

DETERMINATION OF OBJECTIVES

As the definition of management clearly indicates, the purpose behind the management process is the achievement of stated objectives. It is essential, therefore, that we have a clear concept of objectives if we are to understand management.

Importance of objectives

Obvious and trivial as it may appear to some, managers cannot manage effectively without knowing their objectives. As noted in the preceding chapter, objectives are essential to group effort. They are the ingredients which give organizations meaning. They are the reasons why organizations form. Their very status determines whether the organization succeeds or fails, lives or dies. It appears only logical that those who determine the activities within an organization must know the objectives if these activities are to work for the organization's best interest.

Formulation of objectives

Objectives within an organization stem from two sources: the individual members have them; the organization itself has them.

As noted previously, people join organizations because they expect certain benefits from them. That is, the members of an organization have their own objectives—to benefit socially, to gain friendships, and to make money. Organizations, also, have objectives. It may be to make a profit, to produce a product, to serve the public, to get a politician elected, and the like. Obviously, the objectives of these two groups are not the same—at least, not normally.

Even though the objectives of an organization and its individual members normally are different, they must be compatible. One must permit existence of the other. Ideally, one should support the other. For example, in joining a firm the individual worker may have the objectives of financial reward and security. The firm may have profit maximization as its primary objective. By working for their own objectives, however, individuals also work for the firm's objectives. If the firm prospers, so does the worker; and so is the worker's employment security enhanced.

The objectives of the organization

Every business organization has objectives. Their objectives are not always thought out, but they should be. In fact, management authorities generally agree that a business should put its objectives in writing (see Figure 7–2). Using written objectives, managers will know where the business should be going, and they can work consciously to get it there.

The objectives of businesses vary from firm to firm. Determining what should be on any one firm's list is no simple matter, for many possibilities exist. Of course, profit is first to come to mind. Certainly, profit is a universal objective of all businesses in a free enterprise system such as ours. A business is not likely to last long if it does not achieve profits. Nor is it likely to achieve any other objectives unless it makes profits— at least, not for long. Some argue that profit really is the only objective— that all others are related to it. There is good argument for this position. But as we shall see, there are others.

FIGURE 7–2

Statement of objectives of a metals manufacturing company

STATEMENT OF OBJECTIVES

It shall be the objectives of the Company:
1. To manufacture quality products at the lowest cost possible.
2. To sell these products at a competitive price.
3. To gain and hold a position of respect and leadership in the industry.
4. To return a fair profit to the investor.
5. To maintain and increase the value of the owner's investment in the company.
6. To grow at the rate permitted by the company objectives.
7. To provide for the security and health of all employees.
8. To provide fair and reasonable salaries for all employees.
9. To communicate to employees on all company matters of interest to them, confidential information being excluded.
10. To solicit and listen to the opinions and reports of employees concerning company matters.
11. To respect the dignity of all workers.
12. To provide a safe and pleasant work environment.
13. To maintain good relations with the business community, customers, and the public at large.
14. To continually work through research and development to improve products.
15. To continue to diversify production.

Various services to society are objectives often mentioned. By providing employment, by filling needs for goods and services, by giving assistance to community projects, and the like, businesses contribute to the well-being of society. Whether they make these contributions because it is profitable to do so is a matter of some controversy.

Another objective is the quest for power. The history of business contains numerous examples of business people who sought to dominate markets, to drive out competition, and generally to expand their businesses mainly because they wanted power. Victory over the competition is in itself a real goal to the Caesars, Alexanders, and Napoleons who exist in business.

Yet another business objective is security—for the business as well as for those who run it. Thus, a business may forsake profits in order to increase sales and generally to improve the firm's position in the field. Achieving such objectives tends to assure the firm's continued operation, and it assures the management of continued employment.

These are only some of the possible objectives of a business. There are also such goals as achieving social prestige, gaining public recognition, surviving, keeping the business small, developing new ideas and products—even human enjoyment. In fact, just about every strong motivation of human conduct could be a business objective.

MANAGEMENT FUNCTIONS—PLANNING

Having established the proposition that determining objectives is essential, this review now turns to the subject of what managers do as they manage. Specifically, it takes up the management functions separately: Planning, organizing, leading, and controlling. You should recall, however, that the approach of this review has been to treat management as a process. Thus, though the functions are discussed separately, you should keep in mind that they are closely interwoven and interactive. Seldom is it possible in a real-life situation to clearly separate each function from the other functions. For study purposes, however, we must do so.

The nature of the planning process

Before proceeding into a review of the planning function, you should be familiar with the two terms which are basic to this discussion. They are the plan and the planning function. In the words of one management scholar, "A plan may be described as a statement of objectives to be obtained in the future and an outline of the steps necessary to reach them."[1] From this definition you may reason logically the meaning of the second term. Thus, the planning function consists of all those activities involved in making plans. More specifically, these activities comprise the process of evaluating information from the past and present, making an assessment of probable future developments and devising courses of action to meet the organization's objectives.

Planning logically precedes the other functions. The reason is obvious. Before a firm can reach a goal, it must know what that goal is; and it must have a course of action (plan) for reaching it. Of course, it is possible for a firm to achieve goals quite unintentionally. The discovery of radioactivity, for example, was made quite by accident; and so have been many other accomplishments of people. But for the organization, where cooperation and coordination are mandatory for success, such random happenings would not produce satisfactory results. Managers could not organize if they had no purpose in mind. They could not provide leadership if there were no course or direction. And they could not evaluate progress without first knowing where the organization should be at a certain time. Thus, planning must precede all the other functions of management.

The formulation of the plan

Just how one goes about the task of making a plan is not easy to describe. Not all people work in the same pattern; and not all situations

---

[1] Ernest Dale, *Management: Theory and Practice,* 3d ed. (New York: McGraw-Hill Book Company, 1973), p. 300.

provide the same problem of planning. Much of what is done involves the logical and imaginative use of the mind; and as we know, the mind works in ways that defy meaningful description. Nevertheless, it is possible to outline a general procedure for formulating plans (see Figure 7–3). Pre-

FIGURE 7–3

Scientific method in plan formulation

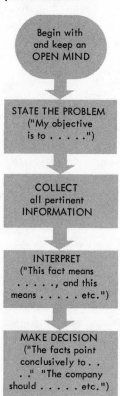

cisely how managers carry out the steps in the plan, however, is a matter for them to work out individually.

In working out the plan, managers make full use of a procedure commonly referred to as the scientific method. It is a logical thought process useful in all forms of decision making, including making decisions about plans. Simply stated, the method involves a thorough and painstaking effort to be objective. In forming this plan, managers keep their minds open. Their goal is to find truth. They will let the facts and figures speak; and they will keep out bias and emotion.

Statement of the problem   A logical first step in the scientific method of forming a plan is to state the problem. On first thought this may appear to be an elementary and perhaps unnecessary step. The truth is, however, that stating the problem serves vital purposes. That is,

1. It helps to get the problem clearly in mind—to determine what it is, where it is, who it involves, and so on.
2. It helps to determine the limits (scope) of the problem—that is, what the problem does and does not involve.
3. It helps to determine whether a problem really exists.

Information collection   After the problem is stated, the next step in the planning process is to collect all available information relevant to the problem. Typically, such data will draw on sources from the past and present and should also include forecasts of the future.

Interpretation of data   Managers take the data collected and logically applies them to the problem at hand. More specifically, they look for meaning in the data. They look for the alternative courses of action available to them. They weigh objectively all of the information, conclusions, and alternatives available and reach logical decisions.

Selection of the plan   From these logical alternatives, managers next select the plan best supported by their judgment. Their selection is the plan for the problem.

The process illustrated   To illustrate this technique, take the case of a manufacturer who must plan the packaging for a new candy product. One part of this plan would involve determining the form of packaging to use. A manager might begin this part of the task by clearly getting in mind just what must be done: "To determine which is the best form of packaging for this candy: box, cellophane, aluminum foil, wax paper, tin cans, glass, and so on." Next, the manager would gather all the information available on each of the forms of packaging. How do they compare on cost? What are the protective features of each? Which makes the most attractive display? What handling problems does each involve? Then, with all such facts in mind, the manager would apply them to the one product. Perhaps, for example, the candy is soft and would benefit from a metal container to protect it. Or maybe the manager feels that the candy's distinctive quality requires a color and design that can best be printed on paper or cardboard. From a careful weighting of such specific interpretations, the manager then arrives at the conclusion: that _____ packaging is best. The manager would develop each part of the plan for packaging similarly.

Criteria for evaluating plans

Evaluating the plan is a vital part of the planning process. As this process clearly is a subjective one, it is difficult to describe. The proper bases for evaluating plans, however, clearly are evident. They are objectivity, structure, and flexibility.

Objectivity of the plan   The more objective a plan is, the better it is likely to be. Objectivity, as you will recall, refers to the degree that the plans are based on measurable and verifiable data. Thus, the more objective is the plan, the less it possesses elements of subjective judgment (feeling, emotion, or hunch). We may conclude that a plan is objective if another logical-minded person working with the same data would reach the same conclusion.

Requirements of structure   The requirements of a good plan are many. And they vary with the facts of the one case. Even so, four basic requirements of structure stand out:

1. *Comprehensiveness.*   The plan should omit no part needed to carry it out.
2. *Time span.*   Whenever time is a factor, the plan should contain a timetable for all parts and a final completion date.
3. *Assignment of duties.*   The plan should assign all tasks to be done to specific people and departments.
4. *Control factors.*   It should contain reviewing and checking procedures over the time of the plan.

These criteria give us a guide to determining how good a plan is. But the final and only meaningful test of any plan is how it works in practice. How a plan works, however, is affected by performance of the other functions. As you will recall, the functions are all closely related.

Need for flexibility   A third criterion for evaluating plans is flexibility. Plans should take into account the possibility that conditions can change and that alternative actions may be required. They should anticipate the likely changes, and they should provide alternative plans for them. In general, the plan should enable the organization to sway with the contingencies that inevitably arise.

MANAGEMENT FUNCTIONS—ORGANIZING

Organizing can mean many things to different people. For purposes of this review, however, attention focuses on the act of organizing. Specifically, this review concerns the approach managers use to organize, their aims in organizing, and the guidelines and rules they follow when they organize. That is, it is not done only when the organization begins. It may be true, of course, that organizing has its greatest scope when an organization is being "set up;" but the process itself continues for the life of the firm or company. As new expansion takes place, as new products are developed, or as conditions change over time, the organization requires patchwork and revision to accommodate the change. Thus, like planning, organizing continuously is in process.

The meaning of organizing

Organizing may be defined as the process of arranging the flows of people, materials, and work so as to accomplish stated objectives with a minimum consumption of each resource. In essence, organizing involves four specific tasks:

1. Arranging work activities to achieve the organization's goals.
2. Grouping activities to use resources effectively.
3. Assigning activities and delegating authority to carry out assignments.
4. Tying all the working groups together to form a coordinated operation.

Steps in the organizing process

So that you may better appreciate the significance of each step, it is appropriate to examine them in turn. As you examine each, however, bear in mind that primarily they concern the initial design of an organization. No attempt is made to evaluate an organization that already exists.

Determining specific work activities The problem of arranging work activities so as to achieve stated objectives involves several subproblems. Foremost among these is the necessity of determining what work will accomplish the objectives. As you will recall, once the objective is stated, a plan should be devised to accomplish that objective. Thus, the first step in arranging work activities is to turn to the provisions of the plan. The plan should tell us what is to be done and, to a limited degree, how it is to be done. The task of the organizer, then, is to translate those plans into concrete performance.

Illustrating this step is the case of a small, new company established to manufacture shirts. Simply stated, this company's objective may be to manufacture a quality line of shirts at a fair profit to the investor. With this objective in mind, the company's managers would look to see what work objectives would be involved. First, they would need to provide for purchasing the cloth, thread, buttons, packing materials, equipment, and such. Then they would need to determine the work activities involved in production—making patterns, cutting cloth, sewing, inspecting, packing, storing, and so on. As the manufactured shirts must be sold in order to bring in profits, they would also need to consider the work involved in marketing—work such as advertising, promoting, selling, and servicing. The organization itself would need some activities performed so that all of the foregoing work could be done; so the managers would provide for such additional work as financing, plant maintenance, and personnel and general administration.

Grouping activities   The second step in organizing is that of grouping the activities for the most effective use of the organization's resources (workers, machinery, space, equipment, money, time, and so on).

In our shirt company illustration, grouping activities would involve selecting from the workers available to the manager those needed to accomplish the work assignments. It would include arranging them into work units, perhaps by work activities (cutting, sewing, inspecting, and the like); or maybe it would entail setting up a form of assembly line for the entire operation. In order to facilitate these work efforts, it would require arranging the machinery for the most efficient operations. And so would it be done for all of the other work activities needed to produce and market shirts.

Assigning activities   Assigning activities to group leaders is the third step in organizing. It consists of two stages. First, the leaders must be given the formal responsibility for the work to be done. This means they must be given (1) full instruction, (2) a complete plan of action, (3) an indication of resources with which they may work, (4) a set of usable alternatives, and (5) an expression of the boundaries of their responsibilities. The second stage involves giving the leaders the authority to carry out their assignments. They must be given the authorization to perform the activities for which they are responsible. Or in other words, they must be given authority commensurate with their responsibilities.

For our shirt manufacturing company, this step would mean giving to those assigned to the various positions of leadership in the organization all the specific instructions, plans, procedures, and so on, needed to do the work for which each person is responsible. Each would then know specifically what work he and his unit must do; and each would know how it should be done. The leader in charge of the cutting operation, for example, would know the specific steps the workers should follow in their work, the margins of error permitted, the quantity of work expected, and such. Perhaps most important of all, the leaders would be given all the authority they need to do their jobs.

Horizontal and vertical structure   Once the managers have determined the specific activities to be performed, grouped these activities in the most efficient manner, and made the proper work assignments, they will then tie these activities or groups together to form a coordinated operation. They do this in two main ways: (1) by establishing clear authority relationships, and (2) by setting up an information system.

In establishing clear authority relationships, managers make certain that each department, division, section, and so on, clearly has the authority to carry out the activities assigned to it. The authority given to one unit must not conflict with the authority granted another. And generally, the authority given one level should not exceed the authority of the next highest level. Also, the authority must be commensurate with responsibility, for there is little point in holding a unit responsible for something it is not authorized to do. Responsibility, however, cannot be delegated and always resides with the person in the top position. That is, managers may hold a subordinate accountable for their action, but the managers themselves are responsible for the subordinate's mistakes.

In organizing for effective communication, the managers' goal should be to provide every segment of the organization with the timely and accurate information it needs to do its work. It should be apparent at the outset, however, that this goal is an impossible one. This goal can never be achieved perfectly; the manager can only work toward it.

The steps managers should take in establishing authority relationships and an information system vary with the size and complexity of the organization. Because organizations vary so much in their makeups, each must be treated as a uniquely different case. The point is illustrated by inspection of the changing authority relationships and communication needs of a business as it grows over time.

Let us use the case of our shirt manufacturer, which we shall assume is a typical one-owner business. In the beginning it may need only a few employees. They all work for the manager. They work directly under him and they communicate directly to him. Obviously, the authority relationships and information system of the organization are clear and simple.

As the organization grows, the manager hires more personnel. In time it becomes so large that the owner-manager can no longer manage all the employees. Thus, the manager may divide them into two groups and appoint managers over each. While still relatively simple, the authority relationships and information flow now are much more complex than before, for now there are two levels of bosses.

As the organization grows still further, the two departments may need to be split; or perhaps a third or fourth department may need to be added. The result is additional complexity in authority relationships and information flow. And so the complexity continues as the organization continues to grow. By the time it has grown to be the typical full-scale corporation, its complexity has become enormous.

MANAGEMENT FUNCTIONS—LEADERSHIP

The third function that all managers must perform is leadership. Some management writers call it directing. For our purposes, however, leadership appears to be the better word. As you will see, the directing that managers do is a direct outgrowth of their leadership style. Thus, if you can develop an understanding of leadership, you will be better qualified to assess the directing that takes place in the organization.

The nature of leadership

Leadership, as it is performed in organizations, is the accomplishment of organizational objectives through the interpersonal relationships between managers and their subordinates. Analysis of leadership can take either of two basic approaches. One is to cover the patterns or types of leadership that exist. By this approach, leadership is classified according to the degree of authority leaders have over those under them. The second approach is to cover the human traits that leaders typically have.

The plan in the following paragraphs is to use both approaches. First comes a review of the primary patterns of leadership—autocratic, democratic, and revisionist. This examination explores the attitudes of leaders to see how they might shape the behavior of leaders. Next, the review shifts to the characteristics of leaders.

Autocratic leadership (Theory X) As the term implies, *autocratic leadership* is the style typified by a strong boss. It is the style in which the leader's role is to make the decisions and give the orders and the subordinate's role is only to obey. It is the style that prevailed throughout the early days of business when bosses expected blind obedience and considered workers as resources to be used effectively. In more recent times, such extreme forms of leadership have all but disappeared. But a milder form of autocratic leadership does exist.

The autocratic style of leadership is based on a set of three assumptions referred to in management literature as Theory X[2]:

1. The average human being has an inherent dislike of work and will avoid it if he can.
2. Because of this human characteristic of dislike of work, most people must be coerced, controlled, directed, threatened with punishment to get them to put forth adequate effort toward the achievement of organizational objectives.
3. The average human being prefers to be directed, wishes to avoid responsibility, has relatively little ambition, and wants security above all.

Clearly, if these assumptions are true, autocratic leadership is necessary. The pertinent question, of course, is are they true in today's society?

Democratic leadership (Theory Y) At the opposite polar end of leadership styles is *democratic leadership.* It is the style which emphasizes the interests of the workers and seeks their contributions in managing the organization wherever they can help. The democratic approach emphasizes the strengths of each member of the organization, and it makes use of all of them. Instead of "cracking the whip," management attempts

---
[2] Douglas McGregor, *The Human Side of Enterprise* (New York: McGraw-Hill Book Company, 1960), pp. 33–34.

to motivate all workers to reach their full potential. When decisions must be made, the workers contribute to them. Instead of making decisions in favor of the organization, management gives equal concern to the workers. As a result of this approach, the workers' needs are satisfied, and they respond by making their maximum contribution to the organization.

At the base of this leadership style is a set of assumptions known as Theory Y. As you will see, they are directly opposed to those of Theory X.[3])

1. The expenditure of physical and mental effort in work is as natural as play or rest.
2. External control and threat of punishment are not the only means for bringing about effort toward the achievement of organizational objectives. People will exercise self-direction and self-control in the service of objectives to which they are committed.
3. Commitment to objectives is a function of the rewards associated with their achievement.
4. The average human being learns under proper conditions, not only to accept but to seek responsibility.
5. The capacity to exercise a relatively high degree of imagination, ingenuity, and creativity in the solution of organizational problems is widely, not narrowly, distributed in the population.
6. Under the conditions of modern industrial life, the intellectual potentialities of the average human being are only partially utilized.

Revisionist leadership It would be rare indeed for the leadership style in a modern business firm to be totally autocratic or totally democratic. Most are somewhere between these extremes (see Figure 7–4). Most companies seek a logical balance between the needs of the organization and the needs of the individual. Out of this effort to compromise has come a third style, revisionist leadership.

Revisionist leadership is a flexible style that shifts toward autocracy or democracy depending on the conditions facing the organization. The organization adjusts as the need arises to both pressures inside and outside its operations.

In actual practice, this style depends not so much on assumptions of human behavior as it does on conditions that dictate the actions of the leaders. For example, economic conditions would force the revisionist leader to move toward autocratic or democratic rule. During periods of prosperity, the leader can afford to relax controls and concentrate on giving subordinates a chance to make decisions. But when prosperity declines, the leader must take charge, for even small errors may be disastrous.

---

[3] Ibid., pp. 47–48.

Illustrating this condition are the widely publicized experiences of Non-Linear Systems, Inc., a San Diego-based electronics company. In the prosperous 1960s, the company altered its leadership pattern to give employees a strong voice in company operations. In general, they revolutionized operations to give employees decision-making powers over their own work operation. For a few years, all went well. Morale was high, productivity improved, and profits were good. But in the early 1970s, an industry recession occurred. Soon the firm found itself in trouble. Its management quickly scuttled its plan for democracy and returned to a somewhat autocratic system. In short time it regained its prosperity.

FIGURE 7–4

Patterns of leadership styles

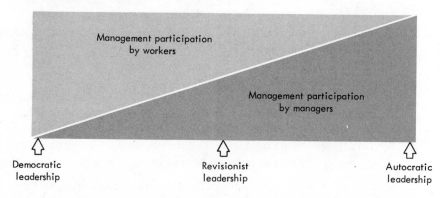

Other conditions may also dictate either a stern or relaxed control. Extreme competition from competitors, the threat of strike by a union, intervention by the federal government, the threat of suits by consumers, pressure from stockholders—all of these to some degree may influence the style of leadership that emerges. Thus, as the managers strive to achieve organizational goals, they are likely to temper their leadership style with the conditions of the moment.

Components of leadership

A second approach to the study of leadership is to isolate the characteristics of the leader. Obviously, this approach serves a most practical need. It permits us to find tomorrow's leaders today. If we know what characteristics of personality are found in the leader, then we should be better able to spot potential leaders of the future. Finding tomorrow's leaders today can be of real benefit to the business firm, as it continually needs to update its sources of workers.

Generally, the traits of a good leader include such qualities as judgment, intelligence, initiative, and perseverance. Other lists include such attributes as emotional stability, maturity, ambition, the ability to get along with others, and integrity. One begins to suspect that almost any human virtue that can be described will sooner or later turn up as a trait of the leader. And this is precisely why the trait approach is criticized. The lists of traits can ramble on and on, seemingly without end.

But the trait approach is also criticized on more legitimate grounds. For one thing, studies of traits do not assign weights to the traits; so it is difficult to determine the value of each. For another, the traits overlap considerably. As an illustration, how does one separate perseverance, aggressiveness, ambition, and drive? A third criticism is that the trait approach ignores the situational factors that surround the leader. Often, contrary to his characteristics, a weak person will rise to the occasion when leadership is needed; and some with all the characteristics of a good leader may fail.

From this review it is apparent that leadership is not the easiest of the management functions. Clearly it requires a high level of ability. Leadership is a most complex subject; and there is much we do not know about it. Even so, managers can profit by understanding and putting to use the information which has developed on the subject.

MANAGEMENT FUNCTIONS—CONTROL

Thus far the discussion has covered the importance of setting objectives, of making plans to achieve those objectives, of organizing activities to put our plans in action, and of providing the leadership necessary to carry out the process. Now it turns to the final function of management—that of evaluating all of this activity to see whether the managers have really accomplished what they set out to do. *Control* is the word for this final function.

The nature of control

The *control function* involves two basic activities. First, it involves checking to find out whether the organization is doing what it planned to do. Second, it involves taking the corrective actions needed to carry out the planning. In other words, the control function is the work of comparing actual performance with planned performance and taking corrective action whenever deviations are found.

This definition gives us two of the steps in the control process—measuring performance and taking corrective action. A third is implied. There must be standards of performance. Without standards we would have no bases for measuring performance; nor could we have a guide for making corrections. Thus the control function involves this three-step process (see Figure 7–5):

FIGURE 7–5

The control process

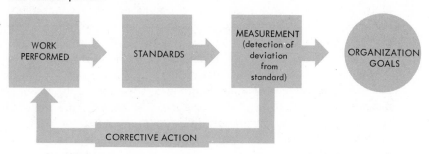

1. Developing standards that tell us where we should be at a given time.
2. Measuring current performance against the standards to determine where deviations have occurred.
3. Taking corrective action.

Setting standards

A *standard* is a unit of measurement selected to act as a criterion for evaluating performance. It is comparable to the 300 points which serve as the standard in bowling. Just as the 300 does for the bowler, standards for control provide managers with a recognized level of performance with which they can compare actual performance.

A convenient way to classify standards is according to *key result areas* of the firm. By key result area is meant the major gauges of an organization's success in operation. For example, one large manufacturing firm identified these key result areas:

Profitability	Personnel development
Market position	Employee attitudes
Productivity	Public responsibility
Product leadership	Balance between short- and long-run goals

The units of measurement used for each key result area depend on the nature of each area. Profitability is measured best, for example, by a dollar-and-cents yardstick. And market position is measured best in terms of units sold as well as by percentage of total market. Obviously, measuring such areas as personnel development and fulfillment of public responsibility is more difficult. In such areas somewhat subjective standards may be needed—in other words, standards based on our best judgment.

A review of the standards used in business shows us that the following three major forms exist:

1. *Statistical standard.* A quantitative measurement based on past information (an average, midpoint, and so on).
2. *Judgment standard.* Measurement based on sound thinking.
3. *Engineered standard.* Measurements based on a quantitative analysis of the work of a machine, person, group, and so forth.

Measuring performance

Once standards are set, it is the task of the manager to periodically measure actual performance and compare it with standards. There are a host of problems that may arise as a part of the measurement step. Chief among these are the timeliness, reliability, and validity of the data derived on the measurement step.

The *timeliness* of measurements can be of crucial importance in the control process. After all, conditions are not static in business, just as they are not static in any area of human activity. Thus, any measurement of deviation from planned performance must represent the point in time when corrective action takes place. To use old measurements simply would not provide an accurate basis for taking correction action.

A second and obvious requirement is that all measurement data must be reliable. *Reliability,* as it is used here, refers to accuracy. And accuracy means that there are neither clerical errors nor omissions. In other words, the data must be consistent and cover all aspects of the problem being considered.

A third requirement of measurement is that it be valid. *Validity* refers to the extent that the measurement actually reflects the phenomena that it intended to measure. For example, in order to assess the performance of a personnel development effort, it would be possible to simply make a head count of the persons who have completed the program. The information derived might be totally reliable, as long as it is accurate. Yet it would also be invalid. A head count is simply not an adequate measure of the efficiency of a personnel development program. Thus, it is quite possible for a measurement to be reliable but invalid. In summary, measuring performance requires that we satisfy the requirements of timeliness, reliability, and validity.

Corrective action

The final step of the control process is to take corrective action when deviations from planned performance are detected. Taking corrective action can be a most difficult step, for almost always it involves telling someone that his performance is not up to par. With respect to this problem, many people are guilty of extremes. They demand such perfection that the slightest departure from planned activities will send them into a frenzy. Generally, managers of this type are ones who become so obsessed with detail and control that they totally alienate their subordinates. At the other extreme are the hail-fellow-well-met types. Their primary concern is making people like them. They are most reluctant to take any corrective action, for it might damage their image. Obviously, either extreme of personality will contribute little to an adequate control process.

Another problem in taking corrective action is finding the source of the deviation. Managers can waste many hours and dollars going after a symptom rather than a cause. One of the unpleasant realities of the control process is that often standards, and deviations from standards, merely tell us that something needs correction. They do not always lead us to the cause of the problem or deviation.

DISCUSSION QUESTIONS

1 What do we mean when we describe management as a process? How is change related to this concept?

2 Select some organization with which you are familiar (athletic team, social club, school, and so on) and list its objectives as you see them.

3 Do businesses really have objectives other than making profits?

4 Do objectives like gaining power, achieving social prestige, and providing human enjoyment have desirable results for society?

5 Are goals such as contributing to the welfare of society just to all concerned?

6 Discuss how you would use the scientific method in developing a plan for improving registration procedure (or some other pertinent problem) at your school.

7 Assume that you are in charge of a party for a social organization. Following the steps in the organizing process, describe how you would organize the work that needs to be done.

8 Assume that you own a small (100 employees) manufacturing plant. Most of your workers are highly skilled craftsmen. What leadership style would you use? Defend your decision.

9 Can true democratic leadership work in a business? In the military? Also in government service areas such as law enforcement and fire protection.

10 Explain the relationship of the control function to the planning function.

11 What key result areas would you use in establishing standards for a large manufacturing company? How would you measure each?

MINI CASES

Three years ago, the Upchurch Manufacturing Company hired Mary Eaton as its sales manager with the understanding that she would be judged in her work primarily by the sales volume generated by her staff. Mary was very ambitious. She hired additional sales people, fired some, and motivated the old sales representatives to greater effort. In a short time, sales increased. At the end of the first year, the total volume was up over 20 percent; and similar increases were recorded for the next two years.

Analysis of the company's financial record at the end of the three-year period showed that profits were beginning to decline. In fact, it appeared that a loss would be suffered for the year. One possible cause of the change in the profit picture was the heavy increase in sales costs. Another was the increased production cost brought about by increased sales: in meeting the demand, below-standard workers had to be used, and costs per unit increased.

1. *Discuss the company's apparent objective of maximizing sales.*
2. *How could proper planning have improved the company's profits in this case?*

Shaka, king of the Zulus of South Africa in the early 1800s, was one of the great military leaders of history. Like Alexander he conquered the world that he knew. His success was in part a result of his military genius, for he revolutionized the technology of warfare in his region. But it was also a result of his leadership abilities.

As a leader, Shaka was among the most autocratic in recorded history. He imposed an iron discipline on his troops. Those who disobeyed any command were put to death. So were those who broke ranks in battle or who received wounds in the back. On one occasion Shaka sought to impress a visiting chieftain with his army's discipline by ordering a squad to march off a high cliff. Each man marched to his death without hesitation. In battle, Shaka always was at the head of his troops. He was never defeated.

1. *Discuss the strengths and weaknesses of Shaka's leadership style.*
2. *Could he have succeeded with another leadership style?*

For seven years Alice Payne served as manager of the Bigg City store of Treasure Island, Inc., a large department store chain. She did a superior job of managing the store and exceeded the quotas set for her every year.

Because of her success, Treasure Island management selected Alice to manage their new store in Muddville. As was the practice with the company, management assigned Ms. Payne an annual sales quota based on population in the trade area. After one full year of operation, Alice's store fell short of the quota by almost 50 percent. It fell short approximately 40 percent for each of the next two years. Treasure Island management became alarmed about this condition and transferred Alice Payne to a lower paying staff assignment at the home office.

1. *Discuss the control procedure used by Treasure Island.*
2. *How would you improve it?*

The name of Elton Mayo is most frequently linked with what probably are the most widely known experiments in the field of management. These are the Hawthorne experiments which were conducted at the Western Electric Company plant in the 1920s. From these experiments emerged the human relations concept of management.

Born in Australia in 1880, Mayo was educated in logic and philosophy. Later he traveled to Scotland where he studied medicine. While there he conducted some clinical research on the treatment of the shell-shock soldiers of World War I and became interested in the study of mental disorders. In 1922 he emigrated to America. And, at the time of the Hawthorne experiments, he was an associate professor of industrial relations at the Graduate School of Business Administration at Harvard University.

In the Hawthorne experiments, Mayo found strong evidence that the human problems in business are as important as are production problems. For example, he found that physical conditions (temperature, illumination, and so on) under which people work have little to do with productivity. Mental attitude, on the other hand, has very much to do with productivity. He found, also, that the worker's social and psychological needs are every bit as important to workers as their pay.

Mayo's work with the Hawthorne studies has made a lasting impression on scholars as well as business executives. To the scholar, the work has meant valuable additions to the knowledge of human behavior. To the business executive it has demonstrated the importance of understanding attitudes and group relations in managing people. Without question, Mayo's work served as a turning point in the handling of workers. Truly he earned recognition as the Father of Human Relations.

Elton Mayo
(1880–1949)

Father of human relations

8

Managing human resources

Workers are not isolated, unrelated animals; they are social animals and should be treated as such.

——F. J. Roethlisberger

Human resources are the primary ingredients of organizations. There are other ingredients, to be sure—land, buildings, money, and machinery. But primarily an organization is people. Thus, managing human resources is a major part of the management of the organization.

NATURE OF HUMAN RESOURCE MANAGEMENT

Human resource management may be looked upon in many ways. In its narrowest sense, it involves the work of a single department or individual in the organization. In this narrow sense it commonly is called personnel management. Most large businesses have personnel management departments. These departments are charged specifically with handling the human resources phase of the organization's management. That is, they do things such as test prospective workers, interview job applicants, maintain employee records, conduct training programs, and administer wages and salaries.

In its broadest interpretation, human resource management is not limited to a single department or individual. Rather, it covers the human resources management functions wherever they may occur in the organization; and they occur wherever managers and workers are involved.

It is this broad interpretation that is used in the following review of human resources management. This review acknowledges that human resources management activities are primarily handled in a personnel management department by specialists. Thus much of its discussion concerns these specialists and what they do. But it also acknowledges that activities can and do take place throughout the organization. When necessary, the discussion reflects this broad scope.

From this discussion it is obvious that *human resources management* is that part of management that is concerned with the human side of the enterprise. The activities it includes span all the human relationships involved in the organization, and there are many. Those that are handled formally by the business generally fall into four broad functional areas: (1) satisfying needs, (2) training and developing employees, (3) providing for the health and safety of employees, and (4) administering wages and salaries. In the remaining pages of this chapter, each of these functional areas is discussed in some detail.

SATISFYING MANPOWER NEEDS

In studying the function of satisfying the manpower needs of an organization, we shall begin with an analysis of such needs. This logical approach will help us to understand how manpower needs come about and why they often fluctuate so widely. Then we shall look to see what one can do to plan for them. Finally, we shall study the specific steps personnel managers take in satisfying them.

Causes of manpower needs

With the exception of firms just starting up, business organizations can attribute their needs for additional work force to four factors:

1. *Normal turnover.* Over time the employees of any business will quit, die, or retire; and sometimes the firm fires them.
2. *Nature of the firm.* By their very nature, some businesses have higher turnover than others. Certain types of restaurants, for example, typically hire young, single women to work as table servers. They work for only short periods of time and must be replaced.
3. *Technological change.* A new product, a new production procedure, or the like can make sudden demands on production. The result is a need for more workers. As an illustration, take the case of a manufacturer of soaps and detergents who has discovered a revolutionary new cleaning product. Rather than cut production of its other products, the manufacturer might choose to add a production unit to make the new product. Thus it would need to add workers.
4. *Normal growth.* Successful companies typically grow. And as they grow, they need more workers.

Need for forecasting requirements

Whatever the reason a business needs employees, it must get them if it is to achieve its goals. In getting the workers it needs, the business' personnel staff follow either of two courses. They may recruit workers on a plan basis—that is, anticipating needs before they develop. Or they may wait until openings develop and then take action. This last approach is the more common one, particularly among smaller firms. Planning manpower needs, however, is the wiser course for the larger organization. The size of their investments in plant, materials, equipment, and people demands a well-planned personnel program that will permit the organization to react quickly to changing conditions. Unless the organization reacts quickly, it is likely to lose to its competition.

Estimating manpower needs

Estimating manpower needs is relatively simple for the firm that knows how much personnel is needed to do each kind of work to be done. The organization begins by estimating the volume of business it will have. Then it constructs a production schedule that will produce this volume. This schedule is a plan for the work to be done in each department. Next, using the information it has on the personnel needed to do each kind of work the company determines the number of employees each department needs to work the schedule. By summarizing department requirements, the company arrives at its overall manpower needs.

While manpower needs for production work can be computed easily, professional and managerial manpower needs often defy computation. Obviously, the work of such specialized people is not closely related to production volume. Thus, in planning for these needs, the personnel staff must rely on judgment and past experience.

Determining qualifications of manpower needed

Besides knowing how many employees may be needed, the personnel staff must also know what skills, talents, abilities, and so on are required in the new employees. These requirements are satisfied by a complete job analysis of each position. The *job analysis* simply is a thorough study of what work is done on each job and what qualifications one must have to do this work. From the job analysis come two documents which guide the personnel staff in the search for workers. One is the job description. The other is the job specification.

The *job description* is a write-up of the work done on a given job. As shown in Figure 8–1, usually it includes job title and number, department duties, machines used, supervision given, and other details. The *job*

FIGURE 8–1

A job description used by a metals manufacturer

JOB DESCRIPTION

JOB TITLE: Thread Press Operator

JOB NUMBER: Unavailable

DEPARTMENT: Secondary

Summary

Operates thread press machine which burnishes parts or threads parts when placed between hydraulically controlled rollers.

Details of Operation

1. Sets up machine for operation according to specification or oral command.

2. Introduces parts into machine by hand.

3. Parts are held in place by hand until burnishing or threading operation is complete

4. Periodically adjusts flow of cutting oil over threading or burnishing rollers.

5. Places completed parts in solvent solution to remove cutting oil.

6. Routes finished parts to shipping department.

7. Consults with inspector periodically to insure production specifications.

8. Provides maintenance for machine.

9. Report time on job on production report.

specification (Figure 8–2) is a write-up of the human qualifications (education, training, skill, and so on) needed to do the job. With the information contained in these two documents, the personnel staff is better able to evaluate those applying for jobs. Also, they can match them better with the jobs available.

Recruitment of the work force

After the personnel staff has determined how many and what kinds of employees are needed, they are ready to begin recruiting them. That is, they are ready to begin the work of attracting applicants to the firm. It is work which may be done in many ways. Best known, of course, is the classified advertising which companies use to make their vacancies

FIGURE 8–2

A job specification used by a metals manufacturer

JOB SPECIFICATION

JOB TITLE: Thread Press Operator

DICTIONARY TITLE: Unavailable   CODE NO. Unavailable

DEPARTMENT: Secondary

Skill

No experience is required for this job. Mechanical knowledge is limited to the use of basic hand tools. Worker must be able to record job time on production report.

Physical effort

Machine is operated in standing position; little or no moving about is required. Job occasionally requires worker to lift moderate to heavy weights. Hand and foot movements must be coordinated to load and activate the machine.

Mental

Repetitive nature of job entails no decision making or independent judgment. Initiative is required at a minimum level.

Working conditions

The conditions of the job are moderately undesirable because worker's hands are continuously emersed in oil. Moving parts of machine pose constant threat to hands. Hands may also come in contact with strong solvents which may cause burns.

Responsibility

The operator is responsible only for complying with oral instructions received.

known to prospective workers. Then there are employment agencies which organizations use to find workers. In addition, many informal efforts typically are used to find employees. For example, industrial managers or supervisors may seek out friends or acquaintances for the vacant positions. Or employees may suggest potential workers.

Societal aspects of recruiting

As they go through the procedure of selecting people to fill jobs, the personnel staff must keep in mind some very real and significant considerations of society. Contrary to what some people may think or wish, businesses are not completely free to hire whomever they wish. They must adhere to certain restrictions and pressures of society.

The major restrictions to their hiring practices are the various laws, executive orders (of the president), and commission and court decisions which forbid discrimination in hiring. Foremost among these is the Civil Rights Act of 1964 and the executive orders relating to it. In general, these documents have established strong and clear rules against discrimination in hiring on the basis of race, color, religion, sex, or national origin. Although discrimination continues in many segments of business, the various legal restrictions and the efforts of government authorities to enforce them have had a significant effect on hiring practices. A review of the most important of these follows.

Adding to the legal restrictions against discrimination are the various social movements which are advancing the causes of groups discriminated against in the past. Unquestionably, the women's rights (women's liberation) movement has been effective in enforcing those parts of the laws pertaining to women. Similarly, the efforts of blacks have served to bring about antidiscrimination legislation and to maintain pressures on enforcing the legislation. Movements of chicanos, American Indians, fat people, old people, and other smaller groups also have been effective.

In general, the legal requirements and social movements have had some effect on company hiring practices. For example, the nation's largest employer, American Telephone and Telegraph Company, has agreed to hire women and minority group members at one and one half times their current representation in the labor force. Universities across the nation have been placed under strong pressures by the U.S. Department of Health, Education, and Welfare to add minority group members to their faculties. Similarly, manufacturers handling federal government contracts have been required to add minority group members to their employment rolls. Few of our larger firms have not felt the effect of these corrective efforts.

In spite of this progress, the pressures to end discrimination remain a matter of some controversy. Some business people argue that these efforts have gone too far. They point out that the employers' rights have been infringed upon—that laws, government agencies, and such dictate to them whom they must hire. And they argue that blacks, women, and other discriminated groups now have the upper hand and that minority or sex status gets more weight in selecting one for a job than do qualifications for the job. The discriminated groups disagree. They point to data showing continued discrimination in virtually all areas of employment. No doubt the controversy will remain with us for some time to come.

The selection process

The actual task of selecting the people to fill the vacant positions is the next subject in this review. In a very real sense, the work of selecting employees is a two-way process. First, it is a process of matching each applicant with the work he can do best. Second, it is the process of matching each job with the person who can do it best. How these tasks are done varies somewhat from company to company. But most follow these general steps:

1. Preliminary interview.
2. Application form.
3. Selection test.
4. Main employment office interview.
5. Investigation of applicant's background.
6. Final selection interview by supervisor.
7. Medical examination.
8. Induction.

The preliminary interview The applicant and employer first come together at a preliminary interview. This interview serves mainly to inform the applicant of the jobs available. Such meetings normally are quite brief and permit the candidate to state education, experience, skills, job interest, and so on. If the requirements of the company and the interest and qualifications of the applicant seem to match after this rough initial screening, the company will ask the applicant to submit an application form.

The application form On the application form the applicants record the information which identifies them and permits the company to make tentative judgment regarding their suitability for employment. Ideally, the information requested on the application form serves as predictors of employment success or failure. And it is the manager's task to use good judgment in evaluating this information and properly matching job requirement and applicant. In making these evaluations, the manager may make use of either of two general techniques: clinical evaluation and statistical evaluation.

The *clinical evaluation* technique involves making inferences from the information on the application form much as a psychologist would diagnose from the words of a patient. Advocates of this technique claim that a properly designed blank can provide clues to the applicant's leadership ability, ability to get along with others, emotional stability, initiative, and the like. For example, they reason that an applicant's energy and enthusiasm are indicated by the number and variety of activities, jobs held, and other interests noted on the application form. Obviously, such conclusions should be considered only tentative. They would need to be verified by further checking.

The second technique, *statistical evaluation,* is the attempt to equate the answers given by the applicant to those given by employees that are proven successes. For example, if it is found that a firm's successful salespeople tend to have a college education, and to be involved in civic and social activities, the firm will seek out applicants whose application forms show similar characteristics.

Both evaluation techniques are subject to shortcomings. One argument holds that managers who apply the clinical evaluation test are pseudo psychologists who in their efforts to analyze are simply projecting their own worlds, values, judgments, and standards onto the applicant. The argument is a sound one, for there is little agreement among personnel managers on the matter of what characteristics are essential for the various jobs in industry.

Likewise, the statistical evaluation technique comes into the line of fire. While there may be some legitimate relationship between character-istics of proven employees, to attempt to equate these traits to a single applicant as a predictor of his probable success would be absurd. Only when dealing with large numbers of applicants can we expect this method to predict accurately. To be statistically valid, this method requires a sizable number of "successful" employees on which to base computation of correlation. Additionally, there is the problem of defining a successful and unsuccessful employee.

The selection test   The third step in the selection process is the selection test. Selection tests, of course, are tests given to applicants to determine their suitability for work. Such tests may measure skills (typing, engine repair, welding, and so on) or any of the human traits considered essential to a job (personality, intelligence, motivation).

How useful tests are in measuring the suitability of applicants is a matter of much controversy. Some managers vigorously support them; some roundly denounce them. The preponderance of management thought probably lies between these extremes. Tests can be valuable aids to subjective evaluation. They can give valuable guidelines to the personnel manager. But they are a long way from being perfected. Until they are perfected (if indeed they ever will be), they should be used only as sup-plementary information to the other factual information available on an applicant.

In recent years, the use of selection tests has been under fire. The critics argue that the only legitimate test for a job is one that shows whether a person can do the work. Some go further, arguing that the test should measure only whether a person is trainable for the job. The critics also argue that tests used in the past have measured educational attainment and have been culturally biased (favoring whites over blacks). These qualities, they say, rarely have an effect on whether one can do the job being considered.

Some proponents of tests counter with arguments that there is more to consider than the specific work of the job. The applicant's potential for advancement, his compatibility with other workers, his ability to make decisions, and such can also be important. Other proponents concede that the tests are culturally biased, but they argue that there is no realistic way of avoiding such bias.

As a result of these arguments, a recent court decision now requires that the tests be related to the applicant's ability to do the one job he is seeking. As you can appreciate, however, determining what is relevant to doing a job is not easy. Thus the arguments are likely to continue for some time to come.

Main employment office interview   The fourth step in the selection process is the main employment office interview. This step remains the single most important phase of the hiring program. In fact, almost every firm that hires employees insists on some form of interview before selecting new workers.

Interviewers serve both the company and the applicant—at least, they should serve both. For the company, the interview permits interviewers to get vital information from the applicants, to assess them, and generally to judge their suitability for employment. For the applicants, it provides the facts about the company and the job which they should have for their decisions. Both the needs of the company and of the applicants should be met.

The fundamental weakness of the employment interview is its subjectivity. No one, no matter how experienced, can determine on first impression a person's suitability for hiring. The interviewer's decisions are shaped by opinions, and opinions are colored by bias and prejudice. Likewise, the interviewee, trying to create a favorable impression in the eyes of the interviewer, may behave in a manner that is unnatural for him. And finally, there are many attributes that simply cannot be measured by the interview. Intelligence, manual skills, strength, health, motor abilities, and other qualities are better measured by other devices. As with selection tests, the interview must be combined with other selection devices if it is to have predictive accuracy.

Investigation   Following the interview comes an investigation of the applicant's background. In this step the personnel staff checks with all sources that can give useful information on the applicant. Typically, this group includes such information sources as past employers, personal acquaintances, clergy, and former teachers. The primary goal of the investigation, of course, is to determine the applicant's suitability for employment. Especially sought is any information which would warn of a possible future personnel problem, such as infractions of discipline, non-payment of debts, low morals, accident proneness, and dishonesty.

This step, also, is the subject of some controversy. The conventional argument supporting the use of recommendation reports, of course, is that prospective employees have a right to know about an applicant's past. Some argue, however, that such reports are an invasion of one's privacy. More specifically, they argue that these reports give an unscrupulous past employer strong control over the life of the applicant. And they point out that even a true report can be unfair to individuals who honestly seek to change their ways. For example, they argue, should an ex-convict be forever penalized for a deed for which he has already been punished?

In spite of these arguments, most employers use references in making their selections. But they use them with some discretion, taking precautions to avoid anything that may be damaging. Even so, the question of fairness of the practice remains unanswered.

Final selection interview After the investigation typically comes the final *selection interview.* At this stage the applicants are called in, this time to talk with managers in the work area for which they are applying. It is here that the decision to hire is made, and normally (and desirably) the manager under whom the applicant will work makes it.

Medical examination Following the hiring decision, usually comes the *medical examination.* This step protects both the organization and the workers. It provides assurance that the health of the applicants equips them to perform on the job in the best interest of themselves, the company, and the other employees.

Whether the medical examination is necessary is another controversial question. Few will argue that it is wrong to check for physical attributes actually needed in performing a job. But many organizations have physical requirements that go well beyond this. In our own military services, for example, Julius Caesar and Napoleon Bonaparte would be rejected for physical reasons. Of course, companies want to hire people who will give them long service and who will not require much sick and early retirement pay. But must one who can do the work be denied the job because of a physical limitation not related to the job? It is a good question for the profit-seeking yet conscientious manager to answer.

Induction The step of *induction* concerns introducing the new workers to the work environment. More specifically, it involves introducing the workers to the workplace, to their fellow workers, and to their close superiors. It includes a briefing of company rules, policies, and employee rights and privileges. It may include more specific instruction on the work they are to do—information on work schedules, standards, procedures, and the like. Usually the employees' immediate supervisors do most of this work, especially that portion pertaining to the work to be done. Overall company matters may well be handled by members of the personnel department.

From a review of these eight steps in the selection process, a very orderly procedure is apparent. At each step, personnel workers gather additional information. They use the information gathered as a basis

FIGURE 8–3

Steps in the employee selection process

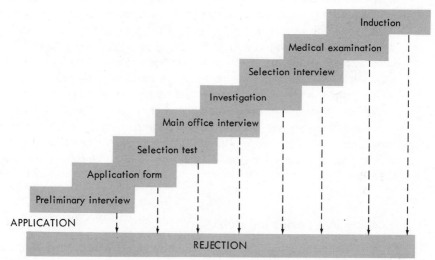

Explanation: As applicants move from step to step, the employers get information about them. The employers use this information to determine whether the applicants should move to the next step or be rejected. The applicants who make it through all the steps are hired.

for moving to the next step or for rejecting the applicant. As shown in Figure 8–3, the applicant who successfully moves through all the steps is hired.

TRAINING AND DEVELOPING EMPLOYEES

The second function of human resource management is the training and developing of employees. Although training in one form or other is about as old as business, it has expanded sharply in recent years. Many reasons explain this accelerated activity, but three in particular stand out.

First, as we all know, technological advances in recent years have made obsolete old skills and knowledge. So, in order to use its old employees, companies have had to reeducate and retrain them. Second, the growth and increasing complexity of organizations have sharply increased the demand for more and better management talent. Because such talent is in short supply, companies have had to train their own. Third, with the prosperity of recent years has come a change in employee demands. No longer content with merely earning a livelihood, employees today are demanding such things as better opportunities, more advantages, and a voice in management. Recognizing the potential of this attitude, companies have responded by providing a broad range of educational opportunities.

In surveying this rapidly expanding function of human resource management, the plan of this review is first to determine just what training involves. In this regard, it covers such matters as what training is, how it differs from job to job, methods used, and the various problems involved. Then because training is a most important and specialized area, the discussion turns to the area of management development. Finally, the review takes up the matter of how to measure employee progress—or, more specifically, the subject of method and technique of employee appraisal.

Generally speaking, employee training falls into two categories. First is the training that will help an employee improve his job skill. Primarily this is how-to-do-it training, although it may cover subject matter related to the job. Second is the wide range of training designed to develop management talent.

Training for specific job skills

Training for specific job skills primarily is the task of teaching someone how to do a job. Although this form of instruction tends to be simple, it can be done through a variety of training methods. Three in particular stand out:

1. *On-the-job-training.* The training one gets by actually doing a task is the on-the-job type. It is often hazardous, but probably it is the most effective. It is especially useful for teaching skills that can be learned quickly.
2. *Vestibule training.* Job training conducted in a classroom equipped with the machines, tools, equipment, and so on found on the job to be learned is vestibule training. It is especially useful in training large numbers of workers at the same time for the same work.
3. *Classroom method.* Training with a teacher presenting instruction before a group is known as the classroom method. It is most useful for teaching high-level material—particularly the theoretical and philosophical.

Managerial development

The task of managerial development involves much more than simply the teaching of job skills. To be sure, job skills are important for them, but managers must also gain knowledge, insight, and attitudes to manage work organization effectively. As was noted in Chapter 7, managers are involved in planning, organizing, leading, and controlling the organization. These tasks are highly sophisticated and complex. They require a great breadth of knowledge, both specialized and general. One does not learn such subject matter routinely. Thus, managerial development is a complex area of training.

Because it is so complex an area, management training covers a multitude of topics. In general, however, most such programs seek similar goals. Three in particular stand out:

1. *To improve administrative and organizational skills.* Such skills cannot be taught as a routine activity—that is, as one would be taught to assemble a rifle or to make a cake. Instead, administrators must be taught the broad management principles and concepts. They must then apply these principles and concepts to fit the facts of each specific case.
2. *To improve technical knowledge and skills.* Because technology changes over time, managers need to be educated to these changes. Such teaching typically is direct, for technical knowledge is likely to be precise and definite. For example, many older managers of today began their business careers before the widespread use of computers. They have had to learn this new technology in order to do their jobs effectively.
3. *To develop attitudes and managerial philosophy.* Probably this goal is the most difficult to achieve. It may take any of a variety of approaches. It may, for example, present information designed to indoctrinate the executive to the company's philosophy. Or it may consist of instruction designed to help the executives understand themselves, to think like an executive, or to see themselves as others see them. Such training programs (for example, sensitivity training) typically are under the direction of psychologists or other specialists. The techniques used are beyond the scope of this review.

Methods of management development   Businesses use a wide assortment of methods in developing their executives. One of the most common practices is to send promising management talent to special short courses for management training. Such courses are offered regularly on college campuses. Also, some professional associations, such as the American Management Association, American Bankers Association, and National Secretaries Association (International) conduct them. So do a number of private organizations.

In addition to training outside the company, much of it takes place within. One method used for inside training is *coaching,* which involves training by having a person work directly under and receive instruction from a superior. Although similar to the on-the-job training method discussed previously, coaching also is quite different. Typically, coaching involves a higher level of training. And it does not involve working on the job for which the person is being trained. Another method is *job rotation* —the practice of moving a person from job to job so that he can get the broad knowledge of the organization an executive should have. Then there is the use of *assistant-to* positions as a training device. This is the technique of using a senior manager to train an assistant to take over the senior manager's job.

Evaluating employee training

Conducting training is but a part of the job. Knowing the success of the training is also important, and for obvious reasons. Training consumes time, money, and materials; and if improperly handled, it wastes all of these. Also, training does not always succeed. In fact, some failures are to be expected.

In evaluating training, one should first establish a time period needed for meaningful measurement. The governing factor here is the nature of the training period. If the training is designed to improve specific job skills, testing can be done at the end of the training period. It is then that the training has had its maximum effect. On the other hand, the results of managerial development may not become evident for several years. Thus, such evaluation must extend over time. Another evaluation problem related to the type of training conducted concerns the use, or availability, of objective data. It is not difficult to collect objective evidence on the improvement in job skills, such as the production output of the piece rate worker. But it is quite another matter to find purely objective data on the performance of the manager. Obviously, to evaluate the training and development of the manager requires qualitative judgment. Even so, such judgment should be made.

ADMINISTERING WAGES AND SALARIES

One of the most important and difficult functions of human resource management is administering a sound wage and salary program. Pay is a personal matter to every member of the business. Each person looks at it from his own viewpoint; and the viewpoints differ. Developing a harmonious compensation plan for all concerned is no simple undertaking.

The following plan of reviewing this most difficult function is first to look at some basic concepts that will help us to understand the significance and nature of compensation. Then the steps one would take in developing a plan for paying employees are summarized. In this part appears in succession a discussion of the steps in determining (1) the general level of pay, (2) the structure of compensation for the different jobs, and (3) the pay for the individual.

Basic concepts about compensation

In developing a plan of wage and salary administration, a firm's managers should understand and appreciate the importance of compensation to all concerned. Also, they should be well aware of the wide differences in how people think about compensation (philosophies of compensation). With this knowledge in mind, managers should be able to develop a wage and salary plan that will be workable and fair to all.

The importance of compensation   That compensation is important to the worker is most obvious to us. Even so, all too often those who work with wage and salary administration tend to forget this vital matter and to treat their work impersonally. The wise wage and salary administrator keeps in mind the basic fact that pay is extremely important to the workers. It determines the workers' standard of living. It establishes their position in society. And it provides a measure of their achievement and their work to themselves, their families and friends.

Wage and salary administrators rarely overlook the importance of compensation to the firm. Quite naturally, they are duty bound to look out for the firm's interests. So they are well aware of the fact that wages paid is a cost. And they know that costs play a direct role in determining the firm's profit. A point they sometimes overlook, however, is that the firm's wages should be high enough to attract, motivate, and keep good employees. Not to be able to do so would hurt the firm's operations.

Administrators should know, also, that compensation is important to groups outside the business—the community, the government, and the country as a whole. Every business plays a role in what goes on in the country. What each does about compensation has an effect on such matters as inflation, prosperity, level of employment, and shifts in the labor force. Thus, managers should look beyond the interests of the company and the workers when they deal with matters of pay.

Philosophies of compensation   In developing a fair pay plan, a firm's administrators should also keep in mind that typically workers and management look upon pay from sharply different viewpoints. The viewpoint of management is a productivity philosophy. In contrast, labor's viewpoint is a purchasing power philosophy.

The productivity philosophy of management is that wages and wage increases are to be viewed as results of the firm's productivity. More specifically, this philosophy holds that as the firm improves its production techniques, the workers will produce more. Then costs will drop, leading to lower prices, greater sales, and higher profits. From these higher profits, the workers' pay can be increased.

Contrasting to this philosophy is the *purchasing power philosophy* typically held by labor. Rather than viewing pay increases as the end result, labor views them as the initial step to profits. Thus, they feel that employers should first pay higher wages. With higher wages, workers would then buy more. Sales would increase. And from increased sales would come increased profits. With higher profits, still higher wages could be paid.

As you would expect, the productivity philosophy is the one most widely accepted in business today. But labor groups challenge it strenuously. Good arguments exist for both sides. Hopefully, in the future managers as well as workers will attempt to appreciate the other's point of view.

Wage payment methods

A basic question to be worked out before determining a wage and salary plan is what should be the basis for payment. Three alternatives

FIGURE 8–4

Percent of pay based on output for production workers
in selected U.S. industries

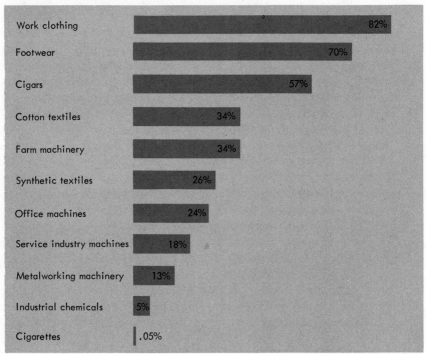

Source: U.S. Department of Labor, 1974.

exist: (1) payment on the basis of output, (2) payment on the basis of time, and (3) a combination of payment by output and time.

Payment based on output If employees' pay is based on output (that is, by the pieces produced in units, pounds, dozens, tons, and so on) and if the employees can earn extra money for producing more than a given quota or norm, then they are operating under an incentive payment method. In short, the employees are paid according to the amount they produce. As shown in Figure 8–4, this method of payment accounts for a heavy portion of wage payments in some industries. But it is insignificant in others.

Payment based on time When a system of payment based on output is unworkable, the employer may pay according to the time the employee works. That is, payment may be for the hour, day, week, or month. The company records the employee's time worked, and at the end of the pay period it multiplies the time recorded by the pay rate.

Combination of time and incentive payment With varying degrees of success, many companies have attempted to combine the incentive and time methods. Some, for example, have offered bonus programs for special tasks or projects not covered in their normal time payment. Some have provided a profit sharing plan, thereby encouraging workers to work harder so that the company may make more money and in turn reward the workers better. And some have used programs of companywide incentive, where technological gains and worker productivity are shared by everyone in the firm.

The wage and salary level

A primary goal of a wage and salary administration program is to establish a level of wages for the firm that will help it to get and keep the production work force. A number of factors influence the determination of the firm's wage level. For the sake of convenience, they are called internal and external influences.

Internal influence Internal factors influencing a company's wage level primarily are two. First is the firm's ability to pay. Obviously, wages are costs to the firm. They have a direct bearing on the firm's profits. Thus, from a very practical standpoint there exists in every case a range within which a company can pay. To go beyond this range would be to endanger its very existence.

The process of collective bargaining is the second factor. Just how much influence it has had over the years in determining wage levels, however, is subject to some argument. Some argue that wage increases have come about primarily through production advancement and not through union efforts. And they cite industry studies to support the claim.

But the argument supporting union influence is equally strong. Both arguments have merit.

External influence Foremost among the external factors is the supply and demand for each of the categories of labor skills (such as machinist, welder, and carpenter). How much of each category is available certainly affects the price. If a particular skill is in short supply, its price logically tends to move up. And if the supply is good, the price tends to decline. A second external factor influencing wages paid is the prevailing industry wage. In most industries, a common wage level exists. Sometimes it is a result of industrywide collective bargaining. More than likely it is the result of company efforts to keep employees from moving to higher paying jobs. In any event, the prevailing wages serve as major influences on a company's wages. A third external factor is the prevailing standard and cost of living. People have grown to expect certain things in life. They expect a certain level of housing, of food, of recreation, and such. Wage payments which do not permit these levels are not acceptable.

Wage and salary structure

In addition to determining the general level for wages, the wage and salary administrators must work out the pay structure for the individual jobs. More specifically, they must determine how much to pay machinists, welders, janitors, typists, and so on. They must work up a ranking of all the jobs done in the business; and they must assign a payment rate for each.

The rankings administrators make should be based on fair and meaningful criteria. The relative skill required for the job is one good one. On this scale, for example, a machinist would rank higher than a worker with a routine assignment on the assembly line. Another criterion is the extent of responsibility involved. An inspector on the assembly line whose decisions are critical to the production process would rank higher than inspectors with less importance. Yet another criterion is the danger involved. Ironworkers who must work at great height constructing tall buildings would get more than those working at ground level. And there are other criteria (i.e., mental and physical activity required, responsibility, working conditions, and bargaining power).

Using such criteria, the administrators study each job carefully. They use their best judgment to determine the relative pay deserved for each job. They may even supplement their judgment with some objective plan of assigning point values to the criteria they use. That is, they may give so many points for job danger, and so forth. However they do it, their goal is to develop a structure that gives each job a fair pay relative to all other jobs.

Individual wage and salary determination

In addition to working out the pay structure for all jobs, administrators must fit each individual worker into the structure. The structure for machinists, for example, may be $7 to $9 an hour. Thus each machinist must be placed fairly in this range. But what should be the basis for this placement? Is time on the job a fair determinant? Or should it be skill? Cooperativeness? Or what?

There are some who argue that no individual differences should exist in pay for the same work. They are critical, for example, of paying men more than women for doing the same work. Or, for another example, they are critical of using time on the job as a basis for pay differences. Some argue that while skill is a legitimate factor, it is difficult to determine. For example, they might point out, how accurately can one measure the skill of a maintenance worker, a receptionist, or a public relations worker?

EMPLOYEE HEALTH AND SAFETY

Providing health and safety for employees is the fourth of the functions in managing human resources. It is a function shared by all management, especially as it concerns safety within the individual departments. But it is the personnel department which must take the initiative and implement a health and safety program for the business.

Probably it comes as no surprise that business firms increasingly are concerned about the welfare of their employees. They simply have to be, and for two good reasons. First, the mood of today's society demands that business do things to promote employee welfare. And much of business accepts this mood. Second, the Occupational Safety and Health Act (OSHA) has forced management to take actions. In fact, so effective has this act been that it deserves a prime position.

Significance of OSHA

Passed in 1970, OSHA imposed stringent requirements that businesses provide safe working conditions. The act's requirements are specific and quite detailed. And its implementation has had strong effects on business. In fact, current industry expenditures for industrial safety amount to more than $3 billion a year. This total represents about 3 percent of the total capital spending by business. Before 1970, these expenditures totaled only 1 percent of capital spending. For some industries the costs run much higher. In the iron and steel industry they exceed 17 percent. In textiles they run about 9 percent.

As you might expect, OSHA has been met with cries of protest. Some of the cries are backed with claims of government interference in private affairs and infringement on freedom. Some executives, while supporting the general goals of the act, criticize specific requirements. They say that OSHA's requirements are infinitely detailed—that many of them are trivial or unnecessary. They argue that few businesses could be expected to know and meet all of these requirements. And they point to arbitrary and unfair decisions and harsh penalties made by OSHA inspectors.

In all likelihood, many of these arguments have merit. But it would be hard to quarrel with the general goal of the act. Many specific facts support this conclusion. In coke-oven plants, for example, studies show that because of coal tar pitch emissions, workers are ten times more likely to get lung cancer than the norm. OSHA requires that these emissions be cut to a safe level. For another illustration, the U.S. Bureau of Mines report on the 1972 fire in Kellogg, Idaho, placed the blame on 17 violations of safety standards. Enforcement of OSHA safety standards would have greatly reduced these hazards. Probably most of the 14,200 deaths resulting from accidents on the job in 1971 could have been prevented by implementation of OSHA safety standards. Hopefully, over time the initial confusion resulting from the act can be overcome.

The nature of accidents

A review of safety programs, of course, must include accident prevention. Before discussing this subject, however, the meaning of the word accident should be made clear. If you are like most of us, probably you think of an accident as an event that causes injury. To businesses, however, an *accident* is any unexpected and unwanted occurrence that interrupts a work activity. Interruption of work is the measure—not injury. For example, if a worker drops a hand tool from a scaffold it is an accident. If it hits someone, it is an accident with injury.

The reason for this distinction between an accident and an accident with injury should be clear. Often pure chance plays a part in determining whether an accident results in an injury. This means safety programs should attempt to reduce the cause of accidents as well as the possible injuries that could, by chance, occur.

Causes of accidents

In designing an effective safety program, managers must first determine what causes accidents. Many, of course, are caused by chance factors that are unavoidable. However, when one digs beneath the surface, usually he finds that accidents occur because of two general conditions: unsafe chemical, physical, or mechanical conditions and personal acts that are unsafe or careless.

Among those conditions where physical or mechanical conditions are at play, some of the following problems are likely to exist:

1. Inadequate mechanical guards or covers over such things as cutting edges, gear boxes, pulleys, and drive belts.
2. Equipment or tools in defective condition, such as cracked ladders, worn electrical installation, or split drive belts.
3. Poor design or construction, such as an overhead winch with inadequate capacity or a chemical vat with leaky valves.
4. Hazardous atmosphere, such as leaky gas lines, poor ventilation, or toxic substances in the air (dust, paint, fumes, and so on).
5. A lack of proper protective equipment, such as gloves, hard hats, eyeglasses, welding masks, and so forth.

Examples of personal acts that cause accidents are the following:

1. Failure to follow established work procedures.
2. Horseplay or fighting.
3. Refusal to use protective devices.
4. Removing safety devices (particularly when repairing a machine).

Not all personal acts, of course, are committed deliberately or consciously. Sometimes a physical or mental condition may cause one to commit them. When workers are emotionally upset, afraid, or inattentive, they might well be candidates for accidents. So are they more likely to have accidents if they suffer from some ailment, are highly fatigued, or are afflicted with some defects.

Implementing the safety and health program

With the causes of accidents and of health problems determined, managers must decide what the company can do about them. This is primarily a process of applying good technical intelligence to each case. The result will be specific plans of correcting each problem. It could be a change in work procedure, a change in equipment design, additional precautions in the work area—in fact, anything that will improve the situation. For specific examples, hazardous walkways may be made safe by adding hand railings; hard hats may be required to protect from possible falling objects; better ventilation may be prescribed to prevent inhalation of toxic fumes.

Typically, implementing safety and health programs requires a formal effort by the company. Safety and health are matters that have to be promoted and need the acknowledged support of top management. Workers simply do not naturally get excited about safety and health.

They are not inclined to go out of their ways to do something about happenings that are seemingly remote. Take, for example, the public's general apathy toward using seat belts. Because people are apathetic, safety efforts should be formally planned and organized. They require that people be assigned to direct them and given authority to enforce them. They also require extensive promotion. In general, like any other operation of a business, health and safety programs require careful organizing, planning, directing, and controlling.

DISCUSSION QUESTIONS

1 What differences in needs for human resources would be likely in these businesses: (a) a large department store, (b) a middle-income restaurant, (c) a large chemical manufacturing company?

2 Write a job description and a job specification for a job you have held or know about. Explain your write-ups.

3 Should owners of businesses have the right to hire whomever they choose? Why or why not?

4 Would it be fair practice for a large manufacturer to use a general intelligence test as one part of the testing procedure for all jobs?

5 Should employers assign more value to the impressions they get from the interview than on test scores?

6 How should a manager handle an inquiry about a former employee who was a good worker but was fired for insubordination? For stealing? For moral reasons?

7 How should physical examinations be used in determining who should be hired?

8 How would you measure the effectiveness of a company executive development program? A short course to teach a job skill? A course designed to update the knowledge of company scientists?

9 Is it the obligation of business to train workers?

10 Contrast the productivity and purchasing power philosophies of compensation. Which do you favor? Why?

11 In the wage structure of the Mann Manufacturing Company, truck drivers, plumbers, and electricians receive much more pay than training specialists and company nurses. Only the last two jobs require college degrees. Discuss.

12 Manufacturers in a certain industry vigorously oppose safety requirements established for them by OSHA. These requirements, they argue, are costly and will force them to raise prices so high that they can no longer compete with foreign companies. Discuss.

MINI CASES

For the past ten years, the A. R. Nobles Manufacturing Company has sent some of its most promising young executives to the State University Executive Development Program. Although the executives usually came back with glowing accounts of the program, there are those in the company who are skeptical. Among the skeptics are A. R. Nobles, founder of the firm and its current president.

So skeptical is the man that he calls into his office Dennis E. Johns, director of training. The following comments to Mr. Johns concisely indicate Mr. Nobles' feelings: "We've been sending men down there for 10 years, and at a heavy cost, too. We don't have a dime's worth of evidence that it is doing any good. The fact is, I can't see any difference in them after they come back. Sure some of the people we sent have advanced. But we sent them because they were our most promising executives; they would have advanced anyway."

1. *Respond to this comment for Mr. Johns.*
2. *How should the Nobles Manufacturing Company evaluate executive training?*

Since its beginning 70 years ago, the management of Central Manufacturing Company has felt strongly that only men should be used in production work. Production work is hard and dirty, they reasoned; and although women are physically capable of doing it, the work is not suitable for women. Only men should be in the production areas, including the clerks who worked in the production departments.

In response to continuing legal and social pressures to hire more women, Central's management weakened. They began to hire women as clerks in the production departments. This work, management felt, could be most easily done by women; and the male clerks who would be replaced could be reassigned to production work.

Soon after implementing this change in hiring practice, Central's management was most surprised when a group of women voiced strong objection and threatened legal action. They charged job discrimination. The company, they said, was only making a token gesture to women, hiring them for low paying work as clerks and denying them the higher paying production work. Management was even more surprised when a group of male clerks voiced strong objection. The clerks claimed that their rights also were being violated—that they were better qualified than the women for the clerk positions and were being replaced solely because of their sex.

1. *How legitimate are the two protests?*
2. *What advice would you give Central management?*

Since Sam Waverly founded it 22 years ago, the Waverly Manufacturing Company has struggled to survive. Little by little this small manufacturing company overcame the obstacles confronting it. Only recently did Sam Waverly begin to feel that his company has made it—that after these years of hard work he would begin to reap the rewards of success. But his viewpoint changed sharply today.

What happened was that the OSHA representative completed his inspection of the Waverly plant. His list of safety violations filled three pages of his report.

To Sam, all of these violations appear trivial. "Any intelligent person can work here as safely as he can work in his own home," Sam reasons. "There's a little bit of danger everywhere."

But trivial or not, Sam must correct these conditions or face the consequences. Correcting them will cost lots of money. In fact, it will just about eliminate his profits for the next few years.

1. *Is there logic in Sam's argument?*
2. *What should be the basis for determining what is too dangerous and what is acceptable?*

Born of Quaker-Puritan parentage in Germantown, Pennsylvania, Frederick W. Taylor rose through the ranks of labor to become the greatest management specialist of his day. But in order to appreciate this man's genius, one must consider the time in which he lived. His period was the late 1800s. It was a time of strong management and weak labor. Management's goal was to produce the maximum output at the lowest cost. Labor was but one of the ingredients used in producing things, and it was to be used as efficiently as any other commodity.

Taylor's contribution to management is that he made a science of getting the most efficiency out of every work situation. His plan consisted of first identifying the elements of each task. Then he studied the motions of skilled workers as they went through these elements. He timed them, and he looked for waste motions. From these observations he attempted to find the very best way of doing the task.

Taylor envisioned that his scientific management would bring about a mental revolution on the part of both workers and management. Such a mental revolution, he reasoned, would be mutually beneficial. Each party would give the other what it wanted: management would get increased productivity; labor would get increased wages.

This mental revolution never took place. Although Taylor's techniques were widely used, many companies did not pass on any of the gain to the workers. Thus, labor tended to look upon Taylor's techniques as ways of increasing production and reducing the need for workers. Even so, Taylor's contributions have made a clear and distinct mark in the development of management thought. Perhaps more important than anything else, Taylor's work tended to make management more scientific and less rule of thumb. For this reason primarily he is generally acclaimed the "Father of Scientific Management."

Frederick Winslow Taylor
(1856–1915)

Father of scientific management

9

Production/ operations management

The principal objective of management should be to secure the maximum prosperity for the employer, coupled with the maximum prosperity for each employee.

──*Frederick Winslow Taylor*

As has been previously noted, business organizations are formed to do things— to manufacture refrigerators, to repair automobiles, to refine oil, to provide health care, and such. Doing these things requires that the organization perform a variety of operations. Precisely which operations are performed in any given case, of course, depends on the nature of the organization. But whatever operations are done, they must be done well.

As you well know, in our competitive economy not to do them well would be to invite failure.

THE NATURE OF PRODUCTION/ OPERATIONS MANAGEMENT

Performing operations well requires careful application of the best management techniques. As you would expect, many of these techniques are technical and require the services of highly trained specialists. Thus, they are beyond the scope of this review. But a summary of some general concepts should give you an appreciation of what operations management is all about. Such a summary follows.

The terms defined

This summary logically begins with a definition of terms. Because most of the early work in the field concerned factory operations, the term *production* management initially was used to cover the subject (thus the reason for using the combination wording, production/ operations). For years, factory production received the attention of managers, and a field called production management developed.

In recent years, however, a broader meaning has been given the subject. Rather than limiting coverage to factory-type production, this broader viewpoint stresses that production types of operations are not limited to factory situations. Rather, they occur in various types of businesses. A hospital, for example, might use production management techniques in operating its emergency room. So might an insurance company use these techniques in operating its mail room, or an automobile agency in operating its service area. This broader approach to

FIGURE 9–1

Illustrated definition of operations production management

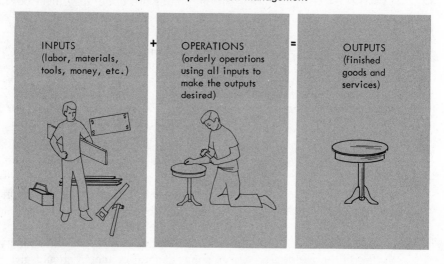

the subject generally is called *operations management.* It is the approach used in this book.

More precisely, *operations management* may be defined as *management of those operations which transform inputs into outputs.* By *inputs* is meant all those things which come into the operation (raw materials, labor, information, money, power). *Operations* are those activities which transform inputs into finished products or services. The finished products and services are the *outputs.*

To illustrate, take the operation of making a chair (see Figure 9–1). This operation obviously requires such ingredients as wood, glue, tools, and labor (inputs). Using these inputs, certain activities are performed (the operation). Through these operations, inputs are changed into chairs (outputs). A similar illustration could be made of a service—an automobile repair shop, for example. Here the inputs are defective automobiles, labor, tools, and so on. The operation transforms these inputs into repaired automobiles.

A three-stage process

The plan in the following pages is to discuss the activities of operations management in the order in which they occur. That is, operations management is viewed as a process—a process with three basic stages. First, there is the initial planning of the production effort. At this stage the organization views its resources, and it works out a procedure for using these resources. This stage is relatively short, for once the plan is put into effect, the organization shifts its efforts to carrying out the plan. Second is the operation stage, which is the stage of doing what the plan set out to do. Of course, what the operation plan set out to do typically is to produce a product or to provide a service. Third is the control stage. This is the stage in which the organization evaluates the effectiveness of the plan and makes corrections, if necessary.

PLANNING THE OPERATION

An organization's initial decision to produce something is a broad subject to begin with. A narrower one could be used. For example, it would be defensible to view operations management only as a manufacturing or service producing activity. In fact, many operations management books do. But such an approach would not cover all the planning steps. Thus, it would not show the complete process of the nature of operations management. Nor would it be true to life, for all producing organizations at one time made the beginning plans for their production.

Planning the product or service

Before a business organization can begin, logically it should have a purpose for being. More specifically, it should have a product to manufacture or a service to perform. Thus, planning the product or service is logically the first activity for a new organization.

This activity need not end after the organization has started. In fact, it is highly desirable that product and service planning continue throughout the life of the organization. An organization's products or services continually should be restudied and improved if the organization is to succeed. In today's competitive business world, the organization that does not do this is inviting failure.

Product and service research All the activity involved in producing new products and services or changing old ones is called product and service research. Obviously, the costs of this kind of research are high. It requires highly specialized personnel and expensive equipment. Thus, only the more affluent and progressive firms are likely to conduct it on a continuing basis. Many of them have departments established to do this research.

Economic evaluation After product and service research has developed a new product or service, or a change in a product or service, the organization must determine its economic value. For a new product or service, this means that the organization first must make certain that the new development will satisfy a need. Then the organization must find out whether it can sell the product or service at a profit. In other words, the organization must find out whether demand for the product or service will be enough to cover the cost of production and produce a profit.

How such an economic appraisal is made is too involved a process to be covered here. It requires the very best of foresight, consumer appraisal, judgment, and economic evaluation. Typically, such decisions are made from a wide assortment of information on the subject. The sales division, for example, may supply information about market and customer reaction. The purchasing department may furnish data on the availability of costs of materials. And the production departments may supply information on production costs. From all such information, management makes its decision.

Product and service development The task of converting these ideas and plans into final form is known as product and service development. This task is typified by comprehensive design and drafting work. It may involve constructing models to work out a production process. And it may involve setting up manufacturing trials designed to cut down errors and point out last-minute corrections. In general, this stage includes all the planning needed to arrive at the final design of the product or service and the plan for producing it.

Product and service specifications The final step in planning the product or service is to provide a set of specifications for production. This step is a logical follow-up to the preceding step, for it reduces the product or service designed to its precise requirements. These specifications literally are the blueprint of the product or service. They give the details. For a product, they describe the materials to be used. They specify the production procedures (sanding, threading, boring, and the like) to be used. They spell out performance standards, tolerances, units to be produced, dimensions, and so on. For a service, they describe the steps in the work to be performed. They make standards for any materials used and for the work done.

Location of the operation

A new organization just beginning production of a good or service will need to select a location for its operation. In making this decision, the organization would do well to consider certain basic factors.

Adequacy of labor supply A factor of paramount importance is the availability of labor. The reasoning is obvious. Any business operation must use labor to some extent. Thus, if labor is not available, the business cannot produce. In assessing the qualification of the available labor force, those making the location decision should consider such facts as the number of people, their skills and training, the competition from other companies for labor, and the attitude of the community as a whole. Usually a company will use local labor for the rank-and-file jobs. Often the management personnel are imported.

Accessibility of raw materials A second basic factor to consider in locating an operation is the availability of raw materials. In fact, in some industries it is the primary factor, especially when the weight and bulk of the raw material would mean high transportation costs. Steel mills, for example, have traditionally located near Pittsburgh because of the huge coal supplies needed to process iron ore. For similar reasons, oil refineries have located in Texas, California, and Louisiana. Availability of raw materials, of course, concerns more than the presence of raw materials in the locality. It concerns, also, the overall ease of getting them to the locality. Thus, a part of this consideration involves transportation costs, availability of transportation facilities, and such. For example, heavy production centers have located along the Mississippi River because of the ease and low cost of shipping bulky raw materials by barge.

Nearness of markets In many instances it is especially important for the firm to locate near its market. The explanation is a practical one. Transportation costs for shipping out finished goods may be greater than for shipping in raw materials. This condition accounts in part for the recent trend toward wide distribution of automobile assembly plants. These assembly plants are closer to population centers than their parent factories. The parts can be shipped compactly and cheaply to these assembly centers; and the assembled and bulky automobiles do not have to be shipped long distances.

Local inducements In some instances, local inducements are major factors to consider. Many states and cities want new industry so badly that they offer a variety of advantages to organizations locating in their area. Some may offer free land, or exemptions from or a remission of a given tax for a certain period of time. Sometimes they offer favorable labor legislation or an expansion of public services. Logically, a company must consider these inducements, but it must also keep in mind the ever present danger that such inducements can be withdrawn at the whim of a legislative body.

Availability of water and power Another important consideration in locating operations is the availability of water and power. Especially is this true in certain kinds of manufacturing. In producing steel, for example, it takes about 65,000 gallons of water to produce a ton; and it takes 800 gallons of water to refine a single barrel of petroleum. In evaluating this factor, a company must consider water availability to meet peak loads in dry spells. Power, of course, is essential in production. It is not uniformly available; nor are the costs the same in all areas. One area may have an abundance of low-cost natural gas. Another may be near a coal-producing area, and another may be near a major source of electricity. The organization must look at its individual production needs and make cost comparisons.

Other considerations   There are other considerations, of course, and these at times may be of major concern to the organization. In some forms of operation, the availability of service and repair facilities may be most important. Community attitude also can be significant, as can sewage disposal facilities, fire and police protection, and climate. In addition, there are the ever present personal considerations, biases, opinions, preferences, and such that influence most decisions.

Properly made, the decision on location is based on a careful evaluation of all the factors that affect the production operation being considered. That is, each of the factors involved is given the weight due it in the one case. The decision is based on an overall evaluation which takes these weights into account.

Plant capacity

In addition to deciding where to locate, an organization planning a new operation must decide on the capacity of the unit. That is, it must determine how much production or service is needed and then build a facility that will produce this quantity. To create more capacity than is needed is costly. In fact, excessive costs at this stage could even prove to be disastrous to the profitable operation of the unit. And too little capacity could lead to a loss in sales, or perhaps to a later expansion of the facility at a high cost. Obviously, the decision is a major one to the organization's successful operation.

Capacity by units of output   The capacity to produce is expressed in units of output and of time. An automobile manufacturer, for example, may have a capacity of 1,100 automobiles (units) per day (time). In some industries, however, measuring capacity is not so simply done, for the units of output are not equal. An illustration is in shoe manufacturing. Some shoes can be made simply and in a minimum of time. Other shoes require much more time. Thus, the capacity of the factory in number of shoes would vary, depending on the kinds of shoes produced at a given time. Only in single-product factories is capacity easy to determine, and such facilities are rare nowadays.

Effects of time   Time, also, provides some problems in measuring capacity. Whether the organization will operate around the clock, will follow a 40-hour week, or will adopt some other work plan is certainly a factor. Production of some products and services requires continuous operation. For example, an open-hearth furnace must not stop, for restarting is time-consuming and costly. With other products and services, management has an option as to work time. Obviously, this option has a direct effect on the plant's capacity.

Pattern and volume of sales The anticipated pattern and volume of sales also must be considered in determining capacity. The volume expected, of course, is a primary guide to capacity needed. Often the problem is complicated by the fact that sales patterns are not constant. With some services and products, sales are seasonal. Thus, the company may need to decide whether to vary its operations to coincide with demand or to produce on a steady basis and store the goods until they are needed. Storing goods is costly; and it is risky, too, for prices can change over time. Likewise, increasing and decreasing production is inefficient. There may be other alternatives, also. The company may work to stimulate sales in the off-season. It may elect to produce other products which have contrasting seasonal patterns. And it may subcontract some of its work in peak seasons. The plan the company selects clearly affects the capacity for which the company must build its plant.

Output of the individual machine Somewhere in the planning for capacity, the work that the individual machines will do must be considered. The calculations here can become quite technical and require the attention of production experts. But some of the major problem areas can be noted. If a machine is used for only one operation, the time required to do that operation (cycle time) must be calculated. Simple multiplication of cycle time by the units to be produced gives an estimate of the machines needed. When a machine is used for more than one operation, however, the procedure is not so simple. First, each cycle time must be determined. Next, a probable use ratio must be established for these operations. From this information should come a measure of the machines needed.

Consideration of scale of operations A final point of concern in determining capacity is the overriding matter of the scale of operations the company wants. Must it be a large plant, perhaps with vast facilities and many employees? Or can it be a relatively small plant with three shifts in continuous operation? A smaller physical layout has apparent operating economies and cost savings. Even so, most companies elect the larger plant with the eight-hour–per-day operation. Probably they do so because most people prefer it that way.

Plant layout

In addition to developing a product or service, locating a site, and determining plant capacity, the organization must consider the design of its plant. That is, it must determine the plant layout. *Plant layout* simply is the arrangement of facilities and services for conducting operations. How well these elements are arranged can have a significant effect on the efficiency of the operation.

Flow of materials Of major concern in developing a layout for most operations is the flow of materials through the work area. Especially is this the case in manufacturing operations. Ideally, the materials being worked on move through the plant in the easiest possible way. Such a movement should be designed to produce the most efficient work arrangement possible. Usually, the ideal layout is a simple one, for simple arrangements are easy to control and supervise.

Although many work arrangements exist, they fall into two broad categories: (1) horizontal and (2) vertical. As shown in Figure 9–2, five

FIGURE 9–2

Five basic forms of horizontal flow of materials in production

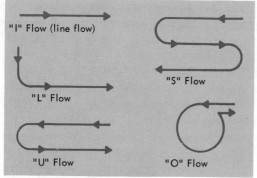

types of horizontal arrangements are most common. The *I* flow (or line flow) is the simplest of these. It is an arrangement of work in a straight line. The materials to be worked on come in at one end; the finished components come out at the other end. The *L* flow is basically identical, but it is used when the *I* flow cannot be adapted because of the accommodations. The *U* flow is convenient to some processes, for it permits both receiving and shipping from the same end or side of the building. When space is at a premium and must be used efficiently, the *S* flow is used. The *O* flow is commonly used when operations are conducted on a rotary table or form of rotary handling system.

In all arrangements, the flow of materials should be unidirectional or retractional. The *unidirectional flow* means the materials do not travel the same path twice. The *retractional flow* occurs when the flow repeats itself—for example, when two or more nonconsecutive operations are performed by the same machine. In the typical, complex plant layout many combinations of flows are possible, such as an *I* plus *U, S* plus *L,* and *I* plus *S*.

In multistoried buildings, vertical flow and handling becomes necessary. In such buildings, most firms will attempt to exploit gravity handling systems when possible by using a downward or an upward processing plan. In downward processing, they take the raw materials and move them downward through the production process. Finished goods come out at the bottom. Upward processing is the opposite, with finished goods emerging at the top. Even though gravity systems can be economical, they are often impractical for certain kinds of manufacturing. In the metalwork industries, for example, many initial machine operations are performed on large raw castings. If downward processing were used, this would mean carrying heavy raw materials and heavy machinery to the top and then using a gravity handling system to remove scrap. Such a setup would be expensive. Installation and foundation costs would be much higher than necessary, and there might be harmful vibrations throughout the structure.

Types of layout   The company's choice of material flow will be worked into one of three general types of layout. More specifically, the layout may be arranged (1) by process, (2) by product, or (3) by taking work to the product.

A layout based on process arranges the work flow around the type of work performed. For example, a furniture manufacturing company would have the sanding done in one place, the turning in another, the painting in another, and so forth.

Contrasting with this arrangement, layout based on product structures the work to be performed by product. Using this arrangement, the furniture manufacturer cited above would perform all of the work operations on chairs in one place, all of the work on chests in another, all the work on tables in another, and so on.

In some types of production, the product is simply too big or heavy to be moved about the plant. Thus, the work must come to the product. When this is the case, the company adopts a static product layout. Typically, shipbuilding operations use this form of layout.

OPERATION OF THE PRODUCTION PLAN

After an organization has worked out the production plan, it puts that plan into operation. This is the stage that most people think of as production management. Generally, it includes two broad categories of activity. First, it includes activities that are supportive in nature—activities of purchasing, control of inventory levels, and maintenance. Second, it includes the task of machine operations and scheduling. The following review summarizes these activities.

Purchasing

As a production management activity, *purchasing* means getting all the goods, equipment, and services the production process needs, when it needs them, and at the best price. By this definition, purchasing is much more than order placing. It is a complex activity requiring a high level of knowledge and job skill. Those who do it must have an intimate knowledge of all that is bought. They have to know their suppliers—what they produce, how they produce, their production limitations and strengths, and the like.

For the best possible production results, those who engage in purchasing have to keep this knowledge current. In this day of rapidly changing technology, new products, processes, and techniques continually appear. And the company that fails to take advantage of a new development may lose a competitive advantage. Thus, it is essential that those engaging in purchasing serve as the eyes of the operators for anything new that would help the product or the production process.

Inventory levels

Maintaining proper inventory levels is a second supportive activity in operating the production plant. A production plant is likely to have several kinds of inventory. In all likelihood, it will have an inventory of raw materials. And it may have an inventory of component parts, some bought from other companies and some produced by its own production facilities. In addition, the firm may have an inventory of the finished goods it is making. This, of course, is the output of the production process which must be kept until it can be sold and delivered.

The importance of proper inventory levels should not be ignored. Decisions concerning the quantities of purchased or manufactured items to be stored involves cost; and costs, of course, are a matter of constant concern in successful production. In considering inventory costs it is significant to note that every unit in inventory decreases the risk of not being able to meet future demand. Any time the firm falls short of meeting demand, it loses sales—and lost sales mean lost profit. On the other hand, every unit costs money to store. The obvious solution to this problem is to find that level of inventory that has the lowest total cost with respect to the cost generated by all other levels. In short, the firm must determine the most economical level for each purchased and manufactured item. Typically it must maintain inventories at these levels.

In determining optimum inventory levels, several relevant factors should be considered. Some of these purely encourage large inventories; others encourage small inventories. Among the factors encouraging large inventories are quantity discounts. These are discounts given by suppliers to those manufacturers who purchase in large volume. Suppliers justify quantity discounts with the reasoning that production handling costs usually are lower on large lots. Thus, they can pass a part of this savings on to the buyer. Another factor encouraging building large inventories is the need to protect against sudden loss in supply (the effects of a strike, for example). Yet another is to guard against price increases. Although one could argue that a price decrease is also possible, the long-run price movement has been upward.

Among the factors serving to work against inventory accumulation is deterioration. Some goods just do not maintain their desired quality over time. Foods may spoil or lose their flavor. Metals may suffer from

FIGURE 9–3

Illustration of general plan for determining inventory level

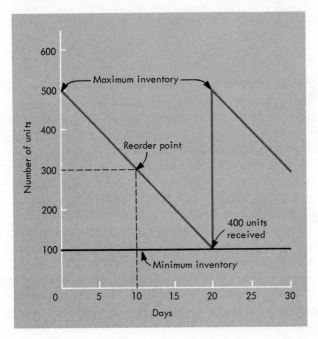

oxidation. Cloth may lose its color. The results are much the same—lost goods and lost money. Similar losses can result from obsolescence. Especially are such losses a threat in industries where technological changes occur frequently, such as in pharmaceuticals. Likewise, it is a threat when style plays a major role. In the garment industry, for example, last year's dresses have little value at the market. Also contributing to low inventories are taxes, interests, and, of course, storage costs. Then there are the natural hazards—fire, theft, floods. All make excessive inventories unwise, to say the least.

A company may use any of a number of methods to determine what level of inventory is best. As these techniques basically are mathematical, they are too involved for detailed coverage here. We can, however, describe generally how they work. First, they determine the maximum and the minimum quantities of an item that can be kept on hand. Then they determine the rate at which the items are used (usually in numbers per day) and the lead time required for filling a new order. With these four items of information known, they then determine the inventory level at which the company should reorder. To illustrate, assume that a company uses 20 items of a certain raw material every day. It computes its desirable maximum inventory to be 500 units and its minimum inventory to be 100. Its supplier needs 10 days to fill an order. As shown in Figure 9–3, the company would need to reorder when its inventory dropped to 300. Ten days after reordering, the new goods would arrive, just as the inventory reached the minimum level of 100 units.

Maintenance

A final supportive activity is maintenance. This, of course, is the activity concerned with keeping all the production facilities running. It is inevitable that even the best of machines will break down. And when they break down, the company stands to lose money for three main reasons. First, when machines are "down," they cannot produce; and lost production may mean missed sales. Second, idle machines mean idle operators that must be paid anyway. And third, failure of one machine may slow down or even stop the production process. Thus, for very practical reasons of economy, maintenance is one of production management's major tasks. Managers must keep the machines running; and they must do it economically, for unnecessary expenditures here can also cut profits.

Usually companies plan the maintenance so that the production process will not come to a complete stop in the event of a breakdown. They may plan the production process so that it has built-in slack. Then, when a machine breaks down, they can continue to operate with other machines. Another plan is to build up inventories between the stages of the production operation. When a breakdown occurs, the other stages of production can continue, at least as long as their inventories hold out. Various other plans may be used, depending on the nature of the production.

A major decision that must be made by every firm engaged in production concerns how much emphasis to place on preventive maintenance and how much to place on repairs. In other words, should the firm maintain all machines continuously, thereby preventing breakdown? Or should it do nothing until the machines breakdown? A firm practicing preventive maintenance will inspect and perhaps replace critical parts in all machines after they have run for a fixed time. The goal is to prevent breakdowns from occurring. The main drawback to this method is that such care is expensive. But the primary question, of course, is whether this cost is more or less than the cost of breakdowns in machinery. To answer this question, the firm must weigh the effects of downtime costs, the ratio of preventive maintenance time to repair time, and the probabilites of downtime under either maintenance system. It is a decision to be made by one thoroughly familiar with all probabilities and costs involved.

Machine operations—Manufacturing

The actual production activities in a typical, modern-day manufacturing plant involve machines, lathes, presses, conveyors, and so on. As we know, we live in a highly mechanized age; and little of our manufacturing is done by human hands alone. Thus, much of production management must concern the management of machines.

So many and varied are these machines that a review of them and their uses would be difficult. It is necessary only to note that in any operation managers should know intimately the operations they perform. And they should know the machines and equipment with which they can perform these operations. They should know what the machines can do; they should know what they cannot do. And they should know how to get the best of output and efficiency from them. Obviously, getting the best efforts out of machines requires a highly technical knowledge.

Scheduling production

In the ideal operation, the work is done in an orderly way. Each form of work is so coordinated with the other forms of work that the overall operation is efficient and smooth. The activity which makes such an operation possible is *scheduling.*

Problems of scheduling For most operations plans, usually several basic scheduling problems exist. One of the most basic of these is the matter of how to schedule production when demand is fluctuating. Most companies attempt to solve this problem by (1) having a static production program coupled with an inventory large enough to satisfy fluctuating demand, (2) varying production so that it parallels demand and using inventory only as a cushion, or (3) using a combination of the above to keep costs at a minimum.

Another problem inherent in scheduling is that of timing the inflow of goods and services bought for production—materials, purchased parts, tooling, and other preliminary work. Closely related to this is the problem of determining the amount of materials and parts that are on hand and available for new work. Still another problem is that of estimating the time required to perform individual production operations, inspections, and the movements of work.

FIGURE 9–4

PERT diagram showing critical path analysis for a simple manufacturing process

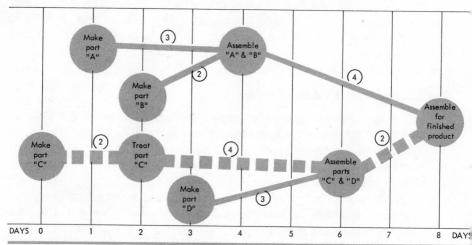

Explanation: The diagram shows all activities involved in making the product. Times in days for each activity are shown in small circles on the paths. The path requiring the longest time (2 + 4 + 2 = 8) is the most critical. It is shown by a broken line (■ ■ ■). This path deserves the most attention in the production process because it has the least slack time.

Methods of scheduling To solve the various scheduling problems, the organization may rely on a variety of methods. But most of them are too technical for this discussion. One that illustrates these methods and is reasonably easy to understand is PERT (Program Evaluation and Review Technique).

Not useful for repetitive activities, PERT has a place in scheduling one-time operations. As illustrated in Figure 9–4, in applying PERT one first determines the sequence of operations that requires the longest time for completion. This sequence, or path, becomes the critical one. Other operations that can be completed before they are needed by dependent critical operations have time leeway and are not critical. Once this critical path is identified, the scheduling of operations becomes apparent. Non-critical operations (those that are nonsequential) can be performed early; or they may be postponed until later. This flexible arrangement frees men and equipment to work on the critical operations and to see to it that the work proceeds on a timely basis.

CONTROL OF THE OPERATION

Control is the final phase of the operations process. In this phase, management checks to make certain that its operations plan has been carried out. It does this primarily by measuring the quality of the output. It makes these measurements by some form of inspection.

Quality assurance

Measuring the quality of the output is a logical means of finding out how well the operations plan is being carried out. If the final output is near that which was planned, probably the operations plan is a good one and is being carried out well. If the output does not meet the standards set in the plan, something likely is awry. The problem may be in the plan or in its implementation. In either event, corrective steps are in order.

Inspection

Measurements of quality are made by some form of inspection. As has been noted, the most meaningful inspection is of the final output of the operation. But other inspections may be needed at various stages of the operation to correct mistakes before they are carried too far. For example, raw materials may be inspected when they first enter the operations process. And each major step in the operations may be inspected. Obviously, a failure to meet quality standards at any of the stages would be critical. The most meaningful inspection, however, is of the final output.

How inspections are made varies by type of operation. In general, however, specific standards are set and tolerances are specified. These standards and tolerances may be in terms of weight, dimension, color, shape, performance, or the like. Inspectors then check a specified portion of the output for these standards; and they note all instances of failure to meet the standards. From these findings, managers can trace errors in the operation. Then they can take the corrective actions necessary.

Our review of operation of the production plan would be incomplete without mention of the role computers are beginning to play in the process. In many industrial operations, mini-computers by the dozens are being used to run machine tools, to keep count of raw materials and finished goods, and to test output. For example, at the Polaroid Corporation, a machine the size of a building works entirely under the watchful eye of a computer. At General Motors, a computer tests carburetors and automatically adjusts them. And at Phillip Morris, computer-controlled stacker cranes without operators identify cigarettes by brands, move them down aisles, and stack them. No doubt the future will bring about even more fascinating production techniques.

SOCIETAL ISSUES OF OPERATIONS MANAGEMENT

To this point, operations management may appear to be a somewhat routine and technical subject. To be sure, much of it is. But this activity involves a number of challenging and exciting societal issues. Management must consider them and solve them in the years ahead.

Job boredom

Perhaps the issue given the most attention in recent years is that of boredom on the job. In producing the most effective operation possible, operations managers have been guilty of assigning workers to repetitive and simple chores. As an example, an assembly-line worker may spend all of every working day doing one simple operation again and again and again. Such assignments may contribute to an efficient operation plan. In fact, the success of the assembly-line technique is attributable to such a division of labor. But workers are beginning to rebel against these boring assignments. They argue that routine work is dehumanizing —that it does not challenge workers or allow them pride in their work.

In an effort to solve this problem, many organizations have taken either, or both, of two general actions: (1) job enrichment and (2) job enlargement. *Job enrichment* efforts are those actions designed to improve the quality of the work. For example, they would include efforts to recognize workers for doing good work, to give workers more responsibility in doing their jobs, and to give workers attainable opportunities for advancement. *Job enlargement* efforts are those which add duties to workers' assignments. For example, instead of doing one routine task all day long, a worker may be given additional tasks. The result would be to make the worker's assignment less routine.

To some extent, job enlargement and job enrichment efforts have been successful. But all too often they have added to the cost of production. Thus, production managers are caught in the dilemma of developing the most efficient operating plan possible or satisfying the needs of their workers.

Decreasing productivity

As a glance at Figure 9–5 shows, over the recent past productivity of American workers has not kept pace with their gains in income. And according to one projection, their productivity will increase even less in the next ten years.[1] In the minds of many, the failure of productivity to keep pace with labor costs is a major cause of inflation.

---

[1] "Forecasting a Decade of Slower Productivity," *Business Week,* January 27, 1973, p. 30.

FIGURE 9–5

Annual percentage increase in compensation and productivity per hour of work in the United States, 1950–73

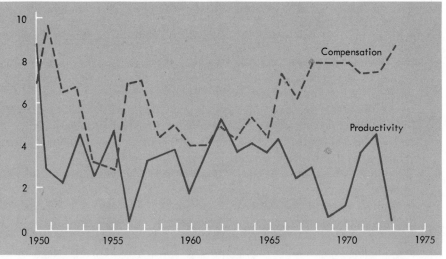

Source: U.S. Department of Labor.

The causes of the decline in productivity are not clear. Probably a major contributor is the declining rate of technological advancement. Although technology continues to improve, its rate of development does not appear to be keeping pace with that of the past. In addition, some people attribute the decline in productivity to a decline in the workers' willingness to work. They see a growing emphasis on personal pleasures, on work satisfaction, on leisure time, and such. Even though these viewpoints have merit, it is obvious that they pose a problem for the competitive organization.

Consumer demand for quality

A very real problem facing the production manager is the consumers' increasing demands for quality. As we all know, in recent years we have had a consumers' revolt. Today's consumers, more than ever before, are concerned about the quality of the goods and services they buy. They are demanding quality. And their demands are being felt throughout business.

To operations managers, these demands mean that quality must be considered more than in the past—that such factors as cost and quantity are not paramount in developing the operations plan. Because most businesses are competitive, the emphasis on quality is not easy to work into the operations plan. Improvements in quality add to the cost of operation. And an increase in operating cost means higher cost to the consumers. Consumers are not always willing to pay the added cost.

Other problems of society

As was noted earlier, the techniques of operations management are not limited to manufacturing production. They are helpful in many other types of operations. There is good reason to believe that they may be useful in solving many of the problems of society.

At this point, one can only speculate on just how operations management techniques may be used in solving society's problems. But it is evident that many of these problems have operations activities in them. Thus, operations management techniques should apply. For example, solving the problem of water supply clearly involves the operation of moving water from one place to another. So does the problem of disposing of garbage involve moving something. Solving the food problem clearly requires producing foods. And so it is with many of the other problems of society. Clearly, the techniques of operations management are likely to make a genuine contribution to the betterment of life in our society.

DISCUSSION QUESTIONS

1 Using the broad definition of operations management, what are some specific operations which are performed at your school? At your home?

2 After extensive research, a group of investors have come up with the idea of building a chain of economy motels. Discuss the additional steps the investors should take in planning this operation.

3 Evaluate your community as a location for (a) a textile mill, (b) a shoe factory, (c) an automobile assembly plant, and (d) a meat-packing plant.

4 A small manufacturer of Christmas ornaments has a plant of 10,000 square feet and works one shift per day. The work is done mainly by hand and requires little skill. Demand has been so good that now he feels that he must expand plant capacity. What should he consider in making his decision?

5 Design a work flow plan for the operation of (a) assembling the mimeographed pages of a 12-page examination, (b) hand assembling a machine comprised of five parts, and (c) manufacturing wooden boxes.

6 Give and explain the examples of products that are likely to require layouts (a) by process, (b) by product, and (c) that take work to the product.

7 What advice would you give to a manufacturer of bakery products on the size of raw materials inventories he should keep? To a shoe manufacturer? To a building contractor?

8 Discuss the nature of control and its role in the operations process.

9 Why are workers today more concerned about job boredom than were the workers of past generations?

10 Some critics say that the declining productivity of labor largely is the result of a growing unwillingness to work. Discuss the merits of this argument.

11 The goal of the operations manager should be to produce the very best product or service. Discuss this statement.

MINI CASES

Superior Manufacturing Company, Inc., is the most efficient in its field. Its wages are the highest, and its profits consistently are good.

Superior's success clearly is a result of the highly automated production system it has developed over the years. This system uses a fast-moving assembly line with workers typically performing simple one-motion operations. Not only does the line move fast, but also it turns out products of unusually high quality.

All had been going well until one day the company's union leader called on Superior's president. "The workers no longer are willing to do this routine work," he reported. "It's not work fit for human beings—makes robots out of them. They demand that this terrible work situation be improved. There will be no new contract until some changes are made."

In studying the union's demands, Superior's president reasoned that to give in to the workers would cut into productivity and reduce profits. But he realized that the workers are serious; and a new contract must be negotiated within the next month.

1. What advice would you give the president?
2. What are the rights of the stockholders in this case? Of workers? Of the public?

Philip Olsen has been chief purchasing officer of the Midway Manufacturing Company for 20 years. "During those 20 years," he boasts, "we never have been short one item of the raw materials and supplies we need for making our products (camping trailers). My secret is to order in large quantities. For most items, I keep enough in inventory to run us six months to a year."

Upon overhearing this remark, Steve Martensen, the new works manager, made this remark: "I have been wanting to talk to you about that, Phil. . . ."

1. *Place yourself in Martensen's shoes and continue the conversation.*
2. *What advice would you give Olsen?*
3. *What should determine the levels of inventory in this case?*

Sunny Hill is a sleepy southern town of about 2,500 people. Surrounded by rich farmland, the little town's economy is almost totally dependent on agriculture. The town has no industry.

Mr. Conrad Pennington, a rich local banker, has a plan to locate a new industry in Sunny Hill—a canning plant. He is attempting to interest you in investing.

1. *What questions would you ask the banker?*
2. *Is this plan in the best interests of the citizens of Sunny Hill? Discuss.*

John L. Lewis was a fiery, powerful leader who worked hard for labor's cause for the first half of this century. Born the son of a coal miner and union organizer, John L. Lewis was conditioned for his assignment from early childhood. He saw his father blacklisted by mining companies for union activities. He witnessed the miseries and horrors of coal mining as it was in the early days. So it was not unexpected that soon after beginning work in the mines at age 15, he became active in union affairs.

Lewis rose rapidly through the ranks of labor. He became president of the United Mine Workers of America in 1920. In this position he gained the attention of the great labor leader Samuel Gompers, founder and president of the American Federation of Labor. Gompers was an advocate of craft unionism, which was the concept upon which the AFL was built. He began to groom Lewis for a leadership role in craft unionism. But Lewis was not to be persuaded. He became an advocate of industrial unionism.

In time, Lewis became the leader in the fight for industrial unionism with the AFL. In 1936, he broke from the AFL and joined others in establishing the Committee for Industrial Organization (later known as the Congress of Industrial Organizations, or the CIO). He became the CIO president; and the organization prospered under his leadership. Following a historic confrontation with President Franklin D. Roosevelt, Lewis resigned as CIO president in 1940. In 1942, he took his United Mine Workers out of the CIO. And in 1946 he took his union back to the AFL. Because of disagreements over the Taft-Hartley Act, however, in 1947 he again moved his United Mine Workers out of the AFL.

Unquestionably, Lewis was one of the most controversial men of his time. But whatever else he was, he most certainly was also a dedicated worker for the cause of labor.

John L. Lewis
(1880–1969)

Founder of the Congress of Industrial Organization

10

Business relations with labor

Industry is a human thing, in which men and women earn the means of life, and from which men and women are entitled to expect the means to a life worth living.
——*Benjamin Seebohm Rowntree*

For a business organization to operate effectively—perhaps even to operate at all—its members must agree to work together. In the typical, modern-day corporation, this statement means that labor unions and management must agree to the terms under which they will work. From the news of the day all of us know that working out such terms and living by them is a most complex activity. These complex activities of management and organized labor are among the most vital to the success of a business.

NEED AS THE BASIS FOR THE LABOR MOVEMENT

This review of business and labor relations logically begins with an inquiry into why labor organized. Probably you know that organized labor has not always been a part of the business scene. In fact, historically speaking, it is somewhat recent in origin. As you will see, it developed for reasons. Specifically, it developed because there were needs for organized labor. Understanding these needs is basic to an appreciation of the complex area of management-labor relations.

Security, protection, and prevention of discrimination

From your study of history, no doubt you know that the attitudes of people change over time. Whereas at one period in time people may willingly accept certain conditions, they can come to regard these conditions as intolerable. So it was with the American workers of the 19th

249

and 20th centuries. In the earlier years, workers generally had no effective means to avoid being the pawns of their employers. When production demands dropped, they expected to be laid off. They accepted the autocratic rights of their bosses to hire and fire indiscriminately. They could not effectively question the employer's rights to show favoritism. They accepted the ups and downs of the economic cycle and its effects on the needs of their services as a fact of life. Although they accepted these ill results, they did not like them. They had a strong need for security, for protection, and for equitable treatment. Not to have these rights was painful, indeed, for the workers' access to the basic needs of life was concerned. At stake were the food on their tables, the roofs over their heads, and the conditions under which they spent a major portion of their lives. It was to be expected, then, that at the right time these basic needs would be voiced.

The right time came with the changing mood of people over the past century. This is not to say that there was not thought or effort in this direction in earlier years. As was described in Chapter 2, history shows that there was. But it was only in the past century that the changing attitudes of the people were such that they could give rise to the labor movement as we know it. It was during this time that the changing spirit of our new country with its emphasis on the individual and his freedom had progressed enough to arouse the workers. They began to voice their long-felt needs; and they organized in an effort to do something about them.

Changing structure of business

Another factor pointing out the need for organized labor is the changing structure of business. Before the Industrial Revolution, skilled craftsmen did most of the work of production. For the most part, they were their own bosses; and they made the basic decisions affecting their work. With the advent of the Industrial Revolution, however, there came a demand for semiskilled and unskilled workers. Obviously, these were workers of lower status. They were not their own bosses. As explained in the preceding section, such workers were subject to the unilateral decisions of their employers. They prospered in good times; they suffered in poor times. They had no protection from the whims of an autocratic management. Their plight was such that organization was bound to come.

Theories of union organization

Perhaps the beginning of organized labor is best explained by a review of certain theories which have been advanced on the subject. This review will be limited to the five that are most generally accepted. All are in some way related to a basic need for organization.

Work opportunity theory   According to the *work opportunity theory,* unions are the workers' attempt to regulate and control competition for work. If the workers are not organized, each of them must compete with every other worker for the jobs available. Obviously, employers are aware of this fact. Thus, they can get cheap labor, for there is always someone willing to accept a wage lower than normal. As a result, employers can draw wages down. And other employers will have to follow, for they must remain competitive. To combat this unfair situation, workers organized. Thus they were able to standardize wages and conditions of employment. As a result, they stopped the employers' practice of bidding wages downward.

Scarcity-consciousness theory   Somewhat similar to the preceding theory is the *scarcity-consciousness theory.* It holds that unions formed because of the scarcity consciousness of employees—that is, the workers' consciousness of the scarcity of jobs. It means that the workers by nature will do what is necessary to keep their jobs. Perhaps it is a matter of self-preservation—survival of the species. But workers will do what they must do. In our society they must work in order to survive. In order to work they must have jobs; and jobs are not always available. Thus, workers formed unions in order to control this scarce commodity—jobs.

Product market theory   The rise of unions is a result of the separation of the threefold function of the craftsman, according to the *product market theory.* The master craftsman of the days before the Industrial Revolution performed three business functions. He was a buyer (of materials), a manufacturer, and a seller (of finished goods). As business grew over time, one person no longer could perform all these functions. Separate manufacturers and merchants came about; and craftsmen became the employees of the manufacturers. As business continued to expand, competition intensified. Manufacturers felt the squeeze, and they in turn squeezed the workers. Workers who once had controlled the product market now saw the chance to control a new material—the labor market. And that is what they did.

Technological theory   As explained by the *technological theory* of why unions formed, the union is the workers' answer to the machine and the dependent role in which the machine puts them. Workers see the machine as a threat to their security. It might even replace them. Thus, they must organize to gain some control over the decisions that could affect their livelihood. The union becomes the workers' power base, and it arises out of their psychological response to their insecurity in our technological society.

Communist theory   Karl Marx in his *Communist Manifesto* advanced a theory explaining the rise of labor unions. According to this *Communist* *theory,* the development of unions simply is another episode in the class struggle between capital and labor. This class struggle, as Marx viewed it, is rooted in the contradiction between social production and private ownership of the means of production. To Marx, the struggle was a political one, led by the political party of the working class. The ultimate goal was revolution and the overthrow of the capitalistic class. Only through successful revolution did Marx see any lasting effect on higher wages and better working conditions for the workers. Thus, he saw unions as a means to improve conditions temporarily—or perhaps as a rallying point from which to advance his cause.

FIGURE 10–1

Theories of why workers organized

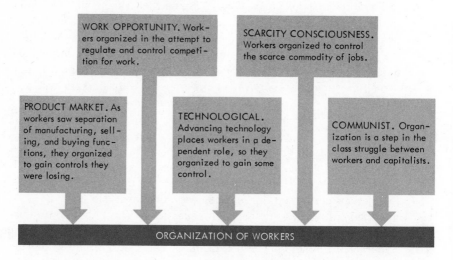

Other explanations of the labor movement exist, of course; but this brief review gives us a broad picture of the more likely ones (see Figure 10–1). But which are correct? The answers are not clearly evident. Perhaps there is a bit of truth in all of them.

STRUCTURE AND FUNCTIONS OF LABOR UNIONS

That labor organized in response to needs is reasonably clear. But how did it organize to meet these needs? It is to answer this question that this text turns next. Specifically, it looks at the structure of the labor union. It views it as it exists at the local level and on up to the national complex organization. Additionally, it looks at the industries unions serve and the effects industry groups have on how unions are organized.

How unions are organized

Typically, a union is a national or international organization of workers who belong to local units. The local units collectively make up the national or international organization. Administration of the organization stems from three levels: local, intermediate, and national. The national administration is the major policy-making body and typically wields the power. Usually there is an intermediate administration designed to handle administrative matters on a regional basis. Local administrations handle the day-to-day affairs of the membership and serve as information and implementation arms of the higher administration.

In all, about 185 national unions exist today. About 135 of these are loosely united in the AFL–CIO, which was founded through merger in 1955 to act as a supernational body. Typical among national unions are the United Automobile Workers, the Aircraft and Agricultural Implement Workers of America, the International Association of Machinists, the United Steel Workers of America, and the International Ladies' Garment Workers' Union. The total number of locals is estimated to be about 78,000. Most of these belong to a national body.

Local unions As has been noted, the local is the basic unit of the union organization. Even though the national level frequently wields great power in negotiations, most negotiations still are conducted at the local level. As a rule, local unions are democratically operated units with each member having one vote. Each local elects its own officers—typically a president, a secretary-treasurer, and an executive board. In addition to these officers, they have the position of union steward. The union steward handles employee grievances, promotes membership in the union, and enforces the provisions of the labor agreement. If there is no payroll checkoff of union dues, then the steward will also collect dues from the members. Unquestionably, this officer is one of the more important cogs in labor-management relations.

Intermediate organizational units Most national unions have established an intermediate organizational unit to coordinate the activities of a number of local unions in a given area. Usually these are administrative offices established on a regional or geographical basis. Their primary function is to serve the locals and to serve as a communication link between the local and national offices. Among the services often supplied local unions is that of furnishing veteran negotiators to conduct bargaining sessions with management.

National unions At the top of the union organization is the national or international structure, such as that illustrated in Figure 10–2. The national organization primarily is responsible for establishing union policy and for establishing uniformity among locals on such issues as wage scales, seniority rules, and group insurance plans. It also provides

FIGURE 10–2

Organization of the AFL–CIO

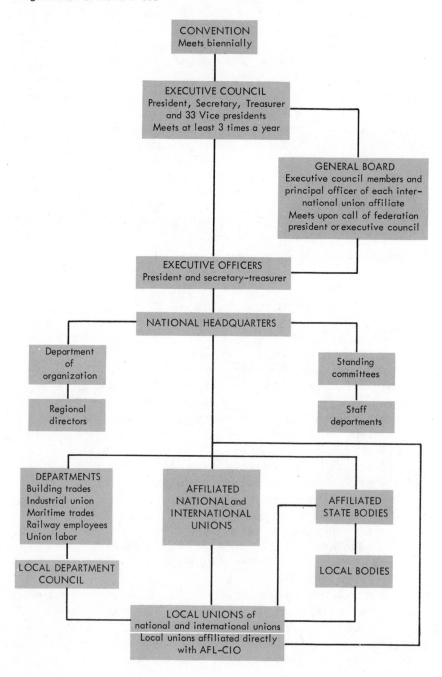

services such as supplying representatives to help in local bargaining and establishing a strike fund in their treasuries. In addition, it may maintain a staff of specialists (lawyers, economists, statisticians, and such) for the use of all levels of the union. Some even have a research department whose function is to supply locals with all kinds of economic data which can be of value in the collective bargaining process.

During the past 20 years, there has been a noticeable shift in power from the locals to the nationals. One reason for this shift is the growing trend toward multiemployer, regionwide, or industrywide bargaining. By concentrating their powers at the top, unions have been able to deal effectively with large corporations. Another reason for this shift of power is the one-party system of electing officials in the union. Since there is no party rivalry for votes, elected officials tend to stay in office once they are elected. They can control channels of union communication; through systematic elimination of opposition they can build a political power structure. Once they have such power, it is most difficult to move them out.

Types of unions

A second way of viewing union organization is by the types of workers they serve. By this classification scheme, two categories of unions exist: craft unions and industrial unions. While these unions are similar in the sense that both bargain collectively to provide security for individuals, some distinct differences exist between them. Generally, they differ in their bargaining strategies, means of protecting individual security, administration, and strike strategies.

Craft unions   Craft unions are organizations of highly skilled workers (plumbers, carpenters, electricians, and so on). Typically these unions attempt to control the supply of craftsmen so that supply will meet, but not exceed, demand. This they do in two ways: (1) they require completion of an apprenticeship program by all members, (2) they maintain hiring halls so that the available work may be spread among union members.

Craft unions bargain primarily for wages. The enforcement of standards of work performance and discipline on the job rests largely with the union—not the employers. Thus, it is quite likely that an employer could have a grievance against a craft union, or vice versa. In any event, the union does not bargain with the employer for work rules. It makes its own, and it enforces them.

The procedure is a reasonable one, since all members are skilled craftsmen. In a sense the craft union has a "monopoly" on skill. And this monopoly provides the union with an economic weapon for winning its ends. Quite simply, highly skilled workers can just go home and wait a while to win a strike. The only substitute for their service is another skilled craftsman. The employer cannot just hire another "warm body"

and train him quickly to do the work needed. He must hire a specialist—
a skilled person. As all are organized, there are no more. Neither can
the employer turn to outside skilled labor (say, from another city) because
these skilled workers also are organized and they will support their
fellow craftsmen. Obviously, craft unions bargain from a strong position
of advantage. Their success over the years makes this strength apparent.

Industrial unions The *industrial union* covers work that generally
is subject to a division of labor. It is work typified by a number of workers,
each making a single contribution to the finished product. Their tasks are
somewhat routine and repetitive—for example, those performed in the
typical assembly line of a manufacturing plant. The bulk of the workers
are nonskilled, although they have come to be called semiskilled. Usually
they receive their training on the job, where the tasks are generally easily
learned. While some workers may develop great expertise as a result of
their specialization, the skills they learn are not often applicable to anything but the particular process of the one workplace.

Because its workers are relatively unskilled and therefore more
easily replaced than craftsmen, the industrial union's bargaining strategy
places great value on the workplace. It is the place to which many members remain attached for life. Thus, a primary issue in the bargaining
process is seniority. They adhere to the principle that the first person
hired should be the last to be let go; and the last person laid off should be
the first to be rehired. Likewise, we can see the reason for the "one shop,
one union" slogan which industrial unions traditionally voice. Obviously,
each union benefits by bargaining as a single unit rather than, for example, allowing the drill press operators to bargain for one agreement while
the milling machine operators bargain for another.

The strike strategy of the industrial union is to prohibit physical
access to the workplace to anyone who might be willing to work while the
strike is in progress. Industrial unions will have, perhaps, hundreds of
members on their picket lines to prevent access to the work area. It is
far too easy for management to find replacements. Unlike craft union
members, the industrial union members cannot just go home and wait
for the employer to accept their terms. If they want their terms accepted,
they must be sure no one gets through the gates. Thus, their strike
strategy is a power strategy, not an economic strategy.

THE FRAMEWORK OF COLLECTIVE BARGAINING

Labor has made its gain largely through negotiations with management. Known as collective bargaining, this procedure is vital to our
understanding of the role of labor in business. Thus, the following discussion examines the structural dimensions of collective bargaining and
explores the procedures involved. Finally, this discourse explores the

legal side of collective bargaining. As you will see, the history of labor law is a rich commentary on the movement of power from big business to labor, from labor to big business, and back and forth again.

The nature of collective bargaining

Collective bargaining is the coming together of union and management to agree on a work agreement. To begin with, there must be a union recognized by management and accepted by the workers. Nowadays, such recognition comes from a secret ballot election conducted by the National Labor Relations Board. If a majority of workers vote for a union, the company must recognize that union and negotiate with it.

The bargaining procedure is a matter of union representatives and company management sitting around a table working out the details of the work agreement (wages, hours, working conditions, and so on). As you would expect, such meetings involve a lot of arguing, haggling, and discussing. In the early stages at least, the workers remain on their jobs and company operations are normal. When the meetings fail to produce results, typically the union calls a work stoppage (strike). As shown in Figure 10–3, work stoppages serve as a good measure of the status of management-union relations over the years. In time, the two sides work out an agreement (contract). After it is approved by the union mem-

FIGURE 10–3

Work stoppages in the United States, 1946–73

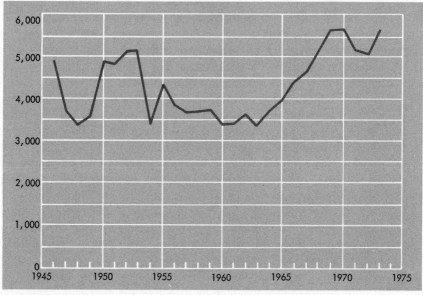

Source: U.S. Department of Labor.

bership, the agreement goes into effect. Usually the contract is for a definite period of time. Shortly before this time period ends, the two sides begin bargaining again.

Major issues bargained for

The work of unions generally is to negotiate and maintain employment relations between its members and management. These efforts concern many matters—in fact, every conceivable item of employer-employee relationship. But primarily they concern five basic issues: (1) union recognition, (2) pay, (3) work rules and time-off policies, (4) job rights and seniority, and (5) grievance procedures.

Union recognition An issue in virtually every case of management-union negotiation is that of recognizing the union as the bargaining agent of the workers. In most cases nowadays, it is a matter of little controversy. Generally management accepts the union. In the early days of labor negotiations, however, the issue was a major one. Perhaps in recollection of these difficult negotiations, unions insist upon contract guarantees that management recognize them as the sole bargaining agents for their members.

In their efforts to gain recognition, unions usually bargain for a *union shop* (an agreement requiring that all workers join the union within a specified time after employment). Before it was outlawed by the Taft-Hartley Act, the *closed shop* frequently was the goal. This was an agreement which required that all workers must belong to the union, even before they were hired. In the minds of some, the requirements of the union shop infringe upon the rights of workers. These critics feel workers should have the right to decide for themselves whether to join. In support of this viewpoint, some states have passed "right to work" legislation to protect the worker's right not to join a union. To say the least, the matter is one of considerable controversy.

Pay Probably on no other issue has labor's influence been felt more strongly than on that of pay. How they are rewarded for their work naturally is of major concern to all workers. And it is quite logical that unions would have a major interest in this matter. In fact, they have made a subject to contract negotiation virtually every area of compensation—across-the-board wage adjustments, labor wage structures, in-grade rate progression, special wages for learners and apprentices, and wage incentives. As a result of the intense efforts of unions on compensation matters, most union agreements have specific clauses that spell out the requirements for job evaluation, time studies, cost-of-living adjustments, and productivity increments.

Making agreements on matters of compensation somewhat difficult are the contrasting viewpoints held by management and labor. As a rule, management prefers to pay the rates prevailing in its own labor market for each job classification. And they prefer to pay according to variations in ability and contribution. In deciding on compensation, management is deeply concerned with its own ability to pay, future business expectations, productivity, and the supply of labor available.

Labor, on the other hand, normally seeks "equal pay for equal work." They feel that persons on the same job should receive the same pay; and they press hard to eliminate wage differentials. Their goal is to achieve wage uniformity throughout an industry for the same class of work. Although management may not think so, there is evidence that labor does give consideration to the company's profit picture, the cost of living, wage settlements in other companies, and the prevailing wage levels in the area.

Work rules and time-off policies Labor's influence is certainly felt on the issue of work rules and time-off policies. Labor strives to regulate work hours to ensure the earnings of all members. If there are layoffs, usually the union seeks an agreement permitting those with the greatest seniority to be laid off last. Likewise, labor strives to balance out the assignment of work duties so that a handful of people do not consistently receive the unpopular jobs. Unions also seek specific regulation of rest periods and meal periods.

Unions also are concerned with overtime regulation, particularly the matter of fair assignment. Sometimes their concern is the question of whether management has the right to make overtime compulsory. The work week is yet another matter of union concern. More and more often the shorter workweek (such as 25 or 32 hours) is becoming a bargaining point. So is the four-day workweek—even the three-day week.

Job rights and seniority Another issue which concerns unions is that of job rights and seniority. Thus, it is a common matter of contract negotiations. Like most matters requiring negotiations, viewpoints on it differ.

The traditional union attitude on the subject is that job changes appropriately are determined on the basis of seniority. Time worked on a job, they reason, is a personal investment. Thus, it should be rewarded. Management usually holds an opposing viewpoint. Their preference would be to have freedom to move workers about unhampered by restrictions. Rigid adherence to seniority rules, they reason, can cause unqualified workers to be assigned to jobs. As they view it, promotion should be based on the worker's ability to handle new and more difficult assignments; the correlation between ability and length of service is far from perfect.

As in most matters of controversy, the end result usually is a compromise between the two viewpoints. The typical management-labor agreement makes some provision for seniority and some provision for ability.

Grievance procedures   A fifth issue of management-labor relations is the handling of grievances. Unions want a well-defined procedure for handling the day-to-day conflicts between management and workers. And they want to make certain that the procedure is followed. Such a procedure is a common part of the work contract.

The typical grievance procedure gives the workers (sometimes the union itself) a step-by-step appeal system for righting wrongs they have suffered. Although such procedures vary from agreement to agreement, the usual plan begins at the lowest organizational level and works up. For example, if an employee feels he has been wronged, he may submit his grievance to the supervisor or shop steward. If he gets no satisfaction here, he then may appeal to higher levels of management. At each step up the hierarchy, higher officials in the union structure enter the picture. If the appeal goes all the way to top management, and the union is still unsatisfied, it may elect to call in an impartial arbitrator who will hear both sides and make the final decision.

Levels of collective bargaining

As was noted earlier, most labor contracts in this country are bargained for by a single company dealing with a single union. This procedure is known as *single-plant, single-employer bargaining.* But there is also found *single-employer, multiple-plant bargaining.* For example, in the field of manufacturing, a company may have contracts with more than one union, perhaps a different union in each of its plants. It would bargain separately with each union.

Somewhat different still is the bargaining done by organizations such as General Motors. Here we have *single-employer, multiple-plant, single-union bargaining.* In the case of General Motors, each local union of the United Auto Workers from each plant elects representatives to what is known as a conference board. This board prepares the bargaining demands and strategy. A master agreement is signed to apply to all General Motors plants. Then each plant negotiates a supplementary agreement with its local union to cover issues that apply specifically to that unit.

Currently the trend is toward multiemployer bargaining. This is the procedure in which employers band together to bargain with one or more unions. The companies set up an employer association, which utilizes a paid, professional staff. This arrangement is common in the construction industry where the unionized contractors will bargain jointly with a building trade council composed of representatives from the craft locals (carpenters, bricklayers, electricians, and so on). There are signs that this form of bargaining may someday occur in the automobile manufacturing industry. Outwardly, the industry has long negotiated on a single-employer basis. Recently, however, the firms have acknowledged meeting with each other concerning labor bargaining matters.[1] Although the companies insist that their cooperation falls short of multiemployer bargaining, their actions may signal a movement in this direction.

Multiemployer bargaining is common in local areas in businesses such as construction, hotels and restaurants, laundries and dry cleaners, retailing, and local delivery trucking. Multiemployer bargaining occurs less frequently on a regional basis. Normally this kind of bargaining includes such industries as pulp and paper, lumbering, trucking, and textile manufacturing.

Multiemployer bargaining is desirable to both employers and unions alike, but for different reasons. Employers like multiemployer bargaining because it takes wages out of competition. To business executives this means that other employers competing in the same product market cannot obtain a price and cost advantage by paying lower wage rates for the same classes of labor. Unions, on the other hand, realize that they cannot force wages up in one firm if that firm is faced with low-wage competition from other firms. Therefore, they press for wage uniformity among all unionized companies in the industry.

One of the main disadvantages of multiemployer bargaining is that a general wage increase is almost always followed by a price increase by all firms. Thus the cost is passed on to the consumer. Also, if strikes occur, the entire industry may close down. Again, the consumer suffers. A final disadvantage is that marginal employers may not be able to afford the wages agreed upon in association bargaining. As a result, they may find themselves placed at a serious disadvantage. They may even be forced to close operation.

Collective bargaining and the law

As labor-management relations are conducted today, they are heavily regulated by federal law. But this has not always been the case. In fact, the past is marked with cases involving long and sometimes bitter struggles. Often the arguments were carried to the very core of constitutional guarantee. On the one hand, management argued that unions challenged the basic rights of personal property—the right to control one's property as one saw fit. Labor, on the other hand, argued that freedom to control one's employment was just as much their "personal property" and thus was equally guaranteed by the Constitution.

In the early 1900s, employers usually had the sympathy of the government and the courts. And they justified their antiunionism to these groups on three grounds: (1) the necessity for preserving free competi-

---

[1] "Auto Makers Grow Less Secretive about Coordinating Bargaining Strategy," *The Wall Street Journal*, August 28, 1973, p. 1.

tion with a minimum of interference in the affairs of business organizations, (2) the sanctity of private property (which they felt unions were
violating), and (3) the right to freedom of individual contract. If unions did
attempt to improve the conditions of employment, usually they were
frustrated by court orders that held their activities to be illegal con-
spiracies. All the employer had to do was get a court injunction to stop
the union. If the union persisted in spite of the injunction, its members
could be prosecuted for refusing to obey court orders.

Norris–LaGuardia Act—1932 With the collapse of the economy
in 1929, and the subsequent increase in unemployment, the attitude of
Congress began to change. Suddenly, it became extremely important to
get workers on the job and to keep them there. The Great Depression, the
massive unemployment (about one fourth of the labor force), widespread
wage cuts, and management's failure to adopt sound industrial relations
policies, all worked to usher in an era of reform. As a result, Congress
passed the Norris-LaGuardia Act.

The main contribution of the act was that it defined permissible
union activities in very broad terms (a significant victory for organized
labor since it meant recognition). But the act did something even more
important. It placed very tight restrictions upon the issuance of an injunction. In fact, for all practical purposes, the court injunction could no
longer be used as a device to defeat union activities (particularly strikes).

The Wagner Act—1935 In 1935, Congress acted even more strongly
in favor of organized labor by passing the Wagner Act (known formally
as the National Labor Relations Act). The act made it public policy to
favor collective bargaining over individual bargaining. In effect, it encouraged unionization by spelling out, point by point, the rights of labor.
Specifically, it included these provisions:

1. Guaranteed employees the right to participate in unions and to bargain collectively.
2. Forbade employers to interfere with or restrain employees who seek
   to organize.
3. Prohibited companies from dominating or controlling unions.
4. Prohibited companies from discriminating against union employees.
5. Made bargaining mandatory whenever a union is involved. (That is,
   it prohibited management from making any companywide wage
   changes without conferring with the union.)

To administer all these provisions, the Wagner Act established the
National Labor Relations Board. It gave the NLRB two primary responsibilities. First, it assigned the Board the responsibility of determining
whether a union or its leaders truly are the chosen representatives of the
workers. Second, it gave the Board the authority to hold hearings on, and
to determine the validity of claims of, unfair labor practice. In cases in-

volving valid claims, it gave the Board the power to issue cease and desist orders and to call on the federal courts to enforce them.

Obviously, this law did much to foster the growth of organized labor. From 1935 to 1947, union membership grew rapidly—from about 3.9 million to approximately 15 million. But there were strong feelings against the law. Representatives from American management vigorously objected to the law on the grounds that it was one-sided and that it tied the hands of management while giving the unions free run to do what they pleased. Along with this tide of opposition, there were great unrest and many bitter struggles. Labor-management relations continued to worsen through 1946, which was a record year for strikes. Congress and the general public became more and more concerned. They tended to place the blame on the unions. The stage was set for a change.

Taft-Hartley Act—1947 As a result of the changed public attitude toward labor, in 1947 Congress passed the Taft-Hartley Act, which amended the Wagner Act. This law attempted to regulate the balance of power in labor relations in two ways: (1) by regulating and restricting the activities of unions, and (2) by protecting individual employees and employers from the power of unions. The act contained many provisions of the original Wagner Act. But in addition to placing restrictions on employers, the act restricted the activities of unions. It did so by guaranteeing the employee the right not to take part in union activity. This guarantee was backed up with these specific provisions:

1. Unions were forbidden from restraining or coercing employees. Thus, unions could not lawfully bar nonstriking employees from the workplace (a provision not fully enforced). Nor could the union resort to violence to enforce picket lines.
2. The closed shop was outlawed. That is, it prohibited agreements which required that only members of the union could be company workers.
3. Unions were prohibited from refusing to bargain in good faith. Thus, unions could not insist on including illegal provisions in the contract, nor could they refuse to make a contract of reasonable duration.
4. Unions were prohibited from taking a number of miscellaneous actions against employers (such as forcing employers not to use products from nonunion companies, and requiring employees of self-employed persons to join unions).
5. Excessive or discriminatory initiation fees for union membership were outlawed.
6. It was made illegal to force an employer to pay for services which were not performed.

As did the Wagner Act, the Taft-Hartley Act specified that the NLRB would enforce its provision. In addition, it gave the president the power to seek injunctions in labor disputes which endanger the nation's safety. In general, the act gave the federal government additional control over union-management relations. Except for the ban on featherbedding, which has not worked, the act has been fairly effective in curbing unfair union activities. Although labor generally has approved its provisions, many impartial observers conclude that the act merely requires unions to exercise the same degree of responsibility previously required of employers.

The Landrum-Griffin Act—1959 During the 1950s, some dramatic exposes were made of racketeering, violence, and lack of democratic procedures in unions. Again Congress reacted—this time by passing the Landrum-Griffin Act. Known formally as the Labor-Management Reporting and Disclosure Act, this legislation provided the following means of regulating the internal affairs of unions:

1. Established a bill of rights for union members. Specifically, the act guaranteed each union member the right to (a) attend, participate in, and vote at union meetings and elections, (b) vote on increases in dues and fees, (c) testify and bring suit against the union for unfair treatment, and (d) receive notice and a fair hearing before union disciplinary action can be taken.
2. Required that union officers and employers periodically file certain administrative and financial reports with the Secretary of Labor. The aim here was to give employees a full accounting of union affairs.
3. Required the union to fully justify a new trusteeship in writing to the Secretary of Labor. (A *trusteeship* is a takeover of operations of a local by its national administration.)
4. Provided for specific rules for election of union officers (secret ballot, three-year terms, fair procedures, and so on).
5. Established the financial responsibility of union officers and provided stiff penalties for violations.

In general, the purpose of the act was to impose democratic operation on the union and to eliminate graft, corruption, and other specific abuses of unions. Congress hoped that with democratic operations guaranteed, union members would see to it that their unions were run properly. This intent, of course, is noble. But there is evidence which indicates that even the supposedly democratically operated unions can become corrupt.

Factors affecting the bargaining process

To this point this review has covered the background of collective bargaining. It has examined its nature, the issues involved, and the levels at which it takes place. It has covered the legal framework within which it works. But what about the bargaining pattern that takes place? What determines the process when management and labor meet at the bargaining table?

As you can easily understand, the pattern of negotiations can vary tremendously. In fact, the possible variations are too numerous for meaningful review. A better way to understand and appreciate the probabilities is to understand the nature of the industry involved. By understanding the factors involved in the specific industry, you should be able to determine for yourself the pattern of bargaining likely to be used in a given case. The following 12 factors should give you the basis for making such determinations.

1. *Size of the industry.* By size of the industry is meant the number of organizations within it. For example, only a handful of companies make up the automobile industry. On the other hand, thousands of firms make up the mining industry. Because of its size, the automobile industry can be expected to push for industry-wide bargaining. Except when unions unite to enforce conformity in bargaining, industries like mining are likely to work for bargaining by company.

2. *Proportion of labor cost.* The percentage of total production cost arising from labor tends to influence union activity. In the oil industry, for example, labor costs are quite a small proportion of the total production cost. As a result, union activity has been nominal. In the building industry, on the other hand, labor costs are relatively large. In such industries, unions tend to be most active.

3. *Degree of competition.* A factor working to the disadvantage of labor union activity is the degree of competition. For example, the steel industry has had administered competition because of federal price regulation—and thus little competition between firms. The garment industry, on the other hand, is characterized by a high degree of intercompany competition. Largely because of this competition, wages typically are much lower in the garment industry than in the steel industry. Obviously, wages will be important in both industries, but steelworkers have a very real advantage over garment industry workers.

4. *Degree of casualness of employment.* The casualness with which the workers enter and leave employment has an effect on the bargaining pattern. Longshoremen typically work day to day for different employers. Newspaper workers may spend an entire lifetime with an employer. Because of these conditions, longshoremen will favor trade-council bargaining and newspaper workers will prefer to bargain directly with their employers.

5. *Stability of employment.* Affecting some industries but not others is the stability of employment. Machinists, for example, must

face periodic layoffs as the economy fluctuates. Because soap has a near constant demand in spite of fluctuations in the economy, soap workers can expect steady employment. Understandably, the more stable the industry, the easier it is to negotiate a contract. In industries that lack stability, the union typically presses hard for security agreements; and security agreements are among the most difficult to obtain.

6. *Location of plant.* The location of the plant also affects the bargaining process. Mining is almost always rural—thus, labor is scarce and the union has a strong advantage. But in the garment industry, where plants have urban locations, labor is plentiful. Thus the garment union will be concerned with controlling access to the labor force.

7. *The changing workplace.* A changing workplace can influence the bargaining pattern. For example, the building trades must go where the work is. Likewise, longshoremen must unload the ship where it is docked. In contrast, an assembly plant stays in one place, permitting work assignments and employment to be more carefully watched by the union. When the workplace requires worker mobility, unions normally insist on hiring halls or some similar work allocation arrangement. When it is stable, they work for means to observe work assignments and employment within the company's facilities.

8. *Diffusion of the work.* Diffusion of work can be a deterrent to union strength. Telegraph operators, for example, are widely separated, and there are few of them at any one place. Thus, they do not have local unions. Such unions would have weak bargaining power. But there are exceptions. Truck drivers are also widely scattered; yet their unions are strong.

9. *Rate of technological change.* The effect the rate of technological change has on union activity is apparent. To illustrate, in the printing industry, automatic typesetting machines and photostatic offset newspaper copying have eliminated many formerly vital jobs. The printers' union has thus had its bargaining power weakened. Quite the opposite result has taken place in the building industry, however. While technological advances have been made here, they have not seriously reduced the need for skill—and the skill requirement is the union's chief bargaining lever.

10. *Skill requirement.* As was noted in our study of craftsmen, skilled workers are always in a stronger bargaining position than are nonskilled workers.

11. *Educational requirements.* Generally, the effect of educational requirements is not strong on union activity. The explanation is simple: most unionized work has no high educational requirement. In recent years, however, professional employees have begun to

form unionlike associations. Such organizations place high stress on educational attainment.

12. *Physical character of the work.* Usually a correlation exists between the physical character of the work and the extent of violence in relationships between management and labor. The most violent relationships have existed in industries like mining where the work is dirty, dangerous, and hard. Seldom are such workers timid about demanding their rights.

Certainly, the relevance of these factors will vary from industry to industry. The reason for this variance should be clear: industries are different. As evidence of these differences we have only to point to the sharply differing records of labor strife by industry. Hopefully, you will be able to detect these differences and appreciate the bargaining strategy that fits each case.

BENEFITS OF ORGANIZED LABOR

From the discussion thus far, it may appear to you that the benefits of organized labor have been one-sided—that only the unions have profited. But such is not the case. As you will soon see, all of the participants have profited—labor, management, and society in general.

How the worker gains

Most of the practical benefits of unions to the workers have been well noted in preceding pages. But there are other, less tangible ones. For one thing, the union satisfies the rather fundamental human drive for self-expression. Most employees like to be able to voice their aims, feelings, complaints, ideas, and such. They want to be more than mere cogs in a large machine.

Unions also benefit workers in a social sense. They give their workers a sense of belonging, of being one of the gang. This effect is desirable, for most people are gregarious, friendly, and sociable in their outlooks. They like to feel that they are "in" on what is going on. Unions satisfy this desire by linking together people with similar ambitions and goals.

Often, membership in a union is the only way an employee can receive restitution for acts of management that he feels are irrational, illogical, or unfair. Often such problems arise out of assignments to jobs, transfers and promotions, or layoffs and rehiring practices. Usually, unions strive for predetermined rules on these matters, thereby protecting the worker from unilateral action on the part of management.

Finally, unions protect their members from economic hazards beyond the workers' control. Workers have no control over economic conditions that bring about a reduction in the labor force. Likewise, workers cannot adequately plan for tragedies such as sickness, accidents, and death. Rightly or wrongly, workers tend to feel that their employers are responsible for helping them to overcome such adversities. After all, if the company can provide for replacement of its capital resources through maintenance of a depreciation fund, then it should certainly do the same for its more valuable human resources.

Benefits to the company

In spite of what you may have thought, companies do reap some benefits from unions. Foremost among these is the fact that unions have forced managements to improve their personnel policies and practices. No longer are managements able to rely on "brushfire" tactics to resolve personnel problems. Rather, they must strive for a program of equality, where rewards and punishments are applied on a just basis. Unions will not accept spur-of-the-moment decisions, and this is good for management. The union's attitude makes it absolutely necessary that management carefully plan labor needs, labor costs, work assignments and scheduling, and package programs of employee benefits. The result is better management.

A second benefit is that through unionization, management can communicate better with its workers. The union structure serves as an orderly and systematic channel for dispensing communications to employees. In addition, the union further simplifies management's communication task by serving as a spokesman for all the employees. By dealing with and through the union, management greatly reduces the number of interactions with its employees. The result is more efficient utilization of management's time and greater uniformity in its dealings with employees. It is significant, however, that the union has the power to edit all such communications. Thus, the benefit may not be so great in cases in which relations between management and the union are not wholesome.

Closely related to the foregoing advantage is the fact that unions provide management with a centralization of labor relations decision making. Management need make only one union agreement, and within that agreement work provisions and rules are carefully spelled out. Management does not, therefore, have to deal with each department separately or with each employee separately. The union acts much as do our selected representatives in Washington—it represents all of the employees and thus centralizes much of the process.

Benefits to society

That society in general benefits from organized labor should be evident from the review to this point. Clearly, organized labor has benefited society by improving the welfare of the working classes. Generally, workers are paid better today than ever before. They are given insurance, retirement programs, and an assortment of fringe benefits. Gone are many of the unscrupulous practices of the 1800s, where labor was considered a mere adjunct to the machine, a replaceable commodity to be quickly put aside when worn out or exhausted. In general, organized labor has achieved a new stature for the workers. It has given them dignity and a voice in the vital decisions that affect our country.

Organized labor has benefited society additionally by uplifting the spirit of the workers. No longer are workers helpless pawns in the hands of an uncaring corporate giant. Rather, they are treated like human beings. They are respected for their contributions and appreciated for the part they play in keeping the industrial machinery of this country going.

ORGANIZED LABOR IN A CONTEMPORARY CONTEXT

This study of labor unions would be incomplete if it did not include some contemporary trends in union activity as well as some permanent issues facing labor today. These are the critical matters of the day. They concern the present and future—not the past. As members of society, all of us will have a role in guiding future development.

The future of unions

A matter of vital concern to us all is the future of the labor union. Opinions vary sharply on this issue. There are those who believe that unions have outlived their usefulness. They argue that the union has become a bureaucratic institution, weakened by its own structure, without purpose or significance.

They cite many causes for this weakening. First, there is the fact that an incessant demand for higher wages has forced management to turn to technology and automation to drive down the cost of production. Along with the technological advance, there has been a significant increase in the number of white-collar jobs. These jobs have developed a new sense of dignity and status among employees, which in turn has led them to resist the lure of unionism.

The critics cite also the fact that this country has experienced a widespread decentralization of business and industry. This change, of course, means that unionizing workers has become much more difficult and costly for the union. Another argument of the doomsday group is that conservatism among aging labor leaders has had its effect. The leaders, they say, have tended to be satisfied with the gains of the past. They have not exercised vision. They have sought no new goals. Without new

goals, labor unions have lost their momentum. Even the workers themselves, they say, have grown complacent. And finally, they argue, the
present level of prosperity has led to an increased middle-class feeling
among American workers. They are well fed, well clothed, and generally
satisfied with their lot. They see little more that the union can do for
them; so, they are less likely to accept unionism.

There are, of course, authorities who argue the opposite viewpoint,
predicting a resurgence of union activites. To support their position, they
cite the fact that young dissidents among labor leaders are calling for
more strenuous, vocal, and active campaigns to organize workers. And
they feel that this young group will give unions the dynamic leadership
they need in order to grow. They argue, also, that there exists in this
country a trend toward social unionism. Another of their arguments
counters one of the opposition. They see the resistance of the white-collar
workers to unionization crumbling. In fact, some argue that the resistance

FIGURE 10–4

Membership in national and international unions in the United States,
1930–75

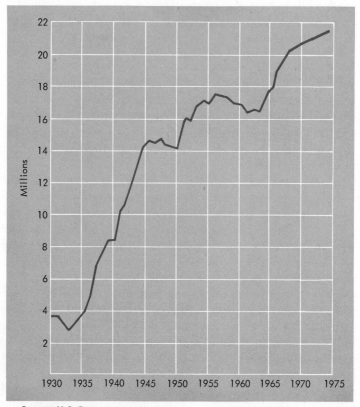

Source: U.S. Department of Labor.

of this rapidly growing group already has been overcome. It is merely a matter of time, they maintain, before most or all white-collar workers will be organized. In support of their arguments, union supporters point to a continuing growth in membership (see Figure 10–4).

Prominent issues in organized labor

In addition to the matter of its very existence, labor faces a number of critical issues in the days ahead. Five in particular deserve mention: (1) rising unemployment, (2) the minority worker, (3) the white-collar worker, (4) a revolutionary movement within labor's ranks, and (5) job enrichment. All five are thorny questions which have no easy solutions.

Rising unemployment   Strange as it may seem, during the past few years we have had rising unemployment and a labor shortage at the same time. How can this occur? The answer is that unemployment has sifted down the occupational ladder. More and more jobs are requiring higher skills and higher education; fewer and fewer jobs are available for the unskilled and the uneducated.

The implications of this phenomenon for organized labor are two-fold. On the one hand, organized labor is going to have a tough fight on its hands maintaining worker security because demand for low-skilled employees is drying up. On the other hand, the fact that technological advances are creating a demand for highly trained employees means the shift will be toward more people going to college. Thus, it appears that labor's future membership will decline. If this is indeed the outcome, organized labor will cover fewer jobs and fewer people.

The minority worker   A second issue that labor must resolve is that of determining what to do about minority workers. Unions, and particularly craft unions, have a history of discrimination, especially against blacks. Many unions simply refused to accept blacks, or they resorted to rigged examinations (mental and academic) to keep blacks out. Some unions even insisted that blacks have separate locals, but that white locals bargain for the blacks. Some craft unions with apprenticeship programs even went so far as to exert political pressure on governmental licensing agencies to see to it that blacks were not accepted. The balance of power, however, is changing. Minority groups themselves have organized and are beginning to wield considerable influence. In addition, a number of new laws have been passed which forbid racial discrimination in labor unions. While enforcement of these laws is difficult, they are having their effect. And labor unions will need to be more flexible and contemporary in their philosophies.

The white-collar worker   A third issue facing organized labor is that of the white-collar worker. The question is whether labor can make headway with this group. In some instances, it already has. Unions have made some success in organizing office workers (the largest white-collar group); but only about 10 percent are now covered. Professional and technical white-collar workers hold even less promise for the labor union. For example, the American Nurses Association has moved significantly in the direction of collective bargaining. But it has done this without developing any formal alliances with organized labor. The same is true for engineers. For the most part, engineers view collective bargaining as having little relevance to their situations. They prefer what they call professional societies. The most prominent of these, the National Society of Professional Engineers, openly and aggressively opposes unionism among engineers. Among schoolteachers there has been a slow drift toward unionism, but the profession's dominant organization, the National Education Association, has been reluctant to embrace union tactics. Generally, professional associations prefer to retain their professional images. They have no wish to be affiliated with organized labor; nor do they want the "manual worker" image that many minds associate with union membership. For many salaried professionals, the status loss suffered by joining a union would never be overcome by gains the union might make.

Internal revolution   A fourth problem facing unions is that of a possible revolution within its ranks. Signs indicate that a somewhat independent and anti-establishment attitude is developing. Some observers note that the changing attitude is the result of a new generation entering the labor movement. The new generation, they note, are not so willing to accept the traditional regimentation of the workplace. In the words of Victor Riesel, an eminent labor reporter, the new workers have "come to the shop with anti-establishment anger, resentment, and bitterness. And rebelliousness against the discipline of any work day."[2]

Although not all observers look upon this issue as angrily as Mr. Riesel, most agree that changing attitudes toward work are beginning to occur within labor's ranks. Some cite as evidence the 1973 veto of the Ford Motor Company contract. This contract had been worked out by old-line leaders who thought they had the backing of their members. But rebellious young skilled workers vetoed it. They refused to accept a contract that permitted management to require them to work overtime. Although such attitudes are somewhat new on the labor scene, it appears likely that they will intensify in the years ahead.

Job enrichment   A major issue with both management and labor is the question of job enrichment. By *job enrichment* is meant improving the quality of work—of making work more enjoyable and less routine and boring. With the technological progress made over the years, much industrial work has become highly repetitive and simple. An assembly-line worker, for example, may spend every working day doing one simple task again and again.

---

[2] Victor Riesel, "Young See Old Union Heads as Non-relevant," *Baton Rouge* (Louisiana) *Morning Advocate,* November 11, 1973, p. 14–A.

Today's better educated and more concerned worker has begun to rebel at such assignments. In response to the worker's feelings, management has begun to take steps to improve work assignments. They have added rewards, improved incentives, increased responsibilities, and generally enriched the jobs. But to date they have only scratched the surface of the problem.

Unions also are concerned about the matter. They are for any action which genuinely enriches the work of their members. At the same time, however, they tend to be suspicious of management's experiments on this issue. Their concern is that management may be more interested in increasing productivity than in enriching jobs. As the issue is one that management and labor must work out in the years ahead, it would be wise if each would look at the matter with the best interests of both sides in mind.

DISCUSSION QUESTIONS

1 Explain how changes in the thinking of workers of the 19th and 20th centuries gave rise to the growth of unions.

2 Which of the theories of union organization do you think offers the best explanation of why unions were formed? Defend your answer.

3 Is the recent shift of power from union locals to their national offices good for the members? For business?

4 Explain the basic difference in bargaining approach taken by craft and industrial unions.

5 Is the union shop fair to all concerned? The closed shop?

6 Are labor's demands for equal pay for equal work fair? Are pay differences for seniority, skill, and attitude defensible?

7 Does an employee have the right to refuse to work overtime?

8 Discuss the question of whether single-employer or multiemployer bargaining is best for all concerned.

9 Review the provisions of the Taft-Hartley Act. Comment on the needs for such measures.

10 Discuss the reasons for the Landrum-Griffin Act.

11 Select some local business and apply to it the factors affecting the bargaining process.

12 The text discusses only benefits of organized labor. Take an opposing point of view and bring out harmful effects.

13 Is the revolutionary movement within labor's ranks good for the nation?

MINI CASES

The Whidden Manfacturing Company has existed for 27 years. Starting as a three-man operation owned and managed by George S. Whidden, the company has grown rapidly over the years. Today it employs 146 workers.

Throughout the company's life, Mr. Whidden has maintained firm control of the organization. He has been a strong leader and has run the company with a firm hand. A rugged individualist, Mr. Whidden is an advocate of free enterprise and a bitter opponent of government intervention in business, of what he refers to as "creeping socialism," and in general of the direction of social and political events in recent years.

Until now no attempt has been made to unionize the company. But today Mr. Whidden learns that representatives of a major national union are in town and that they have talked to some of his employees. They plan to organize the workers. Mr. Whidden is furious. "I built this factory by the sweat of my brow!" he exclaimed. "And no union bosses are going to dictate to me how to run it. I pay a fair wage, and I've been good to my employees. If any of them join, they will be sorry!"

1. *Discuss Mr. Whidden's predicament.*
2. *What advice would you give him?*

At a meeting of stockholders of the Mason-Dier Manufacturing Company one of the stockholders directed these words to the company's president: "I am reliably informed, Sir, that this company was approached by an inventor who has perfected laborsaving machinery that would cut our labor costs about 50 percent and would reduce the cost of our goods to the consumer by 30 percent. If this information is true, doubtless the machinery would also improve our profits. I am also informed that this company considered purchasing this machinery but did not do so because our labor union would not accept it. Now I ask, Sir, who runs this company? Labor or management?"

The president began his response with these words: "Your information is correct. But let me explain our position."

1. *Complete the president's answer.*
2. *Assume that you are an officer of the union and present the union's case.*
3. *Discuss the issue as it affects the whole of society.*

For 40 years, Henry Hess has been a loyal member of his union. As a result of his loyalty, Henry worked up the hierarchy to become president of his local. Henry worked very hard at his new assignment.

When contract time came around, Henry spent long hours bargaining for the best possible results. And he felt that he had succeeded. He got the pay raise the union had asked for, some real improvements in the pension plan, and a number of job safety improvements. He failed only in getting the change some younger members had wanted regarding compulsory overtime. They had wanted it eliminated. But Henry felt this really was a small matter. So he brought the contract to the members recommending that they approve it. To his surprise, they voted against the contract. Then some of the members began a move to remove Henry from office.

1. *Evaluate this action.*
2. *What should Henry do now?*

Frank W. Woolworth was born a poor country boy in upper New York state. From his earliest recollections he wanted to be a merchant. As he explained in his later years, he "envied the young fellows behind the counters in the village store." So it was not unexpected that when he began his working career he sought employment in retailing.

His efforts to enter retailing were not easy. Jobs were hard to find. But finally he landed a position, such as it was. It offered no pay. It was an apprenticeship of sorts which required that he do menial tasks for a dry goods merchant in exchange for training in retailing. Young Woolworth learned his work well. And it was on this assignment that he got his idea for a five and ten cent store.

The idea came to him when he was instructed to sell some unsalable goods. He gathered the goods and dumped them on a table in the store. On the table he placed the sign "Any article on this table five cents." Soon customers were shoving one another to get to the previously unsalable articles.

With this idea in mind, Woolworth borrowed $300 and opened his first five cents store. Although it failed, he made a second effort, and a third. In fact, three of his first five stores failed. Undaunted, he continued to open stores. By 1889, there were 12, and by 1917, there were almost 600. At the time of his death in 1919, the number was 1,050.

Woolworth's success has been credited to a number of factors. Certainly his burning ambition to be a merchant helped. But more probably his vision and ability played the major role. His careful selection of site, his low-cost buying in large volume, and in general his merchandising skills clearly contributed to his success. Perhaps equally significant was his policy that "The customer is always right."

Frank W. Woolworth
(1855–1919)

Chain store magnate

11

Marketing: What it is and what it does

No one returns with good will to the place which has done him a mischief.

——Phaedrus

Of all the fields of business, marketing is likely to be the most vital to an organization's goal of making a profit. Certainly, maintaining an efficient organization is essential; and so is making a good product or providing a good service. But getting these goods and services into the hands of consumers is the activity most likely to make or break a business. It is in this activity that results are least predictable and the most likely to vary. It is here that hard work, imagination, and strategy are most likely to pay off.

The study of this dynamic field logically begins with a definition of the term *marketing.* Like most such terms, marketing means different things to different people. When a sales representative speaks of marketing a product, for example, probably he is talking about selling. When an advertising woman speaks of marketing, probably she means advertising. And when a department store manager refers to marketing, he is likely to mean retailing and merchandising. Actually, each one of these people is talking about a different part of the total marketing activity.

In defining this very broad activity, either of two basic approaches is logical. One, the traditional approach, defines *marketing* as those business activities that direct the flow of goods and services from the producer to the final consumer. Although this definition would be adequate for this review, its emphasis is on the flow of goods and services. Many marketers feel that the emphasis should be elsewhere.

The second approach to a definition of marketing emphasizes satisfying the needs of people. In a sense, it views marketing as a two-way process. On the one hand, marketing involves looking to consumers to determine consumers' needs and wants. On the other, it concerns fulfilling consumers' needs through creating and delivering goods and services. Those who take this approach admit that marketing must work for a profit. But they conclude that profits are but rewards for delivering a standard of living to society. From this viewpoint this definition of marketing evolves: *Marketing* is all the activities in business which work toward satisfying specific customer needs and wants at a profit. Perhaps this definition may appear to be idealistic. But many marketers think it is realistic.

Because both of these viewpoints have merit, the following review of marketing logically combines them. First, this review follows the logic of the traditional definition. It reviews the activities (functions) that take place in moving goods and services. And it covers the types of businesses (institutions) that perform these activities. Then in the next chapter it approaches the subject from the viewpoint of the second definition. Here the review shows how the marketing institutions manage these activities to satisfy the needs of consumers (the marketing management approach). Because the whole area of marketing involves controversy, this review raises criticisms wherever they apply. And it looks at them closely and objectively.

THE FUNCTIONS OF MARKETING

If one views marketing from the viewpoint of the traditional definition, it appears to be the movement of goods from producer to consumer. Thus, distribution stands out as the basic activity of marketing. But if one looks more specifically at what goes on in distribution, a number of more specific activities are obvious. These activities are commonly called the functions of marketing. They are the first subject in this review. Although there are many ways of classifying these functions, the plan used here is a somewhat general and simple one. It divides the total of marketing activities into three broad functional areas: (1) exchange, (2) physical distribution, and (3) facilitating. As summarized in Figure 11–1, the more specific activities of each are emphasized in the following pages.

The exchange function

Perhaps the most obvious of the marketing activities are those of exchanging goods. More specifically, these are the activities of buying and selling. Throughout business, goods are bought and sold. Manufacturers buy raw materials; and they sell the products they make from these goods to middlemen. These middlemen may sell the goods to other middlemen.

FIGURE 11–1

Summary diagram of marketing functions

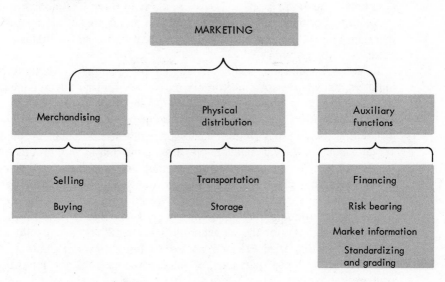

Eventually the goods reach the retailers. And finally they come to consumers.

As you will see in the following chapter, buying and selling goods are not the simple, routine activities they may appear to be. Rather, they involve putting into practice a carefully thought-out strategy. They involve getting a thorough understanding of consumers and of their needs. And they involve developing buying and selling plans to meet these needs.

Buying   In understanding the buying activities of marketers, we should keep in mind that through buying marketers assemble goods. That is, they bring together an assortment of goods, thereby providing a service to their customers. Department stores and grocery stores, for example, bring together a wide variety of goods from a variety of producers. The advantages to the buyer are too obvious to mention.

In buying and assembling goods, marketers must continually keep in touch with their customers' needs, for not to do so can be disastrous. Doing this job satisfactorily, however, is no easy undertaking. It can be hazardous, to say the least; and it requires the utmost in care and skill. Especially is this the case when purchases must be made long in advance of the customers' needs. A clothing store, for example, must order some of its stock a full season in advance—well before anyone knows for certain what the styles will be. The store's wholesalers and manufacturers must anticipate the market for an even longer period. Any errors in selection any one of them makes mean financial losses. To illustrate the point, in the early 1970s the ladies fashion field was in a turmoil concerning skirt lengths. There was the mini, the midi, and the maxi. No one knew what the customers would buy. Yet marketers in the field had to buy their stock in advance. Many of them lost money.

Selling For most businesses, selling is a major part of the goal of the marketing effort. It is the effort that pays off. It brings to a conclusion the other marketing efforts.

In some businesses, selling may take place wholly on the buyer's initiative, as when a customer orders a product from an advertisement or from a catalog. In most cases, however, selling is a personal effort. It involves one human being (the salesperson) working to satisfy the wants of another human being (the customer) with a particular product or service. Just how vital salespeople are in the marketing process is a matter for debate. In this debate, one must answer questions such as these: "What benefits do salespeople provide in the marketing process?" "Are these benefits worth their cost?" "Would it not be better for buyers to select the products they need without pressure and to save the added cost they must pay for the salesperson's service?" These questions are indeed interesting ones. We must answer them in the years ahead.

In answering these questions, we shall need to consider some of the primary benefits salespeople provide to companies and to customers. On the customer side is one paramount benefit. It is that salespeople can and do serve as a vital source of information for buyers. Especially is this true with technical products where salespeople are much more than order takers. Frequently, they are authorities in the field, and their information and advice can be extremely valuable to the uninformed buyer. They can aid buyers in making intelligent choices; and they can make certain that buyers' needs are met properly.

From the firm's point of view, the salesperson's efforts to meet the customers' needs means customer satisfaction. And customer satisfaction leads to repeat sales and future profits. But sometimes, salespeople oversell, and their customers suffer. In general, however, salespeople produce profits for the firm.

The physical distribution function

The actual movement of goods from the point of manufacture to the ultimate consumer is the second of the functional areas of marketing. It involves two basic activities: (1) transportation and (2) storage. Clearly, these activities must be carried on, for goods have to be moved on their route to the consumer. And while they are not being moved, they must be kept somewhere.

Transportation Transportation creates value in goods by giving them place utility. By *place utility* is meant the value added to a good or service by having the good or service where it is needed. For example, if you own a pound of coffee located in Central America, it is of little value to you where you are. If it were moved to you, it would have much more value. Likewise, if you have an automobile breakdown out in the wilderness, you would be quite willing to pay extra to get a mechanic to come to you. Clearly, the cost of moving goods and services to the place they are needed is a legitimate part of the value of goods or services.

In viewing our marketing system, we can see that transportation is a most vital part of it. For one reason, most of our markets are separated geographically from production areas. Thus, manufacturers must move the finished goods to the people who want them. Transportation is especially vital in the production of perishable goods, foods in particular. Milk, for example, must be moved quickly before it spoils; and so is it with meats, eggs, fruits, vegetables, and such. Transportation also is vital in industries where heavy bulk shipments must be made. Steel, for example, is very bulky; and the iron ore from which it is made is even bulkier.

For our purposes, the transportation of goods takes two basic forms: bulk freight and merchandise freight. *Bulk freight* is shipment in large quantity with little or no special treatment needed. Because of the quantity involved, cost is relatively low. Typically it is slow. Goods moved by bulk freight are those that are heavy, that take up space, and that require little service. Typical products shipped in bulk are nonperishable agricultural products (grains, cotton, livestock, lumber, coal, iron ore, and crude oil). *Merchandise freight* is shipment in smaller volume. It is a faster manner of shipping. It is also safer, for the merchandise is given special handling; and it is more costly than bulk freight. Most of our manufactured goods are transported this way.

The freight services available to business generally are well known to us. But some comment about their importance and influence is in order (see Figure 11–2). *Railroads* are our most important carriers of bulk freight. They carry some merchandise freight, but usually in large quantities and for long hauls. Sharing the load of bulk freight shipments with the railroads are our *waterways.* On our major rivers, on the Great Lakes, and on our intercoastal canals, barges and ships carry large quantities of goods, mainly as bulk freight. Another major form of bulk carrier is the *pipeline.* The routes of pipelines, of course, are inflexible. Another major form of carrier is the *motor truck.* They are the most flexible of our transportation forms, for they can go wherever the roads go. They are also fast. Because they are fast and can provide special services, they are primarily useful for shipping merchandise freight.

As in most business areas, transportation has benefited from our advancing technology. One of the most interesting innovations is piggyback transportation. This combination of rail and truck movement gives

FIGURE 11–2

Intercity freight traffic by major forms of transportation, 1950–71

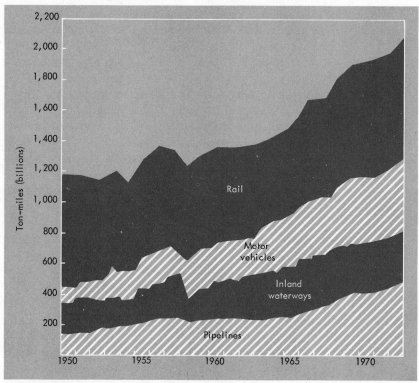

Source: Interstate Commerce Commission, *Annual Reports.*

lower cost transportation to every point the highways go. By this method, truck trailers are shipped by rail to rail points near their destinations. Truckers then move the trailers from the rail point to their destinations. Another innovative system is fishy-back transportation—a similar combination of water and rail or truck carriers. Equally fascinating is the advancing use of computers to route the movements of trucks, rail cars, and their cargos. The result is faster service and generally improved efficiency. Then there are the rapid advances made in airfreight, as larger and larger aircraft are carrying more and more cargo. In addition, seagoing vessels that dwarf any ever made before are making their appearance in the 1970s. Most definitely the transportation field is meeting the challenge of the changing times.

Storage Storage is the second ingredient of the distribution function. From the time goods are produced to the time they are consumed, they must be kept (stored) by someone. Thus, they are kept at all points along the distribution channel—by the manufacturer, the middlemen, the retailers, and eventually the consumer. How long they are kept at any point normally depends on the nature of the goods.

The reasons for storing goods are many, but four in particular stand out:

1. The nature of our marketing system requires it. Businesses must anticipate demand well in advance; and they must hold goods until the demand takes form.
2. Seasonal variations in demand often require storing goods.
3. Storage oftentimes permits economies in production. A manufacturer of nuts and bolts, for example, may find it economical to manufacture one size for a few days, then another, then another, and so on. The resulting large quantity produced would be stored. The alternative would be to make a small quantity of each size every day, but production costs would be higher this way.
4. Storage improves the quality of some products. Cheese, wine, liquor, tobacco, and lumber, for example, all must be aged.

Just how goods are stored logically depends on the nature of the goods. For goods not likely to deteriorate when exposed to the elements (brick, pig iron, sewer pipes, automobiles) *yard* and *ground* storage is likely. That is, they are stored in an open yard on the ground. Another common form of storage is *ordinary warehousing,* which, of course, is storage under shelter. Most of our consumer goods are stored in this way. Some forms of goods require *special* storage facilities. For example, terminal elevators are used for storing grains. Likewise, there are specially designed structures for storing cotton; and the same is true for wool. Often such warehouses perform special services, such as grading, cleaning, and aging, in addition to storing.

In summary, this review shows that our marketing distribution system serves everybody concerned—the manufacturer, the wholesaler, the retailer, the consumer. The plan is such that at every stage of the distribution channel, goods are available when they are needed. As is true with all general marketing activity, our distribution system was not planned; it just turned out this way. Even so, the results are clearly evident. Although many areas of marketing are vulnerable to criticism, it is more difficult to find fault with the physical distribution area.

Facilitating functions

In addition to selling and distributing goods and services, other functions are a part of our marketing system. These functions are not so directly involved in achieving the organization's goals as the two functions discussed. But they are vital to the operation of the marketing system. For purposes of classification, they may be called the facilitating (or auxiliary) functions of marketing. Four of these facilitating functions deserve attention: (1) financing, (2) risk bearing and credit, (3) standardizing and grading, and (4) marketing information.

Finance As we all know, businesses use credit extensively, just as we consumers do. It is a necessary ingredient to modern-day business operations. Many firms simply could not exist without it. Practically all of them would have to curtail their activities were credit to be halted.

Credit for marketing operations comes primarily from two sources: the trade and banks. *Trade credit* is that offered by suppliers on the merchandise they sell. That is, sellers permit buyers to have the goods without payment on the promise to pay in a specified period—typically

FIGURE 11–3

Installment and noninstallment credit in the United States by type of lender, 1973

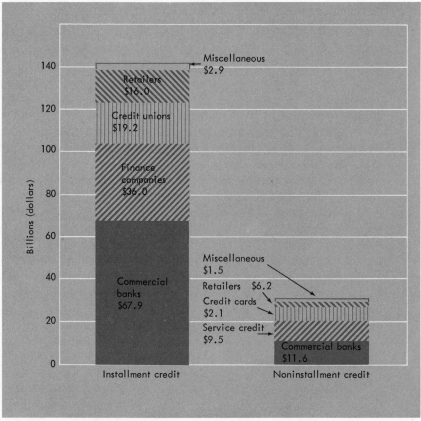

Source: U.S. Department of Commerce.

10 to 20 days. Thus, the buyers get time in which to sell the goods before they have to pay for for them. Often, however, sellers charge interest on the amount owed. And often the interest is high. For this reason and others, many marketers borrow money from banks (*bank credit*) at lower interest rates.

Just as marketers need credit for their operations, so do retail customers need credit. Especially do retail customers need credit when buying expensive goods such as washing machines, refrigerators, automobiles, and furniture. Much of this credit is *installment credit* (repayments made at regular intervals over a period of time); and financial institutions like banks, credit unions, and finance companies furnish the bulk of it (see Figure 11–3). But retailers furnish a significant part, and their share is growing. Over the years, they have developed a wide assortment of buy-now, pay-later plans (open accounts, installment accounts, club plans, and so on). In addition, they widely use the bank credit cards (Bank Americard, Master Charge) that have become so popular in recent years.

Without question, these credit plans have stimulated sales and have led to profits. On the consumers' side, they have made it easier for people to buy; and they have enabled them to enjoy goods that they might not otherwise be able to buy. Some critics of the system argue, however, that liberal credit terms induce consumers to buy more than they can afford. They argue, also, that interest charges for this credit tend to take a major bite out of many incomes and actually reduce the standard of living. But in defense of credit it should be noted that the consumer has the choice of using it or not using it.

Risk bearing   An auxiliary function performed by virtually all marketing organizations is that of risk bearing. To say the least, risk exists in all phases of business operation; and marketing is no exception. A primary risk faced by all marketers dealing in goods is that the value of the goods held may change. Always the possibility exists that natural hazards (fire, floods, storms, and so on) will destroy goods. And there is always the possibility that changes in supply and demand will take place. In fact, such changes are continually occurring with many products. Styles may change suddenly; consumer demands may shift; an improved substitute product may come on the market. The result in each case is the same—a change in the value of the goods held. Thus it is that any marketing organization taking title to goods must bear the risk of price change.

In addition to risks resulting from changes in the value of goods held, firms bear risks merely by being in business. All businesses have some uncertainty concerning their successful operation. Typically, they have investments in machinery, buildings, inventions, and such. For a multitude of reasons, any operation can fail; and as we know, many do.

Defenders of our marketing system point to such risks as justification of the profits a business receives.

Standardizing and grading   A second facilitating activity is that of standardizing and grading the products and services to be sold. This is the activity that classifies or describes products so that customers can select the ones that meet their needs. For example, customers for coats have different requirements. Some need large ones; some need small ones; and others need sizes in between. Efficient merchandising requires that in the manufacturing process such variations in size be standardized —that there be sizes 44, 42, 40, 38, and so on, to meet the needs of every customer. Grocery customers have varying requirements for packaged foods. Thus, package size must be varied, and weights and contents must be reliable. With some types of products, variations in quality are important to the consumer. Beef, for example, is not all alike. Effective merchandising requires that the customer be clearly informed of the differences. Thus, grades of quality must be established (such as prime, choice and good); and the product must be inspected and classified into these grades. To ensure correct grading of meats, federal inspectors regulate the grading operations.

Clearly, standardizing and grading make marketing more efficient. One reason for this greater efficiency is that they make buying easier. When goods are standardized, buyers can buy from description instead of by inspection. They know what to expect when they specify certain standards. And they are better able to compare prices. Perhaps most important of all, standardizing and grading make business more ethical. If there were no clear standards that both buyers and sellers understood, the unscrupulous could take advantage of those who do not understand. The ancient *caveat emptor* (let the buyer beware) rule of the marketplace would prevail.

Most marketers agree that there should be some standardizing and grading of goods and services. But not all agree on how far these efforts should go. It is easy to understand why customers need information such as size for shoes, drill bits, shirts, and the like. But how much more is necessary or desirable? The possible information for some products is vast and complex. Take electronic equipment, for example. How much of its voluminous technical makeup should be described? Or in the case of automobiles, how much of the specific details of each minor part does a buyer really want or need? What should be done with a style product, say ladies dresses? How much does the buyer want to know about technical qualities of the fabric? And how would one describe the style qualities? It is easy to criticize businesses for not giving enough information. But businesses have a genuine problem in determining how much and what information to give.

Marketing information   The progressive marketing firm makes full use of the best information available. Not to do so could be disastrous in our highly competitive and risk-filled business system. Unfortunately, much of the information marketers must know is not readily available. They must gather it themselves.

What a business should know about its market is not easy to describe. Perhaps the best answer is "everything possible." It should know the size, location, and characteristics of the market for its product. It should know its present customers—who they are, their characteristics, needs, buying habits, preferences, and such. Also, it should know its competition —their strengths, weaknesses, activities, and plans. In general, it should have as much of this sort of information as it is able to collect. And it should plan its marketing strategy on the basis of this information.

Marketing executives gather such information in many ways. Some of it they get through informal conversations with other people in business. Some they get from reading trade and business publications, newsletters, and newspapers. Their own salespeople, through written and oral reports, may supply additional specific information about the market. In the largest organizations, they may get information from special research departments or outside research organizations that conduct research to uncover specific marketing information for the firm.

Whatever their sources, marketing executives should make full use of all the available information. Not to do so would be suicidal in today's highly competitive market. Certainly the opposition is using all available information; and the competition in marketing is so keen that the firm that fails to take advantage of any possible information is likely to lose its competitive position.

AN EXAMINATION OF MARKETING INSTITUTIONS

The functions of marketing, of course, must be performed. They are performed by people working in organizations. For a fuller understanding of what goes on in marketing, this review now shifts to the organizations that perform them. This discussion divides these organizations into two broad groups: retailers and wholesalers. Under each is discussed the major subgroups.

Retailing institutions

In reviewing retailing institutions, it may be wise to agree at the outset as to just what the term means. In the minds of most of us, *retailing* suggests a firm that engages in all those activities directed toward selling goods to the consumer. And we think of the consumer as an individual who uses the product himself or who will buy it for the use of his family or friends. But some consumers are businesses or other forms of organizations. A manufacturing firm or a church, for example, may buy office supplies or equipment from a discount house. Thus, a useful definition of a *retailing institution* must be broad enough to cover such practices. This one does the job nicely: a retailing institution is a business open to the public which sells primarily to ultimate consumers, usually in small quantities, from merchandise inventories stored and displayed on the premises.

Within this broad area, a variety of types of operations exist. For our purposes, they may be divided into three groups: (1) independent retailers, (2) large-scale retailers, and (3) nonstore retailers. The principal subtypes in each group shall be examined.

Independent retailers   Although the term does not specifically suggest it, independent retailers are the smaller retail operations. Typically, they are the single-owner or partnership organization. They are likely to consist of a single outlet rather than a chain. They may sell any of the kinds of merchandise normally sold at retail. Examples of typical independent retailers are small dry goods stores, small variety stores (not a Woolworth or Kresge), and specialty stores (those selling a broad selection of one kind of good—such as millinery, lingerie, and bakery products).

Large-scale retailers   The second group of retail outlets is comprised of the large-scale retailers. These firms may be independently operated, and frequently they are chain operations. The main distinction between the large-scale retailer and the independent retailer is size and volume of sales. There are three primary types of large-scale retailers:

1. *Supermarkets.*   Primarily food stores, supermarkets carry a wide assortment of household goods, drugs, hardware, and such. Typically, they are self-service, depend on high volume of sales, and stress low prices.
2. *Department stores.*   These stores carry a number of different lines of merchandise, each sold in a separate department. They stress service over price and enjoy the benefits of mass buying and volume sales.
3. *Discount houses.*   These are high-volume department stores that stress low prices, have low markups, and offer little service.

Large-scale retailers may be single-store operations, or they may be a part of a chain. A *chain* is an organization consisting of two or more centrally owned units which handle similar lines of merchandise. Although chains are centrally owned, usually they are not centrally managed. That is, the actual store management occurs at the store itself. Several advantages to chain store operation exist. Most of them have greater buying power and better buying skill. As a consequence, they are able to offer price appeal. In addition, they have advertising advantages. They can experiment in merchandising, and they can spread or distribute risk. All of these features work to give them competitive superiority.

Nonstore retailers   As the words imply, a *nonstore retailer* sells goods at retail but not from a store. Foremost in this group are these three forms of businesses:

1. *The mail-order house.*   Typically, the mail-order house sells by mail through a catalog or other promotional material. Although the two giants in this field (Sears and Montgomery Ward) are exceptions, mail-order houses usually do not sell from stores.
2. *Direct retailing.*   Selling that takes place in the customer's home is direct selling. It uses various techniques such as telephone, door-to-door, party plan, and delivery route. Some of the better known companies that sell direct are Fuller Brush, Avon, and just about all insurance and encyclopedia companies.
3. *Vending machines.*   Machines that dispense goods when coins are inserted sell a wide variety of small goods—candy, cigarettes, combs, and so on. Although these machines may be placed in a store, usually the store sells goods that are quite different.

Changes in retail institutions   This review of retailing institutions would not be complete without some mention of the changes that are taking place. In a nutshell, the changes are described by one word— bigness. Fading from the scene are the small operations, although in certain specialty areas they continue to be strong. But generally it is the big operation that is able to sell at lower prices, to hire the best managers, to advertise more effectively, and to operate more efficiently.

The declining importance of the small, independent store leaves society with an interesting question to answer. It is the question of whether bigness with its resulting economies justifies the sacrifice of the small retailer. Must the doors of private enterprise be opened only to those who can finance a giant organization? And, if we take the side of the small operator, just how can we justify the less efficient operations? These questions are most provocative, to say the least.

Wholesaling institutions

As contrasted with retailing, wholesaling includes all marketing transactions in which the purchaser buys for a profit. By this definition, wholesaling would include all such profit-motivated purchases regardless of whether the goods are purchased for resale in the same form or for use in a manufacturing process.

By this definition, goods bought by business organizations are bought at wholesale. Buy there are exceptions—or purchases that are difficult to classify. How, for example, would the purchase of automobile tires by a manufacturing firm from a retailer be classified? Or how should we classify curtains bought for a business office from a retail fabric shop? For our purposes, such small purchases by businessmen are retail purchases. All the larger ones are wholesale.

A review of the structure of our wholesaling system shows that it is every bit as complex as is our retailing system. It, too, may be approached in many ways. The plan used in the following summary is first to look at the types of wholesalers in our system. Then it examines the

FIGURE 11–4

Percent of total wholesalers type of operation

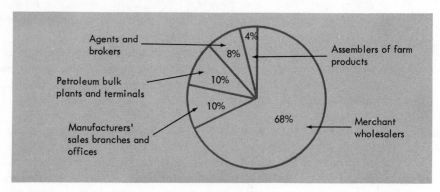

Source: U.S. Bureau of the Census, *Census of Business.*

range of services wholesalers perform. Finally, it discusses a unique type of wholesaler—the functional middleman.

A study of the wholesaling functions reveals that three broad types of organizations perform them: merchant wholesalers, manufacturers' sales branches and offices, and agents and brokers (see Figure 11–4). Two other types are important in terms of numbers and sales—petroleum bulk plants and terminals, and assemblers of farm products. But these two are specialized types dealing in particular products. Thus, this review concentrates on the first three.

Merchant wholesalers   By far the most numerous type of wholesalers are merchant wholesalers. They are wholesalers that buy from manufacturers, farm producers, importers, or other wholesalers. They sell to retailers, institutions, industrial buyers, and even other wholesalers. Typically, they have salespeople who call on their customers. Some of them have their own brands of goods.

Merchant wholesalers may be classified by the services they perform. On this classification basis, two types exist: full-service and limited-service.

1. *Full-service wholesalers* These wholesalers perform all of the principal marketing functions. They buy merchandise on their own account, operate from warehouses and maintain a stock of goods. They also sell through salespeople, extend credit, make deliveries, and assume all the risks normally assumed by businesses. On total, they account for the great bulk of sales volume transacted by all wholesalers. They are traditional middlemen in the sense that they stand between the producer (generally the manufacturer) and the retailer.

Typical of full-service wholesalers are *general merchandise wholesalers*. These are distinctive from other full-service wholesalers because they carry a wide variety of unrelated merchandise lines. These diverse lines might include dry goods, hardware, electrical supplies, sporting equipment, furniture, plumbing and heating equipment, and farm implements. In recent years, the trend has been for general merchandise wholesalers to become general-line wholesalers. General-line wholesalers carry a complete stock of rather closely related product lines. Thus, they can service a particular industry, such as drugstores, grocery stores, or hardware stores. Another full-service middleman is the *specialty wholesaler*. These wholesalers carry only part of a broad, general line. In dry goods, for example, there are specialty wholesalers who carry only shoes, or piece goods, or curtains and draperies, or hosiery and lingerie. Typically, they carry a complete selection.

2. *Limited-service wholesalers* In this group are those wholesalers that perform only some of the functions and services that other wholesalers perform. Typical of these wholesalers are the cash-and-carry wholesalers, rack jobbers, and drop shippers.

The *cash-and-carry wholesalers* sell only for cash and do not deliver the goods. As they offer little service, they are able to offer low prices. Usually these wholesalers are found in the food industry and sell products such as poultry, fruits, and vegetables. They have arisen mostly in response to the independent retailer's desire to remain competitive against the large chain operations. Since cash-and-carry wholesalers perform only limited services, they can sell to retailers on a low-price basis. Because of these wholesalers, independent retailers have managed to remain reasonably competitive.

Rack jobbers supply and service the goods at the point of sale. Typically, rack jobbers operate in supermarkets and deal in fast-moving goods such as housewares, drugs, toiletries, records, and clothing. Their work is to keep their racks in the stores filled with their goods. Rack jobbers receive payment only for the goods actually sold. Thus, they relieve retailers of an inventory and merchandising problem.

The *drop shipper* makes sales for the manufacturer, who ships directly to the customer. The manufacturer bills the drop shipper, who then bills the customer. Thus, the drop shipper does not store or handle the goods.

Such operations usually take place with heavy goods that are expensive to move—such as coal, lumber, and construction materials.

Manufacturers' sales branches and offices   Some manufacturers operate their own wholesale businesses to sell their products. Such branch houses resemble the merchant wholesaler in that they carry a stock of goods, solicit business, and sometimes extend credit. Often these organizations sell the products of other manufacturers in order to be able to offer the customers a complete line of goods. Typically, they sell to other wholesalers, manufacturers, contractors, institutions, and retailers.

Agents and brokers   Agents and brokers differ from other wholesalers in that they do not take title to the goods. Rather, they negotiate purchases and sales between buyers and sellers. They are paid on a fee or commission basis, and they may represent one *or more* buyers or sellers. Sometimes they work for a group of clients. And generally they specialize according to kind of goods. For example, there are sugar brokers, fruit brokers, vegetable brokers, and livestock brokers.

CONTRIBUTIONS AND CRITICISMS

Of all the business areas, probably marketing is the most criticized. The arguments against it are varied and many. As they are vital to your appreciation of this field, the major ones are discussed next. First, presented is the basic question of marketing's contribution. Next comes an examination of some of the criticisms leveled at marketing. Foremost among these is cost, and it is discussed first. Then come the remaining major ones. As most of these matters are controversial, this review will cover all major viewpoints. Hopefully, you will be able to form your own opinions from the information presented.

Contributions of marketing

In appraising the contributions of marketing, it is appropriate to examine the four primary benefits claimed by marketing proponents. They are that marketing (1) adds value to goods and services, (2) provides utilities, (3) performs necessary functions, and (4) has a social value.

Adds value   Perhaps the best way of measuring the contributions of marketing is by determining the value the marketing function adds to the goods (see Figure 11–5). In order to understand the concept of "value added," picture mentally the flow of goods and resources through the process of production in a manufacturing plant. Each good and resource has an individual price; and the total of these individual prices makes up the cost of the item produced. The total cost, however, is somewhat lower than the value of the finished product. This difference is the "value

FIGURE 11–5

Concept of value added by the marketing process

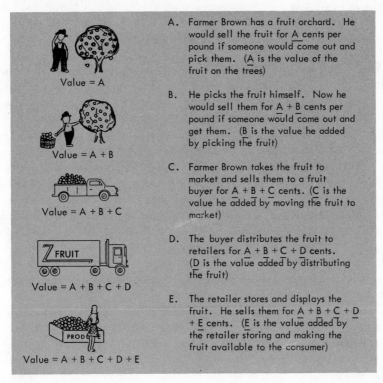

Value = A

Value = A + B

Value = A + B + C

FRUIT

Value = A + B + C + D

PRODUCE

Value = A + B + C + D + E

A. Farmer Brown has a fruit orchard. He would sell the fruit for A cents per pound if someone would come out and pick them. (A is the value of the fruit on the trees)

B. He picks the fruit himself. Now he would sell them for A + B cents per pound if someone would come out and get them. (B is the value he added by picking the fruit)

C. Farmer Brown takes the fruit to market and sells them to a fruit buyer for A + B + C cents. (C is the value he added by moving the fruit to market)

D. The buyer distributes the fruit to retailers for A + B + C + D cents. (D is the value added by distributing the fruit)

E. The retailer stores and displays the fruit. He sells them for A + B + C + D + E cents. (E is the value added by the retailer storing and making the fruit available to the consumer)

added." In other words, *value added* is the difference between the total of costs of all goods and services going into a product and the value of the finished product.

It is easy to see the value added in the manufacturing process. A piece of finished steel, for example, certainly is worth much more than the ore, alloys, heat, and so on, that produced it. It may be more difficult to see how the marketing process can add value in the same way. But it most certainly does; and it is a significant addition.

On the average, the value added by the marketing process amounts to around 40 percent of the final retail price. The percentage varies widely by type of good. For groceries, it is relatively low—around 20 to 22 percent. With department store merchandise, it may run to 40 percent For jewelry items, the percentage often exceeds 50. These percentages, of course, do not represent the payment to just a single marketer. Rather, the payment is shared by all who handle the goods in its route from the manufacturer to the consumer.

Creates utility Another distinctly different way to view marketing's contribution is in terms of the utility that it creates. *Utility* in this particular sense is a term borrowed from economics. It means the capacity of a good or service to satisfy a human want or need. If a given product will satisfy a human want, then that good is said to have so much utility.

One type of utility commonly known is *form utility*. Form utility arises out of the transformation of resources from unusable to increasingly satisfying states. For example, think of a can opener. Does not the utility of a can opener arise out of its transformation from a hunk of metal into an operating tool? And for which would you pay the most—the raw material or the can opener?

Usually we associate utility with manufacturing—not with marketing. Marketing, however, does create other forms of utility. One of these is *time utility*. Or, specifically, marketers make goods available when people need them. Another utility created by marketing is *place utility*. Marketing's major aim is to see that goods are sent where they are needed. Still another is *possession utility*. This utility arises from the fact that transfer of title must take place before a business firm can sell goods to consumers. Marketing creates possession utility by getting the goods into the hands of merchants and consumers.

Time, place, and possession utilities normally occur in sequence. And each adds value to the goods involved. That is, getting goods to their proper place adds some utility. Getting them there when they are needed adds more utility. Finally, putting goods into the hands of retailers adds even more utility. The greater the number of places a good must be sent, the longer the period of time the good must be stored, and the greater the distance the good must travel, the greater will be the utility of the good.

Performs necessary functions Yet another way of assessing the contributions of marketing is to consider the functions performed. As was noted earlier, certain activities take place in marketing. The proponents of marketing point out that these activities are vital—that they must take place in getting the goods from producer to consumer. Goods must be bought and sold. They must be transported. From time to time they must be stored. Risks must be borne. In our economy, all these functions are necessary ingredients. We may improve them, we may alter them, but we cannot eliminate them.

Has a social value A final way to assess marketing's contributions is in terms of its social value. As has been noted, marketing activities are intended to satisfy the needs of customers. By satisfying individuals, marketing thus has a positive effect on the economic well-being of the nation. Just how much marketing contributes to the well-being of us all hinges on the answers to two questions: How much does it satisfy customer needs? and How much of a positive influence does it have on the market?

Certainly the answer to the first question is strongly positive. The U.S. market today is characterized by an abundance unknown anywhere else in the world. While it is somewhat inexact to measure the satisfaction of customer needs by the abundance of goods and services alone, abundance clearly is an outgrowth of marketing's efforts to satisfy these needs.

The answer to the second question is not so clear. Whether our marketing system is the most economically efficient way of satisfying customer needs is debated by critics and advocates. Social value will occur only if the total marketing effort is at least equaled by the satisfaction it produces. Whether or not it is in our marketing system is up to each of us to decide.

In summary, we have seen that marketing provides for "value added" to products in their movement from the producer to the consumer. This value added occurs through the time, place, and possession utility resulting from marketing activities. Marketing provides product utility through the performances of functions; and these functions are a necessary part of our economic system. Finally, marketing contributes to the well-being of society to the extent that it satisfies customer needs on an economically sound basis.

Criticisms of marketing

From time to time in the preceding discussion of marketing it was noted that the field has its critics and that it is vulnerable to criticism. So numerous and involved are these criticisms that limited space permits covering them only in summary fashion. Thus the plan is to cover only the major points and to mention only the key arguments for each.

High cost The most often stated charge against marketing is that it costs too much. In appraising this charge, one needs to look objectively at just how high marketing costs really are and whether these costs are justified.

Looking at how high the costs are is somewhat complicated by the fact that one can view costs in a number of ways. If we look at cost in terms of the final price of goods produced in our economy, we find that marketing makes up about 50 percent of it. If we look at the cost of each function, we have another viewpoint. We find, for example, that selling makes up from 5 to 10 percent of the total value of goods and services and that advertising accounts for 3 to 5 percent. Looking at marketing costs on a product basis, we find a wide range. With meat products, for example, 25 percent of total cost goes to the retailer, 4 percent to the wholesaler, and 5 percent to the manufacturer. Viewing costs by institution shows that overall, manufacturing accounts for 25 percent of the final price, wholesaling 30 percent, and retailing 45 percent.

Whether these costs are justified is a matter for debate. As noted earlier, marketers argue that the costs are justified. They argue that marketing truly adds value to the product—that marketers perform a very necessary function. The argument is a complex one. As the final answer is based on how one thinks about the matter, you will have to form your own conclusion. Perhaps the most defensible viewpoint is that marketing does make a vital contribution but that its costs could be reduced.

Improper allocation of resources One major criticism of marketing is that the allocation of resources to marketing functions actually reduces consumer welfare. Here the argument goes that too much of the economy's wealth is given to marketing. The economy would be better off, the critics say, if its scarce resources were allocated to producing goods, not marketing them. As noted earlier, the critics who take this approach often seize on advertising as a prime example of economic waste. While they admit that the customer needs to be informed about a product, they hold that all noninformational content in advertising is wasteful—that it uses money, labor, and time without contributing to the economic well-being of society.

Inefficiency The critics of marketing attribute some of the cost of marketing to inefficiency in the system. Specifically, they say that in our marketing system, too much repetition occurs—that the buying and selling functions may be performed several times for a single product. And each seller adds something to the price the consumer must pay. Merely by reducing the number of middlemen, they argue, product cost would be lowered.

There is some truth to the argument. From time to time in past years marketers have eliminated some middlemen. In doing so, they passed on savings to the consumer; and they kept some of the savings as profits for themselves. It is with this last point that the critics' arguments are best answered. The profit motive encourages marketers to improve the system—to eliminate some of their members if practical. Thus, in time marketers will find additional places where needless middlemen operate. They will bypass them, just as they have done in the past. They will do so because they will profit from it. In other words, because our competitive marketing system rewards those who can improve the efficiency of the system, we can expect improvement when it is needed.

Social irresponsibility This defense gives rise to another criticism of marketing organizations. It is that since marketing organizations are moved mainly by the profit motive, they are not likely to be socially responsible. Marketing organizations, they argue, must serve not only private but also public interests. They say, for example, that petroleum marketers over the years were concerned primarily with selling and that they gave little or no thought to the long-run national interests. As a result of these irresponsible actions, they point out, the nation suddenly found itself in a serious energy problem.

Another illustration often used to support the social irresponsibility argument is that of how marketers ignore the plight of the poor. The critics point to the fact that typically goods are sold at a higher price and in poor neighborhoods than in rich neighborhoods. They acknowledge the explanation—that frequently rents are higher in downtown poor areas than in the suburbs, that pilferage is higher among poor customers, that poor people buy in smaller quantities. But the results, they say, are unfair. Poor people usually must pay more for their goods. In defense, marketing defenders are likely to point to the taxes they pay from their profits and to the public welfare programs their taxes support.

Unfair Yet another criticism is that our marketing system is unfair. It neither treats it members nor its customers with equal standards. The critics point to many examples in support of this claim. They point out that the system, through its laws, forbids the marketing of some morally or physically dangerous products—for example, marijuana, pornographic materials, and fireworks. But it permits the marketing of some other dangerous products (automobiles, liquor, motorcycles, guns, and such). They point out also that the system gives advantages to the big and the strong. It delivers goods to the big buyers (those most able to pay) at prices below those little buyers must pay. It permits the big marketers to have the best advertising, the best management, and the best facilities. As a result, the big marketers frequently outperform the small ones and drive them out of business.

Dishonest Perhaps the most often heard criticism of marketing is that it is not honest. Certainly no one claims that every marketer or that all of marketing is thoroughly dishonest. But the critics argue that some degree of dishonesty generally is accepted in the marketing system and that the effects are bad.

Most often these criticisms center on the promotional efforts of marketers. Marketers, the critics argue, stray from the truth in promoting their products. Puffery (exaggerated claims) is the rule rather than the exception. They cite literally thousands of examples to support this claim. For one, virtually all makers of aspirin products claim unqualified superiority for their product. In fact, one of them (Sterling) was charged by the Federal Trade Commission with making inconsistent claims for its Bayer aspirin on the one hand and its Cope and Vanquish on the other.[2] The best scientists seriously question the validity of all such claims.

Summary evaluations Evaluation of the arguments of the critics to

---

[2] "FTC Assails Ads for Aspirin Products," *The Wall Street Journal,* April 20, 1972, p. 1.

this point shows that there is some truth to their charges. Marketing does add to the price of a product. It does promote a standard for people to live by. And sometimes it is guilty of the other faults criticized. It appears, however, that the most meaningful measure of the value of our marketing system is how good a standard of living it delivers as a whole. Or, in short, what is the quality of the need satisfiers and want satisfiers marketing creates and delivers to the nation's consumers? The answer appears to be a most positive one. And while some products are marketed that eventually fail (recall the Edsel, packaged cereal with dehydrated fruit, the midi skirt, and the three-D motion picture), there are others that last a long time. If the role of business is indeed to serve customers through satisfying their needs and wants, then the cost of providing those services and satisfactions to consumers cannot be excessive, since they are what consumers demand.

DISCUSSION QUESTIONS

1   Explain the two approaches to defining marketing.
2   Should salespeople be eliminated or reduced in some areas of business?
3   From your personal observations, explain why our physical distribution system is less vulnerable to criticism than the other areas of marketing.
4   Are easy credit terms good for business? For consumers? For the nation?
5   Is the trend toward bigness in retailing good for us all?
6   Select three distinctly different wholesale businesses in the community and classify them by the types discussed in the text.
7   Which of the arguments in support of marketing are most vulnerable? Which are the most valid? Defend your choices.
8   Give your viewpoint of the validity of each of the major criticisms of marketing.
9   What would you recommend as the most important one step toward improving our marketing system?

MINI CASES

Pepe Cardona is a very bright young lad who lives in a remote area in equatorial South America. Pepe works very hard at his studies at the local state school. But because his family is poor, he spends most of his time wading through nearby streams with a dip net catching small tropical fish. These he sells to a tropical fish buyer who comes through weekly. Depending on the size and variety, Pepe gets the equivalent of ½ to 1 cent for each fish.

Although Pepe doesn't understand the fish marketing business, he has heard that the fish are shipped mainly to the United States where people buy them and put them in glass containers. Pepe doesn't quite understand why anyone would want to keep fish in a bowl, but he is glad that they do. He and his family like the money.

Because he is a bright boy, Pepe was singled out of his class to go to the United States on a very special scholarship. Soon after his arrival in the States, he was walking through one of local pet shops where he saw a glass tank displaying tropical fish. They were fish just like those he had caught back home. The sight of these familiar creatures pleased Pepe. His happiness quickly turned to anger, however, when he read the price tags on the tank: "79 cents each."

   1. *Is Pepe justified in his anger?*
   2. *How would a marketing man explain what has happened?*
   3. *Discuss the ethics involved. Make any suggestions for improvement that appear to be practical.*

After ten years of diligent service with East-Beeson Advertising Agency, Caroline Bundy advanced to the position of account executive. As her first assignment, she was given the account of Gann Laboratories, Inc. Gann's major product is a patent medicine for the common cold known as No-Kold. Although the company and its product have existed for 89 years, it had never been among the leaders in its field. No-Kold ranked last among the four smiliar products on the market.

The advertising campaign Caroline developed for No-Kold was built around testimonials of satisfied users. Each person in the ads testified that he or she had tried all the competing products but got relief only from No-Kold. The people used in the advertisements were solicited and were paid by the agency.

From the beginning, the advertisements were successful, and No-Kold's sales moved up sharply. Within a year, the product ranked second among its competition and continued to gain. The Gann executives were elated, and so were the stockholders. And so were Caroline and her agency.

To celebrate the success of the advertising campaign, Caroline's boss held a party. At the party, Caroline was talking to a medical doctor friend who questioned her about her work. "So you got a few million people to use No-Kold, did you?" he said. "Well, it won't hurt them. But there's no scientific proof that No-Kold will help to cure a cold. And that goes for No-Kold's three competitors, too. They all have the same basic ingredients as No-Kold."

1. *What would you say in response if you were Caroline?*
2. *Evaluate the effects of the No-Kold advertising.*
3. *What should be done to ensure truth in advertising?*

For some time now Daniel Harper has been complaining about high prices. Especially has he been critical of the share of each purchase dollar going to the middleman. So fed up is he that now he has decided to do something about it.

A few days ago Daniel called a meeting of his neighbors and friends. Today 50 of them showed up at his house. Dan started off with his often-voiced criticism of our marketing system. He cited all forms of statistics proving its inefficiency and pointed to businesspeople as the villians in the situation. Then he got down to business and explained his proposed solution.

"What we've got to do," he explained, "is to get around the middlemen. That's where the high cost really is. We can do it by forming a buying co-op. We'll operate just like a store. We'll buy from the manufacturers when that's possible—from wholesalers at other times. We can buy most anything—tires, lawn mowers, fishing gear, boats, clothes. And we'll pass the savings on to you. We'll need a little space to store things; and we'll need someone to work for us to make the purchases, take the money, and so on."

Daniel explained many other details of his plans, and soon most of those present were willing to sign up and pay the $50 initiation fee needed to get the co-op going. Before anyone signed up, Warren Huddleston, professor of marketing at the local university, broke into the discussion with these words: "Perhaps you have good cause to be upset. But I wonder whether you have thought this thing out. . . ."

1. *Complete the professor's comments.*
2. *Evaluate this proposal from a national point of view.*

James Cash Penney was indeed unique, resembling more a character from the Main Street era than a merchant prince of the 1970s. A chain of some 1,670 stores bearing his name ranks as the fifth largest merchandising company in the nation. Active into his nineties, Penney never veered from the Golden Rule philosophy instilled in him as a youth.

One of 12 children, J. C. Penney began earning clothes money at the age of eight. The son of a Baptist farmer-minister, young James worked hard on his father's Missouri farm. Life was stern for him, but it provided him with the credo which underlay his great success.

After failing in his first business venture (a butcher shop), Penney worked his way into a one-third partnership in the Golden Rule Store in Kemmerer, Wyoming. Here he introduced a new retailing strategy—strictly cash, low price, low markup, and volume sales. His strategy worked. Through hard work, saving, and sacrifice, Penney was able to open more stores. In 1913, when Penney changed his organization's name to the J. C. Penney Stores, he had 48 locations.

J. C. Penney's revolutionary approach to marketing extended to his employees. From the outset, employees were considered and referred to as associates, and they were permitted to participate in profits. Today, each manager still enjoys the autonomy of a partner.

By the 1920s, the J. C. Penney Company was one of the largest retail organizations. But the 1921 crash brought disaster. Penney lost all his stock. A broken man at 56, Penney entered a Michigan sanitarium. Inspired by the verse of Matthew 11:28, Penney fought back. With borrowed funds, he regained a part of the company. Before long he was again chairman of the board, where he remained until 1958. Under J. C. Penney's direction, the company again prospered, blanketing the nation with its outlets.

James Cash Penney
(1875–1970)

The Golden Rule marketer

12

Marketing management

This company's success is due to the application of the Golden Rule to every individual, the public, and to all our activities.

——*J. C. Penney*

As explained in the preceding chapter, marketing consists of institutions performing the functions involved in getting goods and services to consumers. It is a most complex activity, involving countless people doing countless tasks. As with most complex business activities, the tasks should be planned and executed carefully. That is, they should be managed. This vital area of managing marketing is the next topic for review.

The approach to marketing management used in this chapter places the consumer in the center of things. Instead of the product-oriented approach generally followed by marketers of past years, this modern approach views the marketing situation differently. It views marketing not merely as a means of moving products. Rather, it recognizes the fact that marketing can be successful only if it satisfies consumers' wants and needs. Thus, the entire marketing effort should be planned with consumers and their wants and needs in mind.

With this concept of marketing in mind, marketing managers carry out their work. Like managers of other business activities, they follow the procedures described in our review of management. They carefully develop plans for their work. They use their skills in carrying out their plans. And they exercise controls to make certain that their actions accomplish what they planned to do.

Specifically, marketing managers' activities are concerned with two broad problems. First is the matter of determining the target market. Second is the matter of developing the marketing mix. In the following pages, these two somewhat technical terms are defined and discussed. Also, the procedures marketing authorities recommend for them are described.

DETERMINING THE TARGET MARKET

Determining the target market means finding out who are the people likely to buy a product. Or, in terms of the marketing executive's planning, it means defining the market to which the company should direct its marketing efforts. It should be apparent that the company should not direct its marketing efforts to all customers. Such efforts would be

FIGURE 12–1

Determining the product market

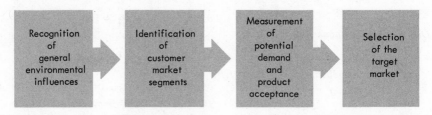

wasteful and ineffective. Instead the company should find out who are its most likely buyers; and it should tailor its efforts for this one group.

In determining the target market, marketers consider all the important information which helps to determine who will buy the product. If they do this job thoroughly, their work follows four logical steps (see Figure 12–1). First, they consider the general environmental influences on customers. Second, from the information collected in the preceding step, they identify and locate potential customers. Third, working with the preceding information, they measure the product's acceptance and potential demand. Finally, from all this information, they determine the target market. A more detailed discussion of this procedure follows.

General environmental influences on target market

The environment in which goods and services are marketed is mainly an environment of people. Obviously, it is people who buy goods and services. Thus, determining environmental influences involves finding information about people. More specifically, it involves finding the information that indicates who are likely to be customers for a product or service. It involves finding such information as who the potential customers are, where they are, what are their attitudes, what are their characteristics, and the like. Using such information, marketers are likely to make good decisions.

In reviewing environmental influences, any number of classification schemes could be used. The one selected for use in the following pages is simple. It covers information about consumers in these categories: population growth, mobility, demographic factors, social factors, and geographic factors.

Population

Although most markets make up only a part of the population, changes in the total are of concern to all marketing managers. Probably you know that the United States has experienced a population explosion in recent decades. As shown in Figure 12–2, the U.S. population increased from 123 million in 1930 to 203 million in 1970. The Bureau of the Census estimate for 1974 was over 212 million.

Just how much more our population will grow in the years ahead is a difficult question to answer. Bureau of the Census experts now project the U.S. total for the year 2000 at 266 million. Only a few years ago (in 1967) their projection was for 360 million—almost 100 million more. This sharp difference is largely a result of the current social movement to

FIGURE 12–2

U.S. population, 1930–70

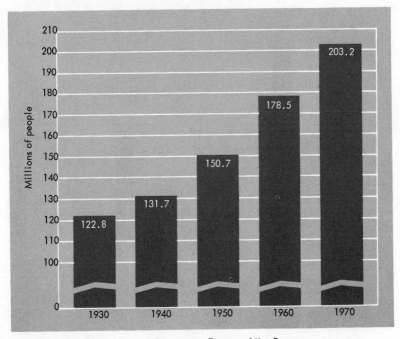

Source: U.S. Department of Commerce, Bureau of the Census.

FIGURE 12–3

Population, 1970,* and percent change, 1960–1970, by region and by state

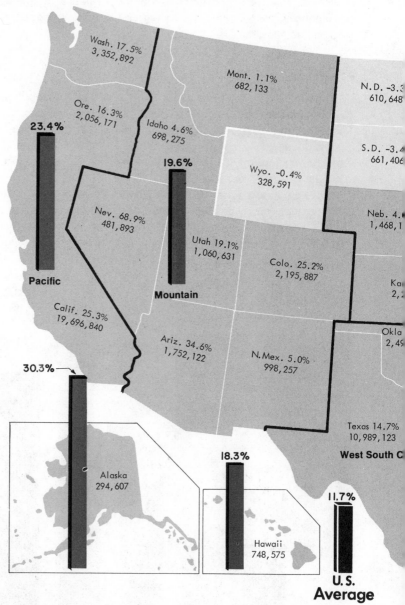

Wash. 17.5%
3,352,892

Mont. 1.1%
682,133

N.D. -3.3
610,648

Ore. 16.3%
2,056,171

Idaho 4.6%
698,275

S.D. -3.4
661,406

23.4%

19.6%

Wyo. -0.4%
328,591

Neb. 4.
1,468,1

Nev. 68.9%
481,893

Utah 19.1%
1,060,631

Colo. 25.2%
2,195,887

Ka
2,

Pacific

Mountain

Okla
2,49

Calif. 25.3%
19,696,840

Ariz. 34.6%
1,752,122

N. Mex. 5.0%
998,257

30.3%

Texas 14.7%
10,989,123

Alaska
294,607

18.3%

West South C

11.7%

Hawaii
748,575

U.S.
Average

* Based on preliminary 1970 census data.
Source: National Industrial Conference Board.

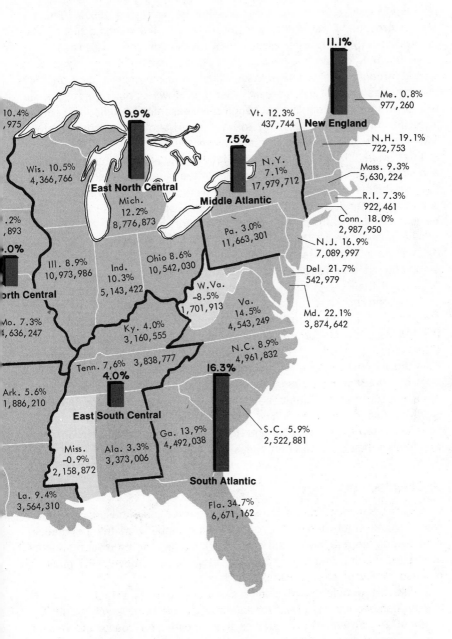

11.1%

Me. 0.8%
977,260

Vt. 12.3%
437,744   **New England**

N.H. 19.1%
722,753

10.4%
,975

9.9%

Wis. 10.5%
4,366,766

East North Central

7.5%

N.Y.
7.1%
17,979,712

Middle Atlantic

Mass. 9.3%
5,630,224

R.I. 7.3%
922,461

Conn. 18.0%
2,987,950

.2%
,893

Mich.
12.2%
8,776,873

Pa. 3.0%
11,663,301

N.J. 16.9%
7,089,997

.0%

Ill. 8.9%
10,973,986

Ind.
10.3%
5,143,422

Ohio 8.6%
10,542,030

W.Va.
-8.5%
1,701,913

Del. 21.7%
542,979

orth Central

Va.
14.5%
4,543,249

Md. 22.1%
3,874,642

Mo. 7.3%
4,636,247

Ky. 4.0%
3,160,555

N.C. 8.9%
4,961,832

Ark. 5.6%
1,886,210

Tenn. 7,6%   3,838,777

4.0%

16.3%

S.C. 5.9%
2,522,881

East South Central

Ga. 13,9%
4,492,038

Miss.
-0.9%
2,158,872

Ala. 3.3%
3,373,006

South Atlantic

La. 9.4%
3,564,310

Fla. 34.7%
6,671,162

reduce the birthrate. Clearly, this movement is having its effect. The 1973 population gain was only 1.5 million—lowest since the 1930s. And the rate of growth, 15 per 1,000, was the lowest in the nation's history. So low was the 1973 birthrate, in fact, that it fell below the death rate.[1]

. As you may know, the movement to limit population has been supported strongly by environmentalists. The world has only a fixed quantity of resources, they argue; and we must hold down population so that we will have enough to survive. Although this reasoning is difficult to refute, a stabilizing population is likely to have some bad effects on marketers. Two possible explanations support these fears.

First, a stabilizing population will tend to stabilize demand for goods and services. In past years, as more and more people entered the population, marketers enjoyed a situation of having more and more demand to satisfy. In general, they prospered. Obviously, such periods of expanding need are filled with profit opportunities for marketers. A stabilizing population will mean that there will not be the great numbers of additional people with needs to satisfy. The effect of this condition on marketing appears to be negative. Even so, manufacturers in the past have used their ingenuity to overcome such problems.

A second possible negative effect of declining population growth concerns the changing proportions of income groups. So far, much of the decline in population growth has come from the educated and professional classes—those of higher incomes. The result is fewer children from the parents in high- and middle-income classes, and more children from the low-income classes. As a result, marketers may need to plan more for the less profitable needs of the poor and less for the more profitable needs of the rich. Although these effects forecast gloom, hopefully marketers will respond to the challenge and overcome the problem as they have so many times in the past.

Mobility factors

Another statistical dimension which marketers may find useful in their work is that which shows the geographical mobility of the population. Where people are located most certainly has a bearing on what marketers must supply them. And any changing pattern in their movements must be planned for by efficient business leaders.

Unlike the population of most other lands, ours is a mobile one. At least, it has become mobile in recent times. In each year since World War II, about 20 percent of our families have moved. As you would expect, this movement has resulted in some rather significant population shifts (Figure 12–3). The Pacific Coast states, especially California, have re-

---

[1] "The Lower Birthrate Crimps the Baby Food Market," *Business Week*, July 13, 1974, p. 45.

corded heavy population increases. So have the Gulf Coast states—especially Florida. Although its numbers have not been so staggering, certain areas of the Rocky Mountain states have recorded very significant percentage increases. Even so, the Middle Atlantic and East North Central areas remain heavily populated.

The effects of such population shifts have significant meaning to the marketer. For one thing, people who move are likely to have expenditure patterns different from other people. There is, of course, moving expense. And according to research findings on the matter, people who move are likely to spend 50 percent more than nonmovers on items such as new homes, mobile homes, furniture, appliances, and miscellaneous home furnishings. Another effect of mobility has been the growth of urban centers. Now about four of every five consumers live in urban markets, and one in five lives in nonurban or rural areas. In 1880, the situation was practically reversed. Then the farm population exceeded 70 percent. As the needs of a city dweller are quite different from the needs of those in a rural area, the effects on business are apparent.

Demographic factors

Various demographic factors help marketers to find their potential customers. Primary among these are education, income, age, sex, marital status, and occupation.

Education   Education clearly is linked with consumer income and thus provides an index of purchasing power. Also, the level of education gives some indication of consumer sophistication. That is, it tells us something about the needs and wants of potential customers.

Compared with people of other lands, Americans are well educated. As you know, elementary education practically is universal; and a high school education is pursued by more and more of our population. As is reflected in Figure 12–4, even college study has become somewhat commonplace. To marketers, the changing educational level of the American consumer has significant implications. They must realize that buyers have become better informed and more sophisticated over the years. They now must adapt their strategy to a better educated consumer.

Income   Without question, income is the major limiting factor in a market. Demand, of course, must be present. But demand does not become effective until there is income, or the power to command credit. Thus, the marketer continually should be informed of the relevant income and debt data.

In examining income as a measure of a market, the marketer may use a number of forms of data. Two in particular stand out. One is gross national product, which is the annual total value of the goods and services produced in a nation. The other is disposable personal income. This

FIGURE 12–4

Number of college graduates in one year, 1930–70

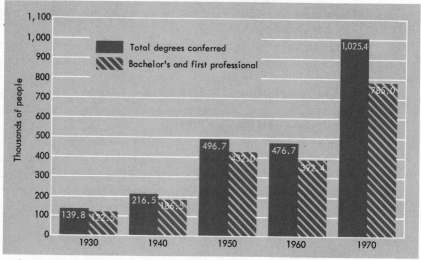

Source: *Digest of Educational Statistics, 1970.*

series is the total annual income available for spending by a nation's people. That is, it is the income received from wages, salaries, private business, farming, investments, social security, rent, and so on, less all federal, state, and local taxes. In examining these figures, we should keep in mind that they are dollars: and as we all know, the value of the dollar has dropped greatly over the years. In fact, it now takes an income of about $15,000 to do what one of $5,000 would have done in 1930. Even so, the data indicate interesting growth patterns to the marketer.

An examination of gross national product (Figure 12–5) reveals that the nation has enjoyed almost continuous prosperity over the years. From levels well under $100 billion in the 1930s, GNP passed the trillion dollar level in the early 1970s. Likewise, disposable personal income accelerated throughout this period. In 1930, the nation's families took in $74.5 billion available for spending. In 1974 they had $967 billion. Of course, these figures exaggerate the differences somewhat because of the high rate of inflation which has taken place. Even so, we have enjoyed great prosperity.

Such increases in income have significant implications for marketing managers. Generally, when a family's income increases above a certain amount, the family spends proportionately less for basic necessities— food, shelter, medical care, and the like. Thus, they have more money available for other things. This extra money, called *discretionary buying*

FIGURE 12–5

Annual gross national product, 1930–74

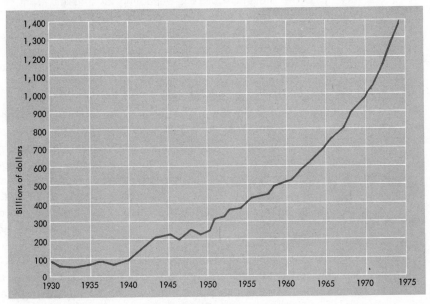

Source: U.S. Department of Commerce, Bureau of the Census.

power, usually is spent on things that consumers want most. With discretionary income people buy vacations, boats, jewelry, fishing equipment, and so on. One of the drawbacks for marketing, however, is that people become much less predictable in what they will purchase with discretionary income. If a person must spend most of his income on basic necessities, then we can well predict what the purchases might be. But discretionary purchasing often is random, unpredictable, and subject to change.

Other demographics Similarly, age, sex, marital status, and occupation influence preferences for products. For example, mothers clearly are the primary buyers of baby food. Men buy hunting and fishing equipment far more than do women. Families with school age children form the base for the encyclopedia market. And mature ladies are the principal purchasers of knitting needles. In like manner, occupation has its influence. The work we do helps to determine our life-styles. And our styles of life determine our product needs.

Social factors

Perhaps the greatest changes in marketing today are attributable to the social forces working in our society. Thus, the marketing manager would be wise to keep abreast of all data pertaining to such changes. As we know from our personal observations, our society is changing before our very eyes. The present society is becoming far different from society of the past; and our future society promises to be far more different.

Social changes The most dramatic of the social changes taking place today is that in the status of women. Time was when a social barrier existed against women working. But this barrier has been broken. Today, the work force contains some 35 million women. In 1950, the number of women working was slightly over 18 million.

In addition to breaking the work barriers, women have broken the social mores binding them to the home. Joining those millions who leave the home to work, millions of other women are spending more and more time away from home. The major explanation, of course, is that modern conveniences have freed the woman from her home duties. With automatic washing machines, vacuum cleaners, dishwashers, ready-made clothing, prepared foods, and so on, to help her do her chores, she now has more time for other activities. Many of these other activities involve goods which marketers must provide.

Among the more significant effects of the changing status of women has been the revolution in the pattern of retail shopping. Time was when the homemaker considered shopping to be a leisurely activity—a pleasant change from household duties. Today, the homemaker tends to look upon shopping as a chore. She prefers to make fewer trips, and she wants to shop on her own terms. She prefers speed and convenience. If she works, she prefers evening hours for shopping. She wants readily available parking space, and she wants quick service. Retailers have had to adjust to these preferences or get out of business.

A social change that is affecting marketing is the general attitude toward leisure time. The old Puritan ethic that idle hands make mischief is crumbling. In its place is a new attitude—an attitude that embraces active leisure as opposed to just doing nothing. Rising incomes have made it possible for people to spend less and less time in work and more and more time enjoying leisure. As a result, people have become active consumers for all of the goods and services that their increased leisure calls for (vacation homes, skiing vacations, boats, stereo equipment, and so on).

Another social change which has had a pronounced effect on marketing is the consumer attitude toward debt. Only a couple of generations ago, debt was something to be ashamed of in the minds of many. There was great pride to be taken in paying cash, and consumers typically saved for long periods for major purchases. Since the Great Depression, however, there has been less and less stigma associated with credit buying. Perhaps during this tragic period people learned that credit buying was not so bad after all. And perhaps so many were doing it that the stigma of credit buying faded away. Whatever the explanation, credit buying has become a way of life for many Americans, including many who could pay cash but prefer credit.

Social group influences Among the influences most likely to affect a person's interest in a product or service are the social groups to which that person belongs. All people belong to a number of such groups—a family, a church, a lodge, a profession, an age category, an economic class, an educational level, a street gang, and so on. And all people are influenced by the groups to which they belong. A person's family, for example, can exert strong influence on product preferences. One reared in a family which placed high value on reading is a more likely consumer of magazines than one from a family of nonreaders. Similarly, one from a nonsmoking family would be likely to have some resistance to smoking.

Since all people belong to many social groups, sometimes the group influences work against each other. The effect could be a mixed-up or neutral attitude toward a product. Or it could be that one influence will stand out well beyond all others. To illustrate, a young man may feel pressure from one group, say, his family, to wear conservative clothing. He may also feel a contradictory influence from his peer groups (classmates, team members, circle of friends, and others) to wear mod clothes. The stronger of the influences would likely determine the clothing he wears.

There is no shortage of illustration for the effects of group memberships on product preferences. From your own experience you know that various groups of people establish codes of dress and appearance. Those who care to belong to the group are likely to conform. Those who do not want to belong, take care to avoid such dress. Members of some street gangs, for example, have a unique manner of dress. Those who belong, conform to it. Most outsiders shy away from these styles lest they be identified as group members.

One of the strongest group influences is the economic class to which one belongs. Traditionally, upper class members display their wealth with big homes, well-kept lawns, and long limousines. The middle class are more inclined to place a premium on education and travel. They tend to be concerned with quality, with time- and work-saving devices, and with security. Members of the lower class, in spite of their needs for the necessities of life, tend to divert some of their limited income to purchase items such as automobiles and flashy clothing. Certainly the knowledge of such influences as these is essential to the marketer who seeks to identify potential customers.

Geographic influences Marketers working to identify their potential customers will also consider the effects of geographic influences. Some products by their very nature are limited to certain geographic areas. Boats, motors, fishing gear, and the like, are natural products for areas where water abounds—not so good for desert areas. Snow skiing equipment is more appropriate for the Rocky Mountains than for Florida. Air conditioning finds a ready market in the deep South; it is not so important to consumers in New England. Water softeners obviously are marketable only in those areas where water is hard. And so it is with many other products. Geography is most certainly a factor to consider in a search for a target market.

Identification of customer market segments

In the preceding stage the marketers reviewed the environmental influences which may tell them who could use the product. But it is not often practical to attempt to sell to everyone who merely could use the product. In fact, the multitudes of could-be users may be well beyond the reach of the company's marketing facilities. Thus, marketers need to limit the market to specific segments. They should base their selections of these segments on three considerations: (1) geographic market areas, (2) socioeconomic dimensions, and (3) buying behavior.

Geographic location　A first step in segmenting a market is to find out where are the likely customers. Are they in cities? In rural areas? All over? In what neighborhoods?

In locating their likely customers, marketers are apt to be concerned with the data on the location of households, for the household is the usual buying unit. Fortunately, they can get such data easily. The U.S. Bureau of the Census compiles a wealth of information by households, with breakdowns by demographic characteristics. With such information as this, marketers have something more specific with which to work in their efforts to identify their customers.

Socioeconomic dimensions　In addition to locating households, marketers should know something about them—educational level, income, occupation, and other characteristics. When they considered the general environmental influences (the preceding step), the marketers did some preliminary thinking on the matter. Now they seek to identify these characteristics in the population—to find out who has what characteristics, and where they are. Statistical information on these data also are abundant. With this information, marketers can compile the data that describes the various segments of the market. They can then compare the various segments found and select those most likely to produce customers for the product.

Buyer behavior　Although location and socioeconomic data do much to inform the marketer about which are the best market segments for a product, they do not tell all. The marketer needs to consider certain factors of buyer behavior before arriving at his final decision. The reason should be apparent. People with all the required characteristics do not all behave the same way at the marketplace. Knowing how they behave can be a major factor in determining who is and who is not a part of the market for a product. It can be most helpful, also, in determining just how a product should be promoted and sold. As consumer behavior is a broad field, there is time only for the briefest of reviews here. There is time only to touch on those parts which are most important to the marketer in evaluating a market segment.

In general, consumers vary in their attraction to a product. Some consumers are moved toward a product primarily by rational motives—that is, by motives the thinking mind can justify (economy, durability, productivity). Some are moved by emotional motives. These are motives that appeal to the nonthinking mind (beauty, sweet sounds, taste). And some are moved by a combination of emotional and rational motives. The matter is made even more complex when we consider the fact that the appeals vary also by product.

Such information on buyer behavior is not easy to get. In fact, usually marketers have to get it through their own research—a topic to be discussed later. However they get it, marketers combine this information with the location and socioeconomic data. And with all of these data they identify the segments of the market which appear best for their products.

Determining product demand and acceptance

Another activity involved in determining the target market is to go to the market itself for firsthand information about it. In this step marketers explore such factors as probable demand for a product, product acceptance, and product changes wanted. The main reason that marketers go to the market for firsthand information is to make certain that the information thus obtained will give them a final measure of the ideal target market.

Marketing research Firsthand information such as that discussed here usually is obtained through the company's own research. Called marketing research, this form of business investigation is carried on in connection with the other marketing management work. Many subsidiary research forms are included under the broad term of marketing research. One is called *market analysis,* which consists of the study of size, location, and characteristics of the market. Another is *sales research,* which concerns analysis of sales data. Another is *consumer research,* which is study designed to learn customer preferences, attitudes, and reactions. Yet another is *advertising research,* which, as the term implies, is research designed to assist the firm in its advertising problems.

The methods marketers use to collect the information previously discussed vary widely. Some are relatively simple, such as that of collecting customer comments or gathering information from salespeople. Other methods are much more sophisticated—for example, the use of surveys and market tests. Typically conducted by research specialists, marketing surveys use interviews with customers, dealers, and so on to gather information about product use, consumer attitudes, and the like. Primarily used to gauge product acceptance, the market test may consist of distributing free samples in a limited area and measuring the effects on sales. It may consist of placing a product in selected areas to determine consumer acceptance.

Whatever the technique used, the goal of marketing research is to gather the information marketers need. With this information, marketers are able to make intelligent decisions in every phase of their work. Identifying the market segment for a product is but one phase of marketing in which the results of marketing research are useful.

Selection of the target market

The final phase in the process of determining the target market is that of actual selection. Ideally, in selecting the target market, marketers select those segments in which their companies and their products can compete most effectively. They take into account all the information from all the preceding phases discussed. Typically, their decision process is subjective. They think through all the data they have assembled, apply them to the one case, and make the decision.

The procedure summarized

Reviewing the discussion thus far, it is apparent that marketers follow a thorough and logical procedure in determining the target market for a product. First, they consider the many environmental influences that operate throughout the market. With this knowledge in mind, they narrow their scope to specific customer market segments. They evaluate these segments in terms of their geographical, socioeconomic, and buying behavior aspects. Next, marketers go to the market segments themselves to analyze demand for and acceptance of the product. With these final data and with the additional information gathered through marketing research in mind, they select the market segments most likely to produce results. These segments are the target market for the product.

MANAGERIAL ASPECTS OF THE MARKETING MIX

Much of the work marketers do consists of developing the best possible marketing mix for their firms. By *marketing mix* is meant the four interrelated areas of marketing strategy: product development, product pricing, product channel, and product communication. In making the right decisions concerning these areas, marketers should thoroughly understand the nature of each of them. A summary description of these four areas follows.

Product components of the marketing mix

In making decisions relating to the product part of the mix, marketers should continually give attention to product planning and development. Additionally, they should view their products in a total sense. They should understand supply-demand interactions, and they should be aware of the nature of the product life cycle. Each of these topics is discussed in the pages ahead.

Product planning and development In planning and developing products, marketers should know consumers well—their likes and dislikes, their shopping preferences, their needs, and such. They should work to improve old products and to develop new ones. And they should combine their knowledge of customers and products to develop products that will sell profitably.

At the manufacturing level, product planning and development involves continuing research. There must be a persistent effort to keep abreast of consumer needs and preferences. And there must be continuing effort to adapt old products or create new products to satisfy the consumer. Not to follow this course is likely to lead to obsolescence of existing products. And it can lead to complete rejection of new products. Both results can be disastrous to the manufacturer.

As has been implied, the task of product planning and development should be performed with the consumer in mind. Certainly, this is the viewpoint held by the progressive, modern marketer. We all know, however, that not all marketers subscribe to this viewpoint. We know, also, that the question of what is in the consumer's best interest does not always have a clear and simple answer. In fact, often what consumers want is contrary to their best interests.

To illustrate the point, over the years many manufacturers have followed a policy of planned obsolescence. That is, they have designed each year's new model to make last year's model appear to be out of date (for example, automobiles, clothing, home appliances, and the like). It is difficult to justify this policy on strictly practical grounds—perhaps also on ethical grounds in some cases. But if we look at the manufacturer's side of the question, we see that the case is not so clearly decided.

The manufacturers claim that they are giving the consumers what the consumers want. They argue that consumers receive emotional satisfactions from the model changes—that these satisfactions are as real to consumers as the practical benefits they get from the products. They point out, also, that manufacturers who do not attempt to satisfy the emotional needs of the consumers are likely to fail. In support they can point to a number of actual business examples. Perhaps the most notable of these is the case of the Chrysler Corporation. In the early 1950s, this major manufacturer decided to go against the style trends of the time and to concentrate on such rational matters of design as comfort, durability, and economy. As a result, Chrysler almost lost its corporate shirt.

In recent times, product planners have been confronted with environmental concerns. Unfortunately, their concerns have come late in some instances. One prime example is the experience of the automobile manufacturers. Over the years they planned their products to satisfy their customers' wants. The ultimate result was a gas-guzzling, luxurious, and beautiful product. As we all painfully know, because of the energy crisis automobile manufacturers have taken a new look at consumers' needs. For other examples, the willingness of fashionable women to buy leopard coats has threatened the existence of this beautiful beast. Plastic, glass, and aluminum containers have met consumers' needs for convenience, but they have produced a gigantic litter problem for us. And phosphates in detergents have satisfied homemakers' desires, but they have polluted our waters.

Just what should be the product planners' responsibilities in such matters is one of the more perplexing business problems of our time. They are pressed by consumer demand. Continually they are pressed by competition to improve their product and to innovate. Marketers are pressed by stockholders to make profits. Not to conform to these pressures would be suicidal. Yet the consequences are not always good for society. The problem is one we must all solve in the years ahead.

Another concern in planning products to meet consumers' needs is that of how good should the product be. As was noted in Chapter 9, some products manufactured are not as safe, dependable, or efficient as they should be. Thus, it is inevitable that sometimes we are disappointed in them. Probably in such cases we place the blame on the manufacturers. Were the manufacturers given a chance to defend themselves, however, they might point out that they have made the products that we want— that we consumers would not be willing to pay the additional cost required to produce better products. They could cite a long list of quality product failures to support their argument. Obviously, this question is not one that can be solved easily.

To this point our concern has been with product planning and development in manufacturing businesses. These activities also take place in other forms of business, but in quite different ways. In wholesale and retail businesses, product planning and development is concerned with finding the best possible selections of goods and services to meet the needs of the business' customers. Retail buyers, for example, perform product planning when they select merchandise for their stores. Grocery wholesale companies engage in product planning when they begin cash-and-carry services. And retail stores that broaden their services by adding new lines of merchandise are also planning their products.

Regardless of the marketing level, however, the effect of product planning and development is the same. It gives customers the goods and services they want. By giving customers what they want, marketers get what they want—sales and, hopefully, profits.

Total product concept In making decisions about products, marketers need to think of them in a total sense. This statement means that products are much more than that which we see or feel. They also are satisfactions or services. To illustrate, a washing machine is not only a combination of nuts, bolts, and other assorted parts, it also is a work saver and a clothes cleaner. A cosmetic is not merely a mixture of chemicals, it also is an aid to beauty. A wristwatch is not merely an arrangement of intricate parts, it also is a timekeeper and an object of beauty to satisfy the wearer's aesthetic needs. And so it is with all products.

By viewing products in this total way, marketers are more likely to give consumers what they want. Specifically, they are likely to give attention to matters such as product installation, instructions on care and use, repairs, and service. They are likely to be more concerned with matters of product size, shape, construction, packaging, and performance. In general, they are more likely to do the things necessary to satisfy consumers. Following this course, marketers are apt to prosper, for satisfied customers mean continuing sales and a likelihood of continuing profits.

Interaction of product supply and demand forces In planning their strategy, marketers should also understand the effects of the forces of supply and demand. Probably you already have a general idea of this basic concept of economics. You know generally that the quantity of goods available and the demand for these goods affects the price of the goods. But let us examine this concept more precisely and relate it to marketing strategy.

Each customer has a set of preferences. And each customer has a certain amount of money to use in satisfying these preferences. Customers tend to use their income to get the greatest possible benefit (called *utility* by economists) from the money spent. Now the utility is directly related to the price they must pay. For example, suppose that a customer has rice high on the preference list. If the price of rice increases sufficiently, this customer's preference would shift to other goods. Or, stated another way, other goods now would provide greater utility. Thus, there is a general interaction between the price of a commodity and the quantity of it the customer will buy.

From this concept, the fundamental law of diminishing demand is explained. According to this law of economics, if the price of a commodity rises, customers will purchase less of it (see Figure 12–6). Likewise, if the price of a commodity falls, customers will purchase more of it. In the latter case, the customers get greater utility (or satisfaction) for a lower cost, and thereby maximize their utility. In the former case, rising prices reduce the customer's utility; so customers look elsewhere for satisfaction.

In summary, to marketers the interactions of supply and demand have important implications. For one thing, they suggest that the demand for a

FIGURE 12–6

Illustration of diminishing demand for a hypothetical product as price increases

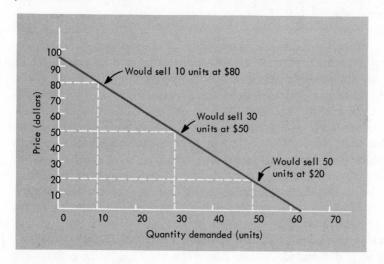

product will be influenced by the price put on the product as well as the prices of competing brands. They also suggest that demand for a product will decline if the product is overpriced.

Product life cycle A product's position in its life cycle also should be considered in developing marketing strategy. For this purpose, the life of a product can be divided into four stages (see Figure 12–7). The marketing strategy needed in each of these stages is somewhat different.

1. The life of a product begins with its introductory stage. During this stage marketers need to work hard and to spend much money on advertising, promoting, and so on to get consumers to accept the product.

2. Next comes the period of market growth. In this stage the competition requires that marketers work to improve their products and to develop new products. This is the time for product variety.

3. The third stage is one of market maturity. Strong competition exists and the market becomes crowded. New firms find it difficult to enter.

FIGURE 12–7

Typical profile of sales and profits for a product through its life cycle

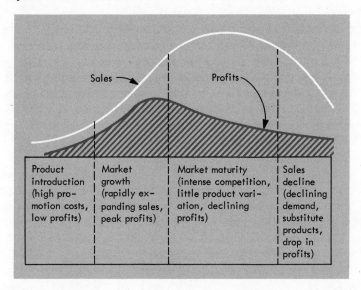

| Product introduction (high promotion costs, low profits) | Market growth (rapidly expanding sales, peak profits) | Market maturity (intense competition, little product variation, declining profits) | Sales decline (declining demand, substitute products, drop in profits) |

Typically, marketers at this stage stress minor differences and advantages of their brands. There is little else to stress for in this stage the products are much alike. Growth and profits slow down.

4. A period of rapid sales decline ends the product life cycle. This is the stage when demand slows down. Perhaps new products now may be substituted for the old ones; or perhaps consumers' needs have changed. Whatever the reason, demand declines. Profits decline until losses set in. It is a time for marketers to be wary.

The price component of the marketing mix

Among the most complex and difficult decisions the marketing executive must make are those concerning product price. Price decisions have not always been viewed in this way. In fact, years ago marketers believed that people bought one product over others primarily on the basis of price. Today the view is somewhat different. Modern-day marketers conclude that the product itself and the promotion the product receives are just as important as product price. They cite three main reasons in support of their viewpoint.

First, in today's mass-production society, supply often exceeds demand. This situation creates excessive competitive pressures and forces producers to use tactics that are not easily imitated. Second, today's customers are more affluent than ever before. Generally, they tend to be more quality conscious than price conscious. Third, it is only through successful selling and promotion that the marketer can achieve any price freedom.

Price can and does play a part in the demand for products; but much depends on the nature of the product. Goods that are very similar in nature will tend to have identical prices. For example, gasoline, toothpaste, cigarettes, and wheat are goods which permit little price flexibility. However, when a manufacturer is able to successfully differentiate his product (either physically or psychologically) he has some freedom to alter his price.

Factors in determining price A variety of factors play a role in determining product prices. Four of these stand out:

1. *Distinctiveness of product* The more distinctive the product is, the more flexible can be its pricing policy. With products that are distinctive (either a new or an unusual product), marketers typically follow one of two courses. Either they price high, so as to "skim the cream." Or they price low in an effort to increase their share of the market.

2. *Promotion* Advertising and developing products cost money. Marketers must set prices to recover these costs.

3. *Choice of distribution* How many and what kinds of wholesalers handle the goods affect the cost of marketing goods. Such expenses clearly must be covered in the prices set.

4. *Cost of production and competition* How much a product costs to manufacture puts a clear bottom level on its price. And how much the competition asks for their products sets a top limit.

Price-making policies In determining product prices, marketers should consider all of the price determination factors as they apply to each product and each situation. In addition, they should consider all the possible pricing policies available to them. They may, for example, need to decide on whether to have one price for all customers or variable prices based on quantities purchased or services rendered. They may need to determine whether there are conventional policies already firmly established in the industry. And they may need to decide on whether to vary costs for faraway places.

In the final analysis, the strategy marketers select in pricing their products depends on the product, the competition, the nature of the market, and the demand for the product. Overriding all of these factors, however, is the necessity of keeping the customers in the forefront. If the price discourages their purchasing, then the loss to the company can be twofold. On the one hand, it loses sales. On the other, it loses the money it has sunk into promotion and advertising for the product. The need for carefully planned pricing is apparent.

The channel component of the marketing mix

Just what channel of distribution to use to get the product to the consumer is another decision area in the marketing mix. A manufacturing company that is near its market is likely to have little concern for a market channel of distribution. It is not likely to need one. Its customers can visit the plant, make their purchases, and carry them home with them. But few manufacturers are so fortunate. Most produce more than the local people can consume and must turn to more distant markets. To reach these markets they are likely to have to depend on other companies (called wholesalers or middlemen). If their demand is over a wide geographic area, manufacturers may use many of these companies to get their products to their consumers.

Two forms of channel The possible channels of distribution are many and complex, but for simplicity they may be placed in two broad categories: vertical and horizontal. A *vertical channel* is one in which there is a similar assortment of goods handled at each step of distribution. For example, a manufacturer of foods sells to a grocery wholesaler who in turn sells to a grocery retailer, who then sells to the consumer. A *horizontal channel* is one in which a variety of goods are sold at each step. A manufacturer of a variety of products, for example, sells various assortments of its products to different middlemen. Or a drug manufacturer who also makes baby food uses one channel for selling drugs and another for selling both drugs and baby food.

Regardless of the category the channel fits into, its objectives are the same. Generally, the firm strives to accomplish the following goals: (1) to move the physical product, (2) to promote the product, (3) to provide market information, (4) to reduce marketing costs, and (5) to increase output and profit. The marketing executive selects that particular channel that best facilitates all of these objectives.

Factors affecting the channel of distribution In selecting the appropriate channel for distributing their products, marketers consider a number of pertinent factors (see Figure 12–8). The most important factors are as follows:

1. *Size and geographic dispersion* If the potential market is heavy with buyers, it may be possible for manufacturers to sell directly to retailers or even to consumers. But when the buyers are thinly spread over a wide area, manufacturers may need to rely on wholesalers.

2. *Product value and* 3. *Frequency of purchase* Although these are separate factors, often they are interrelated. Some low-priced items (milk, bread) that are regularly and frequently bought may be sold directly to customers. High-cost merchandise and those products infrequently bought typically are best sold through wholesalers.

FIGURE 12-8

Decision factors and choices of a manufacturer in selecting for a product

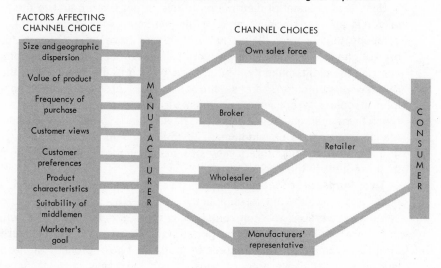

FACTORS AFFECTING
CHANNEL CHOICE

CHANNEL CHOICES

4. *Customer views* How customers view the product is a factor to be considered. Perhaps this factor is explained best by an illustration. At one time new home buyers looked upon home appliances as items to be bought separately by them from appliance retailers. Now they view appliances as a part of the new homes they buy. As a result, such purchases now are made by contractors from wholesalers.

5. *Cutomer preferences* What customers prefer is likely to be a factor only if the customer buys in large quantity. Industrial customers, for example, prefer to bypass wholesalers. If their business is large enough, they are likely to be given their preference.

6. *Product characteristics* Highly technical goods require the knowledgeable salespeople that only certain channels can provide. Perishable products (milk, meats, flowers) require channels with special equipment and fast service. And so it is with many other kinds of goods.

7. *Suitability of wholesalers* Wholesalers who are tied up with competitors, those that do not have adequate personnel, and those without good market coverage may not be the best choices of some manufacturers.

8. *The marketer's goal* Some marketers seek intensive distribution for their products. Thus, they work to get their products sold by all competent middlemen. Some seek selective distribution—that is, distribution only through the middlemen who are best able to take care of the special products involved. Then there are some that prefer a policy of giving certain middlemen exclusive rights to distribute in an area.

As summarized in Figure 12–8, these eight major considerations guide marketers in selecting channels. The channels they select follow five general routes: (1) direct from manufacturer to consumer through the manufacturer's sales force, (2) direct to consumers through manufacturer's representatives, (3) through retailer to consumer, (4) through conventional middlemen (brokers, retailers, consumers), and (5) through conventional middlemen (wholesaler, retailer, consumer). As was noted in Chapter 11, however, many possible types of middlemen may be involved in these last two routes. Thus, the diagrams give only a very general picture of the possibilities.

The communication components of the marketing mix

Product communication is the fourth major area of strategy in the marketing mix. Perhaps you have heard of this activity by its more common term, promotion. By *promotion* is meant all those activities involved in communicating between seller and buyer. Specifically it consists of three basic communication activities: (1) personal selling, (2) mass selling, and (3) sales promotion.

Personal selling as a promotional method   Personal selling is one of the most common promotional methods. As with most activities, it can take many forms. The most common form is retail selling, or across-the-counter selling. Another is door-to-door selling, a form illustrated by the Fuller Brush representative, or the breadman, or even the milkman. Then there is the selling done by manufacturer's salespeople. They call on other manufacturers or middlemen to service accounts or to obtain new business. Another form is illustrated by the wholesalers and agents who call on manufacturers and other wholesalers. Of more recent origin is executive selling, a form of selling that occurs when the home office sends one of its executives to handle a very difficult sales assignment.

Although personal selling is a common promotional method, all too many marketing managers overlook it as a means of promotion. They tend to see it solely as a means for sales and ignore the other possible accomplishments of salespeople. Wise marketing managers recognize the fact that salespeople are a major communication link between company and customer. And they know that salespeople are in an excellent position to do promotion work. Through planned efforts involving training programs, service emphasis, inspirational meetings, and such, they induce their salespeople to be successful promoters of the company and its products.

Promotion through mass selling   *Mass selling* means selling efforts aimed at large numbers of people at one time. Principally mass selling is *advertising,* which is any paid-for form of presentation of a promotional message. As shown in Figure 12–9, advertising continues to grow and by

FIGURE 12–9

Expenditures for advertising and personal consumption in the United States, 1950–74

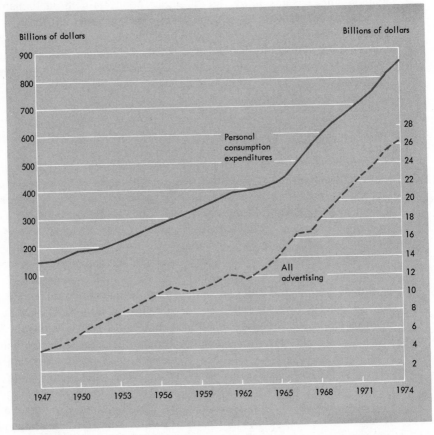

Source: U.S. Department of Commerce.

far outstrips the other forms of promotion. But any form of publicity or public relations effort (nonpaid-for promotion) also applies. Nonpaid-for promotion would include newspaper publicity, articles in trade magazines, contributions to community causes, and such. Although these activities can be extermely effective on occasion, most marketing strategy decisions concern paid-for promotion. Thus, our emphasis centers on this form.

In developing the promotion strategy that will get the best results for their products, marketers must make a number of related decisions. For one, they must decide on the kind of advertising that is best for the one case. In making this decision, they may need to decide whether to promote primary or selective demand. *Primary demand* is demand for a general type of product (such as color TV); *selective demand* refers to the specific brand name (Zenith). They may need to decide on the feasibility of conducting *institutional advertising* (advertising designed to promote the image of the company rather than its products). They may need to decide whether to use brand advertising. In *brand advertising* the company seeks to promote a family of products—such as Campbell soups. And in all cases, they will need to decide on how much to spend. On this point, they may use a fixed percentage of sales, they may be guided by their competitors' advertising, or they may set individual goals for themselves.

In making the decisions on such questions, marketers use all the market information we have discussed. They consider competition, market conditions, newness of the product, size and location of the market, and the customer interest to which the firm wishes to appeal. They consider, also, any information they have on the effectiveness of their past advertising efforts. Such information, however, is most difficult to gather. As with all other matters of marketing strategy, developing a company's advertising requires careful consideration of all pertinent information.

Criticism of advertising Probably advertising is the most criticized area of marketing. Although the criticisms are many, generally they fall into one of three general complaints: (1) advertising often is deceptive, (2) it adds unnecessary costs, and (3) it creates false needs.

1. *Deceptive* The question of deception in advertising is not an easy one to answer. By presenting some facts and leaving out others an advertisement may be deceptive. But as any authority in communications will confirm, any advertising message must be selective; it cannot say everything. Does the fact that it does not say everything make it deceptive? Then there is the matter of whether the advertiser should tell the good with the bad. Should Chevrolet, for example, limit its advertising message to the good qualities—power, economy, style, and such? Or should it also tell of the dangers of using their product—of the injuries, the deaths, and so on, that are certain to occur? We require such a statement from cigarette manufacturers.

Most of the criticism of advertising deceptiveness concerns more subtle techniques than mere omissions. Some contend that advertisers sell qualities that do not exist—catchwords, gimmicks, illogical associations and the like. What, for example, does a picture of a rugged, handsome cowboy in a scenic western setting tell us about the nature of Marlboro cigarettes? Or what does it mean when the makers of Vanish say that their product will "toilet train your bathroom bowl"? And was A&P being deceptive with their WEO (Where Economy Originates) campaign? A *Business Week* price comparison study reported that "the chain's lower-than-rivals' food prices seem more noise than substance."[1]

Although it is apparent that at least some deception occurs in adver-

---

[1] "A&P Counts the Cost of Its Pyrrhic Victory," *Business Week*, April 28, 1973, p. 117.

tising, it is noteworthy that the industry is not without some control. It has established the National Advertising Review Board to police its own advertising. Although the Board has no legal power of enforcement, it has received industry cooperation. In a most significant ruling, it found certain Schick advertisements to be misleading. The advertisements·in question presented test results which measured the weights of whiskers cut by Schick, Norelco, Remington, and Sunbeam shavers. Critics contend, however, that this action actually was a move to discourage the growing practice of referring to competitors by name. This practice had been endorsed by an earlier ruling of the Federal Trade Commission on grounds that it provides the consumer with meaningful purchasing information.

Although industry efforts to control its advertising are increasing, most of the control still comes from two government commissions. The most significant of these is the Federal Trade Commission. This commission is charged specifically with the task of policing deceptive promotions. The Commission has taken some strong actions and imposed stiff penalties on violators. For example, it ordered the manufacturers of Geritol to stop claiming that its product cured "tired blood." When the manufacturer violated the order it was fined $465,000 and its agency $356,000. In late 1973, the Commission's power was blunted somewhat by the results of a historic case involving ITT Continental Baking Company. The case had been viewed as a test of whether the government could clamp down on claims of uniqueness for products that really are not unique. In this case, the Commission dropped six of the most significant charges against ITT Continental. It ruled on only one—that ITT Continental had falsely advertised by claiming its bread would make children grow dramatically. Although the firm was found guilty, no penalty was imposed.

The second federal office active in policing advertising is the Pure Food and Drug Administration. This office has served to control unproven claims about food and drugs. Although few would argue the merits of protecting the public from unsafe food and drugs, many criticize this office for being too zealous in its work. Especially under attack has been the administration's 1969 ban on cyclamates because of a possible link between this artificial sweetner and cancer. As a result, diet drink and food manufacturers lost heavily—over $100 million, according to authoritative reports. In 1973, a thorough German research project found cyclamates to be harmless.

2. *Costly*   A second major criticism of advertising is that it adds to the cost of a product without giving the consumer adequate value for his money. The time and energy spent in advertising, the critics say, could be better spent in productive work—work that would produce additional goods and services, thereby benefiting mankind. The proponents of advertising counter with the claim that through advertising mass sales re-

sult; and with mass sales, mass production is possible. Thus production costs are lower, and the costs of advertising are more than covered. They argue further that advertising provides a valuable information service by keeping consumers up-to-date on the goods and services available to them. And they say that by being better informed consumers have increased their standard of living. To say the least, the argument is a close one.

3. *False* A third major criticism is that advertising creates false needs. The critics point out that all of us enjoy more than the bare necessities of life. We change clothes when our whims or the whims of clothing designers dictate, discarding clothing that still is wearable. For years we used gasoline as if the supply were unlimited, and we put the gasoline in giant automobiles many times more powerful than necessary to move the human cargo they carried. The critics' examples go on and on, but the point should be clear. Such a standard of living, the critics say, is wasteful and unnecessary; and it has been forced on us through advertising. The proponents of advertising must, of course, admit that we purchase many more goods than we really need. But they contend that the results are good—not bad. The results are a higher standard of living, increased production, increased employment, and a generally improved economy.

Sales promotion The third of the promotion methods available to marketers is *sales promotion*. This method covers all activities which are used to aid both personal and mass selling. For example, it may consist of various displays at the point of sale, circulars, sales demonstrations, contests, premiums, and catalogs. As is the case with mass promotion, these activities require the skill of a trained professional. Nevertheless, marketers need to make general decisions about using them.

In summary, we now can view all of the components of the marketing mix. Because this review has been brief, their complexity and broad extent may not have been emphasized sufficiently. But complex and broad are these components. It is the marketer's task to understand this complex and broad area of operations and to seek the best possible blend of components. The marketer should seek the blend that will carry the goods to the right customers, at the right place, at the right time.

DISCUSSION QUESTIONS

1 What should be the attitude of business owners toward the current movement to stabilize population?

2 What kinds of business are affected most by each of these social changes in the United States?

a) Women joining the work force.
b) More positive attitude toward leisure.
c) More positive attitude toward debt.

3 Discuss the environmental influences most likely to determine the target market of these products: (a) perfume, (b) soft drinks, (c) cigarettes, (d) men's shoes, (e) portable typewriters, (f) vitamin pills, (g) water skis.

4 Respond to this statement: "Why go through all the effort to determine the target market for a product? If you just put the product on the market and promote it, those who need it will find it and buy it."

5 Discuss the total product concept of each of the following: (a) automobiles, (b) electric toasters, (c) television sets, (d) accident insurance, (e) breakfast cereals.

6 Do manufacturers really plan their products to satisfy consumers' wants?

7 Give examples of products on today's market in each of the stages of the product life cycle.

8 What should a marketer consider in setting the price for a revolutionary new shaving instrument? This instrument will do the job better than any electric or blade-type shaver on the market; and it costs less than one third as much to make as the least expensive of the competition.

9 For the product described in Question 6, apply each of the factors which affect selection of a channel of distribution.

10 Give some current examples of advertising which emphasize (a) primary demand, (b) selective demand, and (c) institutional advertising. Explain the probable reasons for using these approaches.

11 Would we be better off without advertising?

MINI CASES

AOK Toiletries, Inc., is a newly established company which plans to manufacture a line of men's cosmetics. At the outset they will make a hair spray, a cologne, and a deodorant; but in time they plan to add other related products. All of AOK's products will be of the very highest quality. Also, they will be very expensive. Naturally, the company wants to set up a marketing plan that will produce as much profits as is practical.

1. *Discuss the general environmental influences on AOK's target market.*

2. *What market segments should the firm try to reach?*

3. *Would the products be sold better through rational or emotional motives?*

The Bratten Electronics Company has purchased exclusive production rights to a revolutionary new dictating machine. Compared with other machines on the market, this one is a miniature—so small, in fact, that it can fit easily in a briefcase or coat pocket. It is feather light in weight. In spite of its diminutive size, the machine's quality will match any on the market; and it is so easy to operate that a child can use it. Perhaps most important of all, the machine can be manufactured at a price approaching one half of that required to manufacture competing machines. This dictating machine, is, indeed, a truly revolutionary product.

Although the company manufactures an assortment of electronic goods that do not remotely resemble a business machine, its production facilities are ideally suited to manufacture the new product. It is in the marketing end of the business that the real adjustment must take place. Currently, the company distributes its products through wholesalers who sell to retailers of electronic goods. Typically, business machines are sold to business executives through the manufaturer's own sales organization.

In preparing for the marketing of the new dictating machine, the Bratten Company has a number of basic decisions to make. One concerns price. Some company officials favor pricing high—at about the price of the competition. The small size and revolutionary design will sell the product at the going price, they reason. Another group of officials want to take advantage of the low production cost and sell the machine well under competitor's prices. As they see it, low prices would mean volume sales and greater profits.

Another basic decision is that of deciding how to market the machine. Here, also, the administrators are divided. One group wants to set up a separate sales organization. Another prefers to sell through office supply stores and their wholesalers. Then there is another suggestion to try to work out a distributing arrangement with the sales organization of a competing firm.

Although these two matters are major, the company must make decisions on other matters concerning the marketing mix.

1. *Evaluate the company's decision to manufacture and market this new product.*
2. *What should be the price policy for the new product? Why?*
3. *What recommendations would you make concerning the choice of channel distribution? Defend your answer.*
4. *What other problems concerning marketing the dictating machine do you see for the company? Explain each and make your recommendation concerning them.*

In the mid-1930s, Albert Sanders invented a small household product and started the Sanders Manufacturing Company to manufacture it. From the beginning, the product was a popular one. Sales increased rapidly and the company prospered. As the product was well protected by patent, no significant competition existed from many years. The company charged a high price, and it reaped a large profit. Because its product was well received, the company did little to change it. After the patent rights expired, competition entered the market in great numbers. Company sales and production gradually decreased. So did profits. Losses soon set in. And now it appears that the company must close down.

1. *Explain what has happened in the life cycle of this product.*
2. *What could the company have done to prolong the life of its product?*
3. *What else could the company have done to protect its interests?*

Lynn A. Townsend, chairman of the board of Chrysler Corporation, is a prime example of how a knowledge of accounting elevated a man to the highest pinnacles of corporate success.

Lynn Townsend was born May 12, 1919, in Flint, Michigan. Although his parents passed away early in life, Lynn still managed to attend college. In the fall of 1936, he entered the University of Michigan, from which he received his Bachelor of Arts degree in 1940 and his Master of Business Administration degree in 1941. On graduation, Lynn Townsend joined the Detroit office of the nationally known accounting firm of Ernst and Ernst.

Townsend's career with Ernst and Ernst was short-lived, however. In 1947 he left with one of the firm's partners to become supervising accountant and later partner in a new firm. This firm soon merged with another to become the highly successful firm of Touche, Ross, Bailey and Smart. One of this firm's major clients was Chrysler, and as supervising accountant, Townsend was in charge of this account. In time, Mr. Townsend became highly knowledgeable of Chrysler's affairs. Thus, it was no surprise when, in 1957, Townsend left Touche, Ross to become controller of Chrysler. By 1961, Townsend had succeeded to the presidency of the company.

As controller and later vice president of Chrysler in the late 1950s and early 1960s, Townsend undertook a series of actions that played a major part in saving Chrysler from financial ruin. In just one year, he turned a large deficit into an even larger profit, despite the fact that sales dropped by almost $.5 billion!

Today, Chrysler is a viable, going concern. Although new problems have arisen since Townsend took over the top managerial position, it must still be recognized that this accountant-turned-chief executive played an instrumental role in saving one of America's largest corporations.

Lynn A. Townsend
(1919–   )

An accountant that saved a company

13

Accounting for financial control

Money for which no receipt has been taken is not to be included in the accounts.

——*Hammurabi (c.2000 B.C.)*

Thus far, this review of the functions of the business firm has concentrated on three major activities: Managing the firm's human resources, producing the goods or services that are ultimately sold to create the firm's profits, and the marketing of those goods or services through some channel of distribution to the ultimate consumer. Next in logical order for discussion are those business functions concerned with financing the business enterprise and controlling these activities within the firm. They are the subjects of the following three chapters of this book.

WHY WE STUDY ACCOUNTING

In today's competitive business world, corporate executives, proprietors, or partners make hundreds of decisions daily—decisions that, in some cases, could spell financial ruin for their companies if made incorrectly. This decision-making process wouldn't be particularly bothersome if the executives knew in advance which decision alternative would give them the desired results—that is, if they operated in a world of perfect knowledge. Unfortunately, business executives do not have such knowledge about their alternatives. Usually, the decision-making process takes place with less than perfect information available. When this occurs, the executives attempt to obtain any information they can that might shed light on their predicament. In a business firm, one of the most important sources of information of this sort is the accounting department.

Accounting defined

If you were to ask the average person to tell you what accountants do, probably he would remark, "Oh, they keep the books for the company." Years ago, this probably would have been a fairly accurate definition of the accountant's function. Accountants—or bookkeepers, as they were commonly called—dutifully and meticulously recorded each and every transaction the firm engaged in, in large books called *journals* and *ledgers.* Once the data was recorded, the major financial statements, the *balance sheet* and the *income statement,* were prepared.

Today, however, accountants make extensive use of the computer in the recording of these transactions. The computer can handle these functions with ease; indeed, many firms have the computer construct financial statements on a *weekly* basis, where in previous times these same firms strained to get statements constructed on an *annual* basis! The use of the computer, moreover, has freed accountants to concentrate on the *use* of the financial statistics that have been gathered. Thus, in recent years, the accounting profession has become more information oriented, and less bookkeeping oriented.

As a consequence of this change in emphasis, the definition of what an accountant does has also changed. Today, accounting can be defined as "the process of identifying, measuring, and communicating information to permit informed judgments and decisions by users of the information."[1] This definition differs considerably from what used to be the simple, bookkeeping definition of accounting. In fact, it differs considerably from the conventional definition of accounting as being the recording, classifying, and summarizing of business transactions. Nowhere in the definition of accounting does the word *bookkeeping* appear. Instead, the word *information* has become the key word in defining the duties of the accountant.

Accounting as the language of business   For information to be relayed in an efficient manner and without distortion of its meaning, the terminology used must be understood by all concerned. Over the years, accounting has developed a unique "language" all its own. As the business world has increased in complexity, it has become increasingly necessary for top management to understand the information supplied by the accountant. As a result, accounting has literally become the language of business. The following discussion of the major accounting statements, therefore, gives special emphasis to the language of accounting. Learn these terms, for they shall be referred to not only in forthcoming chapters, but in virtually all of the future business courses you take.

---

[1] Committee to Prepare a Statement of Basic Accounting Theory, *A Statement of Basic Accounting Theory* (Evanston, Ill.: American Accounting Association, 1966).

FIGURE 13–1

Clerks making their calculations on the abacus. The date, 1518, makes this one of the oldest book illustrations of a business activity.

Source: Reprinted with permission from *The World of Business,* Edward C. Bursk et al. (eds.) (New York: Simon & Schuster, Inc.), 1962.

The major financial statements

When information is assembled for transmission to management and other interested parties, it usually takes the form of a financial statement. There are two popular statements that are universally considered as the most important statements of financial condition available. These are the (a) balance sheet and (b) the income statement.

THE BALANCE SHEET

The balance sheet is the financial statement that shows the status of the company at a given point in time. The balance sheet is divided into two parts. One side lists all of the *assets* of the firm, and the other side lists all of the *liabilities* and *owners' investment* in the firm. Assets can be defined as all of those things owned by the firm that have some recognizable value. Buildings, machinery, inventory, cash, and patents are examples of assets. Liabilities, of course, represent all of the claims that creditors have on the assets of the business. Taxes owed the government, money owed to suppliers, and so on, are liabilities. The owners' investment—also called *owners' equity*—consists of all those funds which the owners themselves have invested in the business.

Balance Sheet

Assets	Liabilities and Owners' Equity

It is a fundamental principle of accounting that the totals on each side of the balance sheet equal one another. This is because on one side of the statement are listed all of the properties of the firm, and on the other side of the statement are the claims of those people who have provided the funds necessary to acquire those properties. These claims can only come from two sources: the claims of creditors (liabilities) and the claims of the owners (owners' equity). Therefore, the *balance sheet equation,* can be expressed as:

$$\text{Assets} = \text{Liabilities} \div \text{Owners' equity}$$

We can now see why the statement is called a balance sheet—in a properly constructed statement, the left-hand side of the statement (assets) will always total to the same amount as the right-hand side (liabilities and stockholders' equity).

It is becoming increasingly popular to show the balance sheet in a tabular form, with the assets listed on top, and the liabilities and owners' equity listed below. This type of statement is exactly the same in every other respect as the more traditional statement. The assets must still equal the liabilities and owners' equity. Recent years have seen increased use of this format for balance sheets. For this reason, this form is used in the sample balance sheet (see Table 13–1).

The balance sheet accounts

As has been noted, the balance sheet depicts the status of a business firm at a given point in time. This is an important point to remember. At any given date, the firm can develop a balance sheet. However, it is entirely possible—indeed, probable—that the asset-liability position of the firm will change the very next day, as a result of purchases or the payment of wages, and the like. Thus, a balance sheet always has a specific date to indicate the exact time that the revealed status was verified.

Assets

Assets have been defined as those properties possessing some value that are owned by the business firm. These assets can be further subdivided into current assets, fixed assets, and intangible assets.

Current assets

Current assets are those properties owned by the firm that are expected to be used, collected, or converted into cash in the next accounting period. Since most firms consider their "accounting period" to be one year, current assets are generally thought to be those assets that will be used or converted to cash in one year. Listed in order of their liquidity or expected usage, current assets include the following.

Cash The cash account includes all currency, savings accounts, or checking accounts owned by the firm. Also included in the cash account are checks received from customers which have not yet been deposited in the bank.

Accounts receivable Accounts receivable are those debts owed to the firm by customers of the firm. For a manufacturer, these accounts may represent goods shipped to customers for which payment has not yet been received. For a retailer, accounts receivable may include all of the credit and charge accounts of its various customers.

Notes receivable If a firm has received a written promise to pay from a customer, this written promise constitutes a note receivable and not an account receivable. While this distinction may seem to be a minor one, there is a legal difference between the claims on assets of the two, and therefore they should be distinguished.

TABLE 13–1

THE ABBS MANUFACTURING COMPANY

Balance sheet
December 31, 197–

Assets

Current assets:

Cash...................................		$ 30,000	
Accounts receivable......................	$ 48,000		
Less: Allowance for doubtful accounts............................	2,000	46,000	
Notes receivable.........................		10,000	
Merchandise inventory....................		60,550	
Prepaid insurance........................		3,500	
Total Current Assets..................			$150,050

Fixed assets:

Machinery and equipment................	$ 85,750		
Less: Accumulated depreciation.........	8,250	$ 77,500	
Furniture and fixtures....................	$ 4,500		
Less: Accumulated depreciation.........	2,000	2,500	
Buildings................................	$ 90,000		
Less: Accumulated depreciation.........	12,500	77,500	
Land....................................		121,500	
Total Fixed Assets...................			279,000

Intangible assets:

Patents.................................		$ 5,000	
Copyrights..............................		2,500	
Total Intangible Assets..................			7,500
Total Assets.........................			$436,550

Liabilities and owners' equity

Current liabilities:

Accounts payable........................	$ 18,750		
Federal income taxes payable.............	19,350		
Accrued wages payable...................	6,725		
Notes payable—current installment.......	40,000		
Total Current Liabilities.............		$ 84,825	

Long-term liabilities:

Notes payable...........................	$ 20,000		
Long-term bonds outstanding.............	40,000		
Total Long-Term Liabilities............		60,000	
Total Liabilities......................			$144,825

Owners' equity:

Preferred stock..........................	$ 20,000		
Common stock...........................	250,000		
Retained earnings........................	21,725		
Total Owner's Equity..................			291,725
Total Liabilities and Owner's Equity..............................			$436,550

Merchandise inventory   Merchandise inventory consists of raw materials, partially completed products, and finished goods that the firm has on hand but has not yet sold. Some firms separate these three types of inventory; others merely lump their value together in an inventory account. In any event, the inventory is expected to be converted into finished products, then into sales, and finally into cash in the coming period.

Fixed assets

Fixed assets are properties of the firm that (*a*) have an expected life of more than one year, and (*b*) are not intended for resale but are instead used in the operation of the business. Examples of fixed assets are the following.

Machinery and equipment   Machinery and equipment having a useful life of more than one year are commonly treated as fixed assets. This would not, however, include lubricants, oil, and other supplies needed to make the machinery work or to keep it in good operating condition. These items have a life of less than one year and are, consequently, treated as expenses and are found on the income statement.

Furniture and fixtures   The furniture and all of the removable or non-stationary fixtures in a building may also qualify as fixed assets, providing again that they have a sufficiently long life.

Buildings   The building or buildings in which the business is housed also qualify as a fixed asset. A building normally has a useful life-span, after which it may be torn down, and is necessary for the operation of the business.

Accumulated depreciation   Each of the above-mentioned fixed assets has a reduction to it called accumulated depreciation. This represents that portion of the fixed asset that we estimate has been "used up" in previous years. The exact amount of "depreciation" allowed each year is based on formulas developed by the manufacturer of the asset (who can provide an accurate estimate of its useful life) and the Internal Revenue Service. Thus, if we accurately estimate the life of an asset and depreciate it accordingly, the last year the asset is useful will see its value on the balance sheet drop to zero, meaning that, for our purposes, the asset is now worthless. Most fixed assets that have an estimatable life can be depreciated.

Land   Land is the only fixed asset that is never depreciated. The reason, of course, is that land does not have a limited useful life. It will always be there. Its value to the firm may increase or decrease, but its basic structure and usefulness do not change.

One might argue that for an oil company the value of the land can definitely change. (As oil is pumped out of the ground, the ground becomes less valuable.) However, special types of depreciation exist for natural resources such as oil, minerals, and timber. This special depreciation is called a *depletion allowance.* It covers only the estimated quantity of natural resources involved. In all other respects, however, depletion and depreciation are treated in the same manner.

Intangible assets

Intangible assets are those assets that have no physical substance— that is, they cannot be seen, felt, or heard—but which exist nonetheless. Intangible assets may have a legal document stipulating their existence, but the document itself is not the asset. Examples of intangible assets are patents and copyrights.

Liabilities and owners' equity

Liabilities are the outstanding debts of the firm. These may be of two types: either short-term (current) liabilities, or long-term liabilities. Sometimes long-term liabilities are called *funded debt.* Owners' equity consists of the owners' investment in the business.

Current liabilities

Current liabilities are those debts which the firm expects to have paid by the end of the current accounting period. As such, they almost always have maturities of less than one year, and frequently have maturities of only a few weeks. Examples of current liabilities are the following.

Accounts payable Accounts payable represent monies owed to suppliers of the firm for goods ordered and received but not yet paid for. Whereas accounts receivable represent money owed *to* the firm by its customers, accounts payable represent money owed *by* the firm to its suppliers.

Other payable accounts Many times, a firm will owe money to another party, but will not be obligated to pay that bill until some time in the future. For example, all companies know they will have to pay quarterly income taxes. However, these taxes will not be "officially due" until the end of the period. Under these circumstances, the firm will have on its books an account called "Income Taxes Payable" to reflect the fact that they know they owe taxes, but the bill is not yet due.

Similarly, when the firm closes its books at the end of the accounting period, it will frequently have an account called "Accrued Wages Payable." The word "accrued" refers to the fact that the firm has incurred a debt which it recognizes, but customarily does not pay until later in the period. For example, if the company pays wages every Friday, but in this particular year happened to close its books on Wednesday, it would "accrue" the wages it owes its workers for their work on Monday and Tuesday. By Friday, of course, it would remove the "accrual" by paying the debt in its normal manner.

Notes payable: Current installments   When a firm has a long-term debt which it is required to pay off in installments, the *current* portion of that debt is listed as a current liability, even though the debt itself may be very long term. The remaining portion of the debt, however, is still considered a long-term liability.

Long-term liabilities

Long-term liabilities are debts that are not expected to be paid within the next accounting period. Examples of such obligations are as follows.

Notes payable   These are long-term notes—usually to a bank or some other financial institution—that are not due in the immediate future. Usually, notes payable represent sizable debts when they are incurred.

Bonds   These are very long-term debt obligations, running as much as 20 to 30 years before they mature. Bonds are discussed more fully in Chapter 15.

Owners' equity

The owners' equity section of the balance sheet contains those funds invested by the owner(s) of the business. Such funds are of three types.

Preferred stock   Preferred stock is an ownership security that has some of the characteristics of debt and some of common stock (which is the "real" ownership security of the company). Preferred stock is usually listed in the balance sheet at its *par* value, which can be thought of as the price listed on the face of the stock certificate, on which the dividend paid to preferred stockholders is usually based.

Common stock   This is the basic ownership security of a corporation. If the stock has a par value or stated value, the number of shares times this amount is usually listed on the balance sheet.

Retained earnings   These are the earnings of previous years that have been reinvested in the business. In a growing firm, the retained earnings account will increase steadily from year to year.

The balance sheet is useful for several reasons. First, it tells at a glance just how solvent the firm is, how much it owes in the near term, how large the firm is in total assets, and how much the owners have invested in the business. Moreover, when compared with other balance sheets—both of previous years and of competitors—it tells a lot about the relative efficiency with which the firm is being managed.

THE INCOME STATEMENT

The income statement is a summary analysis of all of the activities of the firm that were significant in determining the annual profit or loss of the business. Known also as a "profit and loss" statement, the income statement covers a specified period of time, say one year. This is in contrast to the balance sheet, which identifies the corporate asset structure as of a given date. A typical income statement is shown in Table 13–2.

TABLE 13–2

THE ABBS MANUFACTURING COMPANY

Income Statement

For the Period Ended December 31, 197–

Sales revenues:
Gross sales....................................	$650,000	
Less: Sales returns and allowances..........	2,000	
Net sales.................................		$648,000

Cost of goods sold:
Beginning inventory...........................	$ 53,450	
Purchases (net)..............................	452,100	
Total Goods Available for Sale.............	$505,550	
Less: Ending inventory........................	60,550	
Total cost of goods sold....................		445,000
Gross profit..................................		$203,000

Expenses:
Selling expenses..............................	$ 52,500	
Administrative expenses......................	60,000	
General expenses.............................	30,500	
Total Expenses...........................		143,000
Net income from operations.............		$ 60,000

Other income and expenses:
Other income.................................	$ 600	
Less: Other expenses........................	500	
Net addition (deletion) from income.......		100
Net Income Before Income Taxes............		$ 60,100
Federal income taxes........................		22,350
Net Income...................................		$ 37,750

Revenues

The typical income statement usually begins by first listing the major sources of revenue for the firm, and then itemizing those expenses incurred in obtaining that revenue. If the firm has any miscellaneous income or expenses, these are listed last.

Sales An income statement begins with the listing of the revenue generated from the primary business operations. For most firms, this is called *sales,* although it may be called operating revenue, revenue, or simply income.

You will notice that on our sample income statement, there appears an account called "Sales Returns and Allowances." This consists of those goods which were sold but for some reason or other, were returned by the purchaser. These, obviously, cannot be counted as sales by the firm, since they were returned. Thus, we adjust the sales figure by deducting these returns. The result is called "Net Sales."

It is customary in accounting today, to adjust the total sales figure for all returns and allowances before recording the sales figure on the income statement. As a consequence, many income statements no longer show "Returns and Allowances," but simply record "Net Sales."

Cost of goods sold

The cost of goods sold section of the income statement indicates the costs incurred by the firm for the materials that were eventually transformed into the goods sold. Specifically, the cost of goods sold section consists of the following.

Beginning inventory At the beginning of most accounting periods, the firm will have some raw materials in inventory. These materials consist of goods purchased in previous periods, but not transformed into sales. Goods that were in the previous period's ending inventory constitute the beginning inventory for this period. These goods should be added to the purchases for this period in order to get the cost of all of the goods the company had available for sale.

Purchases This is the cost of all of the actual purchases made during the period. Usually, purchases are listed as "net," meaning that all purchases that were returned for some reason were deducted from the total purchases figure in arriving at the net figure.

Ending inventory From the sum of the purchases and beginning inventory should be deducted the ending inventory for this period. These goods, again, constitute goods that were not sold this period. Thus, we will not charge their cost against this year's sales, but will instead charge them against the period in which they are sold. The resulting figure is called the total cost of goods sold. This figure is then subtracted from the net sales of the firm to get the gross profit.

Gross profit Gross profit represents what is left over after the cost of goods sold is subtracted from net sales revenues. It is called *"gross"* profit because it does not take into account all of the expenses incurred in getting the goods sold. It merely considers what was paid for the raw materials and what the goods were sold for.

Expenses

From the gross profit is deducted all of the various business expenses. These expenses may be selling expenses, administrative expenses, or general expenses.

Selling expenses Selling expenses include all business expenses directly related to the sale of the product or service. It includes salespeople's commissions, advertising expense, packaging costs, and so on.

Administrative expenses Administrative expenses include those expenses incurred by the management and office personnel of the firm. This might include managerial or executive salaries, secretarial help, office supplies, and the like.

General expenses General expenses include those expenses that cannot be properly charged to one department or functional area of the firm. Such things as property taxes; heat, water, and light; insurance; and so on, might be classified as general expenses.

Net income from operations Once the total expenses are calculated, they are deducted from the gross profit figure. The resulting figure is called net income (or profit) from operations. This figure reveals the profitability of the firm before deducting income taxes or considering nonoperating incomes or expenses. For firms that have earned no outside (nonoperating) income nor incurred any nonoperating expenses, the net operating income can also be called the taxable income.

Other income and expenses

If the firm has earned income from nonoperating assets (such as investments), or incurred expenses that are essentially unrelated to the operations of the firm (such as a loss on the sale of securities), these items are classified as "other" incomes or expenses. The two items are added together, resulting in either a net profit or net loss from "other" sources, and the balance is added to or subtracted from the net income from operations to give us our net income before taxes.

Net income before taxes The earnings before taxes, or taxable income figure, is one of the most important on the entire income statement. It is the figure that a corporation uses to calculate its income tax liability and thence, its net income.

Federal income taxes The final deduction on an income statement is for taxes. Corporations pay a tax of 22 percent on the first $25,000 of taxable income and 48 percent on everything earned thereafter.

Net income The final figure on the income statement is called the net income. This is the figure that reveals how much the corporation earned after all expenses—including taxes. From this figure, management can then pay the dividends on preferred stock and the common stock. Any residual is forwarded to the retained earnings account on the balance sheet.

Usefulness of the income statement

As the other major financial statement prepared under the auspices of the accountant, a properly prepared income statement is as useful as the balance sheet to management, creditors, and stockholders. Unfortunately, there is a wide variety of ways an income statement can be structured, and this tends to lessen its usefulness. Some firms, for example, will group administrative, selling, and general expenses under one category called "expenses." While such a procedure simplifies the statement, it also prevents proper analysis of the exact nature of those expenses. Other firms make use of their ability to alter certain expenses, such as depreciation, and thereby present an artificially high net income. Thus, it can be concluded that the usefulness of the income statement is dependent upon the degree of disclosure and method of reporting that the firm chooses to reveal.

STATEMENT ANALYSIS

The preparation of the balance sheet and the income statement are only the first step in the processing and transmission of accounting information. The data included in the statements needs to be examined and interpreted so that management can use it in modifying its decisions. To some extent, the balance sheet and the income statement provide information even on casual inspection. For example, a glance at the balance sheet can disclose the size of the firm in total assets, the amount of its debts, the size of its cash balance, and so on. Similarly, the income statement not only reveals the net income, but it also shows the total sales, the distribution of expenses among selling, administrative, or general purposes, and the size of the tax bill. Still, these are superficial disclosures, for often the major decisions facing a firm require information of more depth and analysis.

To provide the in-depth information desired by management, accountants have come to rely heavily on the relationships that exist within both the balance sheet and the income statement. Such relationships are expressed by the accountants as *ratios*. Such ratios constitute a very effective way of interpreting these two important statements.

As an example of the usage of ratos, let's reexamine the income statement of the Abbs Manufacturing Company (Table 13–2). Notice that this company had net income of $37,750. Was this good or bad? As a manager, how would you evaluate these earnings? One way might involve looking at the past year's earnings and comparing this year's income with the incomes earned then. On the other hand, the earnings figure itself may be deceiving. It may be that a new competitor entered the field, and as a result, Abbs Manufacturing had to double its sales just to get the same profit it had a year earlier. We could find this out easily enough by merely looking at the percent of sales that are represented by the earnings. If earnings are, say, 6 percent of sales this year but were 12 percent last year, we could indeed conclude that the Abbs Manufacturing Company had to increase its sales drastically just to hold on to its profits. We have just computed, in effect, a ratio—namely, the Net Profit Margin—and this ratio has enabled us to draw conclusions about the health of the company that might not have been apparent from a mere glance at the income statement.

Ratio analysis—Some popular measures

Quite obviously, ratios can be created for and between virtually every pair of items in either the balance sheet or the income statement. In fact, however, no more than 20 or 30 ratios are ever used, and of these only a handful have popular usage by the various users of accounting data. These include the following.

The current ratio   The current ratio is the ratio of the current assets of the company to the current liabilities of the company. In theory, this ratio is designed to reveal the liquidity potential of the firm. If, for some reason, the company were forced to pay off its current debts immediately, could it do so? Quite obviously, a firm faced with this problem would find it easiest to use its current assets (cash, accounts receivable, marketable securities, and so on) to pay off its current liabilities, since these can be converted into cash most easily. Obviously, then, the firm should have at least as many current assets as it has current liabilities, and preferably, the current assets should be twice the current liabilities. This is because one of the current assets, namely inventory, is not as marketable as securities or cash. Any attempt to convert inventory into cash will probably result in a substantial loss for the firm. Thus, 2:1 is considered a generally acceptable current ratio. For the Abbs Manufacturing Company, the ratio is

$$\frac{\text{Current assets}}{\text{Current liabilities}} = \frac{\$150,050}{\$\ 84,825} = 1.76 \text{ to } 1$$

Notice that for this company the ratio falls short of our 2:1 standard. As creditors or potential creditors, we might be a little concerned about this figure, since it creates a question about the firm's ability to pay off its current debts. However, the amount of the deficiency is not great, and therefore we would probably withhold judgment until we investigated further.

The acid-test ratio   The acid-test ratio (also known as the quick ratio), is similar to the current ratio except in one important way. Whereas the current ratio compares current assets against current liabilities, the acid-test ratio compares only those current assets that are cash or "almost cash" against the current liabilities. Those include, besides cash, such "quick assets" as marketable securities, net accounts receivable, and notes receivable. In the case of the Abbs Manufacturing Company, we would have an acid-test ratio of

$$\frac{\text{Cash} + \text{accounts receivable} + \text{notes receivable}}{\text{Current liabilities}} = \frac{\$\ 86,000}{\$\ 84,825} = 1.0 \text{ to } 1$$

As a general rule, the acid-test ratio should be approximately 1 to 1. A ratio of 1:1 implies enough very liquid assets to pay the current debts of the firm in a hurry. The Abbs Manufacturing Company meets this standard, a fact that would improve its credit standing.

It is worth noting that the major difference between the current ratio and the acid-test ratio is the omission of inventory. Inventory is, in practice, one of the most significant of the assets owned by a manufacturing firm. In many cases, inventory is almost as large as all other current assets combined. With an asset this large, therefore, it becomes imperative that management take particular care in managing the investment made in these raw materials. One way to check the efficiency with which the inventory is being managed is to compute the inventory turnover.

The inventory turnover   The inventory turnover reveals the number of times the inventory of the company has been turned into sales. In essence, it counts the number of times the entire "purchase-of-raw-materials-conversion-to-finished-goods-conversion-to-sales" cycle occurs. It is computed by dividing the cost of goods sold by the average inventory.

$$\frac{\text{Cost of goods sold}}{\text{Beginning} + \text{ending inventory}/2} = \frac{\$445,000}{57,000} = 7.8 \text{ turns}$$

The meaning of the inventory turnover is more difficult to interpret. Some businesses, like those in the computer industry, might have a very low inventory turnover. This is because the unit cost of these products is so high that having only a few of them in inventory can result in an unusually high average inventory—which will lower the turnover figure. Moreover, the very nature of computers dictates that we should expect a low turnover. Businesses don't buy computers every day; once one is purchased the customer may go years before buying another.

On the other hand, a food company may have a very high inventory turnover. This is because the unit cost of the product tends to be quite low, the product is subject to spoilage, and therefore the business manager will attempt to sell it as quickly as possible. Also, the nature of the product is such that customers or users of the product will make continuous purchases. For the Abbs Manufacturing Company, an inventory turnover of 7.8 times would probably be viewed as satisfactory, again depending on the nature of the product being manufactured.

When a firm has an inventory turnover that is too low, it usually is an indication that the average inventory balance is too large. When the turnover is too high, it may be that the company is pricing its product lower than the competition, thereby encouraging high sales and a high merchandise turnover. It should also reflect lower profits per unit of merchandise sold. One way to determine whether, in fact, the firm is selling its product at a competitive price is to check the net profit margin.

The net profit margin The net profit margin indicates what proportion of the sales revenues of the firm actually became net income. It is computed by dividing the net income by the net sales revenues. For the Abbs Manufacturing Company, this ratio is:

$$\frac{\text{Net income}}{\text{Net sales}} = \frac{\$\ 37,750}{\$648,000} = .058 \text{ or } 5.8\%$$

The net profit margin is important in that it gives us an indication of the overall profitability of the firm. The 5.8 percent margin of the Abbs Manufacturing Company is not a particularly high return, but neither is it unusually low. For all manufacturing firms in the past few years, the average return on sales was approximately 4.5 percent.[2] If we feel, however, that the margin is too low, we can extend our analysis by checking the gross profit margin.

The gross profit margin The gross profit margin is much like the net income margin except that it compares gross profit instead of net profits to net sales. The gross profit margin for the Abbs Manufacturing Company is:

$$\frac{\text{Gross profit}}{\text{Net sales}} = \frac{\$203,000}{\$648,000} = .313 \text{ or } 31.3\%$$

The gross profit margin indicates how much profit the firm made on the goods it sold—before allowing for expenses of operating the business. The only expense that is considered is the cost of the goods sold. For the Abbs Manufacturing Company, the gross margin may appear to be unusually high; however, a gross margin of about 40 percent is probably quite common.

When this ratio is used in conjunction with the net profit margin, the accountant can gain an important insight into the causes of low or de-

---

[2] "The Fortune '500' statistics," *Fortune* Magazine, Vol. 89, No. 5 (May 1974). See Table 13–3 for details.

clining profits. The reason is that the difference between these two ratios is directly attributable to the expenses incurred by the firm. Considering them together, the accountant can then begin a detailed analysis of the expenses themselves in order to determine where the inefficiencies are occurring.

Checking the profit margins of the firm is not the only means of determining the profitability of the firm, however. Management is obviously striving to increase the firm's profits, for these earnings are the yardstick that the stockholders will judge their performance by. The stockholders, however, are also interested in another measure of the firm's profitability. This second yardstick concerns the rate of return that the company has earned on the money invested by the stockholders in the firm. To determine this figure, it is necessary to compute one final ratio—a ratio that is probably the single most important ratio management can develop: the return on stockholder's investment.

Return on owners' investment The return on owners' investment, also known as the return on equity, is that ratio that shows how much the company earned on each dollar invested by the owner(s) of the business. It is calculated by dividing the net income of the company by the owners' investment in the business. For the Abbs Manufacturing Company, the return on owners' investment is:

$$\frac{\text{Net income}}{\text{Owners' equity}} = \frac{\$\ 37,750}{\$291,725} = .129 \text{ or } 12.9\%$$

This ratio indicates the rate of return being earned on every dollar of the owners' money invested in the business. For the Abbs Manufacturing Company, the rate is quite high, indicating a very efficient use of the owner's money. To gain a meaningful comparison, ask yourself where you, as an investor, would rather put your money: in a bank where you can earn 5 percent on your savings, or in stock in the Abbs Manufacturing Company, where your money can earn over 10 percent?

One word of caution: this does not mean the company will pay you 10 percent on your investment each year! It means the company has earned that much on the money invested by the owners in the past. Hopefully, this kind of earning power will eventually lead to similar increases in dividends in the future, and to the extent that this happens, the stockholders may realize a very attractive return on their investments. In the meantime, however, other investors may find the prospect of ownership in the Abbs Manufacturing Company to be attractive, and offer you higher and higher prices for your stock. This is what lies behind the changes in the price of common stock on the stock market, and leads to what professional investors call "growth" stocks.

A quick glance at the two tables showing return on sales (Table 13–3) and return on invested capital (Table 13–4) should reveal an interesting

TABLE 13–3

Return on sales (industry medians)

Industry	1973	1972
Mining......................................	14.6%	12.8%
Pharmaceuticals............................	9.4	9.1
Tobacco....................................	7.9	8.0
Petroleum refining..........................	7.7	6.0
Soap, cosmetics............................	7.7	7.7
Scientific, photographic equipment..........	7.2	6.9
Broadcasting, motion pictures...............	6.0	5.9
Paper and wood products...................	6.0	4.2
All industries...........................	4.5	4.1

point. Notice that there is a remarkable similarity between the industries that rank high on one category and also rank high on the other. While this finding is not unusual, (since firms that are very profitable tend to show a high return on both sales and invested capital), it is not always the case. Just a few years ago, the two tables had almost completely different industries ranked at the top. Indeed, it might be argued that finding different industries ranked at the top of these two profitability measures is the *usual* situation. This is because firms that require a lot of capital to operate will tend to show somewhat lower returns on invested capital. Conversely, firms that are not so dependent on capital will tend to show somewhat higher returns. Yet, even the slight differences between these two tables does point out the necessity for careful evaluation of all ratios that are calculated, for sometimes even a ratio is misleading. We should always remember that the real value of ratio analysis lies in the composite picture one can get from evaluating all of the ratios, and putting the pieces together in the decision-making process.

As an aid to business executives in evaluating their respective companies, some firms have developed "industry norms" for a whole series of

TABLE 13–4

Return on invested capital (industry medians)

Industry	1973	1972
Pharmaceuticals............................	18.1%	15.3%
Mining....................................	16.1	10.1
Soaps, cosmetics...........................	15.9	16.0
Broadcasting, motion pictures...............	15.3	13.5
Tobacco....................................	14.6	15.1
Shipbuilding, mobile homes, railroad equipment.................................	13.9	12.3
Beverages..................................	13.7	13.1
Paper and wood products...................	13.5	8.6
All industries...........................	12.4	10.3

ratios. These ratios supposedly indicate what an "average" firm in each industry would have as the level for particular ratios. Notable among firms supplying such "norms" is Dun & Bradstreet, which supplies such guidelines for well over 100 different industries.

Other accounting analysis techniques

As important as ratio analysis can be for accountants, it remains only one of the many techniques they use in obtaining the information needed by management. Other techniques include the development of an aging schedule for accounts receivable, and the developing of a sources and uses of funds statement for the financial manager.

Aging schedule of accounts receivable One of the problems usually facing management concerns the development of a credit policy that will

TABLE 13–5

Aging schedule of accounts receivable Abbs Manufacturing Company

Time receivables have been outstanding	Amount	Percent expected noncollectible	Expected bad debts
Less than 30 days...........	$33,500	0.4%	$ 150
30 to 60 days................	7,500	2.0	150
60 to 90 days................	3,000	10.0	300
90 to 180 days...............	2,000	20.0	400
Over 180 days...............	2,000	50.0	1,000
	$48,000		$2,000

ensure the firm maximum sales and yet minimize the number of bad debts it will incur. Accountants can assist in the development of a credit and collection policy by developing an "aging schedule" of the existing or current accounts receivable and those accounts that are already past due. Such a schedule requires that the accountants seperate the firm's accounts receivable according to the length of time they have been outstanding. On this basis, the accountants can then determine the probability of not collecting these particular classes of accounts. This knowledge will enable them to (a) estimate the bad debt allowance the firm should make, and (b) determine whether the firm's existing credit policy is too lenient or not lenient enough.

To illustrate, let's assume that the accountant for the Abbs Manufacturing Company developed the schedule shown in Table 13–5, based on the experience of the past year.

Noting the rapid tendency for bad debts to develop once a receivable is over 60 days outstanding, the accountants may suggest a change in either the credit terms being offered (in order to encourage early payment for goods) or suggest a change in collection policies, particularly for the delinquent accounts.

Similarly, if a firm shows no bad debts at all, the accountant may become concerned that the firm is passing up possible sales by maintaining a credit policy that is too rigid. A firm should expect to have a small percent of uncollectable accounts; the problem is reaching that point where the bad debts are neither too excessive nor so small as to imply a loss of potential sales.

Statement of sources and uses of funds In today's business world, the problem of obtaining funds for use within the business firm has become more and more important. As business has grown in size and complexity, its needs for money have grown proportionately. The problem of obtaining funds and putting them to effective use is the function of the

TABLE 13-6

ABBS MANUFACTURING COMPANY

Sources and Uses of Funds Statement
For the Period Ended December 31, 197–

Sources of funds:

Net income for the year	$37,750
Depreciation	25,500
Bonds sold to the public	13,000
Notes payable to bank	5,000
Accounts payable to creditors	2,700
Total Sources of Funds	$83,950

Uses of funds:

Purchase of building	$40,000
Purchase of inventory	15,850
Increased accounts receivable	13,100
Dividends paid	15,000
Total Uses of Funds	$83,950

financial manager. To facilitate the job of the financial manager, the accountant prepares a statement that specifically shows where the firm obtains its money and where the money is used within the firm. Such a statement is called a sources and uses of funds statement. Using our hypothetical corporation as an example, we might find that an accountant could prepare the sources and uses of funds statement for the Abbs Manufacturing Company shown in Table 13–6.

At first glance, the sources and uses of funds statement given above may appear confusing. How can money owed to a bank, for example, be a "source" of funds? The answer lies in the following explanation. A source and use of funds statement is basically, a comparison of two balance sheets. If we took last year's balance sheet and this year's balance sheet and compared them, we'd find that the only changes that occurred were those involving the accounts listed above. These changes can be identified as sources or uses of funds on the following basis.

If an *asset* account *increased* over the year, it would mean that money was spent to acquire the additional object. This would be a *use* of money. Similarly, if a *liability* account *decreased,* it would mean that a debt of some kind was paid off during the year. This would also be a *use* of money.

On the other hand, if an *asset* account *decreased,* it would mean that some property of the firm's was disposed of, and this would result in an increase of cash to the firm. This is considered, then, a *source* of funds. Similarly, if a *liability* account *increased,* it would mean that the firm increased its borrowing of funds during the year. Additions to borrowed funds are also considered *sources* of funds. Obviously, since any source of funds must be put to some use, the sources and uses of funds in any given year must balance. This particular statement has become so important in recent years that it has changed the entire concept of finance.

In large part, the sources and uses of funds statement is popular because it tells a great deal about the company. Management likes the statement because it shows at a glance where the firm's money is being invested—where, in fact, the financial manager feels the most efficient use of money can be achieved. Creditors like the statement because it shows whether the firm is relying on increasing use of borrowed money for its expansion, or whether the firm is using its available funds to pay off existing debts. Stockholders like the statement because it reveals the growth of the firm—is the firm expanding on a short-run, temporary basis or on a long-term, fixed-asset basis? Indeed, so important is the sources and uses of funds statement becoming, that it has changed the entire nature of finance, as shall be discussed in the next chapters.

Who uses accounting data?

As a final note to this chapter on accounting, you might ask just who actually uses accounting data, and why. Perhaps by now you may feel that this is an unnecessary question. Yet, so important is the accountant's function, that it would be wise for us to quickly review some of the more important users of accounting data. These major users include: (a) the managers and officers of the firm, (b) the stockholders or owners of the firm, (c) the government, (d) creditors and would-be creditors of the firm, and (e) various labor organizations that must deal with the firm's management.

Managers and officers of the firm The primary users of accounting data are the officers and managers of the firm itself. As previously noted, management lacks information regarding the proper course of action to take. That is, most of the time, management is forced to make decisions without knowing all of the possible problems that might arise because of that decision. In order to minimize the uncertainty that surrounds the decision-making process, management finds it extremely useful to examine accounting information. By checking both the past and present financial records of the firm, management is able to get some idea of the trends that exist, and indications of possible future performance. Such information is much like an X ray to a doctor; it tells the manager how the firm's "health" was in the past, and what its condition is today. By comparing the past with the present, the manager can get an idea of where the firm is heading in the future. If interpreted correctly, such data often proves invaluable to a manager about to make a vital decision in a world of risk and uncertainty.

Stockholders or owners of the firm   A second major user of accounting data are the stockholders or owners of the firm. Frequently, in a large corporation, the only exposure stockholders have to the operational aspects of the firm of which they are part owner is through the annual and/or quarterly reports they receive from the company. In the annual report are included the major accounting statements, together with a summary of similar statements from previous years. By examining these statements, the stockholders can ascertain the overall financial strength of the company and determine for themselves the extent of improvement or deterioration that has occurred.

Moreover, potential stockholders in a firm are also recipients of the accounting data of the firm. Although actual stockholders receive the annual report automatically by virtue of their position as owners of the firm, on request, most would-be stockholders can usually obtain a copy of the annual report from the firm or can refer to one of the investment advisory services for similar data. The would-be stockholders can also request a *prospectus* from the company. A prospectus is a legal document that provides financial and operational information similar to that found in the annual report, but it is much more extensive. After examining these documents, would-be stockholders can then decide whether or not they wish to become stockholders in the firm.

The government   Certainly one of the more important users of accounting data are the various levels of government. At the federal level, for example, the Securities and Exchange Commission must approve major changes in the ownership structure of the firm. Also, the Internal Revenue Service expects to see statements that reveal the earnings and expenses incurred by the firm. Income taxes are based on the income of the firm, as disclosed by the income statement. Moreover, certain deductible expenses can be verified by an examination of the balance sheet.

Thus, government is a constant user of the data provided by the accountant.

Creditors of the firm Other popular users of accounting data are creditors of the firm. When a company applies for a loan from a bank, for example, the bank will usually ask to see copies of the firm's financial statements. Analysis of these statements can inform a creditor, such as a bank, of the creditworthiness of the customer. Moreover, after granting the firm a loan, the bank is likely to ask for copies of such statements on a periodic basis, so that it may be able to keep up-to-date on the firm's changing financial situation.

Labor organizations Final users of accounting data are the various organized labor unions. Labor unions are sophisticated organizations today, and when they sit down to bargain with management, they like to know the exact state of affairs of the business. By analyzing the financial records of the firm, the union can determine whether, in fact, the firm can afford to meet its demands before bargaining actually starts.

The complexity of the accounting function

It is apparent that, with all of the above groups interested in the accounting data of a firm, the actual process of identifying and measuring this data can be a complex one. In many firms, this function is divided into specialties, such that in large corporations it is not uncommon to find the following.

Tax accountants They have the responsibility for assembling the necessary information for the various governmental bodies, particularly the Internal Revenue Service.

Payroll accountants When a firm approaches the size of, say General Motors, with nearly a million employees, it is easy to see how a firm may be in need of a whole accounting unit just to handle the payroll.

Managerial accountants These individuals are primarily responsible for providing information for use by management in the decision-making process. Their function may require special analysis of data for management cost studies, profit analysis, and so on.

Auditors Auditors are the watchdogs of the accounting profession. They crosscheck the work of other accountants to see that they have accurately identified and recorded all pertinent information. Frequently, auditors will use advanced statistical techniques, particularly sampling techniques, in their analysis.

Certified public accountants Finally, many firms employ certified public accountants in the various departments of the accounting division. The CPA is perhaps the best known and most widely respected of all the accountants. Their certification by state supervisory authorities is professional recognition that the accountant has attained a level of competency unsurpassed in the profession.

DISCUSSION QUESTIONS

1   Define accounting. What has happened to cause a change in the way accounting used to be defined, and the way it is defined now?

2   What is the balance sheet equation?

3   Why is it incorrect to think of retained earnings as money that the firm has earned and has lying around in some bank account? What really happens to retained earnings in a business?

4   What relationship do you see between the sources and uses of funds statement and the balance sheet? Explain.

5   Why should an accountant compute both the current ratio and the acid-test ratio, when they both seem to tell him the same thing?

6   Distinguish between the return on owners' equity ratio and the return on sales ratio. Why are the two different for many companies?

7   Why might an accountant be disturbed if a firm had no bad debt expense?

8   Why do your authors feel that the "return on owners' equity" ratio is probably the most important of all ratios?

9   We said that an increase in an asset was a "use" of funds. One asset commonly found on the balance sheet is "cash." How can an increase in the cash account be called a "use" of funds?

10 Earlier in the text, we noted that management comprised essentially four functions. These were planning, organizing, leading, and controlling. Which of these functions is probably closest in relationship to the accountant? Why?

MINI CASES

The National Sporting Goods Corporation, a leading manufacturer of equipment for outdoor recreational activities, was contemplating expansion of its equipment manufacturing facilities into the area of indoor sports. Specifically, it was considering entering the home table-tennis market, and later, into the manufacture and supply of billiard tables and related equipment. To accomplish this, however, would require that the National Sporting Goods Corporation obtain a rather sizable source of funds from outside the firm. The board of directors decided that a loan from a large bank in downtown St. Louis would be the most desirable source of those funds.

Accordingly, the firm prepared two financial statements—a balance sheet and an income statement, for delivery to the First National Bank and Trust Company of St. Louis, as part of its application for the loan. Abbreviated copies of those statements appear below.

NATIONAL SPORTING GOODS CORPORATION
Balance Sheet

Cash...	$ 50,000	
Accounts receivable..........................	100,000	
Inventory......................................	150,000	
Total Current Assets..................		$ 300,000
Machinery (net).............................	35,000	
Building (net)................................	75,000	
Land..	50,000	
Total Fixed Assets...................		160,000
Total Assets.........................		$ 460,000
Accounts payable............................	$ 80,000	
Notes payable................................	120,000	
Total Current Liabilities...............		$ 200,000
Bonds payable...............................	100,000	
Total Liabilities......................		300,000
Common stock...............................	100,000	
Preferred stock..............................	25,000	
Retained earnings...........................	35,000	
Total Owners' Equity.................		$ 160,000
Total Owners' Equity and Liabilities...		$ 460,000

Income Statement

Sales:..	$1,080,000	
Sales returns and allowances...............	30,000	
Net sales................................		$1,050,000
Cost of goods sold...........................		625,000
Gross profit..........................		$ 425,000
Expenses		
Administrative............................	150,000	
Selling......................................	75,000	
General.....................................	25,000	
Total...............................		250,000
Taxable income.............................		$ 175,000
Income taxes...............................		80,000
Net income.................................		$ 95,000
Dividends....................................		$ 75,000

1. Assume that you are the corporate loan officer of the First National Bank of St. Louis. On the basis of these financial statements would you grant the National Sporting Goods Corporation a five-year, $250,000 loan?

2. Would you have any reservations about their ability to pay the loan back when it came due? If so, what are these reservations,

and what would you do to preserve the bank's financial position?

3. *Suppose, instead, that the National Sporting Goods Corporation wanted to use the money for pollution control equipment. Would this influence your decision in any way? Why?*

Bill and Frank were debating the merits of two popular accounting measures one day. Bill made the comment that the measure "return on investment" or "return on invested capital" was a more meaningful ratio than "return on sales." Frank disagreed, arguing that "return on sales" disclosed a more meaningful measure of business efficiency, since sales were directly related to profits, while capital was not. Unable to resolve their argument they ask your assistance.

Indicate which measure, if any, you feel is more meaningful and why.

There is an old adage that "figures don't lie, but sometimes liars figure." Perhaps a case in point occurred in the first quarter of 1974. At that time, the following news item appeared in papers across the country:

> Earnings of international oil companies are coming under close scrutiny in light of the fact that for the first quarter of 1974, Texaco reported an earnings increase of 123% over the same quarter a year earlier, Standard Oil of California reported an increase of 92%, Indiana Standard had an 81% increase, Gulf had a 76% increase, Mobil increased 66%, and Exxon increased 39%.
>
> Part of the reason for the large profit figures stemmed in part from differing ways the oil companies valued their inventory. Several of the companies—particularly those that reported very large profit figures—embarrassingly acknowledged that much of their profit was due to the fact that the market price of oil they had in inventory increased substantially in value between the time they produced the oil and the time they sold it. In other words, a large portion of their profit was due to an increase in the value of oil they had in inventory.

In view of the fact that the United States was suffering from an oil shortage during the same period these firms were gaining profits on inventory, some people felt that the oil companies should be taxed extra hard, or at worst, broken up by the government. The oil companies, on the other hand, felt that it is simply good business to keep some oil in inventory, and also noted that if prices had fallen instead of risen, they would have suffered a loss instead of realizing a profit.

1. *Comment on the "critics'" feelings that it appeared to them the oil companies were "ripping off" the American consumer. Do you agree? Why or why not?*

2. What do you see the accountant's role in all of this to have been?

3. To whom do the oil companies (in this situation, particularly) have their first responsibility: their owners who expect them to practice good business, or the consumers, who were screaming about the price of gas?

David Rockefeller needs little introduction to students of American business. The grandson of America's most famous capitalist and the youngest of five sons of John D. Rockefeller II, David Rockefeller today sits as chairman of the board of the Chase Manhattan Bank in New York, one of the most powerful financial positions in the world.

David Rockefeller was born June 12, 1915, in New York. Although his family was worth literally billions of dollars, young Rockefeller was taught early in life to be frugal. At one time, he worked on the family estate raking leaves—a task for which he received $2 for an eight-hour shift.

Upon graduation from Harvard (class of 1936), he attended the London School of Economics and The University of Chicago, receiving his Ph.D. in economics from Chicago in 1940. Following graduation, Rockefeller desired to learn more of how public institutions functioned, and so joined the staff of New York Mayor Fiorello La Guardia as a $1 per year assistant. Eighteen months later, he found himself involved in World War II, where he rose to the rank of captain in military intelligence.

At the conclusion of the war, Rockefeller returned to the world of business. In April of 1946, he joined the Chase Manhattan Bank as an assistant manager of the foreign department. He became vice-president three years later, president in 1961, and chairman of the board in 1968.

During Rockefeller's charge, Chase expanded rapidly. Its total assets increased severalfold, and it is now represented in scores of countries.

Rockefeller has at times, been criticized for his role as chairman of the Chase bank. Many people have charged that his sole claim to the office he holds is because of his family's wealth. Yet, whether one chooses to believe the cynics or not, one fact remains clear. David Rockefeller today stands as one of the world's most powerful men.

David Rockefeller
(1915–   )

"Bankers are just like anybody else; sometimes richer . . ."

14

Financial management: Sources of funds

There have been three great inventions since the beginning of time:
Fire, the wheel, and central banking.

——Will Rogers

Personnel management, production, and marketing can successfully accomplish their goals only if the firm has sufficient funds. Personnel management, for example, will have no one to manage unless the firm can meet the payroll each week. Production will create no new products or services unless the firm can acquire new machinery and equipment to replace equipment which is wearing out or becoming too expensive to operate. And marketing efforts may prove futile unless money is made available to pay for advertising and promotion. In summary, we can see that no business can exist for long unless it successfully resolves the problem of how to finance its operations. Showing how businesses are financed is the purpose of this chapter.

DEFINING THE FINANCING

Defining the finance function is a more difficult task than one might realize. Certainly, the finance function has as a basic objective the obtaining of sufficient funds to keep the business operating. But "finance" encompasses much more than just this objective. Basically, the finance function is concerned with all problems that are associated with the *efficient acquisition and use* of capital. The problems of determining which of the proposed expenditures will best achieve the goals of the firm, and where sufficient funds can be obtained to pay for the expenditure, form the crux of the traditional function of finance. This chapter and the next elaborate on the two key parts of this functional definition: the *efficient acquisition* of funds, and the *efficient use* of funds within a business firm.

The difficulty in acquiring funds

The problem of acquiring funds for the business enterprise to efficiently operate is a highly complex one. Most firms do not generate enough funds from their operations to meet the growing needs of the various departments and divisions within the firm. As a result, the financial manager usually needs to go outside the firm for some of the funds needed by the business. Depending upon the particular nature of a business, the problem of securing funds at a reasonable cost can prove to be a difficult one.

RESTRICTIONS ON SOURCES OF FUNDS

The problems associated with optimizing a firm's sources of funds differ from firm to firm. Not all businesses are able to take advantage of the same sources of funds. For some firms, the organizational structure of the firm tends to restrict the available sources of funds. For other firms, ownership considerations become significant in the choice of their sources of funds. Finally, the eventual use of the funds plays an important role in the choice of a source of funds. An understanding of the nature of these restrictions, therefore, is important for financial managers if they are to efficiently perform their function.

Organizational restrictions

The source of funds available to business firms differs among businesses of varying organizational structures. Sole proprietorships, for example, find the availability of funds sharply different from those available to corporations. Similarly, partnerships have available to them sources of funds which differ substantially from those traditionally used by either sole proprietorships or by corporations. In each instance, however, the particular availability or nonavailability of funds stems directly from the characteristics of the organization. Let us briefly examine these characteristics, particularly as they relate to obtaining sources of financing.

Sole proprietorships   Sole proprietorships, as we have already seen, are characterized by several qualities, among which are: (a) one owner, (b) unlimited liability, (c) small size, and (d) an uncertain life-span. Because a sole proprietorship has only one owner, ownership funds are restricted to what that owner can afford to provide to the firm. Unless the owner is extremely wealthy, the amount of capital available from this source is limited. Moreover, the unlimited liability feature of the sole proprietorship makes it highly unlikely that the owner is wealthy, for if he were, he probably would incorporate in order to protect his personal wealth from possible lawsuits against the business.

Similarly, the opportunity for sole proprietorships to borrow monies tends to be limited. Creditors usually desire some form of collateral for loans—usually a mortgage on property owned by the business—as security in case of a default on the loan. Moreover, they generally want the party requesting the loan to show good faith by providing some portion of the needed funds himself. Since sole proprietors tend to have limited personal resources, they are usually limited in what they can borrow. Also, the small size of most sole proprietorships tends to limit the amount of assets available for collateral.

Partnerships Partnerships have much in common with sole proprietorships, both from a legal and a financial point of view. For example, partnerships are characterized by: (a) the existence of two or more owners, (b) unlimited liability for all general partners, and (c) an uncertain life-span. These characteristics, however, are not as restrictive as they are for the sole proprietorship. Thus, the partnership is able to maintain greater flexibility in its quest for sources of funds.

The availability of ownership funds (i.e., funds provided by the owners of the business) for example, is not restricted to what one owner can provide but instead depends on the number of owners. Many partners would mean greater latitude in the use of this source of funds than would be the case with only two or three partners. Moreover, more owners can usually be added to a partnership, thus enlarging the ownership base.

Similarly, the availability of debt funds (i.e., borrowed funds) for partnerships is dependent upon the ownership base of the firm. The more general partners (all of whom have unlimited liability for the debts of the firm), the more willing creditors will be to extend loans to the firm. Indeed, all things being equal, partnerships—size for size—tend to have the best credit rating of all forms of business ownership. This, again, is due to the unlimited liability of its many partners for the debts of the business.

Corporations The corporate form of business organization is unlike the other two major types of organizations in securing financing. Corporations are characterized by: (a) the existence of many owners, (b) the transferability of ownership, (c) limited liability, (d) unlimited life, and (e) an unusual taxation classification. These five characteristics are particularly relevant in the consideration of sources of financing.

For the most part, ownership funds are readily available to corporations. To raise such funds, the corporation can sell additional stock—either to new owners or to the existing owners. The sale of additional ownership shares is restricted by only two factors, neither of which is difficult to overcome. First, a corporation must appeal to the state authorities for permission to amend its charter. This charter specifies, you will recall, the number of shares of stock the company may legally sell. Second, once permission to amend the charter has been secured, stockholder permission for such action is required. All corporate activity that affects the ownership position of stockholders requires that such activity be approved by the stockholders. Such approval is not usually difficult to obtain.

The availability of debt funds is more difficult to appraise. Small corporations find that the availability of debt funds is sharply limited, primarily because their size implies a lack of assets for use as collateral. Also, the limited liability feature of small corporations works against the best interests of would-be creditors. Large corporations, however, find that their size works to their advantage and far outweighs any considerations about liability of the owners. Thus, large corporations have little difficulty obtaining debt funds. Moreover, it will be seen that the tax treatment of interest payments actually makes the obtaining of debt funds financially attractive for corporations.

Ownership restrictions

Organizational restrictions, however, are not the only limiting factor in choosing a source of financing. A second constraining factor concerns the ownership restrictions. Sole proprietorships, partnerships, and corporations all differ in their ownership characteristics, and these differences may override any other consideration in a choice of financing.

Sole proprietorships   A sole proprietorship could increase its ownership capital by changing its ownership structure to that of a partnership and admitting one or more individuals into the firm as co-owners. This, however, would require the proprietor's sacrificing *sole* ownership and all of the benefits that go with it. This includes full right to profits, undivided control of the decision-making process, and so on. Rather, obtaining the additional capital would mean the owner would have to accept all of the obligations of partnership, including the sharing of profits and control and the responsibility for a partner's actions. Many sole proprietors refuse to pay this price for additional capital. They argue that the reason they formed a sole proprietorship in the first place was to avoid these problems. For sole proprietorships, then, ownership often proves to be an important factor in the quest for a source of funds.

Partnerships   Partnerships face a similar, although less drastic, problem. Additional ownership funds can be obtained by admitting more personnel to the partnership. Such action, however, tends to reduce the proportional benefits of partnership for all of the original partners. While such action for a large partnership may not be significant (an addition of one partner to a partnership of 100 changes the proportional benefits only 1 percent), for a small partnership the action may be as important as the one facing the sole proprietor. A partnership of two, contemplating the admission of a third partner, faces a reduction of benefits for each of the original partners of from 50 percent each to 33.3 percent each, or a one-sixth reduction. Given the additional risk involved (each partner being responsible for all other partners' actions), it is easy to see why a partnership may be unwilling to resort to this method to obtain capital.

Corporations   The ownership factor for corporations is again not easy to determine. Not all corporations are owned by a large number of people. Many corporations, some of them quite large, are owned and/or controlled by families or single individuals. For controlling interest in a company to exist, it is not necessary for all of the stock in the company to be owned by the individual or the family. All that is necessary is the ownership of a block of stock large enough to be dominant in the management of the firm. The Ford Motor Company is an example of such a company. For such firms, certain sources of funds are less desirable than

FIGURE 14–1

General Motors has so many stockholders that to send out one mailing involves a postage bill of approximately $100,000, each time!

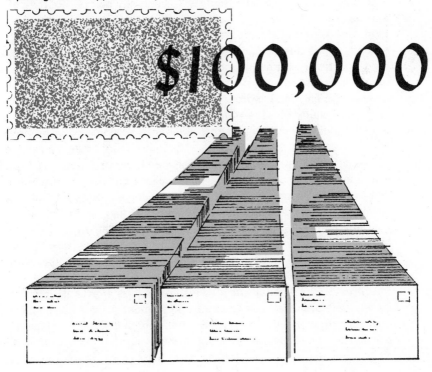

other sources. The issuance of additional common stock, for example, may alter the controlling position of the current owners just enough to allow others to gain control. In such instances, the issuance of common stock as a source of funds may be highly undesirable. The question of control, therefore, may well outweigh all other considerations in choosing a source of funds.

As it is, the vast majority of the major corporations in America are not owned or controlled by families or single stockholders. Most of our largest corporations have stockholders by the tens of thousands. Ownership of the American Telephone and Telegraph Company for example, is so widely dispersed that no one person owns as much as 5 percent of the total outstanding common stock. General Motors, the largest industrial corporation in America, has so many owners that to send out dividend checks or other notices to all of its stockholders involves a postage bill of approximately $100,000 for each mailing! With businesses of such size, it is easy to see why controlling ownership considerations become relatively insignificant for these companies.

Use-of-funds restriction

A final restriction on the sources of financing available to a business firm is the use to which the funds will eventually be put. Sources of funds and uses of funds are generally classified as either long term or short term. Short-term funds are those sought in order to finance current operations of the business, such as meeting the payroll and buying the supplies and raw materials needed to build up inventories. Long-term funds, on the other hand, are needed for relatively permanent investments in new equipment, land, warehouses, plants and so on. The reasoning behind this is fairly obvious—a business firm in the process of constructing a new building would not want to finance the construction by borrowing the money at a bank for 30 days. The bank loan would come due long before the building was finished, and certainly long before the building would ever contribute to the business's profitability. A more rational solution would be to borrow money for a 20- or 30-year period. In this way, the earnings realized through the use of the building could be used to pay the debt incurred in the building's construction. Similarly, the financing of extra inventory, or the financing needed to pay wages to part-time help would more logically be resolved with a short-term loan than with long-term debt.

Unlike organizational and ownership factors, the limitations imposed by the "use-of-funds" restriction are not unique to any particular type of business organization. That is, sole proprietorships, partnerships and corporations—widely held or privately owned—large firms and small firms—all face similar "use" restrictions. For this reason, the following discussions of the sources and uses of funds are limited to those aspects of the problem that concern corporations. Granted, sole proprietorships and partnerships may face similar situations. For purposes of this discussion, however, emphasis is on the financing problems of that business institution that accounts for most economic activity—the corporation.

As has been indicated, sources of funds are usually classified as short term or long term. Short-term funds are those funds that must be repaid in one year or less. Long-term funds are funds with maturities in excess of one year. Occasionally, reference is made to "intermediate-term" sources of funds. Intermediate sources are often listed as those sources of funds maturing in more than one year, but in less than ten years, with long-term funds being those with maturities in excess of ten years. For purposes of this review, however, intermediate-term and long-term sources of funds will be treated as a singular group, with maturities in excess of one year.

SHORT-TERM SOURCES OF FUNDS

Every business firm is faced with the problem of financing its day-to-day operations. Wages and salaries need to be paid regularly, bills come due, supplies need to be ordered and paid for, unexpected emergencies arise, and so on. While most businesses try to finance a majority of these activities out of receipts from sales, sometimes the expenditures exceed the receipts. When this happens, these short-term expenditures need to be financed externally. Such short-term financing usually comes from one of four sources, as listed below.

Short-term sources of funds

Other businesses	Factors
Banks	Government agencies

Other businesses

Trade credit Other businesses are the most popular source of short-term financing. When one business buys merchandise from another, it usually receives a bill (known as an *invoice*) calling for payment in some given period of time after receipt of the goods. This type of financing is called *trade credit.* Thus, a retailer may buy merchandise from a wholesaler and receive delivery on March 1st. The bill accompanying the merchandise may call for payment within ten days after receipt of the goods. The retailer, then, has the "free" use of the merchandise from the 1st to the 10th, at which time he must pay for the goods. During the ten-day period, however, the wholesaler in effect, finances the merchandise inventory for the retailer.

Is trade credit "free"?   There is some question as to whether the use of trade credit is actually "free." It is true that retailers pay the same price for the goods, regardless of whether they pay for the goods on the 1st or the 10th, and that therefore, by delaying payment they could conceivably invest their money in the bank for the ten days and earn interest on it. However, it is highly probable that wholesalers have increased the price of their products to the retailers in order to pay for the financing they are providing. Consider, for example, a wholesaler supplying 100 retailers. If each retailer was given "free" trade credit, the wholesaler would soon face a real financing problem himself. His sales would all be on trade credit—no money would be coming in from current sales until the "free" period ended. The wholesaler, then, would probably be forced to go to the bank and obtain a short-term loan to facilitate his day-to-day expenses. Since the bank would charge him interest, the wholesaler would suffer an added cost. It seems likely, therefore, that the wholesaler would compute this cost in advance and would add it to the price he charged the retailers for the merchandise. In this way, the cost is being "passed on" to the retailer.

Why then, you might wonder, do businesses bother with trade credit? The answer involves several considerations. First, the tradition underlying the use of trade credit is so strong that a firm could find itself in a competitive disadvantage if it ceased offering trade credit. Second, the use of trade credit demonstrates the good faith and trust of one business leader in another. Just as individuals find it advantageous to have a good credit rating with stores, businesses also find it advantageous to have a good credit rating with their fellow business leaders. Finally, retailers don't usually mind paying a little more for goods in order to get trade credit; they merely pass on the added cost to the consumer. Thus, retailers are still able to provide themselves with "free" financing.

Credit terms   To prevent the misuse of trade credit, various incentives are usually built into the credit terms. Typically, billing terms are expressed as "2/10; n/30," or "2/10; n/E.O.M." The first term—the 2/10; n/30—means that the purchaser may deduct 2 percent if he pays the bill within 10 days; otherwise the net (or face) amount is due in 30 days. The second term—2/10; n/E.O.M.—means that the purchaser may deduct 2 percent from the bill if he pays the bill within ten days; otherwise the net amount is due by the end of the month (E.O.M.).

An interesting problem for the student to consider is the effect of *not* taking a discount when it is offered. Consider, for example, a firm that receives billing terms of 2/10; n/30. The financial manager is pondering about whether to pay the bill on the 10th day and take the discount or to wait and pay the full amount on the 30th. What is the cost of not taking the discount? To calculate this, ask yourself the following question: How much extra does it cost if I wait and pay the bill on the 30th? The answer, of course, is 2 percent. How many extra days use of the money did I get by waiting until the 30th to pay the bill? The answer is 20 days. The bill was originally due on the 10th if the discount was taken; otherwise it was due in full on the 30th. A 2 percent cost for 20 days is an expensive loan! On an annual basis, it works out to approximately 36 percent! The business executive could go to a bank and obtain a short-term (20-day) loan for, perhaps, 10 percent. Clearly, the bill should be paid in the discount period, even if it means borrowing the necessary funds from the local banker!

Illustration of the computation of the "real" interest cost

30 days − 10 days = 20 days
360 day year/20 days = 18 "discount periods"
18 periods × 2% = 36% cost.

Commercial banks

The second most important source of short-term funds are the commercial banks. Bank loans are utilized by most businesses at one time or another in the course of their operations. So, too, are financial arrangements known as lines of credit. These are also provided by commercial banks.

Bank loans Bank loans can come in many different forms. Two of the most common are (a) term loans and (b) lines of credit. Term loans are basically, the business equivalent to promissory notes. When a business needs funds for a specific period of time, it can arrange for a loan equal to its needs over that time. At some agreed-on date, the note or loan becomes due. Short-term loans are frequently used by business to finance inventory purchases, to provide working capital, or to pay bills that are coming due. In each case, however, the loan is usually expected to be paid off within a year. Because of the short-term nature of these loans, it is not uncommon to find them granted without the use of collateral. The banker may, however, require that his permission be obtained before the company borrows money from anyone else. This, obviously, is to protect his relative position as a creditor of the firm.

Lines of credit Banks also grant lines of credit to businesses they are familiar with. If a business has a line of credit for up to, say, $100,000, this means that the bank will approve loans to that business for up to $100,000. Whenever the business is in need of the funds, the financial manager has merely to ask for them, and the bank will credit the funds to the business' account. At the first convenient opportunity thereafter, the financial manager will sign a promissory note to formalize the loan. Obviously, for a business to be given a line of credit requires that the owners and/or the financial manager (*a*) have already established themselves and their business as trustworthy and sound, (*b*) show good judgment regarding the use of such funds, and (*c*) be known to the banker.

Term loans and lines of credit usually are granted at favorable rates of interest, particularly when compared with other forms of financing. Indeed, possessing a line of credit is of great advantage to businesses dealing with new suppliers. When suppliers learn of the favored position of the business they are dealing with, they usually are more inclined to grant favorable trade credit and other financing concessions.

Financial instruments honored by banks Banks also provide financing assistance over and above the granting of short-term loans and lines of credit. They assist business leaders in various negotiations by accepting various types of financial instruments that business leaders have agreed to exchange in their dealings with one another. These instruments include drafts, trade or bank acceptances and other, more specialized instruments.

A draft is similar to a promissory note, except that it is an *order* to pay and not a *promise* to pay. In a promissory note, it should be noted, the person incurring the liability creates the note, signs it, and delivers it to the person loaning the money. In a draft, the person to whom the money is owed creates the instrument, and sends it to the person incurring the liability. This person is instructed to pay the sum due to a third party, usually the bank of the person owed the money. If the terms are acceptable to the debtor, he writes "accepted" across the face of the note. Drafts, like checks and promissory notes, are negotiable and can be endorsed over to other parties.

Bank or trade acceptances are, in reality, modifications of the draft. When a time draft (one calling for payment at a specified future date) accompanies an invoice for goods, and the buyer of the goods accepts it, it is generally called a "trade acceptance." In other words, the buyer of the goods acknowledges through acceptance of the draft, the fact that money is owed to the seller of the goods. The seller of the goods can then take the trade acceptance to the bank, and the bank will "accept" it, meaning that it will credit the seller's account for the amount of the sale, and do the collecting itself.

Other specialized instruments frequently honored by banks include bills of lading and warehouse receipts. Both of these instruments are, in reality, title to goods held by someone else—either for storage purposes or transportation purposes. In order for the buyer of the goods to get title, the buyer must go to the bank and "accept" the draft that has been issued against the goods. When this is done, the buyer is given the bill of lading, entitling the buyer to take title to the goods that have been purchased. Until the buyer does so, however, the title to the goods remains with either the warehouseman storing the goods or the transportation company delivering the goods.

Factors

A third source of funds, but one that is significantly less important than the first two, involves the sale of accounts receivables to collection agents known as *factors.* Accounts receivable, you will recall, represent money owed *to* the business by its customers. Occasionally, a firm finds that its accounts receivable represent too large a portion of its sales—the result of too many of its customers postponing payment for goods. When this happens, the firm may run short of cash from receipts needed to handle its day-to-day expenses. It may then be forced to seek short-term financing. To facilitate this financing, the business may turn to a factor. The factor will purchase the accounts receivable from the company for something less than their face value. Just how much depends on two things: (*a*) the quality of the receivables, and (*b*) whether the accounts are sold *with recourse* or *without recourse.*

The quality of receivables When factors evaluate the quality of receivables, they are primarily interested in two things. First, they are interested in knowing how long the accounts have been outstanding. Experience has shown that the longer the accounts have remained uncollected, the more difficult it will be to ever collect their full amount. Thus, a firm whose receivables average 30 days outstanding would receive a larger amount (all other things being equal) for these receivables than would a similar firm whose receivables averaged 60 days outstanding. Second, factors are interested in the nature of the customers involved in the accounts. Customers of the type of IBM or Xerox or General Motors would be considered top grade—very little difficulty would be expected in collecting from them. On the other hand, companies bordering on bankruptcy (such as the Penn Central Railroad) might cause a great deal of difficulty. Similar evaluations can be made on consumer accounts. Stores such as Nieman-Marcus, Marshall Field, and Tiffany Jewelers may cater to better risk customers than stores like some of the discount houses, and their receivables would be evaluated accordingly.

Recourse versus no recourse If accounts are sold with recourse, factors are entitled to return to the business firms any of the receivables that cannot be collected. In other words, factors will keep only the better quality receivables.

Receivables sold without recourse in effect shift the risk of noncollection to the factors—if the receivables cannot be collected, the factor must accept the loss.

Obviously, receivables sold with recourse will bring the selling company higher proceeds than would be the case if the receivables were sold without recourse. Even under the best of circumstances, however, factors will rarely give more than 80 cents on the dollar for the receivables they buy.

Factors are not generally known by the consuming public. For one thing, factors rarely come into direct contact with very many consumers. Usually, a factor will buy a company's accounts receivable, but collection on those accounts may continue to go through the offices of the initial company.

The use of factors, while not overly popular, is not unusual for certain lines of business. The furniture industry, for example, has long used factors as a regular source of financing. The relatively high price of the product sold usually necessitates time payments by the customer. Other considerations include the resale potential of the product (in the event the merchandise must be reclaimed because of nonpayment), and the low merchandise turnover.

Other businesses will, on occasion, turn to factors for emergency financing, although sometimes even factors won't assist in collecting receivables. In the mid-1960s, Brunswick Corporation was forced to write off as uncollectible over $70 million in accounts receivable! The merchandise consisted of bowling alleys and automatic pin-setting machines that had been sold to bowling alley proprietors all across the country. When bowling tapered off in popularity, the proprietors were unable to pay for the alleys and machines. Brunswick could have reclaimed the equipment; it could even have sued to get repossession. But what was it to do with thousands of used bowling alleys and pin-setting machines? Instead, the company tried to sell the receivables to factors. The factors, however, considered the likelihood of collection to be so remote—the quality of the receivables to be so poor—that they would have nothing to do with them. In the end, Brunswick was forced to write off the receivables as a total loss—over $70 million worth!

Government agencies A final source of short-term funds are the many governmental agencies that are in existence. The Small Business Administration, for example, is empowered to make short-term loans to qualified businesses that are unable to get financing elsewhere. The Defense Department has, on occasion, granted advances on government defense contracts to defense-related companies in time of need. Even the Internal Revenue Service serves as a source of financing. While most businesses are required to estimate their next quarter's income, and pay a tax based on that expected income, it is not unusual for such payments to be slightly less than the actual tax due. When this occurs, the company has technically been able to secure the use of the government's money for a short period of time—in effect, a short-term, interest-free loan.

Government agencies, like factors, are much less important as sources of funds than other businesses and commercial banks. Still, they do play a role in the highly complex market servicing businesses short-term financing needs.

LONG-TERM SOURCES OF FUNDS

The importance of long-term financing

Just as short-term sources of funds are commonly used to finance short-term—or current—assets, so too are long-term sources of funds used to finance long-term—or fixed—assets. Naturally, a business firm utilizes long-term financing techniques much less frequently than it does short term. Whereas payrolls need to be met weekly, and other bills are regularly coming due, long-term expansion, such as plant expansion, may occur only once over a period of a few years. It is precisely for this reason, however, that long-term financing decisions require careful analysis. A business may well survive a poor decision regarding its short-term financing. Within a matter of weeks, the problem has been resolved, and another short-term financing decision awaits. But an error in choosing a source of funds for long-term financing could conceivably influence a company's fortunes for years hence—a situation that very few businesses could survive. It is imperative, therefore, that the financial manager give careful attention to the long-term financing decision.

Corporations have available to them, four primary sources of funds for long-term utilization. These are (a) common stock, (b) preferred stock, (c) debt funds, such as bank loans or bonds, and (d) retained earnings. Each of these financial sources has particular characteristics. The financial manager's problem is to determine which blend of these long-term sources of funds will best meet the long-run goals of the firm. To do this, however, requires an understanding of these four sources.

Common stock

Common stock represents the basic ownership shares of the corporation. Each share of stock carries exactly the same rights, privileges, and obligations as all other shares of common stock. These include those shown in the following list.

Characteristics of common stock

Share in earnings	Claim on assets
Voice in management	Permanent existence

Share in earnings The most popular right of common stockholders is the right to share in the earnings of the corporation. Each year, the board of directors of the corporation meet to determine, among other things, the dividend policy the company will maintain for the coming period. If the board decides to pay a dividend, that is, to pay part of the earnings of the company out to the owners of the firm, all common stockholders will receive identical per share dividends. Thus, whenever a dividend is declared and paid, all common stockholders will receive their proportionate share.

It should be emphasized, however, that a corporation is not required to pay a dividend. This policy is determined by the board of directors. If, for some reason, the board decides not to pay a dividend in a given year, the stockholders must accept that decision. Moreover, any dividend paid to common stockholders may be limited by the fact that interest must be paid periodically on any outstanding debts. Also any dividends owed on outstanding preferred stock must first be paid before any dividends can be paid on the common stock.

Voice in management A second right of common stockholders is the right to vote on corporate matters, including a vote on the election of a board of directors. This right has been implied earlier in this chapter. Recall the mention of the problem of control of a corporation, and the way in which the issuance of common stock can sometimes alter this control. This control is effected by means of the vote that each common stockholder has. The greater the number of shares of stock owned, the greater the vote—and thus the greater the control possessed by any given owner or organized group of owners.

It should be noted, however, that the ownership of one share of stock does not necessarily mean the stockholder is entitled to one vote. Sometimes each share of stock entitles its owner to eight, nine, or even more votes! This is because of the existence of two different methods of voting that can legally exist in corporate affairs. Known as *cumulative* voting and *noncumulative* voting, these are discussed in more depth in Chapter 18.

Claim on assets A third characteristic of common stock is the right to share in the assets of the firm upon liquidation. In the event a corporation decides to go out of business, any assets remaining after the liquidation of all debts and prior claims belong to the common stockholders. To illustrate, let us assume that a corporation with assets of $500,000, debts of $250,00 and 25,000 shares of common stock outstanding decided to discontinue operations. The corporation would liquidate its assets and then pay off its debts; in this case it would have $250,000 left. ($500,000 from the assets less $250,000 in debts). The $250,000 would then be divided proportionately among the holders of the common stock. In this case, each share of common stock would be worth $10.

Having a claim on the assets of the firm if and when a corporation liquidates has a very limited benefit to common stockholders, in reality.

Healthy, profitable firms rarely undergo voluntary liquidation. Poor, nearly bankrupt ones almost always do. Consequently, when such an event occurs, it is usually because the company is so overburdened with debt that it cannot pay its interest obligations. Liquidations under such circumstances usually find the company strapped, with more money owed than it has assets to liquidate, and the result is that the common stockholders get nothing. The legal right to share in any remaining assets is still a right of common stockholders, however. It is for this reason that this characteristic is mentioned.

Permanent existence   A fourth and final significant factor that pertains to common stock financing involves the life span of common stock. Once issued, common stock cannot be recalled from the market. It is, legally, outstanding for the life of the corporation. The only way a corporation can regain possession and ownership of its common stock is to repurchase it from the stockholders owning it—which requires meeting the price demands of the common stockholder. For all practical purposes, then, common stock is permanent in its existence.

Preferred stock

A second form of equity or ownership financing involves the use of preferred stock. Preferred stock is a unique and somewhat mystifying security in that it possesses characteristics of both debt funds and common stock. Generally speaking, preferred stock is an ownership security that has special features or benefits that common stockholders do not have. In this sense, it is known as "preferred" or "preference" stock. Specifically, preferred stock has the features listed below:

Characteristics of preferred stock

Dividend features	Longevity of issue
Prior claim on assets	Voice in management

Dividend features   Perhaps the most unique feature of preferred stock concerns the dividend features that may be applicable. Usually, preferred stock carries the right to a fixed, specified dividend and no more. This dividend may be expressed in dollars, such as $5 per share, or as a percentage of par value. As a general rule, preferred stock with a $100 par value tends to carry a dividend expressed as a percent of par; all other preferred issues (i.e., those with par values other than $100) tend to carry a stated dollar dividend.

The fact that the dividend on preferred stock is specified, as opposed to the "residual" claims of common stockholders, is one of the more significant differences between preferred and common stock. Indeed, preferred stock has often been called "quasi debt," because the fixed dividend feature is very much like the fixed interest charge on debt obligations. That is, the firm is somewhat obligated to pay the dividend each year. Indeed, common stockholders are not entitled to any dividends unless and until the preferred stockholder's dividend obligations have been satisfied.

To further complicate the issue, however, are two other features related to the dividend obligation on preferred stock. These other features are conditions that are sometimes attached to the preferred dividend in order to improve the marketability of the preferred issue. These terms are: (*a*) the *cumulative* feature and (*b*) the *participating* feature.

The cumulative feature   Preferred stock is said to be cumulative if nonpayment of the preferred dividend in any given period results in the accumulation of the obligation in the following period. That is, preferred stock is cumulative if this previous obligation must be met before there can be any further distribution of earnings to the common stockholders. Suppose, for example, that a corporation's earnings were so poor one year that the board of directors decided not to pay any preferred dividends. If the preferred stock was cumulative, the corporation would face the prospect of having to pay this previously omitted dividend, plus any other dividend omissions that may have occurred in earlier periods, before any dividends could be paid to the common stockholders.

At this point, it should become apparent that cumulative preferred stock is more like debt than is noncumulative preferred. The dividend on the cumulative preferred becomes a fixed obligation; the firm is forced to pay the dividend or face added problems the following year. In contrast, noncumulative preferred stock is more like common stock. If the dividend is declared, fine. If not, that period's claim is not carried forward.

The participating feature   Another feature relating to the dividends paid to preferred stockholders is the participating feature. While this is a relatively uncommon feature of contemporary preferred stock financing, it does appear on occasion and is one of the most interesting features of preferred stock. Indeed, several large corporations, including Southern California Edison and Litton Industries, have participating preferred stocks outstanding at the present time.

A preferred stock is said to be participating if the preferred stockholders, after receiving their stated dividend, share with the common stockholders in the dividends declared for the common stockholders. While the exact nature of this "participation" may vary considerably from firm to firm, the key element of participation with the common stockholders in the dividends of the firm remains the distinguishing feature of participating preferred stock.

Prior claim on assets   A second characteristic of preferred stock is its prior claim on the assets of the corporation. Like common stock, preferred stock entitles its owners to a portion of the assets of the firm in the event of liquidation. Preferred stockholders, however, are entitled to their share of this liquidating value *before* the common stockholders —they have a prior claim on the assets. Thus, in a corporate liquidation, first, all debts are resolved. Then all preferred stockholders are reimbursed the par value of their stock. And anything that is left is distributed among the common stockholders. Again, it should be noted that this right —preference as to the assets of the firm in the event of liquidation—is a rather dubious one. Rarely does this right assume any meaningful value.

Longevity of issue A third important characteristic of preferred stock concerns the longevity of the issue. Common stock, as has been noted, has the unique characteristic of permanence of issue. Once outstanding, the only way management can regain possession is by buying it back from its owners—at terms acceptable to the owners. This also holds true for preferred stock if it is noncallable. However, sometimes preferred stock is made *callable,* meaning that the corporation reserves the right to redeem the stock whenever it chooses. This right usually allows the corporation to redeem the outstanding preferred stock at its par value, plus a small penalty which usually amounts to an additional 6 percent of par.

It is easy to see how the existence of a call provision has implications for the expected life of a preferred issue. Usually, when a call provision exists, it is impossible to tell just how long the issue may remain outstanding. Thus, a preferred issue with a call provision very closely resembles a bond or other long-term debt issue in that it can be retired at the company's discretion. Moreover, call provisions have an interesting effect on the control of corporations, as we shall see.

Voice in management A final important characteristic of preferred stock concerns its influence on the management of the firm. For the most part, this influence is exercised in any of three ways. These are (a) through voting privileges, (b) through call provisions, and (c) through conversion privileges.

Voting privileges In many states preferred stockholders have the same right to vote on company matters as the common stockholders. In these states, the common and preferred stockholders' voting rights are identical. Indeed, except for the existence of a call provision and possible variations in the dividend policies, practical distinctions between common and preferred stock virtually disappear.

In other states, the preferred stockholders do not have the right to vote unless such a right is specifically indicated in the terms of issue of the security. However, many corporate bylaws require that, in the event dividend obligations for the preferred stockholders are not met for a specified period of time (such as six consecutive quarters), the preferred stockholders would then be entitled to a vote on corporate matters.

Under these circumstances, corporate financial officers may find the potential voting power of the preferred stockholder to be a significant factor in determining who controls the company. Maintenance of the preferred dividend, therefore, becomes more important in the maintaining of control over management.

Call provisions The call provision has implications for the control of a corporation only in those situations where the preferred stock is entitled to a vote on corporate matters. If such preferred stock is callable, management can conceivably determine whether or not it wants the preferred stockholders to exercise their voting privileges. If management feels the preferred stockholders may vote contrary to its wishes, it could conceivably call the stock in, retire it, and thereby remove the potential source of unfavorable votes. Such action, however, would require that the corporation have sufficient funds on hand to be capable of retiring a large block of stock.

Conversion privileges A final feature of preferred stock that has a bearing on the determination of the management of the firm is the convertibility feature. Corporations will, on occasion, issue preferred stock which can be exchanged for common stock in the same company in accordance with the provisions of the preferred stock agreement. Such a privilege is known as the conversion feature. When a corporation issues a convertible preferred stock, it is, in effect, issuing a security that has the potential of permanence of existence, full voting rights, and so on—all of the characteristics of common stock. Such stock, then, has the potential of becoming a major influence in the determination of the management of the firm. This influence, of course, is most apparent in those states where the preferred stock did not have voting rights; the preferred stockholder can conceivably switch from a nonvoting status to a voting one.

Debt funds

A third major source of long-term financing involves the use of borrowed money, or debt funds. Corporations make extensive use of borrowed money in the financing of their activities. The reasons for this heavy usage are sound. Debt money is readily available—banks, insurance companies, individuals and other corporations are always looking for ways to invest their excess cash. Corporations in need of cash—particularly large corporations—offer a very attractive investment medium.

Money borrowed for the long term (over one year) typically takes one of two distinct forms. Funds may be acquired from an institution (such as a bank or insurance company) in the form of a *term loan,* or it may come from the investing public, through the sale of a particular legal instrument known as a *bond.* Before looking at the distinctive features of these two types of debt-financing arrangements, however, we should note some of the unique features of corporate debt.

Characteristics of corporate debt

Corporate debt is distinguished from other sources of financing by the four characteristics listed below.

Characteristics of corporate debt

The interest charge	Tax implications
Claim on assets	Eventual repayment

The interest charge   The most obvious and significant characteristic of all debt financing is the interest charge. Whenever money is borrowed, the lender requires some form of reimbursement for having provided the money. That reimbursement is the interest charged for the loan. Unlike dividends, which are periodic payments of the company's earnings to its owners, interest is a fixed, mandatory expense. A company may omit the payment of dividends; it may *not* omit the payment of interest. Failure to pay the interest on a loan can result in legal action by the creditor and could force the business to sell part of its assets to pay off the debt. In the extreme, the creditor could force the business into bankruptcy.

A claim on assets   All creditors of a business have a legal claim on the assets of the firm. Whenever money is borrowed, the creditor gains a legal right to force the company to liquidate assets in the event it fails to honor the terms of the loan. In the event of liquidation, all creditors have first claim on the assets of the firm. Their claim is superior to that of the preferred stockholders, and obviously, the common stockholders. Rarely, however, does this claim on assets have a significant meaning in practice.

Tax implications   A third characteristic of corporate debt is the tax treatment of the interest expense. Recall the discussion of the income statement in Chapter 13. In calculating its net income, a corporation is allowed to deduct all expenses related to its operations from its revenues. One of these expenses is interest expense. All interest payments paid by a corporation can be deducted from its gross income in arriving at its taxable income. The result is that most corporations are able to reduce their taxes by almost one half of the amount of the interest. Let's examine this again. Assume that we have the following partial income statement:

Partial Income Statement
With Interest Expense

Revenues...............................		$100,000
Less:		
Interest expense.........................	$ 5,000	
Other expenses.........................	45,000	50,000
Taxable income...........................		50,000
Taxes (50%).............................		25,000
Net Income.............................		$ 25,000

FIGURE 14–2

A corporate bond

All other expenses are grouped together in order to draw attention to the "interest expense" item. What effect did the interest expense have on the final net income of the company? Note that the $5,000 interest lowered the taxable income by $5,000. In other words, if there had not been an interest expense charge, the taxable income would have been $55,000. Given a 50 percent tax charge, the final net income would have been $27,500—a difference of $2,500, not $5,000. Why?

Partial Income Statement
Without Interest Expense

Revenues.....................................		$100,000
Less:		
Interest expense.........................	$ 0	
Other expenses..........................	45,000	45,000
Taxable Income............................		55,000
Taxes (50%)..............................		27,500
Net Income...............................		$ 27,500

The reason is found in the 50 percent tax charged by the government. The added $5,000 expense in the first instance forced the government to accept less in tax revenue, solely because the reported income was lower. In other words, the practical effect is that the government absorbs approximately one half of the cost of debt financing![1] The $5,000 interest expense only lowered the net income by $2,500—one half of the actual cost. As you progress in your study of finance, you will learn that this is one of the most important factors in determining the relative profitability of financing decisions. The fact that the government in actuality absorbs almost half of the cost of debt financing makes this particular source of funds extremely attractive to corporations.

Eventual repayment The final characteristic of debt funds that is common to all forms of such financing concerns the eventual repayment of the money. Debt funds—even long-term debt funds—sooner or later need to be repaid. While many corporations are able to refinance their debt (by selling new bonds or obtaining new loans to replace the ones coming due), at some point in time these need to be repaid. Thus, any use of borrowed money in the financing decision must incorporate the problem of how to repay the funds in the future.

Types of long-term debt financing

There are two primary sources of long-term debt financing: (a) bank loans and (b) bonds.

Bank term loans One of the most common forms of debt financing

---

[1] In actuality the corporate tax rate is 48 percent, not 50 percent. Thus the government only foots 48 percent of the interest expense. The formula used to arrive at the true cost of debt to the firms is to multiply the interest by $(1 - T)$, where T is the tax rate.

involves the use of bank term loans. Such loans most frequently have maturities ranging from one to five years, although occasionally a bank will grant a longer loan. Bank loans of these durations usually carry certain restrictions. For example, a bank may require that the amount of dividends the firm pays be limited to some fixed, maximum amount. It may also ask that its permission be obtained before the business firm acquires any other additional debt. Restrictions such as these are designed to protect the bank's investment. By limiting dividends, it helps ensure that money will be available to pay off the loan when the loan comes due. By limiting the acquisition of new debt, the bank has added assurance that its claim on the assets of the firm will not have to be shared with other newly added creditors.

Corporate bonds   The other distinctive type of long-term debt financing involves the use of corporate bonds. Bonds are long-term debt instruments. In many cases they have maturities ranging from 10 to 30 or even 40 years. Bonds are characterized by the promise to repay a principal sum of money at some point in the future and to pay interest on that sum periodically until that maturity date is reached.

The use of corporate bonds has become one of the most popular means of securing long-term financing. Corporations of all sizes and of varying financial strength issue bonds today. Because of the wide variability among issuing corporations, however, some of the bonds are sold with conditions and/or features that other bonds do not have. Most of these special features are found in the corporate document that must be filed with each bond issue. That document is the *indenture agreement.*

The indenture agreement   The indenture agreement is a statement describing the terms associated with a particular bond issue. Many of these terms are similar to the characteristics found in some preferred stocks. For example, bonds may be callable, and they may be convertible into common or preferred stock. They may also have specific assets pledged as collateral as a guarantee for the loan. It is not necessary to repeat the characteristics of the callable feature, the convertible feature, and so on. Figure 14–3 briefly notes some of the more popular and more important types of bonds currently outstanding.

Other features   One final feature of bonds concerns the initial issuing price of the security. If the issuing corporation is a well-known, financially sound corporation, it is entirely possible that buyers of these bonds will find them attractive enough to pay slightly more than face value for the security. If a corporate bond—par of $1,000—sells for $1,020, the $20 excess is called a *premium.* Companies that are very safe can often sell bonds for a small premium.

On the other hand, small, unknown or financially weak corporations may have to sell their bonds at a *discount,* meaning that purchasers will only pay, say, $960 for a $1,000 bond. In other words, they view the company as being risky enough that it no longer warrants the right to sell its

FIGURE 14–3

Types of corporate bonds

Debenture bonds:

No security other than the good name of the issuing company behind them. Very popular with well-known corporations.

Registered bonds:

Owner's name on file at company headquarters. Registering gives owner added protection in case of theft.

Coupon bonds:

In order to collect interest on these bonds, coupons must be cut from the bond itself and redeemed at the local bank. All coupons payable to bearer.

Serial bonds:

Bonds containing a serial number which is related to some retirement scheme. Thus, the company will retire or buy back the bonds in the order of the serial numbers of the bond issue.

Income bonds:

Bonds which pay interest to the bondholder only if the company earns enough money to justify it. This kind of bond is rather rare today.

Chattel mortgage bonds:

A bond that carries a mortgage or lien against specific movable property of the company. Very popular with railroads.

bonds at par. Many smaller corporations are forced to sell their bonds at a discount in the open market.

Retained earnings

Still another source of long-term funds that we need to consider are those funds earned by the business in the course of its operations, but not paid out as dividends to the stockholders. Known as *retained earnings,* this source of funds is used with increasing frequency by large corporations. The advantages of using retained earnings should be apparent: there are no debts to pay back, no interest or dividend expenses to consider, no ownership problems, and so on. However, not all corporations can use retained earnings; and of those that can, most cannot utilize this source as much as they might like. The reason, of course, is that very few corporations earn enough money to be able to pay a dividend *and* have sufficient profits left with which to finance all of their operations.

Depreciation as a source of funds

A last "source" of funds that should be mentioned is depreciation. From Chapter 13, you will recall that depreciation expense is that portion of the cost of a fixed asset that is charged off as an expense each year. Following accounting procedures, a business tries to charge expenses to that year in which the expense was incurred. However, reflect on depreciation as an actual expense. Did the firm actually spend money that year in the amount of the depreciation? The answer, of course, is no. The entire cost of the asset was paid when the asset was purchased. Depreciation merely "spreads" the bookkeeping cost over time. To the extent that "depreciation expense" lowers the reported income, the firm will realize a "hidden" source of funds. In business terminology, depreciation is referred to as a *noncash expense,* and is, consequently, a source of funds.

The problem of finding sufficient sources of funds to finance the operations of the business is, unfortunately, only half of the financial manager's responsibility. The other half of the problem is that of investing these funds. This problem is discussed in the next chapter. In many ways, however, corporations are just like people when it comes to finance. It always seems to be more difficult to obtain funds than it is to spend them. In this regard, an understanding of the sources of funds available to a corporation is critical for the financial manager. Yet, to be successful in the competitive business world, a business must be efficient both in raising its funds and in making use of them.

DISCUSSION QUESTIONS:

1. What is the finance function? What do we mean by the phrase, "efficient sources" of funds?

2. Explain the relationship of the finance function to the other functions of the business enterprise.

3. How can the organizational structure of a business firm limit the available sources of funds for (a) a sole proprietorship, (b) a partnership, and (c) a corporation?

4. Is trade credit free? Explain.

5. What is the difference between receivables sold "with recourse" and those sold "without recourse"? Under what conditions might a firm sell receivables "without recourse"?

6. How does common stock differ from preferred stock?

7. One of the characteristics of common stock is its permanence of existence. Exactly what does this mean?

8. What are different features that are commonly put on preferred stock and which affect dividend policies of a firm?

9. What feature of long-term debt financing makes this a particularly attractive source of funds for large corporations?

10 Why does a large corporation like to have many different sources of funds, rather than just one or two very large ones?

MINI CASES

The Johnston Manufacturing Company was a well-established manufacturer of electric and gasoline motors for lawn mowers and similar garden accessories. Its stock had been listed on the New York Stock Exchange for almost 20 years, over which time it had been a steady, if not glamorous, performer.

About 10 years ago, the Johnston Company issued 100,000 shares of a 5 percent, cumulative preferred stock at a price of $100 per share, in order to finance an expansion program. The preferred dividends have subsequently been paid every year since the issuance of the stock.

At a recent shareholder's meeting, a stockholder asked management why it continued to keep the preferred stock outstanding. The stockholder argued that the dividends being paid on the common stock could be increased if the company would retire the preferred stock and issue bonds instead. The company promised to investigate the matter further.

You have been called in to advise the Johnston Company on the merits of the stockholder's suggestion. To assist you in your deliberations, the company has provided you with the following information: If the bonds are issued as a replacement for the preferred stock, they would carry an 8 percent interest rate. A total of 10,000 bonds, each worth $1,000, would need to be issued. No penalty would be assessed for calling the preferred stock. The corporate tax rate is 50 percent.

1. Determine the feasibility of the stockholder's suggestion. What other considerations should the company keep in mind in deciding on the merits of the suggestion?

2. If the company currently has 5 million shares of common stock outstanding, how much would a switch from preferred stock to debt affect the dividends paid on each share of common stock? In answering this question, assuming the company wishes to keep its total payment of interest and dividends the same, after taxes, as it was before the suggestion came up?

The Major Department Store in suburban Cleveland recently opened a new shoe department. To stock the department, the store ordered approximately $25,000 worth of children's shoes and another $25,000 worth of adult shoes. The goods have just arrived, with invoice billing terms of 5/10; n/90.

The manager of the department store is deeply concerned because he does not have sufficient funds to pay for the goods within the 10-day discount period. He is wondering about the wisdom of borrowing money on a 90-day note from the bank, in order to take advantage of the discount.

How much interest (on an annual basis) could he afford to pay for such a loan and still come out better off than he would be if he disregarded the discount?

Albert Gallatin's career as a banker is particularly impressive, given his birthright and America's own struggling economy. Gallatin was born of wealthy parentage in England, on January 29, 1761. Although he grew up in the aristocratic traditions of his family, Gallatin became enamored with the more radical elements he met while in school. Consequently, Gallatin spurned his grandmother's offer to procure for him a position in the King's army sent to put down the American rebellion. Instead, he set sail for America on his own, hoping to make his fortune.

In America, Gallatin settled in western Pennsylvania, and soon became involved with politics. In 1789–90, he sat in a convention that revised the constitution of Pennsylvania, and by 1794, was elected to Congress. Soon after arriving in Washington, D.C., Gallatin became involved in the Jefferson-Burr deadlock, and as a reward for supporting Jefferson, was named Secretary of the Treasury. He held that post from May of 1801 until February of 1814, the longest tenure of office for any man as Secretary of the Treasury. During that time, Gallatin managed to liquidate most of the debt that had been incurred during the Revolution, and he found the funds to pay for the Louisiana Purchase.

From 1816 until 1823, Gallatin served as ambassador to France. In 1826, despite his pleas for retirement, he acceded to President Adams' request, and became ambassador to England. Finally, in 1831, Gallatin retired from public life to become the president of a new bank. That bank soon became known as Gallatin Bank.

Gallatin's life would be incomplete without mention of his other, societal contributions. He was one of the founders and served as the first president of the University of the City of New York, and was also president of the New York Historical Society. Gallatin died on August 12, 1849, after a long and distinguished career.

Albert Gallatin
(1761–1849)

Financier extraordinaire

15

Financial management: Uses of funds

Never stand begging for that which you have the power to earn.

————*Cervantes*

In the previous chapter, we discussed one aspect of the finance function, namely, how to obtain adequate sources of funds for use within the firm. The business firm, however, faces another problem relating to the financing of its operations. That problem concerns choosing the best *use* of the funds that have been or are about to be acquired. Commonly referred to as the *allocation of financial resources,* this problem concerns the efficient use of capital.

It may seem surprising that determining how to spend money (or allocate capital) can be at least as difficult a question to answer as determining *where* the money (acquisition of capital) is to come from. Yet, this particular aspect of the financing decision is second to none in importance. For it is the wise selection of expenditures and investments that will ultimately determine how well the firm achieves its long-run goals and objectives.

THE CAPITAL RATIONING PROBLEM

If there is one thing the financial manager knows with certainty, it is that someone will be requesting funds for some purpose he or she deems necessary for the successful execution of their job. For example, the marketing manager may want funds to hire additional salespeople, or the production manager may want to buy a new lathe, or the office staff may need a new Xerox machine, and so on. Each of these requests for funds will be accompanied, no doubt, by detailed statements justifying the expenditure involved. Each may appear worthwhile in the eyes of the financial manager. Yet, only one of the requests may be approved. Why? The answer, of course, is a lack of funds. Given that a business firm cannot obtain unlimited funds for use within the firm, it must resort to the only other option available to it—selectively choosing among the worthwhile investment projects that have been proposed. That is, the financial manager must ration his capital resources. The problem of capital rationing becomes, therefore, one of the main areas of difficulty for the financial manager. In this chapter, some of the problems confronting the financial manager as he makes this decision will be examined.

RESTRICTIONS ON THE USE OF FUNDS

We have already seen that the choice of a source of funds is limited at the outset by at least three major restrictions. These are: (a) organizational restrictions, (b) ownership restrictions, and (c) restrictions imposed by the intended use of the funds. Not surprisingly, similar restrictions exist in choosing appropriate uses for funds. These major considerations include (1) ownership restrictions, (2) regulatory considerations, (3) competitive restrictions, and (4) source-of-funds restrictions.

Ownership restrictions

Corporations face ownership restrictions regarding the use to which they put their funds. Usually such ownership restrictions take two forms: the stockholders' demand that the company earn profits, and their pressure on the company to pay out at least part of these profits as dividends.

The demand for earnings   Stockholders of all profit-oriented firms expect their companies to earn reasonable profits year after year. Indeed, when a corporation fails to earn the level of profits expected by the stockholders, top management is usually compelled to explain why at the annual stockholders' meeting. If the explanation is not satisfactory, the company's chief executives may find many of the stockholders unwilling to vote to retain them in office. (Chapter 17 examines the relationship of a stockholder to his company in more detail).

The financial manager, as a result, must be extremely conscious of the earnings potential of all proposed expenditures. All things being equal, a corporation will tend to invest its money in those assets or spend it on those operations that promise to generate the greatest profits. Such a policy, unfortunately, tends to limit a corporation's investment in activities which may be worthwhile but which may have little profit potential. This is one of the fundamental reasons for the reluctance of many corporations to take active steps in eliminating pollution resulting from production. Pollution control equipment is usually nonprofit generating, and, therefore, tends to be less in keeping with stockholder's wishes than more profitable investments.

The demand for dividends As was noted in Chapter 14 one important source of funds is retained earnings. Retained earnings, you will recall, are the earnings that remain after dividends have been paid to the stockholders. Thus, the greater the dividend demanded and paid to the stockholders, the smaller will be the amount available as retained earnings for investment in the firm. We can see, therefore, that the dividend demands of the stockholders place an automatic restriction on retained earnings and, consequently, on the capital available for investment within the firm.

Regulatory considerations

A second restriction on the use of funds is imposed by a wide assortment of laws and regulations. Many firms, particularly large firms, are prohibited by the antitrust laws from using their wealth to buy out their competition. For large, wealthy firms, buying out other companies can be an attractive and easy way to grow. The firm not only can increase its sales and earnings but can strengthen its control over the market for its products by eliminating real or potential competition, in effect creating a monopoly situation. The antitrust laws, however, prohibit this activity when the effect is to eliminate competition for purposes of creating a monopoly. The effect of this legal restriction, however, is to remove a potential use of funds for many large businesses.

Regulation also exists over certain business practices. Various government regulatory agencies oversee business practices to make sure they are not unfair or deceptive and that all business practices are in the "public interest." For example, certain businesses—notably the tobacco and liquor industries—are prohibited from advertising their products on television. Such a restriction automatically reduces the alternative means by which these companies can advertise their products, and thereby influences the expenditure of capital for advertising purposes.

Competitive restrictions

Some firms find their decisions regarding a use of funds influenced by the actions of their competitors. If a firm is in a particularly competitive market, and a competitor decides to undertake certain action (such as introduce a new product line), all other companies in the industry may find themselves forced to spend money to develop similar products, in order to remain competitive. Such "forced expenditures" have the effect of automatically determining the use of funds for some firms.

On the other hand, some firms possess certain patent or copyright privileges which shield them from competitive pressures. Under such circumstances, a firm may feel that it has more freedom, not less, in deciding on the use of its funds. Its legal position may provide sufficient protection from competition to enable the firm to make expenditures it might otherwise forego. For example, the firm may feel that it is sufficiently protected from competition to allow it to invest extra monies in research and development programs instead of increased production equipment. While the research and development may not prove profitable immediately, the firm may feel confident that it will not lose sales to competition by not acquiring additional equipment. Because of its patent protection, the firm can afford to let customers wait for their product, knowing that the customer can't go to another firm for the same product. In the meantime, the research and development program may result in just enough innovation to give the company new patent protection when its old patents run out.

Source-of-funds restriction

A final restriction on the use of funds comes from the source of those funds. This may seem a little contradictory, particularly since we noted in the previous chapter that the *use* of funds acquired by the firm was one of the major restrictions on the *sources* of funds available to a firm. This, unfortunately, is one of the predicaments facing the financial manager. The use of funds helps determine the source, and the source restricts the use. Perhaps an example will help clarify this problem.

Assume that a company obtains a term loan from a bank. As a precautionary measure (to give the bank additional assurance that the firm will be able to repay the loan), the bank may impose a restriction on the amount of dividends the firm may pay. This is a restriction on the use of funds available to the firm. Moreover, the bank may require that the firm maintain at least a 2:1 current ratio (current assets divided by current liabilities) at all times. Such a restriction may limit the firm's ability to use more trade credit in its financing of inventory. Or, it may force the firm to keep larger cash balances than it might otherwise. Finally, the firm must provide for the eventual repayment of the loan. The need to repay will further limit the firm's choices in using the funds, since its choices must now generate sufficient funds to pay off the loan when it comes due.

Similarly, when a firm raises funds for long-term use, it must accept the restrictions imposed by that use of funds. Assume that a business wishes to invest in new machinery. Given the cost of the machinery, the firm knows immediately that certain sources of funds are clearly inappropriate. Trade credit, for example, cannot be used to finance new machinery that has an expected life of, say, five years. Moreover, if the asset is not expected to generate funds for at least one year, it would be

FIGURE 15-1

Constraints on the sources and uses of funds

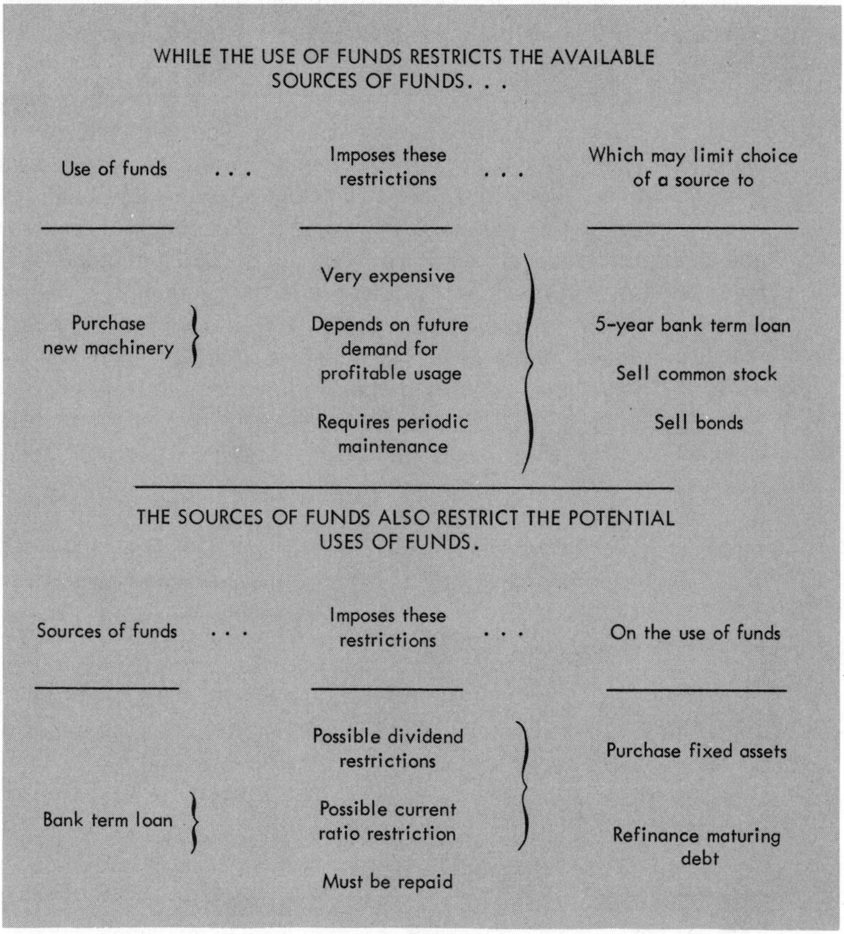

WHILE THE USE OF FUNDS RESTRICTS THE AVAILABLE
SOURCES OF FUNDS. . .

Use of funds . . .	Imposes these restrictions . . .	Which may limit choice of a source to
Purchase new machinery ⎱	Very expensive Depends on future demand for profitable usage Requires periodic maintenance	5-year bank term loan Sell common stock Sell bonds

THE SOURCES OF FUNDS ALSO RESTRICT THE POTENTIAL
USES OF FUNDS.

Sources of funds . . .	Imposes these restrictions . . .	On the use of funds
Bank term loan ⎱	Possible dividend restrictions Possible current ratio restriction Must be repaid	Purchase fixed assets Refinance maturing debt

foolish to search for a short-term loan. The source of funds must be appropriate to its intended use. Figure 15-1 summarizes this important financing rule.

In performing their jobs, then, financial managers must be continually evaluating all possible uses of funds, keeping in mind these various restrictions. Moreover, financial managers must make sure their decisions are consistent with the express goals of the firm.

The financial goals of the firm

In every business firm, problems periodically arise because of conflicts in the goals of the various business divisions. Managers in the personnel department, for example, may be interested in boosting wages for their workers—knowing that higher wages should result in better workers. At the same time, however, they may realize that the firm simply cannot afford such an increase. They are therefore, confronted with a real dilemma: how to keep the workers happy and efficient without causing the company unbearable financial strain.

In finance, a similar conflict can arise among alternative objectives within the division. This problem, which might be termed "the financial manager's dilemma," concerns the unending conflict between *liquidity* and *profitability.* Every firm needs sufficient liquidity (the ability to raise enough cash to pay the bills) to maintain a good credit standing. Inability to pay bills can result in bankruptcy. On the other hand, too much liquidity can result in a loss of profits, since money left idle for use in paying future bills cannot earn profits. As an example, consider a firm facing a decision about how much cash it should keep in its checking account. The dollars kept in the checking account earn no profit for the firm. Yet, to keep a $0 balance by putting every dollar into profitable investments may result in an inability to pay bills when they come due. Because of conflicts of this type, financial managers must pay careful attention to the exact nature of each and every investment (or use of funds) they authorize. Only in this way can managers be sure that they are doing their utmost to achieve the goals and objectives of the firm.

ALTERNATIVE USES OF FUNDS

In Chapter 13, we indicated that sources and uses of funds can be viewed from a balance sheet standpoint as follows:

Uses of funds	Sources of funds
Increase in assets Decrease in liabilities	Decrease in assets Increase in liabilities

That is, any increase in assets or decrease in liabilities constitutes a use of funds, and any decrease in assets or increase in liabilities can be viewed as a source of funds. Thus, a decision by the firm to increase the size of its inventory would constitute a use of funds, since inventory is an asset. In the following pages, we shall examine the various ways a firm may "use" funds, and the considerations that will influence these uses.

Investments in current assets

Typically, business firms have four major items on their balance sheets as short-term or current assets. These are (a) cash, (b) short-term investments, (c) accounts receivable, and (d) inventory. Each of these assets, as we shall see, involves unique considerations in determining the value of increased investment in the asset.

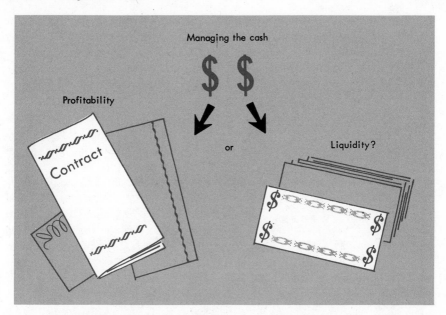

Managing the cash

Profitability

or

Liquidity?

Contract

Cash management In managing the cash position of a firm, the financial manager must pay particular attention to the liquidity versus profitability problem. Too much liquidity, for example, can result in a loss of profits, since assets in the form of cash typically are nonearning assets. Cash does not earn interest. It generates no return. Indeed, if we consider the change in the purchasing power of the dollar (inflation), cash even loses value over time!

On the other hand, too low a cash balance can result in a shortage of funds to pay the day-to-day bills as they come due. This is the liquidity problem. If a firm cannot pay its bills when they are due, the firm may face any number of problems, ranging from a lawsuit to a bad credit rating. At the very least, the firm will find it harder to obtain credit at reasonable rates in the future if it proves negligent in paying its bills.

Short-term investments Most large corporations keep some funds invested in short-term securities or other investments. Such securities usually earn some rate of interest and therefore are considered earning assets. At the same time, these securities are usually marketable on short notice, and thus are also useful as a source of cash when needed. Still, determining the level of funds to invest in this manner is not an easy matter. Companies are limited as to the amount of funds they have available, and so it becomes imperative that they maximize the use of such funds. Investments in securities represent a compromise on both the liquidity and profitability objectives of the firm. Cash is more liquid, and investment of the funds in, for example, inventory can be more profitable.

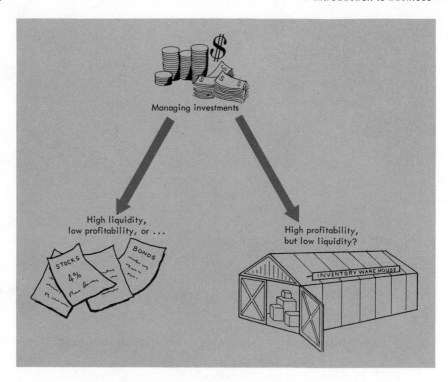

Managing investments

High liquidity,
low profitability, or . . .

High profitability,
but low liquidity?

Thus, for the most part the problem becomes one of deciding which is more important: accepting low profitability and high liquidity, or high profitability and low liquidity? Short-term investments really represent a compromise for the financial manager. They serve as a reserve behind the cash balance in case the firm needs extra cash in an emergency, and yet give a small return in the event the funds are not needed. Most companies combine the management of cash and investments, since they both involve the same basic considerations.

Managing accounts receivable   The management of the accounts receivable of a firm involves two very important considerations. On one hand, the firm may realize increased sales, and therefore, increased profits. On the other hand, the firm may incur increased costs, both because of the poor credit risks it has taken on and because of the investment opportunities lost by not being able to release cash as quickly as before. Let's trace these considerations again.

When a company decides to *increase* the size of its accounts receivable, it does so by liberalizing its credit policy. This can be accomplished in several ways. For example, it may begin to extend credit to customers who have not previously had it or allow more credit to those whose credit has been restricted within certain limits. Or, a firm may begin allowing customers 30 days to pay their bills instead of, say, the 10 days it used to allow. Under such circumstances, two things may take place. First, old customers may increase their purchases, since they now have more time to pay for the goods. Second, new customers may be attracted by the easier credit terms. In either event, the total sales of the firm should increase.

Unfortunately, an increase in sales brought about by a liberalizing of the credit policy of the firm does not always result in increased profits. Whenever a credit policy is eased, certain costs are immediately incurred by the firm. First, many of the new customers gained by the firm may be customers who were unable to get credit under the former credit policy because of their weak financial position. These customers are called "marginal" customers because the possibility of not collecting on their bills is significantly higher than it is for other customers. Thus, when the credit policy is liberalized, more and more bad debts are likely to be incurred by the firm. The financial manager must make sure that any change in the credit policy does not result in more losses due to bad debts than profits resulting from the increased sales.

A second "cost" that is suffered by the firm is known as an *opportunity cost*. This is the loss of profits that could have been earned had the credit policy not been changed. For example, assume that a company had a policy calling for payment within 20 days on all credit sales. In order to increase sales, assume that the company changed the policy to one requiring payment within 30 days. What would you expect the older

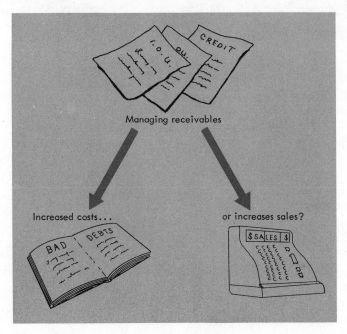

Managing receivables

Increased costs...   or increases sales?

customers—those that were previously paying their bills in 20 days—
to do? Quite obviously, they'll probably postpone paying their bills until
the 30th day. In other words, our company will now have to wait an
additional 10 days to get the funds it used to get in 20 days. The inability
to use these funds for that 10-day period represents the opportunity cost
of the funds.

In summary then, the financial manager needs to pay close attention
to balancing the increased costs with increased sales—and profits—when
revising the level of investment of funds in accounts receivable.

Managing inventory   One of the most important uses of funds in a
business firm involves the investment in inventory. Inventory is important
for two obvious reasons. First, inventory accounts for approximately one
half of the total current assets of manufacturing companies. If for no
other reason, this fact alone makes it imperative that this asset be carefully evaluated for its contribution to the overall profitability of the firm.
A second, and perhaps more important reason, however, is the very
basic relationship between inventory and sales.

Prudent management of inventory requires understanding that raw materials soon become goods-in-process. Goods-in-process, in turn, soon become finished goods. Hopefully, finished goods are then transformed into
sales with a minimum of delay.

The financial manager is only one of several interested parties in-

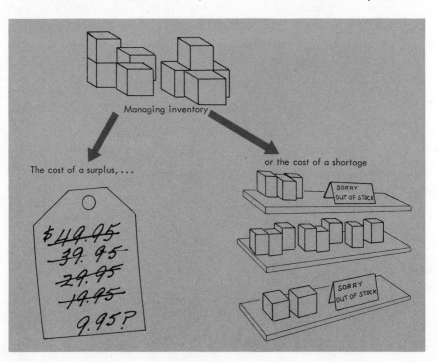

timately involved in determining the amount of inventory the firm will carry. The marketing manager will provide estimates—or forecasts—of expected sales. From the forecasts, the production manager will estimate the amount of raw materials needed to produce these goods. From this estimate, the purchasing agent can then determine how to acquire these materials at the lowest cost to the firm. It is at this point that the financial manager enters the picture.

As has been noted in earlier chapters, purchasing agents are responsible for acquiring the materials and supplies needed by the firm in its operations. While searching for various suppliers, they frequently encounter opportunities to acquire needed items at special savings. Usually, these savings are the result of bulk purchases—buying large amounts of the same product at one time. These opportunities are then related to the financial manager, who must then decide on the merits of the additional investment in inventory.

From the standpoint of financial managers, investment in inventory involves two different risks. If they allow the firm to acquire too much inventory, financial managers may face heavy losses if the goods remain unsold. Unless the inventory can be converted to sales, the goods represent a problem to the firm. Inventory requires storage, and storage—either in the company or in a bonded warehouse—costs money. Moreover, goods in storage are susceptible to spoilage or damage, and general deterioration. Spoiled inventory usually represents a total loss to the firm.

Another problem concerns the possibility of obsolescence. Some goods change markedly from season to season. Unsold goods left in inventory after one season may not be usable in the following year. The goods would have become obsolete and, therefore, worthless.

Finally, the amount of inventory carried by a firm usually influences the cost of obtaining insurance protection. Fire, floods, and thievery all represent perils that the firm must insure itself against. The greater the value of the inventory, the higher will be the cost of insuring against the possible occurrence of these perils.

At the same time, the financial manager must be aware of the risk of not carrying enough inventory. Shortages of raw materials, for example, can prove to be just as disastrous for a firm as the problem of having too much inventory. When the purchasing agent makes a recommendation to purchase additional goods, the financial manager must realize that the purchasing agent has considered many factors in reaching his decision—the possibility of strikes, shipping problems, possible cost savings, and so on. The financial manager, then, must be very careful about disagreeing with the purchasing agent. Nothing would be worse for the firm than to run out of materials or goods to sell. Workers would need to be laid off for a period of time and the plant would be shut down. Moreover, the sales force would find themselves in the unhappy predicament of selling goods that they couldn't deliver. Not only would the firm lose customers, but the morale of the sales force would deteriorate rapidly, causing a major problem for the firm. Indeed, the financial manager will usually attempt to obtain a source of funds to pay for the additional inventory purchase. Failing this, the financial manager then, and only then, will confront the purchasing agent with the need to compromise this use of funds.

Investment in fixed assets

The problems associated with investment in fixed, or capital, assets are much the same as those associated with investments in short-term, or current, assets. That is, the question of liquidity versus profitability is still paramount in importance. The problem of choosing among alternative uses for a limited amount of funds is still evident. And the need for making the correct choice looms just as importantly for long-term investments as it does for short-term investments. Indeed, in some ways, long-term investments are even more important than short-term ones. If a firm errs and makes a poor short-term investment (such as acquiring too much inventory), it may be forced to take a loss. A loss would obviously hurt, but in most cases would not cause the business severe hardship. If, however, the firm errs on a long-term investment decision, the results can be much more serious. As an example, consider the situation facing the computer industry, and more importantly, the fortunes of RCA and its efforts to build a market for itself in this industry.

RCA has been a major company in the electronics industry for many years. It seemed to RCA's management, therefore, that expansion into the computer business would be a logical and ideal area for further growth. Consequently, RCA spent millions of dollars developing a computer technology, building machines and training a sales force. In a matter of years, RCA realized it had made a mistake. For no matter how hard it tried, it was unable to compete profitably with IBM, Univac and other computer companies. The technological lead these other companies had been developing over the years was simply too much for RCA to overcome. Fortunately for RCA, it recognized its error and was able to sell its computer facilities to another firm. As it was, RCA took a substantial loss on the operation. Had the problem befallen any company with less than the financial strength of RCA, however, the error in judgment may well have cost the company its entire future.

Capital budgeting   As the previous example illustrates, decisions regarding the investment in buildings and equipment can be critical to the success of the business enterprise. Indeed, so important are these decisions, that a whole field of study has developed around this aspect of business finance. It is known as *capital budgeting*.

Capital budgeting involves the planning and budgeting of long-term sources and uses of funds. It is complicated, however, by several considerations. In most business situations, we must rely on the profits earned by one investment to help pay for that investment and for other investments. That is, one expenditure decision not only affects that asset, but in many cases it affects all other asset purchases. Complicating the situation is the fact that such decisions are made under conditions of uncertainty about future competitive pressures, stockholder demands

FIGURE 15–2

Capital budgeting considerations

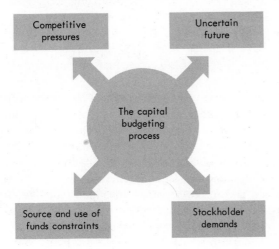

for dividends and the various constraining forces affecting the sources and uses of funds by the firm.

Investment in plant and equipment The restrictions and necessary considerations pertinent to the investment in long-term assets are many and varied. For example, the determining of which investment among many possible investments will yield the highest rate of return is a complex problem. As many as four or five different measures have been developed by business leaders for use in determining a "ranking" of potential investments. Some of these methods consider the uncertainty of future years' incomes and attempt to allow for this added element. Still other methods consider the time value of money, meaning that dollars earned this year or next year have relatively greater value to the business firm than the same dollars earned, for example, 10 years from now. This is because dollars earned this year can be invested to earn interest, while dollars to be earned 10 years from now require waiting those 10 years before the money is even received. Whichever method or methods are chosen, however, is not of immediate importance to us now. Suffice it to say that the problem exists and is quite complex—sufficiently complex to warrant the writing and publishing of entire textbooks on just this aspect of the capital budgeting problem.

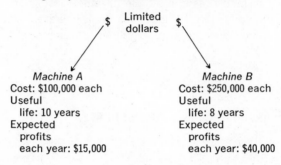

**Investment in plant and equipment . . .
"Higher profits in Machine A or Machine B"?**

Limited dollars

Machine A
Cost: $100,000 each
Useful
  life: 10 years
Expected
  profits
  each year: $15,000

Machine B
Cost: $250,000 each
Useful
  life: 8 years
Expected
  profits
  each year: $40,000

Further confusing the issue is the uncertainty about other factors that will determine the eventual accuracy of our decision. For example, suppose that we decide to invest in Machine A, only to find that two years later another machine appears on the market that makes Machine A obsolete. We now have a new problem. We'll be manufacturing products with an obsolete, slower machine for eight more years while our competitors may be producing on the newer, more advanced machine. Their ability to produce more product at a lower cost could cause us financial hardship, and in the extreme, drive us out of business.

The question might arise as to why the business firm, faced with this unpleasant prospect, doesn't simply buy the new machine and discard the old one. Here again, we see the complexity of the capital budgeting process. First of all, to trade in or sell our old machine would probably result in a terrible loss, since the value of our older machine will fall sharply upon the introduction of the newer, more efficient one. Second, most firms cannot adjust their capital budgets that readily. Most capital budgets are made for periods of 5, 10, or even 20 years into the future. It is extremely difficult to change the budget once many decisions have been made. Where, for example, will the firm get the money to buy the newer machine? All of its financial resources have already been committed to other projects.

Actually, we can put the problem in a more personal framework. Consider the decision by a family to buy a new car. They expect the car to last them five years. One year after they acquire it, a new model comes out that is exactly what they wanted, is priced about the same, is safer, and can be operated for less money than the one they own. What do they do? Most families sigh and wish they had waited, but having failed to wait, continue to drive their old car. There is just no way they can afford to trade in their present car. Their "capital budgeting" decision having been made, they must now live with it. Of course, they might have been smart and waited another year before buying the car, but who is to know when new products, new technology, or unforeseen events will occur that will cause them to regret their ultimate decision?

So it is for the business firm. Not to buy a machine when it is needed will only lead to stagnancy; and stagnant firms soon die. In our profit-oriented society it must be so, for only in this way can we as consumers be assured of continually improved products and services and a constantly rising standard of living.

Decreasing liabilities as a use of funds

Still another use of funds concerns the liability section of the balance sheet. As has already been noted, decreases in liabilities constitute a "use" of funds. This is because, quite obviously, whenever liabilities are reduced, creditors of the firm have been paid what was owed them. That is, funds were used to pay off the indebtedness.

Most business firms require this particular use of funds from time to time. Almost every business owes someone money—whether it be suppliers of raw materials, banks, or the federal government. Periodic payment of these debts is standard business practice and, consequently, represents an important use of funds.

Reducing current liabilities The reduction of liabilities can best be discussed if we distinguish between short-term liabilities and long-term liabilities. The nature of each of these types of indebtedness differs, and therefore the rationale underlying a use of funds in this manner also will differ.

Firms "invest" in a reduction of current liabilities for two reasons. In most cases, the use of funds for this purpose is required by law or by contractual agreement. Thus, if a firm purchases goods on the promise that the goods will be paid for within 30 days, a contractual agreement has been created that requires the firm to spend money—to use funds—within that period. Similarly, the law requires that businesses pay estimated income taxes every three months of the year. This is a legal requirement the firm must abide by—a required "use" of funds that must be provided for.

Insofar as the usage of funds to reduce short-term liabilities is caused by such contractual or legal arrangements, not much can be said. When a debt is incurred, it must be repaid. If the law requires the payment of taxes, the taxes must be paid. However, on occasion a firm will reduce its current liabilities for a second reason, namely, to increase its profits or to increase its financial flexibility. For example, assume that a firm purchases goods on terms of 2/10; n/30. Under such terms, the company will be required to pay for the goods within 30 days. However, suppose that the firm now receives an unexpected cash order for its own merchandise. It now has extra funds on hand—funds it hadn't expected to receive. Since the funds were unexpected, no arrangements had been made to invest the money in the firm. In such a situation, financial managers may decide to use the money to pay for the outstanding liability early— perhaps within the discount period. By so doing, they can save the company 2 percent on its purchase. That saving is as good as earning 36 percent on a comparable investment elsewhere![1]

Similarly, suppose that a firm foresees the need to acquire a bank term loan later in the year. To help improve its chances of getting the loan, and thereby improve its financial flexibility, the business may try to "clean up" its balance sheet. It does this by paying off old loans and debts and trying to bring the current ratio and the acid-test ratio to loftier levels. Thus, if a firm has $100,000 in cash and near-cash items, and $100,000 in current liabilities, it will have a 1:1 acid-test ratio—acceptable, but not exceptional. However, by using an unexpected $20,000 inflow of cash to reduce the current liabilities to $80,000, the acid-test ratio becomes a very attractive 1.25:1. With such an acid-test ratio, a bank may be much more willing to grant an intermediate-term loan to the business.

Reducing long-term liabilities The underlying rationale for the use of funds to reduce long-term indebtedness is slightly more complex. Many firms actually have contingency plans for reducing their long-term liabilities, whereas the reduction of the size of the short-term liabilities may be subject to circumstances unforeseen by the financial manager.

As a general rule, firms undertake to reduce their long-term liabilities because they can (a) increase profits by doing so, or (b) because the debt-equity ratio—the indicator revealing what percent of the business is actually financed by the owners—is getting dangerously out of line in the opinion of other creditors.

To illustrate, consider the action of the J. C. Penney Company in July of 1971. The company announced plans to retire $125 million worth of convertible bonds that were outstanding. Obviously, the company knew that many of the bondholders would convert their bonds to common stock, in accordance with their rights of ownership of the convertible securities. Indeed, the company urged the bondholders to do so. Even though complete conversion (meaning all bondholders converted to common stock) would cost the company an additional $2.5 million annually to maintain the current $1 per share dividend, the company still figured to save money. The outstanding bonds were costing the firm $5.3 million annually

---

[1] Assume that the goods were paid for on the 10th day. Then the firm saved 2 percent by paying for the goods 20 days early. On an annual basis, 2 percent for 20 days approximates 36 percent for a year.

in interest expense. Penney concluded that it could not only save money by forcing the conversion or retirement of the debt, but could also improve its debt-equity ratio in the process.

An interesting sidelight to this action was the impact of this move on the stock market. Although a discussion of the stock market is beyond our purposes here, we should note that stock prices are in large part determined by the forces of supply and demand. The greater the demand for a stock relative to its supply, the higher will be the price, and vice versa. When J. C. Penney announced the forced conversion, the stock market interpreted the move as causing an increase in the supply of stock relative to the demand. As a result, the price of the stock dropped, as the headline in *The Wall Street Journal* indicates.[2] Companies will also redeem or liquidate their long-term debt if it is possible to reissue the debt at a lower interest rate. Thus, in the late 1960s, many firms needed to borrow money and were forced to pay extremely high rates of interest. Later, in the early part of 1971, interest rates fell considerably. Many of these same firms again sold bonds—this time at the lower rates of interest —and used the proceeds to pay off or retire the older, more expensive bonds. Financial managers of the very large corporations are quite adept at arranging such exchanges. However, proper execution of the maneuver requires considerable knowledge of economics, monetary policy, and an understanding of the causes and effects of interest rates and changes in interest rates.

Changing the owners' equity A final balance sheet usage of funds involves changes in the capital investment of the owners of the firm. Consider, for example, a firm that has both common stock and preferred stock on its balance sheet. We have already seen that preferred stock tends to be costly for a firm to keep outstanding. Thus, many times a firm will attempt to call in, or retire, its preferred stock. The rationale, of course, is much the same as that underlying the retirement of long-term debt: namely, profitability and/or financial flexibility considerations.

Corporate dividend policy and the use of funds

A final financial consideration regarding the use of funds within a business firm concerns the dividend policy of the corporation. As will be seen in Chapter 17, one of the major reasons why stockholders buy stock is to obtain the dividend income from the investment. To the extent, therefore, that a company wishes to keep its stock attractive as an investment medium, it will attempt to develop some type of dividend policy. While such a policy is highly desirable from a stockholder's standpoint, it does create problems for the financial manager. Dividend payments constitute

---

[2] "J. C. Penney Calls in Convertible Debentures; Stock Price Plunges," *The Wall Street Journal*, July 14, 1971, p. 24.

an outflow of cash from the firm—that is, they are a use of funds. The more dividends a firm pays, consequently, the more it reduces the available funds for other investment purposes. Dividend payments to corporate stockholders is, in fact, one of the major source-of-funds restrictions limiting a corporation's use of funds today.

CORPORATE RESPONSIBILITY AND THE USE OF FUNDS

Without question, one of the most controversial issues of the day concerns the legitimacy of corporate involvement in philanthropic causes. From a finance standpoint, this issue tends to become centered on the use-of-funds question, and the wisdom of using corporate funds for purposes that will not advance the financial interests of the majority of the corporation's owners.

Financially speaking, the use of funds for nonbusiness activities raises two important issues. First, funds that are used to support nonbusiness activities are funds that cannot subsequently be used for business purposes. That is, a business firm is operating with a limited supply of funds. To the extent that these funds are not used for reinvestment in the business firm, the financial manager will be forced to further restrict his financing activities within the firm. Second, there is the more general, philosophical question about the propriety of corporate involvement in such nonbusiness activities. In theory, the funds being dispersed by the management of the firm belong to the stockholders—the owners—of the business. Management is required by the stockholders to act in the best interests of these stockholders in managing the firm. Financial managers must decide whether contributions to such nonbusiness-related activities as aid to educational institutions, and aid to charities, fall within the scope of the "stockholders' best interest"? To answer this question, let's examine one of these "nonbusiness" related activities, namely, corporate aid to education.

Education: A proper role for corporations?

Should corporations give financial aid to educational institutions? Many of you—as interested parties in the question—probably will respond with a resounding "Yes"! You know all too well the cost of higher education, and probably would be quite willing to see our large corporations "pick up the tab" for your eduaction. Guess what? Many of them are already doing just that! Many corporations have spent millions of dollars on aid to education, through such activities as providing money for new buildings, donating equipment for use in classrooms, providing money for support of libraries and faculty salaries, and of course, student financial assistance. General Electric, for example, sponsored a television program known as "The College Bowl" for many years. On that show, various schools received grants to aid their educational program. Many accounting firms give small cash awards to hundreds of outstanding students at schools across the land every year. And we could go on and on, for the list of corporations giving assistance to education is almost endless. But the questions still remain: *Why?* And *should* they? After all, it is the stockholder's money they are giving away.

Aid to education: A proponent's view Those who express satisfaction with the corporate practice of aiding education rely chiefly on an economic argument. That argument goes like this: "If a society—any society —wants to improve its standard of living, it can do so only by increasing its productive output. Productivity is, by definition, the amount of goods and/or services that society can produce. As we have seen, two of the major components of production (i.e., two of the "factors of production") are labor and capital. Capital, by definition, includes all of those physical items that go into the productive process—including money. Labor is just that—the physical work used in the process. Aid to education involves both of these factors of production. Brainpower, that is, intellect, expert knowledge—these are part of the productive cycle. They are a form of capital. Similarly, a better educated work force means a more intelligent, more ambitious, more resourceful work force. That means improved labor, more productive labor. Corporations are the primary vehicle for employing people. Thus, it is in their own best interest to see to it that the labor and capital they need are going to be available in the coming years. Even if those employees are hired by other companies, at least *that* company will have employees who can contribute to increased productivity. When that happens, everybody gains, including the company that paid for the education.

The reasons for that, of course, is that increased productivity means, among other things, more people earning more income to spend on more goods and services. In a capitalistic society like ours, that is the essence of things.

Corporate aid to education: A dissenter's view Those who argue against corporate aid to education do so on the ground that, regardless of what role others may see the corporation playing in a community, aid to education remains, in reality, a distribution to others of money belonging to the stockholders of the firm. As such, the stockholders of the firm ought to have the final say as to who gets what and why. Indeed, argue the dissenters, if the stockholders truly want financial aid to go to various schools, perhaps the best way to effect this distribution would be to pay out the money to the stockholders as a dividend and let them decide on their own how they wish to disburse the funds. Corporate management, by arbitrarily deciding which school ought to receive the contribution, is usurping the right of the stockholder to decide the disposition of his own wealth. Again, the case has its strength. As we shall see in Chapter 17, the degree of control exercised by management of the firm is in part reflected in management's willingness to disburse stockholder's money at will.

Deciding which point of view is most appropriate is, again no easy matter. The issue, however, cannot be ignored, for it is intimately related to the operation of the business firm and the maintenance of the firm's social reputation.

Another "use" of funds that has sparked some controversy can be seen in the following example.

An illustration   Imagine a company that is the largest employer in a small midwestern community. The company has assets totaling $175 million, and last year earned $8 million after taxes, down from $9.5 million the year before. In its annual report, the company explained that foreign competition and the need to replace outdated machinery was continuing to hurt the profitable growth of the firm. Indeed, the company's fortunes had been steadily worsening over the past six years.

Mr. Jacobson, owner of 2,000 shares of the company's stock, was deeply concerned over the return on his investment. He was retired from his pharmaceutical business and depended on the dividends from this and other investments for his income. This particular year, this company's annual report included notice that the dividend was being cut 25 percent because of the continuing fall in profits.

On reading the annual report, Mr. Jacobson noted that the company gave $2.3 million to charity in the past year. This caused considerable concern to Mr. Jacobson. He had nothing against charitable contributions —indeed, he gave to the Heart Fund and the March of Dimes himself. What concerned him, however, was the apparent willingness of the corporation's officers to continue their charitable contributions in the face of declining profits, and despite their plea that those low profits were necessitating a cut in dividends. He decided to attend the annual meeting and ask management about this particular development.

At the meeting, management pointed out that the contributions included aid to the local hospital (where many of the company's employees were treated when hurt on the job), aid to the local school, and assistance to the local arms of the various large charities. It also included a gift of $800,000 to help support a local symphony orchestra. Management argued that this type of cultural activity was necessary if it was to hold and attract new managerial talent.

Another stockholder, on hearing management's argument, objected strongly, and offered a motion that would prohibit all future contributions until dividends were restored and profits returned to a reasonable level. Mr. Jacobson deliberated on his vote. Question: If you were Mr. Jacobson, how would you vote on the stockholder's proposal?

Such a question has many ramifications. Both sides have a reasonable argument. Can you think of any circumstances under which you might change your vote? Suppose that Mr. Jacobson were not retired, and did not depend on his dividend income for survival. Would that fact change your decision?

Unfortunately, Mr. Jacobson declined to tell us how he actually voted. We do know, however, that the motion was overwhelmingly defeated. The following year, though, the company abandoned the symphony orchestra, thereby cutting its charitable contributions by almost one third.

We have seen that the issues underlying the use of funds by a business firm are many and varied. In some cases, the use of funds is determined strictly on the basis of the contribution to profit of the investment. In other instances, nonprofit considerations become a factor of paramount importance. Whatever the situation, however, it should again be clear that the functional activities of managing a business enterprise cannot be divorced from the broader social impact of those actions on others. Business today is a multifaceted operation; what happens in one area affects what happens to the rest of the firm. Such is the nature of the modern business establishment.

DISCUSSION QUESTIONS

1 Explain why deciding on the uses of funds is at least as important a question as deciding on the sources of funds.

2 What kinds of restrictions does a sole proprietorship face in determining the uses of funds? What restrictions are faced by a partnership?

3 Define "capital rationing." Explain its importance to the financial manager.

4 Can you think of any instances where competition has caused firms to use funds in ways they might not otherwise have done? Think of the automobile, photographic, cereal and household products industries in particular.

5 Distinguish between sources of funds and uses of funds from an accounting standpoint.

6 Is it always in the best interest of a firm to try and get the credit business of "marginal" customers? Why or why not?

7 Explain the concept of an "opportunity cost" that is often associated with a change in credit policies for businesses.

8 Why is inventory such an important asset for manufacturing firms? Do you think it would be as important for service-related firms as well? Explain.

9 What is meant by the term "capital budgeting"? Why is it so named?

10 What do you see as the key mistake made when RCA attempted to go into the computer business?

11 How does conversion of long-term debt securities enter into the capital budgeting decision-making process?

12 Should nonbusiness-related expenditures, such as charitable contributions and aid to education, be treated like all other expenditures —that is, put in the capital budget—or should they be treated as something to be made only with excess or unexpected funds? Why?

MINI CASES

Pan-Caribbean Airlines was a fairly large carrier that served all of the southern United States and Central and South America. It was trying to make a decision regarding the purchase of a new tri-jet airplane that was to begin service in the fall of the next year.

Pan-Caribbean had not been active in the purchase of the jumbo jets that came on the market in the late 1960s and early 1970s. Its executives felt that the added cost of the planes would not be justified by substantial increases in passengers. Accordingly, they had passed up the opportunity to acquire the jets and to this date had been thankful they had.

Now, however, they faced the problem all over again, but with some added complications. Two large international carriers had recently been given approval by the Civil Aeronautics Board to extend service to the areas presently served by Pan-Caribbean. These two carriers had large fleets of the jumbo jets, and Pan-Caribbean saw a serious threat to its market if it suddenly had to compete with these new, fancy jets. Thus, it was considering acquiring the new tri-jet as a suitable counterpart to the other carriers' planes.

One particularly difficult problem, however, centered on the financing of these jets. Because Pan-Caribbean served only South and Central America, it was more vulnerable to expropriation and seizure by an unexpected change in the political structure of any one of the Latin-American countries. Pan-Caribbean officials were concerned that the banks might not be willing to help finance its acquisition. Faced with this problem, you are called on to help Pan-Caribbean resolve its financing problem.

1. *How might Pan-Caribbean resolve its financial problem?*

2. *Should Pan-Caribbean, in your opinion, proceed with the purchase of the new tri-jets? What problems do they face if they do make the purchase? What problems do they face if they don't?*

America's international sports program is unique in many respects, not the least of which is that it is not sponsored or financed by the federal government. Our Olympic teams, for example, are financed entirely out of private contributions—dollars contributed by citizens and businesses across the country.

Knowing this fact, John Boulding had a real problem. He had just been selected by the U.S. Olympic Committee to head its fund-raising program. The committee estimated it would need about $10 million over the next four years to adequately train and develop competitive teams for the next Olympics.

To help his fund-raising efforts, John Boulding decided to search out some way of getting business's support—and money—behind him. He approached you to ask your assistance in securing business's assistance.

1. *How might Mr. Boulding convince business that it ought to aid in financing this endeavor?*
2. *Suppose that a business proves reluctant to contribute without some type of "compensation." Can you develop some means of enabling the corporate contributors to be identified as having provided support?*
3. *Why might business ask for some type of recognition?*

Since the mid 1930s, the automobile market has been dominated by General Motors. Behind GM came Ford, Chrysler, and varying other, smaller manufacturers. The market percentages for these companies has, in recent years, remained fairly stable, with each company usually keeping between 1 and 2 percent of the previous years' market share.

In 1973–74, however, a major problem occurred which threatened to cause major upheavals in the auto industry. That problem was the energy crisis. People began to give serious thought to the kind of gas mileage they were getting on their cars, and began to make major changes in their buying habits. These changing buying habits caused sharp changes in the share of the auto market each of the major companies controlled. For example, GM's market share alone dropped over 4 percent in just one year.

Company	Market shares (percent)	
	1973	*1974 (est.)*
General Motors	51.9	47.7
Ford Motor Co.	27.6	29.3
Chrysler Corp.	16.5	17.7
American Motors	4.0	5.3

Of particular concern to the management of General Motors, was the fact that the combined sales of Buick, Oldsmobile, and Pontiac dropped almost 30 percent from the preceding year. By all standards, it appeared that a major decision would have to be made by GM regarding their future automobile offerings.

While several of GM's competitors were busy expanding capacity for the production of small, compact cars, GM did not do so. Rather, they surveyed the market and became convinced that the real growth market would continue to be in the profitable, medium-sized cars. They reasoned that drivers of the big luxury cars would probably be willing to settle for an intermediate-sized car, but not a compact. Also, GM felt that the oil crisis would subside, and buyers would once again begin to buy larger cars.

1. *Discuss the financial considerations that GM had to make in the above situation. Was this a "capital budgeting" decision?*
2. *Would you say that GM made a wise decision? Why or why not?* (Hint: Auto production figures are usually published weekly in *The Wall Street Journal*.)

Henry Ross Perot is founder and president of Electronic Data Systems, Inc. At the age of 45, Mr. Perot ranks as one of the world's wealthier men, a feat made all the more remarkable by the fact that much of his fortune was created in the short span of only ten years.

Mr. Perot joined IBM as a salesman shortly after his discharge from the Navy. His skill at selling soon became evident. In 1962, he astounded everyone by meeting his annual quota in the first two weeks of January! Encouraged by this remarkable success in selling, Mr. Perot began thinking of forming his own company—one which would provide total computer services, and not just the equipment, to its customers. It was a determined Ross Perot that left IBM on June 27, 1962—his 32nd birthday—and formed Electronic Data Systems, Inc. By November 1968, Mr. Perot's stock in Electronic Data Systems was worth over $300 million. Its value has fluctuated substantially since that time.

Mr. Perot recognized, however, the good fortune he had enjoyed, and was aware of the responsibilities that went with it. The Perot Foundation which he developed has provided aid to minority businessmen in Texas and has been instrumental in aiding education. Recently, Mr. Perot announced that he would endow a graduate school of business at one of five Texas universities—the school to be chosen on the basis of plans for the program that each school was developing.

Today, Mr. Perot ranks among the more influential of all businessmen. Although his efforts at revitalizing the giant DuPont brokerage firm were unsuccessful, he remains an undaunted supporter of the American system. His concern for the welfare of his fellow man, and his ability to incorporate this concern into his highly successful business career, makes him an outstanding representative of the socially minded modern business executive.

H. Ross Perot
(1930–   )

Businessman with a conscience

16

Computers and quantitative analysis in business

Collecting data is a lot like collecting garbage. . . . You've got to know what your going to do with the stuff before you collect it.

——*Mark Twain*

Virtually every aspect of today's complex society requires us to come into contact with computers and computer technology. In school, for example, registration for classes is commonly performed by computer. Records for all of the students' registration and class assignments are processed on the basis of their social security number or some other numerical code. Our everyday lives are similarly affected by computer technology. Most of us use charge plates in making purchases at the store, in buying gasoline for our car, or in arranging for air transportation. Indeed, approximately 10 percent of the total amount of all consumer installment credit is charged on credit cards, meaning that credit cards account for almost $7 billion worth of consumer credit. In virtually every instance, computers are used in the billing procedures for these cards. Typically, we are billed once each month for the amount owed—via a computer-prepared statement. When we pay for these charges, we write a personal check—which has special magnetic ink characters imprinted on it for use in computer scanning and sorting at the bank. When we mail the payment, the post office uses phosphor-coated postage stamps that can be "seen" by computer-controlled equipment, enabling the post office to sort airmail and first class mail with added speed and accuracy. Even in medicine, computers are routinely used to provide rapid analysis and diagnostic assistance in laboratories and hospitals throughout the land.

While computers are widely used in education, science, and government, their widest use is perhaps in business. Initially, computers were used primarily for record-keeping purposes, since the ability to record, remember, and feed back information was an essential need of business. Today, however, industry has greatly expanded its use of computers. Computers have the unique characteristic of being able to process, remember, and manipuate large amounts of quantitative data in an extremely short period of time. To properly utilize this attribute, management has had to learn how to quantify the problems it faces and the alternative decisions available. Management has also found it necessary to learn how to effectively use the vast amounts of statistical data that the computer made available. Most importantly, perhaps, management has had to learn what can and cannot be achieved by using statistics and statistical tools in decision making. The computer and statistics are, in the final analysis, only tools which can be used to crystallize a problem and arrive at a possible solution. The erroneous use of these tools can prove just as harmful as studying the wrong notes in preparation for a major exam.

In this chapter, statistics and the use of quantitative analysis as they relate to the decision-making function of business leaders will be introduced. At the same time, it will be indicated how and why the computer has greatly facilitated the use of these statistical techniques. The purpose, remember, is not to frighten the reader by introducing a series of abstract concepts and ideas. Rather, our purpose is to show how modern business, and subsequently our contemporary society, has been affected and changed by the technology of the computer.

WHAT DOES QUANTITATIVE ANALYSIS ENCOMPASS?

In its broadest sense, "quantitative analysis" refers to the application of science and scientific techniques to the decision-making process. That is, it refers to a method of problem solving that requires decision makers to formulate their problem in very precise terms and to execute the problem's solution in a logical, sequential manner. We commonly refer to such a procedure as the "scientific method."

The method of quantitative analysis

Essentially, solving a problem with the use of quantitative analysis involves a series of four or five steps. These are: (a) *qualitatively evaluating* the pertinent factors surrounding the problem, (b) *formulating* the problem, (c) *performing* the analysis, and (d) *implementing* the findings. Let's look at these again.

Qualitative evaluation The qualitative evaluation of the pertinent factors involves an examination of those factors that would seem at first glance to be of importance in solving the problem. For example, suppose that an executive of a trucking company is considering the purchase of additional trucks and the building of a new terminal in another part of the same state in which he is currently operating. His preliminary, *qualitative* evaluation might well include consideration of the following factors:

1. The amount of business currently existing in that part of the state.
2. The condition of the present fleet of trucks.
3. The amount of competition that can be expected if the company moves into that part of the state.

While this *qualitative* evaluation may raise questions that later prove to be unimportant, it does provide a useful starting point for the rest of the analysis.

The formulation of the problem The second step is formulating the problem. It may seem that the problem has already been developed—that is, deciding on whether to buy new trucks and open another terminal. Consider, however, some of the following, related problems.

It may mean making judgments about the way the business may change if the executive expands the fleet, or the ability of the new trucks to meet these changes. It may mean making certain assumptions about the state of the economy in the future, for surely the success of the trucking business requires satisfactory economic growth. Note that not all of these problems can be answered precisely, nor in fact, are all of them necessarily part of the main problem. The raising of these questions, or problems, however, helps the executive to decide just what the real problem is. Indeed, the real problem may be one the executive has failed to consider. For example, maybe there aren't enough roads and/or gasoline stations located between the customers and the proposed terminal to make such a project worthwhile. In that case, the problem of whether or not to build a new terminal is not necessarily the right question. A more vital question may concern where to locate such a terminal if, indeed, one is to be built. In any event, the process of identifying the problem(s), and ranking them in order of their importance, is the essence of problem formulation.

Performing the analysis In this stage the actual steps are taken that will provide us with an answer (although not necessarily the correct one) to our problem. For example, the executive of the trucking company might survey a number of potential customers to see if they would consider using his service if he decides to branch out to the new area of the state. Some potential customers probably would be uncertain, but hopefully, enough would respond to enable the executive to make an intelligent decision. By obtaining information like this, and by using various statistical techniques and possibly even a computer, the business leader will hopefully improve his chances of making the "best" decision, given the uncertainty he faces.

Implement findings   In this final step we put into practice that which we have learned from the previous stages. This may seem to be a logical, natural step to take. We should realize, however, that implementation can be a disrupting influence on the company. Moreover, the preliminary results of an action may not agree with what we had expected to occur. If this happens, we need to go back and reexamine the four steps we have undertaken to make sure we have correctly executed each step.

The importance of quantitative analysis

Quantitative analysis is useful in business, particularly, for two important reasons. First, it enables business executives to put known information into proper perspective. It minimizes the guesswork, the hunch, the approximation, if you will. Proper quantitative analysis requires that precision be used both in the analysis of data and in the specification or use of words. To illustrate, consider a classroom grading situation in which your professor told you that you had scored an "average" grade on your last examination. What would this mean to you? As will be seen shortly, the word "average" can mean several things. It can mean, for example, that you scored the "middle" score in the class, or that your score was the "most popular" of all the scores recorded. If the professor had specified precisely what was meant by "average," you would have had a much better understanding of your performance on that last test.

On reflection, of course, you probably will note that in many instances, knowledge of the "average" score is really not enough. For example, besides knowing what the "average" score was, you probably would like to know what the highest and lowest scores were. In that way, you could see how you compared with the best and worst scores.

Such information is generally classified as information about the *dispersion* of the scores. Essentially, *dispersion* refers to how much the scores tended to vary from one another. There are many different ways of measuring dispersion. For example, when we seek to learn the highest and lowest scores in a distribution, we are calculating the *range*. The range represents the difference between the highest and lowest scores. The greater the range, the greater the variability or dispersion. As we have noted, there are many other measures of dispersion. Discussion of these, however, can probably await your first encounter with a statistics course.

A second justification for the use of quantitative analysis involves the existence of uncertainty in our decision-making process. We don't know what will happen in the future. If we did, we would have no problem deciding on a course of action. Because we are living in a world of uncertainty, however, we need to learn how to gain as much insight into our future as our available data will allow. The quantitative analysis of a problem allows us to maximize our insight into an uncertain future by putting the known information into different perspectives. Consequently, we can usually make better decisions.

Putting known information into perspective

The first important use of quantitative analysis in business involves putting known information into better perspective. This may require the specifying of a problem in simple mathematical terms and then solving the mathematical equation, or it may involve the use of statistics, and various statistical measures. To clarify, let's examine in detail some of the more popular uses of quantitative techniques in the business world.

Break-even analysis

Every business leader is anxious to learn whether his particular enterprise is going to earn a profit. Unfortunately, this is an answer that only time can provide. By using one of the tools of business analysis, however, he can learn what level of sales he must achieve in order to avoid incurring a loss. That is, by using the technique known as *break-even analysis,* he can determine what level of sales will be necessary, given the selling price of his product, to enable revenues earned to exactly equal the costs incurred. At this point—the point of zero profit—the business executive "breaks even." While this does not tell him his chances for profits, it does *put into perspective* the problem confronting the business executive.

To illustrate, let us consider the problem confronting a manufacturer of television sets. The Abbott Television Company sells its sets for an average price of $300 each. This sales price must cover all of the expenses and hopefully provide a small profit. The owners wish to determine the number of sets they must sell at this average price in order to cover their costs. To determine this point, or sales level, they must first examine the nature of the expenses they will incur in producing the TV sets.

Analysis of expenses   All business expenses can be divided into two groups: "fixed" costs and "variable" costs. Fixed costs are those costs that must be incurred regardless of whether the business sells one unit (or TV set) or 1,000 units. Examples of fixed costs are rent, property taxes, executive salaries, and so on. These expenses must be paid, and they remain constant or fixed, no matter how many units are produced. Rent, for instance, is the same amount, month after month (unless the landlord raises it) regardless of whether the factory is in full production or only partial production.

The other major classification of expenses are the "variable" costs. Variable costs are those whose importance varies directly with the amount of production realized. For example, wages to the workers are a variable expense, since workers get paid only if they are being actively employed in production. Similarly, most of the electric bill is variable. If production slows down, machines sit idle, and consequently consume less electricty. Variable costs are usually zero under conditions of no production and increase rapidly as production increases. Continuing with the example, let us assume that our manufacturer of TV sets determines that it has $300,000 in fixed expenses. This includes the rent, taxes, certain salaries, money owed on machinery, and other items of fixed cost. Further, the manufacturer concludes that it will cost approximately $100 in variable costs to produce each TV. The question, then, is how many units or sets will Abbott Television Company need to sell at $300 each to cover all of these costs? There are two ways this problem can be solved: one is graphically and the other is mathematically.

The graphic solution   Figure 16–1 shows the break-even chart for this particular example. Note in particular, the structure of the graph. Sales in units are listed across the bottom, while dollars are listed up the left-hand side. The total cost line starts at $300,000, since at zero production level, the only costs incurred are the fixed costs. As production

FIGURE 16–1

Break-even chart for Abbott Television Company

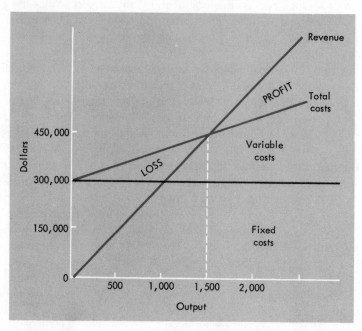

increases, however, total costs increase by $100 for each additional unit.

The revenue line simply reflects the amount of revenue received (as read off the left-hand side) for each $300 television set sold.

Notice that the break-even point—the point where sales revenues will just equal total costs—is 1,500 television sets. The managers of Abbott Television Company can now examine the possibility of earning a profit from a different viewpoint. It is certainly easier to estimate chances for profits if we know the minimum number of units necessary to produce and sell in order to break even.

The mathematical solution   The same results can be obtained by expressing these cost and revenue figures in the form of a mathematical expression and solving. For example, we know that break even is the point where revenue equals cost; that is, the break-even point is that point where:

$$\text{Revenue} - \text{total costs} = \text{Zero}$$

or

$$\text{Revenue} - (\text{fixed costs} + \text{variable costs}) = \text{Zero}$$

Since we know revenue to be $300 per unit, and variable costs to be $100 per unit, with fixed costs equaling a sum of $300,000, we can show the break-even point as

$$300X - (300,000 + 100X) = 0$$

where X equals the number of television sets necessary to produce and sell in order to reach break even. Solving for X, we get

$$300X - 100X = 300,000$$
$$200X = 300,000$$
$$X = \quad 1,500 \text{ units}$$

This is the same break-even point we arrived at earlier by the graphical method.

The use of ratios

Still another instance where quantitative analysis techniques can be used to put known information into perspective is in the use of ratios. In Chapter 13, for example, we saw how various ratios and techniques of statement analysis were used by managment, labor, stockholders, and government to clarify the current financial position of the firm. When used in this manner ratios, too, can be considered a quantitative technique—a means of expressing numerically or graphically some concept, idea, or known characteristic of the firm.

The use of index numbers

Finally, business is a heavy user of a statistical technique known as *index numbers.* For example, we have frequent mention these days of the rate of inflation, and how the dollar's purchasing value is changing when compared with its value a few years ago. Usually, such expressions take the form of index numbers. An index number shows the relative change in some item compared with that item's value in some other period. This other period or year is frequently called the base year. Any year can be a base year. It is simply the value during that year that we are concerned about. We assign a value of 100 (think of 100 percent) to the value of the item being studied during the base year. Then, every other year's value for that same item is expressed as a relative value (or percent) of that base year.

To illustrate, let us consider the prices of food. If we think of the cost of a certain basket of food in 1967 as having a value of 100, we can compare the cost of that same basket of food in other years by means of an index number. In 1971, for example, the food index had a value of 118.4, meaning food that was included in that basket in 1967 at a value of 100 had increased 18.4 percent in those four years. As you can see, index numbers can be extremely useful in showing the change in values for selected items over some time period.

THE USE OF STATISTICS IN BUSINESS

Statistics is a term that has many meanings. It may, for example, refer to a collection of numerical data pertaining to some individual or event. In baseball, reference to batting averages, runs batted in, and earned-run averages are but three types of "statistics." Similarly, in business, the individual items found on the income statement and balance sheet are "statistics."

Statistics may also refer to a broad field or study, one which applies certain principles of science to the analysis of numbers and numerical data. When used in this way, statistics may be defined as a scientific system for the *collection, organization, analysis, interpretation,* and *presentation* of information in numerical form. This definition, obviously, is much more comprehensive than the first one, and in fact includes the first concept of statistics in it.

Statistics as a language of business   The science of statistics has developed as an essentially new language of business. Terms such as "measure of central tendency," "standard deviation," "correlation," and "frequency distribution" dot the literature of statistics. For business leaders who would use the tool of statistics in the decision-making process, an understanding of the meaning and the use of these terms is essential. Accordingly, an effort shall be made in the next few pages to discuss the meanings and uses of some of the major fundamental concepts that give meaning and importance to the field of statistics.

THE BASIS OF STATISTICS

As we have already seen, statistics is a body of techniques that are useful in acquiring information about some problem. To properly utilize "statistical techniques," however, it is usually necessary for us to obtain the basic information which the technique will then be used to analyze. To illustrate, let's consider the case of an advertising executive trying to determine whether he should rent a certain billboard that is located along a major interstate highway. He knows that the billboard advertising, if it is to be successful, must be read by the passing motorists. In order to determine whether the average car is going at a speed that is sufficiently slow enough to allow the driver and passengers to read the message, the executive decides to check the speed of cars passing that location on a certain day.

Let us, for simplicity's sake, assume that the advertising executive knows the average car must pass that particular location at an average speed of not more than 50 miles per hour. If too many cars pass that location at speeds greater than 50 miles per hour, chances are the driver and the passengers won't have sufficient time to read the advertising message. Assume that the executive's survey discloses that cars passed the location traveling at the following speeds:

TABLE 16–1

Observed automobile speeds (in miles per hour)

42.5	46.6	49.5	51.5
43.1	47.3	49.5	51.9
44.0	47.5	49.5	52.3
44.7	47.9	49.7	52.5
45.3	48.3	50.0	53.3
45.8	48.5	50.6	53.6
46.1	48.5	50.6	54.3
46.6	48.8	51.4	55.7

The preceding series of speeds is an example of what is commonly known as an *array*. By definition, an array is a listing of values by order of size, either smallest to largest or largest to smallest. Such a list, however, tends to be cumbersome to work with. Consequently, it is a common practice to group the information into a more organized table of values. When this is done, the data that was formerly presented as an array is now presented in the form of a *frequency distribution*. It tells us the frequency or number of times each of the values was recorded.

TABLE 16–2

Number of cars	Speed in mph
2	42.0 to 43.9
4	44.0 to 45.9
6	46.0 to 47.9
8	48.0 to 49.9
6	50.0 to 51.9
4	52.0 to 53.9
2	54.0 to 55.9

Frequency distributions of data pertaining to some problem are at the heart of the statistical process. Based on the distribution, a whole series of additional tests can be performed, each of which helps us to learn more about the answer to our problem. For example, we can diagram the results shown in our frequency distribution by drawing a *histogram,* as shown in Figure 16–2.

A histogram, essentially, is one way of graphically presenting statistical data. Actually, there is an entire branch of statistics that is con-

FIGURE 16–2

Histogram of observed speeds

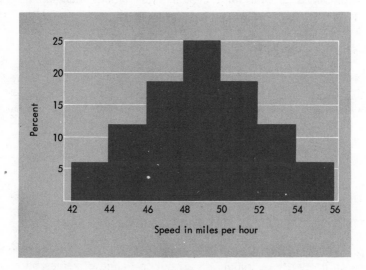

cerned with the use of tables, line or curve charts, pie diagrams, and graphs. This branch of statistics is known as *descriptive statistics.* Descriptive statistics do merely that: describe in picture form what a frequency distribution describes numerically. For examples of the different ways statistics can be graphically described, see the graphs, charts, and figures shown below, as well as figures 8–4, 18–8, 21–2, and 21–7.

FIGURE 16–3

Examples of different kinds of "descriptive" statistics

A. Price changes at the wholesale level
Percent change selected items wholesale price index, 1961–71

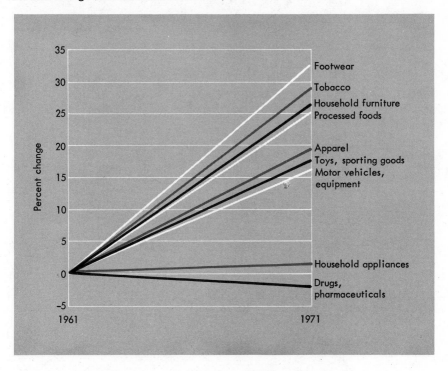

B. College enrollment by age and sex
Percent of each age group enrolled, 1970

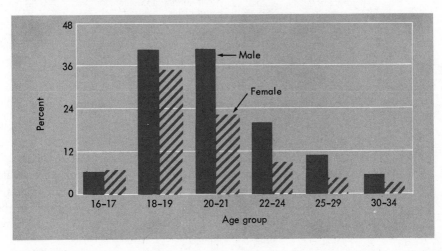

FIGURE 16–3 (continued)

C. Families by income class based on 1970 dollars

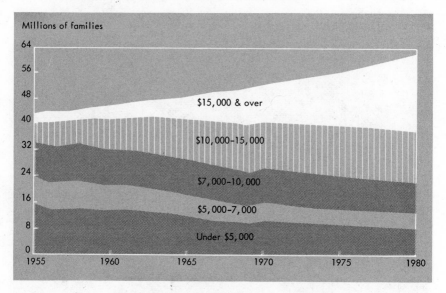

D. Population by residence
Total population each year = 100 percent

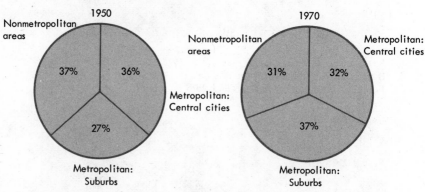

Source: The Conference Board, "A Guide to Consumer Markets," 1972–73.

If, instead of showing our data in the form of a bar histogram, we show our data by means of a curved line connecting each of the values in a frequency distribution, we form a curve similar to that in Figure 16–3. If this curve is perfectly symmetrical—that is, evenly balanced on both sides of the center point—we say this body of statistical data forms a normal distribution.[1] If, however, the resulting diagram is shifted to one side or the other, then we have a *skewed distribution*. Thus, if auto speeds had concentrated heavily at 50–55 miles per hour, with very few cars traveling at speeds lower than 50 miles per hour, we would have had a *negatively skewed distribution*. Had the concentration of car speeds been less than 45 miles per hour, we might well have had a *positively skewed distribution* (one that leans to the left).

FIGURE 16–4

Frequency distribution—A normal distribution

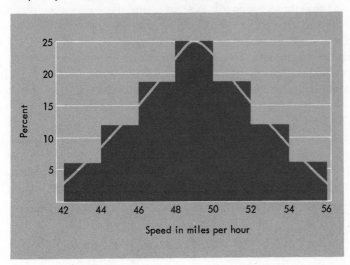

Characteristics of distribution

Each of these three types of distributions[2] have certain unique characteristics or properties, and it is an understanding of these properties that makes a knowledge of statistics the useful tool that it is. Just as an example, let's consider one of these characteristics, namely, that of the *measures of central tendency*.

Measures of central tendency

The word *average* is one that is familiar to all of us. What exactly, is an average? Essentially, an average is that score or number from a set

---

[1] Actually, a uniform distribution (i.e., a straight-line distribution) will also fit this definition, but this is a peculiar case and need not be of concern to us here.

[2] These are not the only possible types of distributions, however. Scientists, mathematicians and economists are constantly uncovering new types of distributions, and new characteristics that are unique to each.

of scores or numbers around which other related scores tend to congregate. For example, a person might say that the "average" score on a test was the middle score. Or, one might use average to mean the most popular or recurring number. Thus, a business leader talking about the average life expectancy of a sole proprietorship may be referring to the number of years such organizations tend to last before encountering problems. In each of these instances, an "average" of sorts was used. In each case, the "average" meant some center score, or predominant score among many. Each was a measure of some central tendency.

Actually, there are three different ways of expressing the term *average.* These three types of averages are the *arithmetic mean,* the *median,* and the *mode.* Let's look at the three of them and see how they relate to the earlier discussion of distributions.

The arithmetic mean   The arithmetic mean is the most widely used of all "averages" or measures of central tendency. It is found by summing all of the scores in a distribution, and dividing this sum by the number of scores. The resulting figure is the arithmetic average or mean score.

To illustrate the various kinds of averages, refer back to Table 16–1. Notice that a total of 32 automobile speeds were observed by the advertising executive. If we add the speeds for all 32 cars, and divide by the total number of cars observed (in this case, 32), we will get the arithmetic mean. That is

Total sum of all speeds observed = 1,567.4

divided by   32

equals = 48.9+ miles per hour

Notice that the arithmetic mean happens to be a score that does not appear in our original list of 32 speeds. This is not unusual, since the mean tends to weight the respective scores by their magnitude in the total distribution.

The median   Another popular measure of central tendency or "average" is the median. The median is simply the middle score. In our example, we have a listing of 32 scores. Obviously, there is no single "middle" score (i.e., a score with an equal number of values above and below it). Rather, the median falls somewhere between the 16th and 17th scores. In our case, the median can be said to be midway between 48.8 and 49.5, or 49.15.

Notice that to calculate the median, it is necessary to put the scores in the form of an array. That is, the data must be listed from highest score to lowest, or vice versa. For the mean, however, this is not necessary.

The mode   A final measure of central tendency is the *mode.* The mode is that number which reoccurs the most often in the distribution.

In our example, the mode is 49.5. This is because the number 49.5 appears three times in the list, whereas numbers 48.5 and 50.6 appear only twice.

On occasion, several classes of numbers will tie for the distinction of modal class. When this happens, we say the list was "multimodal," (meaning it had several modal classes).

A brief comparison of measures of central tendency   Each of the three measures of central tendency—the mean, the median, and the mode—is a statistic that describes some characteristic about the distribution in question. In a normal distribution (such as that in Figure 16–4), the mean, median, and mode are all the same. Notice, for example, that in our distribution of automobile speeds, the mean, median, and mode are all the same class (i.e., the class of speeds ranging from 48 to 49.9 miles per hour). If, however, we had *skewed* distributions, this characteristic would not be true. In a *skewed* distribution, the scores would not be perfectly balanced or symmetrical, but rather, would weigh more heavily toward one side or the other. In such a situation, we would find that these three measures are *not* all the same. Figure 16–5 shows both the positively skewed and negatively skewed distributions, with the mean, median, and mode designated respectively, *A, B,* and *C.* (The readers should satisfy themselves as to *why* these three measures differ in a skewed distribution.)

The discussion over the past few pages might seem like an exercise in mathematics or arithmetic, but it really was necessary. For it is on the foundation just shown that an entire field of statistics has been developed. The point to remember, however, is that statistics is merely a tool—a laborsaving device that can enable an executive to become better informed about his problem and the information available to solve it. Thus, our advertising company now knows what the average speed of cars passing that particular point on the highway is. It can now decide whether enough drivers will be able to read the message, and thereby decide whether to rent the billboard. If the survey had revealed

FIGURE 16–5

Skewed distributions

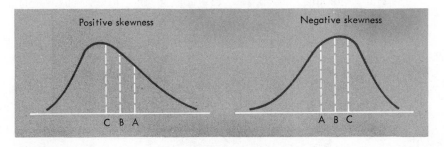

a skewed distribution, however, the advertising executive might have been forced to come to a different conclusion.

We need, too, to be careful in our use of statistical tools. Even simple problems, like finding a measure of central tendency, can be confusing. For example, suppose that our advertising executive had found the car speeds formed a negatively skewed distribution (i.e., one that leaned toward higher speeds). Which average—the mean, median, or mode— should be considered "correct" average? Why?

Applications of statistics to business

The application and uses of statistics in business are endless. Indeed, it is fair to state that modern business could not exist in its present form were it not for the application of statistical techniques to the decision-making process. To illustrate, consider the following typical examples:

1. A soft-drink manufacturer wanted to bring out a new noncola drink. He took his new soft drink and packaged it in 100 unmarked bottles, with only a number identifying the product. He did the same for the products of his leading competitors. One hundred families then tested the soft drinks, and completed questionnaires on which product they liked, why, and so on. After each sample, the formula of the new product was revised, and the entire experiment was repeated on another group of families. Eventually, a formula was developed that was preferred over all other products by the sample families. When the product was marketed, it proved highly successful.

2. In accounting firms, it is a common practice to check only a small number of the invoices or bills received by a firm. By using the statistical technique known as random sampling, the accounting firm can determine with amazing accuracy whether the firm has properly recorded all of its receipts and expenses.

3. Insurance companies have discovered that by insuring larger numbers of people, they can predict with consistency and accuracy the number of claims they will have to pay out in a given year. That is, the distribution that is formed tends to remain very constant over time. For this reason, they are able to offer insurance to young and old alike.

Actually, the use of statistics is so widespread that often we are completely unaware of our role in some statistical study. Telephone surveys, mail questionnaires, refund offers on merchandise we purchase, and the like, all lend themselves to statistical analysis and provide the business executives with information they might otherwise have had to do without.

THE ROLE OF THE COMPUTER IN BUSINESS

In the introduction to this chapter the extent to which the computer and computer technology have penetrated our everyday lives was noted. Also mentioned was the computer's importance to business. The influence of the computer can be seen in the accounting division of all businesses, in the preparation of payroll, in the research departments, and even in the planning processes of upper management.

Factors underlying the importance of computers

The development, application, and use of electronic data processing in business has been of incalculable value to our economic development as a nation. Business 30 or 40 years ago was essentially domestic (restricted to the continental United States), in nature, with foreign trade comprising a relatively minor part of our commercial activity. Today, however, business operates on a worldwide scale. This increase in the magnitude and scope of business operations has led to tremendous increases in people, paper work, and problems for management. The increases in personnel, for example, have greatly increased the need to evaluate and control the activities of everyone, so that a unified business policy may be formulated. Just the payment of wages becomes a tremendously difficult and time-consuming task. Imagine General Motors—with over 700,000 employees—calculating the payroll, payroll taxes, social security, and pension payments without the use of computers!

Simultaneously, increases in paper work have accompanied the increases in personnel. The overwhelming abundance of reports, forms, applications, and information relating to business might well have swamped business executives if it had not been for the development of the computer. This versatile machine enabled order to prevail where once chaos was seen as inevitable.

Finally, the problems of management greatly increased in recent years. As business moved overseas, new types of managerial problems arose. Moreover, the growth of the conglomerate companies greatly increased the needs of management for a streamlined, efficient flow of information for use in the decision-making process. The computer facilitated this development.

Today, of course, computer technology has wide application in business. We have computers performing tasks in minutes, seconds, or even microseconds that previously took people months to do, or which previously went undone completely. For example, the Wharton School of Finance at the University of Pennsylvania has a computer programmed to duplicate the total U.S. economy. Whenever a tax change is proposed, or a major strike occurs, this computer can estimate what the effect will be on the total output of goods and services for every business firm in the country combined. Think how useful this computer usage is for planning long-range developments and government policy. Similarly, the Chesapeake and Ohio railroad, one of the largest railroads in the country, is able to produce a balance sheet and an income statement of the year's activities on the day after New Year's. Just think of the thousands of transactions and items that need to be accounted for in order to produce these two statements. Most firms usually produce such statements, but in February or March, at the earliest!

Finally, some companies utilize their computers to develop "games" for their executives. These games are *simulations,* or replications of the real-life problems facing decision makers. By playing the games, the executives see what the consequences of alternative actions will be long before they actually need to make the decision.

We can see, therefore, that the computer has realized rapid advances in its applications to the business world. Before discussing more of these uses, however, and how statistics has been integrated into computer technology, let's examine some of the fundamentals of what the computer is, how it functions, and the limitations and shortcomings affecting its use.

What is a computer?

A computer is an electronic device that functions much like a human brain. That is, it has the capabilities of receiving instructions and numerical data, processing that data, and providing the user with solutions to the operations it was asked to perform. Specifically, a computer system performs five distinct functions. These are known as (a) the input function, (b) the memory function, (c) the control function, (d) the arithmetic function, and (e) the output function (see Figure 16–6).[3]

Input The input unit of a computer system is that segment of the system that "reads" the instruction and data upon which the computer is to operate. This unit typically receives its input in the form of punched cards, paper tape, or magnetic tape. These cards or tapes are marked with holes or magnetic symbols which the computer input unit can interpret. The instructions are read, and stored in the memory unit of the computer.

Memory The memory unit (or *core*) of the computer is at the heart of the total computer system. This unit contains storage spaces where each "word" or "instruction" is recorded for future use. Various parts of the computer system, particularly the arithmetic unit, frequently

---

[3] The computer system being described here is essentially that of the *digital* computer. Other types of computers, particularly the *analog* computer, also exist, but their role and function in business is minor by comparison.

FIGURE 16–6

The functional stages of a computer system

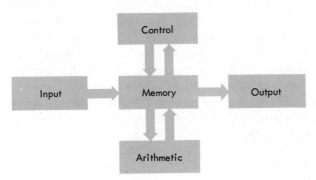

gather information from the memory unit and process it, storing the solution back in this unit.

The memory units of computers, obviously, determine just how useful a system will be. If a system has a small storage or memory unit, or if the time required to retrieve units of information from the memory is too slow, the system is restricted in just what operations it can perform. Computers with large memory units or very rapid retrieval abilities obviously can perform many more functions. Today, of course, it is possible to attach additional memory units to a computer system, thereby making the entire system much more flexible than it would be if the memory unit could not be expanded.

Moreover, the time required to retrieve information from the memory unit has decreased dramatically. Today, computers have the ability to recall information from memory in billionth's of a second, thus demonstrating the fantastic capabilities of these machines.

Control The control unit of the computer contains the logic or "brain" section. This section of the system examines the instructions that have been stored in the memory to see if they can be understood. If errors exist in the input, the control unit will reject the instructions by notifying the operator that an error exists in the instructions. If no errors are found, the control unit then begins processing the data according to the set of instructions.

The function of the control unit really points up the importance of the human brain vis-à-vis the computer. The computer cannot think for itself, but it can only interpret that which it reads. If any instruction is not consistent, the control unit will reject it. If any instruction is not presented in the format or in the exact wording that the computer has been looking for, it will reject it. Thus, if even a comma or period is inserted in the wrong place in an instruction, or accidentally omitted from some place where it should have been inserted, the control unit will not recognize the instruction but will reject it.

Obviously, providing correct and accurate input to the computer is essential to the operation and use of this mechanical brain. Writing these instructions and providing the computer with the logic by which it will execute these operations is the function of a *programmer.* Good programmers are extremely useful in business, government, and other places where computers are in widespread use. For this reason, programmers usually command a premium salary for their work. Recently, it was estimated that the United States was creating a demand for over 100,000 more computer programmers each year than were being trained in schools across the country.

Arithmetic The arithmetic unit performs the actual calculations that have been written for it by the programmer. It can, for example, add, subtract, multiply, divide, and compose numbers. It also examines the problem to determine if the problem can in fact be solved within the limitations of the computer system and the information it has been given. Sometimes, for example, a particular problem will result in an answer too big for the computer to remember. When this happens, the arithmetic unit will either chop off part of the answer or will notify the operator that the solution exceeds the range of the computer's capabilities.

Speed is also a critical factor in the arithmetic unit. The faster the computer can make certain calculations, the more useful it can be for industry. For example, a computer today can take the telephone directory for any major metropolitan city and add all of the numbers found within it, divide by the number of names, and multiply by the number of pages, in just seconds. Think how many months it would take for a person to do the same thing. Indeed, the fantastically complex calculations needed to put our astronauts on the moon and return them safely to earth could not have been performed without the high-speed capabilities of a computer.

Output The final function of a computer system is to provide the output or answer requested by the operator. This output, moreover, must be expressed in terms the operator can understand. That is, the computer may generate the answers on punched tape, punched cards, or by some other means, but these must then be translated into language that the operator can read. To accomplish this, the output units contain high-speed typewriters, capable of printing entire lines at one time. These typewriters print out the required output, even arranging the data neatly on a page if so requested.

The printing of the output is one of the slowest stages of the entire computer system. Even so, great strides have been made here, too. Today, these high-speed typewriters can print in excess of 1,000 lines per minute, far more than the average person can read in that time span. Indeed, one of the biggest problems facing computer manufacturers is trying to figure out how to increase the speed with which the paper can move through the printer. The new high-speed typewriters can print so fast, the paper has begun to burn up from the friction it generates in moving through the typewriter!

THE ROLE OF COMPUTERS IN DECISION MAKING

As has been indicated throughout this chapter, the computer has become an invaluable aid to management in decision making. By carefully combining the use of statistical methods with computer processing, scientific tests can be performed which have greatly improved management's ability to properly chart a course of action. The area of study which thus applies statistical and mathematical procedures to the solution of business problems has come to be known as *operations research* (OR). Today OR lies at the heart of the entire approach to quantitative decision making.

Operations research

Operations research involves the application of mathematical and scientific principles and techniques to the decision-making process. In general, it requires the use of the computer in arriving at the actual solutions. These techniques have proven to be extremely powerful tools in the hands of competent managers. With a knowledge of OR techniques, management can perform analyses never before dreamed of by other managers. Following are examples of such techniques.

Transportation and network problems This OR technique is useful in dealing with problems in the transportation area. Assume, for example, that an oil company has four refineries in the United States and four storage areas to where the oil is to be shipped. Assume that the refineries and the storage depots all differ in size. The question becomes: Which storage depots should be filled or served by which refinery? Operations research techniques will solve the problem in such a way as to minimize the cost of transporting the oil from refinery to storage facility.

Linear programming This is a statistical technique that enables a researcher or executive to solve a problem that has a number of factors influencing the final decision. For instance, assume that a sawmill receives a shipment of logs, 50 of which measure 100 feet in length, 50 of which measure 90 feet in length, and 50 of which measure 80 feet in length. Assume further that it has orders for boards measuring 6, 8, and 12 feet in length. Each of these board lengths will sell for different prices, and therefore, result in different profit levels for the sawmill. The problem, then, is to decide how to cut the 150 logs so as to (a) maximize profits on the boards, (b) minimize the waste remaining on the logs, and (c) still produce enough boards to meet the orders of customers. Linear programming provides a technique to solve problems of this type.

Forecasting problems Business leaders of all kinds perform some type of forecasting or estimating of future sales and costs. This is necessary so that they can properly plan for future business fluctuations. Sometimes, however, the forecasting problem itself becomes a problem of operations research. For example, consider the problem of a manufacturer of women's shoes. The manufacturer cannot know in advance how a particular style of shoe will sell. Yet, because styles change so rapidly, the total production of the shoes must take place even before the shoes are advertised for sale. If the shoe production is too low, the manufacturer will lose profits. If, however, too many are produced, the shoes will need to be disposed of at a loss. By applying the research technique of *probability analysis* to a *dynamic programming problem,* the manufacturer can resolve his situation in such a way as to maximize the chances of profit and minimize the chances of loss. This is, quite obviously, a rather sophisticated technique; but it does point out the usefulness of operations research to decision making.

Simulation As has been indicated earlier, business finds it useful on occasion to "imitate" or "simulate" the real world. Essentially, simulation requires that the business executive carefully note all of the facets of a particular problem, and all of the factors which are expected to influence the problem. The executive then decides which of these various factors can be influenced or controlled, and which cannot. These are then expressed mathematically and fed into a computer, together with the alternative decisions. The computer shows what might happen if each decision was actually made. By looking into this "model" world he has thus created, the business executive can experiment with different decisions until the one that best accomplishes the goal is found. In effect, the executive has performed a "simulation" exercise.

Simulation is extremely difficult, particularly since it requires that every possible influencing factor be accounted for. Yet simulation (and the model building that is associated with it) is perhaps the most powerful tool of all yet developed for use on the computer. For simulation is the only means by which a business leader can actually "see" what will happen if he makes a certain decision—even before he actually makes that decision.

Limitations to computers and quantitative analysis

Despite these many uses of computers and statistical techniques, computers, computer technology, and quantitative analysis have very definite limitations. The rapid increase in popularity of the application of quantitative analysis to the solution of business problems has caused many people to regard the "quantification of problems" as the only reliable and proper way to solve any problem. This approach has become, to some people, the answer to all our problems. Unfortunately, nothing could be further from the truth. Both computers and statistical analysis have limitations—some of these limitations are the result of their improper use. Others are the result of the inherent weaknesses of people. Let's discuss this point a little further.

Limitations to the technique   Computers are great devices for solving extremely complex problems. All too often, however, their use is misguided. In our little example in Figure 16–7, for instance, we show a computer solution to the calculation of an average for a list of numbers. Such a use, in reality, would be quite foolish, for the time spent writing the program and solving the problem probably could not be justified. Time is money—particularly where computers are concerned. It is not uncommon, for example, to be charged in excess of several hundred dollars an hour for the use of computer time. Our purpose, of course, was merely to illustrate a program. In industry, however, many people tend to use the computer in ways that are routinely simple and nontime-consuming by themselves. Such a use is wasteful and demeaning. Moreover, it is a sign of laziness on the part of the executive authorizing such trivial uses. The computer, after all, is a highly sophisticated machine and should be put to work on tasks equal to its potential.

Moreover, statistics, too, are often misused. There is an old adage that goes: "There are lies, damn lies, and statistics." Fortunately, the implication of this adage is not entirely true. Statistics do not lie; only people do. Finally, some people get carried away with high-powered statistical tests to solve problems which may be resolvable with very simple basic tests. Others use the computer for solving problems, not because the computer is necessary, but because it tends to be a status symbol and lends an aura of special importance and glamour to the work being done. Such practices not only are wasteful but indicate a real lack of understanding of the purpose of this useful tool.

Limitations of people   A final limitation, and one that has particular relevance regarding the computer, concerns the limitations of people. A computer is not intelligent. It cannot make value judgments. Nor can it "think" for itself. A computer can do only what it is told to do, and only if it is given the proper information will it give valid answers. In other

FIGURE 16–7

Example of computer program and flowchart
or sketch of steps necessary to execute program

Problem: Find the arithmetic mean of a list of numbers.

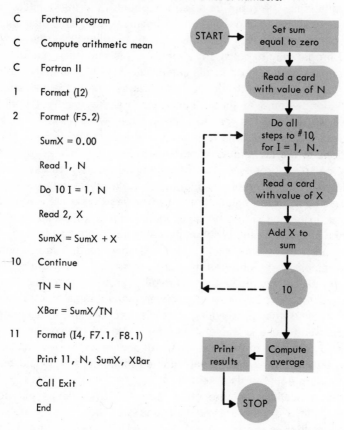

```
C     Fortran program

C     Compute arithmetic mean

C     Fortran II

1     Format (I2)

2     Format (F5.2)

      SumX = 0.00

      Read 1, N

      Do 10 I = 1, N

      Read 2, X

      SumX = SumX + X

10    Continue

      TN = N

      XBar = SumX/TN

11    Format (I4, F7.1, F8.1)

      Print 11, N, SumX, XBar

      Call Exit

      End
```

words, its limitation is that of the human operator. If the operators are not skilled in their duties, the computer's fantastic capabilities will remain unused. The computer is only as good a tool as the operator is a good director—no better, and sometimes worse.

SOCIAL IMPLICATIONS OF COMPUTERS AND QUANTITATIVE ANALYSIS

Finally, mention should also be made of the social influences of the computer and statistics in the world of business. The computer has had a great impact on the everyday lives of people as workers as well as consumers. The computer, for example, has displaced thousands of telephone operators from their jobs and made obsolete the job of thousands and thousands of other workers. The phrase "technical obsolescence" has been coined to describe many business executives who have failed to keep themselves up to date on computer technology. This tremendous displacement of people from occupations has been simultaneously accompanied by the creation of thousands and thousands of new jobs—jobs such as programming, for instance. And thus we find ourselves facing one of the great problems of our contemporary society— one that was, interestingly enough, predicted by John Stuart Mill and John Cairnes several hundred years ago—the immobility of labor. The inability of labor to move from one job to another as technology changes has been one of the great problems created by the computer.

A second problem has been the impersonalization of relations between business and the consumer. How many times have all of us received advertisements, subscription renewals, and so on, addressed to us personally, but which were obviously printed on a computer-controlled typewriter? Moreover, some of the problems that people have encountered as a result of some careless operator who punched the wrong button, are classic. People have literally gone hysterical with their inability to communicate with "the machine." It would seem at times that people exist to serve machines, rather than the other way around. These and many other problems are the result of this fabulous technology of the computer. The mastery of these problems, and the increased usage of the capabilities of the computer, then, must rank among the great challenges facing the business community in the future.

SUMMARY

In this chapter, an attempt has been made to put the role of statistics and computers into perspective as powerful tools in our business society. We have attempted to show how statistics and statistical techniques can greatly assist the managers in their decision-making processes. We have shown, too, how statistics as a science is derived from simple characteristics that are found in groups of data about a given event. These data, when transformed into frequency distributions, form the basis for a whole realm of statistical tests which help reveal aspects of our problem heretofore undisclosed.

Moreover, it has been seen how the computer has greatly enhanced business' use of statistics and statistical tests. High-powered statistical tests never before dreamed of are now being applied to the solution of business problems.

Yet, the development and refinement of these tools has not been without its related problems. The impersonalization of relations between business and consumers has contributed greatly to the lack of respect suffered by business leaders in some quarters. Moreover, the problems of job dislocation caused by the technology of the computer has greatly influenced relations between business and an uneasy and distrusting public.

DISCUSSION QUESTIONS

1 Define "quantitative analysis" in your own words. What are some of the ways you have used quantitative analysis techniques in managing your everyday life?

2 Define break-even analysis in both verbal and mathematical terms. In what ways are the relationships between profit, revenue, variable costs, and fixed costs as developed in our analysis, not indicative of the real world?

3 The scientific method has been described as "doing one's damnedest with one's mind, no holds barred." Explain the meaning of this statement.

4 Why are index numbers useful? Give an example of index numbers in use.

5 Can statistics lie? Explain.

6 Distinguish between "quantitative analysis" and "operations research." How are the two related? How do they differ?

7 What is a histogram? Have you ever used or developed one? Do you find them particularly useful? Why or why not?

8 Distinguish between "normal" distributions, "positively skewed" distributions, and "negatively skewed" distributions.

9 Ask your professor to give you the class grades for the last examination. Do these form a particular type of distribution? What might account for the failure of your class to fall in a perfect, normal distribution?

10 Calculate the mean, median and mode for the scores you used in answering Question 9. Which of the three averages do you consider most meaningful? Why?

11 Describe the five major components of a computer system.

12 Computers have also been called "electronic brains." Do the five major parts of the computer system (as developed in Question 11) have any counterparts to the human brain? Explain.

13 Critics of our society have charged that our technological advances in the use of the computer have led to massive alienation of people from the mainstream of life in the United States. These people, it

is charged—the poor, the disadvantaged, minority groups, and so on—have found themselves unable to cope with the complexities of life that have resulted from this technological age. Do you agree? What does this mean for business, assuming the charge to be true?

MINI CASES

The American Broadcasting System (ABS) was one of the large networks in the United States. In preparing a forecast of its expected revenues and expenses for the fall season of television shows, it noted the following facts:

1. The studio had available for sale, 180 minutes of commercial time each evening. This comprised 18 minutes of commercial time for each hour of broadcasting. The studio's concern is primarily over the "prime" TV times running from 5:00 p.m. to 2:00 a.m.

2. Audience exposure determined the amount of revenue received for each minute of commercial time. In this regard, the studio determined that audience exposure was lowest in the early evening and very late evening, and in fact, followed the pattern presented here:

Millions of Viewers

5 p.m. : 8 million	10 p.m. : 20 million
6 p.m. : 10 million	11 p.m. : 16 million
7 p.m. : 12 million	12 p.m. : 12 million
8 p.m. : 16 million	1 a.m. : 10 million
9 p.m. : 20 million	2 a.m. : 8 million

3. As a general rule, television commercial time was priced between $5,000 per minute and $60,000 per minute.

1. *What pricing schedule would you recommend the studio follow if it is to fairly price each hour's TV time?*
2. *Assuming that the studio follows your recommended pricing schedule, how much revenue could it expect to receive each seven-day week?*
3. *What was the price of their "average" commercial?*

The Charging Ram Book Manufacturing Company has just completed a cost analysis of their operations. The following information was uncovered. The average price of the textbooks they produce is $10. The firm is capable of producing books at runs up to 10,000 copies. When they do, they incur fixed costs of $30,000. These costs do not change if for some reason production is at less than 10,000 units. The firms variable costs are $4 per unit.

1.   *What is the firm's break-even point?*
2.   *What would be the firm's gain or loss if it produced 4,000 units? 6,000 units? Illustrate the 6,000 units of production with a chart.*

part three Business and society

Having discussed the functions of American business, our attention will now be turned to the relations of business with its counterpart publics in American society. Business, we have learned, cannot act in total disregard for the welfare, desires, and requirements of others. Stockholders need to be answered, government needs to be listened to, and the consumer needs to be catered to. Moreover, in our contemporary society, we have reached a point of maturity where *all* people—young and old, rich and poor, business leaders and laborers —need to be concerned with the quality of life. Pollution, for example, is a problem of sufficient magnitude to threaten our very society unless it is halted.

In the following chapters, we will examine business' role and responsibility to its owners, to its customers, and to the government and society that permit it to operate. Lastly, but certainly not of least importance, is business' role in an international community. Hopefully, we will conclude our development with a keener understanding of this dynamic institution we call business.

445

It is one of the great ironies of business in modern society that so few women have ever achieved public acclaim for their accomplishments in the world of business. Perhaps this is because of the fact that this has been a "man's world" for so long. Perhaps too, it is because those women who have succeeded have not bothered publicizing the fact. One woman who qualifies under the latter category is Catherine Blanchard Cleary.

Catherine Cleary was born in 1917, the daughter of the late president of Northwestern Mutual Life Insurance Company. She came out as a debutante in 1935, and proceeded to earn degrees from The University of Chicago and the University of Wisconsin. In 1947, she joined First Wisconsin Trust because, as she tells it, "there were no Milwaukee law firms that wanted a lady lawyer." In 1950, she was made a trust officer of the bank.

Ms. Cleary spent the years, 1953–54, as assistant treasurer and assistant to the Secretary of the Treasury in the Eisenhower administration. In 1954, she became vice president of First Wisconsin Trust.

In 1964, Ms. Cleary was a delegate to the Republican National Convention. Finally, in 1969, she was appointed president of First Wisconsin Trust.

While many careers might well have ended here, Ms. Cleary's career seemed only to begin. In 1970, she became a director of Wisconsin Telephone. Since then, she has been named to the boards of directors of American Telephone and Telegraph Company (A.T.&T.), Kraftco, First Wisconsin Bankshares (the holding company that controls First Wisconsin Trust) and finally, in 1972, to the board of directors of General Motors Corporation. As of this point in time, Ms. Cleary may well be, in the words of *Business Week,* "the most prominent woman director in American business." May she have continued success.

Catherine Blanchard Cleary
(1917–   )

Most prominent woman director in America

17

Business and the stockholder

Business, as we already know, frequently comes under severe criticism for its participation, or lack of participation, in certain commercial and/or social practices. How many of us have driven through any of the large industrial centers of this country and seen smoke belching from large smokestacks, a visible cause of pollution in the air, and asked, "Why?" Why doesn't business do something about it?

Similarly, we continually hear about the lack of safety of certain of our products—for example, automobiles—and the apparent unwillingness of manufacturers to build safer and more easily repairable cars. Rather, they place emphasis on glamorous looks, speed, and power. Again, the question becomes— Why? Why won't business—the institution that profits by making these products—do something about these problems?

Part of the reason is because you and I, or people just like us, don't *want* business to do anything about these problems. This isn't to say we don't care. We do! Indeed, some of the most vocal critics of business practices are the very people who prevent the business firm from doing anything about the problem. Apparently there is a conflict of purpose. Such conflicts occur in many aspects of our lives. To illustrate, consider the following: As consumers, we demand that we get the best product available for our money. We get irritated if we buy something which doesn't live up to our expectations. Yet, as workers on the assembly line of the company making the product, we often fail to be

447

as careful as we might otherwise be. Maybe we had a fight with the supervisor, or maybe we were not feeling well. Whatever the reason, we turn out a product that is not of the best quality. The result—we produce a poor product, and when we turn around and buy it as a consumer, we complain about the shoddy workmanship. There are many such examples of situations where our actions as producers conflict with our interests as consumers.

In this chapter, we shall attempt to shed a little light on the nature of one of these areas of "conflict of purpose." Specifically, the role of the stockholder shall be examined as one of the major forces helping to determine the various actions that are ultimately taken by business firms. The unique position of a firm's stockholders as a potentially powerful force in the shaping of corporate goals and actions will be examined, particularly as those actions affect business and its relationships with other groups in society.

STOCKHOLDERS: SOME SIGNIFICANT QUESTIONS

One of the most important questions of how well business serves society involves the relationship of the business firm to its owners, namely, the stockholders of the firm. Before discussing further the importance of this group of individuals, however, certain questions need to be answered. Just who are stockholders; and what is it that they own? More importantly, how do they come to own what they do? What do they expect to receive as a reward or return for assuming the role of a stockholder? As elementary as these questions may seem, they are fundamental to our understanding of this segment of contemporary business.

Who are stockholders? What do they own?

Stockholders are those people and institutions that own America's corporations. Such ownership usually takes place because people have decided, for one reason or another, that investment in business firms offers the best possibility for achieving their own personal financial goals. Thus, people who wish to receive constant flows of income from their investments, but who feel that bank interest rates are too low, may decide to invest their money in the stock of corporations that have a history of paying large dividends. Similarly, investors who desire to realize a substantial increase in the size of their total wealth, and are willing to assume certain risks in order to have a chance at that large increase, may also find investment in the common stocks of certain companies to be the best investment medium for them.

Whatever the reason, however, the fact remains that more and more Americans are "owning their share of America's businesses" by acquiring common stock. Figure 17–1 shows the extent of this growth over recent years.

Moreover, such increases in the number of stockholders in the country is not the result of increased wealth on the part of any one segment of the population. While over 50 percent of all stockholders have attended college at some time during their lives, we should not infer that only the college educated and professionally employed persons are

FIGURE 17–1

Shareholders in the United States (selected years)

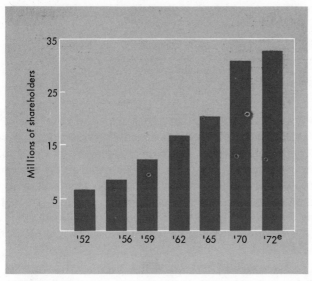

e Estimated.
Source: New York Stock Exchange, *Fact Book*, 1972, p. 47.

owners of common stock. Indeed, over the past 10 years, the largest single group of individual stockholders has comprised homemakers and retired persons! Table 17–1 gives a detailed breakdown of stockholders, by occupation.

Individuals, however, are not the only holders of common stocks. Many institutions, such as insurance companies, banks, pension funds, and others, own common stocks as part of their investments. These institutions moreover, are a growing force in the world of the shareholder. As of early 1971, approximately 28 percent of all of the outstanding shares of stock were held by these various institutions. Later in this chapter, we will extend our discussion of the business-stockholder relationship to include these institutions, for they exert great influence on stock market transactions.

TABLE 17–1

Shareholders of corporations—by occupation

	Individual shareholders	
Occupation	*Number*	*Percent of total*
Professional and technical................	6,320,000	20.2
Clerical and sales........................	4,415,000	13.9
Managers, proprietors, etc...............	3,981,000	13.6
Craftsmen and supervisors...............	1,377,000	4.0
Operatives and laborers..................	849,000	2.7
Service workers..........................	622,000	2.0
Farmers and farm laborers...............	170,000	0.4
Homemakers, retired persons and		
unemployed adults....................	10,320,000	34.4
Minors...................................	2,221,000	7.1
Other....................................	575,000	1.7
Totals...........................	30,850,000	100.0

Source: New York Stock Exchange, *Census of Stockholders, 1970,* p. 7.

Knowing who owns stock, however, does not help us answer the question, "What do they own?" At first glance, this question seems easy to answer. Stockholders own the corporations they have stock in! Unfortunately, owning stock in a corporation does not give the stockholder the same claim on the property of the corporation that a person might have if he owned some other asset. For example, a college student who owns a car has the right to use the car, to change its structure and performance, and to do most anything he wants with it. This is his right, as owner of the car.

Stockholders however, do not have the same freedom with their property. Stockholders may own 5 percent of a company's stock, for example, but that does not give them a claim to the *use* of 5 percent of the company's assets. Only in the event of a liquidation of the company do stockholders actually have a claim against the assets of the firm. Usually, however, the conditions that bring about the liquidation of a firm will probably be of enough significance as to assure that the stockholders' claim will prove worthless. This fact, however, does not really answer our question, namely, *What* do stockholders own? To answer this question, we really need to answer one other question: "How is it that stockholders come to own what they do?"

Why do stockholders own what they do?

Stockholders exist because of the profit-oriented nature of our society. The Protestant ethic (see Chapter 4) that this country was founded under established the tenet that people should work hard to improve their position in life. Consequently, people with income over and above what they need for survival tend to invest that "excess" income in ways which they feel will best enable them to achieve the future financial goals they hold for themselves. Thus, people buy stock in companies because they either desire high dividends (that is, current income) or because they desire large increases in their wealth position (that is, long-term price appreciation), or both. In other words, for most people buying stock is an investment decision. Poor people don't usually buy stock. Most if not all of their income is used to buy the basic necessities of life. As people gain more and more income, however, they find themselves able to save— and invest—more and more of that income. By so doing, they hope to increase the amount of money they will have available to spend tomorrow. This basic law of economics is critical in understanding why people become stockholders.

What do stockholders own?

We have noted that when people invest in the stocks of corporations, they are usually investing "excess" funds or "excess" wealth in the expectation of receiving some kind of financial return. In acquiring stock, these people then become owners of the corporation. However, most of these stockholders find themselves unable or unwilling to manage the firm in which they own stock. They may have other occupations which require their time or they may lack the skills necessary to properly manage the firm. It is for this reason that stockholders elect a board of directors to manage the corporation. It is also the reason why large corporations have a separation of ownership and management.

Much of the reason for the difference in ownership rights between a stockholder and the owner of other property comes about because of this separation of the management of the corporation from the ownership of that same corporation. Most stockholders do not *want* to manage the business. All they want is the right to sell their claims whenever they choose to do so and to receive some kind of return on their investment while they possess that ownership claim.

This is not to imply, however, that legally the stockholders have no ownership or managerial rights. Quite the contrary! Ownership still carries the legal right to vote on major issues and elect the directors and thereby control the management of their property.

If we stop to think about it, we would probably agree that it is a good thing most stockholders do not want to manage their investments. Imagine the total confusion that would exist, for example, if the stockholders of any of the ten companies listed in Table 17–2 decided to take an active part in the management of their company. Can you imagine the telephone company operating with almost 3 million supervisors?

TABLE 17–2

Companies with the largest number of stockholders
of record, late 1974

Company	Stockholders
American Telephone and Telegraph	2,991,620
General Motors	1,306,500
Exxon	720,000
International Business Machines	574,887
General Electric	530,000
General Telephone and Electonic	482,000
Ford Motor Co	342,500
U.S. Steel	311,088
Texaco, Inc	310,698
Radio Corporation of America	298,318

Source: Standard & Poors, *New York Stock Exchange Reports,* July 1974.

To summarize our findings to this point, then, we can state that stockholders are, indeed, the owners of corporations—at least in a legal sense. For the most part, however, stockholders maintain *only* legal title to the company. They do not attempt to manage the firm in which they have part ownership. Rather, they delegate the power of management to others, expecting to hold them accountable for the developments that eventually occur.

This concept of the separation of ownership and management is an important one. In essence, we can state that stockholders "own" but do not "control" the companies in which they hold stock. Rather, this "control" has been given to another group of individuals—the managers of the business—to use for the good of the company.

In theory, of course, this practice seems perfectly legitimate. The managers control the business, and the stockholders control the managers. In practice, however, this does not always hold true. Given the wide differences among stockholders—their geographic dispersion, their educational differences, and the varying degrees of knowledge each has about the business in question—it becomes very difficult for any small group of stockholders to hold the management of the firm truly accountable for their actions.

What do stockholders expect to receive?

As has already been noted, stockholders desire either dividends or price appreciation on their investments. To the extent that the management of a firm desires to keep the stockholders happy, it will attempt to undertake those operations and activities that best enable it to achieve those results. This may mean, for example, that a firm whose management realizes the stockholders prefer price appreciation instead of dividend income will restrict the dividend payout and reinvest all of the profits in the hope of generating greater profits and a higher stock price in the long run. Similarly, if management perceives that the stockholders desire dividend income, policy may be the reverse: paying out large dividends now and not concerning itself with the future. In academic terms, this is frequently called "maximizing shareholder wealth."

From a stockholder's viewpoint, "maximizing wealth" means one of two things. Either the firm maximizes the dividend it pays to the stockholders (thereby "maximizing" the annual return to the stockholder) or it undertakes those activities that will cause its stock to rise in price on the open market (thereby "maximizing" price appreciation). Depending on the philosophy of the management, and what management perceives the philosophy of the stockholders to be, most companies will tend to pursue policies that lead to one or the other of these two objectives.

Maximizing dividends to stockholders Many stockholders invest in firms with the intention of receiving a steady return from their investment. This return is generated from the dividends that are paid on the stock. Some firms have made serious attempts at paying a steady, continuous dividend in both good years and bad years. The companies listed

TABLE 17–3

Companies that have paid dividends for over a century

Stock	Dividends since
Bank of New York Co., Inc.	1784
Morgan (J. P.) & Co.	1840
Chase Manhattan Corp.	1848
Manufacturers Hanover Corp.	1852
Cincinnati Gas and Electric.	1853
Singer Co.	1863
Travelers Corp.	1866
Pullman, Inc.	1867

in Table 17–3, for example, had a record—as of late 1974—of paying dividends every year for over 100 consecutive years.

Maximizing price appreciation The problem of insuring a "maximum" price for its stock is a more difficult task for management. Whether a company's stock can command a high price in the marketplace depends on a number of factors. The more significant of these are: (a) a wide exposure of its stock to potential investors, (b) favorable prospects for the future of the company, and (c) favorable publicity and periodic announcements concerning company activity. Each of these is important enough to warrant closer attention.

Wide exposure of its stock To a great extent, the price of a share of common stock in the marketplace depends on the number of shares of that stock available for purchase and the number of people interested in acquiring it. That is, the price is determined by the laws of supply and demand.

Certainly one of the more significant factors that determine the demand for a company's stock is its exposure to potential investors. This requires that as many investors as possible be aware of the existence of the company's stock and know where and how they can acquire it. For this reason, many companies like to have their stock traded on one of the organized stock exchanges. In this way, maximum exposure is almost guaranteed. Every day, newspapers all across the country publish listings of stock prices of thousands of companies. By listing their stock on one of the major stock exchanges, companies can help broaden the exposure of their stock to the investing public.[1]

Favorable prospects for the future Wide exposure of a firm's stock, however, will not by itself guarantee "maximum" demand for the stock. The firm must also demonstrate that it has a favorable potential for

TABLE 17-4

How growth stocks grow*

	Mid-1953	Mid-1963	End 1966	End 1971
American Cyanamid	$1,000	$ 2,615	$ 2,726	$ 3,038.82
Bristol-Myers	1,000	15,671	34,727	36,857.96
Caterpillar Tractor	1,000	5,356	8,694	11,736.89
Corning Glass Works	1,000	5,548	10,033	6,023.04
Factor (Max)	1,000	23,484	30,188	65,211.71
General Electric	1,000	3,320	3,720	10,529.49
Grumman Aircraft	1,000	2,540	5,619	2,504.12
Gulf Life Insurance	1,000	4,336	2,695	5,067.23
International Business Machines	1,000	14,557	23,256	86,366.37
Magnavox	1,000	18,556	32,458	39,939.84
Minneapolis-Honeywell	1,000	3,500	4,658	9,359.86
Minnesota Mining & Manufacturing	1,000	7,235	9,879	34,196.53
Pacific Gas & Electric	1,000	2,601	2,929	2,652.49
Pitney-Bowes	1,000	7,557	7,442	15,154.61
Polaroid	1,000	33,777	137,700	308,795.00
Procter & Gamble	1,000	5,071	4,887	21,020.79
Radio Corporation of America	1,000	3,106	6,478	5,625.63
Safeway Stores	1,000	4,857	4,070	6,021.08
Texaco	1,000	5,646	6,012	11,561.53
Union Bank (Los Angeles)	1,000	8,681	3,573	8,469.17

* The table shows how a $1,000 cash investment in any of 20 different stocks regarded as growth stocks in 1953 would have grown since mid-1953. Full adjustment has been made in this tabulation for splits and stock dividends. But no account has been taken of cash dividends or rights offerings, and no allowance has been made for brokerage fees.
Source: Merrill Lynch, Pierce, Fenner & Smith, Inc.

[1] Not all companies are eligible for listing on one of these exchanges, however. Each exchange has certain minimum qualifications that must be met by every company that desires to list stock. The New York Stock Exchange, for example, requires among other things that a company meet certain earnings requirements, have a certain number of shareholders, and have reasonable reason to expect its stock to have a national market.

generating earnings in the future if it is to attract potential investors. Firms with bright futures are firms that will, in all likelihood, realize increases in profits, dividends, and consequently, the value of their stock in future years. This is, of course, highly desirable for individuals investing money today in the hope of a larger return tomorrow. Consequently, the managements of these firms are under pressure to make shrewd business decisions regarding their investments in machinery, their marketing policies, and their overall management of the firm.

Favorable publicity and announcements   Finally, a firm desiring to see its stock sell at the highest possible price must generate periodic news releases, publicity announcements, and informational releases to its stockholders. Only by keeping the investing public informed of latest events of importance in the firm can the management hope to create interest in the firms' stock on the part of potential investors.

Having established who stockholders are, what they own or control, and what they expect to receive as a reward for being stockholders, we can now consider the direct interrelationship of the business firm with its stockholders. In so doing, we shall see that the area of business-stockholder relations is an exceedingly complex one, and in many ways lies at the heart of the problems business faces in adjusting to the demands of today's society.

THE RIGHTS OF THE STOCKHOLDER

As owners of the corporation, stockholders are entitled to certain rights. These rights include the right to vote on corporate matters, including the election of the board of directors, the right to receive information about the company's activities, and the right to receive dividends if they are declared. Since we have already discussed this last right, we will concern ourselves with the first two rights of stock ownership.

The right to vote on corporate matters

Ownership of common stock carries with it the right to vote on all important corporate matters, including the periodic election or reelection of a board of directors. Frequently, however, the power and control that the stockholders have relinquished to the management of the firm results in an inability of the stockholders to execute the rights and privileges that are legally theirs. This is particularly true in the area of voting privileges.

Stockholders are entitled by law to have a vote on matters that are considered important enough to directly affect their welfare. Thus, a decision to rehire the present board of directors can only be decided by vote of the stockholders. Similarly, a decision regarding the merger of the firm with another company usually requires the approval of the existing stockholders. Sometimes, however, the management of the corporation has so structured the "voting rules" that the average investors find themselves prevented, for all intent and purposes, from having any real say in the decision-making process. Let's examine the problem in more detail.

The method of voting   Stockholders are entitled to have a vote on all matters of direct concern to them. The exact voting power that any one stockholder has, must—quite logically—be related to, or based on, the percentage of ownership each stockholder has in the firm. Thus, the greater the number of shares owned by a stockholder, the greater is the voting power. However, the voting power does not necessarily have to be in a one-to-one relationship with the number of shares owned. Sometimes each share of stock entitles its owner to eight, nine, or even more votes! This is because of the existence of two different methods of voting that exist in corporate democracy. These methods are known as (*a*) *noncumulative voting,* and (*b*) *cumulative voting.*

Noncumulative voting   Under noncumulative voting, each share of stock carries with it one vote on corporate matters. As an example, assume that you owned one share of stock in a corporation that had noncumulative voting. Further assume that 15 people were running for election to the nine-member board of directors. Under noncumulative voting, you could cast one vote for each of nine candidates running for office. This may seem as though you are, in reality, casting nine votes; however, the key factor is that no one candidate may receive more than one vote from you. You are not allowed to "accumulate" your votes and cast them all for one person. It should be apparent that, with noncumulative voting, a stockholder who owns more than one half of all of the common or voting stock can always elect the entire board of directors. Minority stockholders have no choice but to accept the will of the majority.

Cumulative voting   A second method of voting is known as the cumulative voting method. Under cumulative voting, the restrictions on the number of votes any one candidate may receive from a single stockholder are removed. Each shareholder is entitled to "a number of votes equal to the number of shares owned, multipled by the number of directors to be elected, *and* furthermore, the number of votes possessed by a stockholder may be divided in any desired manner among the candidates."[2] Thus, in our example, if cumulative voting were in existence at this corporation, you would be entitled to nine votes (one share of stock times nine directorships) which you could vote any way you chose. You could cast all nine votes for one candidate, cast three votes for each of three candidates, or even vote for each of nine candidates—just as under the

---

[2] Joseph Bradley, *Administrative Financial Management,* 3d ed. (Hinsdale, Ill.: The Dreyden Press, Inc., 1973).

noncumulative system. The significant factor, however, is that stockholders have the right to accumulate their votes on behalf of one or two candidates. Such a right usually prevents a stockholder who controls most of the company's stock from electing all of the directors. Minority representation is almost always assured.

Should cumulative voting be abolished?

In recent years, many companies with cumulative voting specified in their corporate bylaws have been trying to get stockholder approval to change to noncumulative voting. Management has argued that noncumulative voting will benefit the company—and indirectly the welfare of the stockholders—by assuring that dissidents and others who would be perpetual troublemakers are kept from having undue power to select representatives on the board of directors. This is necessary, says management, if the company is to act quickly and decisively in effecting managerial policy. They argue, and not without foundation, that continued bickering and disagreement on the part of upper management can lead only to poor morale and confusion at the lower levels of management. Such bickering would have obvious adverse effects on the performance of the company. By abolishing cumulative voting, the company could then be assured of the election of a "slate" of officers, all of whom met with the approval of the others. Thus, stockholders would be assured of a unified, cooperative managerial team.

This argument favoring a change in the voting method has brought about a sharp rebuttal from advocates of cumulative voting. Their disagreement is based on two major issues: That of corporate democracy and fair representation, and the belief that some dissent is necessary for good, efficient management.

The issue of representation   The dissenters tend to argue that cumulative voting is necessary if all stockholders are to be assured of their rightful say in corporate affairs. Without the protection that cumulative voting provides minority stockholders, it would be possible for the votes of as much as 49 percent of the stockholders to be totally ineffective. One large stockholder, it is argued, could assure himself of absolute control of the firm by controlling only 50.1 percent of the stock of the company. This, it is argued, is not a very democratic way of managing the stockholders' interest, particularly since the stockholders have no effective check and balance over the actions of the board of directors.

A corollary argument, and one that is probably just as valid as the first argument, concerns the personal motivations of the directors in seeking the abolition of cumulative voting. Many of these directors were elected under the rules of cumulative voting. While candidates for election, these persons were quick to utilize the unique features of cumulative voting to gain election to the board. Once elected, however, these same people fought for abolishment of cumulative voting. Advocates of cumulative voting have charged that the real reason management wants to abolish this voting technique is that, without cumulative voting, the directors of a firm can more easily perpetuate their terms of office. It is much more difficult to vote a director out of office under noncumulative voting than it is under cumulative voting.

The value of dissent   Finally, advocates of cumulative voting argue that dissent among the board of directors may be a good thing. Too many firms, they argue, find themselves facing problems of mammoth proportions because the board of directors failed to be as probing and as inquisitive as it might have been. The classic example used to illustrate this point concerns the Penn-Central Railroad. This multibillion-dollar corporation had a board of directors which, for the most part, consisted of a cooperative team. Indeed, over half of the board of directors were also vice presidents or operating officers of the company. Apparently they failed to ask enough questions to uncover the problems that eventually led to the bankruptcy of the railroad.

Corporate voting procedures

A second issue that has a bearing on the relationship of the voting stockholders and the directors of the corporation concerns the procedure by which the vote is actually taken. As a general rule, corporations vote on the election of the board of directors and on other pertinent issues, once a year at the annual meeting of the stockholders. As might be expected from a glance at Table 17–2, however, not all of the stockholders can or will attend the annual meeting. As a result, corporations have developed a technique, similar to an absentee ballot, that enables stockholders to vote without actually being present at the meeting. This technique involves a legal instrument known as a *proxy.*

The proxy   A proxy is a legal document that allows a person to vote for, or act on behalf of, another person. Thus, stockholders who receive a proxy in the mail will be asked to indicate their voting preferences by a simple "X" in the appropriate square, and then to sign the proxy. The treasurer or other top officers of the firm, are usually named on the proxy as the person or persons who will then be entitled to vote on behalf of the stockholder.

On the face of it, there would appear to be little that seems objectionable insofar as corporate democracy is concerned. The proxy, it would seem, would tend to insure stockholder participation in the vote, rather than the apathy we generally associate with such democratic processes. The problem, however, is more a matter of the way in which proxies are structured and the manner in which they are distributed than of the proxy itself. Let's examine the problem more closely.

Proxies are mailed to all stockholders of record as of the close of business on a stipulated day. To make it as easy as possible for the voting stockholders, proxies usually contain the two or three major items of business that are to be voted on, condensed into a single sentence or two. Next to each item are two boxes, one for a vote "yes" and one for a "no," on the particular issue (see Figure 17–2). Also stated next to each

FIGURE 17–2

A proxy

RICHARD D. IRWIN, INC.

PROXY FOR ANNUAL MEETING OF SHAREHOLDERS, JUNE 5, 1974

Richard D. Irwin, Irvin L. Grimes, and John K. Franklin, or any one of them with power of substitution are hereby authorized to represent and vote the stock of the undersigned at the annual meeting of the shareholders of Richard D. Irwin, Inc., to be held June 5, 1974, and at any adjournment thereof.

1. For ☐ or withhold authority to vote for ☐ the election of directors.
2. For ☐ or against ☐ the appointment of the firm of Ernst & Ernst, Independent Public Accountants, of Chicago, Illinois, with offices at 150 South Wacker Drive, as auditors for the 1974 fiscal year.
3. Any other business that may properly come before the meeting.

(Continued on Reverse Side)

IF NO PREFERENCE IS SPECIFIED, IT WILL BE VOTED IN FAVOR OF THE PROPOSALS OUTLINED IN PARAGRAPHS 1, 2, AND 3 ABOVE, AND DISCRETIONARY AUTHORITY IS CONFERRED AS TO ANY OTHER BUSINESS THAT MAY PROPERLY COME BEFORE THE MEETING.

Name _____

Please sign exactly as name appears hereon. Executors, administrators, and trustees should so indicate when signing.

DATE_____, 1974

This Proxy is Solicited on Behalf of the Management of Richard D. Irwin, Inc.

---

item will frequently be the recommendation of the existing management on how they feel the stockholder should vote. In boldface type will be a further admonition to the stockholder to sign the proxy and to return it to the company by a specified date. Words will also be found to the effect that a failure to indicate a preference, that is, a failure to vote "yes" or "no," will be considered a vote "for" the issue (or against it, if management is basically opposed to the particular issue). For the stockholders added information, a booklet entitled, "Notice of the Annual Meeting for _____ Corporation" will accompany the proxy. This booklet describes in some detail each of the issues that are to be voted on.

Usually, sufficient information is provided to aid the inquisitive stockholder in making a reasonably intelligent decision on the issue at hand. The stockholder, after reading this material, can then sign the proxy, indicate the vote preferences, and return the proxy to the company.

Critics of this aspect of corporate democracy argue that the proxy itself is responsible for the inability of stockholders to exercise more control over their corporations. These critics charge that putting oversimplified and often noninformative labels on the proxy for the stockholder to vote on only confuses the stockholder (who in all probability knows little about corporate affairs) in making a decision. To understand the issue, the stockholder is forced to read through the lengthy, and often technical, documents that accompany the proxy. This, say the critics, just does not happen. People will not read their life insurance policies, let alone a technical financial document ranging from 10 to over 100 pages in length. As a consequence, these stockholders either do not check a box at all (in which case the vote is cast the way management chooses) or stockholders allow themselves to be influenced by the recommendation of the present board of directors, (which is usually displayed prominently on the proxy). In either case, charge the critics, management begins the election with an almost assured majority of the votes.

In defense of the proxy Management tends to defend this voting technique on several counts. First, it is argued, the proxy vote assures that a vast majority of all stockholders will participate in the election. Without the proxy, corporations might be managed by minority parties whose interests might not coincide with the wishes of the stockholders.

Second, management justifies presenting its recommendation on how to vote as being consistent with its position as the duly elected representatives of the stockholders in the management of the firm. The stockholders obviously hired the current board of directors because they felt these individuals were most informed and qualified to manage their company. What would be more logical, then, than for these "representatives" or "trustees" of the stockholders to advise their clients on how they feel the stockholder should vote? If stockholders wish to know why they should vote that way, they can read the proxy material. Moreover, since most stockholders are not interested in managing their investment in the business, they probably will appreciate the assistance of their elected officials. Obviously, the arguments have merit on both sides, and it remains for the readers to think about this issue before reaching their own conclusions.

The structure of the proxy statement, however, is not the only aspect of this voting device that has aroused controversy among those interested in reestablishing the stockholder's voice in the management of the firm. Also criticized is the manner in which the proxies are distributed. Each proxy is sent to the stockholder of record as of a certain date. Included with each is a postage-paid envelope for returning the proxy to the company. All of these expenses—printing the proxies, paying the postage, and so on—are paid for by the corporation. The individual directors, even though they may be running for reelection to the board, incur no expense. As current directors, they have the right to use corporate funds for the proxy solicitation.

Opposition candidates for the board, however, are not able to make similar use of corporate financing. If stockholders or groups of stockholders oppose the reelection of the present board of directors, or if for some reason decide to solicit proxies for their own purposes, the cost of such solicitation must be borne by them personally. Imagine, then, the problem of opposing the management of A.T.&T. With almost 3 million stockholders, the postage alone would exceed $0.5 million! Quite obviously, this cost problem alone can seriously hamper open elections of the directors of many firms.

The right to receive reports

A second right of stockholders is the right to receive reports on the performance and activities of their corporation. Such reports are usually of three types: (a) the proxy statement and other statistical booklets containing information that stockholders will be requested to vote on; (b) quarterly or semiannual performance reports, usually issued in conjunction with quarterly or semiannual dividend payments; and (c) annual reports summarizing all of the year's activities for the firm.

Voting proposals Stockholders are entitled to receive from their companies information on any merger, purchase, or other activity of the firm that will have an immediate effect on the ownership position the stockholder currently enjoys. These reports are usually statistical in nature, and contain summaries of several years' financial statements. They also discuss the history of the business, salaries and other types of financial compensations received by the officers, and so on. Such statements usually require some understanding of basic accounting and finance in order to read. As such they are not frequently consulted or read by the average stockholder. Unfortunately, these documents frequently contain more information than all of the other reports that are sent to stockholders combined. The reluctance of stockholders to read them undoubtedly contributes greatly to the inability of stockholders to exercise more effective control over their corporations.

Quarterly reports Many firms issue quarterly reports to their stockholders. Such reports inform them of results over the previous three months, including a general prediction on the expected performance this year as compared with last year's performance. These reports are quite brief, often running only two to four pages.

The annual report   The annual report is probably the most important report received by the stockholder from the firm. It summarizes all of the activity of the company during the past year. Such reports are often impressive documents, running from 8 to 48 or more pages in length. Multicolored photographs, high-quality paper, and attractive layout and design are often combined to make the physical appearance of the report a pleasing one.

Corporations make a major effort to present a dignified and exciting image in their annual report. The report itself usually emphasizes some theme, or major feature, of the company each year. For example, one year's annual report may emphasize research and development, highlighting the many ways this activity contributes to the company's development. Another year the theme may be new product development, growth, safety, or some other corporate activity. Regardless of the theme, however, the company attempts—through the annual report—to present all of the many activities of the firm in as informative and interesting a manner as possible.

What's in an annual report?   Although annual reports differ considerably in length and attractiveness, the content maintains a fairly close uniformity among companies. Annual reports usually begin with a section of *highlights,* in which the major accomplishments of the past year (if any) are briefly mentioned. This is followed by a *Letter from the President,* explaining to the stockholders what happened in the past year and why. Depending on the profitability of the firm in the previous year, the next 10 to 15 pages discuss various aspects of the company's business.[3]

This is followed by the financial statements of the firm for the past two years (for comparative purposes) and finally, by a summary of past performances (usually for a ten-year period). Occasionally, a firm will issue its annual report in two parts—one part containing the descriptive material and the other part containing financial statistics. The Burlington and Northern Railway and the Georgia Pacific Paper Company are but two companies that follow this practice. Some companies follow this procedure in the belief that individual stockholders would rather read the descriptive portion of the report, while professional security analysts desire detailed financial data. By providing a two-part report, both parties can be satisfied.

---

[3] American Motors Corporation presents an interesting example of how the quality of an annual report can vary with the degree of profitability the firm enjoyed in the previous year. Following the introduction of the compact car in the early 1960s, American Motor's profits steadily decreased, until the company began showing net deficits. The annual reports for American Motors followed suit, going from a glossy-covered, 30-page annual report to a paper-covered, black-and-white statement that ran only 15 to 20 pages in length. As the fortunes of the company declined, so too did the size and quality of the annual report.

The annual meeting

A third right of stockholders is the right to attend an annual meeting of shareholders of the firm. At this meeting, stockholders are given the opportunity to meet with the board of directors and other top-management personnel of the company. Usually, the stockholders who attend hear the chairman of the board and the president of the firm report on the affairs of the firm. The stockholders then have a chance to ask any questions of the board and the officers that they might have.

Generally speaking, the annual meeting is usually a pleasant experience for the stockholder who can attend. Whether a stockholder owns 1 share or 10,000, he usually finds himself treated in a most cordial manner. Companies often provide lunches, tours, and even small gifts as tokens of appreciation for attending the meeting. There is, however, one aspect of the annual meeting which has raised some question about the ability of stockholders to exercise this right. That concerns the *location* of the meeting.

One would expect that corporations would hold their annual meeting in (a) the city in which the company home office was located, or (b) in the city where most of its stockholders lived. In either case, it would seem logical to expect the annual meeting to be held in a large, metropolitan area. Yet, in recent years, Detroit Edison—an electrical utility serving the metropolitan area of Detroit, Michigan—held its annual meeting in New York City. Similarly, U.S. Steel—the largest steel company in the United States—recently held its annual meeting in Sheboygan, New Jersey, at the same time and on the same day that RCA and General Foods were holding their annual meetings in New York City. Obviously, if a stockholder held shares in both RCA and U.S. Steel, he would have to choose between them. Worse yet was the case involving IBM. This gigantic computer company is on record as having held its annual meeting one year under a circus tent on a hot summer day in Texas.

Such meeting locations have the obvious impact of preventing or making it terribly inconvenient for many stockholders to attend the meeting. In recent years, however, thanks partly to the efforts of John and Lewis Gilbert and Mrs. Wilma Soss,[4] corporations have responded by rotating the location of their annual meetings around the country. Thus, one year the meeting may be held in New York, the next year in Chicago, the following year in Los Angeles, and so on. In this way, stockholders who might otherwise not be able to attend a meeting may find themselves now able to attend.

---

[4] These individuals have made careers out of representing small shareholders at annual meetings and pressing for the rights of these shareholders. Often, these "corporate gadflys" engage in antics that border on the ludicrous, but their actions have captured enough publicity that they have enjoyed some limited success in achieving their goals.

CORPORATE RESPONSIBILITIES AND THE STOCKHOLDER

Thus far, we have reviewed the actual interrelationship of the stockholder with his corporation. We can now look at the important area of how and why corporations exercise—or don't exercise—social responsibilities in their day-to-day activities.

Two hypothetical situations

Imagine you have recently inherited several hundred shares of stock in a large industrial corporation. Three weeks prior to the annual meeting, you read a newspaper account of a government claim that your company is guilty of causing massive water pollution in a small river near the company's manufacturing facilities. The company, in response to the lawsuit, has said it cannot afford to provide corrective equipment to halt the pollution, without jeopardizing the return to its stockholders.

Subsequently, you learn that an irrate stockholder is going to request a vote of stockholders on whether, in fact, the stockholders want the firm to acquire the necessary pollution-control equipment. The cost, the company has said, will be so high that no dividends can be paid for the next several years. How would you vote your shares regarding this proposition?

When this question was put to a class of students at a large midwestern university, the students voted heavily in favor of the proposition—even though it would mean receiving no dividends on their stock. They were quite obviously influenced by the growing awareness and magnitude of the problem of pollution. "Besides," argued one student, "since the stock was inherited, the loss of the dividend didn't really cost me anything anyway. I was receiving no dividends before I inherited the stock, and so all I'm losing is something I didn't have before anyway."

The question was then changed slightly. Now, assume that you had been acquiring the stock periodically over a number of years. Further, assume that you are now retired, living on your pension, your social security check, and the dividends you receive on your stock. Now, given the same problem, how would you vote on the issue? Does the fact that the dividend income plays a role in providing you with your income cause the problem to be viewed differently? The class, when asked this question, now divided fairly evenly on this question, with a large number of the students undecided. The class agreed that the new circumstances did, in fact, make a difference. Moreover, one student commented, "If I were retired, I might not be as concerned with the importance of water pollution to future generations as I would be if I were not retired and perhaps 30 years younger."

These examples help put the problem in a clear perspective. Reexamine Table 17–1. Which group of individuals constitutes the largest segment of American stockholders? The answer, obviously, is homemakers and retired persons—the individuals most likely to need a regular dividend check! The pattern that is forming should now become clear. As stockholders, we tend to have certain vested interests that we consider more important than other interests. No one, obviously, wants to perpetuate pollution. But if the elimination of, say, pollution requires us to relinquish certain other rights—such as dividends—it may be that a majority of us would not be willing to pay the price. After all, stock is purchased for investment purposes, and as such it is logical that stockholders expect to receive a financial return on their investment. We can argue that if we ignore the problems of society long enough, we might not have a society left in which a company can earn a profit. Unfortunately, as true as this statement may be, it is also well established that many of us have the attitude once expressed by Lord Keynes, when he said, ". . . In the long run, we're all dead" anyway.

Institutional investors: Another influence

To further complicate the situation is the existence and influence of various institutional investors. In recent years, institutions—that is, pension funds, mutual funds, bank trust departments, foundations, and others—have become major purchasers of corporation stock. Indeed, Table 17–5 shows the true magnitude of these funds as corporate shareholders.

As a general rule, institutional investors vote their proxies in accordance with the recommendations of management. Rarely, if ever, do they attempt to use their tremendous voting power to influence managerial policy. This is because they themselves are in a vulnerable legal position. They are investing money entrusted to them by clients: the insurance companies invest premiums received from policyholders, pension funds invest pension contributions made by workers, and so on. These institutions are required by law to exercise prudence and conservative judgment in the handling of other people's money. It follows, then, that if the large institutions used their influence to change management policy, they might so upset the stability of the corporation's management that the company profits would fall. If the profits fell, the stock would decline in price. If this happened, the institution could be accused of not properly managing its clients' investment. Consequently, these institutions practice a quiet, "get-along-with-management" philosophy, on the grounds that this will be the best way of insuring a profitable company.

We can see, therefore, that the influence of *which* people buy stocks, and the various reasons *why* they buy them, combine to result in a general

TABLE 17–5

Estimated holdings of NYSE-listed stocks by selected institutional investors (in billions)

Type of institution	Year end				
	1949	1962	1971	1972	1973†
Insurance Companies:					
Life	$ 1.1	$ 4.1	$ 16.1	$ 21.2	$ 21.1
Nonlife	1.7	7.1	15.6	18.6	16.9
Investment Companies:					
Open-end	1.4	15.4	46.7	51.4	37.2
Closed-end	1.6	5.3	5.6	6.4	5.0
Noninsured Pension Funds:					
Corporate	0.5	17.9	75.6	98.6	82.2
Other private	*	1.0	4.6	5.9	4.9
State and local government	*	0.6	10.7	13.6	15.5
Nonprofit Institutions:					
Foundations	2.5	8.5	19.3	23.9	19.2
Educational endowments	1.1	3.5	7.4	8.8	7.5
Other	1.0	5.0	10.1	11.8	9.5
Common Trust Funds	*	1.7	5.5	6.8	5.5
Mutual Savings Banks	0.2	0.4	1.5	1.5	1.7
Total	$11.1	$ 70.5	$218.7	$268.5	$226.2
Market value of all NYSE-listed stock	$76.3	$345.8	$741.8	$871.5	$721.0
Estimated percent held by above institutions	14.5%	20.4%	29.5%	30.8%	31.4%

* Less than $50 million.
† Preliminary estimates. Prior data have been revised.
Source: *NYSE Fact Book,* 1974.

stockholder apathy about social involvement by business. While some companies—such as Smith, Kline & French Laboratories and Eastman Kodak—have built reputations on their participation in social action causes, a large number of corporations have been rather reluctant to engage too heavily in this area, primarily because their stockholders haven't indicated a desire that they do otherwise.

In the few cases where an attempt has been made to generate stockholder support for a more socially aware corporation, the results have been astounding failures. The most dramatic of these attempts has been "Campaign GM," an effort that was made in 1970 and again in 1971 to achieve certain social goals (the closing of a South African plant as a means of protesting that nation's apartheid policy was an example). Stockholders voted down such proposals by margins of approximately 98 percent No, 2 percent Yes. Clearly, the conclusions must be drawn that the combined influence of personal stockholder goals, their indifference towards exercising more managerial power, and the various peculiarities of corporate democracy indicates that a long time may pass before a change in corporate philosophy occurs. Indeed, whether a change in corporate philosophy is even desirable is a perplexing problem, and one that the generations of young people in the 1970s and beyond will need to address themselves to.

DISCUSSION QUESTIONS

1   What are the principal reasons stockholders invest in common stock? Suppose that a stockholder buys a stock that pays no dividend. What is the investment objective of that stockholder?

2   What accounts for the large amount of stock owned by retired persons, homemakers, and unemployed persons?

3   Discuss how the Protestant ethic and the spirit of Calvinism can be seen in the ownership of common stock by people today.

4   Differentiate between cumulative and noncumulative voting. Develop an example of each.

5   Do you feel management is justified in attempting to abolish cumulative voting? Why or why not?

6   Suppose that your parents were stockholders in a major industrial firm. Your folks told you that you could have the entire dividend check each quarter for spending money while in college. At present this amounted to several hundred dollars. Now suppose that this company proposed cutting the dividend in half, so that they would have funds to combat their industrial pollution. Would you approve of such a move?

7   Figure 17–1 reveals that a substantial portion of Americans own common stock. What, if anything, does this tell you about the extent to which we as Americans practice the economic doctrine of "capitalism"?

8   It is frequently charged that the really big corporations only serve the interests of a few individuals. Examine Table 17–2. Does this table seem to contradict this charge? If so, in what way? In what way does Table 17–2 tend to create a false impression about these companies?

9   Table 17–5 shows that nonprofit institutions own a substantial portion of their wealth in common stock. Do you feel this is a proper activity for nonprofit institutions? Explain.

10 Examine the list of "growth stocks" presented in Table 17–4. What is the "average" rate of return on these stocks? Check the newspaper for the average dividend paid on the stocks in Table 17–3. Is the average return on these stocks greater or less than the average return on the list of growth stocks?

MINI CASES

Alice Henderson was a student at the Monmouth Valley Junior College. This term she had enrolled in a course on the stock market. As part of the class assignment, Alice had been required to develop a portfolio of stocks to manage. At the end of the term, she had to present a paper to the class in which she explained why the stocks she chose to follow moved in the manner they did.

One of the stocks Alice chose to follow was that of Xenon Corporation. Xenon was the maker of highly computerized printing equipment and had copyrights on several photographic processes. The stock continually sold for several hundred dollars a share and paid very little dividend. In recent years, it had been growing at a rate of approximately 40 percent a year.

One day Alice noticed that the company announced an increase in its dividend from 10 cents a share to 12 cents a share. No other news was forthcoming. Alice felt this ought to drive the price of the stock up, since increased dividends almost always caused this to happen. Imagine Alice's surprise when on the following day Xenon Corporation stock dropped $10 in value! Confused, Alice sought an explanation for this behavior.

   1. *What factors can you think of which might have caused this situation to develop? Which of these reasons do you think was the probable cause of the decline?*
   2. *Comment on the investment characteristics of Xenon Corporation stock. What kinds of investors would probably purchase it? What investment objectives would they probably have? Would this help explain the strange behavior of Xenon Corporation's stock? Why or why not?*

One of the problems that is frequently encountered in the area of business-stockholder relations develops when the stockholder finds himself in a position where he both benefits and suffers as the result of a decision. Such was the situation in the following example.

John Petersen was a noted tax attorney. His life's work had been devoted to finding ways to reduce the tax liabilities of the average person. Mr. Petersen believed in the American concept of paying for services received, but he did not like paying money when it was not really necessary.

Mr. Petersen also believed in the virtues of the capitalistic system, and accordingly, prided himself on the ownership of stock in many of

America's largest firms. Among these was Paxton Industries, a large conglomerate firm that had recently received a multimillion-dollar government defense contract.

One day Mr. Petersen received the annual report for Paxton Industries in the mail. It was an extremely impressive document, running about 80 pages in length, full of color photographs, and embossed in what appeared to be a gold lettering. Two days later, Mr. Petersen saw an article in a leading business journal that discussed the extensiveness and uniqueness of this particular report. In the journal article, it was disclosed that the annual report was indeed embossed in 24-carat gold, and that each report cost a record $2 to produce. Since Paxton Industries had over 500,000 stockholders, this meant the company spent over $1 million just producing the annual report.

Mr. Petersen found himself in a real predicament. On the one hand, he appreciated the efforts of the company to project an image that would probably increase the value of their stock, and consequently, of Mr. Petersen's holdings. On the other hand, however, the idea of spending over $1 million on the report—particularly after receiving a large government contract, raised certain ethical questions in Mr. Petersen's mind. He wondered if he should say anything at the annual meeting, which was only two weeks away.

What is your advice to Mr. Petersen?

One day Jacob Arney had an opportunity to go to an annual meeting with his uncle. The meeting was that of one of the largest food store chains in the country. Jacob found the meeting to be a fascinating experience, except for one thing. After the meeting ended, the company presented boxes of groceries to each of the stockholders in attendance as a gift of appreciation. When Jacob asked his uncle about the reason for this, his uncle replied that it was a gift that was given to anyone who attended the meeting. "You mean," said Jacob, "if I were a stockholder, and mailed my proxy in instead of attending, I wouldn't get a free gift?" "That's right," said his uncle.

Jacob thought about this for a minute, and then made the comment that maybe business wasn't as ethical as he had hoped, but rather that it still was showing favoritism to the rich.

Comment on Jacob's conclusion. Do you agree with him? Was the company doing anything wrong in giving these gifts as they did?

Charles Harting Percy was born in Pensacola, Florida, on September 27, 1919. Early in life, his family moved to Illinois, where Percy attended school. He graduated from the University of Chicago in 1941. Upon graduation, Percy went to work for the Bell & Howell Corporation. However, with the outbreak of World War II, he enlisted and served for two years as an apprentice seaman in the U.S. Navy. He received his honorable discharge in 1943, having achieved the rank of lieutenant.

Following his military service, Percy returned to Bell & Howell. His career there was nothing short of meteoric, and in a few years he was elected the youngest president in the history of Bell & Howell. A few years later, he became chairman of the board. Because of his tremendous business success, Percy received many awards, including designation as businessman of the year in 1962.

Charles Percy had interests in politics as well as business, however. As early as 1946, he began his way in politics by taking a job as a precinct worker. By 1955, he was named president of the United Republican Fund of Illinois. In the next few years, Percy held several high posts in the Republican party.

Although Percy's bid for the governorship of Illinois in 1964 was unsuccessful, he continued to pursue a political career. In 1966, he resigned the board chairmanship of Bell & Howell to run as the Republican candidate for the U.S. Senate. Ironically, the man he opposed, and eventually beat, was then incumbent Sen. Paul H. Douglas, under whom Percy had studied when he was a student at the University of Chicago! As noted, Percy was successful in his senate bid, and to this day, continues to serve in that august body. Periodically, Percy's name is mentioned as a potential candidate for president of the United States. Truly, his is a success story worth emulating.

Charles H. Percy
(1919–   )

Modern day Horatio Alger

18

Business and government relations

You can make even a parrot into a learned political economist—all he must learn are the two words "supply" and "demand."

—*Anonymous*

Since the earliest days of our economy, the responsibility for solving the problems of society has been jointly vested in the two major institutions of our country—business and government. Throughout this text, the emphasis has been on the specific institution of business. We have described and analyzed the privileges and obligations, the rights and responsibilities of this institution in all phases of economic and noneconomic activity. We have not, however, given this same treatment to the role of government in society. Government has always been involved in our commercial lives in one form or another. For example, government has provided us with our currency, established the legal structure under which business functions, and established a standard for weights and measures, to name but a few. However, a detailed development of this topic is perhaps best examined in a political science rather than in a business course. We should, however, remain aware of the interrelationship of these two institutions. Viewed from an historical standpoint, the roles of business and government have become more and more closely intertwined. Today, business leaders are serving in high government positions; and government for its part, has greatly increased its influence on business. This chapter will attempt to examine some of these interrelationships and to provide an insight into their development.

INTRODUCTION

There is probably no single topic that has generated as much interest and concern in the past decade as the subject of business and government relations. For the most part, this interest and concern has centered on three primary areas: taxation, regulation, and government competition with business. Taxation, for example, directly influences the profits that firms make and the prices they ultimately charge consumers for their goods and services. Taxes also influence consumer spending habits. Taxes on certain items, such as tobacco and liquor, play a major role in determining the extent to which consumers purchase them. An understanding of the types of taxes and the reasons for them, therefore, should be of paramount concern to all. Certainly, as business executives of the future we should understand the impact of taxation on business' efforts.

Similarly, government regulation has been of prime concern to the business community. Following a century of essentially laissez-faire economics in the 1700s and 1800s, the United States gradually became a regulated economy. Regulation has ranged from the control of drugs and medicines by the Food and Drug Administration to the regulation of the merchant marine by the Federal Maritime Commission. Indeed, so widespread has government regulation become that today we tend to take it for granted. Yet, to fully understand the reasons underlying this regulation, we should examine the respective laws and the economic and political conditions that led to their passage. Only in this way can we better appreciate the reason for the unique development of our industrial society.

Finally, the critical area of governmental competition with business in the commercial activity of our nation needs to be explored. The federal government runs, or takes active part in running, many businesses, ranging from the Tennessee Valley Authority to COMSAT to the Post Office. The giant federal departments (such as the Defense Department and the Department of Health, Education, and Welfare) are similarly involved in the commercial activity of our country.

Certainly the ramifications of this aspect of business and government relations need to be examined if we are to develop an understanding of the relationship between these two important institutions.

TAXATION

In this country, the power to levy taxes is bestowed upon the government in Article I, Section 8 of the federal Constitution. This section states in part: "Congress shall have power to lay and collect taxes, duties, imports, and excises to pay the debts and provide for the common defense and general welfare of the United States." As the demand for government's services have increased, the various levels of government—federal, state, and local—have been continually beset with the problem of raising new and more efficient sources of revenue. The result has been the eventual creation of the wide variety of taxes that are now levied by all three levels of government.

The nature of taxes

Taxes are usually classified according to their economic impact on the individuals or businesses assuming the tax. There are, basically, three major types of taxes under this system of classification. These are: (a) regressive taxes, (b) progressive taxes, and (c) proportional taxes.

Regressive taxes   A tax is considered to be regressive when the tax itself represents a greater burden for the poor than it does for the wealthy. Thus, a tax which comprises 5 percent of a poor person's income but only 0.5 percent of a wealthy individual's income would be considered regressive; the burden is greater for the poor than it is for the wealthy.

Generally speaking, regressive taxes are not considered particularly "fair" as far as taxes go. Regressive taxes put the burden on those least able to afford it, and consequently, tend to impede the ability of the poor to rise above their poor, unfortunate status.

Examples of regressive taxes are rather easy to find. The sales tax on food, for example, is a regressive tax. This is because people rich and poor alike—tend to spend just so much on food. If one is poor, the expenditures on food constitute a fairly large percentage of income. If one is rich, more dollars will be spent on food, but the percentage will usually be substantially less. A tax charged against food purchases thus constitutes a larger burden for the poor person than it does for the rich person.

The most popular of our regressive taxes, however, is the common payroll tax. Social security is paid by most of the wage-earning public in the United States. As presently calculated, everyone covered under social security pays a percentage of their earnings into social security. Upon retirement they get back a sum—the exact amount of which depends on their income over that time they paid into the system and the length of time they paid into the system. The tax itself, however, is paid out of the *first* $15,000 of income. Thus, the person earning exactly $15,000 pays the tax on the full salary. The person earning $30,000 however, pays the tax on only half of the income. Thus, the tax actually becomes a regressive tax. (See Figures 18–1 and 18–2.)

Progressive taxes   A second type of tax is the progressive tax. This tax is characterized by the fact that it is based primarily on the principle of "ability to pay" (see Figure 18–3). The greater one's income, the greater the percent of that income one must pay in taxes. Our federal income tax is often called a progressive tax, although there is some question about the amount of "progressiveness" of this tax.

Progressive taxes are often termed the most equitable, since they

FIGURE 18-1

A regressive tax (a sales tax on food is a common regressive tax)

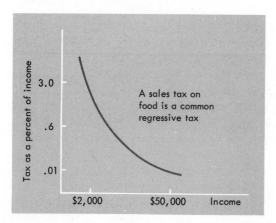

put the burden of taxation squarely on the back of those most able to pay. This argument, however, overlooks the fact that often it is the poor and not the rich that utilize many of the government's services. An old tenet of American society states that each person should pay for what he or she uses. Thus, the question of taxing those most able to pay versus the question of taxing those who use the service the tax is to pay for, becomes an important one.

Proportional taxes The final type of tax under this "economic effect" concept of taxation is the proportional tax. A tax is proportional if the tax itself constitutes a fixed percentage of one's income. Some counties in the state of Pennsylvania have a school tax which is levied against the earned income of the residents in the county. Typically, the tax charge is 1 percent of income earned. Thus, a person earning $3,000 would pay a tax of $30, while an individual earning $30,000 would pay a tax of $300. In either case, the tax payment would amount to 1 percent of earned income. Such a tax is a proportional tax.

Evaluating taxes from the viewpoint of who bears the burden of the tax is, however, only one way of classifying taxes. Taxes may also be evaluated according to the purpose behind the levying of the tax. When evaluated from this standpoint, we find that taxes were created for two reasons. Either the tax was created to raise revenue for the governmental body imposing the tax, or the tax was designed to limit or regulate the use of certain products or services.

Revenue taxes

The best known of all taxes are those that exist for the primary purpose of providing the funds to support the many services provided by govern-

FIGURE 18–2
The importance of regressive and progressive taxes

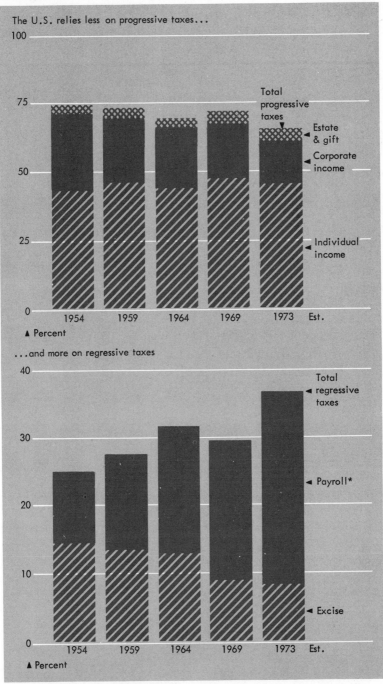

The U.S. relies less on progressive taxes...

Total progressive taxes

Estate & gift

Corporate income

Individual income

1954 1959 1964 1969 1973 Est.

▲ Percent

...and more on regressive taxes

Total regressive taxes

Payroll*

Excise

1954 1959 1964 1969 1973 Est.

▲ Percent

Data: Treasury Department.
* Social Security and unemployment insurance taxes.

FIGURE 18–3

A progressive tax   U.S. federal income tax

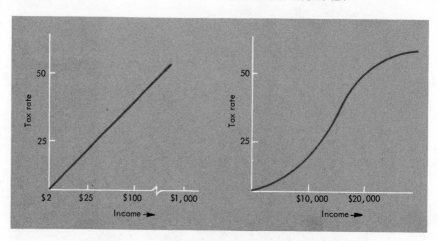

ment. Foremost among the revenue taxes is the income tax. Figure 18–5 shows the importance of this source of revenue to the federal government.

The income tax is really an interesting phenomenon. Until 1913, the United States had no income tax, except for a brief period of time around the Civil War. Indeed, until World War II, the tax rate was so low that many people scarcely worried about it. Today, however, the payment of the

FIGURE 18–4

A proportional tax

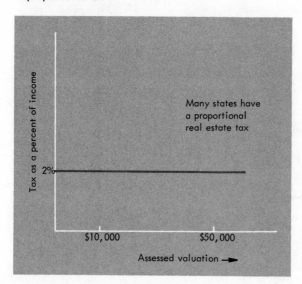

FIGURE 18–5

Federal tax revenues, 1973

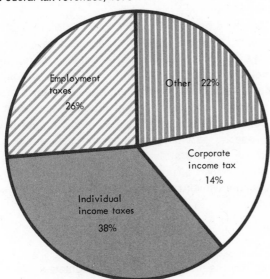

Source: Office of Management and Budget.

income tax bill looms as a major undertaking for both individuals and business.

One point worth mentioning is the fact that the corporate income tax ranks second in importance as a revenue tax, behind the individual income tax. Indeed, when one considers the *number* of businesses that contribute to this tax, versus the *number* of people that contribute to the individual income tax, it becomes readily apparent that corporations pay a substantial portion of the tax burden of the federal government.

An interesting question that is frequently raised regarding the corporate income tax concerns the question of who actually pays the tax? Do the corporations actually sacrifice part of their profits in paying the tax, or do they merely raise the prices on their products and services, thereby effectively passing the tax on to the consumer?

As we have already seen, the tax rate on corporate income is one of the strong deterrents to this form of business organization. Corporations are required to pay a tax rate of 22 percent on the first $25,000 income they earn and 48 percent on everything thereafter. Thus the effective tax rate for a multimillion dollar corporation is almost 50 percent, or one half of their total earnings. Until recently, General Motors paid a tax to the federal government of almost $2 billion, or about 7 percent of the total corporate income taxes paid during those years to the government!

Other important revenue taxes are the property tax, the sales tax, and the estate and inheritance tax. Most of these are taxes that are assessed directly on the consuming public; only the property tax has a direct impact on business firms.

The property tax is a tax assessed on the owners of real property (such as land or buildings), and is usually some proportional amount of the value of the property. This is the most important source of revenue for local government, which uses the funds primarily to finance schools systems in their jurisdiction. The federal government does not levy a property tax. Business is a significant contributor to the property tax collections. Usually, the value of commercial property is substantially higher than the value of residential property, and consequently the tax bill is higher. Indeed, many communities that are attempting to lure business into their locales do so by offering a waiver of property taxes for a period of years. For some businesses, such a waiver represents a substantial savings in its overall cost of operations.

Regulatory taxes

A second reason for the creation of taxes is to regulate certain business practices. For example, excise taxes are a form of regulatory taxation. An excise tax is a tax on the use, consumption, or manufacture of certain products. Taxes that are classified as excise taxes include taxes on cigarettes, liquor, gasoline, and telephone calls. The regulatory impact of these taxes can be most readily seen in the case of gasoline and cigarette taxes. Taxes on cigarettes have gone up sharply since the medical profession began expressing concern about the possible relationship between cancer and smoking. Quite obviously, Congress felt that increasing the taxes on cigarettes not only would bring in additional revenue, but if it succeeded in discouraging the use and/or sale of cigarettes, so much the better.

Similar effects can be seen in the case of gasoline. When the oil companies finally developed a lead-free gasoline in response to the public outcry about pollution from cars, Congress quickly proposed a tax on the sale of gasoline with lead in an effort to discourage its use.

Because of the wide applicability of excise taxes, they have generated a substantial amount of revenue for the various levels of government. The regulatory nature of the tax, however, still is the primary reason for the tax, not the revenue-generating capability.

Another regulatory tax is the tax on imported goods. Such "import duties," as they are called, are designed to discourage competition for American-made goods. This is done by imposing a special tax on goods coming into this country from abroad. Recent years have seen increased negotiations between the United States and Europe (and to a lesser extent, Japan) with the goal of mutual abolition of such duties. Such abolition, however, promises to cause severe repercussions for communities where business would suffer because of the increased competition from abroad. For example, the United States presently maintains rather strict limitations on imported beef. Meat-packers would like to see cheaper, imported beef become more plentiful. So, too, would consumers, assuming the retail price of beef were to fall. However, letting beef into the country at an unrestricted pace would soon destroy the American beef industry. No longer would ranchers be able to raise cattle for slaughter, since the price of feed, land, and labor would make ranching an unprofitable business. Many western communities that presently thrive on the cattle industry would suffer enormous hardships if restrictions were removed. This political impact of such "free-trade" agreements, consequently, has caused such reductions in duties to move at a snail's pace over the years. Indeed, recent problems with America's gold outflow, and the enactment in the early 1970s of various import duties by President Nixon has virtually halted discussions regarding an elimination of trade barriers.

Taxes, however, do not represent the only, nor in fact, the most important means of regulation. To fully understand the regulatory aspects of our industrial society, we need to study the laws that have been passed over the past 80 years and learn of the circumstances that led to their passage.

REGULATION

In our contemporary society, the regulation of business and business practices seems so natural that, on reflection, it appears almost incredible for our business community to have operated virtually free of restrictive regulation for over 100 years. During this period of time, moreover, the business community enjoyed one of its greatest periods of growth. The railroad and steel empires of Vanderbilt and Carnegie were built, as was the oil empire of Rockefeller. The Industrial Revolution truly came of age during this period. But, as Arthur M. Johnson points out:

> As the American economy and society changed in the late nineteenth century [however], the power of some businessmen was exercised in ways that hurt the interests of their fellows or of other groups in society. These elements of the electorate demanded that government do something to right the balance, and the political and legislative processes provided the means."[1]

The federal government had always had the constitutional authority to intervene in the commercial endeavors of the nation. For example, Article I, Section 8 of the Constitution states: "The Congress shall have the power . . . to regulate commerce with foreign nations, and among

---

[1] Arthur M. Johnson, *Government-Business Relations* (Columbus, Ohio: Chas. E. Merrill Publishing Co., 1965), p. 209.

the several states, and with the Indian Tribes." The final portion of this article goes on to state that Congress shall have the power to "make all laws which shall be necessary and proper for carrying into Execution the foregoing powers, and all other Powers vested by this Constitution in the Government of the United States. . . ." On the basis of this constitutional prerogative, the federal government has expanded its role in the regulation of commerce in many ways. Figure 18–6 illustrates the general juris-

FIGURE 18–6

The development of government regulation

Date	The regulation of operations	The regulation of structure	The regulation of finance	D
1887	The Interstate Commerce Commission Act			18
1890		The Sherman Anti-trust Act		18
1913			The Federal Reserve Act	19
1914	The Clayton Act			19
1914	The Federal Trade Commission Act			19
1930	The Federal Power Commission Act			19
1934	The Federal Communications Commission Act			19
1934			The Securities and Exchange Commission	19
1936	The Robinson-Patman Act			19
1950		The Celler-Kefauver Anti-Merger Act		19

diction of major legislation that has been designed to regulate or influence business.

The Interstate
Commerce Commission Act—1887

The first of the major regulatory acts to be passed was the Interstate Commerce Commission Act of 1887. This act created the Interstate Commerce Commission, whose job it was to regulate the operations of the railroads. The creation of the ICC was the culmination of many years of complaining by the farmers and Grange Associations throughout the country about the activities of the railroads. For many years, the rails represented the only means by which the farmers were able to get their products to market. Knowing this, the railroads charged excessively high rates for the farmers. The political power that the railroad magnates possessed stalled any legislation for many years, but eventually the outcry from the public became so great that Congress had to pass some form of

FIGURE 18–7

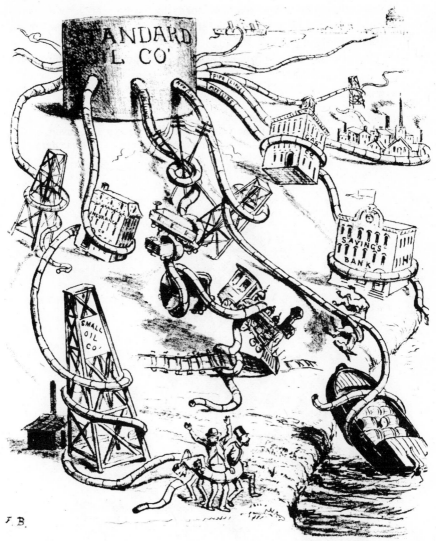

An 1884 cartoon strongly critical of the Standard Oil trust: As antimonopoly feeling grew in the U.S., and as populist politics picked up steam, Congress passed the 1890 Sherman Antitrust Act. but it failed to curb bianess or monopoly.

control. The resulting legislation established the Interstate Commerce Commission, which was given authority to regulate all forms of interstate commerce—a power which has since grown to include bus, truck, and pipeline traffic, among others.

The creation of a regulatory agency to govern the railroad's rates,

FIGURE 18–8

An 1888 barb by Thomas Nast: So many trusts were created in Standard Oil's image that Sherman warned that unless the government acted there would be "a trust for every production and a master to fix the price for every necessity."

The Bettmann Archive.

however, only solved part of the problem. The depression of 1873 had left many scars in the memories of people—scars which were pointedly attributed by writers and journalists of the day to the business excesses which were taking place. Business leaders were depicted as the worst element in society—a breed unto themselves that thought only of making money, and preferably at someone else's expense. Of particular vengence were the cartoons of the day, many of which were very pointed in their criticism of business.

Much of the criticism of the business community was, unfortunately, justified. As one author has put it, "The unhampered pursuit of self-interest has led to riches—but only for the few who could restrain others from similar pursuits."[2]

The economic reins of power had gradually come into the hands of a few. The railroad situation was only one instance of the widespread problem. The attempts by the business titan to justify his actions via a philosophy of Social Darwinism gradually lost its potency. Antimonopoly sentiment grew steadily among farmers, labor, and small business leaders. Slowly but surely, Congress was being forced to respond to the public clamor for regulation. The result was the Sherman Antitrust Act of 1890.

The Sherman Antitrust Act—1890

The Sherman Act was designed to prohibit the formulation of monopolies by business. Specifically, the act states that, "Every contract, combination in the form of trust or otherwise, or conspiracy, in restraint of trade or commerce among the several States, or with foreign nations, is hereby declared to be illegal." The act went on to state that, "Every person who shall monopolize, or attempt to monopolize, or combine or conspire with any other person to monopolize any part of the trade or commerce among the several states, or with foreign nations, shall be deemed guilty of a misdemeanor . . ." Violators of the Sherman Act were subject to a $5,000 fine or one year in prison, or both. It is interesting to note that the Sherman Act is the only regulatory act on the books that carries the threat of a prison sentence.

The intent of the Sherman Act appeared to be obvious. Any arrangement between business leaders that resulted in a "restraint of trade" or constituted an "unfair" method of competition was illegal. The framers of the act thought that it would suffice in controlling the trusts of large business combinations that dominated the country. Indeed, the public appeared to be satisfied, particularly after the quick enforcement of the act against the Sugar Trust.

---

[2] Joseph McGuire, *Business and Society* (New York: McGraw-Hill Book Co., 1965), p. 79.

The Clayton Act—1914

Enforcement of the Sherman Act, however, soon raised as many questions as it was originally designed to resolve. Did, for example, the appointment of the same individual to the board of directors of competing firms represent a "conspiracy" or not? And what exactly constituted "unfair" methods of competition? While these questions did not prevent the eventual enforcement of the Sherman Act against the Standard Oil Trust and the Tobacco Trust, it did cause enough concern to result in the passage of the Clayton Act in 1914.

The Clayton Act was passed as an amendment to the Sherman Act, and attempted to clarify some of the ambiguity in the language of the Sherman Act. Specifically, the Clayton Act:

1. Outlawed price discrimination where the effect was to "lessen competition or to tend to create a monopoly." This section of the Clayton Act was aimed at the ruthless practice of cutting prices in one area and not others, in order to destroy a competitor. The law allowed, however, price differentials to exist if (a) they were based on differences in quantity or quality of goods purchased, or (b) if the price was cut in order to meet competition.
2. Outlawed "tying contracts." Tying contracts were a device in which the manufacturer of a patented item forced would-be buyers of the product to purchase other merchandise as well if they desired the patented item. In this way, the less desirable goods were "tied" to the more desirable goods.
3. The Clayton Act restricted corporations from buying more than a limited amount of stock in competing firms. Such action was deemed to be "tending to create a monopoly" and was, therefore, made illegal.
4. The act outlawed interlocking directorates. This was the situation that existed when one person was serving on the board of directors for more than one competing firm. Since board members are permitted to see confidential information pertaining to a company's business, the act held that such "interlocking directorates" tended toward a lessening of competition. (Recall the situation discovered by the Pujo Committee in its investigations of a banking trust in 1912.)
5. At the urging of several important lobbies, the Clayton Act exempted labor organizations, agricultural associations, and fraternal groups from the rules of the act.

The Federal Trade Commission Act—1914

To assure the enforcement of the Clayton Act, Congress passed the Federal Trade Commission Act. This act created a commission which was empowered to issue cease and desist orders wherever it felt a violation of the antitrust laws had occurred. Over the years, however, the Commission has greatly enlarged its sphere of influence. For example, the FTC today maintains a watch over corporate advertising, and attempts to halt any false or misleading advertisements. It also checks for deceptive practices, whether such practices are the result of misleading packaging or the use of deceiving sales practices. Very recent years have seen the power of the FTC broadened still further. The result has been to turn the FTC into the watchdog of American business practices.

The passage of the Clayton Act and the Federal Trade Commission Act represented the culmination of the move to curb unfair and monopolistic tendencies in the business sector. Indeed, not until the Great Depression did the government actively seek to further extend its influence in the business world.

There was, however, one area of concern to the business community that was restructured by the federal government. That area was the financial system of the United States. For many years, the United States labored under the strains of a diffused banking system. Early attempts to create a national Bank of the United States had met with failure primarily because of the distrust and fear that many people had about putting control of the financial system of the United States in the hands of a few powerful bankers. Events in the late 1800s, however, gave rise to the suspicions of a "banking trust" in America. When the financial panic of 1907 hit, Congress began considering ways of developing some kind of central banking system—one with federal control and stature, but also possessing diffused ownership. The result was the Federal Reserve Act, signed into law by President Wilson in 1913.

The Federal Reserve Act—1913

The Federal Reserve Act represented the first successful attempt by this country to establish a uniform banking policy and system. The act created a system of 12 central banks, each to be located in various commercial centers of the United States. Each member bank was required to hold stock in the "Federal Reserve" bank of its district. The function of these Reserve banks was to serve as a "banker's bank," providing the same services to local banks that the local banks provide to businesses and consumers. Membership in the system was made optional for all state-chartered banks that met certain qualifications, but it was made mandatory for all nationally chartered banks. (See Chapter 3 for details of the operations of the Federal Reserve System.)

The Federal Reserve Act also established a national supervisory agency in Washington, known as the Board of Governors. The seven members on this Board are appointed by the president of the United

States, and operate independently of his control once their appointment is approved by the Senate.

Congress hoped at the time that the establishment of this system of banking would stabilize the financial sector of the economy. In one sense it did; monetary policy and banking practices were unified and equalized throughout the nation. Depositors were given additional assurances about the safety of their deposits. Except for the unique circumstances that surrounded the Great Depression, the system has, in fact, worked fairly well. Evidence of this fact can be seen in the many countries that have since attempted to duplicate this unique system of central banking.

Federal legislation tapered off after 1914, partly because the nation as a whole was absorbed with other events, notably World War I, and also because the country began to enjoy the prosperous decade of the 1920s. New legislation was, therefore, minimal until the Great Depression.

The regulatory commissions

The Great Depression of 1929 afforded the federal government an unprecedented opportunity to correct a number of abuses and practices that had existed for some time. These abuses involved such widely diverse areas as finance, communications and power, among others. As part of the "New Deal" package put forth by President Roosevelt, Congress quickly passed a series of legislative acts that brought these abuses to a halt.

Among the acts passed at this time were (a) The Federal Power Commission Act in 1930, (b) The Federal Communications Commission Act in 1934, and (c) The Securities and Exchange Commission Act, also in 1934.

The Federal Power Commission   The Federal Power Commission was really set up under the Federal Water Power Act of 1920. This act was passed as part of a conservation movement in the early 1920s. Later, when Congress saw fit to broaden its control to include electric power and natural gas, as well as water power, the Federal Power Commission was established and given jurisdiction over these power sources.

The Federal Communications Commission   Similarly, the Federal Communications Commission Act, passed in 1934, was designed to place federal regulation over a vital aspect of American life—communications. The Commission was given power to license and regulate radio, telephone, and telegraph companies throughout the land. Later, this commission was given the power to regulate television transmission as well.

The logic behind the establishment of special commissions to regulate power companies and communications companies is easy to appreciate. Both of these areas of activity require large markets for efficient operation. Indeed, they almost require a monopoly situation if chaos and confusion are to be avoided. But we have already seen that monopoly situations were specifically outlawed by the Sherman Act. Thus, by placing these particular industries under special governing commissions, the Congress was able to exempt these companies from the Sherman Act and at the same time protect the consumer from the abuses that usually follow from monopoly situations.

The Securities and Exchange Commission   The Securities Act of 1933 was passed in order to prevent a recurrence of some of the practices that helped lead to the crash of the stock market in 1929. This act required, among other things, full disclosure of all pertinent data relating to new securities issues. Enforcement of the act was left to the Federal Trade Commission. In 1934, the Securities Exchange Act was passed, which established the Securities and Exchange Commission, which was created to enforce the Securities Act of 1933. Upon passage, control reverted from the FTC to the Securities and Exchange Commission.

The Robinson-Patman Act—1936

As the economy struggled to pull itself out of the stagnant postdepression period, another abuse of business power came to light. Retail merchandise stores, most notably the chain stores, had grown considerably in size and importance. Some of these chains had become so large that they dwarfed the companies that supplied them with the goods they subsequently resold to the public. As a consequence, many of these large retailers began demanding special price discounts from the wholesalers that supplied them. Because the retailers used the threat of buying from another wholesaler if they didn't get their way, the suppliers were helpless—they had no choice but to comply with the unreasonable demands of the large retailers. Moreover, such *buyer* discrimination was not illegal; the Clayton Act only outlawed discrimination on the part of the *sellers* of goods. To correct this situation, Congress passed the Robinson-Patman Act of 1936. Specifically, this act not only outlawed price discrimination on the part of the sellers; it also outlawed such discrimination on the part of the buyers of goods. Enforcement of the act was also given to the Federal Trade Commission.

Following passage of the Robinson-Patman Act, legislation to control business activity again tapered off. World War II and the postwar problems of shifting from a wartime economy to a peacetime one were the primary concerns of the government until 1950. However, in 1950, Congress again turned its attention to the antitrust laws, and finally closed a loophole in the law that had been in existence for almost 25 years. The result was the passage of the Celler-Kefauver Antimerger Act of 1950.

The Celler-Kefauver Antimerger Act—1950

Recall that one of the provisions of the Clayton Act restricted the amount of stock that one company could purchase in a competitive company. This clause was aimed, obviously, at the holding company—companies that attempted to control or monopolize industries by owning large amounts of stock in the various competitive firms. During the legal enforcement of this clause, however, the courts ruled that, while the Clayton Act specifically outlawed large *stock* purchases in competing firms, it did not outlaw large *asset* purchases in competing firms. This interpretation of the Clayton Act had the immediate effect of negating the value of the entire clause as far as enforcement was concerned. The act specifically prevented one company from gaining control over another through stock purchases but was not enforceable against a company which literally bought for cash the assets, or properties, of another company!

While Congress had been aware of this loophole for many years, it wasn't until 1950 that it passed a law to correct the problem. Since the Clayton Act could not be used to regulate or prevent companies from merging (via an outright purchase), Congress passed a law which gave general enforcement authority over all mergers to the Federal Trade Commission. This law was the Celler-Kefauver Antimerger Act of 1950. Under the terms of this law, the FTC and the Justice Department had the right to give tacit approval to all merger plans of companies *before* the actual merger took place. In this way, companies were informed of the opinion of the enforcement agencies regarding the legality of all merger plans.

Recent developments

Since the Celler-Kefauver Act, no major legislation affecting the government-business relationship has occurred. What has taken place has been a gradual broadening of the interpretive powers of the regulatory agencies. Today, for instance, the FTC has an influential voice in a multitude of areas of business activity. The Clayton Act's language has been so broadened as to *presume* intent of companies that merge, and not just wait for monopolistic tendencies to take place. Indeed, one of the most interesting developments in the past ten years involves just such a broadening in the interpretation of the Clayton Act.

Recall the development of the General Motors Corporation back in the early 1920s. When Durant was attempting to enlarge the scope of General Motor's operations, he ran into some financial difficulty. The rich Du Pont family offered him financial aid, in exchange for stock in the corporation. Throughout the next 40 years, the Du Pont Corporation kept its stock interest in General Motors. After various splits the value of the stock by 1960 was well up in the hundreds of millions of dollars. At this point, the Federal Trade Commission, which had been studying the automobile industry, noted that a large number of Du Pont products were used in the manufacture of General Motor's products. The FTC ruled that a possible restraint of trade was in existence, since Du Pont held a large amount of General Motor's stock. The courts agreed, and ordered Du Pont to rid itself of its interest in General Motors. The subsequent divestiture of the stock took several years to complete—so large was the amount of GM stock owned by Du Pont.

More recently, the merger wave that occurred in the 1960s, particularly among conglomerate-type corporations, resulted in the creation of several interlocking directorships—situations which the directors themselves were unaware existed until the FTC brought it to their attention!

Perhaps the most significant and important antitrust action ever embarked upon by the federal government, however, is an action that is even now still in the courts, and promises to remain there until, perhaps, 1980. That action is an antitrust suit lodged against the fifth largest and second most profitable corporation in America—IBM.

The United States versus IBM

The case of the *U.S.* v. *IBM* is by all dimensions, a landmark case in antitrust legislation. No one disputes the fact that during the past half century, the data processing industry has been the fastest growing, most remarkable industry of them all. Many large companies—Sperry Rand, RCA, Bendix, to name but a few, have tried to compete in this industry. All have failed to do so. The reason, in one simple—perhaps over-simplified—word, is IBM. IBM, otherwise known as the International Business Machines Corporation, has managed to achieve a position as the unrivaled leader in this field. Combining a top-notch management team with a company that has registered a growth rate of 20 percent per year over its life, IBM has become the nation's leading producer of computer-based equipment. Indeed, so powerful and successful has IBM become that the Justice Department, in an action filed in 1969, charged IBM with violation of the Sherman Act. Specifically, the government has charged IBM with monopolizing the market for general-purpose digital computers, and also of using its market power to extend and perpetuate its dominance. IBM has, of course, denied the charge, claiming that it is neither a monopoly nor does it seek to use its powerful position to perpetuate its dominance.

The case of the *United States* v. *IBM* is made both more interesting and more complex by a related matter. That matter concerns several other lawsuits that have been pressed against IBM. Table 18–1 provides a concise summary of these other lawsuits. Of particular concern to us is the Telex suit filed in 1972. In that suit, Telex charged that IBM had made certain changes in its equipment that effectively destroyed Telex's ability to develop competing supplementary equipment for use on IBM's computers. This, Telex charged, was an attempt by IBM to destroy its competition by the use of its vast market power to dominate the industry. The courts reached a judgment of guilty as charged in September of 1973, and awarded Telex damages of over $350 million.

The specific charges that the judge ruled IBM had violated are of interest only because they have a strong bearing on the status of the other charges currently pending against IBM. In the Telex case, the judge claimed that IBM had deliberately changed its pricing policies and the

TABLE 18–1

Lawsuits filed against IBM

Plaintiff	Date filed	Status
Control Data Corp.	1968	Settled
Data Processing Financial & General Corp.	1969	Settled
Justice Department	1969	Active
Applied Data Research Inc. and Programmatics, Inc.	1969	Settled
Levin-Townsend Computer Corp.	1969	Settled
Greyhound Computer Corp.	1970	On appeal
VIP Systems Corp.	1970	Active
Memorex Corp.	1971	Active
Itel Corp.	1971	Settled
Telex Corp.	1972	Guilty, 1973 Reversed, 1975

nature of its machines so as to destroy competitors such as Telex. The judge could find no basis for IBM's having made the structural change in its equipment other than for this purpose. He further said IBM's actions were in no way related to technological advances, skill, or customer benefit. In other words, said the judge, IBM was trying to put its competitors out of business by using its vast market power to force them out. This was in violation of the Clayton Act. IBM appealed the decision, and won a reversal in early 1975. Telex has since appealed to the Supreme Court.

The Telex ruling, of course, has strong implications for the government's case against IBM. If one company can prove correct in its charge that IBM violated the Clayton Act, the government's case becomes much more powerful. In the government's case, however, the implications for IBM are much more important than a mere $350 million. The government wants to break up IBM into as many as five separate companies! Moreover, a legal battle between the U.S. government and the fifth largest, second most profitable company in the country has simply got to take on dimensions that stagger the imagination. In this particular case, IBM delivered to the government literally millions of documents. Indeed, one estimate placed the number of documents alone that changed hands during a recent hearing relating to the Control Data lawsuit at 27 million. Of these 17 million were delivered at one time. These 17 million documents weighed 87 tons, and would have filled a file drawer two miles long! Such are the things major lawsuits are made of.

The implications for all of business, of course, goes much farther than the sheer size and complexity of these lawsuits. For the real basis for the government's claim against IBM really boils down to an issue of size: Can a company get too big? Recall our discussions in Chapter 5 about "bigness in business." At that time, we noted the problem of defining "bigness." Another problem related to bigness, however defined, concerns the implications of big business on society. Is big business inherently bad? The government's argument seems to imply as much. They are claiming that IBM is using its vast market power (developed as a result of being the largest—or biggest—computer manufacturer in the world) to continue itself in power. That amounts to saying that bigness is bad. But isn't that what businesses are supposed to do? Get big, grow rich, and provide a fair return to its owners? The arguments almost seem to say that if a business gets too successful, it runs the risk of violating the law! That seems like quite a contradiction for a capitalistic society to take.

On the other hand, the government has some very solid arguments in its favor. When a company gets so large that the Department of Justice is literally outnumbered in the courtroom by the corporation's lawyers, something is drastically wrong. If the government can't put some bounds on these companies, and competition is suffering because none of the other firms can possibly compete on the same scale, who is to be the watchdog of business practices? The caption on Figure 18–8 may be more prophetic than we realize.

Yet, one must look with some degree of puzzlement at the large number of lawsuits that have been pressed against some of the largest of corporations and wonder just what the basis of antitrust activity really is. For example, the government has sued Kelloggs, General Mills and Quaker Oats for anticompetitive practices in allowing route representatives to arrange the position of their cereals on store shelves. Xerox has been accused of monopolizing the office copier business; and General Motors, Chrysler, A.T.&T., and Exxon have all been charged in recent years with various violations of the antitrust laws. While some of these charges are, no doubt, well founded, one must wonder what this nation would be like if all of the real large corporations were, in fact, broken up. Would we still maintain the creative genius that has made our nation great? It's a question to ponder in the months and years ahead.

FIGURE 18–9

IBM versus its competition

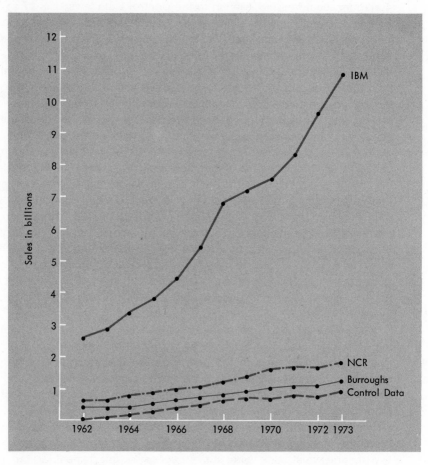

THE INTERACTION OF GOVERNMENT AND BUSINESS

The basis for government intervention

A third significant area of government-business relations concerns the subject of governmental involvement in the business sector, and alternatively, business' involvement in the public, or governmental sector. Government has always been involved in economic activity; indeed, the Constitution of the United States specifically authorized the government to establish a postal service, mint coinage, and provide for the general defense and welfare of the United States. Moreover, legislation over the past 100 years has considerably broadened the government's role in the economy. For example, the Federal Reserve Act put the banking system under quasi-governmental control. The regulatory acts of the 1930s furthered the government's influence in the economy by establishing "ground rules" for business activity. Perhaps the most significant single government act, however, was the Employment Act of 1946. In this act, the government took as its responsibility the maintenance of maximum employment, production, and purchasing power. The basis for this act, of course, stems from the "General Welfare" clause in the Constitution. Numerous activities, including highway construction, federal office building construction, aid to education through the National Defense Loan Act, and many, many more programs, were initiated under the general conditions of this 1946 act.

In some ways, however, the government has attempted to lessen its influence in the private sector. For example, both Presidents Wilson and Truman found it necessary to seize, or nationalize, important segments of American industry during times of a national crisis. Wilson took control of the railroads during a short phase of the World War I, and Truman did the same thing with the steel companies during the Korean War. Yet, as soon as the crisis abated, both presidents quickly initiated steps to return control of these companies to their rightful owners.

Similarly, when World II broke out, only one company in the United States was engaged in the production of aluminum. Because of the peculiar properties of this metal, it quickly became a strategic material. To assure itself of an ample supply, the government moved into the aluminum business—building factories, hiring workers, and so on—literally becoming a major "business" itself. At the conclusion of the war, the government then sold its aluminum interests to private parties, thus "creating" a competitive industry, where before there existed only one company.

Finally, the wide dispersion of nuclear reactors for the generation of electrical power represents a third example of government's positive interface with industry. Immediately after World War II, all nuclear power facilities and know-how were securely vested in the U.S. government. Yet, in the 1950s, the government took steps to disseminate the use of nuclear power for peaceful purposes—thus providing a new source of competition for the power companies and enabling the private sector to improve its competitive structure for the benefit of all Americans.

Noncompetitive
business-government involvement

The interaction of government in business, however, is not the only aspect of this question we should consider. Business has exerted, and continues to exert, a strong influence on government operations. For example, business leaders have served in presidential cabinets, as ambassadors to foreign nations, as members of regulatory commissions, as congressmen, and indeed, as presidents themselves. More recently, business has acted in cooperation with the federal government in trying to find solutions to mutual problems. The most apparent and successful of these interactions is probably the National Alliance of Businessmen. This is a voluntary business organization, operating with limited federal financing, that is attempting to retrain and employ the previously "hardcore" unemployed. The program has been successful in helping to eliminate some of the frustration of unemployment that has continually befallen those lacking in training and skills.

Business and government have also become partners in other ventures. For example, COMSAT—the Communications Satellite Corporation —is an international communications network operated jointly by the U.S. government and private enterprise. Each owns stock in the corporation, with business providing the vast management and operational skills and government providing the necessary rocketry and satellite construction facilities.

SUMMARY

We have seen, at least to this point, that the issue of business and government relations is a complex one. There are no simple rules or guidelines governing the relationship of these two institutions. If anything, it would seem that what really determines the degree of exchange or interface between business and government depends upon several other factors. For example, taxation is really dependent upon the demands society makes upon the government to provide certain goods and services. If society deems it wise to increase defense spending, someone must pay for the expenditure, and usually, business is one of those asked to pay in the form of higher taxes.

Similarly, government involves itself in several businesslike operations simply because there is no one else to provide the particular good or service. Some things, such as the building of the TVA (Tennessee Valley Authority) required such massive expenditures of funds that no business could afford to build the dams and other supportive projects. Consequently, government moved in and soon became a provider of electrical power to society, in competition with private industry.

Finally, the role of government in the area of regulation really depends on the actions of business executives themselves to set the limits of government intervention. If business leaders were 100 percent ethical, perhaps a great deal of the legislation that has been passed concerning the regulation of business activity would not have been necessary. But as we all know, no single group within society is 100 percent ethical. Indeed, the mere task of *defining* ethics and ethical behavior can be an exceptionally difficult task.

What is meant by "ethics"?

Ethics is generally considered to be concerned with the value judgments, actions, and conduct of individuals in their relationships with others. That is, ethics is concerned with moral judgments about what is right and what is wrong, given the standards of society at that time.

Ethical standards exist for practically all aspects of life. Government employees are required to uphold certain codes of conduct in the performance of their jobs. Senators and Congressmen are urged to make public disclosure of their financial assets, in the belief that this will prevent them from making decisions that involve a "conflict of interest." Schools, too, have ethical standards, and like other institutions, sometimes have trouble enforcing them. For example, the various service academies of the Army, Navy, and Air Force practice—try to practice—their ethical standards in their honor systems that exist in the classroom.

The nature of business ethics

Just like individuals, business and business leaders are constantly faced with the need to make ethical judgments. Consider, for example:

. . . . The bank loan officer, who has access to confidential information about his various customers, and who is conceivably in a position to pass this information on to his bank's Trust Officer, thereby enabling the bank to make a great deal of money in its Trust Department; even though such transfer of information is of questionable ethics, and may even be illegal.
. . . . . The employee who is in a position to profit personally from a decision he makes on behalf of the company he works for. For example, the purchasing agent who receives a "kickback" or free gifts for buying items from a certain supplier.

As you can imagine, business finds the problem of ethics to be a perplexing one. Business firms are made up of many individuals, each of whom has his or her own moral and ethical standards. Consequently, the interpretation of what is right and what is wrong is subject to a variety of responses. Some firms have tried to establish ethical codes of conduct for their employees. To a large extent, these have been successful in solving most ethical questions. But even here, problems sometimes arise. For instance, in 1972, many corporations made secret contributions to political campaigns, after having been "told in not so many words" that unless they did make contributions, their business contracts with the government might be jeopardized. Put yourself in the shoes of the business executive, then, and try to decide what *you* would do. If you go along and make the contribution, probably no one will find out, and your company can continue to receive its share of government business. Refuse to go along, however, and you may be accused of not acting in the stockholder's best interest, which, as we have seen in the preceding chapter, is to act in such a manner as to maximize the profits of the company.

Such examples, of course, can and do occur, and it is only unfortunate that business leaders sometimes do not have the ethical standards to stand up to the challenge. It is particularly unfortunate because, historically, business leaders have never been seen as having much of a set of ethics. Indeed, as Chapters 2 and 3 point out, business leaders have, at various times in our history, enjoyed much praise, respect, and prestige. But usually, they were considered to be of only modest ethical standards, and were usually thought of as putting profits ahead of ethics.

Much of this feeling, of course, stems from the very basis and objectives of business. Business is essentially a profit-oriented institution, and profitability is taken as the measure of the degree to which business succeeds at its role. Thus the question becomes: Can profits and ethics exist side by side?

Profits and ethics

Can a business executive earn a profit and still be ethical? As surprising as it may seem, many people no longer believe that the answer is yes. In a great many sections of society today, profits are no longer viewed as being the "just reward" that Smith, Ricardo, and Mill accepted as proper several centuries ago. Rather, profit is viewed by some as being the re-

FIGURE 18–10
Can a good business leader be a good American?

If your biggest single interest is your company's profit, and if you have to spend eight, ten, twelve hours a day to make it, how can you call yourself a good citizen?
Look at it this way:
Good Profits enable your company to offer more jobs.
    And more secure jobs.
Good profits make your company an attractive investment which gives you more capital to expand to offer still more jobs.
    And even more secure jobs.
Good profits enable your company to design and manufacture better products.
    And provide better service to your customers.
    And make your company a better place to work.
Good profits enable your company to make meaningful bequests to community projects such as new hospitals, new schools, new recreational facilities.
And of course, good profits make it possible for your company to pay your full share of the cost of government—at all levels. The bigger your profit, the bigger your tax contribution.
Come to think of it, maybe one type of ugly American is the businessman who constantly loses money.

Source: *The Wall Street Journal*, Advertisement for Marsteller, Inc., New York, in March 1, 1966, p. 17. Reprinted with permission.

ward for trickery, deception, and concealment—something earned only at someone else's expense. Thus, if a business executive raises prices, the action is viewed as "unfair" or "unethical," since it may result in higher profits for the business executive at the expense of the consumer. Similarly, if a business executive discharges or lays off an employee, this, too, is seen as unfair. The worker is deprived of the chance to earn a living, simply because the business executive desired more profit. Rarely, if ever, however, do these same critics examine the consequences of *not* taking those actions. If business *didn't* earn a profit, there would soon be no business. Without business, where would the employee find any work at all? Perhaps the defense of profits—ethically, morally, and economically—was best summarized in an advertisement that appeared not too long ago in *The Wall Street Journal* (see Figure 18–10).

Business leaders' views on business ethics

Having noted that business ethics can and should exist, and that they are not necessarily inconsistent with profit goals, perhaps we should examine the way business leaders feel about their ethics, and look at a few instances of practices that might not be condoned by all business leaders.

Increasingly, business leaders are becoming more and more concerned that the actions they take not only be consistent with good ethical standards, but that the public perceive them as being so. In the wake of various business scandals and collapses such as the Penn-Central, and the revelation of the numerous corporate contributions to political campaigns in the 1972 presidential election, business leaders are becoming increasingly criticized for actions that even seem to be questionable. As one authority has put it, "Business, to survive, must merit the confidence of its customers. . . . As business people, we cannot afford to close our eyes to violations of sound business principles, and there is much evidence that the business community is accepting increasing responsibility in this direction . . ."[3]

For instance, a few years ago, American Airlines discovered that its in-flight magazine, *American Way,* was being published by a firm that apparently had connections with several officers of the airline. In subsequent action, the airline has charged one of its vice-presidents and a former sales promotion manager with receiving kickbacks from the firm doing the printing. American Airlines tried to exercise good ethical judgment in this matter, however, as witnessed from the following. After the alleged scheme was uncovered by its own in-house investigators, American Air-

---

[3] Mercedes S. Wood, "Business and the Consumer," *The Journal of Business* (published by the Bureau of Business Research, Seton Hall University, Vol. 10 (December 1971), pp. 23.

lines turned the information over to federal law enforcement officers for prosecution, and openly acknowledged the situation in its next annual report. No attempt was made to "whitewash" the incident.

Still, much remains to be done, and business practices still abound that leave much to be desired. One such incident was reported in the *Wall Street Journal* of July 9, 1974. The case involved the manufacturer of boiler controls, and the society that governed the code of standards for that particular profession.

As reported in the *Journal,* a small manufacturer of boiler controls in New York developed and marketed a particular boiler control that apparently was more versatile—and possessed capabilities that other competitive controls in the industry lacked. Sales boomed, although the company's share of the market was still small next to the sales of the major company in the industry. Suddenly, however, customers of this small manufacturer began to cancel orders, and raise questions about the products' quality standards. It seems that the Society of Mechanical Engineers (which was the governing standard-setting body of the industry) had circulated a letter raising questions about the particular control, and noting that the control might not meet industry standards. The small company was amazed that such a report could be issued by its own society, and investigated further. It found out that the report had been issued by the chairman of the Standards Committee of the association. The chairman also happened to be a vice-president of the largest competitor of this small company. The chairman readily acknowledged that, perhaps the report wasn't printed in total candor and honesty, but that he considered such action to be "fair and honest competition."

The president of the small company appealed to the Federal Trade Commission, but to no avail. The FTC simply said the matter was really one for the courts to decide. The president, however, has dim views of going to court. His small company, he feels, has little chance of going to court against the larger firm, fighting a lengthy court battle, and coming out of the dispute with a solvent company. His company is so small he simply can't afford a lengthy court battle. Certainly the small company has been a victim of some rather shoddy ethical practices.

CONCLUSION

We have seen that the ethical questions confronting business are not easily resolved. Many problems remain to be corrected. And yet, one must be encouraged by the actions of an increasing number of business leaders to adopt strict and admirable ethical standards. After all, every segment of society has its ethical dilemmas, and in this regard, business is no different than any other sector of society. The place to begin correcting the problem, however, is by first acknowledging that a problem does exist, and focusing in on ways to resolve it. Business has made that beginning. But it has a long way to go. It remains for the present and future generations of business leaders—you in particular—to accept the challenge, and advance the cause of high ethical standards in the years ahead.

DISCUSSION QUESTIONS

1 Distinguish between regressive, progressive, and proportional taxes. If your state has an income tax, determine the extent to which it is progressive, proportional, or regressive.

2 Import duties are one form of tax that is imposed on goods coming into this country from abroad. Would you consider import duties to be primarily a revenue tax or a regulatory tax? Why?

3 The progressive tax is often said to be based on the principle of "ability to pay." Comment on the strengths and weaknesses of this tax.

4 It has often been said that every law that exists regulating the business firm was passed because business misused some privilege that it had. Is this true for the Federal Reserve Act? The Robinson-Patman Act? Why?

5 Define ethics. How does ethics differ from morals? Explain.

6 What occupations do you consider "unethical"? Why? Which occupations do you consider most ethical? Why?

7 Discuss the merits and demerits of the case of the *U.S.* v. *IBM.* Do you think a company should be broken up simply because it has achieved a position in its industry as the unquestioned leader?

8 Consider the case of the small manufacturer of boiler controls. If you were the owner of that firm, what might you do to counter the "unethical" acts being imposed upon you?

9 Most people would agree that a business leader can be both ethical and successful. Yet, surveys show many people are suspect over possible collusion of business leaders to monopolize, fix prices, or in some way conspire to cheat the public. Can these two views on business be consistent? That is, can a business leader be ethical in a world of unethical competitors and still be successful?

10 It is often said that business policy reflects the ethical standards and conduct of the top management of the firm. If this is true, what can we say about the ethics of young people going into business and who will, in a few years, be the top executives of those firms?

MINI CASES

Anita Michaels was in the process of negotiating the purchase of a new car. She had culminated her negotiations with a trip to the local bank to see about financing costs. The banker assured her that the car could be financed and that the interest cost would be "a simple 6 percent —add on." Anita didn't quite understand what this meant, so she asked for a clarification. "Well, it's really quite simple," said the banker. "We charge you a straight 6 percent on the loan, but since you are required to make monthly payments on it, your interest cost is slightly higher. But it's all disclosed in the contract you sign and is in full accord with Truth-in-Lending requirements."

Anita felt relieved and signed the contract. Later, she looked again at the contract, and noted that the "slightly higher" interest rate she was paying was actually 11.08 percent, not the 6 percent she had thought it was. Moreover, the banker charged her $75 additional for life insurance on herself. Anita was disturbed at this factor and complained to the banker. The banker explained that it was bank policy to charge for additional life insurance. Anita still disagreed, and questioned the "ethics" of the bank's practices.

1. Do you agree with the "ethics" of the banker's action? Present an alternative way that the banker might have proceeded in the negotiations with Anita.

Roger Mountain was an honor student at a large eastern university. As a graduating senior, he was engaged in taking several job interviews with various companies. One in particular interested Roger, and invited him to the company's headquarters for an in-depth interview.

Part of the interview included a psychological test. One question on that test asked him to check which of the following magazines he read occasionally, and which ones he read regularly. The list of magazines included: *Reader's Digest, Time, Fortune, The New Republic, Oui, Ramparts, The Nation, Sports Illustrated,* and *U.S. News and World Report.* Roger's reading tastes were quite broad, and at one time or another he had read most of the magazines listed. However, he was a subscriber to several, including *Time, Fortune,* and *The New Republic.* He was also an avid follower of *Oui,* and purchased it regularly at the newsstand.

Roger wasn't sure if his interest in *The New Republic* would necessarily find favor with the management of the company, and he had a good suspicion that his interests in the pictures in *Oui* would be frowned upon. He wondered what he should do.

1. *If you were Roger, how would you respond to the question?*
2. *What ethical questions would be raised by your answer to question 1?*

Bill and Mary Freeman, both age 20, had taken a trip to Europe for their honeymoon. Because both were under age 21, they were able to take advantage of the student rates that the airlines offered for such flights.[1]

On their return flight, they sat near an elderly couple who were returning from a similar trip. The elderly couple had gone to Europe for their 50th wedding anniversary. They had, moreover, been saving for this trip for years, since their pension benefits were not large enough to enable them to afford such a trip on short notice. Their tickets, after all, cost twice as much as Bill and Mary's, even though the accommodations were identical.

Bill began to contemplate the "fairness" of the airlines' policy regarding student fares. Was it fair, he wondered, for students—himself included—to receive lower rates for travel, while an elderly couple had to pay the full rate? After all, the elderly couple could no more afford the fare than could Bill and Mary. Moreover, Bill reasoned, this might be their only chance to take such a trip, whereas Bill and Mary had their whole lifetimes ahead of them.

1. *Comment on the airlines policy. Do you feel it is a "fair" one? Why or why not?*
2. *Suppose that the airline offered reduced rates for the elderly. Would this then resolve the ethical problem that Bill saw?*

---

[1] At the time of this case, most major airlines offered student discounts. These have since been abolished.

On some occasions, the role of government in business causes mixed feelings on the part of those affected by the action. The following is an abstraction of a true incident in business and government relations that expresses that predicament.

In the late 1960s, the federal government announced further tightening of the federal antipollution laws. As a consequence of these new restrictions, many businesses were faced with the choice of modernizing their facilities or shutting them down.

In one small Pennsylvania community, a large, antiquated paper mill was the sole employer of people in the town. Virtually 50 percent of the total population worked in this single mill. Moreover, the families of this town had resided there for generations—many families traced three and four generations of relatives that worked for this plant.

When the new federal regulations were passed, the managers of this plant were faced with a real dilemma. The plant was old and would require massive expenditures to bring it up to the standards dictated by the new law. Such expenditures were far in excess of the profits earned by the firm. There was no way the firm could be expected to recover its costs.

At the same time, however, the managers knew they were the major employer in a town surrounded by vast, hardcore unemployed. To close the plant would impose major hardships and difficulties on all of the residents of that small town.

1. *Discuss the problem facing this paper mill.*
2. *What would you do if you were the manager of the mill? Do you feel the role of government in this particular situation was beneficial to all concerned? Why or why not?*

Once the most famous saleslady in the United States, Betty Furness became the official champion of the American consumer, with her appointment in 1967 as President Lyndon Johnson's special assistant for consumer affairs.

Betty Furness was born on January 3, 1916, in New York City. Educated at the Brearly School in New York City, and at Bennett Junior College in Millbrook, New York, she soon embarked on a career in the movies. Miss Furness appeared in 35 motion pictures from 1932 to 1937. In 1937, she left Hollywood to perform on the live stage. Discouraged by her lack of success in the theatre, she returned to New York and employment in the infant industry of television. It was in this media that Betty Furness was soon to become a nationally recognized personality.

From 1949 until 1960, Miss Furness was employed by the Westinghouse corporation, and soon became one of the highest paid salespeople on television. She also had several small television shows of her own during the latter part of the 1950s. Her television career came to a fitting conclusion when, in 1961, she was appointed president of the New York chapter of the Academy of Arts and Sciences, a position she held for two years.

In 1967, President Johnson appointed her to the position of special assistant to the president for consumer affairs. Although this position may well have been politically motivated, Miss Furness soon earned the respect of friend and foe alike for her aggressiveness on behalf of the consumer. She resigned from the post in 1969, when the change occurred in political administrations.

In 1970, Miss Furness was appointed chairman and executive director of the New York State Consumer Protection Board, a position she still holds. Since 1969, she has also been a member of the Board of Directors of the Consumers Union, publishers of *Consumers Report*.

Betty Furness
(1916–   )

Champion of the consumer's interests

19

Business, the consumer, and the quality of life

*Good intentions are very mortal and
  perishable things;
Like very mellow and choice fruit
  they are difficult to keep.*

——*C. Simmons*

The role of consumers in our business society is one with which we are all familiar. As consumers, we have occasion to deal with business firms on a daily basis. It may be as consumers of food in the local restaurant, the purchasers of new appliances for the home, as car buyers, or as consumers of needed drugs and medical care. When we make such purchases, moreover, we make them in the belief that they are everything the manufacturer and retailer have made them out to be. Yet, on occasion, such is not the case. One needs only to examine the popularity over the years of such critics of business practices as Thorstein Veblen, John Kenneth Galbraith, and Ralph Nader to realize that shortcomings exist in the business-consumer relationship.

Partly as a result of such criticism, government has expressed an interest in the role of consumers in our economic society and has taken legal measures to protect them. Even so, the laws passed have been sporadic and generally poorly enforced. Not until the 1960s did *consumerism*—concern over safety of product, truth in packaging, truth in lending, and so on—become a household word. Only then did business and government become actively concerned about the problems facing the consumer.

Concurrent with the problems of consumerism, however, has been a growing concern about the general question of the quality of our life. Technology has caused many changes in our way of life; and as consumers, we have been greatly influenced and affected by it. Many new products, new chemicals, new fabrics, and so on, have been introduced in the past ten years. These products have not only influenced the business-consumer relationship, but have also had an important impact on the environment in which we live. Pop-top cans and disposable, nonbreakable plastic containers greatly simplified the life of the average consumer; but their use ultimately created massive problems of refuse disposal. Increased production of automobiles, trucks, and jet planes demonstrated the potency of our industrial productivity. But the noise and pollutants they emitted have created health problems and have been damaging to the environment and to the quality of life.

As society became increasingly concerned about the state of our environment, business found itself confronted by a dilemma. On one hand were consumers, demanding more and more goods with convenience characteristics and low prices. At the same time, however, society was asking business to help preserve and protect our environment. It is this state of affairs that presently faces the business community. In this chapter, we shall take a closer look at how this situation came into being and what response business has made to this challenge.

BUSINESS AND THE CONSUMER

Materialism and the consumer in society

Consumers in our contemporary society have been and still are, something of an enigma. On one hand, the term *consumer* refers to practically everyone. In our own way, all of us are consumers of one sort or another. At the same time, however, the *consumer* is a nobody. Consumers are the only large interest group in America that until recently lacked an advocate, a common grievance, and an effective means of displaying their dissatisfaction. Indeed, it has not been until the past 15 years that consumers have even had an advisor to the president, or that magazines and journals purporting to represent consumer interests have become popular national news vehicles.

Why this has been the case is difficult to answer. Partly, one might suppose, it stems from the basic ideas and attitudes of independence that have long been ingrained in the American mind. Consumers long have been content to acquire their goods and services by bargaining for them as individuals. Thus, the consumer cooperatives that one sees in Europe have never achieved a similar degree of lasting popularity here in the United States.

Then, too, the traditional working philosophy of business known as *caveat emptor*—let the buyer beware—has been well indoctrinated in both the consumer and the business executive. From the days of the Yankee peddler to the present-day age of the used-car salesman, the unwritten code for business-consumer relations has been precisely that— let the buyer beware!

Finally, the unceasing quest for material wealth that has distinguished American society is partly to blame for the lack of a proper consumer voice. In their quest for more and more things, consumers have been willing to sacrifice quality for quantity, necessary goods for superfluous ones, long-lasting goods for rapidly deteriorating ones. Price, not quality, has been the key bargaining point. Consequently, business sought to satisfy the demand by producing goods that met the wishes of the consumer. People needed transportation; so business gave them a low-priced car and relatively inexpensive airplane travel. In the process, however, the air was filled with noxious fumes; and an unending cycle of repetitive production was created as used cars were traded in on newer ones. Consumers desired low-cost, convenient communications; so business gave them the telephone, the radio, and television. As a consequence, however, the consumer was forced to suffer through an unending barrage of commercial messages and solicitations.

Technology further complicates the consumer life

Our age of technology, moreover, has further increased the new products made available to the consumer. Synthetic fabrics abound in our clothing; plastics are found in our homes and offices; even artificial sweeteners and preservatives are used in our foods. Consumers, already somewhat overwhelmed by the tremendous number of choices of products available to them (over 300 makes and models of automobiles alone), began to find themselves more and more at the mercy of the business leader. They did not know what was in their products, how safe they were, or what dangers might arise because of their use. What had started out as an effort by business to satisfy a materialistic desire on the part of society had suddenly mushroomed into a mountain of new products and services, many of which were totally unknown just a few years earlier. Clearly, consumers were in need of some kind of assistance. But lacking an appropriate consensus voice, they were forced to withstand the onslaught of new technology as best they could. Sometimes they made wise purchases, and sometimes—as in the case of the drug Thalidomide[1]— they made tragic choices.

This discussion of the effects of technology is not meant to imply that the consumer was totally ignorant or unable to intelligently choose among products. Consumers learned from experience, for example, what

---

[1] Thalidomide was a drug developed in the early 1960s whose use by expectant mothers resulted in scores of cases of deformed births. The drug has since been removed from the market, but its memory remains a reminder of the tragic consequences that can result from consumer and industrial ignorance of the effects of new products.

products were good and which were not. They also learned from friends, whose buying experiences were relayed to others. Television, newspaper, and radio advertisements similarly helped "educate" the consumer as to the values of certain products. Each of these vehicles played—and still play—an important role in the consumers' decision-making process. The problem, however, is that each of these lacks a certain sureness; each lacks the objective standard that the typical consumer desires. Experience, for example, is a good teacher. But when models and designs change so rapidly, is it really a fair criterion to use? Can we, for example, say that the new model of a particular car is no good just because we did not like the 1970 model we owned previously? Engineering features can change substantially in a few years.

Similarly, friends may very well provide a biased opinion on new products. Some people, for example, may like or dislike a certain laundry detergent because of the "colored crystals" it contains, or the amount of suds it makes. Accordingly, they might rave about the detergent to their neighbors. Lost in the argument is the question of just what those colored crystals add to the detergent, or whether the quantity of suds has anything to do with the function of a detergent—namely, to get the wash clean. Finally, the advertisements that bombard us daily are obviously biased. Granted, advertising has an educational value, and when properly presented it can be a credit to both the company and the product being advertised. But some commercial messages are clearly exaggerated—and proclaim qualities and benefits that, on reflection, are dubious indeed.

Consumerism as a national issue

Faced with the problem, then, of intelligently choosing products in an increasingly complex marketplace, consumers began to cry for help. They were finally heard in Washington in the early 1960s, when President Kennedy sent Congress his "Special Message on Protecting the Consumer Interest." In his message to Congress in March of 1962, President Kennedy spelled out what he believed were the basic rights of all consumers. These were (a) the right to safety, (b) the right to be informed, (c) the right to choose, and (d) the right to be heard. Although none of these rights was new, Kennedy's message was the first time they were spelled out as part of a national effort which sought to protect the interests of the consumer.

The right to safety   The right to safety is one which has been of increasing concern over the past 15 years. Ralph Nader's crusade against the Corvair and the Surgeon-General's investigation into the harmful effects of cigarette smoking are but two signs of the concern over this aspect of the business-consumer relationship. Cigarettes, for example, present an interesting example of how products are occasionally developed and used for years before their real effects are known. As recently as 1929, cigarettes were actually being advertised and sold on the grounds that they were beneficial to one's health! One very famous advertisement proclaimed that people should smoke rather than eat sweets that made them fat. Today, of course, the emphasis has changed. Even tobacco company executives acknowledge that cigarette smoking is not beneficial. One executive, for example, has said that the purpose of contemporary cigarette ads is not to lure more people into smoking but rather to convince smokers to switch brands. Regardless of the validity of this comment, however, one fact remains clear: None of this attention to potential hazards to health would have come about had it not been for the consumer movement and the concern of our public health officials for the safety of consumers.

Other products have been similarly examined for their implications for consumer safety. The Pure Food and Drug Act of 1938 was amended in 1962 to strengthen the enforcement of these standards. For example, the 1962 Drug Amendments established federal standards for new drugs, for the testing of drugs, and the labeling of possible injurious side effects from the drug's use. Similar efforts were made by the National Safety Council in obtaining laws requiring seat belts, shoulder harnesses, head rests, and stronger bumpers on automobiles. And more recently, Congress created a Consumer Product Safety Commission to coordinate many of the safety laws that were already on the books.

What has this push on product safety meant for business? For one thing, it has meant higher prices for the goods we buy. Adding new equipment to automobiles, for example, means higher costs for the manufacturer and subsequently higher prices for the consumer. Increasing the laboratory tests of new drugs and medicines increases their costs, and similarly, increases the costs to doctors and hospitals and, ultimately, to consumers.

More significant, perhaps, is the impact that the safety push has for the number and types of products we have available. The number of new drugs introduced in recent years has been sharply reduced because of the requirement that they undergo additional testing. Car designs have been affected by the safety requirements. The 1969 ban on DDT and other insecticides has had a marked effect on the productivity of farms and on the preservation of our national forests.

Still, much remains to be done. Each year, an estimated 20 million Americans are injured seriously enough in product-related accidents to require medical attention. Of these, an estimated 30,000 die and another 110,000 are permanently disabled. Partly to combat these statistics, Congress passed, in 1973, the Consumer Product Safety Act. This act created the Consumer Product Safety Commission, and gave it power to enforce the many acts already on the books. The Commission's real power, however, comes from its power to levy fines and prison sentences on offenders of the statutes it enforces. In the first year of its existence, the Commission moved vigorously in the direction of enforcing consumer safety. It forced major revisions in washing machines sold by Sears and television sets produced by Philco-Ford. It even ordered the removal from the shelves of a small import store in San Francisco small paperweights that were designed to look like light bulbs.

FIGURE 19-1

Today's top hazards

Estimated injuries 1973*

Bicycles and bicycle equipment.............................	372,000
Stairs, ramps, landings (indoors, outdoors)...............	356,000
Nails, carpet tacks, screws, thumbtacks..................	275,000
Football-related equipment and apparel...................	230,000
Baseball-related equipment and apparel...................	191,000
Basketball-related equipment and apparel.................	188,000
Architectural glass.......................................	178,000
Doors (other than glass).................................	153,000
Tables (nonglass)..	137,000
Swings, slides, seesaws, playground climbing apparatus...	112,000
Beds (including springs, frames).........................	100,000
Nonupholstered chairs....................................	68,000
Chests, buffets, bookshelves, etc........................	68,000
Power lawn mowers.......................................	58,000
Bathtub and shower structures (except doors, panels)...	41,000
Cleaning agents, caustic compounds......................	35,000
Swimming pools and associated equipment (in-ground only).....................................	32,000
Cooking ranges, ovens and equipment....................	25,000
Fuels, liquid, kindling, illuminating.....................	25,000
Space heaters, heating stoves...........................	22,000

---

* Based on injuries treated in 119 hospital emergency rooms.
Data: Consumer Product Safety Commission.

The right to be informed The right to be informed is a right that society has enjoyed in one way or another for the past 100 years. In 1872, for example, mail fraud was prohibited by federal law. Other laws regulated securities, weights and measures, and advertising.

In very recent years, the emphasis on informing the public has taken the direction of enacting laws governing packaging, labeling, and most recently, disclosure of true annual interest rates charged on various types of credit. The laws are better known under the names "Truth-in-Packaging" and "Truth-in-Lending." They require more complete disclosure of the actual package content and actual costs of borrowing money. They have also required the contents of various products to be prominently displayed on the package itself, so that the consumer will know exactly what is being sold. Efforts have been under way, too, to have products priced in a manner which will enable consumers to do comparative pricing. Thus, instead of having a 64-ounce box of laundry soap sell for $1.89, and a 24-ounce box sell for 84 cents, each would also carry the cost *per ounce,* thereby enabling the consumer to determine just what savings can be realized by purchasing the larger size.

Business has reacted to these various laws and movements with mixed emotions. In some instances, the requirements were quite easy to meet and posed little difficulty. Indeed, many businesses were pleased at the passage of the Consumer Credit Protection Act of 1968, otherwise known as the Truth-in-Lending Law. This law helped unmask the unscrupulous or unethical business leader who gained an unfair advantage by hiding exorbitant interest rate charges on credit sales behind vague descriptions of the terms, thereby preventing the consumers from actually learning what rate they were paying. In other cases, however, the stringency of the laws, as, for example, Truth-in-Packaging, created a real problem. Potato chips, for example, are packaged while still warm in order to assure freshness. However, on cooling the chips tend to settle in their package, resulting in a bag or box that is half filled with air. This was interpreted at first as a violation of the Fair Packaging and Labeling Act of 1966, otherwise known as the Truth-in-Packaging Law, since the package gave the impression of a greater quantity of chips than was actually there. No intent to deceive was ever planned by the manufacturer; indeed, the contents in ounces was still accurate. The product, however, had peculiarities which tended to cause untold grief for the well-intentioned business executive.

The right to choose   The right to choose is perhaps, the oldest enforced right of the consumer. Essentially, this right is another way of saying competition should be encouraged and not stifled. The antitrust laws of the United States have over the past 80 years attempted to assure competition in most fields of commerce, from transportation to communications. Even here, though, problems tend to arise. Often various nations find themselves facing an undesirable amount of competition in the world marketplace. Other nations' businesses are taking markets from them, with a resulting loss of income for the country's business firms. When this happens, nations often impose artificial barriers, such as taxes and tariffs, on goods from other countries. This limits the amount of foreign goods coming into a nation, and, consequently, reduces the choice for individuals.

The right to be heard   The final right of consumers that was specified in President Kennedy's message was the right to be heard in the councils of government. Until 1962, consumers had enjoyed only fleeting moments of access to the high policy-making offices in Washington. These few instances, moreover, tended to occur during moments of national emergency, and as such did not give the consumer a permanent, substantive voice in Washington. For example, an Office of Consumer Counsel was developed within the Department of Agriculture in 1933, along with a Consumer Advisory Board. The Advisory Board, however, was developed as a part of President Franklin D. Roosevelt's famous National Recovery Act. When the NRA was ruled unconstitutional in 1935, the Advisory Council came to a quick end. In the meantime, the Office of Consumer Counsel continued an uneventful existence, until it, too, was eventually terminated in 1945.

At other times, too, consumer influence has been minimal at best. The Bituminous Coal Commission of 1937 had a Consumers Counsel advising it, but its influence was slight. The National Defense Advisory Commission of 1940 similarly had a consumer commissioner on its board, but he was strictly a minority member. The Office of Price Administration that began in 1941 was supposedly to consider the consumer's welfare among its many and varied functions, but given the state of emergency that existed then, it is doubtful that such an interest was really observed. Finally, President Truman's Council of Economic Advisors had a Consumer Advisory Committee giving it recommendations. However, the Council of Economic Advisors was itself a new creation at that time and did not possess the degree of influence that it possesses today.

Thus, we can see why President Kennedy's message was so significant. For almost 40 years, consumers had enjoyed very little influence in determining the rules, terms, or conditions under which they were expected to function in the marketplace. This Congressional Message for the first time expressed the desire that consumers be able to enjoy a constant voice in government.

To help ensure the right of consumers to a voice in policy-making, Kennedy's message called for the creation of a Consumer's Advisory Council. The Council came into existence in July 1962, and promptly identified ten areas that it felt were of pressing interest to consumers. These were:

1. Standards, grading, and labels.
2. A flow of information between government and consumers.
3. Representation in government.
4. Consumer credit standards.
5. Improvement in the relationships between and among various federal and state consumer agencies.
6. An accelerated economic growth.
7. Improvement in the level of consumption for the low-income groups in society.
8. Regulation and prevention of price fixing.
9. Development of adequate housing.
10. Improved medical care.

Of these ten points, the Council felt strongly that the first six needed immediate implementation. As it developed, however, great strides have been made on almost all of these points. The following are examples.

Standards, grading, and labeling The passage of a Truth-in-Packaging law was a significant development in the improvement of standards for packages and rules for labeling. Meaningless phrases like "Giant Quart" and "Giant King Size" were prohibited from advertising and packaging labels. "Cents-off" sales were required to actually *be* "cents-off," and not just an advertising gimmick. Packages were required to be as nondeceptive as possible, given the limitations of the product contained therein.

A flow of information and representation in government The creation of a Special Assistant to the President for Consumer Affairs by President Johnson has been the foremost advance to date toward creating a permanent voice for the consumer in government. This office, moreover, has been continued by Presidents Nixon and Ford, and has had an active voice in the councils of government during the few years of its existence.

Consumer credit standards The passage of a Truth-in-Lending Law was the first significant step in the development of standard credit laws throughout the country. Under the provisions of the law, business was required to disclose annual interest charges on all credit sales.

Improvement of the level of consumption for low-income groups The War-on-Poverty programs begun in the mid 1960s illustrate the degree to which government has undertaken this important task. For example, in 1962, the Manpower Development and Training Program was passed. This act was intended to help develop marketable job skills among the disadvantaged. Later, Job Corps and Title II and Title III programs were established to further the fight against poverty. Increases in social security, increased aid to the unemployed, and joint efforts by business and government to improve job opportunities and housing all reflected the steps made in implementing this point. Unfortunately, much of the early gains made in this regard were countered by the hyperinflation (excessively rapid increases in the cost of living) that occurred in the late 1960s and early 1970s.

Improved medical care The delivery quality and price of medical care has been a major problem of increasing concern to all in the past decade. Passage of medicare and medicaid bills by Congress has greatly advanced the ability of all segments of our society to receive better medical care. Medicare, for example, covers a major portion of the hospital expenses for those over 65, and makes available a system of medical insurance that helps cover doctors' fees, outpatient expenses and some home health services. Medicaid provides similar protection, but is not restricted to the elderly. Rather, it is designed to aid those who, regardless of age, are too poor to afford proper medical care. Perhaps the greatest strides in this regard, however, will be those that come about because of the National Health Insurance Program.[2] While the authors intend no personal viewpoints regarding the advisability or undesirability of such a program, they do concede that the program as envisioned will probably provide health protection benefits to many who previously were unable to afford it.

What does this mean for business?

It is obvious from the above discussion that consumerism has taken on new importance and dimensions in the past 15 years. Much of this new importance, however, has been due to the stimulus of government rather than of business. Business has been noticeably weak in furthering the cause of consumerism. This is probably because of two factors: first, the historic role in business and consumer relations has been one of *caveat emptor*—let the buyer beware. Many business leaders have been reluctant to abandon this philosophy. Second, consumers have traditionally lacked the means to persuade business to be of more assistance. As a consequence, many practices still exist which irritate the business-consumer relationship. Warranties and guarantees, for example, are still written in fine print, and lack a clear and concise explanation of what they cover and what they do not cover. Dealers, moreover, have been notorious in their reluctance to correct faulty merchandise under warranty. Indeed, quality repair service for many products—notably automobiles—still exists more often in the advertisement copy than it does in the auto service departments.

In the case of drugs and medicines, problems of information exist. Most drugs are sold under some brand name—a name that is licensed and protected by patent for 17 years. These drugs and medicines are heavily advertised, and usually are quite expensive when purchased in the local pharmaceutical. Yet, often the same drugs are available under another name—either its chemical or generic name—at a fraction of the cost. Aspirin tablets are a classic example of this problem. Some brands sell for 10 to 15 times the price of others, even though they consist of the same chemical ingredients, mixed in the same government-controlled proportion. Consumers, however, are rarely told this fact, nor are they assisted in determining the lowest priced product available for any given ailment.

Finally, business has been accused (although these accusations are highly debatable) of generating a demand for goods that consumers previously neither wanted nor needed. This "demand creation" is the result —so it is claimed—of advertising. John Kenneth Galbraith is perhaps the

---

[2] As of this writing, a bill was pending in Congress to establish this program. It was viewed by most observers as having a good chance of passage.

best known of the critics who have leveled this charge. Galbraith's argument, in essence, is that business creates a demand for its products, which it then proceeds to fill, rather than filling the legitimate needs and wants of society. He claims that business, not the consumer, determines what will be produced and consumed.

Such an argument, of course, has a certain intuitive appeal, and no doubt is true in certain situations. The hula hoop and the skateboard, for example, are undoubtedly the result of some imaginative business leaders who created a product, advertised it heavily, and consequently "created" a demand for the product. It must be recognized, however, that limitations exist on the extent to which this procedure can be effectively used. Despite all the money, time, and research that went into the development of the Edsel automobile, for example, it still became one of the greatest failures in the history of American business. Similarly, the dismal performance of the maxiskirt and midiskirt a few years ago shows that for some products, no amount of advertising will guarantee the creation of a "demand" for that good. Advertising is an extremely valuable tool for use by a business firm, but it cannot replace the logic and reasoning of the American consumer.

What is business doing to correct the problem?

Although business was slow in recognizing the legitimacy of consumer complaints, there are signs that business leaders are moving to correct this problem. Automobile manufacturers, for example, are taking steps to simplify the coverage and interpretation of their warranties and are also making efforts to improve dealer cooperation in enforcing these warranties. Corporate presidents and other high officials of commerce are indicating an increasing interest in obtaining customer satisfaction—even to the point of encouraging calls directly to their offices or other upper echelon offices specially developed to handle such conplaints. Ford Motor Company is one example of a firm with such a policy.

Still, much remains to be done before business can be said to have satisfactorily resolved the problem of protecting and safeguarding the consumer's interest. It remains one of the areas still awaiting the challenge of corporate officials.

THE ENVIRONMENT AND THE QUALITY OF LIFE

One area of concern to consumers, to government, and to business alike is the quality of life in our society and the implications that our life styles hold for the continued survival of our natural environment. In the quest for survival, and later for a higher standard of living, human beings have managed to denude the forests, plunder the oceans and streams, poison the air they breathe. They have polluted the rivers and the landscape with garbage and refuse, and slowly altered the delicate balance of nature.

Such a development has been a long time in reaching this critical stage, for traces of people's negligence go back far beyond the time when Indians and buffalo roamed the plains of America. Today, however, we are finally facing up to the problems for the first time. Such an awareness, moreover, is happening none too soon. Wildlife species are disappearing with increasing regularity, and in some of our major industrial and metropolitan areas, the streams have literally died from an overdose of pollution. The Cuyahoga River in Cleveland, Ohio, for example, has the dubious distinction of being perhaps the only flammable river in North America—one summer night in 1969, the river literally burst into flames, so thick was the oil scum on it. That such a situation was ever allowed to develop is a travesty whose blame must be shared by all. Governments pollute, as city after city dumps its sewage in rivers, lakes, or in open dumps. Business pollutes, as a ride near any steel town or paper mill factory will amply disclose. Individuals pollute, as is evidenced by the litter existing on the sides of virtually every major highway in the United States. Indeed, in some ways technology itself is to blame, as the throw-away bottles and pop-top aluminum cans in which we buy beverages make it easier for us to litter the highways and rivers. Yet, business must share part of this blame, for in developing such containers, it failed to consider the ecological consequences of its actions. This is also true of the soap manufacturers, almost all of whom were heavy users of phosphates in their detergents. When phosphates were identified as a pollutant, these firms complained about the need to change their formula.

Indeed, some writers have recently been particularly critical of the roles played by business and government in perpetrating the pollution problem. Charles A. Reich's *The Greening of America,* for example, develops an argument which criticizes the corporate state (the alliance of big business and government) for determining how our scarce resources should be allocated. Reich claims that the decision as to who gets what and why is determined in an uncontrolled manner. As a consequence, the quality of life deteriorates, machines injure and destroy human life, the environment is polluted, and individuals become unable to determine how their own life can be lived.

We can see, therefore, that the problem of the environment has a particular relevance insofar as business is concerned. As whales and fish are eliminated from the seas, business is forced to look elsewhere for its necessary sources of supply. As leopards and jaguars disappear from the jungles, the pressure on business to quit manufacturing fur coats of these skins begins to grow. What really complicates things, however, is when business gets caught in the middle of a clash between consumers on one hand and environmentalists on the other. The case of the fur coats is an example of such a situation.

The problem that exists regarding wildlife extermination, however, is only a small part of the environmental problem. Perhaps the biggest environmental problem that exists is one that is not related to the whales in the ocean or the game in Africa, but rather concerns the survival of humanity itself on the face of the earth. The threat that humans face is that of pollution, and in the next few pages, we will look more closely at the problem of pollution, and business' role and responsibilities regarding it.

POLLUTION AS AN ENVIRONMENTAL PROBLEM

Pollution is both a relatively new concept and at the same time a very old one. People in England suffered from the effects of pollution centuries ago. Yet, until 1961 very little attention was paid to it, and not much was known about it. Not until that year were instruments available that would enable people to decipher the chemical content of pollution and denote its effects on them.

Today, of course, the situation is entirely different. We know that pollution is a major problem; we know its causes and we know its effects. The literature of the day abounds with hair-raising tales of what might conceivably happen if the pollution problem continues unchecked. Consider, for example, the plight of the oceans. The oceans represent perhaps, the ultimate collector of all pollution. It is so because in the final analysis, everything in the way of waste material that is not in some way accounted for by humans, finds its way to the oceans. They are the world's greatest sewer. They are also the primary source of oxygen for the world. If—or when—the oceans become so polluted they cannot continue to produce oxygen, life as we know it on earth will cease to exist. The possibility of this happening, moreover, is not as remote as one might think. Jacques Cousteau, the noted ocean explorer, has stated that if nothing at all were done, the world had, perhaps, another 50 years of survival. Needless to say, the problem is a serious one.

Who causes pollution?

As has already been noted, pollution is caused by all of us. Yet, even though we recognize this fact, most of us have a tendency to single out one or two major sources of pollution, and thereby create a "stereotype" of the real culprit. Moreover, it happens that business is the party most frequently identified as being the prime offender. For example, the automobile industry is frequently singled out as being a major polluter, simply because the automobile is itself an obvious source of pollution. Similar criticism befalls steel companies and paper mills, primarily because their products frequently pollute. Such criticism, interestingly enough, arises primarily because of the products that are produced, and not necessarily because of the industrial processes itself. The question becomes, consequently, one of determining the validity of these criticisms. Are automobile manufacturers, for example, really the ones to blame for the pollution autos create? Are the paper companies really responsible for the fact that so much litter is allowed to clutter our streams and highways? Let's look at some of the particulars and see if we can't better clarify this problem.

Types of pollution

Essentially, there are four basic types of pollution that are of concern to business leaders and consumers. These are: (*a*) air pollution, (*b*) water pollution, (*c*) refuse disposal, and (*d*) noise pollution.

Air pollution   It is an established fact that automobiles are the single most important contributor of pollutants in the air. In 1970, for example, 263.9 million tons of pollution were spewed into the atmosphere, of which 47 percent or 123 million tons came from the automobile. More significantly, perhaps, was the automobile's contribution of carbon monoxide and hydrocarbon emissions. Figure 19–2 shows the automobile's share of

FIGURE 19–2

The automobile and air pollution

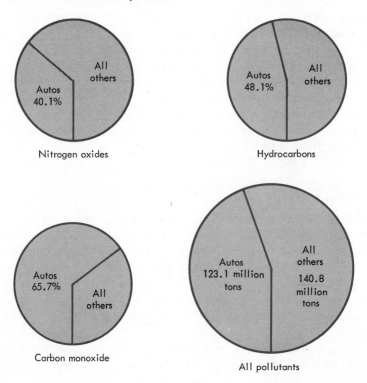

Nitrogen oxides

Hydrocarbons

Carbon monoxide

All pollutants

FIGURE 19–3

Air pollution in the United States, 1970

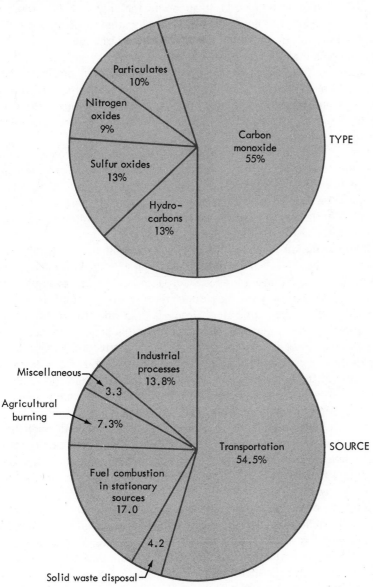

the total amounts of various pollutants spewed into the air from all sources.

Before we reach any conclusions about the guilt of the auto, however, perhaps we ought to give the auto industry a chance to tell its story. According to the automobile industry, the implications of the "total pollution caused by cars" is completely misleading. One Chrysler engineer, for example, noted that although the automobile accounts for over 40 percent of all atmospheric pollutants, it accounts for only 4 to 6 percent of all *harmful* pollutants! Although this engineer's statistics disregard the effect of concentration of cars in cities, and similarly disregards those respiratory ailments that might have been caused in part by the rest of the pollutants, his statistics are certainly noteworthy. Indeed, one scientist at a leading eastern university medical school claimed that more exposure to carbon monoxide comes from smoking a package of cigarettes than one would obtain from breathing the air on a typical city street, automobiles not withstanding!

The automobile, moreover, is not the only source of air pollution. Air pollution results from many practices, not all of which are the result of business activities. Municipalities, for example, are a leading source of air pollution, particularly in reference to their handling of sewage disposal. Even farmers cause air pollution when they spray insecticides on their crops.

Water pollution   A second major type of pollution is water pollution. Water pollution is similarly caused by many factors: industry, government, individuals, and others. Steel companies, for example, pollute streams and waterways if they dump the "pickling liquor" (a mixture of sulfuric acid, hydrochloric acid, iron sulfates and chlorides) from their steelmaking processes into streams. Although such practices are now illegal, sometimes such developments occur inadvertently. One company decided to dispose of its pickling liquor by pouring it into a deep hole in the ground. Such a procedure might have worked, had the solution not seeped down and contaminated the water table for the nearby town.

Other types of water pollution are caused by industry. Electric power companies use tremendous amounts of water to run and cool their turbines. When the water leaves the utility, it contains a major type of pollutant: heat. Warming up the water in a stream or river just a few degrees is enough to alter the balance of life in the river sufficiently to ultimately "kill" the river.

Another major polluter of rivers and streams is the unsuspecting farmer. Irrigation leads to pollution of the streams into which the water used eventually flows, as does the rainwater after it erodes cultivated land. Indeed, one authority has noted that more damage has been caused Illinois' rivers by well-meaning farmers using nitrogen fertilizers than by any other source. This fertilizer accelerates the growth of plant life in the river, starves the water of oxygen, and thereby kills certain bacteria in the river that are vital to a proper ecological balance.

Still other sources of water pollution are offshore oil rigs that go out of control, oil spills, and dumping of refuse from ships at sea. Oil slicks occurring from shore facilities or from ships create a terrible ecological hazard. All of us can recall, for example, the pictures that were flashed around the country of birds by the thousands that had been caught in the oil slick off the coast of California. Table 19–1 puts the importance of this source of pollution in better perspective.

TABLE 19–1

Polluting spills in U.S. Waters—1971

Total spills reported............................		8,496
Source:		
Vessel.......................................		2,086
Tanker.....................................	380	
Tank barge...............................	816	
Other......................................	890	
Transportation related facilities..............		1,932
Pipelines..................................	1,446	
Other......................................	486	
Other..		4,478

Source: U.S. Council on Environmental Quality, *Environmental Quality,* 1972.

Refuse A third major type of pollution is solid waste disposal. Perhaps the most obvious source of pollution, solid waste exists as a visible source of pollution in practically every town and village in the country. Our roadsides are cluttered with aluminum cans, paper, plastics, and automobile tires. Indeed, in 1971 alone, there were 44 billion throw-away beverage containers manufactured! Moreover, there were 60 million tons of paper consumed during that year, of which a large portion ended up as roadside litter. What can possibly be done to eliminate such a situation? The answer seems to hinge on whether industry and the consumers are willing to cooperate in improving the situation. Some companies have tried to recycle the glass bottles and aluminum cans, but have found the recycling process is too expensive. Still, efforts are continuing in the quest of an economical solution. The aluminum ring on the neck of twist-off bottles has made it uneconomical to grind the glass up for use in highway construction, unless consumers cooperate by removing the metal beforehand. Paper, too, can be recycled, but such a procedure requires the cooperation of all society. To date, 20.3 percent of all of our paper is recycled (used again). In Japan, by contrast, the figure for recycling is closer to 50 percent. And in Western Europe, almost 28 percent of their waste paper is recycled. It would appear that, although a start has been made, we have a long way to go.

Some metropolitan areas have been forced to find unusual ways of disposing of their trash. In Chicago, for example, garbage has been used for fill in Lake Michigan and has been the object of recent discussions relating to a pipeline that would transport it to agriculturally poor areas for use as fertilizer. Even the U.S. Department of Fisheries is finding an interesting use for one of the worst sources of refuse pollution—automobile tires. The fish service has begun experimenting with the sinking of old tires on the continental shelf in order to provide protection for the smaller fish living there.

Still, much remains to be done both by government and by business. Business cannot go on creating massive amounts of waste materials as a result of inefficient production facilities. Nor can government continue to ignore the threat that refuse poses for our way of life.

Noise Another type of pollution, and one we don't hear much about, is noise pollution. Noise, however, is on the verge of becoming a source of one of our most troublesome types of pollution. Table 19–2 shows, in

TABLE 19–2

Noise pollution tolerance levels (in decibels)

	150	
	140	
		Painfully loud
	130	Limit of range of amplified speed
Jet takeoff at 200 feet	120	
Discotheque		Maximum vocal effect
Riveting machine	110	
Jet takeoff at 2,000 feet		
Shout at a half foot	100	
New York subway station		Very annoying
Heavy truck at 50 feet	90	Hearing damage (8 hours or more)
Pneumatic drill at 50 feet		
	80	Annoying
Freight train at 50 feet		
Freeway traffic at 50 feet		
	70	Telephone use difficult
Air conditioning unit at 20 feet		
	60	
Light auto traffic		
	50	Quiet
Living room		
Bedroom	40	
Soft whisper at 15 feet	30	Very quiet
	0	

decibel levels, just what problems noise pollution poses. As the decibel level of noise in general increases, more and more concern is being expressed about the impact of noise on the human nervous system, on hearing, and indeed, on mental health in general! In fact, it was this type of concern that helped terminate the development of America's supersonic transport plane in the early 1970s.

Much of the problem surrounding noise pollution is that no one really knows the "safe" noise limit for the average worker. Because each individual has a different tolerance for noise, scientists cannot pinpoint the danger level. However, it is known that prolonged exposure to high noise levels can cause psychological and physiological problems. One study of weavers in a jute mill found that, although the weavers were exposed to 98 decibels of noise, during the first year their hearing remained unimpaired. However, after ten years, the same weavers had become partially but permanently deaf. And in Germany, a study concluded that workers subjected to the most noise on the job tended to be more prone to heart disorders and circulatory problems than other workers.

Unfortunately, corrective action does not seem to be on the near horizon. Technological advances have, in the past few years, greatly accelerated the use of power in our everyday lives—power which, when harnessed for use by humans, invariably results in more noise.

Land use Finally, various kinds of pollution are caused by the many ways people use the land. In this sense, land use may not be a unique "kind" of pollution. Yet, in some instances the very way land is used *is* a form of pollution. For example, consider the oil shale exploration currently being undertaken in Colorado, Wyoming, and Utah. The process of extracting shale oil is unique in one very important respect. The residue—that is, the waste or leftover material after the oil has been extracted—is actually larger in volume than the rock was when it was in its original state. Moreover, one of the most popular ways of extracting shale oil results in that residue being left in the form of a powdery black substance, totally void of any usefulness. It won't grow anything, it tends to be too powdery to build on, and so forth. Moreover, the residue is high in salt content. Consequently, when the powdery ash finds its way to the various rivers and streams (particularly the Colorado River, which is already very high in salt content), they become polluted with the saline solution.

Another kind of pollution—or perhaps we should say environmental impact—that has resulted from shale oil exploration, is the threat that development poses for the wildlife of the region. At the present time, one of the major sites for shale oil exploration lies in the heart of the largest grazing area in the country for mule deer. This animal could face a serious threat to its existence if adequate steps aren't taken to protect it. Moreover, that same area is habited by one of our few remaining flocks of eagles. We can see, therefore, that the problem of environmental control, and/or pollution, is a serious one, and is not one that will be solved very easily. Trade-offs must be necessary. American consumers desire a plentiful supply of oil; but are they willing to pay the price that must be paid to get that oil? American workers desire to have a job; but are they willing to live in the soot and water pollution that may result? These are questions that have no easy answers.

WHAT IS BEING DONE?

Given this brief background to the problem facing business and society, we can ask the logical question: "What's being done about it?" Fortunately, the answer is, "Considerable." Government has recently been exceptionally active in passing laws and regulations that will help alleviate the problem. New regulations regarding automobile emissions, for example, went into effect in 1973; and still others go into effect later in the decade. With full implementation of these laws, emissions from automobiles should drop rather sharply (see Figure 19–4).

Congress also passed the Federal Water Quality Act in 1965. This act authorized the creation of a Water Pollution Control Administration in the Department of the Interior. This law gave the states two years in which to establish standards and procedures for enforcement. Also, the government has begun to enforce Section 407 of Title 33 of the Refuse Act of 1899. This old, almost forgotten law prohibits deposit of "any refuse matter of any kind" in navigable waters.

Government, however, has not been the only segment of society that has been active in pollution abatement. Business, too, has tried to make improvements. The most publicized efforts, of course, have been the rather extensive attempts by the automobile companies to answer the criticism that has been leveled against the automobile. Ford and General Motors have both increased their spending on pollution research severalfold in the past few years.

Moreover, in September 1971, the Environment Protection Agency a recently created agency that has powers and responsibilities in broad sectors of the area of environmental control—and Ford jointly announced that an experimental engine had been developed. This engine would

TABLE 19–3

Pollution control expenditures, 1971 and 1981

	1971 total costs	1981 est. total costs
Air pollution:		
Public	200 million	1.2 billion
Private	1.9 billion	16.2 billion
Water pollution		
Public		
Federal	n.a.	n.a.
State and local	5 billion	9.6 billion
Private	1 billion	6.2 billion
Radiation	n.a.	200 million
Solid waste		
Public	1.2 billion	2.1 billion
Private	2 billion	3.2 billion
Land reclamation	n.a.	800 million
Grand Totals	11.3 billion	39.5 billion

Note: n.a. means data not available.

allow the auto manufacturers to meet the rigid standards that the new laws are going to require. The engine is still experimental, and some concern has been expressed about its availability by 1975. Still, however, the prospect is promising that in the not-too-distant future, this major source of pollution will be controlled.

Other industries, moreover, have achieved equally impressive results. The steel industry has been working on pollution abatement for almost 20 years. Today, the industry is beginning to reap the benefits of some of its research. U.S. Steel, for example, recovers almost 60 tons of sulfur daily from one of its Pittsburgh plants. Indeed, the area of pollution control has grown so rapidly that whole industries are developing as a result of it. As

FIGURE 19–4

Vehicle emissions

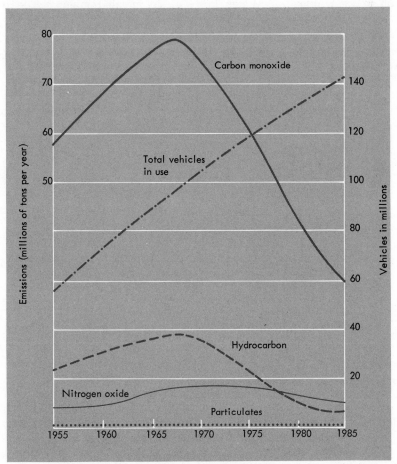

Source: Environmental Conservation, *The Oil and Gas Industries*, Vol. 1 National Petroleum Council, June 1971.

industry increases its efforts—particularly in air pollution control—it seems likely that more profitable means will be discovered to aid business in resolving this problem.

In other ways, too, business has been active in pollution control. Weyerhauser, the large paper and pulp company, has spent millions developing a "laboratory in the woods" in the state of Washington. Florida Power and Light has shown its concern for the environment by building a wildlife refuge around one of its nuclear power plants in southern Florida. Anaconda Copper has even planted shrubbery and trees around some of its dumping areas near Tucson, Arizona, in an attempt to hide from view the unsightly picture that most dumps and dumping areas present. Even newspapers have gotten into the act. Two in particular—the *Milwaukee Journal* and the *Louisville Courier-Journal*—were cited for their efforts at preventing strip mining. In all, industry spent an estimated $1.86 billion on treating industrial wastes in 1974. Yet much remains to be done.

FIGURE 19–5

Cost of treating industrial waste (capital investment* and operating expenses, 1971 dollars)

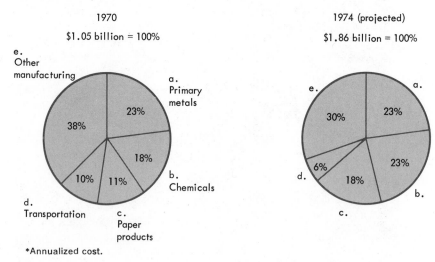

1970
$1.05 billion = 100%

1974 (projected)
$1.86 billion = 100%

*Annualized cost.

Can business solve the problem alone?

The degree of involvement by business in the resolution of this problem is really quite significant. In a recent survey by *Fortune* Magazine, it was revealed that a full 10 percent of the capital budgets of large corporations is being used for pollution control equipment. Still, great doubts remain—both in government circles and among the average consumers. A recent survey of the largest corporations in America showed that most business executives felt the government would have to do more to assist corporations in solving the problems. Many of the executives wanted, for example, some kind of tax adjustments made for the expenditures they incurred in abating pollution. The costs of developing pollution abatement equipment is quite high, and given the competitive nature of our society, has resulted in a reluctance by some business executives to spend the money necessary to control pollution.. Many executives fear that competitors might not use their funds in a similar manner and would thus gain a competitive advantage. Moreover, most of these executives did not feel that the answer was to pass the costs on to the public in the form of higher prices.

Consumers take a somewhat different view of the whole problem. Many of them feel businesses *have* passed the cost of pollution equipment on in the form of higher prices. Moreover, many of them are not at all convinced that business has done all it can to help solve the problem. In a recent poll, people felt the four major problems currently facing the American consumer were (*a*) air pollution, (*b*) water pollution, (*c*) inflation, and (*d*) litter and solid waste disposal. These same individuals felt —by a five-to-one plurality—that business firms were not doing a very good job at controlling pollution. While this is a disturbing statistic to say the least, it is worthwhile to note another aspect of that figure. Consider, for a moment, what the state of concern was just a few short years ago. A few years ago, many people were learning what pollution was for the first time—no one really cared before. This was true for business firms as well as consumers. Just think how far we as a society have come in just a few short years. Business has made great strides at solving the problem. And the mass population has made great strides in understanding the seriousness of the problem, as is evidenced by their unwillingness to settle for anything less than full control of the problem. What we need now, perhaps, is a better understanding of the problems business firms face as they attempt to continue to solve the pollution problem. Perhaps the difficulty they now confront can best be portrayed by two quotes: one from a leading environmental advocate, and the other from a leading industrialist:

> When effluents from a paper mill can be drunk and exhaust from factory smokestacks can be breathed, then man will have done a good job in saving the environment.
> *Jacques Cousteau, Los Angeles Times, November 23, 1971*

> Cousteau himself, breathes in air with 21% oxygen and exhales it with 17%. He drinks water with perhaps 20 ppm. dissolved solids and releases it with perhaps 20,000 ppm. No living animal can meet his criteria. It is equally unrealistic to expect it of industry.
> ——*E. G. Lowell, Los Angeles Times, December 30, 1971*

One final consideration: Profits

Regardless, however, of the method employed to achieve an effective pollution-controlled society, most executives felt it was necessary to get involved. Indeed, over 80 percent of them put the protection of the environment over and above the earning of higher profits as desirable and necessary goals. This is particularly interesting, given the role and interests of the stockholder affecting the practices of corporations in society.

This last point brings out an interesting question regarding the real motivation behind business' involvement in the pollution abatement problem. That question concerns the issue of profits. Many people believe that business has been a reluctant partner in the fight on pollution, primarily because investment in abatement equipment tends to be nonprofitable. A recent survey, however, has cast serious question on the validity of that belief.

In August 1971, *Business Week* reported that a survey of 17 companies in the paper and pulp industry showed that companies with low profits tended to be high polluters, while companies that have been active in pollution control have also been among the leaders, profitability-wise, in the industry. This is certainly an unexpected development, at least as far as many in our society are concerned. Apparently, concluded the article, those businesses that showed and demonstrated a social concern for the environment possessed managers who were progressive and forward looking—managers who saw problems as challenges and not as obstacles. This attitude, of course, is essential to all successful business executives, not just those interested in the environment. However, by possessing such intelligent and aggressive officers, these socially progressive firms were also the marketing progressive ones—the businesses that thought first of the customer and strove in every way possible to win the customer's allegiance. Herein, perhaps, lies the reason why we have bothered to introduce these "social problems" in a business context after all. By becoming aware of the broader problems facing society and business, we may all gain the ability to recognize the problems facing society today as challenges that will face the business community tomorrow. If so, then all society—business included—gains.

DISCUSSION QUESTIONS

1 In what way has the "consumerism" movement created a dilemma for business?

2 What is the meaning of *caveat emptor*? Is it a meaningful business practice or code today?

3 In what ways has technology complicated the life of consumers? In what ways has technology caused problems for the maintenance of a clean environment?

4 Do you think we as consumers would be better off if our society was less technology oriented? Why or why not?

5 Land use is a term that only recently has come into popular usage. Identify instances in your community where "land use" is an important ecological factor.

6 Why have consumers lacked, from a historical standpoint, an effective advocate in Washington? Is the situation different in our present-day society? Explain.

7 The automobile is often singled out as the largest single source of air pollution. Do you agree? In what ways might such a statement be misleading?

8 Why has business been slow in recognizing and correcting the problems of pollution?

MINI CASES

William C. Barton, president of Barton Cake Mixes, was attempting to find a way to cut costs for his business. Profits had been declining in the past few years, primarily because of the increased popularity of frozen cakes and pastries. As a result, Mr. Barton saw a program of cost cutting as being one way to improve his company's profitability.

One cost-cutting technique that had particular appeal to Mr. Barton involved the standardizing of all cake mix packages. At the present time, his cake mixes came in 14 different-sized packages. This was because of a difference in the ingredients in each cake mix. Some cake mixes, for example, required two eggs and one cup of milk, while others didn't. Consequently, the sizes of the packages needed tended to differ.

Mr. Barton, therefore, proposed developing one size of package for all the cake mixes. Although some of the packages would have less content in them than others, he felt it really didn't matter, since the package ingredients would, in each case, make up into a standard-sized cake.

On checking with various package suppliers, however, Mr. Barton discovered that what he proposed doing was in violation of the Truth-in-Packaging law. Those packages that were not full would be deceptive, and therefore illegal. Mr. Barton protested furiously at what he considered an unfair law.

1. *Do you agree with Mr. Barton's feeling about the fairness of the law?*

2. *Can you think of any way Mr. Barton might solve his problem and still develop a uniform-sized package for all of his cake mixes?*

In the late 1960s, Procter & Gamble Company, the world's largest manufacturer of soaps and detergents, found itself confronted with a major problem. The government had just determined that one of the major ingredients in detergents—phosphates—was a prime cause of water pollution. Given the state of concern over pollution at that time, numerous zealots were proposing legislation to force the removal of all products containing phosphates from the market.

To protect itself, and to answer the critics' objections to phosphates, Procter & Gamble spent large amounts of money on a crash program to find a substitute. So, too, did the other large soap manufacturers. In the early 1970s, they finally uncovered a substance known at NTA. NTA had all of the qualities of phosphate insofar as a detergent additive was concerned but none of the drawbacks. Relieved at the prospect of a solution to their problem, the manufacturers quickly substituted NTA for phosphate in their detergents.

In late 1971, two scientists—operating independently in their own lab—injected NTA into a large group of rats. The experiment resulted in the death of the rats. The scientists concluded that, because NTA was harmful if taken internally, soap manufacturers should not be allowed to use NTA in their product.

Discuss the "social responsibility" of the soap manufacturers in finding chemical ingredients for their product.

The business incident that follows is a true—although tragic—story. It actually occurred in early 1972.

There is, in the city of El Paso, Texas, a small section of the city that is commonly known as "Smeltertown." The name is really quite apt, for it is the home area for one of the nation's largest copper and lead smelting complexes. In the vicinity reside approximately 600 Mexican-Americans. The area has long been poverty-stricken, and lacks paved streets, garbage collection, sewers and street lights. The City Fathers of El Paso have long ignored the area. The only assistance the residents of the area have received have come from the smelting complex, which has provided water to the community, rebuilt its church, and in other ways tried to help the residents.

Pollution from the smelters has long been a problem for the company. Indeed, the efforts at cleaning the environment trace all the way back to 1917, when the company first installed air pollution equipment. In just the recent past, the company has made even greater strides. Lead emissions have fallen over fivefold just since 1970, and were promised to fall another fivefold later in 1972, when a new $18 million addition went into operation. None of this, however, was able to avert a real tragedy from occurring in Smeltertown.

In early 1972, 70 children in the Smeltertown region were found to have abnormally high levels of lead in their blood. In effect, they had acute lead poisoning. The company was shocked, for it thought adequate safeguards against air pollution had been taken. Then it discovered the shocking truth: the lead poisoning was not a direct result of air pollution from the company's smokestacks. Rather, it was caused by the wind stirring up the accumulated lead that had fallen to the ground over the years. In effect, it was a kind of "soil pollution" that was causing the trouble. The company and the town wondered what to do about the problem.

1. *What would you suggest be done to solve the problem?*
2. *Was the company negligent for not protecting against this problem?*

Hallmark Cards, Inc., is a classic example of a large, profitable corporation that has decided that being a good corporate citizen is a responsibility that goes hand in hand with profitability.

Hallmark Cards was the outgrowth of an early wholesale business begun by Joyce Hall and his two brothers in 1910. During that time, Joyce Hall became intrigued with the idea of making greeting cards that the average person could afford. Until that time, greeting cards were trimmed in lace, engraved, and generally expensive. Hall persuaded a bank to loan him $25,000 to recover from a disastrous fire in 1915; and thus was born the Hallmark Card Co. By 1930, the company had sales of $3.5 million. At the present time, annual sales are estimated to run $350 million.

Hallmark Cards remains today one of the largest privately held corporations in America. As such, the company is relatively free to pursue those practices of corporate citizenship it deems worthy, regardless of cost or stockholder concern. And Hallmark has done just that. Since 1951, Hallmark has produced a series of television specials known as the Hallmark Hall of Fame. The cost to produce this series has run over $50 million, and despite relatively mediocre ratings, the company announced in 1972 plans to continue the series for at least ten more years at a cost estimated at $60 million.

Perhaps the greatest achievement, however, has been the creation of Crown Center in Kansas City. This $400 million real estate venture involved the redevelopment of 23 square city blocks, and houses office buildings, banks, apartment houses, stores, a 730 room hotel and more. It has won praise for its architectural beauty. Eventually, the project will become profitable, but officials estimate it will take at least twice as long as most real estate ventures. Hallmark is convinced of its merits, however, and the project is given credit for sparking a plan to revive Kansas City's decaying downtown area.

Hallmark Cards, Inc.

A company with a social conscience

20

Contemporary problems in business and society

*Before I built a wall,
I'd ask to know what I was
walling in or walling out.*
——*Robert Frost*

The preceding 19 chapters of this book have attempted to put into perspective the problems, challenges, and opportunities facing the modern business establishment. We began by examining the historical development of business. Our attempt to put business into a philosophical framework consistent with the philosophies that have been, and still are, prevalent in society. As we approach the close, we have been looking at the issue of "social responsibility" in detail. Indeed, societal considerations have constantly reemerged throughout the text as we discussed questions relating to businesses ethics, philosophies, and practices. In the last three chapters, we have attempted to explore the specific responsibilities facing business in its relations with its most important "publics," namely the stockholders, the government, the consumers, and labor.

In some ways, however, a discussion of these "publics" and their relationships with business does not fully reveal the scope of business in our modern society. We need to look beyond the isolated relationships of one interest group with another and examine the broader problems that confront all of these publics simultaneously. For they have the potential of pulling down the entire economic, political, and societal fabric of our society unless they are resolved. These problems—the problems of the hardcore unemployed and racial discrimination; of business' involvement with rural poverty and urban decay, and of the problems facing our many social institutions, such as education and the arts—are the fundamental problems facing our society today. As such, they are the basic problems facing business. For as we have seen, business is inseparable from our complex social network. An examination of these problems, therefore, and their particular challenge to the business community, is the objective of this chapter.

THE PROBLEMS IN PERSPECTIVE

Most of us are already all too familiar with the problems we are about to discuss. Substandard housing, lack of jobs, racial discrimination, poor education, and the like, have been in the news constantly. Since the riots in the Watts community of Los Angeles first shook the country in 1965, attention has been focused on the plight of minority groups. Government has poured billions upon billions of dollars in recent years into discovering the factors that were responsible for this tragedy, and into the search for a cure of these causes. To date, its efforts have been highly publicized, but the results have been meager, at best. Indeed, in some ways, the problems have worsened, as the best laid plans of humans have gotten hopelessly enveloped in the red tape of bureaucracy. We have seen countless government agencies and projects come and go over the few years since the problems of our domestic society have been made apparent. Each time, the project or program seems to have the highest of ideals and goals. But, each time the glamour and hopes of the agency seem to fade into obscruity.

It is at this point that society, government, and the business community have found themselves wondering why these massive projects haven't worked. Why have they, with just a few notable exceptions—all ended in much the same way as the hopes of those the programs were intended to help, ended?

This is a question we are still trying to answer. Parts of the answer are known, of course, and it is because of those "part answers" that business has suddenly found itself thrust into the center of the effort to resolve these issues.

Identifying the problems

Identifying the real problems facing our society is not quite as easy as it may at first seem. Certainly housing, jobs, racial discrimination, and so on, are problems in society—problems which we all recognize. Indeed, it is these problems and their relationship to the business community that we are going to examine in more depth. This does not, however, preclude the possibility that other problems exist which underly the more obvious and visible ones of poverty, unemployment, and the like. In some ways the new technology that we are witnessing in business and government is itself at fault. This technology has given us many benefits, to be sure. But it has also resulted in large-scale impersonalization in society. And it has contributed to the insecurity felt by many in society as they see their jobs made obsolete by machines. It has also led to greater consumption of goods and services than we have been able to provide.

This technology, moreover, has had as a by-product an increasing alienation of various people in society. As machines are developed that can perform more and more jobs, people find themselves shifted to new positions, retired early, or in some way removed from the productive mainstream of society. Even the young find it increasingly difficult to relate to the demands of our new technological age. Where once a college degree was considered a noteworthy achievement and a ticket to economic success, today it is a necessity—particularly in society's view. Indeed, even with a college degree, graduates have seen with dismay in their eyes, the signs go up announcing the fact that their degree alone no longer guarantees them a position as productive members of society.

Put in this perspective, the problems facing our society seem impossibly complex. How does one train a hardcore unemployed person, for example, to compete effectively in a world where college graduates can't find work? Yet, start we must, and the place to begin is most logically with those who have been most alienated from our economic society: the poor, the disadvantaged, the unemployed.

The poor Perhaps the best way to begin to understand the difficulties we face in resolving some of these problems is to try to determine who the poor are. We begin by trying to define poverty.

One way to define poverty is in terms of the population as a whole. That is, we can say that 30 percent of our population is poverty-stricken. The trouble with this idea, however, is that if we only isolate a set percentage at the bottom, there will *always* be 30 percent of the population so classed. Whenever we determine who is poor by comparing them with others who are not poor, we are making the question of "poverty" a relative one. Someone will always be "poorer" than someone else.

We may also define the poverty-stricken in terms of dollars and cents. If, however, we do, then many retired and elderly people who sustain themselves quite nicely on a minimum income will be classed as poor. So too, will numerous young people, particularly college students who maintain their own residences—with their parents' help—in dorms or apartments. Yet, a glance at many student parking lots quickly belies the "poverty" of this class of citizens. They may not be rich, but most cannot be considered "poor" in the social sense.

Although the problem of identifying the poor is a real one, and subject to considerable debate, government has been forced to assign an arbitrary definition to the term *poor* in order to put its programs into effect. The guidelines as developed by the Council of Economic Advisors, and in use in 1973, can be seen in Table 20–1. Using these guidelines,

TABLE 20-1

Low income levels, 1973

Household characteristic	Low income line
Nonfarm households:	
1 member	$2,044
Under 65 years	2,092
2 members	2,534
Head 65 years and over	2,349
Head Under 65 years	2,619
3 members	3,113
4 members	3,970
5 members	4,684
6 members	5,263
7 members or more	6,486
Farm households:	
1 member	1,697
65 years and over	1,597
Under 65 years	1,778
2 members	2,138
Head 65 years and over	1,996
Head Under 65 years	2,225
3 members	2,635
4 members	3,387
5 members	4,002
6 members	4,491
7 members or more	5,521

Note: Unfortunately, these guidelines are expressed in terms of dollars. One could just as easily construct a set of guide lines identifying the poor on the basis of age, education, sex, health, and numerable other characteristics. The reader is. therefore, cautioned about the limitations of judging the poor on the basis of any one criterion.
Source: U.S. Bureau of the Census.

we will be able to see more clearly the extent of poverty in our society (see Figure 20-1).

The poverty problem, moreover, merely underscores still another problem in our society: that of racial discrimination. While over 70 percent of all poor families were white, the fact that there are predominately more whites than other racial groups far outweighs that statistic. Actually, the incidence of poverty among white households is one in seven, while that among nonwhite households is one in three. Indeed, the racial lines among people at the poverty level have been rather sharply drawn. Puerto Ricans, for example, constitute only 8 percent of New York's population, but comprise 33 percent of its recipients of welfare.

The disadvantaged Poverty in our society can also be seen as a characteristic of those deemed *disadvantaged*. This term has been much abused in recent years, but still is perhaps the most succinct word to describe those who have lacked—*for reasons not of their own making*—the same opportunities and advantages as the majority of our society. Generally speaking, people termed *disadvantaged* usually have been

FIGURE 20–1

Number of poor persons

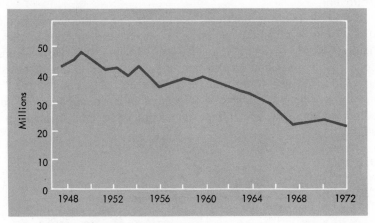

Source: *Economic Report of the President.*

"socially disadvantaged." That is, usually the nature of their handicap is due to societal causes rather than biological or mental. Such people, for example, have never been exposed to the cultural enrichment of the arts and sciences or enabled to develop marketable skills. Nor have they been taught the requisites of life in our society. Rather, they have grown up somewhat isolated or removed from the mainstream of the dominant culture. They have developed their own code of social conduct, and frequently it is at odds with that of the majority in recognized society.

Most often, the "disadvantaged" are members of minority races. Thus, we hear frequent mention made of the problems confronting the urban blacks or Mexican-Americans, whose lives have been one of survival on a day-to-day basis. Meanwhile, their white counterparts have enjoyed the benefits of a stable home environment, good clothes and food, and cultural enrichment brought about because of their parents' social acceptance. Who can deny the difficulties that face minority groups today? How many well-known blacks, Mexican-Americans, or American Indians can you name whose fame was earned in something other than sports or entertainment? Where are the "idols" that small kids of minority groups can look up to? What is the heritage of the blacks and Mexican-Americans in the area of business? Yes, a disadvantaged people do exist, and the depth of their disadvantage underlies still other problems, in particular, that of employment.

The unemployed A third major problem confronting those at the poverty level is that of unemployment. If people are unemployed or unable to find work, they have in effect been rejected as useful components in the productive processes of our economy. Unable to find employment, these people become wards of the state, diverting tax dollars from other uses, such as finding a cure for cancer, or the advancement of education.

Although it might seem that identifying the unemployed would be the easiest task of all, problems exist which tend to conceal the real difficulty. Who, for example, qualifies as "unemployed"? Do we consider college students seeking employment in the summer as unemployed? Do we consider the well-to-do and the retired as being unemployed? How about those who are seeking employment in an occupation no longer needing workers, but who refuse to accept other jobs in lower paying positions?

TABLE 20–2

Selected unemployment rates (percent)

	All workers	White	Nonwhite
1950.....................	5.3	4.9	9.0
1952.....................	3.0	2.8	5.4
1954.....................	5.5	5.0	9.9
1956.....................	4.1	3.6	8.3
1958.....................	6.8	6.1	12.6
1960.....................	5.5	4.9	10.2
1962.....................	5.5	4.9	10.9
1964.....................	5.2	4.6	9.6
1966.....................	3.8	3.3	7.3
1968.....................	3.6	3.2	6.7
1970.....................	4.9	4.5	5.2
1972.....................	5.6	5.0	10.0
1974 est..................	7.1	5.0	9.8

Again, the federal government has had to compromise these various classes of "unemployed" persons. In so doing, it has resolved to consider as unemployed all able-bodied men and women actively seeking full-time employment. Such a definition excludes students who are seeking part-time employment. Also, it omits those who are retired or otherwise not seeking jobs. It also leaves out those who have given up all hope of finding jobs and who have consequently stopped looking. And it disregards those who had to settle for part-time work. Part-time employees are not considered unemployed, even if they are earning a wage so low as to abort all attempts to rise above the poverty class.

Unemployment, like poverty and economic disadvantage, tends to follow racial lines also. The rate of unemployment among nonwhite is more than twice the rate among whites. Further, the changing technology we mentioned earlier tends to work more against the nonwhites than the whites, primarily because of differences in income and the degree of social advantage enjoyed by the whites.

Perhaps the best summary of just how complex the problem really is was given by the late Whitney Young, who once described his efforts at finding a beginning or starting point to the problems facing society. Seeing the poor state of the average housing lived in by the black man, Mr. Young went to the real estate agent to see why the blacks didn't have better housing. He was told it was because they couldn't afford better houses. The logical place to inquire about the low pay—and subsequently the inability of the black to buy a better house—was with business. Mr. Young, therefore, went to an employer asking why the employer didn't give the poor black man a higher paying job. The business leader replied that he would, except that the black man lacked the education necessary to meet the job requirements. This seemed logical enough, so Mr. Young then went to the school, where he sought reasons for the black man's relative inability to improve himself educationally. He was told that the cultural disadvantage borne by the blacks was too great to overcome; that the blacks would need to move out of the central city to a new home and a different cultural environment.

But that, said Mr. Young, requires that he have better housing, something he can't get because he lacks money, which he can't get because he lacks skills, and so on. A vicious circle has been formed. This fact must be recognized as business attempts to help solve this most urgent problem of our society.

BUSINESS AND OUR URBAN PROBLEMS

Given this preliminary introduction to the complex problem we face, we can now begin a detailed examination of the part business has played thus far in the search for answers to these problems. In so doing, we shall examine several company cases of actual business involvement. These cases are mentioned, not because they are unique, for they are not. Rather, they are presented as mere examples of what industry can do, is doing, and may do in this vital area of concern.

Minority groups and the business community

In 1882, a southern white journalist and novelist by the name of George Washington Cable observed that at the rate the racial problem was being handled we would get to the moon before we reached a solution.[1] Mr. Cable proved to be an excellent prophet. Blame, of course, cannot be thrust upon any one institution or segment of society, nor should it be. All segments have contributed to racial difficulties—business, government,

---

[1] Eli Ginsberg, "American Democracy and the Negro," in Eli Ginsberg, ed., *The Negro Challenge to the Business Community* (New York: McGraw-Hill Book Co., 1964).

labor, the whites, the blacks, and others. All segments of society, however, are not as equally endowed with the ability to overcome the difficulties. Only a few of these groups or segments actually possess the power and strength to make a significant start. Business, as it develops, is one of those few institutions.

Early background   Prior to the Watts riots of 1965, few businesses concerned themselves about the plight of the minority worker. This apparent neglect was not, understand, a deliberate callousness on the part of business executives. Rather, this indifference existed because executives thought of the problem as one that fell outside the proper scope of business activity. It was a moral issue, and as such one to be resolved by churches, schools, and private or government programs. For this reason, most executives tended to consider racial inequalities as outside the scope of their activity.

Actually, it's hard to fault business for this lack of concern, for this attitude was prevalent throughout all of our society. Educational institutions did little or nothing about overcoming the cultural biases of their I.Q. tests and entrance examinations. Governments, too, did little in the way of developing programs to help minority groups improve their station in life. Even churches reacted rather passively to racial injustices. Indeed, business—with its impartial approach to the problem—may well have been the most equitable of the institutions just named in their treatment of minority groups. Business executives, after all was said and done, were still prone to act in a way that would enable them to earn more profit. If they could see gains for themselves in providing opportunities for minority groups, they were quick to do so. The dollar sign proved to be a powerful equalizer to racial prejudice. Kenneth Clark, noted black psychologist, confirms this conclusion. Business, he has said, is perhaps the least segregated, least discriminatory and most fair of all the areas of our society —including government, unions, schools and churches.

Business motives for social involvement

Business' motives, to be sure, are not all altruistic. Business has a lot to gain by aiding the minority groups. Minority groups, of which the two largest are the blacks and the Mexican-Americans, constitute a large potential market. By improving the lot of these people, business gains in many ways—not the least of which is profit. Consider, for example, the problems confronting the minority group members living in the inner city. Slums and the problems that go with them tend, over the years, to siphon off corporate profits via higher tax bills and higher insurance rates. By correcting the conditions in these areas, business not only can realize increased sales, but lower taxes as well. It has been estimated that city ghettos alone will require 10 million new homes between now and the year 2000.

Such a private motivation by various sectors of our economy may prove more successful than government efforts, which seem to some to foist charity on members of minority groups. Mexican-Americans, blacks, the American Indian, and other ethnic minorities—just as the average white—resent the belittling that accompanies such charitable actions. Pride is a powerful motivator among people, and business' motives in aiding the minority groups is consistent with that pride. It's not a question of "What do you expect out of it?", but rather, one of . . . "You know what I'm after—if you gain, I gain." One thing business can't be accused of is having ulterior motives. It wears its motives on the last line of 'its income statement.

As we have said, business senses a large market in the improvement of the minority groups. Blacks, for example, constitute some 14 percent of our population—roughly 30 million people. Mexican-Americans constitute another substantial portion. Any improvement in their standard of living would have significant meaning to business. The average Mexican-American, for example, earns an income that is less than 70 percent of that earned by the average (median) in the United States as a whole. Yet, their unemployment rate runs double the national average—as does that for the black citizens of our country. Most significantly, perhaps, is the fact that the Mexican-American citizens possess no significant middle or upper class, as does the black. There are literally no precedents for success in business. Consider, for example, the fact that of 13,500 banks in the United States, only a handful are owned by Mexican-Americans! Moreover, only 1 percent of the nation's business as a whole are owned by them—and these are all small. Small wonder that the Mexican-American feels alienated from society! So rare are occasions where Mexican-Americans achieve business success that when a MacDonald's hamburger franchise was granted to a Mexican-American in San Antonio, Texas, it was hailed as a major breakthrough.

Why business needs to get involved

As has been indicated, business has historically approached the spectrum of social involvement from the viewpoint of self-interest. Today, however, more and more business leaders are realizing the need to transcend the profit motive in business. As Henry Ford II said in an address at the Harvard Business School Public Affairs Forum in 1969:

> Industry has succeeded by specializing in serving one narrow segment of society's needs. We have bought labor and material and sold goods, and we have assumed that our obligations were limited to the terms of the

bargain. Now we are being asked to serve a wider range of human values and to accept an obligation to members of the public with whom we have no commercial transactions. We are being asked to contribute more to the quality of life than mere quantities of goods.[2]

THE PROBLEMS FACING MINORITY GROUPS

Urban dwellers at the poverty level usually are confronted with three distinct, yet interrelated, problems. These are (*a*) a lack of employment, (*b*) poor housing, and (*c*) lack of an education. Whitney Young's commentary on the vicious circle illustrates how these problems are related. Yet, for business or, indeed, for any institution to find satisfactory answers to these problems, they must be examined on an individual basis.

Employment, jobs, and black capitalism

Unemployment is one of the big problems facing our society today. The experiences of the early 1970s have made all Americans conscious of its seriousness. What is perhaps most tragic, however, is the fact that unemployment has fallen disproportionately on those people that can least afford to be unemployed: the blacks, the Mexican-Americans, and the uneducated in our society. The unemployment rate among blacks, for example, runs well in excess of 20 percent in many parts of the country today. The situation is even worse among the Mexican-Americans who, it has been estimated, suffer an unemployment rate as high as 40 percent in some parts of the Southwest.

Such conditions obviously must be corrected, and it would seem that business is in the best position to aid. It is comforting to note that business has willingly accepted this responsibility and has made major steps toward providing solutions. In 1966, for example, the Watts riots startled our sleeping society into a realization of the extent of joblessness among blacks, particularly the young. Immediately thereafter, Aerojet-General Corporation helped establish a manufacturing business in the heart of Watts. This business—operated by and for blacks under the guidance of Aerojet-General—began doing contract work for Aerojet and other businesses. Within five years, the Watts manufacturing company was operating on its own, free of Aerojet-General's influence, and was employing over 350 people from the Watts community. The company stands today as an outstanding example of corporate assistance in the providing of respectable employment for minority groups. It also serves as an example of one type of "Black Capitalism" in entrepreneurship of, by, and for blacks. Since then, of course, numerous instances of business' assistance to various minority groups can be found. Scores of companies

---

[2] Speech titled "Business, the Environment and the Quality of Life," delivered in Boston, Mass., December 2, 1969.

now provide "seed money"—initial capital aimed at enabling small businesses to get started—to various minority interests. Even banks have become involved, with one large bank going so far as to make an admittedly very risky loan of over $5 million to a Chicano organization for the construction of low-cost housing.

These examples notwithstanding, business' real involvement with jobs for minorities began in 1968, following a meeting between top business leaders and the president. The meeting resulted in the creation of the National Alliance of Businessmen, a private-public cooperative effort to place 500,000 of the hardcore unemployed (those lacking the educational skills and suffering the cultural disadvantages that often restrict social acceptance) in jobs in industry by 1971. The program proved to be a tremendous success. Over 20,000 business firms joined the effort *the first year* and pledged over 300,000 new jobs! Almost 270,000 people were put in these jobs, and over 142,000 of them remained on the job after the first year—a retention rate that equaled that of the non-disadvantaged, new white employee. In other words, business had successfully found ways of overcoming many of the unusual problems and obstacles that had previously hampered the employment of these people. What is interesting, too, was that the cost of training and hiring the hard-core unemployed, although high (often running as high as $3,000 per employee), was borne primarily by business. Three-fourths of those placed in jobs were placed there at company expense.

While this major effort was going on, other businesses and business-related organizations were making their own efforts at solving the problem. Ford, in an attempt to alleviate the condition that resulted in Detroit's massive riots a few years ago, announced it would hire inner-city people for jobs at its plants in southeast Michigan. Expecting 100 people to apply, Ford was shocked when over 4,000 applied on the first day. Bethlehem Steel Corporation hired virtually all of the workers at its Burns Harbor, Indiana, plant from those totally unskilled in steel work. Today, it is finding several lines of unskilled production workers outperforming engineering specifications for their jobs. Similarly, New York Life Insurance Company developed a program to train keypunch operators. While it had need for only a few of those people it trained, the Urban League easily found jobs for the rest.

Still, problems exist that hamper the achievement of full success in this massive employment effort. Operation Bootstrap, an effort designed to train Watts area blacks in the professions, found that jobs were being filled by whites who had become unemployed as the economy dipped into the recent recession. Although such competition for work is the ultimate aim of these programs, the failure to immediately place a large percent of the newly trained blacks created a morale problem for the endeavor.

In Chicago, business executives active in the Alliance of Businessmen programs designed to attack the problems of welfare and unemployment, found themselves confronting unexpected obstacles, such as the lack of transportation facilities and the lack of day-care centers. To overcome these obstacles, some executives provided bus service to get inner-city blacks to the suburban factories. Creation of day-care centers proved more difficult, however, because of state and local zoning laws, ordinances, and code requirements. Indeed, problems concerning child-care or day-care centers can prove particularly troublesome, since many inner-city families require the employment of the mother in order to lift the family out of the poverty class. Sometimes it requires a particularly novel approach to correct some of these obstacles. In Brooklyn, for example, one group of homemakers that formed their own child-care, day-care center, soon found themselves in the restaurant business. As their initial activities expanded, suddenly an eating facility became a profitable business enterprise.

Job requirements, and the red tape necessary to create new jobs and fill them, similarly has taken its toll on the ultimate success of business' endeavors. The director of Chicago's "Jobs Now" program once griped that he had kids who could strip a car in 10 minutes but couldn't pass the written test for a mechanic apprenticeship program. Indeed, the resistance of many craft unions to the admission of inner-city minority groups to their ranks has been a major problem. Kenneth Clark, in fact, openly criticized organized labor a few years ago for its lack of help in the providing of jobs and apprenticeships. Now, however, even labor is getting actively involved. The East Los Angeles Community Union, a self-help association sponsored by the United Auto Workers, has developed a small but growing business in the heart of a sprawling Mexican-American community known as the *barrio*. This business endeavor today counts a mattress manufacturing company and a service station among its many activities.

Finally, many firms are discouraged from engaging in job training efforts for basic reasons of business. In Watts, for example, a large industrial park stands empty of major businesses—simply because no business wants to accept the high insurance costs that location in that area would entail. Moreover, some companies have been concerned about the reaction of their stockholders, many of whom have become particularly resentful toward the racial conflict that exists in some parts of the land.

Housing and urban development

A second area that business has become active in is the area of housing and urban development. At first glance, this might appear to be one aspect of the total problem that is of least concern to business.

Rather, it might seem to be the particular area of interest for cities and other governmental associations. After all, business pays taxes to help government at all levels solve the problems facing it. Isn't urban renewal, then, one of these areas? Certainly, a strong case can be made for this point of view. Indeed, some business leaders have echoed such sentiments, particularly in view of the fact that they pay approximately 50 percent of their total income as taxes.

For the most part, however, business leaders today have ceased to oppose urban renewal. Cities have proven themselves unable to satisfactorily solve housing and other problems of disadvantaged groups. And problems exist! Urban transportation, housing, slum clearance, poor schools, lack of police protection, and more, make demands on the limited resources of the cities. As a result, the efforts of municipalities have, for the most part, gone unnoticed over time. The problems remain, and indeed, have been growing steadily worse.

Business, beginning to experience a desire to improve its own future prospects, has witnessed firsthand the consequences of urban decay. As cities deteriorated, more and more businesses began leaving the city, leaving behind large numbers of now unemployed people, higher welfare costs, and higher taxes for those businesses that remained. Eventually, these firms would run out of places to go. Realizing this, businesses all across the country began to look anew at the problem, and in so doing, undertook still another challenge to the American enterprise system.

Early business involvement Ten years ago, few businesses engaged in any type of effort to alleviate the problems of the urban poor. For the most part, these problems were left to government and private organizations. Business exercised its role as a good citizen by dutifully contributing to the known and respected private organizations—the YMCA, the Boy Scouts, the Urban League—and left it to them to decide how to resolve these problems. Gradually, however, business came to realize that its "investment" in these fine groups wasn't generating the expected rewards. When Watts finally erupted, business realized—as did everybody else—that conditions of a substantial proportion needed desperately to be improved. Accordingly, business began searching for answers.

Actually, business has played a big role in accomplishing much of the progress that has been and is being achieved. As the largest taxpaying bloc in the inner city, many businesses find they are able to exert great pressures on local government to effect changes. Moreover, business leaders possess the one talent most needed in all of the various projects that have been developed to aid the urban poor—the talent of management. Business-sponsored organizations tend to be the most efficient of all such organizations at obtaining the desired results.

Recent developments In the last few years, scores of businesses have become active in trying to solve some of these problems. In the area of housing and urban development, numerous companies are active. General Electric has been trying to apply its aerospace technology to housing materials. Coca-Cola has provided low cost housing for the hundreds of migrant workers it employs in the Florida citrus belt. B. F. Goodrich has contributed over $4 million to the development of Opportunity Park in Akron, Ohio, a development area near its home quarters. Other companies, such as Armstrong Cork, Reynolds Metals, U.S. Steel, and Rockwell International, are also active in this regard. Also active with its own unique program is the Smith, Kline & French Laboratories in Philadelphia. Smith, Kline & French is unique in that, of the firms mentioned, it is one whose product line is not directly connected with housing. Smith, Kline & French, moreover, is managing a total program of urban renewal; the others are active in smaller, although just as meaningful, programs.

The Smith, Kline & French story Begun in the mid 1960s, Smith, Kline & French has attempted to provide housing, education, training, and information to residents of a neighboring section of Philadelphia known as Spring Gardens. As one of the largest taxpayers in Philadelphia, the company was able to pressure city officials into modifying its urban renewal programs in order to obtain certain economics and speed. Smith, Kline & French discovered, for example, that a good many of the houses in Spring Gardens were solid structures that had been allowed to fall into poor condition. It, therefore, acted as a liaison between contractors and the city to get the homes rennovated. Starting with an abandoned home, Smith, Kline & French arranged for it to be repaired, after which a neighbor was moved into the unit. (In this way, dislocation of people from their neighbors and friends was avoided.) The neighbor's house was then fixed, thereby freeing still another home to move local people into. Smith, Kline & French absorbed part of the financing costs of the repairs, with the city arranging for low rent payments to be made by the residents. The company also undertook the training of residents for new jobs and held classes on the fundamentals of reading and writing after hours in its plant. Why did Smith, Kline & French do all of this? Primarily because they found that their contributions to the various charitable causes weren't making any headway. They resolved that they could do just as well on their own. The results of this program show they were correct.

Smith, Kline & French is not the only firm with a real understanding of, and devotion to the solution of social problems. Hundreds of businesses all across the country have made similar commitments. Kodak and Xerox in Rochester, New York, have long been known for their concern over social conditions, and for the steps they have taken to alleviate problems in that city. Indeed, Xerox provides time off from work to employees wishing to become active in social causes. Leaves of absence can be given to as many as 40 employees annually, for periods of six months to one year. Xerox guarantees them their jobs on returning and will pay them their salary for the period of their leave. Elsewhere, U.S. Steel and the Urban League participated in the construction of a 550-unit housing development in Gary, Indiana. We could, of course, go on and on, but this would not further the point we are making. That point, of course, is that business *is* making an effort. Surprisingly, however, business has not been particularly quick to publicize that fact. Indeed, a group of graduate students from Stanford University recently sought to find out what business was doing in this area. When they discovered the extent of business' involvement, they were so stunned they set up a voluntary group that sought to aid other businesses in finding ways of helping. What had started off as a critical examination ended up as an assisting venture.

Problems encountered Business encountered many problems in this venture into the world of urban renewal, some of which led to great frustration. Although some of these problems were rather humorous, others were not quite so. For example, one company that was attempting to utilize modular room units in housing rehabilitation found—after having gutted the old buildings—that the streets were too narrow to get the giant cranes down them with the new room units. In another case, the trees and telephone wires caused massive problems in moving workers and machines. On the other side of the spectrum, moreover, are the very real problems of conflict between races and natural groups. In many neighborhoods where urban renewal projects are underway, tremendous rivalries and jealousies exist among the whites, blacks, Mexican-Americans, and Puerto Ricans. Businesses that get caught up in this conflict often show the scars of battle for some time to come. As former Health, Education, and Welfare Secretary Robert Finch put it, many businesses reacted with more energy than discretion to government pleas for help. Even the most resourceful and powerful companies have encountered difficulties.

Yet, the results of corporate participation are clearly evident. In a recent survey of 247 of America's largest companies, 201 currently had under way some form of urban affairs program. Figure 20–2 shows the organizational programs.

Business aid to education

A third aspect of business efforts to upgrade conditions in society concerns the area of education. Many businesses found themselves thrust into this area somewhat unexpectedly, as their training programs for the hardcore unemployed revealed a basic lack of education among those they were trying to train. Business was caught somewhat off guard by this problem, since it had little or no exposure to techniques for teaching elementary skills. The need, however, was obvious, as Kodak discovered

FIGURE 20–2

Location of urban affairs in the corporate organization chart

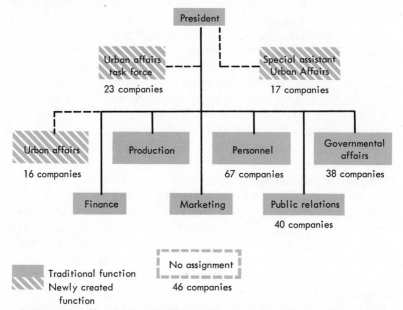

Source: Jules Cohn, "Is Business Meeting the Challenge of Urban Affairs?" *Harvard Business Review,* Vol. 48, No. 2 (March–April 1970), p. 78; based on McKinsey survey of 247 companies. Reprinted with permission.

early in its program. One employee to whom Kodak was giving on-the-job training was told to drill some holes in a piece of material, so that the holes were 1 foot apart. The employee was puzzled: he didn't know what a "foot apart" meant! Still another employee had to be taught how to use a ruler. As a result, businesses all across the land are today offering remedial classes in the three R's. This remedial educational assistance, moreover, is having an effect. Mr. Roger Cellar, former Civic Affairs Administrator at Smith, Kline & French, tells of one man who commented on his new "education." "This one fella said; 'I haven't had any opportunity to put this new arithmetic learning to use on the job, but I can tell you one thing. My wife spends a lot less money at the store because I go with her.' "[3]

Other companies are equally committed to improving the working skills of various minority groups. IBM operates a manufacturing facility in Brooklyn's black ghetto to provide jobs and executive training. Quaker Oats provides training to inner-city residents that will enable them to be-

[3] Quoted with permission of Roger Cellar and Smith, Kline and French, from a speech given at a Conference on Business and Society, at Northern Illinois University, February 27, 1969, the proceedings of which were subsequently published by the university.

come store managers. And Polaroid operates a subsidiary in Boston's black ghetto of Roxbury where over 243 "unemployable" workers have learned enough skills to move on to further employment with Polaroid and other firms.

In other ways, too, business has begun to aid education. Of course, we all know about corporate giving to institutions of higher learning. Corporations all across the land offer scholarships to colleges, match alumni donations, and provide financial grants to local colleges and universities. Such aid, of course, is vitally needed by colleges and universities today, and such corporate efforts as these certainly speak well of the caliber of people managing today's industries.

In examining their newfound responsibility to education, however, businesses active in the training of the hardcore unemployed have begun to look closely at their previous commitments to education. Many firms, for example, have grown critical of the educational system itself and point to the weaknesses of these hardcore unemployables in the basic skills as verifying that fact. Other businesses have seen education move farther and farther away from a meaningful role in solving society's needs. These business executives see a strong need for business guidance of educational institutions back toward a relevant role in society. As one executive has said: "Business leaders must take an active role in helping educational institutions relate to the community in the most desirable way."

What business has discovered, in fact, is that in our society, we have a situation where two different cultures are attempting to learn from a single educational system. Quite often, the inner-city youth possesses a value structure and social background completely different from that of the student from a suburban neighborhood. Since schools tend to emulate the suburban schools in philosophy and development, business saw that most of the inner-city schools were contributing to the "alienation" process, by teaching a culture that had no meaning to the students in the inner city. Business, as a consequence, began exploring new patterns of involvement in this area. Michigan Bell Telephone, for instance, found that a strong lack of association existed between what went on in the classroom of one Detroit High School and what the students really wanted to know. Consequently, it began offering classes of its own in the school, emphasizing job application techniques. In no time at all, the classes were jammed with students who wanted to get their first taste of "relevant" information from school.

In still other cases, business has developed radically new teaching aids for use in the classroom. Corn Products Corporation, Xerox Corporation, and many others have been instrumental in developing techniques for increasing a teacher's effectiveness. Unfortunately, many of these new techniques are still costly, and in some cases have actually put a strain on the financial resources of the school systems that have acquired them. Yet, it is a start, and one that has greatly broadened business' role in solving social problems.

We could, of course, continue indefinitely with our discussion of this important aspect of business' involvement in society. The law clinics that have been developed to aid the poor are but another example of the concern of business in this area. The point, however, has been made rather abundantly clear. Business *has* been active in the search for solutions to many social problems, and if its past abilities in the commercial fields are any indication, business will prove similarly successful in accomplishing its goals in the societal area as well.

BUSINESS AND THE ARTS

Providing aid to minority businesses, however, and contributing to the solution of problems of unemployment, housing, and education are not the only areas in which business has begun to exert an influence. It has also become a great benefactor to the arts and humanities of this country. In 1965, for example, business contributed almost $50 million to the support of the arts. By 1970, this support had reached $100 million. Today, businesses support symphony orchestras, provide concerts and art shows, and—to the extent that it can be considered a "cultural" event —finance and support professional sports teams.

Why does business support the arts?

To the skeptic, business supports the arts for one very tangible reason—it can be treated as a tax deduction. Closer examination of this aspect of corporate support of the arts, however, raises clear questions about the validity of this skepticism. It is true that contributions to qualified cultural organizations are tax deductible within certain limits. But from a corporate viewpoint, why should management be any more interested in supporting an opera, let's say, than supporting its government in Washington? Let's look at what admittedly is a hypothetical situation. Suppose for a moment that every large corporation in America decided to try to reduce its taxes by making large contributions to the support of the arts. If this happened, two things would immediately result. First, the arts would enjoy an unprecedented era of prosperity, and our society would probably witness a second "Renaissance." Second, corporate tax revenues received by the federal government would fall sharply, as this second most important source of revenue suddenly diminished in size. This second development would probably force one of two other developments to occur. Government, faced with a reduction of its revenues would have to (*a*) cut its support of projects aimed at helping the unemployed, the poverty-stricken, or the uneducated, or (*b*) it would have to seek a tax increase to make up for the lost revenue. Whichever result occurred, business would be the loser. Neither development would work in the best interests of business; indeed, it would make business problems all the more serious!

Another reason why the argument regarding the tax reduction of corporate support for the arts is weak or erroneous concerns the corporation itself. Can you conceive of the stockholders of a firm willingly foregoing larger dividends so that the corporation could give its profits away to the arts? When put in this perspective, the tax argument for support of the arts becomes tenuous at best, and falls apart completely in the ultimate analysis. Indeed, so suspect is this argument that a recent survey found many business firms were totally ignorant of the tax-deductible nature of their support for the arts!

How has business supported the arts?

Business support of the arts has taken many different forms. Some businesses have provided managerial talents for various art associations. Thus, the B. F. Goodrich Company provided urgently needed accounting aid to the troubled Akron Art Institute. In other instances, business has assumed an interest in supporting the arts in their own local areas. The Chase Manhattan Bank, for example, has sponsored art exhibits in Harlem and has aided in introducing talented but unknown inner-city artists to the circles in which they might be "discovered." Perhaps, however, the prime example of business support of local art was the support provided the Philadelphia Civic Ballet by the Philadelphia Gas Works. The Philadelphia Gas Works decided a few years ago to "adopt" the ailing Philadelphia Civic Ballet. It provided funds for new costumes and sets and also aided in the hiring of additional performers. The Gas Works then "put the show on the road" by sponsoring free neighborhood performances of the ballet. It advertised these performances by enclosing circulars with its gas bills that were mailed to customers. Soon, the ballet began to realize an increase in popularity. Today, the Philadelphia Civic Ballet operates totally free from the aid of its corporate benefactor. The free performances so stimulated interest in the ballet that now the ballet is able to support itself through the increased sales of tickets for its regular performances.

More recently, the Los Angeles County Museum of Art sponsored an "Art and Technology" project, part of which was exhibited at Expo '70 in Osaka, Japan. The museum arranged for the financial and technical assistance of nearly 40 corporations, over half of which agreed to take the artists into residence for a three-month period in order to make ambitious works of art. Although some of the works are spoofs of our technological age, business' contributions of its time, money, and facilities to the support of the project illustrates the extent of business' involvement in the arts.

Inflation: A barrier to still more involvement

Despite what is generally conceded to be a sincere and earnest effort by many companies to assist in the development of a better society, many firms are stopped short of doing as much as they might like. The reason is simply one of survival—and the culprit threatening their survival is inflation. Many corporations have found themselves "up against the wall" insofar as competing with other firms in its industry. As costs have gone up and profits down, many of these firms have had to make the hard decisions to cut back on some of their more benevolent works. U.S. Steel, for example, has decided that, however reluctant it is to do so, it must close a plant it has located in Ellwood, Pennsylvania. This might not sound like much of a decision, until one realizes that this plant employed almost one-third of the town's labor force. U.S. Steel says, however, that the costs of producing steel today are such that it simply is uneconomical for it to continue to operate the Pennsylvania plant, when similar products are made more efficiently at its Gary, Indiana, plant.

U.S. Steel is not leaving the town of Ellwood holding the proverbial bag, however. It has promised to turn the 125-acre mill site into an industrial park and will assist the town in finding new industry.

In other ways, too, inflation has hurt business in its social activities. Many youths, particularly inner-city youths, look forward to part-time employment in the summer months at various companies. In these recent inflation-ridden years, however, many companies have cut back on their employment policies. As the coordinator for a Boston antipoverty summer job program explained, ". . . the Chamber of Commerce felt that the business community had its own problems . . . It couldn't see pushing for summer jobs for kids when so many parents were out of work."[4]

NEW COMMITMENTS AND RESPONSIBILITIES

Finally, business has broadened its influence to include still other areas of responsibility and has further intensified efforts to develop and refine a firm philosophy of operations for the remainder of the century.

To strengthen its understanding of the problems of minority groups, urban problems, and racial bias, more and more businesses are beginning to seek the advice and counsel of noted members of the minority groups. A prime example is the appointment of the Reverend Leon Sulli-

---

[4] *Business Week*, June 29, 1974.

van to the board of directors of the General Motors Corporation. Dr. Sullivan has established himself a leader in the area of corporate involvement in urban renewal, and in fact, was involved in the Spring Garden project of Smith, Kline & French Laboratories. Similar moves were made by Scott Paper Company, IBM, and the National Bank of Washington, all of which appointed Mrs. Patricia Roberts Harris to their boards. Such appointments were made, not in an attempt to practice "tokenism," but to bring, as the chairman of Scott Paper Company said, a personal perspective to help anticipate and fulfill the social responsibilities of business.

This then, is the response of business to the new challenges of society. Business has already done much to relieve and correct the problems facing our society. There remains, however, much to do. Business must continually strive to achieve a better understanding and feeling for the plight of others, both in its own organizational structure and in those institutional forces with which it comes into contact. After all, business is, in the words of Kenneth Clark, the last hope, in that it is the most relevant structure in our society. If it doesn't do the job, who will?

Perhaps the best summary of the reason why business *must* engage in coping with social problems is indicated in two quotations from the leaders of two of America's largest corporations. Speaking at different times and under different circumstances, the two leaders nonetheless pinpoint the nature of the problem.

> "Man does not live by bread alone"—but he has to have bread before he begins to think of other things.
> ——*Henry Ford II, Ford Motor Company*

> We're the cats with the bread.
> ——*Lewis W. Moore, American Oil Company*

DISCUSSON QUESTIONS

1   Why should business get involved in resolving the great social issues of our time?

2   It has been argued in some quarters that the reason for the existence of so many social problems stems from the fact that the institutions of our society have failed to restrict themselves to doing that which they were originally intended to do. That is, schools were developed to educate, churches were developed to provide a place of worship, and business was developed to facilitate the movement of goods and services between peoples. Government, it was argued, was developed to handle all other problems. Thus, the way to solve the great social issues of our time is for business, education, labor, and all of

the other great institutions to remove themselves from this area of concern, and leave it to government. Do you agree? Why or why not?

3 Who are the poor in America? Does the term *poor* carry a stereotyped image that may be misleading for some people? Explain.

4 Your text defined the "disadvantaged" as comprising those segments of society that have lacked—for reasons not of their own making— the same opportunities and advantages as the majority of our society. Elaborate and clarify just what this means.

5 In the text, we have concentrated on two specific minority groups: the Mexican-Americans and the blacks. Can you think of other minority groups that also fit the problems discussed in this chapter?

6 Whitney Young discussed the "vicious circle," and noted the problems associated with any attempt to break the circle. How does the highly controversial issue of busing fit into a potential plan for breaking the circle?

7 Should business provide aid to education? Does business provide aid to any schools that you know of?

8 What is the business of business?

MINI CASES

The question of business' role in resolving the urban problems of our society is certainly an important one. Some people feel quite strongly, for example, that business has a duty—an obligation—to assist in resolving the problems of unemployment, poverty, housing, education, and so on. Still others, however, are quite convinced that business' responsibility in these areas is minimal—that its primary objective is and ought to be, to earn a profit. Advocates of both of these varying points of view, however, usually agree that business ought to pay a reasonable wage— one that will enable a person to live in reasonable decency.

Thus, it was with surprise that Paul Short read about a large conglomerate firm that had recently diversified into agriculture. The report that had appeared in the local paper mentioned that this conglomerate was paying $1.75 per hour to field hands working the farms that the corporation owned. Paul thought about this for a moment, did a few calculations, and discovered a disturbing fact. Assuming a 40-hour workweek, and 52 weeks in a year, a worker could earn as a gross wage only $3,640 per year! Such a wage could actually put a worker with a wife and five children below the poverty income lines set by the government, even though the person would be considered a full-time employee!

Paul decided to check further into the agriculture industry itself. He discovered that wages had, previous to this company's action, been considerably lower than $1.75 per hour. Moreover, he found that agriculture ranked traditionally at the bottom of the profitability scale. The high cost of machinery, the high cost of land, the need for large amounts of manual labor, and the low prices that were received for agriculture crops, all combined to keep this a relatively unprofitable industry. Paul sat back for a moment and began to reflect on the "social responsibility" dilemma facing this particular company.

1. *What is the dilemma that Paul saw existing?*
2. *Does the company appear to have any other choice in its labor practices?*
3. *Can you suggest ways such a dilemma might be overcome?*

One minority group that is probably more in need of assistance than any other is that of the American Indian. The plight of the Indian is a sad blemish on the pages of American history. What was once a proud independent people now are forced to the sad state of life on a reservation, with high illiteracy, unemployment, and sad health standards. The reservation roads are overwhelmingly inadequate. In bad weather, the roads are impassable, preventing kids from going to school, hampering decent medical care and creating shipping problems for companies operating on the reservation. Among the Navajo indians, for example, most people live in one-room "hogans," or houses, with dirt floors, no telephones, and no electricity. Some of the older people speak only Navajo, and the unemployment level hovers at the astronomical level of 65 percent. Moreover, the population of the Navajo is increasing at over 4 percent per year, one of the fastest growth rates in the world. Thus, even though in 1972 over 700 jobs were created on the reservation, the labor force increased by over 2,000. Presently, more than 25,000 are believed waiting to obtain employment.

Things show some sign of changing, however. In 1973, the Navajo tribal council obtained exclusive right to decide how $110 million of federal funds was to be spent. Previously, this money was spent by the Bureau of Indian Affairs. It is the council's hope that, within ten years, the reservation will be brought up to 20th-century standards.

Suppose that you have been called in as an advisor to assist in the spending of this $110 million to be received each year for ten years. What would be your priorities? How would you entice companies to locate in the reservation? What kinds of businesses would you seek out?

For the most part, the concept of a multi-national corporation is a phenomenon of the post-World War II period. Some companies, such as IBM, Colgate-Palmolive, and Unilever, for example, have been operating overseas for some time. But none of these companies can compare in age to the multinational industrial complex now headed by Michel Fribourg.

Known historically as the House of Fribourg, this industrial complex was started by Michel's great-great-grand-father, Simon Fribourg. In 1813, Simon founded a grain trading company in Arlon, Belgium. Since then, the company has expanded and prospered. It wasn't until 1922 that they expanded into the United States by setting up an office in Chicago under the name of the Continental Grain Co. In 1944, Jules Fribourg died, and René became Chairman of the Board. René, however, was more interested in art than grains, and thus left the operations of the company to a young ex-Pfc. of the United States Army, Michel Fribourg.

Michel was born in Antwerp, Holland, and raised and educated in Paris. He had immigrated to the United States and become a naturalized citizen. Assuming the presidency of the family operations, Michel expanded the families operations to all parts of the globe. The family now owns or controls at least 100 companies, manufacturing all types of consumer goods in the United States, controlling vast real estate holdings in France, Morocco, Switzerland and the U.S., raising large herds of cattle in Argentina, and operating several ski slopes in Spain. The company is also active in Thailand, Japan, and Korea. At the present time, Michel Fribourg owns about 90 percent of Continental Grain, one of the world's largest grain companies. Today, Michel ranks as one of the richest, and yet least known, men in America.

Michel Fribourg
(1914–   )

Descendent of one of the world's first multinational families

21

International business

No nation is capable of maintaining a high standard of living independent of other nations in the world. Over the years, a complex web of economic dependence has been built up, such that today virtually every nation in the world has economic ties with other nations of the world. These ties, moreover, have become well ingrained in the living pattern of the average world citizen. Even in America, a country that has more economic independence than most, the amount and number of goods that are of foreign origin and are used by the average citizen is staggering. Consider one typical American morning: A man wakes up to the alarm from his Japanese-made radio, shaves with razor blades made in England, and dresses in a suit made of wool from England. He breakfasts with cereal topped with strawberries from Mexico or bananas from Costa Rica, and puts a teaspoonful of sugar from the Philippines in his coffee from Colombia. After checking the time on his Swiss watch, he heads for work in his automobile from Germany, France, Japan, or Italy.

The amazing aspect of this vast economic complex, however, is not the magnitude or amount of world trade, but rather the fact that so many goods from such a variety of sources are so readily available. The average consumer of foreign products rarely stops to reflect on the process by which such ownership arose. Political and economic treaties had to be negotiated; the goods had to be produced, transported to this country, financed by specialized dealers in international finance, serviced by subsidi-

557

ary companies and finally, sold to the consumer. It is a remarkable tribute to the international economic system that quality goods can be produced and sold at prices that are attractive enough to induce their purchase by discriminating consumers all over the world.

Yet, international trade is not without its problems. As trade has increased, some nations have seen their domestic economies become virtual captive markets for the goods of foreign producers. As a defensive gesture, these nations have imposed a variety of controls, regulations, and taxes on goods from other countries. Similarly, nations have formed regional trading blocs, designed to promote trade within the group of nations, while simultaneously keeping goods from outside from entering their markets. The European Economic Community, better known as the Common Market, is but one such group. Finally, political unrest, wars, and revolution have continually disrupted the economic processes.

Major aspects of international business will be examined in this chapter. We shall discuss some of the problems and challenges facing the American business executive overseas, and shall examine in some depth the question of business' international social responsibilities. This will put into clearer perspective the role and philosophy of American business in the international community.

WHY NATIONS TRADE

Nations trade with one another because they have come to realize that it is usually in their own best interests to do so. Such a realization, however, has not always existed. Recall that in the days of Adam Smith and other early economists, England and other nations wanted to buy raw materials but not finished goods from their colonies. Under the economic doctrine of mercantilism, a nation sought to control the sources of materials needed for its survival. That is, each nation sought to become self-sufficient. Sales of goods to other nations were allowed, as this increased the national wealth. Purchases of other's goods, however, was to be avoided at all costs. The fallacy of such a doctrine should be readily apparent. It is logically impossible for all nations to sell goods without some other nation(s) buying those goods. When the nations of the world realized this impossibility, their attitudes toward world trade underwent a sharp reversal. Today, international trade that makes more and better goods available to all has become of paramount importance both to American business executives and business leaders from other lands.

THE IMPORTANCE OF WORLD TRADE

Figure 21–1 shows that the total value of the goods and services traded internationally exceeds $300 billion annually and is growing rapidly. This

FIGURE 21–1
World trade and U.S. imports (billions of dollars)

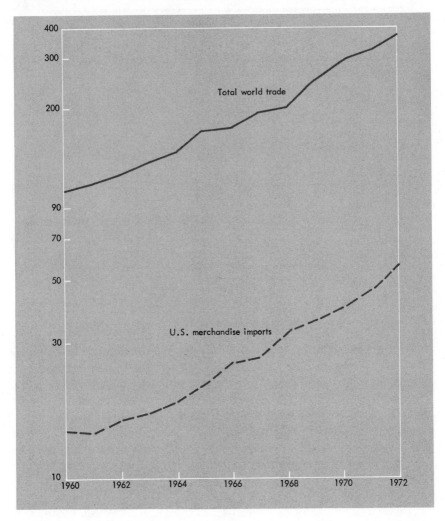

is a remarkable total, to say the least, and what is most remarkable is the extent to which the U.S. business leaders participate in that $300-billion-plus amount.

From the standpoint of American business involvement in international trade, an even more revealing figure can be seen. Of the top 200 industrial companies in the United States, over 80 of them—a full 40 percent —receive over 25 percent of their sales and earnings from overseas business. Indeed, some companies—such as the Colgate Palmolive Company—actually do more business overseas than they do in the United States.

TABLE 21–1

Foreign operations of American businesses*

Company	Foreign sales as a percent of total sales (approx.)	Foreign earnings as a percent of total earnings (approx.)
American Brands....................	39.2	16.6
Avon Products......................	30.0	19.3
Burroughs..........................	32.3	45.4
Dow Chemical......................	40.4	44.5
Eastman Kodak.....................	31.4	19.0
Heinz (H. J.).......................	44.5	46.7
Honeywell..........................	33.1	37.0
IBM.................................	39.1	50.4
I.T. & T.............................	42.0	35.0
Merck...............................	38.0	38.0
NCR.................................	45.2	50.9
Otis Elevator.......................	60.9	35.0
Pfizer...............................	47.3	54.8
Philip Morris.......................	35.0	24.8
Warner-Lambert....................	33.3	33.3
Xerox...............................	30.1	38.3

* Oil companies excluded from this study.
Source: *Business International*, selected issues.

CHARACTERISTICS OF INTERNATIONAL DEVELOPMENT

Not all nations of the world are capable of developing economically in the same way. Some nations are larger than others; some are richer. Some nations possess very stable governments; others do not. Moreover, each nation differs in its available supply of the factors of production necessary to produce the goods desired by its society. That is, certain characteristics of each nation largely determine the types of goods that nation will produce. Among these characteristics are those discussed in the following paragraphs.

Climate Some nations have a climate that is more suitable for growing certain agricultural products than others. The climate in Central America, for example, is ideal for the growing of bananas. Similarly, the warm, tropical climate of Brazil and Colombia is ideally suited for the growing of coffee.

Occasionally, countries possess sufficient land space to enable them to produce crops that require a variety of climates for success. The United States, for example, has sufficient geographic dispersion to enable it to produce virtually any agricultural crop it desires.

Natural resources The existence of natural resources is extremely critical in determining what goods a nation will produce. Bolivia, for example, is the world's foremost producer of tin, a raw material which is found in abundance in the mountainous regions of that part of the world. Similarly, the vast oil fields of the Middle East are the primary source of trade and production for countries such as Iran, Iraq, and Saudi Arabia.

Skilled labor supply   The existence of a skilled labor supply is also essential to the determination of a nation's output. In the United States, there exists a substantial supply of highly skilled workers. The presence of these workers has helped make possible America's leadership in the production of technological equipment, such as computers, automobiles, aircraft and machinery. Japan and the major countries of Western Europe are similarly endowed with a skilled labor supply.

In contrast, many nations are lacking in this vital resource. India and Pakistan, for example, lack many of the labor skills found in the Western world. However, these nations have an abundance of unskilled laborers, something which is lacking in many Western nations. Accordingly, production in these countries tends to emphasize products that require very little skilled labor but many hours of unskilled labor.

Another aspect of labor supply that can influence the production of a given country is labor cost. The United States, for example, is highly efficient at producing steel, but until recently has had difficulty com-

FIGURE 21–2

Percent of world exports from selected countries

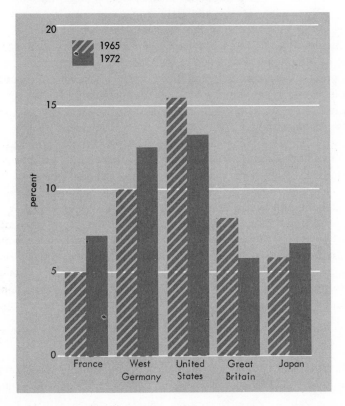

peting on world markets because its labor costs are so much higher than those of other countries. By way of illustration, Japan recently had labor costs in the iron and steel industry that were approximately 40 percent less than comparable costs in the United States. Moreover, the productivity of Japanese workers (the ability of Japanese labor to produce steel in a given length of time) was almost 80 percent of that of the American worker. Small wonder, then, that U.S. steel companies were finding it increasingly difficult to compete with Japanese steel. Japan was capable of producing almost as much per worker but paid those workers less than half the wage the American worker was receiving. The United States was virtually priced out of the market by the high costs of labor.

Fortunately for American steel companies, something completely unexpected occurred that helped to revive the prospects for U.S. steel producers. That event was a sudden worldwide shortage of shipping capacity. As a result, the cost of shipping skyrocketed. The result was that U.S. steel suddenly was priced competitively with steel from Japan, which had to be shipped halfway around the world.

Available capital resources   Closely associated with the problem of labor supply as a determinant of a nation's output is the availability of an adequate supply of capital. Remember that capital refers to those items that are used in the production of other goods (such as plant and machinery). Possession of an adequate supply of capital enables a country to use its labor force in the most efficient and productive way possible. In the United States, for example, the vast supply of capital permits the development of all kinds of technological and research equipment, and greatly expands the productivity and the resulting standard of living of the average worker. By way of contrast many nations of the world lack a capital base, and are compelled to use their manual labor force in less efficient ways.

Proximity to markets   In some instances, what a nation emphasizes in production will depend upon where the particular market for the good is, particularly in reference to the area of production. Prior to World War II, for example, the major supplies of rubber in the world were the countries of Southeast Asia, Burma, and Indonesia. When World War II began, these sources of supply were endangered, thereby necessitating that the United States find a new source of rubber—one whose location was more suitable for its needs. Natural rubber, however, did not exist in abundance throughout the world. Ultimately, the United States developed a synthetic rubber to replace its former dependence on a supply source located halfway around the world.

The principle of comparative advantage

It should be obvious at this point that sharp differences exist among the production outputs of various nations. Some countries—particularly the economically underdeveloped countries—may be sharply limited in what they can produce. They may be limited to just one or two products, commodities, or raw materials. Other nations—such as the United States —are blessed with an abundance of the factors necessary for production of virtually any good or service. The United States, for example, could conceivably produce virtually any product desired. Crops of bananas and coffee could be grown in New England merely by building a vast array of hothouses—buildings with temperature and humidity controlled to duplicate the conditions found in Central America. Given this abundance of wealth, then, the question might well be asked: Why does the United States bother trading for goods if it is capable of producing everything it needs? The answer lies in a concept of international trade first advanced by David Ricardo concerning the production of goods. This concept has two important parts: the concept of *absolute advantage* and the concept of *comparative advantage.*

The theory of absolute advantage   If a nation happens to be the sole producer of a particular good, that nation is said to have an *absolute advantage* in the production of that good. A nation can also be said to have an *absolute advantage* in the production of goods if it can produce something more efficiently—for less cost—than another country. Let's examine these again.

It is obvious enough that if a country enjoys a monopoly in the production of a particular good, it will concentrate its efforts on the production of that good. Thus, South Africa produces natural diamonds because it is the only place in the world where they can be found in abundance. Similarly, Brazil and Columbia concentrate in the production of coffee, while little Costa Rica concentrates on supplying the world with bananas. In each of these instances the nations involved enjoy unique characteristics that give them a natural advantage over other nations in the production of these goods. They have an *absolute advantage* in the production of these goods.

What happens, however, when one country is capable of outproducing another country in a given product? In such an instance, we say that the more capable country also has an absolute advantage in the production of that product. This does not mean, however, that these two nations will not find it profitable to trade. The theory of absolute advantage merely indicates which nation is most capable of producing a given good. It does not state, however, whether in fact a nation should produce *all* of those goods in which it has an absolute advantage. This is left for the theory of comparative advantage to resolve.

The theory of comparative advantage   The theory of comparative advantage states that a country with an absolute advantage in the production of goods will tend to concentrate its efforts on the production of those goods in which its advantage is greatest. The other nation—the one facing an absolute disadvantage in all goods—will tend to concentrate its efforts on producing those goods in which its absolute disadvantage is smallest. Let's consider an example to clarify the situation. Suppose that we have two countries, Country A and Country B. Both Country A and Country B produce products 1 and 2, but Country B can outproduce Country A in both goods, Thus,

Production and consumption of goods by Countries A and B

	Product 1	Product 2
Country A.......................................	80	30
Country B.......................................	100	60
Total Output.......................	180	90 = 270

In the absence of any trade, the two nations will produce and consume 270 units of products 1 and 2.

Suppose, however, that each country decides to specialize in just one of the products and trade the surplus of their production to the other in exchange for the surplus produced by that other country. That is, Country B specialized in the production of that product in which its comparative advantage was greatest, while Country A specialized in the production of that product in which its comparative disadvantage was least. Then Country B would produce product 2 (it can outproduce Country A by a ratio of 2:1) while Country A will concentrate on producing product 1 (Country B's relative or comparative advantage is only 1:25:1 for this product). Assume that Country A, by concentrating its productive resources on just product 1, can produce 200 units of product 1, while Country B is capable of producing 100 units of product 2. Now the advantages of trading can be clearly seen.

If Country A requires only 80 units of product 1, it can trade 120 units to Country B. But Country B only needed 100 units of product 1. An

TABLE 21–2

The principal imports and exports of the United States reflect the principle of comparative advantage

Imports	Exports
Bananas	Aircraft
Tea	Computer equipment
Diamonds	Cotton
Natural rubber	Sewing machines
Coffee	Textiles
Oil	Wheat
Spices	Soybeans
Asbestos	Tractor parts
Tin	Chickens
Cobalt	Mining equipment
Cacao	Lumber

excess of 20 units exists. In the meantime, Country B needed only 60 units of product 2; it will therefore have a surplus of 40 units of product 2 to trade to Country A. However, Country A only required 30 units of product 2. A surplus of 10 units of product 2 exists. In actuality, the total production of both products 1 and 2 has increased because the two countries were able to specialize. By doing so, they increased their production, and now have more goods for their respective economies. Their standards of living can increase as a result of following the principle of comparative advantage.

TRADITIONAL PROBLEMS IN INTERNATIONAL TRADE

Despite the extent of international trade and the obvious advantages that exist for nations that encourage it, many problems arise that are peculiar to this aspect of business. Some of these problems are cultural in nature, deriving from the fact that trade is occurring between peoples of different societies and backgrounds. These questions include considerations of language, customs, and manners. While these may not all seem to be of significant importance to the American business executives, frequently an appreciation of such national characteristics means the difference between success and failure in international trade.

A second type of problem that is frequently encountered can be called operational in nature. Buying and selling goods to an unknown party 5,000 or 10,000 miles away can be much different from buying or selling goods to someone in another state of the United States. Transportation problems and currency problems can exist. Indeed, the area of international finance is of extreme importance, for the problems of obtaining credit overseas can be much more complex than the "signature only" approach we see so often in the United States.

Given, therefore, the general importance of these issues, it might prove useful to discuss a few of them in more depth.

Cultural problems

Cultural problems, as noted, can arise when peoples from different societies come in contact with one another. The major types of cultural problems arise out of differences in language, customs, manners, and tastes.

Language Differences in language is a problem that has always been confronted whenever people engage in international trade. Communication is, after all, the heart of any business transaction. Buyers and sellers must agree on terms, on price, indeed, on the nature and quality of the good itself.

In years past, American business leaders relied on interpreters as a means of overcoming the language obstacle. This tended, however, to remove the privacy and intimacy from the negotiations that many people felt belonged there. Moreover, there was always the slight possibility that something might not be understood or interpreted correctly, thus weakening the bonds of trust between buyer and seller that are so essential to successful trade.

A classic example of how language can sometimes cause problems or embarrassment for an American company concerns the recent problems of a well-known American airline. This particular airline operated jet service to Brazil. One of its advertising campaigns played up what the airline called its "rendezvous lounges," only to discover later, much to its dismay, that "rendezvous" when translated into Portuguese meant a room hired for love-making.

Fortunately, problems like these are becoming fewer and farther between. Gradually, the major nations of the world have come to accept English as the language of business. Moreover, American business leaders have been stressing the importance of their chief negotiators understanding the language of the country they are dealing with. Finally, American businesses with overseas divisions have been hiring local personnel to manage those divisional operations. Each of these factors has helped remove some of the traditional problems associated with language.

Customs A second major cultural problem encountered in international trade is that of varying customs. For instance, Americans are accustomed to conducting business in settings other than the office. It is not uncommon for an executive to be invited out for dinner, or to invite a potential customer to his home for dinner. This may not seem like a terribly significant fact in itself, until one realizes the importance that customs play in the success of the business relationship. In Japan, for example, the home is never used to entertain for business. Rather, business associates are treated to an evening on the town.

Sometimes a company can suffer substantial financial losses as a result of its failure to consider cultural differences between nations. General Mills once attempted to capture a large portion of the British breakfast cereal market. Part of its attempt involved the use of an advertisement in which the main character was a small, freckled-faced redhead boy. The child was, essentially, the "All-American" kid. Much to the surprise of General Mills, the cereal failed to sell well. Upon further investigation, they discovered that the British tended not to be as child-oriented as American families. Indeed, when the British do use children for advertising purposes, they prefer the children to be somewhat aristocratic in their manners.

And finally, Pepsodent toothpaste had a serious, although funny thing happen to it. Pepsodent tried to launch a major campaign to push its well-known toothpaste in a country in Southeast Asia. Imagine the shock that executives of Pepsodent suffered when they discovered that their campaign promising whiter teeth fell flat on its face. It turns out that this particular country viewed *black* teeth as a symbol of prestige. The local natives were fond of chewing a particular native substance that helped turn their teeth black. And you can well imagine how Pepsodent's famous, "You'll wonder where the yellow went. . . ." commercial went over. An understanding of customs, consequently, may prove more important than managers realize in successfully executing an international business transaction.

Manners Manners—the little characteristic ways of behaving unique to the people of a country—often play a decisive role in the success or failure of international business transactions. Most manners are the result of some cultural or societal trait that is found in all people of that society. A failure to appreciate them can lead to a lack of respect, a failure in communication, and even a breakdown in negotiations. Examples of manners are easy to come by. For instance, the English are known to dislike meetings before 11:00 a.m. The French, Swedes, and South Africans are known to expect promptness when going to a meeting. Indeed, the French are known to keep a tardy visitor waiting in an outer office for the length of his tardiness, plus five minutes, as a means of showing their displeasure.

In communication, similar characteristic patterns exist. Mexicans, Spaniards, and Arabs prefer close, face-to-face negotiation. The story is told of the American who kept walking backwards around a room while negotiating with a Mexican business executive. He wanted to negotiate at arm's length; the Mexican, however, liked to negotiate at virtually nose-to-nose contact. The Mexican couldn't understand why the American kept walking away, and the American couldn't understand why the Mexican wouldn't stay put.

By way of contrast, the Japanese prefer keeping a discreet distance in communication. Indeed, doing business in Japan can be particularly delicate, since the manners of the Orient are much more complex and subtle than those of Europe.

Style and taste A final cultural factor that can be considered a problem peculiar to international business is that of style and taste. Very few products or business techniques are successful in all countries of the world. One of the few exceptions is Coca-Cola—perhaps the most universally accepted product yet developed. Other products, however, need substantial changes before some countries will accept them. Coffee is a prime example. Nestlés, Switzerland's big multinational firm, makes over 40 varieties of instant coffee for the various markets in which it sells. Helene Curtis, the noted cosmetic company, markets a black shampoo in

Thailand, after it discovered that Thai women felt the black shampoo made their hair feel glossier.

Style and taste differences extend to the packaging of products as well. In Germany, menthol cigarettes in a brown package sold better than the same cigarettes in a blue package. The color blue, in fact, can itself be controversial. In Holland, blue is considered to be a warm, feminine color. In Sweden, however, blue is characterized as being masculine and cold.

Operational problems

The second major type of problems encountered in international trade are those that are operational. These problems are the result of difficulties within the business transaction process itself or are the result of government intervention. Examples include the problems of monetary standards, transportation costs, ownership of foreign business, and governmental controls.

Monetary standards When a company does business overseas it must be prepared to deal in the currency of the country involved. Thus, in England, the pound is the standard monetary unit, in France it's the new franc, in Germany it's the mark, in Sweden it's the kronor, in Japan it's the yen, and so on. The American manufacturer of computers selling in Japan, for example, will receive yen as payment for the computer. The computer manufacturer, however, desires dollars. He must, therefore, take the yen to the bank and request conversion into dollars. In some countries, however, the central banks have a shortage of dollars, and cannot or will not exchange dollars for their own currency. This can create a serious problem for the American manufacturer. Indeed, on occasion American manufacturers have been known to take payment in merchandise, which they can then sell in the United States for dollars.

This entire problem of currency exchange is a complex one. Indeed, in 1971, the United States undertook major changes in its policy with reference to the dollar overseas, and these had a major impact on business. This problem will be examined in more detail later in this chapter.

Transportation costs Another obvious operational handicap to world trade concerns the problem of transportation costs. Quite frequently, this is the most important barrier to further trade. An earlier international trade example showed how the cost advantage enjoyed by Japan in the manufacture of steel was recently eliminated by the increased cost of transporting that steel to the United States. Occasionally, however, the problem of transportation costs backfires on some governments that attempt to use it as a means of extracting concessions from American businesses. For years, the Suez Canal was responsible for the low cost of transporting oil from the Middle East to Europe. When the canal was closed almost a decade ago, the major oil companies began work on a pipeline across the desert, and simultaneously began building huge tankers capable of sailing around the cape of South Africa. In the late 1960s, the Arab nations attempted to extract higher taxes from the companies for use of the pipeline. They implied that future use of the Suez Canal might depend on the willingness and cooperation of business in paying these taxes. The tactic might have worked had it not been for the giant tankers. These huge ships were so successful that they resulted in lowering the cost of transportation below that possible when the Canal was open. Now, many of the major oil companies don't care if the Suez Canal ever opens.

Finally, companies may miscalculate when attempting to cut transportation costs. Many companies find transportation costs to be one of the major costs they face in the entire cycle of getting product from source of manufacture to the consumer. Consequently, they occasionally place too much importance on cutting transportation costs, and too little importance on other aspects of the problem. An example of this situation is a recent problem that confronted the Del Monte Food Company.

Del Monte maintained large pineapple acreages in Mexico. The company found, however, that the transportation costs to and from the cannery were rather high. In an effort to cut those costs, Del Monte arranged to build a cannery at the delta of a river in Mexico. It planned to process the pineapples at that cannery, and then use barges to ship the product to ocean liners for shipment to the United States. Things would have worked out well, had Del Monte considered factors other than transportation costs. It seems that just at the time the pineapple crop matured in that part of the world, that particular river the cannery was located on happened to reach flood stage. The barges couldn't get through to the cannery. Del Monte eventually sold the cannery to a Mexican group for pennies on the dollar. The Mexicans promptly disassembled the plant and moved it away from the river.

Ownership of foreign business   Another operational obstacle to international business involves the ownership of foreign business enterprises. Many countries are just beginning to develop themselves economically, and are, consequently, prime candidates for expansion of U.S. businesses. These countries, although they appreciate the innovation and technical abilities the Americans bring with them, are quite concerned about the ownership of their businesses and industry by "foreigners." This has culminated in a good many disputes, ranging from the prohibition Japan places on foreign ownership in its businesses to the outright seizure of U.S. business enterprises by Chile, Indonesia, Bolivia, and many other countries.

Governmental controls   Government, too, plays a part in creating operating obstacles for business overseas. As a means of protecting its national interests—meaning its domestic businesses—governments impose taxes, tariffs, and quotas on goods of foreign manufacture.

Tariffs Tariffs are taxes or duties levied on goods that are imported into a country from abroad. Most governments impose tariffs on some goods of foreign manufacture, primarily as a means of keeping low-cost, foreign-made goods from competing with domestically produced goods. Although tariffs are occasionally used to provide revenue for the government, in today's world this reason or justification is hardly noteworthy. Rather, government uses tariffs as a means of limiting imports into the country. It does this because it fears that too many of its dollars may flow out of the country as payment for the cheaper imported goods, thereby depriving the country of the use of that money for other purposes. Other arguments or justifications for tariffs are the following.

The home industry argument The home industry argument states that tariffs provide a wall of protection for domestic industry. Without such a protective wall, it is argued, many businesses would close or fail because of their inability to compete with foreign producers. This would lead to unemployment and eventually destroy the domestic economy of the nation.

Examples of tariffs that have been imposed for this reason here in America are rather easy to find. Beef, glassware, shoes, and automobiles are all protected to some degree by tariffs imposed under the home industry argument. The argument for protecting home industry appears at first glance to be a legitimate one. After all, no one wants to cause massive unemployment and chaos in the economy. This argument is particularly true for other nations. A study of Table 21–3 shows the size of the largest, non-American corporations. A comparison of this table with Table 4–1 illustrates the justification for the fear that many foreign nationals have about their native industries. On the other hand, the protection of home industry runs counter to the principle of compara-

TABLE 21–3

World's largest industrial companies outside the United States
(in billions of dollars)

Company	Country	Industry	1973 sales
Royal Dutch/Shell..............	Netherlands–Britain	Gas, oil	$18.672
Unilever.......................	Netherlands–Britain	Food, household products	11.009
Philips Lamp...................	Netherlands	Electronics	8.108
British Petroleum..............	Britain	Oil, chemicals	7.725
Nippon Steel...................	Japan	Iron and steel	7.628
Volkswagen....................	Germany	Automobiles	6.412
Hitachi........................	Japan	Electrical equipment	5.971
Farbwerke Hoechst	Germany	Chemicals	5.590
Daimler–Benz..................	Germany	Automobiles	5.550
Toyota........................	Japan	Automobiles	5.547

tive advantage. If a nation's businesses need protection, maybe these businesses shouldn't be in existence in the first place. Moreover, when inefficient businesses at home are protected, the consumers are forced to pay a higher price for goods. Unable to get the cheaper foreign goods, they must purchase the more expensive domestic product.

Finally, tariffs designed to protect home industry frequently are countered with similar tariffs by other countries on the goods of the first country. In other words, if Country A applies a tariff on products from Country B, Country B might well retaliate with a similar tariff on goods from Country A. Then, no one gains.

The infant industries argument Tariffs are also justified on the grounds that they are necessary to protect new or infant industries. In the early days of the United States, tariffs were imposed on foreign goods as a means of aiding new business development at home. The concept worked. Unfortunately (and this is the major drawback to this argument), it has been hard to decide when an industry loses its infancy. Many tariffs that continue to exist started originally as tariffs designed to protect an infant industry. As the businesses grew, however, their political contacts and influence grew also, such that the tariffs were never removed.

The military preparedness argument A final argument used to justify the existence of tariffs concerns the military preparedness question. Some industries, skills, and raw materials are vital to the national security in time of war. These, it is argued, should be protected from foreign competition during peacetime, so that they will be available for use in the event war breaks out. An example of such an industry is the watch-making industry. Timing devices are of critical importance in missiles, torpedoes, and other weaponry systems. Unless a country maintains a supply of craftsmen knowledgeable in these skills, there will be a void of these necessary talents in the event of war.

The military preparedness argument is a difficult one to repudiate, for even though none of us wants war, it is nonetheless advisable to remain prepared. Often, however, this argument is used as an excuse by business to obtain a protective tariff and thereby perpetuate what is essentially an inefficient industry.

Other governmental barriers to trade Other governmental barriers to trade include taxes and the outright prohibition of certain goods from being imported into the country. Many countries impose a tax on all profits that are taken out of the country. This creates a particularly interesting problem. What does a company do if it earns a profit in an overseas nation but is unable to transfer that profit to the United States, where it can be paid to the stockholder? Quite obviously, the company reinvests the profit in the country in which it was earned. When this is carried on long enough, the company may soon become one of the largest economic units in that country. This brings up the question of foreign domination of domestic business, and often results in expropriation—the seizure of

FIGURE 21–3

U.S. exports and imports

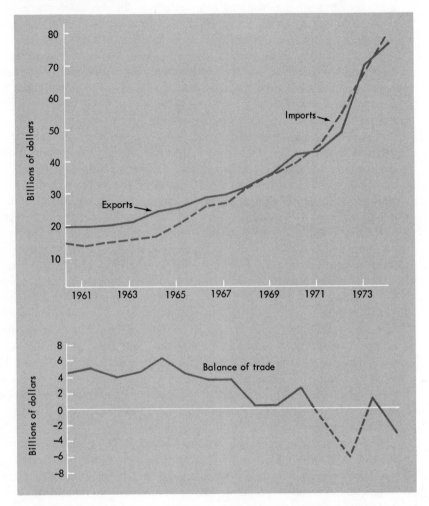

the company by the local government. Although the problem of expropriation has not yet been resolved, steps have been taken to minimize the threat. Reciprocal tax agreements have been passed between the United States and most other nations of the world, allowing some, if not all, of the profits earned by U.S. business overseas to be returned to the home country.

Finally, some goods are simply barred from entry into the country. Opium from Turkey, for example, can be imported only under the strictest government controls—and then only by qualified drug companies, doctors, and health institutions.

Balance of trade   A final area of governmental concern that causes problems in the area of international business is the effect such trade will have on a nation's balance of trade. All nations of the world desire to have a favorable balance of trade—that is, they strive to export or sell to others more goods than they import or buy from others. Obviously, this is a goal that cannot be achieved by all nations. For every nation that has more exports than imports, there must be another nation with more imports than exports.

Government frequently uses the power of tariff-levying or taxing as a means of keeping imports down, thereby maintaining a reasonably favorable balance of trade.

THE COMPLEXITY OF INTERNATIONAL FINANCE

Earlier, it was noted that one of the more complex aspects of international business concerned the financial aspects of trade overseas. Some of the financial problems that are typically encountered—these include the problem of money and monetary units, and the problem of maintaining a favorable balance of trade. To put the role of finance in its proper perspective, however, it is necessary to diverge just slightly from the previous line of discussion and examine the overall, worldwide financial picture. Later, the role of the business firm can be related to this complex arrangement.

Principles of international finance

As explained earlier, nations of the world trade with one another in order to obtain those goods which they themselves cannot produce or are at a comparative disadvantage in producing. The acquisition of these goods usually occurs through private business firms—each buying or selling those goods that it was organized to handle. Thus, if consumers in the United States desire products made of mohair, such as sweaters, it is private industry that acquires this material, fabricates it into sweaters, and sells it to the American consumer. Government plays a passive role, for the most part.

Moreover, we have seen something of the problems associated with differences in the world's currencies. Until recently, the American business executives buying mohair would pay for their purchases in dollars. The merchant in Afghanistan that sold them the mohair, however, had need of rupees, not dollars, and so exchanged the dollars for rupees at the local bank. The bank took the dollars and either kept them for use in buying American products, or it shipped them back to the United States and asked for rupees or gold. As long as America was ready and willing to pay gold for dollars held by foreigners, no problem existed other than determining the value of gold in relation to the various currencies. Foreigners readily accepted dollars for payment instead of their own currency, for they knew they could get rupees, pounds, marks, or whatever by simply converting the dollars to gold and then using the gold to acquire rupees or marks, and so on.

From an American viewpoint, the exchange of dollars for gold created no real problem, for America had always managed to sell more goods to others (thereby obtaining claims against their gold supplies) than others sold to the United States. Gradually, however, the picture began to change. West Germany and other industrialized nations of Europe,

FIGURE 21–4
Industrial production (indexes 1958–100)

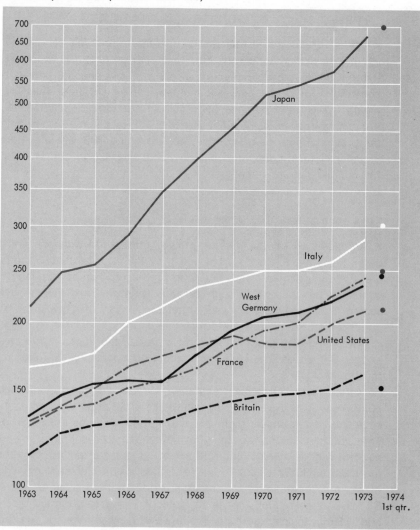

and Japan, grew and prospered at an unprecedented pace (see Figure 21–4). Assisted by American foreign aid (gifts of American goods and dollars with which they could acquire more goods or obtain gold), these nations quickly attained a high level of productivity. This enabled them to compete effectively with American business in the United States and on the world market. Moreover, wage rates in these countries did not advance as rapidly as they did here in the United States. As a result, America found itself buying more and more of the cheaper, foreign-made products, while simultaneously exporting fewer and fewer of its own goods. America's favorable balance of trade began to fall to historically low levels (see Figure 21–3). In mid-1971, the inevitable happened. America realized an unfavorable balance of trade—the first since 1893. We were buying more from others than we were selling to them. Translated into financial terms, this meant the United States was granting others more claims against its gold supply than we had against their gold stocks.

By itself, this created no special problem. As possessors of a large portion of the world's gold stock, America could easily afford to lose a little because of an unfavorable balance of trade. However, America was losing gold long before it lost its favorable balance of trade. The developments regarding the trade balance only accelerated the outflow of gold and brought to a head the problems of the U.S. balance of payments.

The balance of payments

As noted earlier, the balance of trade refers to the net balance of a country's exports minus its imports. If exports exceed imports, the balance of trade is positive, or favorable. American claims against the gold supply of foreign countries is larger than the claims of foreigners on the American gold stock. If on the other hand, the balance of trade is unfavorable, then the reverse is true—foreign claims on America's gold exceeds America's claims on their gold. If the only exchange of currencies among countries was the result of exports and imports, this would constitute the *balance of payments* for the country. That is, American payments to others would consist of payments for the imports purchased, and receipts would comprise payment received for goods sold or exported to others. However, other factors also enter into the net exchange of funds between nations (see Figure 21–5). For example, tourists cause a change in the balance of payments. When Americans go abroad and spend money, these funds find their way into foreign banks and eventually become claims against the United States. People from other countries come to the United States to be sure, and to this extent, help offset American expenditures overseas. However, as the world's most traveled people, Americans vacationing abroad far outnumber the foreigners vacationing here.

FIGURE 21–5

Balance of Payments

Receipts (billions)	Payments (billions)
Exports	Imports
Transportation, tourists	Transportation, tourists
Income on foreign investment	Investment abroad
	Military expenditures
	U.S. government grants and aid
Other	Other
SURPLUS	or *DEFICIT*

Two other factors which represent payments, or outflows of cash, are military expenditures and foreign aid. These constitute substantial items in our balance of payments. Finally, investments by businesses overseas cause an outflow of American dollars, only part of which is offset by the returns earned on that investment. When the effect of the unfavorable balance of trade was combined with the continued outflows resulting from the rest of our payments accounts, major trouble loomed for the United States. Claims against our gold stock exceeded by four times the amount of gold the United States possessed.[2] Merchants, bankers and government officials of other countries began to wonder what would happen if the United States were to run out of gold. Until this point, most banks had kept the dollars they received, primarily because of their assurance that the U.S. Treasury would always be willing to give them gold if they really needed or desired it. Their newfound fears grew, however, and soon there was a tremendous rush by banks, foreign business leaders, and speculators to convert their dollars to gold. As a result, the U.S. gold supply dropped sharply. To halt this "run on the dollar," President Nixon took the historic step of refusing to honor requests of gold for dollars at the fixed rate of $35 per ounce of gold. Rather, he decided to let others (speculators, foreign merchants, and so on) decide what the value of the dollar would be. If one merchant felt an ounce of gold was worth $40, and he could find a seller, then that would be the dollar "float"—seek its own level in relation to gold and, consequently, the other currencies of the world. In the months and years immediately following this action, the dollar's value in terms of gold dropped to an

---

[2] In 1949, the U.S. gold stock was the largest in the world, totaling over $24 billion. By 1974, it had fallen to approximately $1 billion.

official value of $38 per ounce of gold. In effect, the dollar had been devalued by almost 8 percent.[3]

What did devaluation mean to the business executive?

Now that we have completed our short course on international finance, we can ask ourselves what this means to the American business executive —particularly the executive engaged in international trade.

FIGURE 21–6

The changing value of the U.S. dollar

| | One dollar on | | |
Equaled	3/31/70	7/24/73	9/3/74
German marks.....................	3.7	2.3	2.7
Swiss francs......................	4.4	2.9	3.0
British pounds....................	.42	.39	.43
Japanese yen.....................	360	265	314

When President Nixon devalued the U.S. dollar from the previous exchange rate of $35 per ounce of gold to the new value of $38 per ounce of gold, two things immediately happened. First, the dollar in relation to all other currencies of the world assumed different values depending on the particular currency it was being evaluated against. In Japan, for example, the dollar suddenly equaled only 308 yen instead of the previous 360 yen. This happened because people of the world saw the American dollar as being slightly weaker relative to the yen than it had been previously. Accordingly, they were only willing to give 308 yen for $1 instead of the 360 yen of earlier days.

A second event that happened was that American-made goods suddenly became cheaper for foreign buyers. This, too, was because the dollar had dropped in value. Perhaps an example will clarify why this happened.

Consider an American manufacturer selling industrial machinery in Japan. Assume that the machinery sells for $5,000. Before the change in the value of the dollar, this machinery sold in Japan for 1,800,000 yen. Now consider what happens when Japan reevaluates the dollar vis-à-vis the yen, such that it now considers the dollar worth only 308 yen instead of 360 yen. The price of this machinery in Japan will drop—from 1,800,000 yen to 1,540,000 yen. The machinery is still valued at $5,000. But now a

---

[3] Devaluation can be viewed as the lessening, or lowering, of the value of a currency vis-à-vis some other currency or medium of exchange. Thus, where one ounce of gold had previously been "worth" $35 (American), following the devaluation, the same ounce of gold was now worth $38. In other words, the value of each dollar in terms of gold had dropped. The present value of an ounce of gold approximates $200 per ounce.

Japanese desiring to buy this equipment doesn't need to spend as many yen. The American machinery is suddenly cheaper, and hopefully, more competitively priced on the world market.

For a business executive, of course, this is a significant development. The executive can now sell more goods overseas, increase the profits, and by selling more goods to others, help resolve America's balance of trade deficit. Just imagine, for instance, what potential this has for the enterprising business executive. In the United States, we have approximately 6 percent of the world's population. By selling to this 6 percent, firms like GM, Ford, Standard Oil, and others, have been able to earn profits of over $1 billion annually. Imagine what possibilities exist if they can now compete effectively for the sales dollars of the other 94 percent (or a substantial portion thereof)! Certainly, if business ever faced an exciting challenge—one that offered potential profits far beyond the imagination of most of us—this is it. No wonder American business leaders are so anxious to move into international markets. Despite the problems— and some of them are substantial—the potential rewards are simply staggering.

BUSINESS AND ITS INTERNATIONAL RESPONSIBILITY

As one of the most important members of the international trading community, American business executives are confronted with a variety of questions relating to their role and contribution to world development. We have already seen, for example, how the simple matter of earning profits and reinvesting them in the country in which they were earned can result in eventual domination of the economy of that country. Should this be allowed to happen? Should American business be permitted to grow unchecked in foreign lands? On the other hand, what would be the consequences of *not* permitting such expansion? Could the world community survive without the presence of the American business executive? These are but a few of the questions that come into focus as we attempt to determine the role and responsibility of American business leaders in the international community.

The multinational corporation

The increased activity of American business overseas has resulted in the development of a new type of business corporation: the *multinational* corporation. Basically, the multinational corporation is characterized by two elements: (a) it has a manufacturing base or investment in at least one country other than its home country, and (b) it has a managerial philosophy regarding management, marketing, production, and finance that is global in nature. Thus, all decision making considers not only the domestic economy and competition but the global positions of the firm. Most of the large corporations in the world today are multinational corporations.

In many ways, the multinational corporation is a natural phenomenon. As businesses grow and expand, they begin to sell their products or services to ever-increasing markets. Eventually, some of these markets become international in scope. At first, most companies establish an overseas branch or subsidiary. This subsidiary usually has a manager, who frequently carries the title of vice-president for international operations. Soon, the company finds its sales abroad increasing at a far greater rate than its sales at home. So, the company begins to expand its international operations. Only instead of adding more plants in the same foreign country, the corporation opens offices in other countries. In effect, the company begins to view the *world* in the same way it used to view the home country. Where before it routinely made decisions about locating plants, say, in New York and California, now it *routinely* makes the same decisions about locating plants in London and Tokyo. To paraphrase William Shakespeare, "All the worlds' the stage, and all the people and countries are the markets."

The multinational: An imposing example

Perhaps the best way to describe the nature of the multinational corporation is to examine one of the largest and most successful of all such companies; the Unilever Corporation.

Unilever is a particularly interesting illustration because it is *not* an American corporation. Rather, the company is jointly managed by two identical boards of directors, one in England and the other in Holland. Yet, many of its products are familiar to most Americans, including such well-known brand names as Lipton Tea, Wisk, Lifebuoy, Knox gelatine, Pepsodent, All detergent, and Imperial margarine.

Unilever was formed as a multinational corporation in 1929, when a major producer of margarine in Holland merged with a soap manufacturer in England. Since then, the company has grown and expanded, such that today the statistics on Unilever are staggering. *Some* of its activities include the following:

1. Detergent:
    (It supplies approximately 20 percent of the market in *all* of the world's major industrialized countries.)
2. Ice cream:
    (It is the largest manufacturer in the world.)

3. Frozen foods:
   (It supplies about 70 percent of the European market.)
4. Margarine:
   (It supplies again, about 70 percent of the European market.)
5. Dried soups:
   (It has 70 percent of the market in the United States.)
6. Tea bags:
   (It has more than 50 percent of the U.S. market.)

Other activities of Unilever include such diverse operations as salmon farms in Scotland, logging operations in Indonesia, chocolate production in Ireland, a chain of 86 fish restaurants in Germany, the A&W Food Service chain in Canada, and several yogurt companies in France, to name but a few. Until recently, it also owned a paper mill in Germany, an animal foods plant in Spain, a plastics packaging company in Britain, and several operations in Mexico and Peru. And the company also has an African subsidiary that is also expanding around the world.

It should be apparent that managing a company as large and as diverse as Unilever requires some original thinking and managerial skills. Unilever recently, for example, abolished the idea of having a manager in charge of each country's operations. Instead, Unilever has created brand managers, whose authority crosses national boundaries. Thus, the market for any particular product in the various countries where it is sold is viewed exactly as another company might view the market in various cities for its products.

To add still another perspective to Unilever, one needs only look at how well the company has done. In 1973, Unilever chalked up net profits of $395 million, on sales of $10.4 billion! Over the past three years, net income has increased over 110 percent. One executive of Unilever was recently quoted as saying, "If our profits continue to grow at their present rate, we'd wipe out the world."

Presently, Unilever considers the worldwide inflation that exists, to be its number one problem. Its problem is complicated somewhat by the fact that many of the countries in which it operates have passed price controls, thereby preventing Unilever from increasing its prices as its costs rise.

Multinationals: Their impact on the world

As the above discussion shows, Unilever is quite a corporation! Now consider the fact that as impressive as the above statistics are, as a corporation, Unilever is *less than one-third the size of General Motors!*[4]

Quite obviously, the potential for the misuse of power—both political and economic—is substantial. In the early 1970s, rumors abounded about

---

[4] As measured by dollars of sales.

an attempt at an overthrow of the Argentinian government by I.T.&T. And who hasn't given thought to the possibility that some kind of collusion existed among the oil companies when the gasoline shortages of 1973–74 occurred?

Moreover, the tendency of these large multinational firms to take actions *without concern* for the impact of that action on any given country is growing daily. For example, Unilever recently attempted to cut costs in its British operations. It did so by making certain economy moves that enabled it to fire 11,000 workers. That meant a cut in expenses for Unilever, probably an increase in profits, and possibly an increase in the dividends paid to the owners. But what about the British economy? Britain was in the midst of severe economic problems. It was suffering, as most nations were, from high unemployment and high inflation. The last thing the country needed was to have 11,000 of its wage-earning, tax-paying, citizens suddenly lose their jobs.

These economic issues and the issue of power potentials of the multinationals is of concern to American citizens as well. Opinion Research Corporation ran a survey in 1973 of American opinion about the multinational companies. The findings were disturbing, to say the least. By a margin of almost 2 to 1, people felt that the government should do something to prevent American corporations from expansion overseas. Almost two-thirds of the people surveyed felt that such foreign expansion resulted in fewer jobs for Americans, and also resulted in a loss of tax dollars for the American government.

These findings are, of course, disturbing to advocates of the American business system. But what may really be disturbing is the impact these companies are making on other nations of the world. The United States, after all, is an extremely large and affluent nation. We are used to companies such as IBM, General Motors, and A.T.&T. But what about other, smaller nations? Envision, if you will, General Motors opening a plant in tiny Belgium. GM's total sales constitute a larger figure than the combined value of all the goods and services produced by all companies in the entire country of Belgium in a single year. If you were an influential citizen in Belgium, would the presence of a General Motors in your economy cause you some misgivings? No doubt it would. And Belgium is only an example. GM's total sales exceed the total national production of goods and services of all but a handfull of countries in the free world!

This isn't to say that American business isn't welcomed abroad. Quite the contrary. American businesses have introduced new products and new managerial techniques and have offered new jobs to thousands of people overseas. The problem is that no country wants to be dominated by business firms from another country. Consider, for example, the computer industry. The graphs in Figure 21–7 illustrate the extent to which American computer companies, and particularly IBM, dominate the

FIGURE 21–7

American computer companies dominate the world market

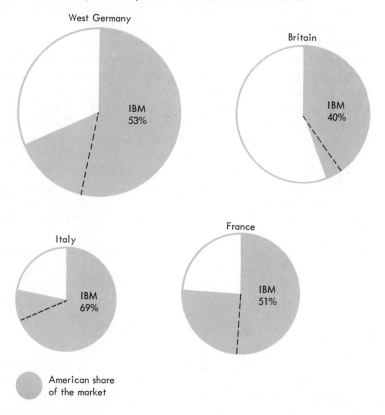

 West Germany, Britain, Italy, France pie charts. IBM 53%, IBM 40%, IBM 69%, IBM 51%. American share of the market.

world's computer market. Small wonder that the late President of France, Charles de Gaulle, attempted to keep General Electric from buying controlling interest in France's largest computer manufacturer. In the end, however, he reluctantly gave in, primarily because he could find no non-American business that had the funds necessary to rescue the French company. Even the national government of France was unable to save it!

International contributions of the multinationals

Lest we draw the conclusion that multinational corporations are all bad, we should give proper exposure to some of the benefits these large corporations have bestowed on other countries. Many American businesses, for example, have made major contributions to the betterment of the standard of living of peoples of other lands. Consider, for example, the following situations:

1. An American company opens a canning factory in South America. This factory imports raw materials—vegetables, fruit, and so on—and exports to the United States the finished canned goods. The South American country benefits from the jobs provided to its people and from the contribution this factory makes to its balance of trade.

2. An American airline once helped the African nation of Ethiopia to establish its own airline. The American firm provided planes and personnel to get the airline started. It charged the airline for the costs incurred, and as the airline prospered, it began to take part of the profits as payment for the aircraft, plus a small profit. It trained Ethiopian personnel to manage the airline. Over time, the American firm disassociated itself from the venture. Today, the Ethiopian Airlines is one of the most profitable airlines on the African continent. The American firm no longer has an interest in it, but is rewarded by the ability to now provide connecting flights for Ethiopians and other Africans who wish to travel to places not served by Ethiopian Airlines.

The above examples are just illustrations of the many ways American business had aided the economic development of peoples around the world.

THE QUESTION OF INTERNATIONAL BUSINESS ETHICS

As might be expected, the question of ethics arises on the international scene with increasing frequency. Often, we hear the complaint that goods are "dumped" on various markets by overzealous merchants. "Dumping" refers to the selling of goods abroad at lower prices than equivalent merchandise sells for at home. It has been charged, for example, that Japanese automobiles cost the average Japanese as much as $700 more than Americans pay for the same car. The purpose behind dumping of goods, of course, is to gain an advantage in the foreign market. In Japan, particularly, it is extremely difficult to market automobiles of American manufacture. Thus, the Japanese have their domestic market all to themselves. They are free to charge what they please, knowing that foreign companies won't prove too competitive. At the same time, however, they are free to cut prices on their cars sold overseas. Here, they must compete with others, and consequently seek to gain an advantage by selling the goods at extraordinarily low prices. What they lose on cars sold overseas they make up for in cars sold at home. This is dumping, and has been of considerable concern to American business executives. Many executives have expressed concern over the "ethics" of this situation.

Finally, there is the question of international cartels, or monopolies. With no central governing body to regulate conspiracy by international business, the opportunities for practices that we would consider "unethical" abound. How to cope with such practices is a question facing all business executives, and one that desperately needs to be resolved.

Laws and treaties   Finally, the American government has aided businesses overseas in their attempts to develop themselves. Were it not for a variety of federal institutions and trade agreements, many of these international business activities would never have been possible. Underdeveloped nations need assistance in exporting their goods. They also need capital—funds—with which they can buy the necessary materials to improve their way of life. Several important agreements and institutions have thus been created to assist this development.

1. *The European Recovery Plan.*   Better known as the Marshall Plan, this historic plan was instrumental in aiding the rebuilding of Western Europe after the close of World War II. Although it is no longer in effect, it was perhaps the first of the important steps taken by the United States to improve the world community and, particularly, set the stage for increased world trade.

2. *The Export-Import Bank.*   This is a federally sponsored agency that is empowered to lend funds to exporters and importers who are unable to obtain financing privately. On occasion, the Export-Import Bank will also loan funds to foreign governments.

3. *The International Monetary Fund.*   This international association has been primarily responsible for stabilizing the exchange rates among the currencies of the world. By so doing, it has helped build confidence in the international financial circles and has caused people all over the world to more readily accept foreign currencies in payment for goods. It, too, can make loans to foreign nations temporarily suffering from an adverse balance of payments.

4. *The General Agreement on Tariffs and Trade.*   GATT is an international agreement signed by almost 100 countries, in which the signatories agree to work to reduce tariffs on imports, and thereby promote world trade. Every few years negotiators from the various countries meet together to bargain for tariff concessions.

International trade associations   The recently created trade associations also have played a role in the economic and social development of foreign countries. The best known of these is the European Economic Community, better known as the Common Market. The Common Market is an economic association of the major countries of Western Europe, specifically, Belgium, France, West Germany, Luxembourg, the Netherlands, Great Britain, Italy, Denmark and Ireland. The Common Market has as its objective the establishment of a free-trade community, a society whose members are free of tariffs, taxes, or other influences from member states' governments. To promote internal growth, the EEC has established stiff tariffs for all goods imported into the Common Market. In effect, it

FIGURE 21-8

The European Common Market

Key:
1. Belgium   7. England
2. Netherlands   8. Luxembourg
3. West Germany   9. Ireland
4. Denmark
5. France
6. Italy

resembles a United States of Europe, where trade can take place freely *within* the community, but outsiders must pay to get in. Similar associations exist in South and Central America, but these associations have not been successful in actually establishing free trade among themselves.

Trade associations of this type are significant for the economic development of nations. By combining forces, smaller countries may be able to nurture and develop business institutions which will be capable of competing on an equal scale with the business firms of other lands. If this does, in fact, occur, perhaps some of the fear and misgivings others have of the multinational corporation will disappear.

CONCLUSION

In this chapter, we have obtained a glimpse of the complex world of international trade. We have seen how the welfare of the United States and the role of American business overseas are unalterably intertwined. The problems faced by both government and the businesses in the international community are many and difficult, to be sure, but so, too, are the potential rewards. Several billion people wait to be served, and whole societies remain untouched by the great business advances realized by America. It is this challenge that makes international business exciting. It is the promise and excitement of being able to better the living standards of not just hundreds, but billions, of people, that lures business—America's peace corps—overseas.

DISCUSSION QUESTIONS

1   What is the principle of comparative advantage? Why is it a useful principle insofar as international trade is concerned?

2   What types of problems exist in developing trade between countries?

3   Discuss the arguments used to justify tariffs on imported goods. What arguments can you raise that would negate these justifications?

4   What is the balance of trade? Account for the gradual worsening of America's balance of trade.

5   What is meant by "the balance of payments"? Distinguish the balance of trade from the balance of payments.

6   Name an industry that you feel is probably qualified for tariff protection under:
    a.   The infant industries argument.
    b.   The military preparedness argument.
    c.   The home industry argument.

7   Figure 21–6 shows the changing value of the dollar over time. Why do you think recent evidence shows the dollar regaining some of its earlier strength?

8   Many people are concerned about the multinational companies' growth, especially in regards to the loss of tax revenues for the parent country. Do you feel this argument has merit? In what ways do the multinationals help offset this loss of tax revenues?

9   Does American business have an international social responsibility?

Why or why not? (Consider the role of the stockholders in your answer.)

10 What do we mean by "dumping" of goods on the international market? How can such practices be prevented?

MINI CASES

Following the close of World War II, the United States had maintained a highly restrictive trade policy toward the Soviet Union. The sale to the USSR of any machinery or other heavy-duty equipment that had possible military value was generally prohibited by the U.S. government. The decade of the 1960s, however, saw that trade policy change. More and more goods of an industrial nature were approved by the authorities in Washington for sale or trade to the Soviet Union. Still, the process for arranging such trade was a highly complex one. The Commerce Department had to issue licenses, the State Department and the Defense Department usually had to give their approval, and financing arrangements —usually through the Export-Import Bank or some other world agency— had to be arranged.

One day in the late 1960s, representatives of the Soviet Union approached several major American automobile manufacturers about the possibilities of having an American firm build a large truck plant in the Soviet Union. Several of the auto manufacturers expressed an interest in the project, and indeed, it appeared that such action would materially advance the government's new policy of relaxed trade with the Soviets. However, objections arose from within the Defense Department to such a transaction, and the negotiations were subsequently broken off. The Defense Department was particularly sensitive to any attempt at aiding the Soviet Union in developing an advanced transportation network, particularly in light of the problems the United States faced in Southeast Asia.

The Russians, however, were persistent. Within a year, they had reestablished contact with another well-known and respected American truck manufacturer. This time, however, they offered the American firm the chance to head a project that had an ultimate value of over $1 billion.

The American company that had been approached suddenly found itself in a quandary. It was keenly interested in the billion-dollar deal. This would give it the chance it had been seeking to become one of the world's great automotive producers. However, the Defense Department had again raised objections to the transaction. Although the opposition of the Defense Department by itself would not necessarily terminate the transaction, the American firm had been doing substantial business under various defense contracts. The company didn't want to lose these contracts, and disregarding the advice of the Defense Department might well lead to such a loss.

To further complicate the matter, the company's possible involvement with the Soviets leaked to the press, who quickly gave it nationwide coverage. Many stockholders had begun to question the wisdom of such a transaction, with some of them openly questioning the wisdom of "aiding the enemy." Although the company knew that many of these stockholders were well intentioned in their advice, they were also relatively uninformed as to the complexities of this transaction. For example, the approval of the Commerce Department to the transaction was hardly mentioned in any of the newspaper stories. Yet, the company did not want to risk irritating its stockholders to the point of causing them to be irate at the next annual meeting. A decision had to be made, however, for the Russians were getting impatient and wanted to get construction started.

1. *Summarize all of the factors favoring the acceptance of the Russian contract.*
2. *Summarize all of the factors that did not cast favor on the contract.*
3. *If you were the president of this company, would you accept the contract to build the truck factory for the Russians? Why or why not?*
4. *Comment on the social responsibilities of this company, particularly regarding (a) government policy, (b) the stockholders, (c) the American economy, and (d) international relations.*

Don Kolbe was a student of business history at the local community college. One day, while he was reading *The Wall Street Journal,* he came across an editorial in which the writer was discussing the multinational corporations. This writer was particularly concerned that the multinational firms were contributing to the unemployment problem in the United States. The writer argued that as wage rates have gone up in the United States, many businesses have begun opening manufacturing facilities abroad, where they can produce the same products for less money. This, the writer argued, resulted in a loss of jobs for the American worker.

Don reflected on the writer's argument, and pondered the suggested solution, namely, that Congress prohibit American companies from opening plants overseas. As Don pondered the question, he reflected back on the history of this country, particularly the history of organized labor in the United States. It was rather ironic, he thought, that in some ways organized labor itself contributed to this very problem.

1. *What did Don refer to when he noted that organized labor may have contributed to the problem?*
2. *Do you agree with him? Why or why not?*

appendix

Appendix:
Business careers

Training is everything. The Peach was once a bitter almond; cauliflower is nothing but cabbage with a college education.
———Mark Twain,
in Pudd'nhead Wilson

CAREERS IN BUSINESS

As a concluding comment on this introductory study of business, it is appropriate that something be said about career opportunities in the world of business. A satisfying career, after all, is the ultimate goal for all of us, at least as far as our productive contribution to society is concerned.

Career opportunities in business

It can be safely said that the career opportunities for young people in the world of business are virtually unlimited. For the enterprising and imaginative student, moreover, the career opportunities that are just now opening promise to be among the most exciting and challenging ever posed to anyone. Most businesses today, except for the smallest, need people versed in the technicalities of high finance, computers, and statistical techniques. Business also wants people concerned with, and interested in improving the state of the environment and with bettering the relationships between the business community and the various publics with which it must coexist. Indeed, if challenging employment is to be found anywhere, it is most likely to be found in the world of business, for it is here that the action is. Business, even more than government and educational institutions, has the know-how and financial resources to effect changes and improvements rapidly. And it has the motivation (via the profit motive) to suceed in improving our society.

What are the jobs that exist in business? Specifying the jobs that exist in business today would be an impossible task. We would no sooner complete our list than new job opportunities would suddenly appear. A few years ago, for example, hardly anyone was concerned with problems relating to the environment. Today, however, many businesses have whole departments that specialize in learning new ways that business can effectively help to preserve the environment and, in the end, the quality of our life. Indeed, finding profitable ways to accomplish these tasks may be among the most challenging tasks business faces today. As the goals and aspirations of Americans change in the future, moreover, business will similarly be motivated to resolving new problems, and in the process, new job opportunities will develop. Such is the way of business in a dynamic society.

As a bench mark, however, to guide you in narrowing your choices in the coming months and years, consider the following exercise. Go back to the Table of Contents of this text, and construct an organization chart of a hypothetical business. For each of the functional chapters in Part Two, list at least six different career positions that were discussed or alluded to in the text. It's quite a list, isn't it? And it's only a beginning. As your study of business continues in more advanced courses, you should be able to further divide these areas into still more career choices. It's a complex institution, American business, and preparing for a career in it is no easy task.

What to look for in a career

As your search continues in the next few years for that particular job you would like to engage in, you should attempt to resolve in your own mind those things you would most like to achieve or realize in your career. Do you desire a high salary above all else? If so, your career selection will be narrowed to certain professions or occupations. Do you wish to travel? If so, then maybe international business or a career as a sales representative will have a certain appeal. Do you want to settle into a community, raise a family, and become a civic leader? If so, then occupations that tend to emphasize travel, sometimes to the detriment of a quiet home life, will not be for you. Thus, you should begin to specify, to your own satisfaction, those features of a prospective career that you would most like to see, and those characteristics that do not appeal to you. By so specifying the characteristics of your job, you will help assure that the position you ultimately take in business will be one that is consistent with your goals in life, and one in which your happiness will be greatest.

Considering the future potential of your career

One factor that many students fail to consider when choosing a career is the future growth potential for their chosen area. In the early 1960s,

Where corporate chief executive officers come from

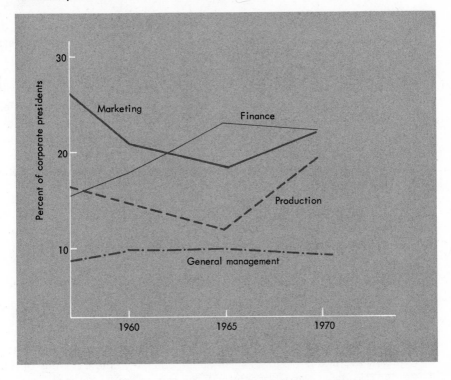

for example, the nation faced a severe shortage of qualified teachers, at all levels of education. As a consequence, salaries rapidly advanced, and teaching positions rapidly gained favor as a career choice for new students entering college. The result was a heavy shift of people into educational careers, a shift that was so great that by 1972, many new teachers found themselves with teaching certificates but no place to gain employment. In a relatively short period of time, a shortage of teachers had turned into a surplus.

This is not to imply, of course, that all shortages today will become surpluses tomorrow. Computer programmers have been in short supply for 20 years and will probably remain in short supply for the rest of this century. What the example does reveal, however, is the need for each of us to appraise the potential of the career we are considering. The surplus of teachers might have been predicted, if the students had only considered what factors would force school systems to restrict employing new teachers. Education is a heavy burden on our tax dollars. To employ all of the new teachers that were being turned out by our universities would have put an unbearable burden on the taxpayers, a burden they were unwilling to accept. As a result, many new teachers, although needed by the school systems, could not be hired because of a lack of funds.

In business, certain fundamental changes that are occurring in society promise to have broad ramifications. For example, consider the question of population growth. Will the population explosion continue, or are we approaching ZPG, zero population growth? If ZPG did in fact come about in the reasonably near future, what changes could you foresee in the business services and product lines that business offers? With a little imagination, it is easy to see whole industries changing, and entire careers being drastically shifted as the population being served undergoes a marked change. Such projections into the future are a necessary part of selecting any career, and in the foreseeable future each of us should carefully consider the long-run prospects for our career choice.

The job market at the present time

Job opportunities for young people trained in business subjects has been exceptionally bright for over ten years, and indications are that prospects will continue to look good in the foreseeable future. While the American economy has undergone some fluctuation in recent years (such as the recession of 1974), business has continued to actively recruit new college graduates for positions in their respective firms. Usually, the job opportunities for those students whose grades and accomplishments are below average tends to diminish as the economy enters periods of recession. No doubt this will continue to be true in the years ahead. However, the market for the better than average student continues to be bright. Even the student of average accomplishments should find the prospects favorable. Corporations, after all, cannot afford to consider only the state of the economy at the present time. The large companies realize that the economy will, periodically, go through periods of prosperity and recession. They also realize that, if they are to be successful in the long run, they must continue to provide for new managerial skills and talents, even if the state of the economy at any point in time is not favorable. Because the large corporations view skilled labor as a vital, scarce resource, they usually continue to seek out the good students and train them for positions in their companies.

Two questions that frequently are asked by young college students concern, first, the types of jobs that are in demand, and second, the salaries that are being offered. The first of these questions is, perhaps, somewhat easier to answer than is the second.

What types of jobs are in demand? As we have noted, business is constantly recruiting new people for positions in their firms. As a general rule, these people tend to have interests that span all aspects of business. Firms periodically are hiring accountants, sales personnel, production people, and so on. However, we can note the tendency for firms to hire certain kinds of people, depending on the nature of the company and on the state of the economy in future years, as the executives see the problem.

Year in and year out, accountants are perhaps in demand as much as any single career position. However, most firms are looking for the above-average accountant—one capable of earning a CPA, or who has shown a marked ability in the area, by getting good grades in school. And, as a general rule, accountants typically command a fairly high starting salary vis-à-vis other business positions.

Two other skill areas that typically enjoy a good job market are the areas of finance and computer and/or quantitative skills. Finance positions are not always easy to identify, inasmuch as many firms consider accounting and finance work as part of the same division. Consequently, many of the job requests that indicate companies are looking for accountants could also be filled by finance people. Finance also enjoys its own select market. Just as accountants are usually the only people sought by the large public accounting firms (giving accounting students an automatic marketplace), banks, real estate firms and brokerage firms usually seek out finance majors. Consequently, finance people also enjoy a good marketplace, most of the time.

People trained in the quantitative skills, or knowledgeable of computer programming, usually are in demand by all kinds of businesses. Indeed, over the past ten years, the demand for people skilled in these decision-making areas has probably grown faster than the demand for any other skill. It has been estimated that, no matter what effort we expend to resolve the problem, the nation will face a shortage of computer programmers for at least the next 25 years.

Marketing skills are constantly needed by firms that sell products for general consumption. The large firms—such as General Motors and Procter & Gamble, whose primary objective is to sell products to consumers—are constantly looking for marketing people. Many times such firms advertise for people to fill sales positions—and this tends to cause some students to shy away from them. These students, often erroneously, assume that the company is simply looking for salespeople. Sometimes the firm is. But keep in mind one thing. Salespeople—particularly good salespeople—can rise to the top positions in a company probably quicker than any other person. Moreover, many companies like their people to work in sales for a short period, so that when they move into management, they will have an understanding of just how difficult the salespeople's job is.

General management and general business positions are perhaps the most difficult to discuss. The reason is that many firms will interview people with a business background, regardless of their specific training.

These firms are looking for good people to put into their training programs, and subsequently move into various management positions within their firm. These firms are not as concerned with the type of business education the student has acquired, but rather are concerned that the student has obtained a reasonably good business background in all subject areas.

What about salaries? A discussion of salary levels being offered to students of business is always a dangerous thing. The reason is that the salaries being offered are constantly changing. Moreover, the actual cash salary may not be the proper measure of compensation. Many firms may offer better hospitalization and insurance plans, better pension benefits, and so forth. Some firms offer to pay all or most of the costs for those interested in continuing on in college. All of these "noncash" forms of compensation need to be considered when evaluating the salary offer of any firm. Even such things as a company car can be worth several thousands of dollars a year for some people.

To discuss cash, however, consider the following bench marks. In 1974, the "typical" business graduate was being offered salaries ranging from $9,000 per year to $12,000 per year. These offers were probably 5 percent higher than the year before. And they were probably 5–10 percent higher than the year before that. Now, before you go and calculate what you can expect when your turn comes, consider the following. More and more firms are no longer specifying a salary figure that they will hire at. Rather, they are basing their salary offers on the individual involved. The very best students can expect salaries considerably higher than these "typical" figures would indicate. Similarly, the marginal student had best be prepared to accept salary offers somewhat lower than the average.

Having considered, then, the current state of the job market, let us return to our earlier suggestion of preparing in advance for your job opportunities. How well you do in school is a matter to be determined solely by you. Assuming, however, that you do your best in school, there are some things about getting a job that you should be aware of, and might not get exposed to in some of your courses. These things relate to the job interview itself.

THE JOB INTERVIEW

No study of career opportunities in business would be complete without a discussion of the proper way to take a job interview. The job interview, after all, is where the door is either opened or closed on the career opportunity of your choice.

A successful and satisfactory job interview can go a long way toward assuring you of employment in the type of firm that will prove to be compatible with your long-term goals in life.

We realize, of course, that as beginning college students, you will hopefully have a few years remaining before you will need to confront an interview with a prospective, permanent employer. However, we also realize that many students will not complete a four-year college degree, and that many who do will continue in pursuit of higher educational goals. In either case, knowledge of how to take a job interview will not be wasted. Moreover, for the students leaving school permanently, a knowledge of job interview technique is particularly essential if he or she is to obtain gainful employment.

The material that follows is condensed from a widely known pamphlet titled *Making the Most of Your Job Interview,* published by the New York Life Insurance Company. We believe this small pamphlet is one of the finest interview guides available today, and with the permission of the New York Life Insurance Company, have reproduced a large portion of it here.

PREPARING FOR THE INTERVIEW

The employment interview is one of the most important events in a person's experience, because the 20 or 30 minutes spent with the interviewer may determine the entire future course of an individual's life. Yet interviewers are continually amazed at the number of applicants who drift into job interviews without any apparent preparation and only the vaguest idea of what they are going to say. Their manner says, "Well, here we are." And that's often the end of it, in more ways than one.

Others, although they undoubtedly do not intend to do so, create an impression of indifference by acting too casually. At the other extreme, a few applicants work themselves into such a state of mind that when they arrive they seem to be in the last stages of nervous fright and are only able to answer in monosyllables.

These marks of inexperience can be avoided by knowing a little of what actually is expected of you and by making a few simple preparations before the interview.

The following are some of the things you can do to get yourself ready.

The time and the place

Find out the exact place and time of the interview. This may sound almost too basic for mention, but it's an unfortunate applicant who assumes that the interview is to be held in a certain place ("All the others were!") and then discovers two minutes before the hour that the appointment is somewhere else. Write the time and the full name and address of the company down and keep the notation with you. Don't rely on your memory. Be certain you have your interviewer's full name and find out how to pronounce it if it looks difficult.

Above all, be sure to be on time, because late arrival for a job interview is almost never considered excusable.

Research

Do some research on the company interviewing you. Try to find out how old the company is, where its plants, offices, or stores are located, what its products or services are, what its growth has been, and how its prospects look for the future.

Prepare any questions that you might have before you go in for the interview. Bring a pen and a pencil with you and have some kind of notepaper with you out of sight. You may be asked to take something down. If not, you should make a few notes immediately after you leave the interview.

To help you research a company, there are a number of publications which provide such information. Most of them can be found in any good-sized college or public library.

a. *College Placement Annual,* by the College Placement Publications Council.
b. Thomas' *Register of American Manufacturers.*
c. Moody's *Manuals.*
d. Fitch *Corporation Records.*
e. Standard and Poor's *Corporation Records.*
f. Poor's *Register of Directors and Executives.*
g. *Dun & Bradstreet Reference Book.*
h. Company annual reports.

Your school's placement office is an excellent source for booklets and other material prepared by various firms for recruiting purposes. You may find detailed information in the company's own literature that is unavailable in general registers.

Personal appearance

The importance of neatness and cleanliness scarcely need to be mentioned.

With regard to clothes, let your own good taste be your guide. Simply remember that you are looking for a job—not going to a ball game or a party.

The above suggestion is meant to be helpful, but it would be a mistake to become unduly worried over too many details. A genuinely attractive personality and a good school or employment record will overcome most small errors. Be friendly, honest, and sincere and you will always make a good impression.

THE INTERVIEW

You cannot rehearse your role in an upcoming interview because you don't know what cues will be given to you. Your best guide is to rely on your own courtesy and good sense. There are, however, some basic rules and situations common to most interviews which may help you if you know about them ahead of time.

Relax!

It is normal for many people to be nervous, particularly during an interview. A little nervousness is to be expected. Experienced interviewers discount a certain amount of nervousness, but try to avoid doing things with your hands which might make your nervousness more obvious. If you don't know where to put your hands, leave them in your lap and keep them still.

The interviewer on your campus is there because he wants to hire people—not because he wants to trip them up or embarrass them. Your interviewer wants to hire you if he thinks you have something definite to offer the company and that you will fit into the organization.

Initial tips and possible questions

Greet the interviewer by name as you enter the office if you are sure of pronunciation. Take your cues from the interviewer at the start. Shake hands, but only if the interviewer makes the first gesture. Normally wait until he offers a chair before you sit down and don't smoke or chew gum unless invited to do so.

You should be ready for at least one surprise question right at the start. A few interviewers favor one of the following openers:

a. What can I do for you?
b. Tell me about yourself.
c. Why are you interested in this company?

If you think these are easy questions to answer without some previous thought, just try it. This is where preparation will count.

If you are asked what the company can do for you, be prepared to say that you would like to apply for a job in a certain operation of the company, with an idea toward progressing into some more advanced phase. Be as specific as you can.

Suppose you are asked to talk about yourself. You have found out what the company sells and a little about how it operates. If you are wise, you have thought, "If I were in the interviewer's place, working for this company, what would I like to know about an applicant?" Tell those things about yourself which relate to the situation—your background, your education, and your work experiences, if any. Don't learn a speech by memory, but have a number of points in mind.

As for the third question, why are you interested in the firm—if you have studied the company's literature you will not be at a loss for words.

Answering questions

Most interviewers will follow a rather simple question-and-answer formula. If such is the case, your ability to answer quickly and intelligently is of great importance. If your answers are confused and contradictory, your cause is lost. The best guard against contradictory answers is the plain, unembroidered truth. A frank answer, even if it seems a little unfavorable to you, is better by far than an exaggeration which may tangle you up in the next question.

Often a frank admission can be turned to your advantage. Frankness is admired, and you may be able to recover in this fashion: suppose you are asked if you always pitch right into an assignment and get it done ahead of time. You answer, "I'm afraid I don't always get assignments done before they are due. I sometimes have a tendency to put a thing off until it has to be done. However, I never turned in a major assignment or term paper that was late."

Keep following the interviewer's lead. Don't answer by just saying yes or no. On the other hand, don't talk too much. Be informative without boasting or telling your troubles. If you find yourself talking too long, give the lead back by saying, "Perhaps you have some other questions to ask me?"

A few interviewers like to do most of the talking and judge you by your reactions—the interest, comprehension, and intelligence you show. Others hardly speak at all, and for an amateur these are the hardest to deal with. Their attitude is that it is your job to sell yourself. That is where you will have to call on your knowledge of yourself and your interest in the work the company does. In any interview, in the last analysis, you will have to sell yourself.

Even if the recruiter does much of the talking, remember that you can lead by asking questions which call in turn for a question you want to answer. Example: You are strong in extracurricular organizations. The interviewer hasn't mentioned that point, and you want to go into a little detail you couldn't cover fully in your résumé. You simply watch for an opening and ask, "Are you interested in my extracurricular activities?"

Make sure that your good points get across. The interviewer won't know them unless you tell them—but try to appear factual and sincere, not bloated with conceit. If you can mention your best qualities in relation to something concrete, so much the better. For example, saying

"I paid for 75 percent of my college expenses" is better than saying "I am a hard worker and I want to get ahead."

Be ready with an answer to the question, "What do you plan to be doing ten years from now?" It's a favorite. A popular alternative question is, "How much money do you expect to be earning in ten years?" The purpose is to determine your ambition, ability to plan ahead, and the soundness of your thinking. Conduct yourself as if you are determined to get the job you are discussing. You have other irons in the fire, of course, and the recruiter is aware of that but still wants to think that you want a job with this company. Wherever possible, apply for a specific job or field of work. If there is no opening in the line you suggest, the way you present what you have to offer may well lead the interviewer to suggest another job or department, perhaps even better than the one you are seeking. For this reason it is not advisable to get too far out on a limb by saying you will not consider anything but one certain job.

Questions about your salary objectives some years into the future are among the most difficult to answer. One recent survey of top business people, however, provided a clue to how to answer that question. The survey noted that executives on the rise within a firm are typically earning $1,000 per year of age up to the time they reach 40. Thus, if you are asked how much you expect to be earning in 10 or 15 years, this little study might provide you with a guideline.

If the courses you took have not led you into preparation for a specific field of work, don't, on that account, pass up chances for interviews. But research on a company will better help you present your broad qualifications in the light of the company's needs.

Be careful not to make a slighting reference about a former employer or professor. If something went wrong, suggest that at least some of the blame must have been your own.

If you are asked if you've ever been fired—and you have been—frankness again is the answer. Admit you've learned from your mistakes. Also, there is the possibility you got into a wrong job through a misunderstanding.

Show the interviewer that you are interested in the company by asking some definite questions. Don't ask so many that the recruiter thinks you are afraid of work or are hesitating at the thought of joining the company. Before you report for the interview, have in mind two or three questions you want to ask about the company. Also keep in mind two or three good reasons why you are interested in this particular employer. The chances are excellent that you will be asked for your reason. If so, stick to the subject at hand. Don't let yourself wander away on a tangent because you like the sound of your own voice.

Should you get the impression that the interview is not going well and that you have already been rejected, don't let your discouragement show. You have nothing to lose by continuing the appearance of confidence and you may gain much. The last few minutes often change things. Once in a great while, an interviewer who is genuinely interested in your possibilities may seem to discourage you in order to test your reaction. If you remain confident and determined, you will probably have made a good impression.

Miscellaneous pointers and questions

Don't take notes during an interview if you can help it. This is annoying and distracting to some recruiters. The best policy is to note on paper immediately after the interview everything you want to be sure to remember.

If you are given applications forms, be certain that they are filled out completely and neatly. A messy application form can creates as bad an impression as personal untidiness.

What if you so impress the interviewer, or the company is in such need of recruits, that you are offered a job on the spot? This is rare, but you should have an answer prepared. If you are absolutely sure it is the job you want, accept with a definite yes. If you have the slightest doubt or do not want to accept without further thought or further interviews, play for time. You must not embarrass the person who has made you the offer. Be courteous and tactful in asking for time to think it over. Try to set a definite date when you can provide an answer. This will reassure the recruiter you are giving this offer serious consideration.

On the other hand, don't be too discouraged if no definite offer is made or no specific salary is discussed. The recruiter almost always wants to communicate with superiors first or interview more applicants before making any offers.

If you accept more than one job offer, you will reflect badly upon yourself and your school. If you have accepted one job and a chance turns up suddenly to interview for a really irresistible position, turn to your placement officer for advice. Job engagements have been broken before. But the way it is done is most important. It frequently happens that in your job with Company B you will have dealings with Company A. Hard feelings are best avoided.

Don't make appointments in which you are not interested. You will find yourself in an extremely awkward position, and you stand to lose the confidence of everyone involved.

You may be asked why you left your last two or three jobs. Return to school, better pay, more responsibility are acceptable reasons. Be careful, however, not to give the impression that you are a job jumper or shopper.

What about salary? Many people believe that an applicant has to ask for as much as the traffic will bear, or more, in the hope of gaining a bargaining position. They feel that companies always offer as little as they can. However, where most college interviews are concerned, the company representative has arrived on campus with a certain number of jobs to be filled in definite salary brackets. The interviewer may not choose, unfortunately, to tell you what there is to offer. You may be asked how much you want. The usual answer in that case is to indicate that you're more interested in a job where you can prove yourself than you are in a specific salary. This politely passes the question back to the interviewer. In most cases, reputable corporations will offer the standard salary for the type of job in question. It is in your interest, of course, to have found out what the rate is. You know, also, the level beneath which your needs and responsibilities will not permit you to go. Your placement officer can tell you what the normal range of starting rates is for a person with your background.

Most interviews last between 20 and 30 minutes. Don't go on talking and talking. Some applicants talk themselves into a job and then right out of it. Be alert to signs from the interviewer that the session is almost at an end. (Watch-looking is a sure one.) If you still want the job, sum up your interest briefly, say you are interested, and stop.

Be certain to thank the recruiter for the time and consideration given to you. Resist the temptation to flatter. Even if the interviewer is the most fascinating person you've ever talked to, don't say so. You may be misunderstood. Smile, and show as much confidence in leaving as you did in arriving. Say something like: "If you have any other questions, or if there is anything you want me to do, I hope you will get in touch with me." Then say thank you and leave.

If you have answered the two questions uppermost in the recruiter's mind: (1) Why are you interested in my company? and (2) What can you offer? Then you have done all you can.

Should you write a thank-you letter? Ordinarily, no. You will have noted, soon after the interview, any further contact your interviewer suggested. Follow the instructions exactly and don't send unrequested correspondence.

The interviewer may have indicated that you would hear from him or that he truly seemed interested in you. Wait about a week and then write a brief note to remind the recruiter of your talk. Express appreciation for the time given you and explain in as few words as possible your continuing interest in the company. You have little to lose by refreshing his memory, and you might get a favorable response.

In any event, if you do not get a flat rejection, or the polite no expressed in the type of letter that says, "We will keep your letter in our files and let you know if anything . . . ," keep in touch. Unless you make a nuisance of yourself, you will thus be able to stay in the foreground if a vacancy appears.

As other questions or problems arise, take them to your placement officer. They work with all types of business, governmental, educational, and other organizations and can be of great help to you if you work through their office. Be certain to notify them when you take a job or change your job.

If you don't connect immediately, remember that interviewers, companies, and jobs differ greatly. You will learn much from your first interview, and you will almost certainly do better in succeeding ones. The important thing is to keep trying.

QUESTIONS FREQUENTLY ASKED DURING THE EMPLOYMENT INTERVIEW

The following are examples of the types of questions asked, as reported by Frank S. Endicott, Director of Placement, Northwestern University.

1. What are your future vocational plans?
2. In what school activities have you participated? Why? Which did you enjoy the most?
3. In what type of position are you most interested?
4. Why do you think you might like to work for our company?
5. What jobs have you held? How were they obtained and why did you leave?
6. What courses did you like best? Least? Why?
7. Why did you choose your particular field of work?
8. What percentage of your college expenses did you earn?
9. What do you know about our company?
10. What are your ideas on salary?
11. Do you prefer any specific geographic location? Why?
12. How much money do you hope to earn at age 30? 35?
13. What do you think determines a person's progress in a good company?
14. Why do you think you would like this particular type of job?
15. If you were starting college all over again, what courses would you take?
16. Do you prefer working with others or by yourself?
17. How did previous employers treat you?
18. What have you learned from some of the jobs you have held?
19. Can you get recommendations from previous employers?
20. What interests you about our product or service?
21. What kind of boss do you prefer?
22. Have you ever changed your major field of interest while in college? Why?

23. When did you choose your college major?
24. Do you feel you have done the best scholastic work of which you are capable?
25. What do you know about opportunities in the field in which you are trained?
26. What have you done which shows initiative and willingness to work?
27. Which of your college years was the most difficult?
28. How do you feel about overtime work?
29. What are your own special abilities?
30. What types of people seem to rub you the wrong way?
31. Are you eager to please?
32. Do you demand attention?
33. Did you enjoy your four years at this university?
34. What size city do you prefer?
35. What is your major weakness?
36. Do you have an analytical mind?
37. Define cooperation.
38. Have you had any serious illness or injury?
39. Are you willing to go where the company sends you?
40. What job in our company would you choose if you were entirely free to do so?
41. What types of books have you read?
42. Have you plans for graduate work?
43. Have you ever tutored an underclassman?
44. What jobs have you enjoyed the most? The least? Why?
45. What job in our company do you want to work toward?
46. Would you prefer a large or small company? Why?
47. Do you like to travel?
48. What kind of work interests you?
49. What are the disadvantages of your chosen field?
50. Are you interested in research?

Note: If you take the time necessary to write out brief answers to each of the questions in the list, it can help you clarify your own thinking and establish ready answers.

YOUR RÉSUMÉ

Your school placement office may use a standard data sheet which you will be asked to fill in so that it may be used as a résumé of your activities and work experience. Some companies also may ask you to fill out such a sheet. In either case, be certain to do so accurately, fully, and neatly. Your data sheet will represent you to people who have never met you. If it is untidy you will be judged accordingly.

Some schools, and a number of companies, prefer you to develop your own résumé as a supplement to the face-to-face interview. For this reason we have included the following material on the résumé with the thought that it might be of help to you.

A self-prepared résumé becomes increasingly important if you change jobs in the years after graduation. In certain instances it is almost indispensable, such as application by letter, off-the-campus interviews, or an intensive job-hunting campaign in a major city.

The résumé must be neat. Careless erasures and misspelled words are inexcusable, and the latter, particularly, may cost you a good chance at a job.

A good résumé will go a long way toward helping you make a good impression. A bad résumé can seriously hurt the chances of an applicant who may seem desirable in every other way.

Contents and layouts of résumés vary as widely as the different individuals who apply for jobs. Interviewers and companies, also, differ as to what they want to see on a résumé. You will be safest, however, if you keep it simple and keep it on one page.

Your résumé should be typed. Multilithed, mimeographed, or otherwise duplicated copies are acceptable if they are well done.

Be sure to use a good-quality bond paper and keep copies to save yourself a rewriting job if the original is lost.

Organization

Your use of white space is most important in creating an impression of neatness and orderliness. Space can be used to isolate important points to which you want to draw attention. Sufficient spacing between all elements helps to create a clean, pleasing impression. Crowding too many details too close together results in an untidy appearance, as well as a fine-print look that repels a reader.

Your method of organizing the separate elements of your résumé is not as important as the fact that you show some kind of orderly, reasonable process. Unless you have proved that you have a better idea, it is wisest to stick to a rather conventional layout with straight lines and non-erratic paragraphing. Gimmick-type résumés have occasionally caught the interest of companies, but these are best left to the professionals. Gimmicks can backfire.

Reproduced in this section are two sample résumés. Each is a little different in its makeup. Each reflects a different personality and background. Each seeks to highlight strong points in an honest, straightforward fashion. It is as natural for a laboratory technician to emphasize lab experience, high grades, and professionalism as it is for one who expects to work with people to stress extracurricular activities and broad experience.

PERSONAL DATA SHEET

Name: John R. Richards
Address: 1201 Senator Place, Cincinnati, Ohio (to June 5, 1975)
Telephone: AVon 1–5000
Home Address: 12 River St., Portsmouth, Ohio
Home Telephone: 3–4832
Age: 22   Height: 5'9"   Weight: 159
Education: University of Cincinnati
                         Degree: Bachelor of Science, 1975
                         Major: Business Administration

Major Subject	*Minor Subjects*
Quantitative analysis & Computer programming	Finance, Economics

I received two scholarships to the School of Business which paid part of my tuition expenses.

Extracurricular Activities:

　Member of American Management Association
　Independent Student Association

Work Experience:

　1971–73: General Chemical Laboratories, 3455 Woodburn Ave., Cincinnati, Ohio. As part of my cooperative education program, I have been working full-time, alternate six-week periods as a program analyst.
　Summer: Ajax Laboratory Supply Co., Portsmouth, Ohio. Inventory clerk.
　　1970: Promoted from shipping department after first month.

References:

Ms. Jane A. Neff	Mr. Walter J. Schapp	Dr. John O. Ryan
General Chemical Lab.	Ajax Lab. Supply	Professor
3455 Woodburn Ave.	Portsmouth, O.	School of Business
Cincinnati, O.		U. of Cincinnati
		Cincinnati, O.

If you make use of a résumé in a job hunt a number of years after graduation, your work experience will, of course, be highlighted. College activities will then ordinarily be reduced in the résumé to a statement of your university's name, the year you graduated, your degree, and possibly your major.

Your own situation may dictate a different approach from the examples given here. What is important to remember is that you must sell your value to a company as surely as that company sells its own products to the public. You must appeal to the employer's interest in what you have to offer. Never emphasize your personal problems or the personal advantages you will gain from employment.

References

References may or may not be included. Some interviewers prefer to see them on your résumé. Others assume that you have them readily available. References related to your work experience are preferred to those of social acquaintances. A professor in your chosen field of interest is a good choice if you are known well. (Not all of your references should be teachers, however). Courtesy dictates that you ask your references' permission before using their names. Relatives' names are never used.

Work experience

Work experience is an essential ingredient of any résumé. Dates should be given, along with company addresses and a brief description of

---

PERSONAL DATA SHEET

Name:
Jane E. Doe
1000 University Ave.
Minneapolis, Minn.
University 1–4296
(to June 5, 1975)

Home Address:
3414 Nicollet Ave.
Minneapolis, Minn.
Minnetonka 1–3689

Personal Data:
   Birth Date: February 27, 1953
   Height: 5'1"   Weight: 110
   Health: Excellent

Occupational Goal:
   My goal is a job in the field of sales promotion, with the eventual aim of a management position.

Educational:
   University of Minnesota
   Degree: Bachelor of Arts, 1975
   Major: Psychology
   Minor: English literature
   Major subjects:
      Industrial psychology, general psychology, English literature, economics, history.
Grades:
   Good to excellent in major subjects; average to good in others.

Extracurricular Activities:
   Secretary, Alpha Pi Zeta, honorary social science fraternity.
   Member of Student Industrial Relations Society.
   Vice-president and social chairman of the ABC social club.
   Swimming team.

Work Experience:
   Summer, 1974   Gunderson Manufacturing Co., 1203 Ryan Ave., St. Paul, Minn. Payroll clerk. While working for Gunderson Co., I received a cash award for a payroll procedure suggestion which resulted in saving time for the company.
   Summer, 1973   Wearever Aluminum Co., door-to-door sales in Minneapolis.
   Summer, 1972   Lifeguard, Camp Chippewa, Lake Bemidji, Minn.

the work you did.

Your job list should ordinarily begin with the last job you held. It should include listings in reverse order, ending with the earliest. Some applicants have made strong cases for themselves because they have held jobs with a company for a considerable length of time. If you have been asked, for example, to return to the same company several summers in succession, by all means say so.

Other applicants, who have had successively more responsible jobs should emphasize that growing responsibility.

Since any company considering you likes to think that you will be a success, it is also good to note a promotion or recognition that has come your way as a result of success in a job. Be frank about your accomplishments, stating them briefly and factually. It is better, for instance, to say that you began as a shipping helper and were promoted to inventory clerk than just to list the latter position. Demonstrated ability and progress may mean more to an interviewer than the simple fact that you held a certain job. Also, significant minor experience, if it relates in any way to the job you are seeking, may help you, and should be included.

Since your major courses in school and your showing in those courses indicate your interests and abilities, you should have a section in your résumé touching on the highlights. Frankness is the wisest policy. Most companies do not limit themselves to seeking only students with stratospheric grade averages. Grades are an important part of the picture —but not the only part.

Extracurricular activities

Include your extracurricular activities. Many jobs are especially fitted for a well-rounded individual. The fact that you have been chosen as a member by honorary groups or elected to professional societies in your field speaks well for your future in that field. If you belonged to purely social organizations, list them. A large part of anyone's success in a new job grows out of his ability to get along with fellow workers. A demonstrated social awareness can be a point in your favor. Further, if you participated in activities to an extent that you were recognized by awards or offices, mention those, too. Leadership quality will be welcome everywhere.

It is understood however, that if you worked your way through school and maintained good grades you had little time for extracurricular activities. You should definitely state what percent of your college expenses were personally earned, and how many hours a week were usually devoted to working.

Everyone has something to offer: analyze your abilities, talents, and interests correctly and stress strong points as they relate to the job you are seeking.

Do that successfully in your résumé and follow through with it in your interviews. Sooner or later, you will find the organization which has been looking for you.

glossary

Glossary

absolute advantage, theory of The theory which explains the economic advantage one country enjoys when it can produce products that other countries cannot duplicate.

accident, industrial Any unexpected occurrence that interrupts the regular progress of an activity.

accounting The process of identifying, measuring, and communicating information to permit informed judgments and decisions by users of the information. Also defined as the recording, classifying, summarizing, and interpreting of financial data.

accrual accounts Those portions of income and expense accounts which are incurred during the current period, but which will not be paid or received until the next accounting period.

acid-test ratio A ratio to measure the liquidity of a business firm. It is calculated by dividing cash and near cash items by current liabilities.

advertising Nonpersonal selling technique designed to inform customers and to induce them to buy the product or service advertised.

agent Middlemen who negotiate sales on a fee or commission basis without taking title to the goods.

alien corporation A corporation chartered in a foreign country.

annual reports Summary reports of the preceding year's activities that are provided to all of the stockholders of a corporation. The annual report also includes the major financial statements of the corporation.

arithmetic mean The arithmetic average of a distribution of scores or values, obtained by summing all of the values and dividing by the number of scores or values in the distribution.

array A listing of all values in a statistical study, frequently from lowest to highest.

assets Those properties (both tangible and intangible) of value that are owned by a business firm or other legal entity.

assistant-to training The training method using a senior manager to train an assistant to take over the senior manager's position.

auditors A specialized type of accountant who inspects the records of companies and individuals and verifies the accuracy and honesty of the data recorded therein.

authority The delegated power to take actions within an organization.

autocratic leadership A style of leadership in which the leader makes the decisions alone and the subordinate's role is only to carry them out.

autocratic management The strong ruler viewpoint of management.

balance of payments The net effect of a nation's trade, travel, and other international financial activity. A favorable balance of payments means a country received more financial remuneration from others than it sent to others. An unfavorable balance of payments means the reverse occurred.

balance of trade The difference between a country's imports and exports. If exports exceed imports, the balance of trade is favorable; if imports exceed exports, the balance of trade is unfavorable.

balance sheet   The primary financial statement of a business firm. The balance sheet shows the type and dollar value of all assets owned by a business at a given point of time, and also the debts and owner's investment at that same instant.

bimetallism   The name attached to the period of time when the financial system of the United States had two metals—gold and silver—as the standard out of which money was coined.

blacklist   The name attached to the lists of individual names of union sympathizers that were circulated among business leaders during the early days of the union movement. The blacklist is now illegal.

board of directors   The elected representatives of the stockholders of a corporation whose responsibility includes the management of that corporation.

bond   A long-term debt instrument issued by corporations or governments. These may be secured by collateral, such as a mortgage bond, or they may be secured only by the faith that the corporation will pay the indebtedness, as with a debenture bond.

break-even analysis   A quantitative or statistical technique used to determine that level of output or sales that is necessary in order for revenues received to equal the total of all fixed and variable expenses incurred in making those sales.

broker   A middleman who acts as an intermediary between buyer and seller for a commission.

bureaucracy   A highly structured form of organization.

business   The economic activity of providing goods and/or services to others for a financial return.

business functions   The activities that take place in a business organization.

call provision   A provision occasionally found in preferred stock and in bonds that allows the issuing company the right to retire or redeem the particular security in advance of its stated maturity date.

Calvinism   An early English philosophy that stressed hard work and savings as virtuous aspects of life.

capital budgeting   That aspect of the study of finance that is concerned with the acquisition of major assets. This study particularly concerns the acquisition of the funds to make the purchases, and the choice of the particular asset that is to be acquired.

capitalism   An economic system that allows for the private ownership of all of the factors of production. It also allows the decisions of what is to be produced, where, and how, to be determined by that private sector.

cash-and-carry wholesaler   Wholesaler who sells for cash, does not deliver, and offers low prices in lieu of services.

caveat emptor   A phrase that means "let the buyer beware." It was liberally applied to the business leaders of the 1800s.

Cellar-Kefauver Act   Law passed in 1950 that gave the Federal Trade Commission authority to rule on all mergers. The law authorized the Justice Department and the Federal Trade Commission to give tacit approval to mergers before they actually occurred.

channel of distribution   The route which goods travel from producer, through middlemen, to consumer.

charter   The legal document that must be filed by each corporation with the authorities that approve the creation of the corporation. This document specifies the areas of activity that the corporation may engage in, and spells out all of the constraints that exist on the corporation's activities.

chattel mortgage   A type of bond that carries a mortgage on specific movable property of the issuer of the bond.

circular combination   A combination of two or more firms that operate in related, but not competitive industries.

Clayton Act   An antitrust act passed in 1914 as an amendment to the Sherman Act. The Clayton Act outlawed tying contracts, interlocking directorates, and in other ways redefined restraint of trade.

clinical evaluation   A method of evaluating application forms which is like that of a psychologist diagnosing a patient.

closed shop   A labor-management agreement whereby the company is prohibited from hiring anyone who is not a member of the labor union.

coaching   The training method involving employees working directly under and receiving instruction from a supervisor.

collective bargaining   The process in which labor representatives and management representatives arrive at a settlement of their differences.

commercial paper   Very high grade promissory notes issued by large corporations and secured with only the promise of the corporation to pay the indebtedness.

common stock   The basic ownership security of a corporation.

communism   An economic system in which, theoretically, all of the factors of production are owned jointly by all of the people. In practice, such a system is characterized by a group of individuals who make all of the decisions regarding economic priorities and who supposedly act on behalf of all of the people.

comparative advantage, theory of   The theory of international economics which states that a nation will tend to concentrate its production on those goods in which its advantage of production is greatest.

computer   An electronic device which, through the transmission of electronic impulses, is capable of making calculations and choice decisions (given a predetermined set of choices) almost instantaneously; often referred to as an electronic brain.

computer core   That section of a computer system that makes the rest of the system work. It contains the memory unit, which records all of the instructions and remembers or stores all of the relevant information.

conglomerate combination   A combination between two or more firms operating in unrelated industries.

conspicuous consumption   A label given to the belief that many people were spending their wealth, and consequently, the resources of the country, on items that lacked any real economic necessity, but were designed to show off their wealth.

consumerism   A term used to describe the attitude of consumer protection and concern that has taken hold in recent years.

consumer research   Study designed to learn customer preferences, attitudes, and reactions.

controlling   That function of management concerned with coordinating and regulating activities to assure performance in accordance with standards and plans.

convertible stock   A type of preferred stock that is exchangeable for common stock at the option of the holder of the convertible security.

coordination   The assignment of tasks to provide a smooth working operation.

corporation   A legal entity or artificial being created by law and endowed with certain characteristics as specified in its charter. Corporations are created only with the consent of a government body.

coupon bond A bond with small, detachable coupons, each of which is redeemable for the interest payable on the bond.

craft unions Labor organizations based on crafts (plumbing, carpentry, welding, and so on).

culturally disadvantaged Those people who, either because of their socioeconomic status or because of discrimination, have been deprived of the opportunity to participate equally in the fruits of our society.

cumulative voting A technique whereby one stockholder can accumulate the votes he has on behalf of one or a select few candidates. Cumulative voting almost always assures minority representation on the board.

current assets Those properties owned by a business or person whose usefulness or value will be consumed or used up within the span of one year.

current ratio A popular measure of liquidity, the current ratio is determined by dividing the current assets of a firm by its current liabilities. A two-to-one ratio is considered normal.

debenture An unsecured corporate bond.

decision theory The management technique that bases decisions on mathematical computations.

demand creation All that marketers do to make consumers want their products.

democratic leadership A style of leadership which considers the interests and seeks the contributions of the organization members in decisions concerning them.

depreciation The decline in value realized on all assets of a long life. This decline in value is the result of wear and tear and use. In accounting, depreciation is treated as a reduction to a fixed asset, the charge being made annually.

depression A period of economic stagnation characterized by high unemployment, low levels of output, and a generally deteriorated state of economic welfare.

descriptive statistics That branch of statistics that concerns itself with the graphic presentation of quantitative data.

evaluation The process by which the price of the monetary unit, expressed in terms of gold, is increased. Thus, the monetary unit becomes worth less relative to what it had been worth before.

direct retailing Selling that takes place in the customer's home.

discount The deducting of the interest charge on a loan from the principal proceeds paid to the borrower. Thus, the borrower receives the amount requested, less the interest charge, and must repay the full amount originally contracted for.

discount house A retail outlet that sells in high volume at low unit profit.

discount rate The rate of interest charged by the Federal Reserve Bank when it makes loans to the member banks.

dispersion The degree to which scores or numbers in a distribution tend to differ from one another.

dividends That portion of a corporation's earnings that are distributed to the stockholders—the annual return on a stockholder's investment.

domestic corporation A corporation doing business in the state in which it was chartered.

draft A financial instrument involving an order to pay a certain sum from one party to a third party.

drop shipper A limited service wholesaler who gets orders from customers and then passes the orders back to the manufacturer.

dumping The practice of selling manufactured goods in other countries at lower prices than are charged for the same goods at home.

ecology The study of the environment in which people live.

economics The study of how people and society choose, with or without the use of money, to employ scarce productive resources, which could have alternative uses, to produce various commodities over time and distribute them for consumption.

economies of scale The decline in cost of units produced as the quality produced increases.

elastic currency A currency that has the capabilties of being expanded in amount to meet the seasonal and cyclical needs of a nation.

entrepreneurship One of the factors of production, this characteristic refers to the managerial skill and talents needed to bring the other three factors into order.

ethics The art or science concerned with the social justifications, mores, and practices of humans in their environment.

European Economic Community The formal name for the common market; Europe's free trade community.

excise tax Specialty taxes designed strictly for revenue-raising purposes and commonly levied against expensive, luxury items.

exports Those goods produced in one country and shipped to other countries.

expropriation Seizure of property owned by foreigners by a government. Such seizure may or may not be compensated for.

factor evaluation A method of job evaluation which determines the basic requirements (factors) for performing a job.

factors A financial agent that specializes in buying and collecting accounts receivable.

factors of production The essential elements for the production of goods or services. The common elements or factors of production are land, labor, capital, and entrepreneurship.

Federal Reserve System The central banking system of the United States. It was developed in 1913 and comprises 12 regional banks and a central Board of Governors.

fiduciary A person entrusted with the property of another.

finance That aspect of the study of business that is concerned with the efficient acquisition and use of capital within the firm.

fixed costs Those costs incurred by a business firm whose magnitude does not change regardless of the level of output.

floating the dollar The actions of the federal government which allow the value of the dollar (as expressed in gold) to vary from day to day and from currency to currency.

foreign corporations Corporations operating in states other than the one in which they were chartered.

formal organization The planned structure for coordinating the activities of two or more people working toward a common goal.

franchise A licensing agreement between an operator of a business and the owner of a particular idea and distribution center.

frequency distribution An ordered array of numbers, with the frequency of occurrence for each number or score noted.

full-service wholesaler Middlemen who take title to goods purchased, operate from warehouses, sell through sales representatives, extend credit, make deliveries, and assume the risks attendant to business operations.

functional middlemen Middlemen who negotiate the buying and selling of goods without taking title to the goods.

general line wholesaler A wholesaler who carries a complete stock of closely related product lines.

general merchandise wholesaler Full-service wholesalers who carry a wide variety of unrelated merchandise lines.

general partner An active partner in a business firm. He is subject to full liability for all of the debts incurred by the business.

greenback The name attached to America's first national currency. The money was called greenbacks because the color of the paper on which it was printed was green.

Gresham's law "Bad money will drive out good money." This law was developed in conjunction with the period of bimetallism and indicated the essence of the problem facing a country with two or more standard currencies.

gross national product The total dollar value of all the goods and services produced in a nation in a given year.

gross profit The profit realized on the sale of goods after accounting for the cost of the goods sold, but before considering all other expenses that may have been incurred.

guilds The predecessor of the labor unions, guilds were organizations of skilled craftsmen designed to assist them in improving their trade and standard of living.

histogram A diagrammatical presentation of statistical data.

holding company A company whose assets consist primarily of the stocks of other companies. Holding companies usually do not deal in any product or service but rather earn their profits by collecting dividends from the companies whose stock they own.

horizontal combination A combination of two or more firms that previously had operated at the same level in a channel of distribution; a combination of former competitors.

human resource management The application of managerial skills to the direction of all human activities occurring within the business environment.

import duties Taxes imposed on selected goods coming into the country from abroad in an effort to discourage their purchase. Such duties are usually imposed on those goods that compete with goods of domestic manufacture.

imports Goods purchased from other countries. The opposite of exports.

income bonds Bonds that pay interest to the bondholder only if the firm earns enough money to enable it to do so.

income statement One of the two major financial statements of any business. It reveals a summary of the income or loss resulting from the business transactions of the preceding period.

indenture agreement That aspect of a bond issue that spells out the rights of the bondholders and the obligations of the issuing company.

independent retailer Typically the small, single owner or partnership retail operation.

index numbers The presentation of time-series data expressed as the relative change from some designated period within that series.

induction The process of bringing a job applicant into the employment of the company.

industrial unions Labor organizations based on industries (petroleum, aircraft, automotive, and so on).

inflationary economy An economy in which increases in the gross national product are the result of increases in the price level and not the result of an increase in output.

informal organization The structure of an organization that comes out of the socialization process.

insolvency A condition in which an individual or business finds itself with more debts than it has ready funds to pay them off with.

integrated business A business firm that controls all aspects of the production and marketing cycle relating to a particular product or product line.

interlocking directorates A situation in which the same individuals are members of the board of directors for competing corporations.

international unions Labor organizations with memberships covering two or more nations.

Interstate Commerce Act The first major piece of regulation, this act was passed in 1887 to provide regulation over the railroads.

inventory The volume of goods on hand.

inventory turnover A ratio that measures efficiency within a business firm. This ratio shows how many times the average inventory balance of the firm is converted into sales in the course of one accounting period.

investment banker A specialized financial institution that assists large businesses in obtaining financing funds.

invisible hand of competition The unseen force that Adam Smith felt would assure that an efficient economic system prevailed.

job analysis The process of determining by observation and study and of reporting pertinent information relating to the nature of a specific job.

job description A listing of the elements involved in performing a specific job.

job enlargement Adding tasks to a worker's assignment.

job enrichment Improvement in the quality of a job (by actions such as increasing responsibility, recognizing good work, and providing for advancement).

job rotation A training method involving moving a person from job to job so that a broad knowledge of the organization is gained.

job specification A listing of the human qualifications needed for performing a specific job.

joint venture A short-term, partnership type of agreement between two or more firms in which the two firms agree to work jointly toward some common, specific objective.

journal A book of entry or account in which all of the financial transactions effected by the business are recorded. From the journal the various account balances are then transferred to ledgers and finally are used to construct the financial statements.

Knights of Labor Predecessor to the American Federation of Labor, this labor union was one of the first to achieve national prominence.

labor, organized The total of the work force belonging to unions.

laissez-faire A phrase meaning "nonintervention by government in the affairs of business."

leadership The human qualities that cause one person to follow another.

ledger Individual account books that keep a running balance of the status of each account.

liabilities The debts incurred by a business firm or by an individual. Also refers to one of the three major sections of a balance sheet.

limited liability One of the characteristics of ownership of a corporation, or corporation stock. Such an owner's liability for losses is limited to the amount invested in the stock, and no more.

limited-service wholesaler Wholesalers who perform only some of the functions and services typically performed by wholesalers.

limited partner A partner who assumes a relatively inactive role in the affairs of the partnership and who enjoys a limited legal liability for the activities of the partnership.

linear programming The name given to a class of mathematical techniques used to solve certain problems in business. The technique assumes that the elements of the problem can be expressed as a system of linear equations.

line authority The authority an executive has over the people under him.

line relationship Relationship between the people or units in an organization in which the boss-subordinate roles are clear.

liquidity The quickness and ease by which an asset can be converted into cash.

Machiavellian A term that is used to describe crafty or deceitful motives. The word derives from the name of Niccolo Machiavelli, a Florentine statesman and political philosopher who lived by the principle that "the end justifies the means."

mail-order house A retailer selling by mail, usually through a catalog.

management All those activities involved in running an organization.

managerial development Training aimed at improving the administrative abilities of executives and potential executives.

manpower Total quantity of workers.

margin requirements Requirements set by the Securities and Exchange Commission regarding the percentage amount of down payment that an investor must make to purchase securities.

marginal customers This phrase is used to describe customers whose credit standing is relatively poor.

market analysis The study of size, location, and characteristics of the market.

market segment A part of a larger market distinguished by characteristics such as geographic area, buying behavior, or socioeconomic factors.

marketing The interaction of multiple business activities with a view to satisfying specific customer needs and wants at a profit.

marketing management The approach to marketing that holds that the activities of marketing should be managed with the goal of satisfying human wants and needs in mind.

marketing mix The combination of four interrelated areas of marketing strategy used by an organization (product development, pricing, channel, and communication).

marketing research Any research which obtains information useful in a firm's marketing-management work.

maximizing shareholder wealth This phrase describes the corporate objective which, rather than maximize short-term profits, seeks to maximize the long-term benefits which accrue to its ownership.

measure of central tendency A measure such as the mean, median, or mode which tries to express the average of a group of numbers.

median A measure of central tendency which is found by locating the middle number of a series of numbers that are arranged in order of increasing values. Ideally, 50 percent of the numbers in the series will have a value lower than the median.

mercantilism A political philosophy held by many countries during the 18th century which placed a high value on the economic wealth of the nation.

merchandising A broad, functional area of marketing including all those activities involved in determining, creating, and satisfying consumer wants.

merchant wholesaler Middlemen who buy from manufacturers, farm producers, importers, and other wholesalers and sell to retailers, institutions, industrial buyers, and other wholesalers.

merger The type of business combination by which one of combining firms survives the combination (for example, $A + B = A$).

middlemen Those business executives acting in some capacity within the channel of distribution between the producer and the consumer of goods.

military-industrial complex A term which is used to refer to the relationship which exists between the business and military establishments.

mobility of labor Describes the degree to which the labor force is able to respond to changes in the labor market.

mode A measure of central tendency which is found by locating the number(s) which occurs most frequently in the group of numbers.

monopoly The economic situation under which a company is able to exercise some degree of control over the market for its good or service. A pure monopoly refers to the situation in which there is only *one* firm (or labor union, or any economic unit) which can provide the good or service to the economy.

multinational corporation A corporation whose activities cross international borders.

national union Labor organizations with memberships restricted to one nation.

net profit margin The ratio of net income to sales.

New Deal The name given to the program of President Franklin D. Roosevelt, designed to lift the nation out of the depression of 1929.

nonstore retailing Retailing that is not conducted at a store (such as mail order, vending machine).

normal distribution A common pattern that is formed when statistical data previously arranged in a frequency distribution are plotted on a graph. All normal distributions are symmetric and all have the property that the mode = the median = the mean.

on-the-job training The method of teaching workers a job while they are working on that job.

open market operations One of the tools used by the Federal Reserve System to control the money supply. These operations involve the purchase and/or sale of government securities to member banks in the system.

operations Those activities which transform inputs into finished products or services.

operations management Management of those operations which transform inputs into outputs.

operations research A term which refers to the application of the scientific method to the decision-making process.

opportunity cost. This term refers to the theoretical cost of forgoing a profitable investment.

organization A system of concisely coordinated activities or forces of two or more persons. A group of people working together for a common objective.

organization chart A diagram showing the formal authority relationships between the components (workers, departments, divisions, and so on) of an organization.

organizing   The process of arranging the members of an organization and the organization's activities for achieving the objectives of the organization.

OSHA   The Occupational Safety and Health Act, passed in 1970, and designed to provide safer working conditions for workers.

owner's equity   This term refers to the net worth of an enterprise to its owners after all debts have been paid. The balance sheet equation holds that owner's equity = total assets − total liabilities.

participating stock   This feature gives the owner of the security the right to either share in the earnings of the firm, or to vote on important issues facing the enterprise—or both.

partnerships   A legal form of business organization in which the business enterprise is owned by two or more persons. Generally speaking, the law does not distinguish the income of the partnership from the income of its owners.

par value   The stated value on a stock certificate. It has little use except in the taxing of a corporation upon chartering.

planning   The act of determining the course of future actions.

plant layout   The arrangement of the facilities and services within the work area.

pragmatism   A philosophy that emerged toward the end of the 19th century which held that the validity of a concept can be tested only by its practical results.

preferred stock   A type of ownership certificate in a corporation whose owners have a preference to either dividends or to assets upon liquidity, or both.

production   The sequence of operations that transforms something (such as raw materials) into a desired form (such as a finished product).

production scheduling   Coordinating the activities involved in production so that a smooth output results.

productivity   The ability of a nation's work force to produce goods, measured in units of work per unit of time.

product life cycle   The time period from the time a product is first manufactured to the time it ceases to be manufactured.

product planning and development   The activity of making what one has to sell conform to the consumer's needs and desires.

profits   In the general sense of the term, profits refer to the return expected by the entrepreneurs engaged in some business activity.

program, computer   A coded set of instructions which direct the computer's operations.

progressive tax   A tax structured so that the rich are faced with a relatively greater burden than are the poor.

promissory note   An unsecured, short-term debt instrument in which the maker promises to pay a specific sum upon a certain date.

proportional taxes   Those taxes which have one tax rate that is applied to the incomes of the rich and poor alike.

prospectus   A statement which outlines the major financial and economic features of a business.

proxy   A document which transfers the rights of one person to another. In particular, a document which transfers the voting rights of a stockholder.

public relations   All the activities an organization engages in which influence the viewpoints the public has of that organization.

Pujo Committee   A congressional committee formed to investigate the existence of a banking trust. The committee's findings led to the eventual creation of the Federal Reserve System.

quality assurance (control)   A system of inspection designed to assure prescribed levels of quality in production.

quantitative analysis As opposed to qualitative analysis, seeks to quantify the information relevant to a decision and to determine a mathematical solution for the decision.

rack jobber A wholesaler who places goods in the retailer's store, keeps up the stock, and is paid only for the goods sold.

rag merchant An individual popular in the early 1800s, who traveled the country in search of out-of-town bank notes, which he would buy for a fraction of their face value and then redeem on his travels around the country.

range A statistical term, referring to the spread between the largest and smallest score in a distribution.

recourse This legal term refers to the right to hold the endorser of a note responsible for its payment.

registered bonds Bonds whose rightful owners are recorded as such by the corporation. Registered bonds differ from other bonds in that registered bonds have the protection of this record as a safeguard against theft.

regressive tax This tax is stuctured so that the poor bear a relatively larger tax burden than do the rich. An excise tax is an example of a regressive tax.

regulatory tax The general classification for taxes whose primary purpose is to regulate or restrict certain economic activity.

responsibility The accountability for actions in the operations of an organization.

restraint of trade A legal phrase descriptive of any behavior which tends to reduce the level of competition.

retailers Middlemen who sell goods to the final consumer.

retained earnings Those profits earned by a business firm, but which have been reinvested in the business rather than being paid to the owners as dividends.

retractional flow A production arrangement in which the flow of materials repeats itself (goes over the same path more than once).

revenue tax The general classification of taxes whose primary function is to raise revenue to finance the various government programs that have been legislated.

revisionist leadership A style of leadership which combines the democratic and autocratic forms.

risk That level of uncertainty in which a decision maker knows, at least, the possible outcomes of an action and can assign subjective probabilities to them.

Robinson-Patman Act Passed in 1936, this act was concerned with unfair marketing practice. Its most important provision outlawed monopolistic behavior on the part of the buyer.

salary Fixed compensation for work or services, regularly paid.

sales promotion A form of demand creation which includes all of those activities which supplement and facilitate personal selling.

sales research Research involving the analysis of sales data.

scientific management The management viewpoint that seeks the most efficient way of doing things.

scientific method A method of investigation which is based upon the empirical verification of predictions drawn from theory.

sectionalism This term refers to the condition which existed during the 19th century in which each region of the country developed its economy along different products and technological levels.

Securities Act This act created the Security Exchange Commission, which was given the authority to regulate the practices of security selling and exchange.

serial bond A type of debt security whose maturity and retirement dates are sequentially determined, usually by means of a serial number.

Sherman Antitrust Act Passed in 1890, this act was created to control business growth where it threatened to hurt competition. It provides a jail sentence for those convicted of acting to create a monopoly.

silent partner A partner who assumes an inactive role in the management of the enterprise and whose ownership status is often kept secret. This partner may enjoy a limited liability legal status.

simulation This term, in a statistical sense, refers to the construction of a scale model of a real-world situation which can be used as a learning or teaching device to allow participants to see how they would fare if they exercised various options in decision making.

skewness A term which refers to the degree of asymmetry in a distribution.

Social Darwinism A political and social philosophy of the 19th century which held that the "survival of the fittest" law of nature should be equally applicable to the world of business.

social responsibility A moral or legal obligation to society as a whole that a business or individual will behave in a manner which is acceptable to that society.

socialism A form of economic organization in which the government itself owns the basic industries in the economy.

sole proprietorship A business that is owned by only one person. This person, known as the sole proprietor, is fully responsible for the affairs of the business and is sole recipient of all profits earned. It is the most popular form of business organization.

span of management The number of subordinates a manager can supervise effectively in a given situation.

specialization of labor A breakdown of a job by the tasks performed and assignment of these tasks to individual workers.

specialty wholesaler A wholesaler who carries only a part of a broad, general line.

staff authority The authority of an advisory position.

staff relationship An advisory relationship between the people or units in an organization as contrasted with a boss-subordinate relationship.

standard A predetermined level of performance.

statistical evaluation A method of evaluating application forms which equates answers given to those given by workers who have been successful in the same work.

statistics The branch of mathematics which involves the collection, analysis, interpretation, and presentation of masses of numerical data.

stockholders Those individuals who hold stock in a corporation and who are its owners.

strike A deliberate stoppage of work in an effort to force management to grant union demands.

subsidiary A company which is owned by a parent company.

syndicate A type of business combination in which several companies combine their resources temporarily toward the accomplishment of a stated objective. This form is most commonly found in financial markets where several companies may enter into a syndicate to float a security issue for another company.

target market The people most likely to buy a product—the group to which the company should direct its marketing efforts.

tariffs Taxes placed on imported goods.

term loan A loan which is made for a specific sum of money over a specific period of time.

time value of money A concept which acknowledges that money changes value over time; that a sum of money today is worth more than the same sum of money received at a future date, because the money received now can be invested to earn interest.

total product concept The marketing concept that products should be viewed in a total sense—as satisfiers of wants, as well as objects with physical characteristics.

trade acceptance A draft drawn by the selling party asking the buyer to accept the terms of the credit. Upon such acceptance, the trade acceptance becomes another draft.

trade credit The credit which a seller of goods gives to a buyer.

trust A combination of companies in the same or allied industries formed to administer prices and reduce competition.

tying contracts A contract which requires the recipient of goods to accept other goods as part of a "packaged" arrangement.

unidirectional flow A production arrangement in which materials do not travel in the same direction twice.

union shop A labor-management agreement requiring union membership as a condition of employment.

utility An economic term referring to the capacity of a good or service to satisfy a human want or need.

variable costs Those costs whose magnitude changes with the level of output. Together with fixed costs, they comprise the expenses of the business firm.

vertical combination Combination of business firms within a channel of distribution. Such combinations are usually depicted as being between supplier and customer.

vestibule training Job training conducted in a classroom which duplicates actual working conditions and equipment.

wage and salary administration The process of establishing and implementing sound policies and methods of employee compensation.

Wagner Act Often called the Magna Carta of unionism, this act gave workers the right to organize and required employers to bargain with these organizations.

Wealth of Nations Abbreviation of the title of the famous book written by Adam Smith in 1776 in which Smith spelled out the virtues of the private enterprise, free capitalistic system.

wholesaling All marketing transactions in which the purchase is for a profit.

indexes

Name index

A

A & P, 327
Aerojet-General Corporation, 542
Aircraft and Agricultural Implement Workers of America, 253
Akron Art Institute, 551
Allen, Frederick Lewis, 106
American Airlines, 497
American Bankers Association, 213
American Broadcasting Company, 443
American Chiclet Company, 135
American Federation of Labor (AFL), 44, 248
American Federation of Labor–Congress for Industrial Organization (AFL–CIO), 253–54
American Management Association, 213
American Motors Corporation, 462 n
American Nurses Association, 272
American Telephone & Telegraph Company, 48, 116, 118, 125, 206, 368, 446, 491, 581
American Tobacco Company, 41, 54–55
Anaconda Copper, 526
Aristotle, 27
Armour meat-packing company, 40
Armstrong Cork, 546
Avis, Inc., 136
Avon, 289

B

Bailinson, Frank, 78 n
Beecher, Henry Ward, 85
Bell, Alexander Graham, 116
Bell & Howell Corporation, 470
Bell Telephone Company, 116
Bendix, 489
Berle, Adolf, 108
Bernard, Chester I., 154 n
Bethlehem Steel Corporation, 543
Biddle, Norman, 35–36
Boulding, Kenneth E., 161 n
Boy Scouts, 545
Bradley, Joseph, 456 n
Briscoe, 56
Brunswick Corporation, 374
Bryan, William Jennings, 46
Buick Motor Company, 56
Burger King, 139
Burlington and Northern Railway, 462
Burr, Agnes Rush, 97 n
Bursk, Edward C., 100 n, 337 n
Business Publications, Inc., 138

C

Cable, George Washington, 539
Cairnes, John, 90–91, 441
Calvin, 88
Campbell soups, 327
Carnegie, Andrew, 39, 41, 54, 82, 92, 94–96, 479
Carnegie Steel Company, 41
Cellar, Roger, 548
Cervantes, 391
Chandler, Alfred D., 56 n
Chase Manhattan Bank, 362, 551
Cheit, Earl F., 107 n
Chesapeake and Ohio Railroad, 434
Chevrolet, Louis, 58
Chrysler, Walter P., 55, 60–61
Chrysler Corporation, 60–61, 318, 334, 413, 491
Churchill, Winston, 69
Clark, Kenneth, 6, 540, 544, 553
Cleary, Catherine Blanchard, 446
Cochran, Thomas C., 61 n
Cohn, Jules, 548 n
Colgate Palmolive Company, 556, 559
Columbia Motor Company, 59
Communications Satellite Corporation (COMSAT), 78, 125–26, 472, 494
Congress of Industrial Organization (CIO), 248
Consumers Union, 504
Continental Grain Co., 556
Control Data, 491
Conwell, Russell, 97
Cooke, Jay, 47
Coors Banquet Beer, 84
Coors Co., Adolph, 84
Corn Products Corporation, 549
Cousteau, Jacques, 517, 527
Couzens, 56

D

Dale, Ernest, 173 n, 183 n
D'Alembert, 2
Darwin, Charles, 95–96
Dayton Motor Company, 59
de Gaulle, Charles, 582
Del Monte Food Company, 569
Detroit Edison, 463
Dewey, John, 98
Dickens, Charles, 92
Dickson, W. J., 102 n
Dodge Motor Company, 61
Douglas, Paul H., 470

Subject index

Sixty years of the consumer price index, "the cost of livi

Percent, 1967 = 100

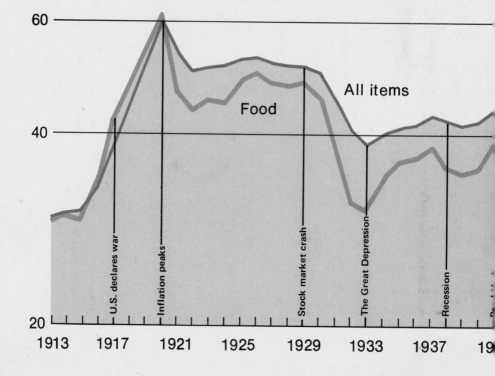

Ratio scale

All items

Food

U.S. declares war

Inflation peaks

Stock market crash

The Great Depression

Recession

1913   1917   1921   1925   1929   1933   1937   19